The People Of Ocean County

A HISTORY OF OCEAN COUNTY, NEW JERSEY

by David D. Oxenford

Edited by: Vilma B. Oxenford
Illustrations: Sheila Mickle Kierce

The Valente Publishing House, Inc.
Point Pleasant Beach, New Jersey

Marianne,

I hope you enjoy this book as
much as I did preparing it.

David D. [signature]

Library Of Congress Catalog Card Number 92-81379
ISBN: 09632906-06

First Edition, May 1992

Published by
The Valente Publishing House, Inc.
Publisher: George Valente
Graphic Design and Production:
Dawn Turner, Timothy John, Jennifer John, Diana DePrizio, Judy Cardella
Offices: 306 Route 35 South, Point Pleasant Beach, New Jersey 08742
Mailing Address: Post Office Box 176, Bay Head, New Jersey 08742
Telephone: 908-892-8021 • Fax: 908-899-3477

Proudly printed in the United States Of America.

Table of Contents

CHAPTER IV - Patriots or Loyalists

CHAPTER V - Wreckers or Lifesavers

CHAPTER VI - Travelers

CHAPTER VII - Toilers

CHAPTER VIII - Tourists

CHAPTER IX - Citizens

CHAPTER X - The New Natives

Epilogue

Annotated Bibliography

Bibliography

Photograph and Illustration Index

Index

A Native

I am indeed fortunate to have lived all my life in Ocean County. I was born and grew up in Point Pleasant Beach and was a part of the Point Pleasant Beach Schools for fifty years, first as a student and then as a teacher of senior American History. When my wife and I established our home in 1951, we chose a place on the banks of the Beaver Dam Creek in Brick Township and have lived there ever since. This choice enabled me to qualify as both a "Piney," a resident of the Pinelands, and a "Clamdigger," a native of the shore. These terms have been used to identify natives of the county in both a literal and figurative sense. Clams and oysters were attractions for people coming to the shore in the early days, thus, "Clamdiggers," while the term "Piney" was first used extensively at the end of the nineteenth century for those living in the Pinelands.

Point Pleasant Beach High School. Only public high school building in Ocean County currently in use that was built prior to World War II.

When I taught, my students often kidded me by saying, "No wonder you can teach American History. You have lived a quarter of it." Well, since Ocean County was only established in 1850, I have lived almost half of its history. During these years I have witnessed many events that have shaped the area, and, as a history buff, I have learned many interesting facts. In this book I will attempt to share with you this information and hopefully help you to expand your knowledge of Ocean County.

I have a vivid memory of many things with which you may be unfamiliar. I can remember, as a child, walking across the Manasquan Inlet. No, I can't walk on water. The inlet, which had shifted again and again over the years, was closed entirely by storms after the opening of the Point Pleasant Canal. This canal gave the Manasquan

River another outlet. The tides, which rushed in and out, had helped to keep the inlet open over the years. I can remember seeing rocks, which were taken from the excavation of the New York subway system, being unloaded from flat cars on a siding in Point Pleasant Beach. These rocks were then taken to the shore, where they were used to form the seawalls which have protected the inlet.

Many times my bike was caught in the trolley tracks that still remained on Arnold Avenue in Point Pleasant Beach. I can remember the crowded Central Jersey and Pennsylvania trains taking tourists home from a day at the shore. There was even a shore train that originated in Point Pleasant Beach, traveled down the beach strip to Seaside Heights where it crossed the Barnegat Bay to Ocean Gate, Toms River, and continued to Camden.

Manasquan Inlet - Closed by sand. Dredges begin the slow process of opening the inlet in the 1930's.   Joe Eid Collection

When I traveled Route 88, no cars passed for long periods of time.

Forge Pond-Where the salt waters of the Metedeconk meet the fresh water of the upper branches. Now the partial source of drinking water of northern Ocean County communities.

We played softball in the center of Laurelton Circle without fear of traffic. The circle was replaced at the end of the 1980's by a complicated system of lights and new lanes to handle the greatly increased traffic. Not far from this intersection was my favorite freshwater swimming spot, Forge Pond. I learned to dive from the second wooden bridge where the Metedeconk River joined Forge Pond and I collected arrowheads from the trails along its banks.

I viewed silent movies in the old Grove Theatre in Point Pleasant Beach. Once in a great while, I traveled to Lakewood to visit the beautiful Strand Theatre to view new sound films. I can remember attending Big Band concerts at Jenkinson's Pavilion, which were carried over WOR radio, each Sunday afternoon. On other summer evenings, for ten cents, you could dance to the music of the Sammy Kaye Band or other name bands.

I played high school basketball against the other county high schools: Barnegat, Toms River, Tuckerton, and Lakewood. Today there are sixteen. Traveling south seemed like going to the end of the world, for south of Toms River very little of the land was occupied year round.

I watched the Morro Castle and the Hindenburg burn. These two disasters in the 1930's made Ocean County famous throughout the country.

I viewed many of the major hurricanes. I played "King of the Boardwalk" during the 1938 hurricane, one of the major storms to hit this area. This violent storm sent the boardwalk, hotels, and plenty of water rushing down Arnold Avenue in Point Pleasant Beach. I recall

Storm Waves-Atlantic Ocean sweeps down Bridge Avenue in Bay Head during the 1938 hurricane, chasing the usual sightseers.   W.E. Hess Collection

sitting on the front porch of the Old Cook House in Point Beach, which served at that time as the clubhouse for a nine hole golf course, to hear the radio announcement of Hitler's invasion of Poland which began World War II. During the war years, while I was lifeguarding at Jenkinson's, I watched bathers use kerosene to remove tar from their bodies and suits after swimming in the ocean. This tar resulted from the sinking of Allied ships by enemy submarines in the nearby shipping lanes. The boardwalk lights had the sides toward the ocean painted black to prevent these lights from outlining ships sailing a short distance off the coast. I remember being denied access to the beach after dark while soldiers with dogs patrolled the sand to prevent the landing of spies and saboteurs after a rumored story of a successful landing on Island Beach.

When I returned from military service, I viewed first hand the tremendous changes that were taking place in Ocean County. I observed the influence of north Jersey's urban problems, the construction of the Garden State Parkway, and the establishment of retirement communities. I saw how these events contributed to the county's becoming one of the fastest growing areas in the nation.

This book is not intended to be a work of original scholarship. It attempts only to gather in one book information on people, places, and events in Ocean County history from my personal experience and from the experiences and research of others. It is designed primarily to help high school students overcome the major weakness of many who have come before them: knowing more about the history of their nation and the world than about the county in which they live. Others may find the book interesting in recalling many of the events of their lifetime and that of their ancestors. This source will help natives and visitors alike become better acquainted with this county by the sea.

I have given much thought to how to tell the history of Ocean County. A chronological presentation offers a simple organizational structure but often makes it difficult for the author to determine which facts should be selected and for the reader to see a relationship between the past and the present. I have always felt that a thematic approach develops a clearer understanding of history, and that is the approach I have taken.

The theme of this book is based upon the variety of people who have contributed to the history and development of the county and who have given it its unique character. Beginning with the terms "Piney" and "Clamdigger", I have tried to trace the history of the county through the various roles and occupations of its residents. The "people of Ocean County" themselves provide the structure for this book.

Chapter I establishes the stage or setting for that history. Subsequent chapters will examine its players: the native Americans, the first settlers, the Loyalists and Patriots during the Revolution, the citizens who established its government, the toilers who worked the land and the sea, the travelers and the tourists who helped shape the character of the area and, finally, the new residents, each of whom added a new dimension to the county. Understanding the roles of these people over the years will not only offer an overview of the county's past but will also provide a greater understanding of Ocean County today.

CHAPTER I

The Setting

Tucker's Island (The Disappearing Island)

Looking southward today from the Holgate Section of the Edwin B. Forsythe Wildlife Refuge on Long Beach Island you will see a two mile stretch of open water, Little Egg Harbor. What you will not see is Sea Haven, Short Beach or Tucker's Beach. All are names for Tucker Island, an area that now lies under water.

Tucker's Island Lighthouse as it stood with many other buildings on this island in the early part of the 1920's.

In The Disappearing Island, Pauline Miller traces this 600 acre island from its purchase in 1725 by Reuben Tucker until its disappearance in 1939. In colonial days, a body of water separated it from the southern tip of Long Beach Island. This passageway allowed ships to enter Little Egg Harbor and the port of Tuckerton. Shortly after the Revolutionary War, this inlet filled with sand and Tucker's Island became part of Long Beach Island. However, storms and tides continued to change the topography. The inlet reappeared during a storm in 1840 and lasted until 1874 when it again disappeared. In February of 1920 a severe northeast storm again reopened the inlet and recreated Tucker's Island. This passageway became wider and wider, washing away so much of the island that it became nothing but a sandbar.

Over the years the area served as one of New Jersey's earliest seashore resorts, Tucker's Beach, and was the sight of Little Egg Harbor lighthouse, a school, a lifesaving station and a small community of vacation cottages and homes of government workers. Not a sign of this community remains today.

As with Tucker's Island, physical changes have had a profound effect on the history of Ocean County. By describing the physical *features of the county and some of the changes in environment made both by nature or man, this chapter will attempt to lay the groundwork for the story of the people of Ocean County.*

The Shoreline

In 1850, when Ocean County separated from Monmouth County, it became the second largest county in area in the state. Centrally located, 62 miles south of New York City and 54 miles east of

Philadelphia, it is one of four New Jersey counties to border the Atlantic. Just off its shore is one of the busiest sea lanes in the world, and this fact, along with its central location, has influenced the county's development.

One of the dominant geographic characteristics of Ocean County is its shoreline. During the ice ages, when the level of the ocean was much lower than it is today, the land extended 90 to 100 miles eastward. Today this area is known as the continental shelf. Findings of mastodon bones and other fossil remains on the seabed support the claim that this area was once dry land.

Tucker's lighthouse pictured here toppled into the ocean in 1927. It was only fifty feet above sea-level and was visible for twelve nautical miles.
Ocean County Historical Museum

Although the present-day coastline seems relatively stable, changes are continually occurring. According to the Beach Haven Times, " In 1856, a geologist said that he had evidence that land was sinking at the rate of 1/4 inch a year." Whether the land is sinking or the water is rising, as other authors claim, Ocean County's shoreline is moving inland.

New Jersey's coastline today stretches 127 miles from Sandy Hook to Cape May. Ocean County makes up 45 miles of this coast. The coast of most of New Jersey and all of Ocean County is formed by low barrier islands. These islands were formed by strong ocean currents cutting away large amounts of mainland and gradually forming offshore underwater ridges. Over the years, waves deposited loose bottom material on these ridges until they eventually rose above ocean level. Thus, a series of offshore islands were created. A visit to the shore after a major storm where a strong coastal sweep has formed a sandbar off the beach might help conceptualize this process.

Barrier islands are separated from the mainland by bays, channels, sounds, salt marshes, and a canal. The Ocean County coast is formed by two of these islands. The northern barrier island was a natural peninsula made by man into an island with the construction of the Point Pleasant Canal. In its early days this land was known as Squan Beach and Island Beach. The southern barrier island is Long Beach Island. The only shoreline where the mainland is directly on the New Jersey coast is from Long Branch to Manasquan and at Cape May.

The Inlets

The inlets which connect Barnegat Bay with the Atlantic Ocean have played a vital role in the development of Ocean County. Each had a particular influence on its surrounding area. At various points in the history of the county there were at least ten passageways across the county's barrier islands. Three are still in existence; Manasquan Inlet, Barnegat Inlet, and Little Egg Harbor Inlet.

The Manasquan Inlet gained importance as a direct result of the building of the Point Pleasant canal. The present site of the canal was chosen over two other sites. The first proposal, in 1903, was a plan to

Manasquan Inlet - Modern fishing boat returning to port.

link Barnegat Bay with the Manasquan River by connecting Twilight Lake in Bay Head with three lakes in Point Pleasant Beach. A 1920 proposal to connect the bay and river by using the waters of the North Branch of the Beaver Dam Creek was also dropped when the owner of Pine Bluff Inn, a resort along the river in Point Pleasant, donated land for the present canal site to the Army Corps of Engineers. The canal was finally completed in 1925 allowing boats to gain easier access to the ocean from the northern end of Barnegat Bay.

The opening of the canal, however, contributed to the filling of the Manasquan Inlet with sand. In 1930 a joint federal, state, and local project began to dig a 400' wide opening through the sand. Rock jetties

Point Pleasant Canal - Dredge engaged in digging the canal in 1923.
W.E. Hess Collection

were placed along its sides to keep the inlet open. This effort, along with constant dredging and the addition of concrete "jacks" (artificial rocks), has kept the channel open and has today created one of the safest entrances to the Intercoastal Waterway to Florida.

Barnegat Inlet, on the other hand, is one of the more difficult crossings of the barrier islands. It serves as a passageway between the bay and the ocean for central Ocean County. Its location has changed little in the past 400 years, but its channels and sandbars have shifted constantly. Although a tremendous amount of water flows through this inlet, the depth of water is a constant problem because of the changing channel.

The first recorded sighting of this inlet is found in the log book of Henry Hudson's First Mate, Robert Juet. In September of 1609 he wrote of Barnegat Inlet, "The mouth of the lake has many shoals, and the sea breaks upon them as if it is cast out of the mouth of it". Foaming breakers caused Cornelius Mey, explorer of Barnegat, to name it "Barendeget" (breakers inlet).

Many attempts have been made to control the shifting sands at the mouth of this passageway to the sea. Today

Cement Jacks - In recent years these artificial rocks have been used to strengthen jetties protecting Manasquan Inlet.

the Army Corps of Engineers is again trying to improve this entrance.

Eighteen miles south of Barnegat Inlet is Little Egg Harbor Inlet. This inlet helped Tuckerton become one of the major American ports during our nation's early history. Tuckerton, along with Philadelphia and New York, was made an official port of entry in 1787 by President George Washington on the recommendation of Thomas Jefferson.

Two early inlets were Herring Inlet and New Inlet. Both existed during the early part of the 1700's. Herring Inlet stood opposite the Metedeconk River and enabled Brick to serve as a port for ocean-going ships. The New Inlet cut through the barrier island near the present day entrance to Island Beach. These two inlets were filled with sand during the storms of 1740 and were never reopened. However, this same storm opened Cranberry Inlet which played an important role in the history of the county.

Map of Early Inlets.

Cranberry Inlet was located on the border of Dover Township and Seaside Heights. It enabled Toms River to function as a major port during the Revolutionary War, and contributed to the prominence of Toms River in Ocean County. This inlet also filled with sand during a storm in 1812. Two attempts were made to reopen it. Michael Ortley, who at one time owned the area known today as Ortley Beach, attempted to reopen the inlet in 1821 and failed. In 1850, a fifteen foot channel was created permitting three ocean-going ships to sail up the Toms River. However, it was closed almost immediately by a storm.

The story of these inlets shows the constantly changing nature of Ocean County's coastline with both storms and man contributing to this process. Today, man is working to protect what remains of the dunes and to fight erosion by building jetties and planting dune grass.

Coastal Wetlands - Any bank, marsh, swamp, meadow, flat or low land subject to tidal action at or below elevation of one foot above local extreme high water mark which is capable of growing salt meadow grass, black or salt marsh grass or spike grass.
(N.J. Coastal Wetlands Protection Act 1970)

Wetlands

During the Ice Ages the forming and then the melting of the glaciers caused the level of the sea to fluctuate hundreds of feet. At times, water covered much of the mainland of Ocean County. As the sea retreated, it left a series of salt marshes and tidal waters along the inland side of the barrier islands and along the edge of the mainland, forming what are now called coastal wetlands. These wetlands, once referred to as just a "smelly, mosquito-infested swamp", serve a valuable purpose. They provide a buffer zone to absorb high water caused by storm and wave action and they act as a filtration system to dissolve and remove many pollutants brought in by the tide. The wetlands also serve as a nursery and feeding ground for 70% of the fish and ocean life of the area and provide a home for numerous species of wildlife.

Wetlands can also be found inland. Inland wetlands lie between the better drained uplands and the deep water lakes and rivers. In the pinelands, where many of Ocean County's inland wetlands are found, they form shallow depressions covering large areas with only little changes in elevation.

Inland Freshwater Wetlands-A variety of marshes, bogs, swamps, and bottom land forests that are saturated for "sufficient duration" to grow vegetation adapted for life in saturated soil conditions. (U.S. Army Corps of Engineers,1982)

Today Ocean County has 150 miles of bay front and estuaries. Barnegat Bay is 72 square miles of brackish shallow water. The property along these waterways was once thought to be of little value in spite of the fact that the water was rich in fish, crabs, eels, and in beauty. Today these same lands make up some of the most valuable real estate in Ocean County. There remain only a few acres of sensitive undeveloped land along the banks of Barnegat Bay. Because of the limited area remaining and its sensitivity, much of the remaining waterfront is regulated by Fresh and Salt Water Protection Acts.

The Pinelands

Another area of Ocean County once thought to be of little value except for its timber is the Pinelands. Most of the mainland in Ocean County is known as the Pinelands or Pine Barrens. Twenty-three percent of land in New Jersey is classified under this label. It covers portions of eight counties: Atlantic, Burlington, Camden, Cape May, Cumberland, Gloucester, Monmouth, and Ocean. This triangular shaped area starts just south of Long Branch and extends 80 miles to the Delaware Bay where, at its widest point, it reaches 50 miles. The Pinelands form a unique ecosystem characterized by an unusual blend of soil conditions, forest areas, ground vegetation, and water resources. This unique ecosystem attracts researchers from around the world.

Poor acidic soil and low water retention influences the type of vegetation grown in this area. The forest in the Pinelands first contained fast growing pines. As these matured and died, hardwoods began to dominate. However, most of the larger hardwoods fell victim to colonial industries. This, along with periodic fires, tended to eliminate hardwood seedlings and promote pine seedlings. The acidic soil and the accumulation of forest litter which did not decompose, prevented the enrichment of the soil and created an environment in which mainly pitch pines grew.

A "miniature forest" of approximately 12,000 acres of dwarf pitch pines and scrub oaks is found along Route 72 near the Burlington/ Ocean County border. Frequent fires have kept this growth young and small. Not only are the stands of pitch pines slow growing but they tend to also be misshapen since many grow out of stumps and decayed matter resting on the forest floor.

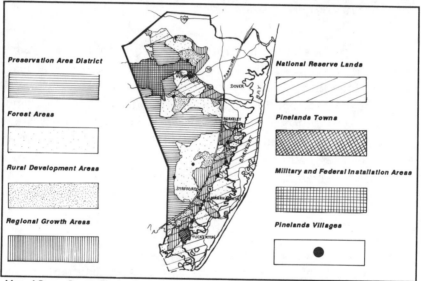

Map of Ocean County Pinelands.

On upland sites, huckleberries and low bush blueberries grow under the pine stands in areas free from fires. Cranberries, white cedars and swamp hardwoods grow in low level areas along with many types of grasses. Over 850 different species of plant life have been identified. An abundant variety of wildlife also exists in the Pinelands. Some 350 different types of birds, mammals , reptiles, and amphibians reside in this area. Raccoons, squirrels, beaver, field mice, skunks, and muskrats still abound and over forty-eight species of birds have been reported nesting in tidal marshes.

Surprisingly enough, this area known as the Pine Barrens because of its impoverished soil, produces over 1/4 of the state's agricultural income. Because of its yearly harvests, Ocean County has made New Jersey the second state in the United States in the production of blueberries and third in cranberries.

Dwarf Pine Forest.

Cranberries

At first glance, the Pine Barrens seem dry. On the contrary, lying a few feet under the surface of unconsolidated sand and gravel are 17.7 trillion gallons of fresh water, known as the Cohansey Aquifer. Used as a source of drinking water by some of the communities bordering the area, today it represents the largest reserve of fresh water in the eastern United States. This shallow aquifer pushes water to the surface producing bogs, swamps, marshes, creeks, lakes, and major waterways such as the Toms River, Metedeconk, Manasquan, and the Wading River. The rich organic contents seeping out of the soil give Ocean County's lakes, creeks, river narrows, and even Barnegat Bay a tea color.

Embracing most of Ocean County, the 1.3 million acre pinelands represents the largest open space in the Boston-Washington corridor. In the 1870's, Joseph Wharton, a mineralogist and financier who founded the *Wharton School of Finance* in Philadelphia, recognized the value of the Pinelands. From 1876 to 1890 he gradually acquired a hundred thousand acres. He hoped to establish a series of reservoirs to store and transport clean drinking water to the Philadelphia area. The state passed a law blocking Wharton's plan, and in 1955, the State of New Jersey finally

The Pinelands - As viewed by canoers paddling Cedar Creek on trip from Double Trouble Park to Route 9.

purchased this land.

In recent years almost all levels of government have acted to protect the environmental integrity of the Pinelands. Today one third of the land is publicly owned. The Pinelands National Reserve Act, passed in 1978, covers about 1.1 million acres or 1,700 square miles of land in 56 municipalities of which 75,000 acres are federally owned. Two hundred and seventy thousand acres of state owned lands are included in the 933,000 acres protected by The New Jersey Pinelands Protection Act of 1979. In 1983 the United Nations also designated the area as an *International Biosphere Reserve.*

Public Lands

In addition to the shore and the pinelands, Ocean County's most valuable resource is its open space. The 116,000 government owned acres in Ocean County are used primarily to provide active and passive recreation, to protect migratory birds and endangered species of plants and animals, to provide a home for fish and mammals, and to protect pure air and water.

New Jersey owns most of the open space in Ocean County, 78,678 acres. Most of this land is under the control of the New Jersey Fish, Game and Wildlife, and Parks and Forestry Services. The state park system of New Jersey is the third largest in the nation and almost one fifth of New Jersey's parkland is in Ocean County.

The largest single block of open space in Ocean County is owned by the Defense Department. The Fort Dix/Lakehurst NASC military reservation controls 23,000 acres. Only a few of these acres are intensely developed. Added to these military lands, in 1984 the United States government created the Edwin B. Forsythe National Wildlife Refuge. The Barnegat Division of this refuge placed over 10,000 acres of open space in Ocean County under the protection of the Department of the Interior. Over two thousand acres of Reedy Creek and Herring Point in Brick Township, as well as other sensitive areas along Barnegat Bay, are now in the process of joining this very important reserve.

In addition to open space, the Reedy Creak area will protect the Swan Point Shellfish Relay Station, which lies directly opposite its mouth.

Great Blue Heron - Enjoying the protection of Ocean County's open space.

Comprising over 70 acres of Barnegat Bay, these clambeds purify over five million clams yearly. Clams gathered from polluted waters further north are placed in the harvest plots opposite the creek to be cleansed naturally by the waters of the bay. The need to protect this area from further development is imperative in order to preserve the relatively unpolluted waters in the Barnegat Bay. (The saving of Reedy Creek came too late for Swan Point. As this book goes to press, the state has just announced that Swan Point Relay Station must close as a direct result of the growing pollution.)

Reedy Creek - Newest addition to Forsythe Reserve.

In recent years local park and recreation sites have kept pace with other levels of government. Many of these sites have been aided by the granting of matching funds by the state Green Acres program.

Citizen environmental groups of Ocean County, such as the Izaak Walton League, The Citizens Conservation Council, and Water Watch, are working to guard the important natural resource of open space. One of the most recent Green Acres Projects to be approved in Ocean County, is the Murray Grove Project in Lacey Township. In October of 1991, William deCamp Jr., president of the Izaak Walton League, described this project as "by far the most significant piece of unprotected open space available in one purchase along Barnegat Bay." The undeveloped lands contain not only the homes of many migratory birds and other endangered wildlife, but also wetlands, fields and wooded areas. The Murray Grove site, along Stouts Creek, also is an historic site, the birthplace of the Universalist Church in America.

Other County Resources

Ocean County also contains a small amount of fertile farm land. Located in the northwest section of the County, New Egypt, in

Plumsted Township, is the center of this farming area and is also the geographic center of the state. In 1699, twenty-seven hundred acres of land were granted to Clement Plumsted. It contained most of present-day New Egypt. Plumsted, a Quaker, was one of the original proprietors of New Jersey. There is no official record of when the town was first called New Egypt. One story tells of a mill owner who stocked his bins and storage areas so that he could supply farmers with corn during bad times, hence the name New Egypt. This fertile farm land is fast disappearing, as is much of the unprotected land. It is being subdivided and used for shopping malls and housing developments.

Climate is also an important county asset. The unequal temperatures of water and land make this region cooler in the summer and warmer in the winter than its neighboring urban areas. The pines are also said to be warmer in the winter. During World War II, rather than travel to Florida, the New York Giants baseball team took advantage of this warmer climate to hold their annual spring training camp in the area now known as Ocean County Park in Lakewood. Many tourists, before and after the Giants, have come to this area because of these attractive weather conditions.

Other natural advantages of Ocean County include its clean air and clean water. The sea breezes provide a healthy atmosphere and relief from the densely populated surrounding areas. Most major river systems, and many minor ones, in the United States have been polluted for many years, but in Ocean County most of the small rivers and streams were drinkable until recent times. The county rivers rise in the pines. They do not flow through urban and industrial areas as do many of the other rivers along the Atlantic Seaboard. This relative absence of pollution is a major attraction of the county.

Nature's Obstacles

Two natural threats faced people choosing the shore as their permanent residence: mosquitos and storms. A Philadelphia newspaper in 1858 complained that "there is no peace in the place because of the mosquitos." This condition continued to be of

Mosquito Drainage Ditches - These ditches are part of the Cattus Island State Park in Dover Township.

concern well into the 20th century. To combat this problem, starting in 1912, many miles of drainage ditches were dug in Ocean County to drain the swamps. Examples of these ditches are exhibited in the wetlands of Cattus Environmental Center in Dover Township. In the 1950's, increased use of D.D.T. and other sprays improved the situation, but the toxicity of these sprays and the growing immunity of these insects led to more drainage projects. The filling in of many wetlands, and the construction of homes were major factors in the reduction of mosquito breeding areas and mosquitos are no longer a major threat.

Long Beach Island after 1962 storm.

Storms, however, have always constituted a threat to those living near the beaches and wetlands. The hurricanes of 1938, 1944, and 1951, along with the northeaster of 1962, caused major damage to homes in Ocean County. The leveling of the dunes to construct homes, hotels, boardwalks, and businesses contributed to this damage. Even though the storm of 1962 destroyed many of the homes in Harvey Cedars, it failed to discourage rebuilding in that area and future building along the shore.

In spite of these natural obstacles to settlement, the geographic setting of Ocean County is still very attractive. That setting has contributed to a tremendous increase in population in recent years. Since the end of World War II, federal, state, county and local governments have acted to protect Ocean County's natural resources from the threat of overdevelopment and nature. The success of these efforts require the constant support of all its citizens in order to maintain the area that prompted Robert Juet to write in his journal on September 2, 1609: "This is a very good land to fall in with, and a pleasant land to see."

CHAPTER II

Native Americans– Lenape Indians

William Penn (Indians' Friend)

Historians must be thankful to William Penn, who established the colony of Pennsylvania, for the fairest and most comprehensive picture of the Lenape Indians. Penn, a Quaker, had been given the land by Charles II of England to settle a debt owed his father. He was determined to settle the land as a refuge for God-fearing people, where tolerance and freedom would exist. He felt, as a proprietor, that he had every right to govern as he saw fit, but at the same time he recognized the property rights of the natives. His land purchases from the Indians were characterized by negotiated agreements.

Lapowinsa - Lenape Indian Chief signed with William Penn the Walking Purchase Treaty which gave Penn the right to all land as far north as a man could walk in three days. Using three runners, Penn's successors gained all the land from the Delaware to the Pocono Mountains.)

He was respected by the natives and knew them as well as any man of his day. In his writings he described the Indians as generally tall, straight, and well built. He found them to be handsome people with many having noses similar to the Romans. He respected their character and defended their religion, which he believed was, in many instances, similar to the Europeans. He and many authorities considered their language beautiful and fluent.

Unfortunately, Penn's view of the Lenape Indians was not shared by many of the white settlers. Only recently have people in the county come to appreciate the culture of the Indians and to form a more accurate picture of their place in Ocean County history.

The Origin Of Americans

The origin of the first Americans is the subject of debate. Theories have been introduced by laymen and scientists alike. One thesis is that man originated in this hemisphere. Roberta Miskokomn, a Canadian Munsee, at a symposium in 1981 declared, "Our Indian ancestors did not come across the Bering Sea as anthropologists and archaeologists theorize. We were always here as my elders have told me." She is supported in this idea by scientists from Mexico and Argentina who claim that man originated in their nation.

Another theory, in the 1500's, was advanced by Bartolemeo de las Casas, a Spanish bishop horrified by the treatment given the Aztecs, who dedicated his life to protecting them from the Spanish conquistadores. He stated that the first Americans were descendants of the Lost Tribe of Israel. This position was supported by William Penn as well as by *The Book of Mormon*. Many of these theories run contrary to genetic, linguistic, archaelogic, and historic evidence. However, no single answer seems to fit all the characteristics of the Native Americans. Even the date of the appearance of the first humans in the Americas is the subject of controversy. At one time, 10,000 B.C. was accepted as the date of the earliest American. However, evidence suggests that our first Americans could have been here as early as 35,000 years ago.

Diomede Islands.

Today most anthropologists support the theory that the first Amerinds (scientific name for the first Americans) were Paleolithic-Mongoloid-Asians who came from Siberia to Alaska via a land bridge connecting the two Diomede Islands in the Bering Sea over 25,000 years ago. During thaws, this crossing may have been made with small kayak-type water craft. The migration continued southward from Alaska via gaps that existed in the glaciers and during interglacial periods. Most found their way into Latin America with some remaining in the Western United States, and an even smaller number migrating eastward.

The story of that eastern migration is said to be described in a series of pictographs on wood known as Walum Olum. Constantine Samuel Raffinesque, a French scholar and professor of historical studies and natural science at Transylvania University, first published a translation of this record. He received some of these wood tablets from a Dr. Ward, who in turn had received them from a Delaware Indian he had treated. These pictographs relate the history of the New Jersey Indians from their origin until 1600. It describes the long and difficult journey of the Lenape Indians from the cold north country, their spiritual and cultural beliefs, and how they lived. Herbert and John Kraft in their book, *Indians of Lenapehoking*, state that this story cannot be considered either ancient or reliable, and that Walum Olum was never part of the Delaware tribal lore. Although there is some controversy over the date that these pictographs were written and their accuracy, they remain an attempt by some Delaware Indians to relate their history.

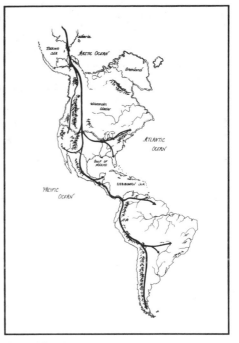

Indian Migration.

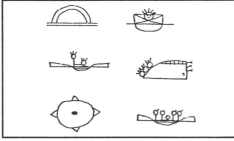

Walum Olam.

Earliest Ocean County Natives

The history of Native Americans in New Jersey dates back to at least 10,000 B.C. From 10,000-5,000 B.C. these people wandered through the east coast relying on nature's bounties to supply their needs. About 1000 B.C. small groups began to settle in the area around the Delaware River. The majority still lived inland and only visited the shore during the summer months. However, each year some remained living in caves in the cliffs of Island Heights, at Indian Hill near today's Hooper Avenue and in the Forked River Mountains.

Lenape Indian Shelter.

These early residents of Ocean County were called Lenape Indians. Roughly translated the name means "Common or Ordinary" people and their land was called "Lenapehoking" or Land of the Lenape. With the arrival of the white man they also became known as Delawares as that was the name used by the English to identify people living along the Delaware River. The name Lenape or Delaware was then extended to include all the Indians living in New Jersey and surrounding areas.

The Delawares were not a tribe in the common usage of the term. They were not a unified group of people with a common language and a common political and social structure. Rather they were more like a collection of small groups, not much larger than an extended family, with each group responsible for its own care. They were a mobile society and moved where food and other supplies could be found.

The Lenape Indians lived in a matrilineal society. In this form of society the inherited power was passed on through the woman's clan. The women would select the men who would exert the actual legislative power and handle relations with other tribes. This increased the respect for women in this society.

The lifestyle of the Lenape began to change sometime about 900 A.D. Farming was added to the traditional hunting, fishing, and gathering as a basis for livelihood. More enduring homes were built and land and resources, although not individually owned, were subject to "use rights." This meant that property belonged to those who occupied it until they no longer wished to use it.

Prior to this period, the Lenape were known as fierce warriors but as they became more settled, it was evident that they preferred to live in peace. Their homes and gardens were rarely fortified and they became more dependent on agriculture. The reason for this change in attitude is the subject of historical debate. Some sources feel that this attitude was forced on the Lenape by the more militant Iroquois who wanted a buffer on their southern border and a mediator in their disputes with other tribes. Robert Hamilton, a contemporary historian better known as Greywolf, in his article in *The New Jersey Ethnic*

Experience, feels that this change in lifestyle was a conscious choice made by Delaware.

With agriculture as the foundation of the economy, the Delaware became more attached to the soil. Principal crops included corn, beans, pumpkins, and squash. The Delaware's diet also included fish, animals, and fowl. This made it necessary for the Indians in the interior to be away from their homes on fishing and hunting expeditions.

Way Of Life At The Shore

Ocean County's first Indians were truly its first "tourists." The women of the tribe planted maize in their plots in the interior before the family traveled to the shore. It would take about a week to reach the shore. They set up temporary wigwams along the banks of the rivers or streams and began gathering oysters, scallops, clams , sea snails, crabs, and fish. The shore offered not only a change in diet but also supplied food for the winter months. While the men gathered the seafood, the women prepared the summer meals, took care of the children, gathered wood to cook the daily food, and smoked and dried seafood for their return home in the fall.

C.A. Weslager in his book, *The Delawares*, stated that Europeans would have found Indian women very shy, modest and desirous of pleasing their men. Of their appearance he stated, "...the young women would have been highly attractive to the white visitor." Women were not slaves of their men but shared with them the responsibilities of survival. Their responsibilities included planting, harvesting, preparing food, care of children, weaving baskets and carrying supplies during a journey. Men were responsible for felling trees, constructing dugouts, trapping animals, fishing, hunting, and protecting the family.

The Delaware female was respected and recognized for her authority in the home and community. Weslager goes on to say that they were often held in greater respect than women in European society. Because of this, he stated that, surprisingly, white women captured in war often chose to remain with their Indian tribe.

The Atlantic coast offered an important commodity: wampum. At first wampum was a necklace made by stringing wooden beads together. It was used to support treaties or agreements or to express friendships. The substitution of shells added to the attractiveness of the wampum

Wampum - Herbert Kraft in his book *Lenape* questions the Lenape role in the making of this product.

and placed an added value to it as a medium of exchange. A number of different types of shells were used. Some were polished and some were made with holes bored by a flint splinter. Black or white shells were used, with black the more valuable. Also used were mussel shells that were black on one side and mother of pearl on the other. These were most prized in wampum form since they were most difficult to use. Shell gathering was an important part of the natives' visits to the shore, a practice continued by most visitors to the shore in years to come.

Indian artifacts discovered in Ocean County give us the most accurate picture of how the Lenape worked and lived. These artifacts were found in mounds of shells as well as in sites along the rivers and

Tuckerton Indian Shell Mounds - Pictured as they stand today.

stream banks. The most famous mounds of shells were located in the sedge grass near Tuckerton. At its peak, 2000 years ago, this mound was estimated to have been over 12 feet high, 100 feet long and 50 feet wide.

The artifacts found along the inland streams tell us of the patterns of settlement in Jackson, Plumsted, Manchester, and Berkeley Townships.   The artifacts found at the shore indicate that tools were formed of bones and shaped stones and that the Native Americans in Ocean County had no knowledge of metals prior to the arrival of the first Europeans. Tools found included stone axes, anchors, sinkers, and hammers. Steatite (soapstone) was used for pendants and gadgets, and as parts of nets. Canoes were made from fallen trees hollowed out by fire and axes. Fragments of pottery, pestles, pots, and ritual objects such as a turkey shaped in stone were discovered in Island Heights. The pottery was made from clay available along the river banks. Homes and meeting houses were made of skins, trees, and the plentiful sedge grass. The discovery of many arrowheads indicates the importance of hunting in the nearby pinelands.

Contacts with Europeans

Early Europeans were more interested in exploring, gathering furs and skins, or in fishing and whaling than in settlement. The first white settlers in Ocean County were squatters, who set up their homes near their work, and were welcomed by the natives.

Unfortunately, the Iroquois nickname for the peaceful Lenape of "women in petticoats" and "honored women", along with the matrilineal structure of society, gave the new settlers a mistaken impression of the Lenape Indians. They were frequently taken advantage of in trade and when Indian demands increased, the white traders used rum to sweeten the bargain. The spectacle of the drunken Indian added to the prejudice that the white man developed toward the Indian.

In the opinion of the early settlers, these natives lacked a language, customs, a culture, or spiritual values. Early settlers were unaware of the Indians' belief in one Great Spirit, whose home was in the heavens, or the "Manittos" (Manitos) who were lesser spirits in nature. Many were pleased by the peacefulness of these natives even though there were stories of a massacre on Mystic Island before their arrival in a struggle between Indian groups. The killing, in 1609, of one of Henry Hudson's crew, John Coleman, by a native arrow, and the attack on a young couple marooned in a shipwreck in 1640, also made the settlers uneasy.

The settlers misinterpreted the Indian views of property ownership and failed to recognize how the white man's trade in tools, liquor, and land was destroying Indian society. The white man also brought disease that threatened the already small Indian population.

Indian Tales

Since only a handful of Indians were residents of Ocean County after the arrival of the white man, the few that lived in the county were the subject of many legends. Most of these stories were not very complimentary. The yarns told here were taken from nineteenth and twentieth century writers.

Many stories are told about Indians in one of the most respected books on Ocean County, *The History of Ocean and Monmouth County,* written by Edwin Salter in 1882. The tales about Indian Will are an example.

Indian Will lived on the Cook Homestead on the banks of the Manasquan River, first in a wigwam and later in a cabin that Thomas Cook helped him build. Will was described as stocky, broad shouldered, wearing a ring in his nose, earrings, and dressed in a cocked hat and long crimson coat.

The story goes that Indian Will found Captain Kidd's treasure on the beach at Manasquan. Not knowing the value of his find, he gave it all to the Eaton family who gave him the red coat and hat and jewelry in exchange for this treasure. Another version of the story is that after finding the treasure he gave the gold to the Longstreet family and kept only the silver.

Another story associated with Indian Will concerns the naming of Will's Hole, a channel of the Manasquan River which separates Gull Island from Point Pleasant Beach. The legend goes that Will asked his wife to cook a muskrat and when she refused to join him in the meal, he believed that she had poisoned the food. He killed her and dropped her body in Will's Hole.

Another legend is about Indian Peter who moved from Toms River to Imlaystown. The story goes that when his wife died, he was so upset he refused to bury her. To preserve the body he placed her in a nearby lake. After a period of time he noticed that the body attracted eels which he promptly sold in town. He had a good business until the citizens discovered the source of the eels.

These stories of Indians reflect the lack of sensitivity of many past writers and show a stereotype of Indians that is unacceptable today.

Will's Hole today.

Indian Lands

Early settlers in Ocean County, as well as the rest of New Jersey, took great pride in the claim that they didn't seize Indian lands. In 1685 the proprietors purchased the property from Manasquan to Little Egg Harbor from the Indians even though few settlers arrived before 1700. Land purchased from the Indians was usually gained in barter for tools, trinkets, clothing, and other goods. The Indians, however, failed to understand the real meaning of land sale and felt that they were only granting "use rights of the land to the white man." As a result, they returned to their land again and again to the dismay of the white man. In an interview reported in *Down Barnegat Bay*, written by Robert Jahn, an old time resident told of a hanging of six Indians in the 1850's in Ocean County because they refused to move away.

The lack of understanding on the part of Indian and settler alike over property ownership and hunting rights and problems arising from the native use of alcohol led the Governor of New Jersey to call two conferences in neighboring Burlington County. In 1758 these conferences, "designed to protect the Indians", the Indians agreed to abandon claims to the land between the Metedeconk and Toms River. In return they received 1000 pounds in English currency and the creation of the first Indian Reservation in the United States. This 3284 acre site was called Brotherton, and was located in Burlington County near today's town of Indian Mills.

There were only about 350 Indians left in New Jersey when the reservation was first established. Its first superintendent was the Reverend John Brainerd, and the Reservation land included a saw mill,

a cedar swamp, and hunting grounds. In addition to purchasing the land, the government helped build a grist mill, a blacksmith shop, a school, and a house of worship.

Site of Brotherton Indian Reservation today. - First home built on reservation land after the Indians left for New York.

Money was a problem from the beginning. By 1796, Brotherton was so destitute that it had to lease some of its land to raise money. There were never more than a few hundred Indians on the reservation. By 1801 these last remaining reservation Indians joined the Mohicans near Lake Oneida in New York State. As a part of President Jackson's "Removal Policy", these Indians were again moved west of the Mississippi, and in 1832 most joined the Mohicans in their move to Green Bay, Wisconsin. Later most moved again into the Indian Territory in Oklahoma. The 1890 census reported that only 84 Indians remained in New Jersey.

Indians Today

The departure of the Indians from Brotherton did not end the Indian story in New Jersey. Many of the individuals and families who remained were absorbed into the white or black society. A group living in Monmouth County met regularly until 1953 to preserve their culture. Many Indian organizations are still active nationally: The American Indian Movement (AIM), The National Congress of American Indians, United Native Americans, American Historical Society, and the First American Caucus of New Jersey. Of the 615 Indians remaining in Ocean County (1990 census), only a few take part in Indian affairs. The national revival of interest in Indian affairs is just beginning to be felt in Ocean County. With this revival will come more knowledge of the history of Ocean County's first immigrants.

CHAPTER III

Early Settlers And Explorers

Captain Cornelius Hendricks (Explorer)

Captain Cornelius Hendricks was the son of one of the first five Dutch captains sent to the New World by the Dutch West India Company to follow up the Henry Hudson expedition of 1609. His purpose was to map the coastal region of New Jersey and to investigate the possibility of establishing trading posts in the area.

He charted Barnegat Bay, the Metedeconk River, and Little Egg Harbor, as well as other rivers along the coast. He sailed up the streams and deep into the pine and oak forests. His report to the Lords' Estates General of Holland stated that he "traded with the inhabitants; said trade consisting of sables, furs, robes and other skins." His report also observed that he found "the country full of trees; to wit: oak, hickory, and pines...bucks and does, turkeys, partridges." He judged the climate to be "as temperate as that of this country Holland."

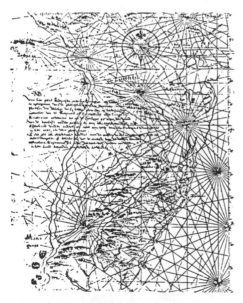

Cornelius Hendrick's Map.
Ocean County Cultural Heritage Commission

One of the most important recent contributions to Ocean County history can be credited to Pauline Miller and Dr. Susan Halsey. In 1988, Dr. Halsey, a coastal geologist and Pine Beach resident, following a lead from Mrs. Miller, found the map that Hendricks had drawn in 1616 in a museum in The Hague, Netherlands. This map demonstrated that he did survey the coastal region, back bays and streams of Ocean County. It confirmed the claim that this Dutch Captain was the first European in the post Columbus era, to set foot on what is today Ocean County.

This recent discovery also demonstrates that much of Ocean County history is still to be uncovered.

Unlike the South and New England, many of the early settlers of what was to become Ocean County were second and third generation Americans. These people were seeking to escape religious, economic, and political problems in the more established colonies rather than problems in Europe. It is important to understand these first residents, not only to gain a wider knowledge of the history of Ocean County, but also to gain a better view of our national background.

Explorers

Although Christopher Columbus spent most of his four voyages to the New World looking for a passageway to the Far East, his trips did publicize the existence of a vast land across the Atlantic. Immediately after his trips, both Spain and Portugal established settlements in Latin America. John Cabot sailed the North Atlantic coast for England, and in 1497, his son Sebastian Cabot took a more southerly route. He was probably the first post-Columbian European to view New Jersey. The voyage of the two Cabots served as the basis for the British claim to North America.

A firmer claim to the title, "First Explorer of New Jersey," belongs to Giovanni Verrazano. He sailed for the French as the pilot of the ship, *Dauphin*. He reported to the French King, Francis I, about his entrance into New York Bay in 1524. The French, however, who for many years prior to Verrazano had fished off the Grand Banks, concentrated their

Half Moon.

exploration in that area and penetrated the interior via the St. Lawrence and Great Lakes.

In 1609, Henry Hudson sailed on the *Half Moon* from Delaware Bay, along the coast of New Jersey, to the river that bears his name. Robert Juet, his first mate, gave a glowing description of land that may now be part of Ocean County. This report led the Dutch Estates General in 1614 to pass an ordinance authorizing the exploration and settlement of these new lands. As a result, the Dutch West Indian Company was formed and Dutch captains, including Cornelius Hendricks, were sent to establish trading posts and to map the area. Nine years later, Cornelius Mey brought a shipload of settlers to South Jersey. The expeditions of the Dutch captains formed the basis for Dutch claims to parts of Connecticut, New York, Pennsylvania, Delaware and New Jersey.

Finns and Swedes, as well as the Dutch, laid claim and were rivals for control of Delaware and New Jersey. In 1655 Swedish royal influence ended with the Dutch winning control of the forts along the Delaware. Less than nine years later, the Duke of York received title to the Dutch land from his brother, Charles II. A fleet was sent by the British to take control of the area under the leadership of Governor Richard Nicolls. Without a shot being fired, he gained the surrender of New York (New Amsterdam) and New Jersey from the Dutch Governor, Peter Stuyvesant.

The British were very generous in their surrender terms, granting the Dutch settlers all the religious freedom, property rights, and trade privileges that they had enjoyed under Dutch rule. The Duke of York then gave the land between the Delaware and Hudson River to two friends, Lord John Berkeley and Sir George Carteret. The Duke named the area New Jersey after the Isle of Jersey, Sir George's birthplace and site of one of his military achievements.

Early Settlements

Prior to the establishment of British control in New Jersey, there were very few permanent settlements. Most of these were in or around trading posts or forts along the Hudson and Delaware Rivers. The first communities in New Jersey were Bergen and Hoboken. Prior to the 1700's, most of the people of Ocean County were seasonal squatters using the land as a base for carrying out their work. As the Indians before them, many lived in dugouts or caves in the Forked River Mountains and the hills east of Hooper Avenue.

Forked River Mountains

Are there really "mountains" in Ocean County? Approximately three miles west of Forked River, several distinct peaks can be noticed rising above the flat pinelands. At one time, these hills were recorded at 211 feet above sea level. This figure was changed somewhat during World War II when the area was used for a military proving ground.

During the War, the U.S. Signal Corps used the area for communications and, later, scientists from Princeton University used it for military research. The area was off limits to local residents and explosions were heard emanating from the mountains. After the War, evidence was found in the form of concrete bunkers and small buildings which, evidently, had housed explosives.

Wartime occupation also eliminated most of the Indian mounds that had been in the area. The Indians has used dried clams, oysters and mussels for food as well as for flavoring in lieu of salt. The shells were also used for wampum and for fertilizer for farming. They were probably kept in piles and covered with dirt for convenience, as well as for sanitary reasons. The only remaining evidence of mounds now exist in Tuckerton on Great Bay Boulevard.

Those who did settle in the area preferred to live on the mainland and were mainly fisherman, whalers, subsistence farmers, and those making a living from lumber. Some also raised cattle in the meadows along the shore. Travel was done mostly by boat and homes were built of wood covered by sod, dirt, salt hay, or shingles. Some of the earliest settlements were in the Tuckerton and Manahawkin area and along present day Route 9.

One of the earliest grants in New Jersey was the Monmouth Patent. Richard Stout settled the area around Middletown in 1648. At the time only six families lived in the settlement, and they withdrew in a short time to New York because of an Indian threat.

Stout and his new wife, Penelope Van Princis, returned to New Jersey in 1668 armed with the Monmouth Patent. This land grant was dependent on the attraction to the area of 100 families in three years. It also guaranteed "free liberty of conscience without any molestation or disturbance whatsoever in the way of worship." In 1673 Monmouth County was officially named. The northern section of the county became Middletown, the area south to Little Egg Harbor was called Shrewsbury, and the interior of Monmouth County was called Freehold. All of what is now Ocean County was then in Shrewsbury Township. Stafford Township separated from the southern part of Shrewsbury in 1749. The creation of Stafford by Charles II become the first official document relating exclusively to the area that was to become Ocean County. This document is now located in the County Clerk's office.

Penelope Van Princis

Newly married Penelope Van Princis, and her husband, while sailing to New Amsterdam (New York), were shipwrecked near Sandy Hook. Most of the other shipwrecked victims were able to make it to New Amsterdam but Penelope remained with her husband in New Jersey as he was too weak to travel. Not long afterward they were attacked by Indians and her husband was killed. Left for dead by the Indians, she survived by hiding in the hollow of a tree until she was rescued by friendly Indians and nursed back to health.

Word reached the settlers in New Amsterdam that a white woman was living among the Indians and an expedition was sent to Middletown, where she was held, to trade "beads, scissors, cloth and bracelets," for her release. Finally reaching New Amsterdam, she met and married Richard Stout, and returned with him with the Monmouth Patent. Penelope lived a long life, 110 years, and boasted at the time of her death that the couple had 502 descendants.

Settlers

Humpback Whale - The tendency of the 45 ft. Humpback Whale to cluster around islands and hug shorelines has made it one of the easiest whales to hunt. About 1,000 now range the northwest Atlantic.

The earliest settlers of Ocean County probably were fishermen who landed to cure their fish and to obtain oil from whales. In 1623, a Dutch navigator for the Dutch West Indian Company, David DeVries, spotted whales off the coast of Ocean County. A whaler, Aaron Inman, was the first to claim land on Long Beach Island in 1690. Inman and his family were later joined by other whalers at a place called "Harvey's Whaling Quarters", in the area known today as Harvey Cedars. Whalers operated mainly off Island Beach and Long Beach Island where whales were found closer to the shore than in New England. They might average two whales during the whaling season

(February and March). The increasing demand for whale oil led to an increase of whaling, which caused the supply of whales to diminish off New Jersey by the turn of the eighteenth century.

The first settlers reached the mainland of Old Shrewsbury Township during the period between 1660 and 1730. Many came from New England and Long Island to escape taxes and restrictive practices in their former settlements. The tax rolls of Long Island reveal many names of old families of Ocean County such as: Hulse, Havens, Salmon, Tilton, Johnson, Bailey, Horner, Osborn, Townsend, Woolley, Cox, Platt, Falkinburg, Lippincott, Hazelton, Cramer, Grover, and Cook. These are but a few of the many early native families that helped to build this area.

Described by Leah Blackman in her book, *History of Little Egg Harbor*, the area, at that time, was vastly different than it is today. It was heavily wooded with thousands of stately pines interspersed with giant oaks. In the lowlands cedar, sweetgum, and maple trees abounded. The forests were home to the bear, panther, wolf, deer, fox, wild cats, and other smaller woodland creatures. Eagles built their eyries in the tall  pines and turkey, quail, pheasant, and grouse made nests among the dead leaves on the forest floor. The salt marshes and local waters were stocked with a variety of fish and shellfish as well as with duck and other water fowl.

Families needed to be self-sufficient as there were no stores, no grist or sawmills and no roads except for Indian paths. Men hunted and fished for food but also needed to be proficient in carpentry, blacksmithing, coopering, and tanning. They grew their own vegetables as well as corn and rye for grains. Women, besides cooking and baking, helped on the farms, spun wool and flax, dyed the yarn, wove it into cloth and made all the family's clothing and bedding. Little time was left for activities not directly related to home and family.

Slavery

Slavery existed in Old Monmouth County from its early days. Dutch settlers brought slaves with them when they came to the county from Long Island. As early as the 1660's, Monmouth attracted younger sons of Barbadian planters who owned larger numbers of slaves. However, since most of the farms in the county were small, only a few slaves were needed, with an average of 1.6 slaves per estate.

During the latter part of the seventeenth century, most slaves were brought from the West Indies in small groups, sometimes only one or two at a time. They experienced vastly different travel arrangements than the slaves who arrived later on large slave ships. Ships bringing one or two blacks used them as members of the crew. As a result, they not only learned seamanship but also developed a special relationship with the white sailors.

During the early part of the eighteenth century, slave ships began arriving from Africa with 100 or more blacks on each ship, landing in New York and in Perth Amboy. Many of these slaves were undoubtedly purchased by farmers in Old Monmouth County. The colonial census in 1745 reported that in eastern New Jersey there were 513 male and 386 female slaves, which, at the time, was about 10% of the total population.

Since most of the slave holdings were small, slaves had many demands made of them. The range of their talents is best described in Graham Hodges, *African-Americans in Monmouth County During the Age of the American Revolution,* "Men understood all kinds of husbandry, and were skilled as blacksmiths, coopers, carpenters, farriers, or could work on privateering or fishing boats." A woman, advertised for sale in 1734, does "all sorts of housework, she can brew, bake, boyle soft soap, wash, iron, and starch...she can card and spin...she neither drinks rum nor smokes tobacco."

New Jersey had some of the most repressive laws enforcing slavery in the east. Blacks were forbidden to own property and special courts for blacks were in effect until after the Revolution. Any owner who wished to manumit (free) his slave had to post a bond of 200 pounds. This all but ended voluntary emancipation. It also ensured that any blacks who were freed had a difficult time supporting themselves. By 1770, only about forty of the over 900 African-Americans were free blacks.

Unable to gain freedom in other ways, slaves often attempted to run away to New England or to New York where they worked on the wharves or as privateers. Later, many joined the British forces during the Revolution since the British promised freedom to any slave joining their forces. Ironically, these blacks, to obtain their freedom, were forced to fight against the Patriots who, in turn, were fighting for their freedom from the British.

Pirates

Some of Ocean County's earliest visitors profited from illegal activities. At the end of the 17th century, some of the most famous pirates in American history practiced their profession off our shore. Reports of pirate crews being seen in Ocean County were common. Captain William Kidd was one of the most famous. He was commissioned by England to fight the pirates, but soon after capturing a pirate ship, which he renamed the *San Antonio,* he become a pirate captain himself. He was rumored to have courted a girl from Barnegat.

Treasure hunters have looked for Captain Kidd's hidden treasure chests from Manasquan to Cape May. Richard Harding Davis, a well-known author and summer visitor to Point Pleasant Beach in the 1890's, in *Buried Treasure,* wrote about a treasure hunt in the Point

Pleasant area. The clarity of the description made some feel it was autobiographical. Many local residents claim that Robert Louis Stevenson, who summered along the Manasquan River, used the stories of this hidden treasure and Osborn Island in the Manasquan River, as a model for his novel, *Treasure Island.* But in fact, it was the other way around. According to a friend of the author, Stevenson indirectly named the island by carving the name "Treasure Island" on a bulkhead on the island after he had written his book. According to another legend, Money Island, in the Toms River, is another possible site of Captain Kidd's buried treasure. Rumors persisted and in 1954, newspapers carried the story that "no pirate treasure was uncovered in the excavation for the Garden State Parkway." Some still believe that pirate gold is just waiting to be discovered in Ocean County.

Robert Teach, better known as Blackbeard, was said to have sailed into Barnegat Bay when escaping from the British. Richard Worley, a pirate, terrorized shipping off the New Jersey shore for six weeks in 1712. Other equally ruthless pirates raided the shipping lanes off the mid-Atlantic coast. Many of the pirates were protected by local citizens and bribed public officials who helped piracy reach large proportions. As a result, in 1690 Britain made piracy a capital offense. Captain Kidd was captured and hanged in 1701, while Blackbeard and Worley, along with 50 others, were killed in the Charleston area. Many also sought amnesty, bringing to an end this form of piracy off the New Jersey shore.

Smugglers

Some of the earliest settlers of the interior of Ocean County were known as Swamp Angels or Swamp Men. They were a hardy bunch of traders, seafarers, and trappers. Many had come from New England and Long Island to take advantage of the natural environment in Ocean County. The county's remoteness from custom officials, its rivers that enabled small crafts to carry goods inland, and its established well-traveled trails gave smugglers obvious natural advantages. Smuggling was generally accepted by the British in the 13th century when they engaged in illegal wool trade with the continent. However, the British felt differently about the practice 400 years later when the colonists used smuggling to avoid British taxes.

In the 1600's, the British passed Navigation laws to force colonies to trade with the mother country. The early attempts to enforce these measures were not very successful and Ocean County became a smuggler's paradise.

Religious Toleration

Although most early settlers came to the New Jersey shore for economic reasons, some came to enjoy the religious freedom that was not offered in other colonies. The Monmouth Patent in 1648 was the first to guarantee broad religious freedom. Rhode Island's charter excluded Catholics from its provisions for religious freedom, Maryland's Toleration Act extended only to those who believed in Jesus, and William Penn did not begin his Holy Experiment until the 1680's.

The northern part of Monmouth County was populated mainly by Puritans while Barnegat and Little Egg Harbor contained many Quakers. Although

Tuckerton Meeting House. Rebuilt on the site of the 1704 Meeting House on Rt. 9

most were Quakers, missionaries of other faiths were welcome. From 1702-1740 Thomas Thomason was one of the missionaries from the Church of England to travel to this area. After traveling often from Barnegat to Manasquan, he spoke of the settlers as "obstinate and lacking in religious discipline."

In the early 1700's, the Quakers and other religious groups met in individual homes or designated meeting houses. Many of the early white settlers were suspicious of group worship since they had come to Ocean County to escape harsh narrow teachings. The Quakers, in particular, were the subject of abuse in their former homes. Edward Wharton was given 20 lashes for his Quaker beliefs in Boston, and William Reape was arrested for being a Quaker in both Rhode Island and Long Island. Both became recruiters for settlement in the area that was to become Ocean County.

The establishment of churches was also delayed because of the sparse population. The distance between population centers made it difficult for regular visits of preachers. Few formal churches were established until the middle of the 18th Century. The first organized church was a Quaker Meeting in Tuckerton in 1704 with a meeting house built in 1709. The Rogerine Baptists, a group that did not believe in medicine, the sanctity of the Sabbath, a marriage ceremony, or in oral prayers, established a church for four years in Waretown in 1737.

During most of the eighteenth century, the Quakers or Friends were the predominant religious group in the Tuckerton-Little Egg region. The land of the Friends Meeting House and burying ground was deeded to them by Edward Andrews in 1708 and the Meeting House, built in 1709, served a community as well as a religious purpose. Since there were no taverns or public buildings at that time, the Friends' meeting house was also used for public meetings. The building was a plain, one-story structure with a hipped roof and covered in cedar shingles. There were only four windows in the building since glass was precious and had to be imported from England. Seats were long benches with two rows of slats for backs. A small structure o.1 the west end of the building was for the use of women.

Every year, Friends came from distant areas for a yearly meeting. Leah Blackman, in a *History of Little Egg Harbor Township,* describes the yearly meeting as having a social as well as a religious side. Families could meet and, often, marriages were arranged.

1850   1950

OLD POTTER CHURCH
Built by Thomas Potter in 1760 for the preaching of the Gospel of Universal Salvation. In 1770 the Rev John Murray came ashore for help for the stranded Brig 'Hand-in-Hand' at Potter's request he preached in this Meeting House the first Universalist sermon in America. Annual Methodist pilgrimage here each July.

Ocean County Board of Chosen Freeholders

Old Potter Church Sign.

Young people went courting at beach parties on Tucker's Beach, often to the dismay of their parents.

Potter Church.

Because of the sparse population, the practice of building Free Churches came into being. This meant that the building was open to the use of many different faiths and, often also used as a school. One of the first of these churches open to all was built in 1758 in Manahawkin, closely followed by the one built by Thomas Potter, in Lanoka Harbor. He had visions of a church where all could worship. A stranded sailor, John Murray, from the ship *Hand in Hand,* became its preacher and he established the first Universal Church in America.

These churches and others provided for shared pulpits, although not without problems. Preachers often argued over the order of their services and the taking of collections. Gustave Kobbe, in 1888, wrote that "itinerant ministers would of a Sunday morning come to blows for the right to hold service and the accompanying privilege to take up a collection." The religious diversity evident in the county, and this early practice of differing religious groups using the same building, were part of Ocean County's contribution to the establishment of religious freedom in the colonies.

The early settlers of Ocean County were few in number, and came for a variety of reasons. Most chose to settle in the area to make a living from its natural resources. The sea, lands, and forests offered the settlers a greater degree of economic self-sufficiency than practiced in the more

Old Quaker Meeting House, Manasquan N.J. Orignimal Meeting House built in 1701. House shown here was built in 1884.

developed colonies. Many came to be free of restrictive measures in Europe and in the colonies. The region's remoteness, and the scattered rural population, permitted the newcomer to follow his own beliefs. Many of these practices were to be challenged as the county matured.

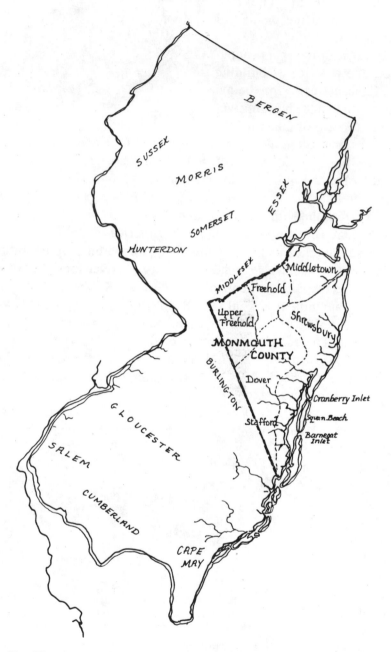

Map of New Jersey 1775.

CHAPTER IV

Patriots or Loyalists

Joshua Huddy (Patriot)

The most famous "patriot hero" of the Revolutionary War in Ocean County was Joshua Huddy. His defense of the Toms River blockhouse was one of the many skirmishes that took place between those supporting the British and those fighting for independence. Huddy's story clearly raises the question about the war in Ocean County: Was it a revolution or a civil war?

In 1792 William Franklin, illegitimate son of Benjamin Franklin and former Royal Governor of New Jersey, working with those loyal to England, ordered an attack on "a nest of pirates" in Toms River. He sent the ship Arrogant *with a force of eighty British and forty colonists loyal to England. Defending this famous privateer center were Joshua Huddy and his men. In the battle, on March 24, the blockhouse, twelve houses, a tavern, two sawmills and a salt warehouse were destroyed. When those in the blockhouse were asked to surrender, Huddy answered, "Come and take it." Nine men were killed, twelve were wounded and Huddy was captured.*

Huddy was taken to New York and less than a month later, he was transported to Atlantic Highlands and executed. His execution was considered to be revenge for the killing of two Loyalists in which Huddy had been implicated. Loyalists felt that Huddy's execution was giving the Patriots a "taste of their own medicine." They felt that Loyalists captured by the Patriots were treated as criminals while Patriots captured by the British were treated as prisoners of war.

The manner of Huddy's death stirred up the Patriots. They demanded that those responsible be punished. Captain Lippincott, who directed the execution of Huddy, was found innocent of any wrongdoing by a British court martial. He claimed he was acting under orders. General Washington, meeting with his officers at West Point, decided to retaliate by selecting a British prisoner of war of similar rank. If the British refused to punish those responsible for Huddy's death, that officer would be put to death. The officer selected was Captain Charles Asgill. The British refused to take any action. However, Asgill was released because of appeals from his family and from our ally, the French government. Huddy was honored by both President Washington and, later, by Congress. In 1837 a Congres-

sional report stated, "Over fifty years later, those of much less merit have been made the theme of biographies and poems. His country, it would seem, has outlived the recollection that such a victim was sacrificed for American Liberty."

Huddy's story suggests an alternate way of looking at the war. A revolution is a struggle of citizens to overthrow the existing authority. The Revolutionary War was more than that. It was also a civil war. It included a clear division among the people of the country as to how they were to be governed.

Huddy Park today, site of the Toms River Blockhouse.

Causes Of The Revolution

The colony of New Jersey suffered more than any other area during the war with over 238 engagements fought on its land. This number included major battles between the British and Colonial forces as well as fighting between Loyalists (those loyal to the King), and Patriots (those fighting for independence). Although most of the people of the colony rejected British policies, they were sharply divided on the question of independence. In New Jersey there was more loyalist sympathy than in any colony except New York.

The Revolutionary War had its origin in the change in British policy following the French and Indian War in 1763. This war resulted in the end of French control on the North American continent enabling the British to enforce many earlier laws restricting trade. The British also felt that the cost of administering and protecting the colonies should be shared by the colonists. The British felt that Parliament represented Englishmen everywhere. The colonists, on the other hand, felt they should be directly represented and they cried, "Taxation without representation."

The British also limited the colonists' rights to print their own money, creating a shortage of cash that led to bankruptcies and foreclosures. In major ports, the British enforced the Navigation Acts, passed a century earlier, which restricted colonial trade to benefit the British Empire. Goods which the Crown considered important to the empire, such as tobacco and sugar, could only be traded to England or to other English colonies. Goods not considered important, such as corn, could be traded to anyone. These laws restricted colonial trade and upset the people of New Jersey.

Protest Meeting.

Meetings of colonists were held throughout the state to protest British legislation. Most of these gatherings condemned the actions, but, at the same time, continued to express loyalty to the King. In "Old Monmouth County" citizens gathered to denounce the obnoxious acts of the British and to begin a movement toward independence. Monmouth County, at that time, was composed of three sections: Middletown, Freehold and Old Shrewsbury. Although Middletown and Freehold became centers of Patriot agitation, most of Old Shrewsbury was slow to support this effort. They sent petitions urging the Provincial Congress to remain neutral. One of the reasons for this position was the large number of Quaker residents in the area, who were noted for their opposition to violence. Another voice speaking out against independence was the royal governor of New Jersey, William Franklin. He continually spoke against the secessionist views of many in the Provincial Congress. John Witherspoon, the President of the College of New Jersey and Chairman of the Committee of Correspondence of New

Jersey, held a caucus of its thirty-six members to urge independence. Only three joined him in support.

Although many residents of Old Shrewsbury did not push for independence, they did effectively protest British taxes and trade restrictions through smuggling. This practice, described in Chapter III, not only was a very profitable business for the residents, but it also enabled the county to defy the laws which they felt were unjust. At the same time, they were not cutting their ties with the mother country. This area, although slow to support independence, through the practice of smuggling, was actually the forerunner of active rebellion.

The Outbreak Of War

As economic problems grew and British restriction of colonial rights increased, sympathy for independence grew. New England, which led the colonies in protests and boycotts, felt the brunt of British enforcement measures and experienced the first outbreak of fighting. The British brought Hessians, German mercenaries, to help enforce their laws and to stop the move toward independence. Instead, as stated by Tom Fleming, an authority on New Jersey and the Revolution, the sending of this Hessian force did more to promote the Revolution than Thomas Paine's book, *Common Sense* .

The spread of fighting to the Middle Colonies increased the pressure on New Jersey to make a decision. Early victories by the British in New York, and the subsequent retreat of Washington's army across New Jersey, led to a weakening of Patriot support. Washington's successful attack on Trenton on Christmas and his later victory at Princeton, reversed this trend and led to New Jersey's commitment to

American Rifle (also called Kentucky Rifle or Pennsylvania Rifle).

independence. In 1776, Governor Franklin was forcefully removed as the last royal governor. William Livingston, who had commanded the New Jersey militia, was appointed governor by the legislature. Franklin was arrested, forcefully detained by the colonists, and eventually handed over to the British in exchange for the Governor of Delaware.

During most of the war the British Army had more fighting men in New Jersey than in any other colony. It maintained its headquarters in New York City and Sandy Hook became a center of the Loyalist forces. When William Franklin moved to New York, he became president of The Board of Associated Loyalists which had been formed by the king to organize Loyalist forces. Earlier, in 1777, New Jersey Governor Livingston supported the creation of the Council of Safety to fight against those loyal to the British. Monmouth County went even further when the County Association for Retaliation was formed by 436 residents to punish and execute Loyalists. "Old Monmouth County" then truly became the site of a civil war.

Privateers

When New Jersey made its commitment to independence, Shrewsbury Township was ready. Encouraged by profits, private investors, and by the Continental Congress, many made the easy transition from smuggler to privateer. These privateers were granted Titles of Marque by Governor Livingston and by the Continental Congress to act as legalized pirates. They were given the power to raid British shipping and to sell at auction the captured ships and their contents. The profits were divided among the investors and the privateers.

Many prominent colonists sponsored privateers. Robert Morris, Treasurer of Congress, made a fortune on his investments, earning between $300,000 and $400,000. Joseph Bull, the owner of Batsto and Silas Deane, the first American Representative to the French Court, as well as many Congressmen, were heavy investors. Perhaps the most famous sponsor was Ben Franklin who used his profits to ransom American captives held by the British.

Toms River and Tuckerton became major harbors for captive ships. At one time Tuckerton harbor contained over thirty armed ships. Toms River, with the narrow Cranberry Inlet, was used mainly by whaleboats and smaller privateers. These men of the sea not only disrupted British shipping but were responsible for the capture of needed supplies and manpower. Privateering alone was responsible for the capture of 1600 men and over 1200 enemy ships. Over seventy-seven naval battles took place off "Old Monmouth County's" shores.

Privateers not only raided British shipping but Loyalists' as well. Many Loyalists, seeking profit, smuggled food and supplies to New York. Patriot patrols continually seized the cargoes of these ships causing British and Loyalist forces to lose supplies that they sorely needed.

Cranberry Inlet.

The Battle Of Monmouth

One of the most important land battles of the war was fought at Monmouth County Court House, now Freehold, in 1778. Even though troops from Ocean County played only a minor role in the fighting, the battle belongs in a history of the county because of its importance in the Revolution and the fact that Ocean County was, at that time, part of Monmouth County.

The British, after occupying Philadelphia, were forced to return to New York when France entered the war on the Patriots' side. Fearing a French blockade, the British, under the command of Sir Henry Clinton, decided to cross New Jersey to return to New York. After a severe winter at Valley Forge, Washington felt that he should attack General Clinton's retreating forces. Many of Washington's officers, including General Charles Lee, Washington's second in command, opposed any attack feeling that the colonial forces were not ready.

Monmouth Battlefield, Freehold.

General Charles Lee

Lee is one of the enigmas of the Revolution. This general resigned his position as a British officer to join the newly formed Continental forces. After serving with distinction early in the war, he was captured under questionable circumstances. In fact, Henry Beck in his book, *The Jersey Midlands*, quotes a contemporary newspaper article, "A tryst with an attractive widow in a Basking Ridge tavern is blamed for the downfall of Continental Army's General Charles

General Charles Lee.

Lee." Washington, although troubled by the circumstances of Lee's capture, worked for his release. While a prisoner of General Howe, Lee became convinced that the British would defeat the American forces and he proposed a plan to protect the army by withdrawing it to the West. Upon his release, and despite his belief, Lee was made the American Commander at the Battle of Monmouth, one of the turning points of the war.

Washington decided to attack and appointed Lee to command the attacking forces.

The Jersey Brigade, was ordered to Mount Holly to destroy bridges and cut down trees to delay the British column. Monmouth County troops were held in reserve. Lee's plan was to send General Anthony Wayne to attack the rear of the British forces while he pulled his troops to the right flank where he felt he had the advantage. Washington, viewing this move as a retreat, ordered Lee to attack. Lee ignored the request to take offensive action, and ordered the retreat of his troops to the right. Washington was furious. General Lafayette, a French general fighting with the Patriots, said that it was the only time he heard Washington swear. Washington rallied the troops, but it was too late to gain the advantage that day. That evening the British forces escaped to Sandy Hook and Washington lost the chance to deliver a decisive blow which might have ended the war three years before Lord Cornwalis' surrender at Yorktown.

Lee was blamed by Washington for the failure. Lee demanded an apology for the way he was treated on the battlefield. Washington called a court martial which condemned Lee and removed him from any command. Lee died in 1782 in Philadelphia, a broken and poverty-stricken man.

Molly Pitcher

The Battle of Monmouth was fought on Sunday, June 28th, 1778, which was said to be the hottest day that New Jersey ever experienced. Mary Hayes, the wife of John Hayes, an American private, was carrying water to the troops. Rushing back and forth to a nearby spring she was nicknamed "Molly Pitcher." While on the battlefield she witnessed her husband fall wounded and she rushed to his side. Hearing a call to remove the artillery piece from the line because there wasn't anyone to replace him, she took his place and helped to load the gun during the remainder of the battle. Washington recognized her heroic action, expressing a generous thanks for her service.

British Raids

Old Monmouth County, prior to the Battle of Monmouth, was considered neutral ground by both Loyalist and British forces. Later, the British seized control of the Raritan River, making raids both north and south possible. The British attacked the northern part of the county looking for grain and stock, and the southern part looking for salt works and privateering centers.

The extensive coastline of Old Shrewsbury left it open to attack. Many important raids occurred in 1778. In that year, the British successfully destroyed a privateering base at Chestnut Hill, just south of Ocean County and attempted to seize Tuckerton. The attack on Tuckerton was halted by a force of 300 men under the command of Count Pulaski. British raids continued well after the Battle of Yorktown with the emphasis shifting from fighting battles involving mainly British forces to fighting between British Loyalists and Patriots. Much of the fighting was centered in Ocean County.

Pine Robbers

Following the Battle of Monmouth, the stage for battles between British and Continental forces shifted to the South. The last major battle of the war was fought in 1781 at Yorktown, Virginia. However, this battle did not end the fighting. Negotiations for peace dragged on. During this period, in Shrewsbury Township, civil war replaced direct clashes between British and Continental forces. The Pine Robbers of the area played a major role in this conflict.

Throughout history, forests have been a refuge for criminals and those seeking asylum. The Pine Robbers in Shrewsbury were no exception. They ranged from dedicated Loyalists to criminals using the Loyalist label to gain respectability. Anthony and Lewis Woodward were examples of true Loyalists who became known as Pine Robbers. They were Quakers, threatened with the seizure of their land because of their loyalty to the British. They captured wagons, arms, provisions, and were among the first Pine Robbers to seek refuge in the Pinelands.

William Gilbertson, another Pine Robber, resigned his commission in the Continental Army when Congress issued the Declaration of Independence. He became the symbol of the many Loyalists who had to make a choice when faced with the question of liberty or loyalty. He was referred to by many in the Little Egg Harbor area as a Robin Hood.

Not all Pine Robbers were men of true conviction. Many were brutal criminals who attacked Loyalists and Patriots alike. Jacob and

Lewis Fagan and their accomplices were typical of this type of Pine Robber. They were young, violent, and of ambiguous allegiance to any cause. One of their most famous raids was the attack on the home of Captain Dennis, a patriot leader. Dennis's wife was able to successfully hide the children, but she herself was threatened by the invaders. Eventually, a fellow by the name of Smith, who had infiltrated the gang, helped arrange an ambush of the Fagans. David Fowler's doctoral thesis on the Pine Robbers illustrates the reaction of Patriots to this type of insurgency.

"When Patriots learned that the infamous robber had been slain and buried...They assembled, disinterred the remains, after heaping indignities upon it, enveloped it in tarred cloth and suspended it in chains, with iron bands around it, from a large chestnut tree about a mile from the court house, on the road to Colts Neck. There hung the corpse in mid-air, rocked to and fro by the winds, a horrible warning to his followers and a terror to travelers until the birds of prey picked the flesh from the bones and the skeleton fell piecemeal to the ground."

Another Pine Robber who became famous because of his brutality and his wide range of activities was Captain John Bacon. His gang raided from Middletown to Long Beach Island. Coming from the Manahawkin area, he was engaged early in the war in smuggling goods to the British in New York. Once he was stopped by Captain Joshua Stutson who patrolled the Cranberry Inlet for such smugglers. Stutson was shot and killed by Bacon.

Perhaps Bacon's most famous exploit occurred on October 25, 1782, when he was responsible for what is known as The Long Beach Massacre. Captain Andrew Steelman and his twenty-five crewmen on the *Alligator*, captured a British ship that had run aground off Barnegat. His men worked the entire day to unload the cargo on Long Beach Island and, at night, settled down among the dunes. That evening Bacon and his forces attacked, killing Steelman and most of his men. Only five managed to escape. Such butchery, coming as it did when the war was almost over, intensified public hatred of these so called Loyalists. Governor Livingston placed a reward for Bacon's capture. An attempt to apprehend him at Cedar Bridge failed. He was finally located by a posse at the tavern between West Creek and Tuckerton where he was shot and killed.

Titus Corlies/Colonel Tye

With the British offer of freedom to all slaves and indentured servants who joined their ranks, slaveholders attempted to keep their slaves at home by passing restrictive laws forbidding blacks to meet at night or to carry any weapons. However, these laws encouraged, rather than diminished, the slaves desire for freedom and many escaped behind British lines. One of these was Titus Corlies, born a slave on the estate of Quaker John Corlies in Shrewsbury. In November, 1775, Titus fled to Virginia to join Lord Dunsmore's Ethiopian Regiment.

Titus become known as Colonel Tye and in 1776 he returned to New Jersey as a member of the Black Brigade. His first action was at the Battle of Monmouth where, it was reported, he captured Elisha Shepard, a captain of the Monmouth Militia. For the next two years, Tye was part of the group of black and white Loyalists who conducted raids on the Patriots in Shrewsbury. According to Graham Hodges, Tye and his men would surprise Patriots in their homes, kidnap soldiers, carry off valuables and secure cattle and food badly needed by the British troops in Staten Island and New York. His forces became increasingly effective in raiding and destroying Patriot property and forces.

Tye's most famous feat, however, was his capture of Captain Joshua Huddy. Huddy was a prime target because of his raids on Loyalists positions on Staten Island and his part in the capture and execution of captured Loyalists. On September 1, 1780, Tye came by boat and led a small group of blacks and white Loyalists to Huddy's house in Toms River. After a two-hour battle, Tye set fire to the house and flushed Huddy out. As Tye was leading his band back with Huddy, Patriots, who had heard the shooting, intercepted. Huddy jumped overboard and swam to safety but Tye was shot in the wrist. Without proper medical attention, lockjaw set in and Tye died.

Tye's memory, however, lived on. Salter concludes that, "Like our ancestors (on the Patriot side), he fought for his freedom." Even Patriots admired his military skill. Even after Huddy's eventual capture and execution, Tye was remembered as a "brave and courageous man whose generous actions placed him well above his white companions." Tye and his fellow black Loyalists served as a symbol to blacks in the Monmouth area. Their struggle and the British support for their safe passage to Nova Scotia after the war, brought the whole issue of slavery into question. As a result, appeals for the end to slavery grew stronger.

Black Loyalists

It was not unusual for blacks to join the Loyalists forces in their raids on Patriot positions. In addition to serving with Bacon, forty blacks joined Davenport in his raid on Forked River and were part of the group that attacked the blockhouse in Toms River. Slave owners in Old Monmouth lost about twenty-eight slaves to the British Army, and to freedom in New York. Eventually many of these blacks moved to Nova Scotia where they tried to set up a free society.

Many blacks fought with the Patriot cause, but not in New Jersey. Massachusetts and Rhode Island promised, and later purchased freedom for the many who fought on the colonial side in the war. New Jersey refused to follow this practice. Edwin Salter points out that Monmouth County found this grant of liberty too costly. He states, "Our ancestors, in the more selfish view of dollars and cents, were clearly the losers by their policy."

Independence

The Peace of Paris of 1783 was finally signed to bring an end to the Revolutionary War and to grant independence. The feelings that the war generated, especially the division of the citizens, did not end as quickly. After the war, the petitions that were circulated in Shrewsbury asked the state legislature to bar ex-Loyalists from the area. "Those blood-thirsty robbers and murderers" was a typical label for those who had supported the British during the war. Many Loyalists left for the Bahamas, Nova Scotia or England.

The British and the Americans were to fight a second war of independence, the War of 1812. However, Ocean County did not play as major a role in this conflict as it had in the Revolution. Only a few of the county's citizens were drafted to protect the coastline. During the war the British staged raids for supplies, patrolled the waters off Long Beach Island, and forced two ships aground off the Manasquan Inlet. During the attack off Manasquan, shells fell on what was to become the Cook Homestead in Point Pleasant Beach.

The struggle for independence and the creation of a new nation did not come easily for the people of Ocean County. Understanding the Revolutionary War as a civil war as well as a revolution helps to develop a more complete understanding of the part played by the people of Ocean County in the process.

CHAPTER V

Wreckers or Lifesavers

The John Minturn (Shipwreck)

On February 13, 1846, a violent northeast storm accompanied by snow and freezing weather, struck the shipping lanes off Ocean County. Nine ships were wrecked on the beaches of New Jersey in what some oldtimers referred to as one of the worst storms of the nineteenth century. Two of these ships, the Alabama *and the* Minturn, *went down three miles apart within hours of each other. The first, the* Alabama, *was beached near the Manasquan Inlet, where rescue efforts failed to save the crew. Hours later many of the same shoremen were involved in the rescue of the* Minturn. *This second shipwreck and its rescue attempt was to affect the history of lifesaving efforts throughout New Jersey and the nation.*

Sinking of the John Minturn.

Leaving New Orleans on the 28th of January, the square-rigger, John Minturn, carried 51 passengers and crew and a cargo valued at over $80,000. Among the passengers were twenty victims of an earlier wreck, the Cherokee, *as well as the family of Captain Stark, the skipper of the* Minturn. *With the ship in danger of sinking and with shredded sails, the captain attempted to save those on board by sailing his ship onto the beach. This failed when, 300 yards off Mantoloking, the ship struck a sand bar created by the storm. Rescue attempts were hampered by the intensity of the storm, the freezing water, and the power of the surf. Lifeboats overturned in the rough seas and attempts to throw lines or launch boats from the shore failed. A human chain of* *courageous surfmen did succeed in saving a few from the sea but failed to reach the ship. After eighteen hours of struggle, over thirty lives had been lost, including the Captain, his wife and their two children. Bodies were washed ashore south of the wreck for days afterward.*

Following the storm, sensational stories about the shipwrecks dominated the national news. In spite of the heroic rescue efforts of local surfmen of the area, charges were made that numerous robberies of bodies and ships stores had occurred. The public outcry led New Jersey's Governor Charles Stratton to establish a special Commission on Shipwrecks. After a study of several wrecks, particularly the Minturn, *the Commission rejected all charges of wrongdoing. The report, in fact, praised the efforts of lifesavers such as Hugh Johnson, wreckmaster of the area, James Dorsett, John Van Note, and Joseph Borden who entered the icy waters several times to help survivors. Of the $84,000 of cargo, it was estimated that only $300 was unaccounted for.*

In addition to rejecting the cries of land piracy, the two wrecks of the so-called "Minturn Storm" led to demands for improved lifesaving equipment and skills. However, there continued to be heavy losses of life and property and the shoreline of Ocean County became known as "The Graveyard of the Atlantic." The history of Ocean County would be incomplete without an understanding of the contributions of its lifesavers.

The lifesavers saved many shipwreck victims by using a lifecar, a watertight, metal-covered boat which could carry up to seven people. (Print from Frank Leslie's llustrated News, 1868.)

Reasons For Shipwrecks

There are many legends and stories about the reasons for the large number of wrecks off the coast of Ocean County. One tells of land pirates who lured ships from the seas. Typical of these were stories of pirates who tied lights to the backs of donkeys and walked the beaches on Long Beach Island and Island Beach to simulate shipping lanes. There are also stories of scavengers robbing bodies cast ashore after shipwrecks. One legend tells of a daughter of one of the scavengers helping her father search bodies for loot. In this process, she found that the body she was to rob was that of her lover whom she had watched go to sea a few months before. It was said that her ghost still walks the sands of Ocean County beaches on foggy nights. In spite of these legends, "Barnegat pirates" were not the major causes of the many wrecks off Ocean County shores.

Leland Downey in his book *Broken Spars, New Jersey Shipwrecks 1640-1935*, lists the following causes of ship-wrecks in this area:

(1) Long Island formed a dead end to this major sea highway. Sailors became careless as they reached this end of their trip;

(2) The coastline of Ocean County bulged out into this important sea lane;

(3) Many hidden and shifting sand bars caused by tides and storms lay offshore threatening passing ships;

(4) There were few warning lights to mark the dangerous spots;

(5) Violent storms occurred frequently;

(6) Many ships that were old and had developed leaks were abandoned to become floating derelicts and a danger to other ships.

The number of wrecks that occurred off Ocean County's coast is difficult to determine. The book *Broken Spars* contains a partial list with dates and locations. Gordon Bishop, in his book, *Gems of New Jersey*, places the number lost off the entire New Jersey coast at between 3,000-4,500. Debbie Whitecraft, in her manuscript, *Biography of the New Jersey Coast*, has set the number at 5,000. The number of wrecks that occurred before 1700 is especially hard to determine because smaller wrecks were so common that they were rarely recorded. One of the earliest recorded shipwrecks off New Jersey is the one that marooned Penelope Van Princis and her husband at Sandy

Hook in 1620. (See Chapter III) The first newspaper account of a wreck off Barnegat was in 1705.

Shipwrecks became more numerous after the War of 1812. This date marked the beginning of unrestricted foreign trade for the United States with the rest of the world and a time of increasing immigration to the newly established nation. This period was also noted for many violent storms. A Reverend Brown of Point Pleasant estimated that over 125 ships were lost between Point Pleasant and Barnegat between 1830 and 1837. Robert Jahn reports that over 1,093 seamen lost their lives off New Jersey between 1800-1871. These facts support Jahn's claim that New Jersey was the shipwreck capital of the world.

Lifesavers

Authorized wreckmasters were established as early as 1795 by New Jersey's provisional government. Most were volunteers, typically fishermen and bay people capable of handling boats in the surf. Some earned a small income by helping to salvage wrecks for the owners. The first crews paid by the government were not until the middle of the nineteenth century. During the early part of that century, the government did provide some crude shacks with very limited equipment, but many of the crews continued to use their own equipment in rescue attempts. In the wreck of the *Minturn,* Dorsett rowed his own boat from the Beaver Dam Creek across the Bay, and then had to pull it across the barrier island to the wreck.

Early wreckmasters and surfmen in Ocean County, with names such as Chadwick, Maxson, Dorsett, Johnson, Borden, and Wardell, were all responsible for saving many lives and a great deal of property. They were recognized for their skills and courage, and the position of wreckmaster was not only coveted but considered an honor. Female members of these lifesaving families also aided the rescuers.

Robert Jahn in his book, *Down Barnegat Bay*, gives these two descriptions of early lifesavers:

"No man except my father-in-law John Maxson has done more to save drowning than I have. I tell you it's an awful sight to see poor drowning creatures clinging to rigging or bowspirit, to see them washed ashore before your eyes, sometimes next to you, without being able to help them. And their bodies thrown on the sand. You don't feel like stealing or murder at such a time. And besides I never knew a dead man come ashore that had anything in his pocket." William Chadwick

William Brown, Ocean County Assemblyman, is quoted as saying, "If the benevolent and heroic deeds of these men entitle them to be called Barnegat Land pirates, then may Barnegat pirates be inscribed on my brow."

The Government's Role

Ocean County led the nation in making major changes in lifesaving techniques. The first of these changes involved government financial support. A leading advocate was Doctor William Newell, who at the age of nineteen witnessed the sinking of the ship, *Terasto*. Newell practiced medicine in Manahawkin and then moved to Allentown where, in 1848, he was elected to Congress. He led the fight for government action. He spoke to Congress about the heavy loss of men and ships during the previous ten years and introduced a resolution calling for $10,000 to subsidize the establishment of a paid lifesaving

service. Congress approved the construction of seven new stations along the coast to replace the old keepers-shacks plus a salary of $40 a month paid to lifesavers during the six stormy winter months of the year. New equipment was also provided by the government including rockets, surfboats, and cannonades.

Bay Head Life Saving Station in 1890's.

President Lincoln recognized Dr. Newell by appointing him as head of the newly established Lifesaving Service. Later, as governor of New Jersey, Newell continued his efforts and, by 1882, the government played a major role in the training of crews and in the or-ganization of stations. By 1900, forty-two sta-tions had been autho-rized with improved equipment and with crews paid on a fulltime basis. The Lifesaving Service, established in 1848, united with the U.S. Rescue Service in 1915 to form today's Coast Guard.

Point Pleasant Coast Guard Station today.

Lifesaving Equipment

The growing role of government was accompanied by a tremendous improvement in equipment. Here again William Newell played a major role. Remembering the wreck of the *Terasto*, he developed a small gun or mortar which could fire a projectile that carried a light line from the shore. This line, once secured to the ship in danger, could be used to bring heavier lines to the ship. This gun was the forerunner of the gun designed in 1878 by D.A. Lyle, an improved bronze gun which was lighter and could operate at a longer range.

Another vital lifesaving tool was designed by Toms River resident

Life-car.

Joseph Francis who decided to build a non-destructible lifeboat. Earlier boats were mostly

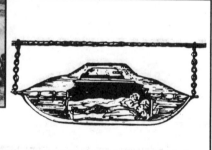

Life-car cut away.

whaleboats and, when not in use, frequently dried up and leaked. Francis's first improvement was placing cork and air pockets along the sides of the old boats to increase buoyancy. In 1843 he constructed metal boats to replace the older wooden boats. The first metal boat was too heavy and was replaced by corrugated material that was both lighter and stronger. In 1844, a covered top was added and it became known as "The Life Car." Joseph Francis was honored internationally for his work by the Shipping and Humane Society.

The value of these two major inventions, the Lyle Gun and The Life Car, was proven when they were used together for the first time. *The Ayrshire,* a ship carrying 200 English and Irish immigrants and crew, ran aground in a gale about 160 yards offshore at Manasquan. The lone fatality mistakenly rode on the top of the life car and was swept away in the heavy sea. Without the new equipment those on board would have suffered the same fate as most of those on the *Minturn*. The *Ayrshire's* rescue marked the beginning of new techniques that were to save over 2,000 passenger lives in the next ten years.

Chadwick House - Early boarding house.

Ann Maxon Chadwick 1833-1898

Ann Chadwick's father, John Maxon, was a well-known waterman who ran a tavern and gunning club in what is now known as Chadwick Beach. Ann helped her father in the tavern as well as in his life-saving efforts. On January 12, 1850, in the midst of a snowstorm, Ann, her sisters, young Bill Chadwick, and a handful of others helped her father rescue more that 200 passengers and crew members from the Scottish ship, Ayrshire. It was the first major use of the life car. John Maxon received a gold medal from Congress for his part in the rescue.

Ann married Bill Chadwick and, together, they turned her father's gunning club into the Chadwick House, the biggest and busiest inn along the coast. Since her husband remained in the life-saving service, the running of the inn and the farm, which produced most of their food, was left to Ann. Her cooking, cleanliness and reasonable prices were praised nationally by journalists and famous guests who included Presidents Ulysses Grant and Theodore Roosevelt.

Ann gave birth to ten children, six of whom lived to adulthood. She died at 65 and is buried in the Methodist cemetery in Point Pleasant. (from the Doctoral Thesis of Marilyn Kralik)

Lighthouses

Lighthouses were also constructed in an effort to protect shipping. The first of these was built on Sandy Hook to mark the entrance to New York harbor. Constructed by New York merchants in 1761, it was later turned over to the federal government. The first lighthouse built by the government was built in 1823 at Cape May. Ocean County's own lighthouse, Barnegat Light or "Old Barney", was built in 1834 on the north end of Long Beach Island. It contained a whale oil light located atop a fifty foot tower. The original lighthouse was destroyed by a storm in 1856, but the light was maintained by the keeper on the top of a wooden tower until the present structure was built in 1859.

Barnegat Light.

George Meade, soon to be famous as a Civil War general, supervised the construction of the present Barnegat Lighthouse. The tower is 165' high. Its light revolved every 4 minutes and flashed every 10 seconds. The light was visible to ships for over sixty years. Although the light atop no longer works, the sides of the tower are now lit with floodlights to serve as a symbol of its many years of service. This entire structure was built at a cost of $60,000. It was singled out by Boris Blair, Dean of Tyler School of Fine Arts at Temple University, as a "great piece of American sculpture, with the power to move men's minds and seize their hearts." This structure has become the symbol of Ocean County, and graces most publications of the county and of the state. In 1951 the state assumed control of the lighthouse and incorporated it into a 20,000 acre park.

Shipping During the Wars

Ocean County may have been connected with the most famous submarine attack of World War I, which eventually led to our entrance into World War II. In May of 1915, a German submarine attacked the passenger ship, Lusitania, off the Irish coast.   Many believe that a coded message, "Get Lucy", was sent from the Tuckerton Wireless Tower to the German Government.

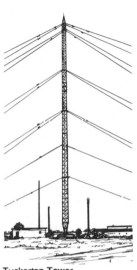

Tuckerton Tower.

The Tuckerton Tower, 680 feet tall and one of the tallest structures ever built to that date, was erected just before the war by the German government on Hickory Island, now Mystic Island.   It dominated the landscape and maintained the highest voltage of any such tower in the world.   Kaiser Wilhelm, German Emperor, in speaking over the tower wireless, said the "station would become a new link between our countries."

The tower was taken over by the United States Navy on orders from President Wilson in September of 1914, but a German station manager and his staff continued to handle maintenance duties.   Dr. F. Lee Terry, who as a boy lived in Tuckerton, has given evidence that the Germans may have continued to use the station to send coded messages.   The station continued to operate until 1917 when The United States entered World War I.   The German nationals were removed and were held as prisoners of war.   The tower was never used again and it was dismantled in 1950.   However, the tower's huge cement foundations still remain today amidst housing developments on Mystic Island.

Submarine warfare was heavy off Ocean County shores during both World War I and II. In World War II casualties were especially heavy. During a short period in 1942, twenty-four ships were sunk by the Axis powers off New Jersey. Two ships, *"The Razor"* and *"The Gulf Trade,"* were sunk near the Barnegat Inlet sending over seven million gallons of oil onto the neighboring beaches.

Tuckerton Tower Mooring - This concrete structure stands today in the middle of a street in a Mystic Island housing development.

The Morro Castle

Perhaps the most famous disaster along Ocean County's shores was the sinking of the *Morro Castle*. This 11,500 ton luxury liner was built in 1930, and was know as the *"Havana Ferry"* since it shuttled between New York and Havana, Cuba. In September, 1934, the *Morro Castle* was completing a trip, carrying 318 passengers and a crew of 258.

While in Cuba, the ship had been threatened with a strike, and the Havana police had also warned of a Communist plot to attack either the ship or the captain. Shortly after the ship left Havana, the captain's body was discovered in his cabin. The cabin was sealed for investigation until the ship reached New York. The first officer assumed command and that evening a fire, which seemed to break out in the library or in the paint locker, quickly spread throughout the ship. The order to abandon ship and to send out an SOS was issued about 3:30 a.m. on the morning of September 8, 1934.

By this time, the *Morro Castle* was already in New Jersey waters and the burning ship was visible from local beaches. First Aid services from Point Pleasant to Asbury Park were alerted. Rescue attempts were conducted by nearby ships, by charter boats and by other private ships in the area. Life boats from the burning vessel were also launched by the crew.

All of the rescue attempts were hindered by the rough winds and surf from a strong northeaster that had developed during the night. The crew was poorly organized and were also guilty of cowardice. When the first two lifeboats reached the shore, eighty of the eighty-five survivors were crew members rather than passengers. Another lifeboat, capable of holding fifty people, landed carrying only four crew members. Because of the heavy surf, the Coast Guard brought most of the lifeboats into the Manasquan Inlet. The skippers of the fishing boats were the real heroes of this disaster, for they pulled many survivors out of the water despite the rough seas. John Bogan's *Paramount* was one of the first charter boats to reach the scene and played a major role in rescue efforts. Nevertheless, 134 lives were lost.

Several investigations into the disaster have suggested some probable causes. Leland Downey summarizes the diverse reaction of passengers: (1) "The crew behaved splendidly; (2) "The crew was drunk"; (3) "The fire was deliberately set"; (4) "The fire was caused by lightning"; (5) "The fire started in the library"; (6) "The fire started from the oil rags in a supply closet"; (7) "The fire was started by Reds."

Later events seemed to point to one of the crew as the cause of the disaster, radio operator William Rogers, who at first was hailed as one of the heroes of the day. His arrest and conviction of arson and murder in connection with another case years later led to a more thorough investigation of his role in the *Morro*

Morro Castle.

Castle disaster. This examination supported the theory that Rogers was not a hero but the one who set the fire.

The Sea Today

Since the last century, improved ship construction, navigational markings, radar, radio and new lifesaving techniques have resulted in a tremendous decrease in the loss of ships and their cargo. However, today, with the increase in pleasure boat traffic and amateur sailors, accidents at sea still occur. Boat inspections, classes in seamanship and strict enforcement of safety regulations are carried on by both the Coast Guard and Marine Police, and by volunteers in the Coast Guard Auxiliary. These programs, along with better weather forecasting and improved mapping of shipping hazards make the oceans off Ocean County safer.

The wrecks which still exist off Ocean County shores do have some value. The hulls of these ships, resting on the bottom of the ocean, serve as protection for sea life. Charter boats and private crafts travel to these sites to improve their catches. Many of these sunken ships still may contain precious cargo. Gordon Bishop states that only about 10% of these wrecked ships have been located and new discoveries are made frequently.

Today, as in the past, the sea contributes to the economic, social, and recreational life of Ocean County. The threat to shipping and boating is always present, but thanks to the efforts of many of the people of Ocean County, both in the past and in the present, the seas are much safer than they were in the past. A new name has replaced the old title of "Graveyard of the Atlantic", and today these waters are known as "New Jersey's Playground."

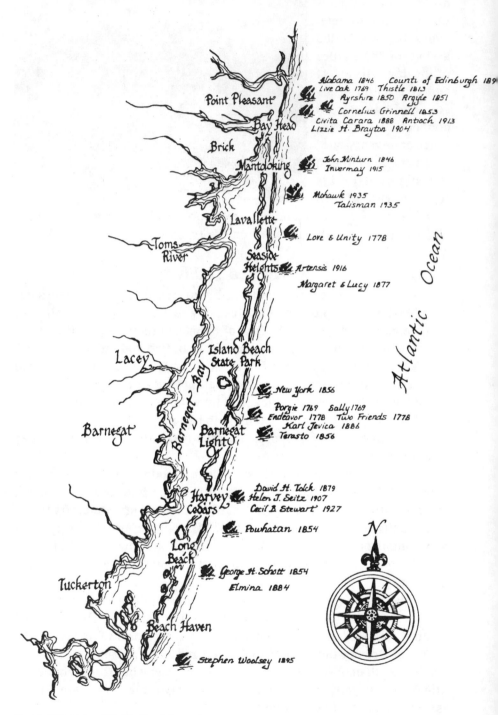

Known shipwrecks off Ocean County's coast.

CHAPTER VI

Travelers

Maja Leon Berry (Bridge Builder)

The year 1914 was important for travelers to Ocean County because two major highway bridges were opened linking the barrier islands with the mainland. One connected Long Beach Island with Manahawkin, and the second connected Seaside Heights and Island Heights. Both not only provided direct access to beaches, but also stimulated further land sales and construction from Point Pleasant Beach to Beach Haven. In 1914, Ocean County beachfront was booming, booming because of these new bridges.

Maja Leon Berry, a native of Ocean County, played a significant role in this growth. Born in West Creek in 1877, Berry went to school in and then became a teacher in that community. Later, he became a lawyer and a judge. He was instrumental in promoting and raising money for both bay bridges and the connecting roads necessary for the bridges to be effective.

In an article published in the Ocean County Observer in March of 1991, Don Bennett describes Berry's role. Berry, at 36, was practicing law in Camden. He formed a stock company to raise the $80,000 needed to build a toll bridge to Seaside. At the same time, he pushed for the construction of a bridge to connect Long Beach Island with the mainland. As secretary of Beach Haven Realty Company, he helped to raise the $90,000 necessary for that bridge which was completed in 1912.

Seaside Toll Bridge.   Photo - Ocean County Observer

This new bridge, however, was "a bridge to nowhere" because there were no roads on either end. Unable to encourage contractors to build the necessary roads, Berry used his personal and political connections. With the help of his brother-in-law, Captain Thomas A. Mathis, he succeeded in having the roads built through the combination of county and state funds.

In 1914 the roads were passable enough for the official opening of the Long Beach Island bridge. In that same year, the Seaside bridge was also opened. At first, both bridges operated as toll bridges. Less than a decade after the building of these two bridges, the state acquired title and the $.25 toll became a thing of the past.

Automobiles and bridge and road improvements were to revolutionize the development of the county. Over the years, the different forms of transportation such as boats, wagons, stagecoaches, railroads, dirigibles, trolleys and automobiles were important not only in the types of travelers who came to the county but also in determining its growth. Berry's role in the construction of these bridges is but part of this history.

Waterways

Early travelers to Ocean County used the waterways. The Indians who visited the shore each summer used the streams to travel from the interior to the shore. Bill Hess, in his book, *On History's Trail*, observes that Indians had no need for roads before the coming of the white man as they had no beasts of burden or cattle. Foot paths were sufficient and those trails usually paralleled the streams.

The earliest white settlers also reached the county by sea. Following the original explorers, settlers came from New England, Long Island and other colonies by way of the Atlantic Ocean. Barnegat Bay and streams feeding into it were used by most of the settlers to reach the mainland where they established their homes. Products sent to market were sent by these same water highways. Unlike many other counties, Ocean County had an abundance of these natural waterways and did not require much in the way of canal construction. The only major canal in the county was not to be built until the 1920's, and, only to complete the Inland Waterway from Florida to the Manasquan River for pleasure boating. Until the Civil War period, waterways continued to be the dominant means of travel both to and within the county.

Roads

Early roads supplemented rather than replaced water routes. Most of them followed old Indian trails and many road and place names can be traced to our Indian ancestors. Few dependable records exist of these early Indian trails, since many of the original paths were built over and widened by the early settlers. The old Laurelton Circle in Brick was the spot where some of these trails crossed. These early roads were used to connect neighbors, to bring produce from the fields to towns, to bring wood from sawmills to ports, and charcoal to furnaces. This explains why many of the older roads in the county are so meandering. Early paths were also used by itinerant preachers and peddlers who, often became their most frequent users. These travelers helped widen and improve the routes. One preacher described the area south of Freehold, later to become Ocean County, as a wilderness.

Shore peddler, traveled up and down the coast with his wares.   W.E. Hess Collection

By 1765, New Jersey probably had more roads than any other colony. Along the way over 400 taverns cared for the weary traveler. Roads were first constructed of sand and dirt. They were dusty in the summer and muddy during the rainy periods. In the winter they were filled with ruts. Some of the roads over sandy areas or swamps used rough logs or planks to improve the traction. One of the earliest "plank" or "corduroy road" connected Lakewood with the Metedeconk River, about where Cedarbridge Avenue is today. There it joined the old Toms River Road, today's Old Hooper Avenue.

One of the major roads connecting the county with its markets was the Old Tuckerton Road. This road was first built to bring Quakers to

the Meeting House in Tuckerton and
goods to market. It took travelers and
goods through the pines via Batsto,
Atsion, Ten Mile Hollow, and
Medford. In 1816 it was used as the
first stagecoach route from Philadelphia to the shore. The trip took two
days each way and was traveled once
each week. In 1833 the stagecoach

Oyster Wagon.

service was improved by scheduling trips on Monday, Wednesday and
Friday. In the western part of the county, New Egypt became the hub
of overland transportation.

Prior to the establishment of regular stage routes, travel to the
shore was done in oyster wagons or "Jersey Wagons." These wagons
carried oysters to market and passengers on the return trip. These
visitors to the shore carried their own blankets and food. They not only
were exposed to poor road conditions, and poor vehicles, but also to
swarms of green flies and mosquitos. Those taking a stagecoach were
subject to many of the same conditions. It is no wonder that most of
these early travelers to the Ocean County area were sportsmen rather
than families.

Prior to the 1860's, tourists reached Ocean County by water,
wagon, or stagecoach. Visitors from New York traveled mostly by ship
to Monmouth County then south via stagecoach. Those from Philadelphia and inland traveled overland by stage. Because of the poor travel
conditions and because New Yorkers had easier access to Long Island
and north Jersey beaches, Ocean County was most influenced by
Pennsylvania tourists.

Shore Stage Coach.

W.E. Hess Collection

Railroads

During the last half of the nineteenth century, an important advancement in transportation came to Ocean County. Prior to that time tourism was limited to those areas easily reached by boat, while the rest of the shore was left to the hearty souls that were willing to brave the rigors of overland travel. Railroads were to change all that.

The first railroad to operate in New Jersey joined Camden with Perth Amboy in 1834. The 1830's and 1840's saw the growth of railroads in North Jersey. However, Ocean County was neglected. John Cunningham in

Railroad Round House turn table in Point Pleasant Beach where New York and Philadelphia trains met.   Joe Eid Collection

his book, *New Jersey: Mirror of America*, said that railroad builders at the time felt that the Shore was a wasteland.

Ocean County waited until the 1860's for rail service when a spur of the Delaware & Raritan Railroad (New Jersey Southern) was extended to the Bergen Iron Works in Lakewood. Later this line continued south to Lakehurst. In 1866 a spur of this line reached Toms River. By 1871 a second line was built from Tuckerton to Edge Cove on the bay. Docks were built at that point for steamers to carry guests to the shore resorts on Long Beach Island.

CNJ station and post office at Beachwood. This building was built by the town in 1922. It was razed in 1967.

Between 1880 and 1883, the Pennsylvania Railroad extended its Pemberton branch through Whiting to a trestle crossing the bay from Berkeley Township to Seaside Park where it turned north to Bay Head. Three years later, in 1886, a railroad bridge was built crossing the bay to Long Beach Island to join a spur running from Beach Haven to Harvey Cedars.

The New York and Long Branch Railroad (Central Railroad) finally crossed the Manasquan in the 1870's and built a roundhouse to handle shore trains at Point Pleasant Beach. Half the stock of the New York and the Long Branch Railroad was sold to the Pennsylvania Railroad. The Pennsylvania then joined with the branch which crossed the Pinelands to provide a daily rail trip to Camden.

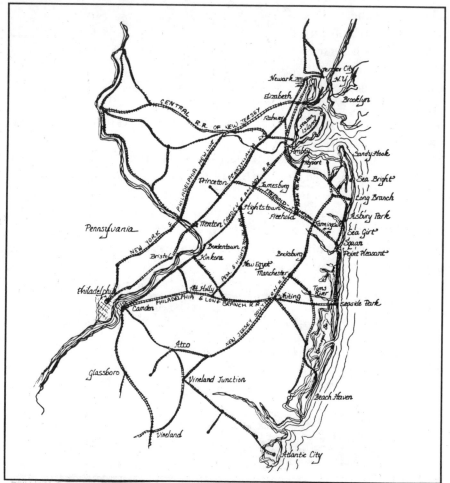

Rail Lines of Central Jersey.

Harold Wilson in his book, *The Story of the Jersey Shore*, writes of the railroads: "no single influence, except the evolution of the gasoline engine and thus automobiles and trucks, proved so catalytic an agent in the development of the Shore." He also cites an article in the Woodbury Constitution which stated that "never had there been a time when the resorts on the New Jersey coast were so easy to access...such facilities placed a trip to the seaside within reach of every class of person." The two-day trip by stage had been shortened to two hours.

Railroad crosses the bay.

Early railroad riders did not travel in much greater comfort than early wagon travelers. Many rode in coaches, open to all the elements of weather, bugs, smoke, poor roadbeds, and crowded conditions. As the quality of railroads improved, so did the number and types of travelers. Families now joined the men to enjoy the beauty and recreational benefits of Ocean County, and the population of the shore doubled in the next three decades. New towns were incorporated including Bay Head (1886), Island Heights (1887), Point Pleasant (1886), Seaside Park (1889), Lavallette (1887) and Long Beach Island, Barnegat City (1887), Long Beach Township, Beach Haven (1890), and Harvey Cedars (1894). Lakewood, although not a beach resort, was to become a nationally famous winter resort at the end of the nineteenth century.

The railroad was a major contributor to the increasing population and accessibility of Ocean County. However, at the turn of the century with the increased popularity of the automobile, the decline of railroads began. Many of the lines were merged and many of the spurs were abandoned.

The Sailcar

An interesting sidelight of Ocean County history deals with the Edge Cove spur in Tuckerton, which had transported people from the main railroad line to the bay. This line was abandoned when the railroad bridge was completed. Enterprising fishermen of the area were said to have used the spur by building a "sailcar" to cheaply transport boxes, barrels and sacks of their water harvest to the mainline. They reclaimed a flat car, rigged a mast, and sailed with their catch on the abandoned spur. This original and inexpensive transportation was used for some time until some older boys raced the sailcar on a Halloween evening. They got up too much speed and it jumped the track into a ditch. Thus ended the days of the "Clamtown Sailcar." John Brinkman, author of *The Tuckerton Railroad,* points to another version of the use of the line. He states that the flat car may have been pulled by horses. Both versions, he acknowledges, may be correct since the one may have preceeded the other.

The Great Depression further shortened the life of many spurs and mainlines. Although World War II and gas rationing did extend the life of tourist travel on the railroads, immediately after the war, this decline continued. Many of the old shore lines were discontinued, tracks torn up and property sold for housing. The line from Mantoloking to Seaside Heights, for example, became Route 35 South. The few remaining railroads are now operated by The New Jersey Transit and Conrail. The recent growth of population and the problems created by heavy traffic conditions are causing a new look at railroads as a means of county transportation.

Clamtown Sailcar.

Trolleys

Railroads doomed schooners, wagons and the stagecoach as ways to reach the shore, but the new railroads didn't solve the immediate problems of travel within the community. Local transportation was still dominated by the horse and leg power. The first attempt to fill this need was the trolley. Trolleys differed from the railroads in that they were able to operate on local streets and, in later days, were powered by electricity. Point Pleasant Beach was the first Ocean County community to have a horse drawn streetcar. As Joseph Eid states in his book, *Trolleys, Across the Sand Dunes,* only 300 cities in the nation had trolleys and the trolley made the town fashionable. The line ran from the Resort House, which now would be located on Route 35 South, to the ocean. Ortley Beach and Long Beach Island later were to have similar lines connecting their railroad stations with beach hotels.

Beach Haven Horsecar.

In 1894 the horsecar in Point Pleasant was replaced with an electric trolley system as developed by Frank Sprague in Richmond, Virginia. New Jersey's first electric streetcars carried passengers from the railroad station to the beach in Asbury Park in 1887. Plans called for Point Pleasant Beach and Asbury Park to be part of an intercoastal trolley system to service the Shore.

Point Pleasant Beach hoped to complete its system by running a line into Bay Head. The original charter defined its line from Bay Head to Clarks Landing, a popular resort on the Manasquan River. However, when the line opened, it ran only from the railroad station at Point Pleasant Beach through the town to the Bay Head boundary. Bay Head refused permission for the trolley to enter its town.

Point Pleasant Beach Powerhouse - Need for a market for surplus electricity led to "Electric War."
W.E. Hess Collection

Point Pleasant found itself in competition with other communities for tourists. Bay Head, on the other hand, founded by a group from the Princeton area, wanted to keep the town as an old-fashioned retreat, free from the pressures of "modern" living. Point had trolleys and a new powerhouse with surplus electricity. Bay Head leaders wished neither. Since the trolley system was run during the summer season only, it was financially essential for the Point system to have a wider market. Some in Bay Head were interested in providing that market. The Grenville Hotel, in particular, wanted to offer these facilities to their guests when it opened in 1901. Thus began the famous "electric war."

On the morning of Sunday, June 15th, 1901, Mayor Pennington, of Bay Head, awoke to find that during the evening, workmen from the neighboring town had erected poles and electric wires to the new Grenville Hotel. Four workmen were discovered completing the job. Two were trapped up the poles and arrested, while the mayor and councilmen chopped down the poles. This led to a series of court actions and finally, two years later, electricity and trolleys came to Bay Head.

Trolley arrives in Bay Head.   Joe Eid Collection

Point Pleasant Beach changed overnight from a sleepy little fishing village with a few small farms and boarding houses offering limited services to a modern resort with both a railroad and trolley system. During the next four years, promoters eyed the town as the site for the terminus of a trolley system connecting the shore with Trenton.

The chief promoter of this trolley expansion was George Vanderbilt, a former State Legislator, lawyer, postmaster, and Treasurer of the Democratic Party. With trolley fever sweeping the state, he saw Trenton as the hub of the biggest trolley system in the United States. In 1903, Vanderbilt, familiar with Point Pleasant Beach as a tourist resort, filed for a charter connecting its trolley system with Trenton. A year later a contract was signed to clear land between Point Pleasant and the developing winter resort at Lakewood. However, problems such as difficult negotiations with the communities involved, finances, contractors, and questions concerning the role of Vanderbilt and other investors, led to a decade of frustration. In 1916, with only the land cleared to Lakewood, the plans for such a route ended. The line was extended only to the Pine Bluff Inn, near the site of the present Point Pleasant canal. The Point Pleasant Beach trolley system operated its last car on Labor Day of 1919 and the right of way to Lakewood was sold to the Jersey Power and Light Company.

Dirigibles

Most seniors who have lived at the Shore remember what they were doing on four memorable days in history: December 7, 1941, when Pearl Harbor was attacked, November 22, 1963, when President Kennedy was assassinated and, locally, when the *Morro Castle* burned, and when the Hindenburg exploded. Each of these events shocked the nation and each had a profound effect on the shore. The Morro Castle and the Hindenburg influenced passenger travel. The Morro Castle brought national attention to the need to improve the safety of luxury liners, while the Hindenburg ended the use of the dirigible as a means of travel.

A dirigible is a rigid, lighter-than-air craft. This type of craft was first built in Germany in 1900 by Count Ferdinand Von Zeppelin and was used and improved in World War I. Following the war, the United States, France, Great Britain and Germany competed in developing these ships for both military and civilian use. The United States seemed to assume the leadership role in the field when, in 1920, it built the *Shenandoah*, an improved version of a captured German dirigible. The use by the United States of helium gas as the lifting power instead of hydrogen was a major advance, as it ended the threat of fire, a major concern of the past.

Lakehurst Naval Air Station in the 1930's.
Ocean County Historical Museum

The *Shenandoah* was built in 1920 at the Philadelphia Naval factory and was assembled and based in Lakehurst. It excited the world by its accomplishments until it crashed in a violent storm over Ohio. Later, the crash of the *Akron* off Barnegat Light and its sister ship, *Macon*, off the west coast, ended the United States' experimentation with dirigibles. However, it was the dramatic end of the *Hindenburg* that ended Lakehurst's hopes to be the center of national and international passenger travel.

On May 6th 1937, the *Hindenburg*, a luxurious and highly publi-

Hindenburg explodes.   Ocean County Historical Museum

cized German passenger dirigible was landing in Lakehurst on the first
trip of its second season. It was delayed in landing from its trans-
Atlantic voyage by afternoon thundershowers. When it prepared to
make contact with the mooring tower in Lakehurst, it suddenly exploded and fire enveloped the ship. Unlike United States ships, it used
hydrogen to keep aloft. Those watching the fire were helpless as the
dirigible crashed and 37 of the 125 passengers and crew perished. The
description by a radio announcer of what had occurred provided one of
the most dramatic broadcasts ever heard by the listening public.

The cause of the disaster was never established. Some stated that
the failure of the United States to sell helium to the Germans as a
national security measure was a contributing factor to the disaster.
Some suggested that lightning or sabotage was responsible. Regardless of the reason, the very spectacle of the fiery crash brought to an end
lighter-than-air passenger travel. Hangar #1, built at Lakehurst to
handle these large airships, is now a National Monument. During
World War II, Lakehurst became the site for the operation of smaller
non-rigid blimps that were used for antisubmarine patrol. Today it
serves as a testing area for many other aspects of naval aviation.

Early 1900's Electric Automobile.   W.E. Hess Collection

The Automobile

By 1900 the automobile reached Ocean County. Tire care and service were handled by bicycle shops and blacksmiths. Gasoline was sold by the general stores. One of the first local owners of an automobile was Captain Thomas Mathis.

At first, the automobile was mainly used for "touring." *The Asbury Park Press*, in an article on August 30th, 1904, tells the story of the "Tally Ho Auto Trip." The news story describes the big machines which left Ocean Grove for Lakewood at quarter past three in the afternoon, amid cheers of guests and neighbors. The route taken passed through Belmar and Point Pleasant, to return by way of Allaire, which at the time was called the Deserted Village. Seventeen people took this trip. The article went on to say, "Words failed to express the delight of the party as they arrived home at 6:30 PM from their 'flying' trip." Refreshments were served on the automobile.

Thomas Chadwick is at the wheel of one of his rental cars in this 1914 photo. Hotel guests were his tour passengers.

W.E. Hess Collection

THOMPSON'S LAKEWOOD AND POINT PLEASANT STREET CAR LINE

Lakewood Street Car - Took the place of the transit connection
when the planned trolley system failed.   Joe Eid Collection

By the 1920's the automobile was common at the shore, although roads were still a problem. The first gravel road in Ocean County joined Lakewood and Point Pleasant and was built in 1904 by the Board of Freeholders. This was followed soon afterwards by roads connecting Point and Seaside Park and one traversing the length of Long Beach Island. The 1920's and 1930's saw a continued improvement in road surfacing in Ocean County and in roads leading to the shore. The major roads to the county included Routes #34 and #35 from the north, Routes #70 and #72 from the west and the north-south Route #9. These highways continue to service the county today.

The highway which made the most impact on the shore area was the Garden State Parkway. In April of 1952, a bill was passed by the State Legislature of New Jersey to establish the Garden State Parkway Authority. This authority was to construct a self-supporting toll road to run along the shore line and to develop recreational sites along its route. The first toll section was opened in 1952 and the entire length of 173 miles was completed by August, 1957. Approximately forty miles of its roadway is in Ocean County. This modern, carefully landscaped highway had an amazing effect on the county's population. It increased the county's role as a bedroom community for north Jersey and New York City workers and also made it easier for tourists to reach the shore.

The problem of traveling to the shore continues today. The Parkway has recently been supplemented by the construction of I-195 and Route 18. These highways, however, still are insufficient considering the numbers who use them to reach their work or to visit shore resorts. The poorly maintained, and far from updated local and county roads are also a problem. The absence of a viable mass transit system and the weak county and local infrastructures demonstrate one of the major problems facing the county today. This, along with the bottlenecks provided by nature in the form of rivers, lakes, streams, and Barnegat Bay, provide a great challenge to the Ocean County traveler.

Bergen Ironworks.   Ocean County Historical Museum

CHAPTER VII

Toilers

Joseph Brick (Businessman)

Bog Iron or limonite, the Pinelands ore used in the production of iron, was known to exist in the Lakewood area of Burrsville as early as the middle of the 18th century. In 1815 the Washington Furnace was built in this area. After operating successfully during its early years, Washington Furnace ran into hard times and was not in operation when it was purchased in 1833 by a former clerk of Batsto, Joseph Brick. Paul Axel-Lute, author of Lakewood in the Pines, refers to Joseph Brick as the most important man in the history of that community. His Bergen Iron Works, established on the site of the old Washington Forge and Three Partners Mill, was named after the north Jersey town which produced a superior type of iron. The Bergen Iron Works of Lakewood was to become the most successful iron works in the county.

Brick was joined by his financial partner and father-in-law, Riley Allan, a wealthy New Egypt farmer. They employed over 200 workers at the ironworks and provided many services to these employees. At Brick's death in 1847, the Bergen Iron Works was a thriving community which included: a sawmill, grist mill, pattern house, carpenter and wheelwright shop, machine and turning shop, blacksmith shop, furnace casting house, a big house, office, and a single's house that served as a store, church, and school. Iron products were taken by plank road to the mouth of the Metedeconk River where they were shipped by boat to New York or northern New Jersey. Later, a rail line was built to carry material to the Bergen Iron Works and products from it to the north. The iron works produced many products including the pipes for the utilities and gas lines of New York City.

In the decades following Brick's death, the growing shortage of charcoal and the competition with Pennsylvania led to the closing of the Bergen Iron Works, the last of the furnaces in Ocean County. However, because of the presence of the railroad, and as a direct result of Joseph Brick's investments, Lakewood had the capital for the beginnings of a tourist industry.

Burrsville become part of Brick Township when Ocean County was created in 1950. The town at the Bergen Iron Works became Bricksburg *in 1865, and later, in 1880, became Lakewood. Lakewood, however, remained part of Brick Township until 1892 when it formed a separate township. Joseph Brick was remembered not only for giving his name to the area and his daughters' nicknames to Lakewood's major lake, Lake Carasaljo,(Carrie, Sally, Josie), he also demonstrated that business and employment opportunities in the county were possible in areas other than just shore related industries.*

Iron Makers

The making of bog iron and the production of iron products played a major role in Ocean County, not only during the Revolution, but for the next fifty years. This industry provided employment for many workers in the Pinelands and contributed to the establishment of new centers of population. Some of the iron workers were indentured servants and some were former English criminals but most were ordinary citizens attracted to the area because of the availability of work. Besides the Bergen Iron Works, other forges included the Stafford Forge, the Federal Forge in what is now Lakehurst, and the Ferrago Forge in Lacey.

An understanding of the way bog iron was made in Ocean County is essential to understand why the industry prospered in this area. John McPhee in his book, *The Pine Barrens*, provides an excellent description of this process.

Ocean County rainwater, soaking through pine needles and other forest materials, leaches iron out of the sands. This dissolved iron moves underground and gradually into the streams where it oxidizes.

On contact with the air, it forms a partly brown rust and partly iridescent blue-colored scum that resembles an oil slick. Drifting to the edge of the stream, this film permeates the sand and gravel to form a sandstone mix known as bog iron ore.

This ore is then brought to furnaces where charcoal provides the heat necessary to purify the ore. The smelting process also required flux which, when combined with impurities, floated to the top. This flux was readily available in the area in the lime of oyster shells. The heating of the ore, flux, and charcoal resulted in a

Iron Furnace - The furnace was the heart of the ironworks operation.
Russ Seuffert, Coast Magazine

melted mass which, when the slag was removed, became pig iron. The pig iron was then transported to nearby forges to be further refined into wrought iron.   Most of the forges were build near water so that waterwheels could provide the power to operate the bellows necessary for the blast heat of the forge.   The production of iron was a rural industry in Ocean County, but it required a large workforce and a considerable amount of capital.

The bog iron industry reached its peak in the 1840's. Each furnace, to make the necessary charcoal, burned one-thousand acres of pines each year. The dwindling supply of timber, along with the superiority of Pennsylvania coal and iron ore, ended the bog iron industry in Ocean County. By the end of the Civil War no furnaces were left in the Pinelands. The shortage of fuel also doomed an attempt to replace the iron industry with glass making.

The end of these industries had a profound effect on the Pinelands and its people. Near the end of the 19th century Gustav Kobbe described Brick Township as "a landscape of deserted and decaying shanties grouped around abandoned furnaces." Land lost its value and in later years, land in the Pinelands and in Brick, in particular, was offered free with newspaper subscriptions.

Millworkers

Mills provided many jobs during the early days of the county. These mills provided lumber for local industries and also shipped lumber and cedar rails to city markets. Some of the first saw-mills were built in the 1740's and were important to communities such as Stafford, Toms River, Lakehurst, Barnegat, Brick and Jackson. Clusters of homes around the mills demonstrated the importance of these sites. The end of the sawmill industry coincided with

Saw Mill at Double Trouble Park today.

the end of the availability of hardwoods. Double Trouble State Park in Berkeley Township today includes the old sawmill. It serves as an example of this early colonial employment.

Grist mills were more important to the farming areas of Jackson and New Egypt. At one time at least 25 sawmills, planing, and grist mills operated in Jackson Township. Its economy was dominated by mills, none of which remain today. However, some of their mill ponds and dams remain to serve as evidence of the early days.

The salt industry also was important during colonial days. During the Revolutionary War, the salt supply from New England, Europe and the West Indies was cut off. The colonists needed salt not only for the preservation and flavoring of foods but also for the production of gunpowder. The process of making salt at the shore was quite simple. Seawater was fed into reservoirs, which naturally evaporated leaving brine which was then boiled to produce salt. Forked River had a saltworks as early as 1754. With the demands of the Revolutionary War, saltworks were built in Squan Beach, Toms River, Tuckerton, Barnegat and Waretown.

The production of salt attracted many workers to the county. Workers were needed so badly that the New Jersey Legislature granted exemption from the war to some workers and Continental Army troops were sent to help. Heat, insects, and poor roads all became problems of the saltworks. During the war, many of the saltworks were attacked and destroyed by the British. Attempts to rebuild the industry met failure when the French, opening the blockade, allowed imported salt to reach the colonies.

Boat Builders

One of Ocean County's earliest industries was shipbuilding. A larger portion of the work force of Ocean County was engaged in shipbuilding than in any other county. By 1790 the industry flourished in Tuckerton, Waretown, Forked River, Barnegat, and Toms River. At one time the Barnegat area was noted for its cedar trees. However, by the 1880's, hardwood timber became scarce. The decline of available lumber and a lessening of demand for coastwise vessels led to a decline in this industry for

Sneak-box.

a short period of time.

Later, during the nineteenth and twentieth centuries, sportsmen and amateur sailors filled the bay with garveys, rowboats, and catboats. The Bay Head area became the construction center for these popular bay boats. In 1815 Hazelton Seaman of West Creek invented the sneakbox for duck hunting. It was originally powered by poles or oars. The design was improved by John Cramer and Samuel Perrine to include a short mast and sails. The sneakbox was from 12-17 feet in length, with a light, low deck and sharp bow. By the end of the century the sneakbox became the most popular sailboat on the bay. Ben Hance, Morton Johnson, Howard Perrine, and later, Hubert Johnson became the builders of many of these sailboats. By the end of the 19th century the sneakbox became the most popular sailing boat on the bay.

Charles Hankins, (left), of Lavallette, works on a Sea Bright skiff with help from Mike Franzoso, also of Lavallette. Mr. Hankins is one of the last wooden boatbuilders in New Jersey.   The Review

The Sea Bright Skiff was another famous boat constructed in Ocean County yards. This flat bottom boat with rounded sides was first built in Sea Bright in Monmouth County. It was constructed to meet the needs of an area where there were few inlets or calm waters as it could be launched directly into the surf. In the 1800's the boats were popular in both the fishing industry and in lifesaving. As the demands of this area changed from fishing to tourism, the boat was modified to meet the needs of lifeguards. Although most boats today are made of fiberglass, this craft is still made of white cedar. Since World War II, the late Charles Hankins Sr. and his son, of Lavallette, have supplied Jersey Shore lifeguards with these wooden skiffs.

The percentage of people engaged in the boating industry remains high and it continues to make up a large part of the county's workforce. However, the major business of today's boatyards is to handle sales and servicing of pleasure crafts.

Fishermen and Whalers

Whaling and fishing were important occupations in the early history of the county. However, both were mainly seasonal occupations. It wasn't unusual for fishermen to also work in lumbering, shipbuilding, farming, lifesaving, or part-time, at mills or furnaces.

Fishermen over the years had restraints placed upon them by the government. As early as 1719, the General Assembly of New Jersey passed laws regulating the gathering of food from the sea. Oyster-raking and gathering were limited to the season from September to May since poor transportation during other times of the year might cause the oysters to spoil before reaching the market. Since that time, many other steps have been taken to regulate the fishing industry and to protect the consumer. Today, laws regulate the types and size of fish that may be harvested, where and when fishing is allowed, and the issuing of licenses.

The methods of gathering products from the sea has also changed over the years. In addition to hooks, lines and nets, pounds were used off the beaches of Ocean County. Pounds were nets up to 50 feet square held in place by poles, some as much as 60 feet deep. These long nets stretched under water to trap fish into an area from which they could easily be gathered. Each day men from the beach would row out to the pound to harvest the fish. By 1914 there were over 112 pounds off the

New Jersey coast. However, by the 1940's, hurricane damage and new technology virtually ended this passive form of fishing.

Commercial fishing still is an important occupation in the county. However, commercial fishing has been challenged during the nineteenth and twentieth century by the sports fishermen. Famous surfmen and fishermen piloted eager sportsmen to favorite fishing spots in the Atlantic and on Barnegat Bay. John Dorsett of the

Fishermen and Their Catch.   W.E. Hess Collection

Beaver Dam Creek area was one of the many who used his knowledge of the bay and his schooner to conduct trips to this wonderland for those sportsmen who were seeking refuge from the pressures of the day. The bay, mostly salt, and fed by many slow moving rivers and streams, offered both crabbing and fishing and was easier to access than the ocean. Today, the guided fishermen have been supplemented by many tourist and local residents who use the water for pleasure boating. The servicing of these amateur sailors has provided year round work for many shore residents.

Hunters and Guides

The eastern flyway along the Atlantic coast lies directly over Barnegat Bay and early settlers took advantage of this readily available supply of food. Hunters trapped or shot large numbers of duck, geese and other waterfowl and sold them to local residents and to city markets. Many of these hunters also hired themselves out as guides to wealthy sportsmen. This practice

Duck Hunters at the Shore.   W.E. Hess Collection

led to related industries in boatbuilding, innkeeping, and in providing necessary hunting equipment.

By the middle of the 19th century, several boarding houses for sportsmen were established. They were mainly ramshackled complexes built low and sweeping to withstand the Atlantic storms. These were scattered along the barrier beaches of the county and usually included unpainted barns, privies, sailsheds, doghouses, icehouses and worn-out wagons. A typical trip from Manhattan to Long Beach Island took six to eight hours. A train would be taken to Sandy Hook and then a catboat to the Ashley House in Barnegat City, to Double Jimmy's at Loveladies, to the Harvey Cedars Hotel, or to Chadwick's in Bay Head.

Professional hunters helped sportsmen construct duck blinds, artificial islands, and sink boxes. Sink boxes were coffin-like floating structures that held one or two hunters level with the surface of the water. Decoys were also a part of a hunters' equipment and the production of these decoys became an important industry as well as an art form. The design and sale of decoys and other hunting supplies employed many in the county. All of these aids enabled hunters to increase their catch. The bagging of 25 to 100 birds in a day was not unusual.

As the number of hunters increased, hunting, as with fishing, became subject to government regulations. It is estimated that when the first settlers arrived, there were 500 million ducks making their annual flight and by 1934 that number had dropped to 30 million. Commercial hunting was outlawed by the Federal Migratory Bird Act of 1918. Artificial islands and sink boxes were outlawed in the next two decades, and hunting seasons and areas are now carefully regulated.

Lawbreakers

The county's location on the water also created the opportunity for some occupations that were outside the law. Some of the earliest settlers in Ocean County were smugglers and, later, privateers. (See Chapter II, III) However, the ending of the war and the removal of obstacles to trade directly with the cities under British control eliminated the need for smuggling or privateering.

During the Prohibition Era, the waters of Ocean County again experienced a short revival as a center of illegal trade. During that period, major ports were closed to the importation of illegal alcohol. The more isolated shores of Long Island and New Jersey were used for landing illegal liquor which was then trucked to the cities. Those engaged in this trade were called bootleggers. Attempts to stop bootlegging in Ocean County were largely unsuccessful. Many citizens criticized both the Coast Guard and the county government for their failure to stop this illegal activity. At one point, illegal alcohol which had been seized by the authorities disappeared from the county jailcell in Toms River where it was stored. The confiscated liquor included 287 cases of scotch and whiskey. The goods and those responsible for the theft were never found. Speakeasies were also open in Ocean County to serve illegal alcohol to their customers. Many of these early bootleggers and speakeasy owners were among the first to apply and receive liquor licenses after the repeal of Prohibition in 1933.

Farm Workers

Agriculture provided some of the earliest jobs in Ocean County. Salt hay grew without cultivation along the edge of the bay. Harvested, it could be used for packing glass and china, stuffing mattresses, thatching early roofs, insulation, feeding cattle, and even stabilizing roads. Cattle grazing was also common in the meadows near the shore. It wasn't unusual for operators of boarding houses to conduct both of these farming operations while they were serving as hosts to their guests.

Harvesting of hay on Cook Farm.   W.E. Hess Collection

The northwestern part of the county was the site of the best farm land. In this area, stretching from Lakewood to New Egypt, corn, wheat and a variety of farm products were grown. In most of the Pinelands, however, the soil was too sandy to provide other than subsistence farming. It would be a mistake, however, to deny the agricultural value of the county.

Wild blueberries and cranberries had long been products of the pines. With the end of the iron industry many of the old cedar swamps, abandoned by the iron ore industry, became sites for cultivated berries. Elizabeth White and Frederick Colville developed the world's first cultivated blueberry in the early 1900's. By the 1970's there were over 100 cranberry bogs in Jackson, Berkeley, Manchester, and Brick Townships and in other areas of the county.

Blueberry.

Picking of commercial berries provided many jobs for county residents. However, most pickers were from Philadelphia. It wasn't unusual for busses to cruise the city for workers and then transport them to the county to harvest the crop. At the end of the day the workers would be transported back to the city. This practice was followed by hiring migrant workers who lived directly on the farms. In recent times these migrants have been replaced by local day workers who are often black, Puerto Rican, Haitian, or Cambodians who recently moved to the area. Also, today many bogs are opened to consumers who pick their own supply.

Cranberry growers harvest their fruit from Pinelands bogs each fall.

Nineteenth Century Women

Women rarely worked outside of the house in this period. They were kept busy with the daily demands of cooking, cleaning, child-care, making cloth and their families' clothing, and day-to-day chores such as filling oil lamps and bringing in water. They also helped on the farm with such chores as milking, collecting eggs, planting a kitchen garden, canning or preserving food, and making butter, cheese and bread. It is estimated that they worked two to three hours longer than men of the day.

As Marilyn Kralik observes, women were also mainly responsible for their families health. Doctors were only called as a last resort and hospitals, as we know them, did not exist. Women were also often pregnant. It was not unusual to have a child every eighteen months, usually born at home. For the average woman, this left little time for social occasions.

Women on the farm in the nineteenth century (Cook Homestead)   W.E. Hess Collection

Egg farming also became an important industry in Ocean County. In the period from 1909-1920, this industry attracted immigrant workers, followed by Jewish businessmen and professionals ruined by the depression. These newcomers chose egg farming because it required little previous farming experience and little capital. In one five year period the county gained five poultrymen a week. Rutgers University had to select a farm agent with special language skills to communicate with these new farmers.

By 1935 the poultry industry became big business in Ocean County. Many of the new Jewish egg farmers maintained their contacts with the city and brought with them their experiences in marketing. Apartment-like structures that could hold up to three thousand chickens and the installation of electric lights to keep the chickens laying twenty-four hours a day were a few of the new techniques that were introduced. World's Farm was one of the largest farms in the county with over 35,000 layers. Lakewood, Jackson, and Toms River became the poultry centers of the county.

Chicken farming in the county reached its peak in the 1940's. Overproduction and higher costs for both land and feed, along with a sharp drop in prices, contributed to this decline. By 1980 only about a half dozen small commercial farms remained in Ocean County. Poultry farming, however, did not die out in New Jersey. In 1990 Ise Farms, a Japanese company, owned more than 10 million egg-producing chickens in Warren County, while it maintained its headquarters in Lakewood.

Chicken Apartment House.

The Military

The military services have employed many residents of Ocean County. Two major military bases were located in the Pinelands in the 20th century, providing many civilian as well as military jobs. Camp Dix, built on the edge of the Pinelands during World War I, grew into

U. S. Navy Dirigible Hangar

U.S. Navy Dirigible Hangar.

one of the largest military reservations in the nation. McGuire Air Force Base, in neighboring Burlington County, grew out of a single airstrip at Fort Dix. McGuire is the largest military air command in the east employing over 5,200 military and 2,000 civilians in the 1980's.

Lakehurst Naval Engineering Center, situated on 11.5 square miles of flat Pinelands adjacent to Fort Dix, was most famous for its years as the dirigible base for transatlantic travel. It possessed some of the largest hangars in the world, and in the 1980's, was the most expensive naval operations base in New Jersey. It is the largest single employer in Ocean County (1986), employing over 3,700 military and civilian employees. With the end of the Cold War and with strong public demand for reduced military spending, the area may see a reduction in employment in the 1990's. Lakehurst, however, seems to be the exception. Plans are now being made to increase its use as a Naval Air Research Center and for the construction of a new airship for Westinghouse. It may also enter the educational field. Once the site of Shore Conference Indoor Track Meets, it may soon furnish classrooms for vocational education.

Industrial Workers

The largest single private employer in Ocean County in the 1960's was the Toms River Chemical Company or CIBA GEIGY. In the late 1940's, CIBA States Limited purchased 1,243 acres in the woodlands of Toms River to construct a vat dye plant. Built in 1952, it expanded to include dyes, plastics, and chemical additives as well as other supportive services. By the 1970's it employed 1,400 workers, and during the next decade, plans were made for even greater expansion into the field of pharmaceuticals.

CIBA, during the 1980's, became the center of a growing concern over compatibility of the chemical plant with the shore environment. Public protests over the plant's outfall line, which enters into the Atlantic Ocean, and the past and present disposal of hazardous waste subjected the company to a hail of public criticism. As a result, the company decided to transfer the dye and plastics production to the southern part of the country. The pressure of environmental groups was also influential in a decision to review plans for operating a pharmaceutical plant on the same site.

The CIBA story illustrates the strong tie between nature and employment practices in Ocean County. This plant chose the site in Ocean County because of the attractiveness of the site and the accessibility to water. CIBA's problems and its eventual decline were brought about by the desire to protect that same environment.

Oyster Creek Nuclear Plant is another major industry in Ocean County subject to many of the same conflicts as CIBA. Construction on this Lacey Township plant was started in December, 1963, and was in operation six years later. It supplies enough electrical power for 200,000 homes. It was built at a cost of $96 million dollars and employs about 900 workers, most from Ocean County.

The water that cools its condensers is taken from Barnegat Bay via the South Branch of Forked River. It is returned to the bay via Oyster Creek. Many concerns have been raised by the public since it began its operation. Fish kills led to a continued study of the water discharge. The issue of radiation and its effect on employees and the community created an even greater concern. As the plant has aged, and with the accidents at Three Mile Island in neighboring Pennsylvania and in the Chernobyl Plant in the USSR, questions have been raised about the safety of the Lacey plant. Although the plant's power has enabled this area to meet the demands of population growth, and has contributed to tax revenue, continued operation of the plant in the 1990's must again be decided by balancing the needs of the population versus that of the environment.

Job Diversity

Ocean County has always had job diversity. Jobs ranging from the selling of pine snakes to the drilling of oil in Jackson were available in the county. Glass making at Barnegat's Atlantic Coast Glass Company and Brick's Van Wickle's Pottery Works were also early examples of this variety.

Meat Market - Peddlers of food, wares, and news were common at the Shore during 18th, 19th and early 20th century.   W.E. Hess Collection

When Toms River became the county seat in 1850, a construction boom was set off. This industry continued to grow in the latter part of that century as towns became established up and down the coast. This post-World War II population growth in the county created an even greater building boom. Brick Township grew from a population of 4,000 in 1950 to 66,473 in 1990 with 28,843 homes. Construction of homes, offices, schools, and buildings became a major economic force in the county.

The railroad and the automobile brought a new designation to the county. In the twentieth century Ocean County became known as a bedroom community for people working in more urban areas. Railroads provided the transportation necessary for those who worked in the city but wanted a permanent home at the shore. The building of the Garden State Parkway, not only tremendously expanded the population of the county, but also was responsible for the growth of industries along its route, providing county residents with closer places of employment. Lakewood Industrial Park and other such industrial centers in the county, along with businesses by Routes #287, #34, and #35 in neighboring counties are examples of employment opportunities for county residents. Toms River Chemical and the Oyster Creek plant earlier, and Great Adventure Amusement Park in Jackson, a major seasonal employer of the county's youth, are other examples of local job opportunities.

As more people moved into the area the need for service industries grew. The professional field employing the most workers in Ocean County today is education. For example, one school system, the Toms River Schools, employs over 2000 people.

Early Store.

W.E. Hess Collection

Retail businesses have also grown in importance as major employers. Giant shopping centers along with strip malls opened during the post World War II years. They rivaled, and in some cases exceeded, the business centers in more urban areas. These retail shops and professional offices are located along most major traffic arteries in the county. In 1986 the Ocean County Mall alone provided over 2500 jobs. The importance of construction and retail employment was apparent in 1991 when slumps in these areas caused Ocean County's unemployment rate to quickly exceed most of the rest of the nation.

The work force in Ocean County has also changed with most women in the County now employed. According to a survey conducted

in 1986 by the Ocean County Advisory Commission on the Status   and
Needs of Women, four out of five top issues were: employment
concerns, day care for children, balancing home and job, and equal pay
and job responsibility.   These concerns reflect the changing roles of
women in Ocean County and, in fact, the entire nation.

The most significant labor trend in the country has been the
increase in numbers of working women.   According to the United
States Department of Labor, in 1988, 65% of the nearly thirty-three
million women with children under the age of eighteen work.   About
47% of the total workforce are women and they represent 67% of all
women, ages 18-64.   This number is equally representative of white,
black and Hispanic women.

These changes in the job market and the workforce have had a
profound effect on the growth of Ocean County.   It has brought great
opportunities for young residents to obtain good jobs and to still enjoy
the good life at the shore.   It has also contributed to many problems.
The tremendous growth in year-round population has placed a major
strain on the county's infrastructure and its environment.   The need to
provide governmental and educational services for the increased population, although creating extra employment opportunities, has also
tremendously increased the cost of living in the county.   Many of the
problems that caused the exodus from the urban areas in the north and
the west are now the problems of Ocean County.   The natural benefits
of the shore and pines are now being threatened by those attracted to
the area by them.   The reconciling of the environment with the increased population remains one of the most important questions facing
Ocean County citizens today.

Christmas Shopping in Bay Head.

Point Pleasant   Lionel Barrymore

Building on Curtis property painted by its most famous guest, actor Lionel Barrymore.

CHAPTER VIII

Tourists

The Cook Homestead (Boarding House)

In 1792, Thomas Cook, a Quaker immigrant, and his wife came to Point Pleasant Beach and purchased 300 acres of land from William Curtis. On the property, Cook built a one-story farmhouse that eventually became the center of the Cook Homestead. The major crops of the farm were corn and hay, but the income from the crops were not enough to carry the property. In 1831, to supplement their income, the Cooks decided to operate a boarding house. The homestead was expanded to include several cottages, a barn, an icehouse, a carriagehouse and a pumphouse.

Cook Homestead.   W.E. Hess Collection

Thomas Cook Jr. took over the boarding house and operated it until the 1880's. Rates for summer guests were between $12 and $15 dollars a week. Swimming and fishing were available in the Manasquan River, in Cooks Pond (today's Lake Louise) and in the Atlantic Ocean. Guests could also enjoy the beauty of the Cedars, a picnic grove in the *center of the property. In the evenings, Thomas Cook entertained his guests with stories of personal experiences with Indian Will, who had lived on the property, and of shipwrecks, such as that of the John Minturn. The homestead also served as a center for an art colony that existed in the Cedars, presided over by Mrs. Carrie Cook Sanborn. One of the writers to frequent this group was Robert Louis Stevenson.*

The Cook Homestead, at one time, encompassed about half the area which was to become Point Pleasant Beach. It extended from the Manasquan River on the north to the ocean

Carrie Cook Sanborn, nineteenth century Quaker, artist and hostess.   W.E. Hess Collection.

on the east. Reporters visiting the boarding house wrote of its great beaches and superb hospitality. The property prospered, and other boarding houses soon opened. However, by the 1880's, other large farms began selling out to a newly formed land company which laid out streets and divided the properties into small plots in anticipation of the arrival of the railroad.

In the years that followed, prosperity ended and the town took over the Cook property. At the end of the century it was purchased by the Reed family who sold off some lots and turned the remainder into a golf course. In the 1920's the Manasquan River Golf Course was located on the site but, in 1925, it moved to its present site across the river. A nine-hole golf course continued to operate on the Cook Homestead site until World War II when the original farm house (the golf clubhouse) burned. The town again inherited the property and much of the land was purchased by the Board of Education. The site of the old farm house became the site of the G. Harold Antrim School and the old "Cedars" became the location of the high school athletic field.

Group of guests on the south porch of the Cook Homestead .   W.E. Hess Collection

The story of the Cook Homestead is representative of the boarding houses and sportsmen's clubs in the county that played a major role in the attraction of tourists to the area during the nineteenth century. One of the most famous boardinghouse for fishermen and gunners was the Chadwick House.   The Shore Heritage Newsletter reports that former President Ulysses S. Grant, George B. McClellan, and Samuel Tilden registered at the Chadwicks in 1878 and "They were drunk as owls."   Other guests included Theodore Roosevelt, Horace Greeley, and Francis Elliot. Elliot reportedly killed "a total of 890 birds during the season." These guests helped to publicize the attractiveness of the county and helped to make tourism a major source of income.

Art Colony in Cedars. Carrie Sanborn's art class.   W.E. Hess Collection

Curtis Homestead.   W.E. Hess Collection

Phoebe Doolittle Curtis

Phoebe Doolittle Curtis was born in New England in 1832 where she completed her education. She moved to Point Pleasant Beach when she heard that it needed a school and she set about creating one. Her students included children of sea captains, farmers, boarding house operators, trades people and merchants. Their names included Mounts, Chadwicks, Formans, Havens, Tiltons, Cooks, Curtises and Herberts.

Although Phoebe was not a Quaker, many of her students were. Ebenezer Curtis was a Quaker who began a boarding house in 1828. Phoebe boarded there and eventually married Captain William Curtis, Ebenezer's stepson. Phoebe helped to manage the boarding house for most of its forty years of operation. Besides raising a large family, she cooked, cleaned, and played hostess to the guests. She entertained many famous artists and writers of the day including Richard Harding Davis, Robert Louis Stevenson, and the Barrymores.

Phoebe joined the art colony that met at the Cedars on the Cook Homestead and she even wrote and published a book of daily verses. In 1894 Phoebe and her husband donated the land for the Baptist Church and helped to found the Point Pleasant Library. In an unpublished biography, her great, great-granddaughter, Virginia Curtis Lee states, "creation of the Point Pleasant Library was an extension of her desire to provide her literary and artistic guests with **food for thought** as well as body."

Early Tourists

Early tourists came to enjoy the ocean, air, and resources just as their Indian predecessors. As the Lenape before them, they packed their own blankets, cooking stoves, and other provisions. In the early days they were mostly men who could face the rigors of travel: poor roads, dusty conditions and mosquitos. They also didn't mind the primitive housing conditions and enjoyed outside life.

As forms of transportation improved, more families began to arrive. These new tourists demanded better housing and a greater variety of activities. Sportsmen's lodges were replaced by larger more elegant hotels with a diversity of activities. The earliest hotel was built in the 1830's in Cape May followed, in the 1840's, by several hotels in Long Branch.

The Mount Vernon Hotel, built in Cape May in 1853 and locally called the largest hotel in the world, had 432 rooms and a dining room that could seat 750 guests at a time. This hotel helped make Cape May the fashionable summer resort of the wealthy. Cape May reached its peak of popularity just before the Civil War when over 17,000 summer visitors filled the community.

Imposing structures were built in Long Branch in the 1840's to house the increasing number of summer tourists. In 1869 General Ulysses S. Grant "discovered" Long Branch. Tom Fleming in his book, *New Jersey*, quotes Grant as saying he had never seen a place in his travels better suited for a summer residence.

Resort House.

The Resort House.

During this period, most towns in Ocean County were still small fishing and farming villages and most tourist lodgings were still of the boarding house variety. Although the number of fishermen and hunters increased, there were limited facilities for female guests. The new enlarged "hotels" that were built

Baldwin Hotel, Beach Haven.   Joe Eid Collection

in Waretown, Barnegat, Tuckerton, Manahawkin, and West Creek were little more than enlarged boarding houses.

The Resort House in Point Pleasant Beach became one of the first modern hotels in the county. Following the example of the elegant hotels in other parts of the state, the Resort House provided private rooms, indoor bowling, ocean bathing, boating, lawn tennis, regular musical recitals and a horsecar line. Hotels in Lakewood, Long Beach Island, and Seaside Park soon opened with similar amenities.

Hotel registers that have survived from the late eighteen hundreds reveal the names of only a few single ladies. At that time women rarely traveled unaccompanied and few

Horse Trolley to Baldwin Hotel.   Joe Eid Collection

women could afford the trainfare and hotel costs. Women traveled with their husbands or as part of a family group. Meals were one of the highlights of these new resorts. The dining rooms became more formal and became a place for visitors not only to eat but also to display the newest styles and manners of society. By the end of the nineteenth century, most of the shore communities in Ocean County had their share of these "centers of civilization."

Inland Resorts

During the same period, Lakewood was also growing as a tourist resort. Railroad construction in the 1860's made Bricksburg easily accessible to north Jersey and New York City. In 1866 the Bricksburg Land and Improvement Company was incorporated to promote Lakewood as a winter tourist and health resort. By the end of the 1880's, three hotels were built: the Laurel House, the Lakewood Hotel and the

Laurel in the Pines. The next two decades saw construction of thirty-three hotels and guest houses with Lakewood becoming nationally famous as a winter resort.

John D. Rockefeller Summer Residence - At his death, Rockefeller's heirs donated the land to Ocean County.   Ocean County Historical Museum

In the 1890's wealthy vacationers began building their own "cottages" and estates. The Ocean Hunt and Country Club of Lakewood, founded in 1894, was sold to John D. Rockefeller, the oil magnate, for his winter vacation home. At his death, the property became Ocean County Park and his house was torn down by the Board of Freeholders in the 1950's to save the cost of improvements and upkeep. Jay Gould, wealthy financier, joined Rockefeller in establishing his home in Lakewood. His magnificent estate and his famous casino today serve as Georgian Court College.

The mansion of George Gould. Kitchen at the far left. Conservatory at the right. The master bedroom was upstairs at the right end. Most of the estate could be seen from there.
Ocean County Historical Museum

New Egypt also tried to become a summer resort at the turn of the century. Taking advantage of Mill Pond, now Oakland Lake, bathhouses, boat rentals, a hotel and a dance hall were offered to summer visitors. The Philadelphia Inquirer advertised this area as the ideal vacation spot. However, swimming ended with the growth of Fort Dix during World War I as the lake was used for sewage disposal by the Fort. Most of the land was later purchased by the government in an attempt to unite the Fort Dix and Lakehurst facilities. Harkers Grove in New Egypt, used as a picnic area and playground, is all that remains of the planned tourist area.

Resort Activities

Improvements in transportation and the arrival of more families changed the character of vacations in Ocean County. Swimming became the center of attraction. Volunteer lifeguards protected swimming areas as early as 1860, relying on contributions of those

Bathing group at Point Pleasant Beach.

using the swimming areas. Twenty years later, Atlantic City became the first city to employ paid lifeguards.

Swimming attire changed slowly. In neighboring Ocean Grove, swimmers were separated by sex. Men went a distance away, left their outer clothing on the beach and went for a dip. Women, on the other hand, found a secluded spot where they enjoyed the surf in garments whose "days of usefulness had passed." In 1870 local governments passed legislation requiring all ocean bathers to wear clothing that covered their bodies from the neck down. In 1924, in Atlantic City, a law was passed permitting stockingless women on the beach but not on

Old Boardwalk to Inlet in Point Pleasant.   W.E. Hess Collection

the boardwalk. "Beach nudists", in the 1930's, were men bathing without tops. As late as 1938, men were arrested for swimming without tops. Most beach resorts in Ocean County passed similar legislation.

Early boardwalks were just that—boards laid on the sand and removed at the end of the season. Cape May was the first seashore to build a boardwalk in 1868 with Atlantic City following in 1870. The first boardwalk built on piling in Ocean County was built in Point Pleasant Beach in the 1890's. However, as late as 1915, planks across the sand dunes still served as the boardwalk north of Central Avenue. At its peak, the boardwalk in Point Pleasant extended from the inlet to the Beacon Manor Hotel. Permanent boardwalks were also constructed at Seaside Park, Bay Head, Lavallette, and Beach Haven, and some short boardwalks were built on the bayfront by the respective towns. Many of the permanent boardwalks, however, were not very permanent as the storms of 1929, 1938, 1944, and 1950 took their toll.

Early bathhouses were also temporary in nature. They were rough and un- attractive shacks erected

on the beaches for only the summer. These were later replaced by pavilions which housed bathhouses, rocking chairs, refreshments and, often, amusements. Many were specifically for guests at hotels, most of which were built inland. The first pavilion in Point Pleasant Beach was built in the 1880's at the foot of Atlantic Avenue for guests of the Resort House. This pavilion was followed by a similar structure on the Manasquan River called Clark's Landing. The first inlet pavilion was built by the Cook family in 1898.

Risden's Casino and Johnson's Bath House Point Pleasant Beach .   W.E. Hess Collection

During the 1920's, commercial pavilions for day bathers blossomed all along the coast. The most famous in Ocean County was Jenkinson's Pavilion in Point Pleasant Beach which not only included bathhouses, refreshments and amusements, but also a saltwater pool and dance hall which attracted major bands during the summer months. Another major dance hall was located in the Seaside Casino and it attracted tourists from the Philadelphia area.

The first boardwalk amusements were built in the 1870's in Atlantic City. This was soon followed by fishing and amusement piers. Rides, games and a variety of foodstands also attracted visitors to the shore. Point Pleasant Beach and Seaside Heights became important tourist centers offering this type of beach entertainment. Although Long Beach Island did construct some boardwalks, their beaches remained free of commercial amusements.

Resort Communities

As the resort industry expanded, more and more visitors sought permanent housing at the shore. Paralleling the growth of hotels, developers began dividing up tracts of land for the construction of summer cottages. In the nineteenth century most of the houses built in the county were built to house workers. In the early part of the twentieth century, most construction was designed to provide for the tourist, first as summer residences and later as year round homes, as tourists became permanent residents.

Prior to 1920, tents were set up among the dunes to house visitors in Point Pleasant Beach, Seaside Park, and Barnegat Light. In the 1870's, the population of Long Beach Island expanded because of railroad construction. As tourism increased, so did the construction of homes on Long Beach Island. This nineteen mile long island, with no boardwalks or amusements, attracted families who wished to spend their time enjoying the sand and surf. Other Ocean County communities soon followed suit. Businessmen from Trenton formed the Point Pleasant Land Company and purchased the Forman Farm for the construction of a hotel and a "city" of small summer cottages. John Arnold, a member of the Land Company, donated the land that was to become Arnold Avenue so that residents could reach the ocean. Until then residents had to pay a toll to use the path running through the farm to the ocean. Arnold also donated land for the railroad to be built into town. The joining of the rail line from New York and Philadelphia to Point Pleasant Beach made this community into a popular tourist area almost overnight.

Seaside Park, Island Heights and Barnegat Light were first formed as havens for those "seeking escape from the evils" of urban life. With this objective, in 1874, the Seaside Baptist Association planned to build a 300 acre resort and, four years later, the Reverend John Simpson started a Methodist Camp Meeting center on the Toms River in Island Heights. The Island Heights camp meetings continued until the 1920's and are still held once a year. The conservative nature of these areas weakened the "hotel trade" in those communities by discouraging Philadelphia tourists who were seeking a "fun" resort. However, Seaside Heights benefited from its location at the head of the bay bridge and became the center of tourist trade from Philadelphia while a section of Island Heights later became a summer resort for employees of John Wanamaker's famous Philadelphia store.

John Wanamaker Commercial Institute, Island Heights, New Jersey, August, 1916 .
Ocean County Historical Museum

Harriet Smart Simpson

Nineteenth century women, besides taking care of their homes and families, were often also expected to help their husband with his business or occupation. Harriet Smart Simpson is an example of such women.

Harriet married the Reverend John Simpson who was appointed the supervisor of the Methodist Camp Meeting in Island Heights. In 1878 Harriet moved her five children from the comfortable farm on which they were living to a tiny attic above her husband's Island Heights offices. From here, she prepared meals for the distinguished guests who attended the summer camp meetings.

Harriet also ran a boarding house, taught Sunday School, helped to establish a local postal service and worked to establish the First Methodist Church of Island Heights. She also taught her own children who all went on to receive advance degrees. Later, when her husband become the first mayor of Island Heights, she continued to assist him. (from the doctoral thesis of Marilyn Kralik)

Long Beach Island, in the 1920's was noted for its summer camps. North Beach Haven offered a camp for underprivileged women, and Harvey Cedars had one for young working women which later became a Bible conference center. There also was a Y.M.C.A. camp, Miquin, a camp for rich boys and the most famous, Dune By the Sea, a noted music camp for girls. Long Beach Island wasn't the only site for youth camps in the county. In the 1930's a young boy's choir camp was held in Nejeco Beach in Brick. The camp's name, Nejeco, was an acronym for "New Jersey Choir."

Marguerite Silbey & Agnes Reifschneider

John Lloyd tells in his book, *Six Miles At Sea*, of Marguerite ("Sibby") Silbey, daughter of a wealthy Philadelphia dentist, who inherited two large oceanfront cottages on Long Beach Island. In the 1920's she and her cousin Agnes, known as "Auntie Riffles", used the houses to establish Dune By the Sea, a camp for girls ages 7-13. Agnes was well known as a voice teacher who had instructed Marian Anderson, the first black woman to have a starring role at the Metropolitan Opera and in Washington, D.C.

The camp these two women established was known not only for its musical training and recitals but also for an excellent sports program. The older girls were allowed to bring their own sailboats or horses, shipped by train from their homes. The camp also sported a mahogany Chris Craft boat and a 1919 Model T station wagon used to transport the girls.

The ladies emphasized good breeding and social skills. The Dune, and its neighboring camp, Miquon, were established as exclusive camps for wealthy families from New Jersey and Philadelphia. However, the hurricane of 1944 and the growing population at the beaches, brought the camp to an end in 1947.

Prior to 1870, the Chadwick House, near today's Chadwick Beach, was the largest structure between Point Pleasant Beach and Seaside Heights. As the railroad brought in more visitors, larger and more permanent homes were built. These structures were mostly designed by developers from Philadelphia or west Jersey. Two communities, Bay Head and Mantoloking, possessed an atmosphere unique along the coast. The homes built among the dunes had, according to John Cunningham, "the ivy look", a combination of conservatism and wealth.

"The Springs" - Island Heights - 1920. Religious Girls Summer School.   Ocean County Historical Museum

The Bay Head Land Company was formed in 1879 by David Mount, Edward Howe and William Harris, all officers of a Princeton bank. The 157 acres they purchased from Elijah Chadwick extended from the ocean to the bay and was first occupied by alumni and faculty from Princeton. Frederick Downer of New York, purchased most of the land comprising present day Mantoloking in anticipation of railroad construction. John Arnold, who originally started to develop the town with his Sea-Shore Land Company, contributed to the growth of the community by importing topsoil from the mainland to grow grass on this strip of sandy soil.

Lavallette was developed earlier than Bay Head or Mantoloking. Albert Lavallette, who named the resort after his famous father, Admiral Elie Lavallette of Baltimore, divided the town into squares for development. Maps of 1870 show only Lavallette By the Sea, Seaside and Point Pleasant Beach as towns on the peninsula. As the railroad extended across the bay, other towns were established, but it was the advent of the automobile that truly opened up the barrier islands to tourism. After World War II, in towns such as Ortley Beach, small cottages were built on extremely small lots, making them affordable to even the most modest families.

Many other towns had grandiose plans to become famous resorts that never materialized. Electric City, on the outskirts of Lakewood, was one of these sites. Its roads, named for famous inventors, were overgrown with grass in less than a decade. Several attempts were made to develop Crystal Lake in Pinewald. It was advertised as a "new

Royal Pines Hotel today in Pinewald.

type of residential, recreational city of the sea and pines." A golf course, some homes, and the Royal Pines Hotel, a seven-story modern hotel with an open pavilion on the bayside, were built. Fire and the Great Depression led to its failure, although the hotel still stands and is used as a nursing home.

Shore Baseball

A favorite pastime of native and summer visitor alike during the first half of the twentieth century was semi-professional baseball. Teams representing Beach Haven, Tuckerton, Toms River, and Point Pleasant Beach played regularly from July through September. Rivalries between neighboring communities were strong and fields such as Clayton Field in Point Pleasant Beach and Walsh Field in Beach Haven were filled with cheering fans.

Games were also held with traveling teams. Many of these teams featured retired major league stars as well as good black players. Since major league baseball was closed to black ballplayers until the end of World War II, these traveling teams brought high quality baseball to the shore. Teams with unusual competitors also played against the community teams. One team, the House of David, featured ballplayers with rabbinical beards. Another, called the Bloomer Girls was made up primarily of girls (only 2 boys permitted). The Shore's most famous ballplayer, Roger "Doc" Cramer, played on such a club after he retired from the majors.

Doc Cramer at bat in the Twenties.
Beachcomber

Doc Cramer was born on July 22, 1905 in Beach Haven. In the 1920's he played with Philadelphia, Detroit, Boston, and the Washington Senators. His major league career batting average was 296. He played on two World Series teams and was selected for five All Star Teams. Many other local ballplayers played in the major and minor leagues, but none matched his record. One local player made a name for himself, Al "Peanuts" Gray. He played on the Point Beach team and later became the United States Marines Corps Chief of Staff.

Unlike most other things in Ocean County, baseball did not grow in the postwar years. Walsh Field became a National Guard Camp during the war and Clayton Field became the site of a traffic complex. Easier access to major league facilities and the broadcasting and televising of major league games helped spell the end of this semi-pro sport in the county.

Ocean County Parks

In 1890, the Seaside Realty Company made plans for the development of a summer resort in the northern section of Island Beach to be called the "Cottage City of New Jersey." Streets and 25' by 100' lots were laid out and were put up for sale at $600 for waterfront and $200 for inland lots. Anyone purchasing ten lots was to be given a free cottage. The project was never started, however, because of the depression of 1893, and because the railroad, which was supposed to

Missile launcher.   Ocean County Observer

make the area accessible, turned north instead of south after it crossed Barnegat Bay at Seaside Park.

In 1925 Henry Phipps, a steel magnate and partner of Andrew Carnegie, purchased over 2000 acres in the area known as Island Beach for $600,000.

He planned to develop the property into wide boulevards and estates. One hundred twenty-five foot lots were sold, but Mr. Phipps's death and the Depression of 1929 aborted these plans for a "high-class private development." However, many shacks were built on the property by squatters and by sportsmen who leased the property.

In 1945 Island Beach was to play an important role in the United States missile program. Allied forces, attempting to end World War II, were faced with the threat of the German V-2 long range rockets and Japanese kamikaze suicide pilots. Some way had to be found to combat these weapons.

Experiments were made to develop a new supersonic missile for this purpose. The Cedar Creek Coast Guard Station was chosen by a group of Johns Hopkins scientists as the site for testing these weapons. This ten month project, called Project Bumblebee, resulted in the testing and development of supersonic missiles. Early in 1946 the

Island Beach site was abandoned for areas that could provide for longer range missiles. Don Bennett, in the *Ocean County Observer*, wrote, "tens of thousands of visitors come to bathing pavilions that surround the old missile site each year and leave without ever knowing what happened in the nearby sand dunes in World War II." Attempts to turn the area into the Coast Guard Training center following the war failed.

In 1953, the state purchased 2,694 acres of the property in Island Beach for $2,750,000 with plans to protect the natural beauty of its sand dunes and to maintain its vegetation. The state expanded plans for the usage of the area and opened Island Beach State Park to the public in 1959. The northern part of the park is open for swimming with the southern ten miles open only to fishermen and to visitors wishing to see examples of pristine beaches and sand dunes with their natural flora and fauna.

Squatters Shack - Island Beach.

In 1953 over 80 squatters' shacks remained, and their claims were still in dispute when New Jersey purchased the estate. The state worked out a compromise with the owners of the shacks so that they could continue occupancy of their properties until their deaths at which time the state would assume ownership. The Phipps home near the entrance today serves as the summer home of the governor of New Jersey.

The area was described by Frances Freeman, manager of the Phipps estate, as an area whose assets are measured "not in the number of streets, or new citizens, or in the number of feet of boardwalk, but in acres of heather and holly, in sand dunes left as God made them, in beach grass holding the shifting sands and offering a haven to numbers of birds, rabbits and other wildlife. No jetties, bulkheads or other beach protective devices to mar the beautiful shoreline." The park today provides the best example of the attraction of the Ocean County shore.

Island Beach is not the only park for visitors to view. Barnegat Light, which from 1857 to 1943 faithfully guided ships around this treacherous part of the shore, was opened to the public in 1953. Double Trouble Park in Berkeley, with its 2000 acres of pines, cedars and oaks surrounding large cranberry bogs, offers an excellent view of the industries of the pines. On display is a one -room schoolhouse, a sawmill, a cranberry processing plant, workers' cottages, and a general store.

The Ocean County Parks System continues to grow. Lakewood Park and Shenandoah Park are examples of both active and passive recreational facilities with the attraction of the pines. Cattus Island Environmental Center in Toms River demonstrates the natural wetland environment with a nature center, trails, and an environmental education program. The County also has several golf courses and offers many other recreational and sporting facilities. All of these add to the attractiveness of Ocean County not only as a place to visit but a place in which to live.

1.   A. Paul King Park
2.   Berkeley Island Park
3.   Cattus Island Park
4.   Cedar Run Park
5.   Forge Pond Recreation Area
6.   Gull Island Conservation Area
7.   Jackson County Park
8.   Lake Shenandoah Park
9.   Metedeconk River Recreation Area
10. Ocean County Park
11. Parkertown Park
12. Robert J. Miller Airpark
13. Riverfront Landing Park
14. Shenandoah Sports Field Complex
15. South Green Street Park
16. Stanley H. "Tip" Seaman Park
17. Wells Mills Regional Park

Map of Park System.

CHAPTER IX

Citizens

Thomas Mathis (Politician)

Thomas A. Mathis was one of the most successful politicians in the history of Ocean County. Born on June 7, 1869, in the rural community of New Gretna, he become the undisputed leader of Ocean County for over half a century. Like many in his family, he first made his living

Republican Party Club Card.

from the sea, becoming a captain at the age of 19. At the turn of the century, he developed an active interest in politics when he took part in the separation of Tuckerton from Little Egg Harbor Township. In 1904 Thomas Mathis was elected to Tuckerton's first city coun-cil. Four years later he moved to Toms River where he assumed a position in county government. In 1913, he won the seat he was to occupy for many terms in the New Jersey Senate, becoming its President in 1928.

"Captain Tom," as he was known, was not only an elected official, he was also the Republican party "boss." Even though he was the leader of a lightly populated county, he was the "Mayor Hague" of rural New Jersey, influencing national as well as state affairs. His complete control of Ocean County was exerted through the many "TAM" (Thomas A. Mathis) Republican Clubs. His favors to all citizens in need, regardless of party, and his political skills were the source of his great power.

With power came controversy. He was either loved or hated. There was no single person in the county's history to receive greater honors nor greater criticism. His machine was accused of providing protec-tion for a gambling ring in Point Pleasant and granting safe passage through the county to those shipping illegal liquor during the Prohibi-tion Era.

His power grew in spite of these charges, and his strength waned only when he opposed the growth of population in the county. In 1958, disheartened by his declining power and poor health, he committed suicide. The strong feelings that he provoked and the influence he exerted were far greater than expected considering the size of his constituency. His supporters can point to his ability to build a strong party organization in the county, while his detractors can single out the dangers of one individual or group making decisions for the entire county. His service to the county and to the state was recognized by the placement of a plaque in his honor in the lobby of the Ocean County Court House and by naming the Seaside Heights bridge, The Thomas Mathis Bridge.

Politics have always been important to the people of Ocean County. The views of its citizens have not always been in agreement with their neighbors or with others in the state or nation; but like Captain Tom, they have never hesitated to take a position. On many issues, such as support for England during the Revolution, opposition to Lincoln, women's suffrage, and the slavery issue, Ocean County has differed from its neighbors. Although these issues have, in many instances, resulted in violent conflicts, the county has been able to resolve most of the issues through the political process.

The laws and institutions that define the role of Ocean County citizens have evolved over the years. Many of its institutions were patterned after the mother country, England. Many were the result of the colonial experience. A review of this process will enable the reader to gain a better view of the county's political history.

Early Government

In 1702, East Jersey and West Jersey were united and New Jersey became a royal colony. This, however, did not end citizen unrest. Taxes were to take the place of the land-use rent paid to the proprietors. The expansion of taxes, the new restrictive measures enforced by the courts, and the cry of "taxation without representation" led to demonstrations and, finally, to the independence movement.

During the Revolution, New Jersey was governed by the State Constitution of 1776. This government was designed to make the transition from the colonial period to the end of British rule. It, however, remained the Constitution of New Jersey until 1844. It reflected the unpopularity of the office of governor as it granted all power to the State Legislature, including the choice of governor. One of the major weaknesses of this constitution was its lack of flexibility as it had no amending procedure.

During the last years of the Revolutionary War, the colonies formed the government under the Articles of Confederation. A representative of New Jersey, Elias Boudinot, who was recognized for his contributions in settlement of western land claims and his help in drafting the Articles of Confederation, became its first president.

Some claim that this position could justify his being called America's first president.

New Jersey, during that period, had considered becoming an independent nation. It went so far as to coin its own money, establish its own courts and defy the government under the Articles. It soon recognized, however, that it was too weak to survive independently and joined the other colonies in Philadelphia to write a new constitution for the nation.

New Jersey played a leadership role in helping to shape the new federal constitution in 1789. In 1844 and again in 1947, it revised and strengthened its own state constitution. These actions provided the outline of government for the citizens of Ocean County today.

Women's Rights

New Jersey has a checkered history in the area of women's rights. Under Dutch rule women had many rights not granted women in other colonies. Women were able to own their own business, to own and inherit property, to retain their names after marriage, and to vote. Many of these rights were revoked under British rule. Voting rights for women were restored in the Constitution of 1766 which gave these rights "to all inhabitants of full age." It was said that New Jersey became the first state to extend these rights "to all women, freed slaves, aliens and Philadelphians."

The power of women's vote was shown in an election in Little Egg Harbor in the early 1800's. Thomas Osborn, who during the Revolutionary War had been forced by the British to accompany them on the raid at Tuckerton, was running for office. His opponent was very vocal about Osborn's Loyalist sympathies. Leah Blackman, in her writings in 1880, stated that, "At the time a privileged class of female was allowed the right of suffrage." Tom Osborn campaigned among the women voters and "on the day of the Town Meeting the women marched up to the polls and each of them deposited in the ballot box a ticket bearing the name of Tom Osborn". Osborn was elected!

In 1807 voting rights for women were again revoked as a result of a controversy in the selection of the county seat of Essex County. The women's support of Newark as the site for the county seat cost them

Women Suffrage - Women joined men in the right to vote with the passage of the 19th Amendment in 1920.   W.E. Hess Collection

their vote. It was not to be restored until the enactment of the nineteenth Amendment in 1920. An earlier attempt to pass an amendment had failed in New Jersey with Ocean County the only county to support its passage.

African-American Rights

One of the critical issues facing the citizens of Old Monmouth after the Revolution was the rights of the African-Americans. Prior to 1804, New Jersey was the only state north of Maryland without a law abolishing slavery. The 1810 census listed in Monmouth County 1504 slaves and 632 freed blacks. Since slaves represented a large financial investment, there was little enthusiasm to end slavery among many of the landowners.

Over one hundred Quakers and one freed black sponsored a petition to the state legislature "to lay a foundation for the gradual emancipation of slavery and to bring an end to the system that forced thousands into a life of bondage." Those opposed to abolition claimed that the Quakers and Anglicans who were behind the anti-slavery movement were Loyalists who had supported the British, and thus, were not to be trusted.

The 1804 New Jersey Legislature passed a bill stating that all slaves born after that date were free but that their masters had to be compensated for their loss. The compensation was in the form of labor by the to-be-freed slave until the age of twenty-one for women and twenty-five for men. The bill also allowed owners to "abandon" their slaves to the state which, in turn, paid the owners for the slave's care. These measures placated the slave owners but certainly did not end slavery in New Jersey. However, it did begin the process of gradual emancipation.

The 1804 legislation did affect the area which became Ocean County. In the 1820 census, Dover and Stafford registered one female slave. By the 1830's, most slaves in Old Monmouth had been freed. In 1846, the Legislature turned the remaining slaves into "lifetime apprentices" and gave all future blacks their freedom.

Freed blacks lost their right to vote along with women in 1807. In the 1830's, a number of petitions by freed blacks was sent to the Legislature asking for a return of the vote. The Negro Convention of the anti-slavery movement, composed of freed blacks and many white supporters, continued these efforts without success.

During this time a new black leadership emerged, the black preacher. W.E.B. DuBois, in his book *Souls of Black Folks*, describes black preachers as "the most unique personality developed by the Negro on American soil." They were a leader, a politician, an orator, a "boss," an intriguer and an idealist.

Before the Civil War, New Jersey had an active underground railroad to smuggle slaves to freedom. However, it was the only northern state that failed to condemn the National Fugitive Law which required states to capture and return runaway slaves. New Jersey also was the only northern state that failed to give Lincoln all of its electoral votes in both of his presidential elections. The bombardment of Fort Sumter changed the attitude of its citizens. Some 88,000 residents of New Jersey fought in the Civil War and the majority of the population supported the Fifteenth Amendment that freed the slaves. However, it wasn't until 1875 that the state amended its constitution to permit blacks to vote. It was not until 1947 that the present Constitution of New Jersey formally outlawed segregation.

History of County Government

County government in the new nation was patterned after the British system of shires. England had established shires or counties to locally administer and manage the king's laws. They had been established as early as 1682 in the colonies, and every colony except Rhode Island had instituted them. Monmouth County is one of the four oldest counties in New Jersey. It grew out of the old Monmouth Patent, and it extended forty-four miles south of the Manasquan River to Beach Haven and Little Egg Harbor.

Since colonial times, many in the southern section of Monmouth

County had objected to the travel distance between their homes and the county seat in Freehold. They also felt they hadn't received their fair share of the tax dollar. As early as the 1700's, petitions were circulated to make the southern part of Monmouth County a separate county. Stafford was the name suggested for the new county. However, it wasn't until the middle of the 19th century that Joel Hayward of Stafford Township wrote to the State Legislature about his objections to unequal funding of area roads and aid to the poor. His efforts and the pressure of others led the State Legislature, on February 15th, 1850, to establish the county of Ocean. The new county covered 637 square miles and had a population of 10,043. Toms River was designated as the new county seat.

Earlier, county legislative functions had been performed by the courts, but in 1798 the state established the Board of Chosen Freeholders to handle legislative and administrative matters in the counties. The term "freeholder" was used only in New Jersey, and came from English and colonial times when only persons who were owners of property free from debts or other legal claims could vote or run for office. At one time, there were two representatives from each township in Ocean County on its Board of Freeholders. Today, there is a total of five representatives, each Freeholder representing the county at large.

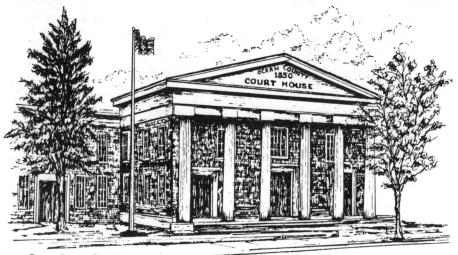

Ocean County Court House.

The first meetings of the Board of Chosen Freeholders in Ocean County were held in taverns and the first court session was held in the Mormon Church in Toms River. During the first meeting on May 10,

1850, the location and construction of a courthouse was discussed. Many sites in Toms River were considered. The present location was chosen although some claimed "it was located too far from the center of town." This claim is hard to believe, since, at that time, the town center was only two blocks long. A rival owner offered to supply 60,000 bricks for the selection of a site south of the river. Finally, Joseph Conrad donated the property at the present site. The property committee chose to pattern the courthouse after one in Hudson County. The first meeting in the new courthouse was in September of 1851.

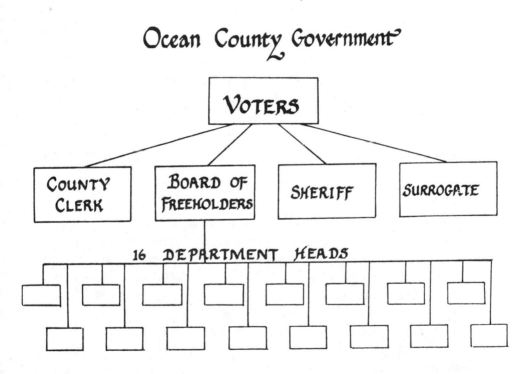

Ocean County Government

Structure of County Government

In Ocean County, each Freeholder is charged with the chairing of a specific area of county government such as: transportation, human services, and environmental resources, administration, finance, parks and recreation, law and public safety, and public works and county operations. One member of the Board of Freeholders serves as the Director each year.

The state mandates that each county must provide courts and law enforcement, education, election, roads and social services. The county also has powers to provide parks, libraries, planning, colleges, health care, and solid waste management.

The county has three constitutional officers required by the state constitution and elected at large by the voters of the county. The County Clerk and the Surrogate have terms of five years while the Sheriff is elected for three years. The County Clerk, one of the most important county offices, keeps county records, serves as the county court clerk, and assists in county elections. The term, sheriff, comes from "shire-reeves", the chief law enforcement officer of the English shires. In the county today, the sheriff does not have as extensive a role in law enforcement as in the olden days. Most law enforcement functions are now handled by local and state police. The sheriff handles custodial tasks concerning prisoners and the courts, serves civil and criminal warrants, and runs the jail. The surrogate is charged with the processing of wills and the supervision of trusts and estates.

To manage its many functions, the County employs an extensive staff. They include civil service employees and political appointments. In addition, Ocean County is fortunate to have many volunteers to supplement the paid staff. The largest share of county operating expenses comes from local property taxes. County taxes are usually second only to education in demands on the local tax dollar.

List of County Officers 1890's.

For much of New Jersey's history, the county served as the election district for state legislative representatives. Since lightly populated Ocean County had equal representation in the state Senate, Ocean County's small population had a disproportionate share of political power. As a result, it held leadership positions in the state legislature for much of the 20th century. In 1964, the Reynolds vs. Sims United States Supreme Court ruling required that the state legislature be based on population. Today, all legislators are selected from districts of equal population, and in many cases, these districts cross county lines. Nevertheless, Ocean County representatives during the 1980's continued to hold leadership positions in the State Legislature.

The Court System

The Court system of New Jersey was one of the most complicated state court systems in the United States. To address this problem, the 1947 Constitution of New Jersey made radical changes, putting into effect a more logical system of county and state courts. In the 1960's, the courts again were streamlined by merging the county courts into one state court organization.

State Court System

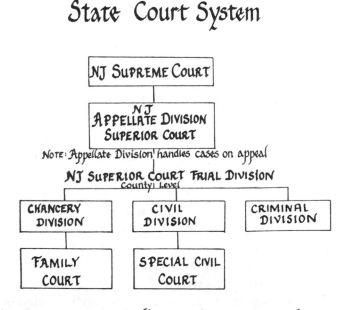

NJ SUPREME COURT

NJ APPELLATE DIVISION
SUPERIOR COURT

NOTE: Appellate Division handles cases on appeal

NJ SUPERIOR COURT TRIAL DIVISION
County Level

CHANCERY DIVISION

CIVIL DIVISION

CRIMINAL DIVISION

FAMILY COURT

SPECIAL CIVIL COURT

Note: Chancery Division handles special Equity cases - such as foreclosures. land disputes. right- to- life cases - courts do not require jury action. Special Civil Court handles small claims courts, landlord problems. etc.

In each county, Superior judges, appointed by the governor with the consent of the Senate, preside over the trial courts. Municipal judges, appointed by local municipalities, handle traffic violations, disorderly conduct complaints and other minor violations. They may also be the first to hear more serious cases which are then referred to the appropriate Superior Court.

Citizens, over the age of eighteen, play a role in the justice system as jurors. Jurors are randomly selected by computer from the county voting rolls and motor vehicle drivers license records. Jurors are chosen for three types of juries. The Grand Jury hears charges and determines if there is enough evidence for trial, the Petit Jury tries the cases, and the State Grand Jury investigates illegal activities.

However, not all court cases require juries. In local matters, the magistrate decides, while many other cases on the Superior Court level are handled by judges without the assistance of juries. Nevertheless, the jury system is the cornerstone of democratic government and, in the late 1980's, Ocean County, aware of its importance, established a Citizens' Advisory Committee to improve conditions under which the jurors serve.

The Ocean County Court system is under the direction of the State Chief Justice and his staff who work through an Assignment Judge and his staff. Together, judges, the administrative staff, and the jurors of the county are responsible for the functioning of the judicial process in Ocean County.

Local Government

The type of government for each town is spelled out in a charter granted by the state. These state charters also spell out the community's boundaries, services, offices, and functions. The State Legislature enacted the Home Rule Act in 1917 to help protect the independence of the local municipalities.

The Town Meeting was the earliest form of local government in Ocean County where decisions were made by all of the property owners of the community. In later years, as population grew, the Township Committee became the form for most rural areas. A township was a subdivision of the county, existing outside of cities or towns. The number of people serving on Township Committees varied depending on the size of the community. Today, the Mayor and Council form of government is used by most county municipalities.

Typical Mayor & Council Form

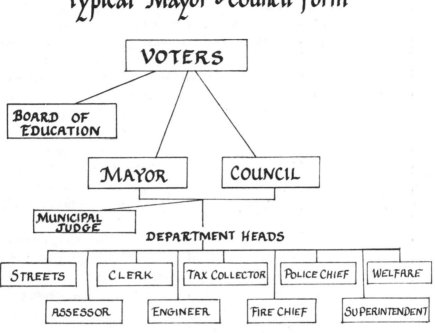

Note: Duties of the Mayor differ in the county municipalities. Council members in many communities are divided into permanent committees which supervise certain functions.

Local municipalities vary in physical size. The Township of Jackson is the largest with over one hundred square miles, while the borough of Seaside Heights is the smallest at .25 square miles. Dover Township has the largest population with 76,371.

The first two townships established in Ocean County were Stafford in 1749 and Dover in 1767. The Township of Jackson was established in 1844. By the time Ocean County became a county in 1850, six townships had been established: Jackson, Dover, Brick, Stafford, Plumsted, and Union. All municipal governments enact laws and conduct functions which directly affect their people. Views on the method of handling such functions as road construction, education, health, sanitation, fire, and safety differed widely in each community. These differences led to the development of thirty-three separate local governments in Ocean County today.

A confusing fact to many new residents and visitors to Ocean County is that many separate communities exist within each township, but do not govern themselves. Brick Township, as an example, has within its boundaries: Cedarcroft, Midstreams, Laurelton, Osbornville, Shore Acres, Herbertsville, Breton Woods, Curtis Point, Normandy Beach, South Mantoloking, Lake Rivera, and a number of senior citizen communities and housing developments, each identified by a particular name. Most of the thirty-three municipalities in Ocean County separated from larger townships, but many more communities have remained part of a township. Several of these small communities, today, feel that they are under represented as part of a large township and, as the County itself had done, are now petitioning to become self-governing.

Another area of confusion in Ocean County is that many communities have been known by several different names during different periods of history. For example, Lakehurst was known as Wrights' Forge, Federal Forge, Phoenix Forge, Dover Furnace and Manchester before it formed a separate borough in 1921. Names of towns have had a variety of origins. Some are Indian names (Manahawkin), some are descriptive of the land area (Ocean Gate, Pine Beach, Surf City), many are named for early settlers (Tuckerton, Plumsted) or towns in the mother country (Stafford, Manchester), and some are named for important figures in history(Jackson, Berkeley). Union Township was named in the pre-civil war era for its loyalty to the Union cause. In many cases, it is difficult to determine exact origins. The naming of Toms River is one example.

Salter offers Indian Tom as one source of the name. Indian Tom was a resident of Island Heights and Dillon Island, noted for his role as an English spy during the Revolutionary War. The name may also have come from Captain William Tom, who, according to Salter, served as a representative of the Duke of York and collected rents in the area. Pauline Miller, Toms River historian, questions whether Indian Tom was alive when Toms River was first named, and she states that records confirm that Captain William Tom never reached this area. She suggests that the town and river were named for Tom Luker. Luker and his Indian wife operated a ferry crossing the river. The crossing was referred to as Tom's Crossing or Toms River.

County Politics

General elections for local, county, state and national offices are held the first Tuesday following the first Monday in November. Elections on the national level are held in even numbered years, with state elections in odd numbered years. County Freeholders are elected for a three-year staggered term. Primaries, non-partisan, and Board of Education elections are held in the spring.

New Jersey has permanent registration. A citizen registers by completing a form issued by the County Board of Elections twenty-nine days before the elections. The only time a voter must re-register is after a change of name, a change of address or failure to vote for four years.

Primary elections select candidates who will run in the general election in November. To run in the primaries, one must be a registered voter and must file a petition with the local clerk. A candidate may run as an independent, filing a petition with the County Clerk by the same time as the party candidates. To vote in the primary, a citizen must be registered with a party. The first time a citizen votes in the primary, he declares his party. A citizen may change parties by notifying the Board of Elections before the next election.

Elections in Ocean County are supervised by the County Election Board composed of two members from each party appointed by the governor and supported by a staff and the County Clerk. The Clerk receives petitions, certifies candidates, places them on the ballot, and certifies election results.

Over the years, Ocean County has acted to improve the election process. Property ownership has been removed as a requirement of voting and seeking office. The registration process has been simplified, and recently, schools have been authorized to register students at the age of eighteen. A shorter period for registration before an election has also been instituted. All of the measures were designed to encourage citizens to vote.

People of Ocean County have never failed to voice their opinions when they differed from their neighbors. It is important that they continue this role. Today, county and state leaders are taking leading roles on issues such as taxes, education, and the environment. Active citizenship on the part of voters will continue to make Ocean County a better place to live.

New Jersey's Voter Registration Application.

REGISTRATION INSTRUCTIONS

**Print in Ink—
Use ball-point pen or marker**

Qualifications of an eligible applicant

By the time of the next election, you must be 18 years old and a United States citizen. You must also be a resident of New Jersey and of your county for at least 30 days before the election.

1 Name of the applicant (Please print):

LAST   FIRST   MIDDLE

RESIDENCE: STREET ADDRESS AND P.O. BOX   APARTMENT NUMBER

2 CITY. TOWN OR BORO   COUNTY   ZIP CODE   PHONE
Rural Mailing Address (if any):

R.D. NUMBER   BOX   CITY, TOWN OR BORO   ZIP CODE

3 This form is being used as (Check One):

☐ New Registration ☐ Change of Address ☐ Change of Name

Date Moved _____
          Month   Day   Year

4 Birth Date:
MONTH   DAY   YEAR

From what address did you last register to vote, and under what name?

5 LAST NAME   FIRST   MIDDLE

STREET ADDRESS   APARTMENT NUMBER

CITY, TOWN OR BORO   COUNTY   STATE   ZIP CODE

6 I am a ☐ native born ☐ naturalized citizen (Check One):

I was naturalized:

MONTH   DAY   YEAR   CITY. TOWN OR BORO   STATE

7
A. By the time of the next election I will be at least 18 years of age.
B. I will be a citizen of the United States and will have lived in this State 30 days and in the above named county at least 30 days.
C. To the best of my knowledge and belief all of the above statements made by me are true and correct.
D. I understand that any false or fraudulent registration may subject me to a fine up to $1,000, imprisonment up to 5 years or both pursuant to R.S. 19 34-1.

SIGNATURE OR MARK OF THE APPLICANT   DATE OF SIGNATURE

I, being a registered voter in _____ county in the State of New Jersey, witnessed the making of the above signature or mark.

SIGNATURE OF THE WITNESS   DATE OF WITNESSING

8 NAME OF THE WITNESS (PLEASE PRINT):

STREET ADDRESS OF THE WITNESS   CITY, TOWN OR BORO   COUNTY   ZIP CODE

☐ Marque aqui si usted desea recibir sus materiales electorales en Español.

CHAPTER X

The New Natives

Father Alphonse Stephenson
(Priest/Musician/New Native)

Ocean County has come a long way since 1780 when its population reached 2,000 residents. In fact since 1960 the county has added 100,000 "new natives" each decade. One of these new natives is Father Alphonse Stephenson.

Reverend Alphonse Stephenson.

Father Stephenson, like most Ocean County residents, grew up in North Jersey (Paterson). As a youth he spent summers at his grandparents' home in Point Pleasant Beach, the house in which he now resides. He attended Montclair State College. While there, the church became an extremely important element in his life and he became an ordained priest in 1975. Music was also always important to him. He taught music, formed a private orchestra and even served as music director of over 3000 performances of "A Chorus Line", one of Broadway's most popular musicals.

His love of music and his priesthood finally came together in Ocean County with his formation, in 1986, of the Orchestra of Saint Peter by the Sea in Point Pleasant Beach. This forty-five member ensemble is believed to be the only such orchestra which plays solely to raise funds for churches and non-profit groups.

In 1989, Father Stephenson founded the Festival of the Atlantic. Over 10,000 people assemble on Jenkinson's Beach in Point Pleasant every Wednesday night during the summer months to hear his free concerts. This "adult Woodstock" of the 1990's provides one more cultural event now available in Ocean County as it makes its transition from a rural to a suburban society. The variety of music, from popular to classical, presented at the Festival mirrors the variety of people and interests in today's county. The difficulty of handling the large number of people attending the concerts parallels the problems faced by the county in the post World War II era such as traffic, policing, clean-up and environmental concerns. The number of those attending these concerts continues to grow, just as the number of "new natives" continues to increase.

The Reverend Stephenson is one of the "new natives" who has enriched the history and contributed to the character of the county. This chapter will examine the history of many such residents of Ocean County.

The Pineys

The population of Ocean County is often separated into two classifications: those living on the mainland among the pine forest (Pineys), and those living along the shore (Clamdiggers).

House in Double Trouble Park.

In 1859 the population of the pines was about as large as it was to become until recent years. Lumber and its related industries and the production of iron helped to swell the population of the pines with hardworking and productive people. The end of the iron industry, along with the loss of timber, had a profound effect on the population. Many of those who had formerly made a living from these industries moved, and the few remaining took jobs that provided only a bare subsistence. This led to a decrease in contacts with people outside the area. Over the years, many became fearful of outsiders, thus further increasing their isolation. This, added to a natural shyness, was often misinterpreted as hostility. The attitudes of visitor and Piney alike led to a wider cultural gap and to greater isolation of the people of the Pines.

John McPhee, in his book, *The Pine Barrens*, tells about the 1913 report of Elizabeth Kite which, he maintains, contributed to much of the negativism associated with the term "Piney." Kite was a psychologist who worked for the Vineland Training School, a school noted for its work with the retarded. It was felt, at that time, that some of the people of the Pines, because of their isolation and inbreeding, were mentally deficient. Therefore, Kite decided to study the "Piney." For two years, clothed in a spotless white dress, she rode her wagon through the pines visiting cabins. Her concern for the people was obvious and her visits were welcomed. Her research traced family ties and living conditions of people in the area. She described continued inbreeding and isolation and their effect on the mental health of the people. Her work resulted in a planned program for care of those with mental health problems.

The report, unfortunately, was publicized in the newspapers of the day, and the negative stereotype which developed was reinforced by the study conducted by her superior, H.H. Goddard. This study traced two branches of the family of Martin Kallikak (a pseudonym). One branch was descended from a feebleminded barmaid and the other of a "worthy" Quaker. In describing the succeeding generations, much illustrative material described the feebleminded side of the family. The publicity generated by the two reports led the governor of New Jersey, James Fielder, to call for the segregation of the Pinelands. It is not surprising that the people of New Jersey came to view the Pinelands as "dark backlands inhabited by hostile and semi-literate people who would just as soon shoot an outsider as look at him." This stigma on the term "Piney" has remained, and people living in the area have resented the negative connotation given the term by outsiders.

In 1940, Ms. Kite wrote that "nothing would give me greater pleasure that to correct the idea that has unfortunately been given by the newspapers regarding the Pines." The people described in her report were only a small fraction of the people of the area. She went on to say, "The families that were not potential state cases did not interest me as far as my study was concerned." Further studies have shown that, even within families in the pines where intelligence levels were deficient, there were many individuals of high intelligence. Ms. Kite also concluded that "I have no language in which I can express my admiration for the pines and the people that live there."

Recent research has further discounted the "Piney myth." Evidence was found which shows the Goddard study was a hoax. Pictures were doctored and the family in the study lived in Hunterdon County, not in the Pinelands. In fact, people in the Pinelands were not much different from rural people in neighboring New York, Pennsylvania or New England.

The post World War II years have brought many changes to the pines. Ocean County and the northern fringes of the Pinelands became the fastest growing area in the nation between 1960-1980. This growth has drastically changed the character of those living in the Pinelands and the attitudes of those on the outside. No longer is it an area to be avoided or ignored. Government has become increasingly active in protecting the environment and a new interest in the culture of the Pinelands has become popular.

Albert Hall in Waretown.

The Pinelands Cultural Society, founded to preserve the cultural heritage of the Pinelands, has established Albert Hall in Waretown as a center for music, books and artifacts of the Pines. Albert Hall, an old warehouse on Route 9, now has weekly musical programs. These shows are similar to earlier gatherings where local musicians got together in a cabin in the Forked River Mountains to play folk songs. A new pride and interest in the culture of the Pinelands is being developed, and this unique way of life has added to the heritage of Ocean County.

Clamdiggers

During the early years of Ocean County, the shoreline had a limited permanent population. There were a few small fishing villages with sportsmen coming as seasonal visitors. The post Civil War period brought an accentuated period of growth. Improvements in transportation, along with the problems facing many urban areas, led people to look for a more rural atmosphere. The shore area benefitted from these conditions. In contrast to the Pinelands, the shore areas increased in population, and its new residents more closely resembled the rest of New Jersey.

Being equidistant from two of the nation's largest cities, New York and Philadelphia, the shore was said to have a split personality. Most of the early visitors and developers came from the Philadelphia area. The coming of the railroad and later advances in the automobile, however, brought about increased influence from New York and north Jersey. The "new Clamdiggers" were a diverse group including immigrants, minorities and senior citizens, all having an impact on Ocean County.

Immigrants

New Jersey is probably as ethnically diverse as any state in the union. This was reflected in those who moved to Ocean County in the latter part of the nineteenth century and in the beginning of the twentieth century. Newcomers included many who were born in other countries and who were formerly residents of urban areas.

The shore's fishing and boat building industries attracted many Latvian and Norwegian immigrants during the nineteenth century. In the 1930's and 1940's they were joined by Estonians who purchased land in Lakewood and Jackson. Groups such as the Lakewood Estonian Association were formed to promote their social, cultural, and religious heritage.

St. Vladimer Russian Church.

Russian immigrants came in three waves; in 1870-1914 they came to improve their economic situation, in 1917-1934 to escape from Communism, and in the post World War II era they left the USSR to find a new home after being displaced from their own. Each of these waves contributed to the establishment in Ocean County of one of the largest Russian communities in the United States. Following World War II, one group settled near Cassville in an 1,200 acre area called Rova Farms. Over 5,000 Russians attended the dedication of their cathedral, the Church of Saint Vladimer. This cathedral serves as the international shrine to Saint Vladimer, the founder of Russian Christianity. Another community, called Rodemic, was established near-by in the 1930's. The surrounding areas today feature a Russian Museum, two Russian churches, a cemetery and a Russian restaurant. All of these are open to the public and display Russian art, folklore and ceremonies.

The first Jewish settlers came to Lakewood during the first decade of the twentieth century. During the period between World War I and the depression, the Jewish population of this winter resort increased greatly. Paul Axel-Lute described Lakewood, at this time, as having over 100 hotels "with Jewish management and Kosher cuisine serving an increasing large Jewish clientele." Many of these visitors, hotel staff and clientele remained to settle in this resort. During the Great Depression in the 1930's, Lakewood experienced another wave of Jewish immigration when jobs in the cities become scarce. Many of this group become egg farmers. In the 1940's over two-thirds of the egg production of the county was controlled by the Jewish residents.

Today, the Ocean County Jewish Federation, as well as many Jewish cultural groups, are active in interpreting and promoting Jewish heritage. Beth Medrash Govoha, one of the most important Rabbinical colleges in the east, was established in Lakewood to train future leaders of the Jewish faith.

Few Italians lived in New Jersey prior to the Civil War. However, toward the end of the nineteenth century, a combination of poor economic conditions in Europe and the need for agriculture workers in this county, encouraged many Southern Europeans to emigrate. By 1930 Italians formed the largest group of foreign-born residents in New Jersey.

Although most Italian immigrants come from agricultural areas, few became farmers in the United States. Many preferred to remain in the cities but with a lack of specific job skills they were forced to take menial jobs. Poor wages and crowded living conditions led some into illegal activities. Some noted figures were involved in racketeering and in violation of the Prohibition laws. The sins of the few tarred the many, and this association of Italians to crime and to low paying jobs led many at the Shore to discriminate against them.

In the early 1900's, Italian immigrants made their way to the shore. About thirty settled in the Toms River area. Sam Christopher, in an article entitled *"Italian Immigrants, Early Settlers in County"*, tells the story of early Italian immigrants to Ocean County through the eyes of Joseph Citta. Citta's father, James, came from Italy to Ocean County in 1912. After working in New York, he moved to the Manitou Park section of Berkeley Township. He was attracted by the open space and by land that could be purchased for $2.00 down and $1.00 a month. James established one of the county's first poultry farms, worked as a laborer and as a mason and made shrewd property investments during the depression. Joseph Citta, the son, become one of Toms River's community leaders.

After World War II, middle and upper class Italian families began to move in large numbers to the suburbs. In Ocean County they became an important segment of new natives. According to the 1980 census, Italy led all ethnic groups as the ancestral home of Ocean County residents.

Minorities

In the first United States census, in 1790, there were about 15,000 black in New Jersey with 3,000 being freemen. The number reached

25,000, eighteen of whom were slaves at the start of the Civil War. However, it was not until the first World War that large numbers of blacks were attracted to the North. Racial tensions, poverty, and restrictive legislation in the South, as well as the more attractive job market in the North, led to the migration. The black population of New Jersey expanded during the first half of the twentieth century. The black population tripled in New Jersey during this period, with New Jersey experiencing a larger increase than any other northern state. In 1930's about 90% of the state's black population lived in urban areas.

Industrial jobs that were plentiful during the war disappeared at its close, and many blacks faced some of the same problems they had faced in the South. Employment opportunities centered around domestic and part time labor. Ocean County's new resort industry offered such jobs. With the increase in population, the defacto segregation that was practiced in urban areas found its way to Ocean County. One form of segregation following World War II was the conversion of many public beaches into "private clubs" with membership limited to whites. This practice was abolished, along with many other forms of discrimination, during the Civil Rights drive of the 1960's and 1970's.

Paul Axel-Lute, in his book, *Lakewood in the Pines*, describes racial incidents that occurred in Lakewood in the 1970's. As in other urban areas throughout the nation, there were protests about housing practices and unfair treatment by the police. Looting and violence also took place in Lakewood. Ocean County was no longer free from the tensions found in the urban world.

Schools in Ocean County also reflected the racial tension of the community. However, schools made a concerted effort to ease this tension. In 1971, Lakewood's school population was 35% black or Hispanic but all teachers were white. As a direct result of a recruitment drive, by 1973 Lakewood had a staff of 15% minority teachers and a black principal. During that same period the Ocean County Social Studies Project, a project designed to improve the teaching of United States History, worked with teachers and the Black community to improve minority studies in the schools.

The Hispanic population in Ocean County grew from 8,444 in 1980 to 13,950 by the end of the decade. During that same period the Black population in Ocean County grew by 83%. During the 1980's, increased job opportunities occurred for all minority groups in Ocean County as well as in the nation. This, along with progress in schools and the enforcement of equal opportunity laws, led to a reduction in tension and an improvement in the position of minorities in the life of the county.

Senior Citizens

During the 1960's, Ocean County became one the first areas in the country to introduce adult communities. Residents in these adult communities were mostly middle class, over 50, and had grown children. They were attracted by the need for security and for neighbors of similar view. One of the first of these senior housing projects was Leisure Village in Lakewood. In 1963, Robert Schmertz, its builder, revealed his plans for a "total retirement community designed to meet the broad spectrum of recreational, physical, social and cultural needs of its residents."

During the 1960's, Manchester Township became one of the fastest growing communities in the nation. Seniors had gained an alternative to Florida and Arizona that was nearer to their families and friends. By 1980, Crestwood Village in Whiting was the second largest senior community in the nation with only Sun City in Arizona larger.

New tax incentives by the state and national government and special zoning privileges resulted in over fifty such developments. Ocean County became the "adult capital of the East." These new natives brought significant changes to the character and personality of the county, and senior problems became a major concern of local government. These new natives demanded the same services they had enjoyed in their previous homes and they had the political clout to accompany these desires. The senior vote had become an important determinant in both school board and municipal elections.

"Bennies"

The term "Benny" is a post World War II term applied to summer tourists in Monmouth and northern Ocean counties. The origin of the term is a matter of speculation. *The Dictionary of Regional English* defines it as a label for a tourist in Point Pleasant Beach and Toms River derived from a term used for Jewish workers in urban areas. Others say it may have been an acronym for the tourists' cities of origin: "B" for Brooklyn, "E" for Elizabeth or Edison, "N" for New Brunswick or Newark or "NY" for New York. Another source suggests that the portrait of Benjamin "Benny" Franklin on a hundred dollar bill might have been applied to free-spending tourists.

In a similar way, "Shoebees" was used to refer to visitors to the

Long Beach Island area. Shoebee was derived from those who carried their beach needs in shoeboxes,or to those who wore their shoes to the beach.

Both "Benny" and Shoebee" were primarily used as negative terms. Tourists placed tremendous demands on the people, environment and facilities of resort communities and, although welcomed economically, natives usually breathed a sigh of relief when the tourist season ended. However, tourists were beneficial to the area. Not only did they provide employment and generate income for residents, they often liked the area so much that they, too, became permanent residents.

Ocean County Educators

Formal education in New Jersey began quite late in comparison with other states. Although the General Assembly of East Jersey passed the first public school law in 1693, private schools and tutoring programs assumed the major responsibility for education in Ocean County until the middle of the 1800's. The 1693 law required that each community choose three men to establish a house or room for a school and required the residents to share the costs. This law set the precedent followed in New Jersey today with each district electing its own school board and with funds coming from taxation.

School in Double Trouble Park.

One of the earliest schools in Ocean County was built in Waretown in 1744 and remained in operation until 1957. In 1846 the position of Town Superintendent of Schools was created by the state, which, in Toms River, was rewarded with a salary of $1.00 a day. In 1867 William F. Brown of Brick was selected as the first County Superintendent of Schools. In 1906 Charles Morris assumed these duties. As County Superintendent, Mr. Morris inherited a county with a sparse, scattered population, and with slow economic growth. During his thirty-eight years as superintendent, his strong leadership skills and educational background established the basis for a growing school system.

38

ANNUAL REPORT *of the Teacher in School No* 49 *County of* Ocean *for*
the School Year beginning July 1st, 1896, and ending June 30th, 1897.

1. Number of days the school has been kept open...... 185
2. Number of children between five and twenty years of age enrolled during the year...... 40
3. Number of boys enrolled...... 17
4. Number of girls enrolled...... 23
5. Total number of days present (all pupils)...... 487l.5
6. Total number of days absent (all pupils)...... 795
7. Average number on roll (no fractions)...... 31
8. Average daily attendance (no fractions)...... 27
9. Percentage of attendance (use decimals)...... 87
10. Number of pupils who have not been absent or tardy during the year......
11. Total number of times tardy...... 26
12. Average number of cases of tardiness per day (use decimals)... .14
13. Number of children suspended or expelled during the year...... 0
14. Grade of school...... Gr. + H.
15. Number of classes in school...... 16
16. Average number of recitations heard daily (no fractions)...... 12
17. Number of pupils enrolled in "Primary" grade...... —
18. Number enrolled in "Grammar" grade...... 33
19. Number enrolled in "High School" grade...... 7

20. Date of opening school...... Sept 134
21. Date of closing school...... June 18
22. Annual salary of teacher...... 750
23. Grade and kind (State, County or City) of certificate held by teacher...... College Diploma and State
24. Length of time in present school...... 1 yr.
25. Total experience in teaching...... 5 yrs.
26. If normal graduate give name of school......
27. If college graduate give name of college...... Dickinson
28. Amount raised during the year for school library...... $10
29. Amount previously raised...... 40
30. Amount received from the State during the year...... 10
31. Amount previously received from the State...... 30
32. Number of books purchased during the year...... 30
33. Number of books previously purchased...... 19
34. Amount expended for apparatus during the year......
35. Amount previously expended for apparatus......
36. Number of books now in the library...... 49
37. Number of books taken out during the year......
38. Present value of school library...... $60
39. Present value of apparatus......

	Male	Female
Number of pupils between 5 and 6 years of age		
" " " 6 " 7 " "		
" " " 7 " 8 " "		
" " " 8 " 9 " "		
" " " 9 " 10 " "		
" " " 10 " 11 " "		
" " " 11 " 12 " "	1	2
" " " 12 " 13 " "	1	4

	Male	Female
Number of pupils between 13 and 14 years of age	1	2
" " " 14 " 15 " "	2	6
" " " 15 " 16 " "	5	4
" " " 16 " 17 " "	2	3
" " " 17 " 18 " "	3	2
" " " 18 " 19 " "		2
" " " 19 " 20 " "		

17 23

School Annual Report 1896 - This report gives an excellent picture of schools in 1896.

Because of the widely scattered population, each community established its own school district. This resulted in numerous small schools with 90% of them being one-room schoolhouses. Many of these schools were limited by shortages of teachers and money. In 1832 Dover Township recognized the need for public education by appropriating $300 for education. The Township Act of 1894 required each township to form a single school district which led to the elimination of many of these small districts.

A compulsory school law, passed in 1885 in New Jersey, required all students, age seven to twelve, to attend school. In an 1892 report, 89% of the school age population attended school with an average attendance of 55%. Only 33% were still enrolled at age 12. Education was free but books and many other educational needs were paid by the parents.

Admiral Farragut Academy, Pine Beach - One of the five private schools offering a high school education in Ocean County.   Ocean County Historical Museum

Today, almost all expenses for an education are assumed by the taxpayers. Today, 65.2% of Ocean County residents over the age of twenty-five have graduated from high school. The county school population in 1991 reached 61,000. This growth is not only the result of new residents of the county but also of the requirements of a more sophisticated society. Schools today offer improved materials, require a greater educational background of teachers and administrators, and present a variety of curriculum offerings. They also possess modern facilities. The opportunities for learning have increased in Ocean County along with the school population.

In March, 1917, Charles Morris, the County Superintendent of Schools, wrote a letter describing the influence of a $25 victrola on

Cedar Crest, a small community between Toms River and Tuckerton. Only two houses existed between the town and Toms River and no means of communication. He wrote, "I wish I could picture to you just how this little instrument is brightening the lives not only of the children in school but of that whole rather desolate community." What a change has taken place in 70 years!

Myrtle Moore - Educator

Women have played a major role in the educational process in Ocean County. Although early teachers were mostly men, by the end of the eighteenth century, women outnumbered men as teachers. In 1931, of the 234 teachers in Ocean County, 197 were women.

Myrtle Moore is typical of the many women who devoted their lives to the children of Ocean County. As a child, she attended one-room schools in Plumsted Township. She attended high school in Allentown and Hightstown, completed courses in education and began teaching in New Egypt. She strongly believed in practical as well as intellectual education and frequently took her students on field trips to widen their horizons . She eventually moved to Brick Township where she taught fourth grade and became teaching principal of the Herbertsville School until she retired in 1961. A plaque at that school pays tribute to her dedication of children and to her friendship to all.

Besides teaching, Myrtle Moore was also interested in the history of the area. Involved in the Brick, New Egypt, and Ocean County Historical Societies, she worked diligently to preserve records of the past. She willed her books and papers to the reference section of the Brick Library and she left a sizable bequest to the Ocean County Museum. The Museum recognized her varied contributions by naming an exhibit area after her.

Social and Cultural Experiences

In the early days, the family, church and school provided most of the social and cultural experiences in Ocean County. The changes in population have dramatically increased the number and variety of experiences now available. In addition to Albert Hall, the Festival of the Atlantic, and the ethnic programs mentioned earlier, there are many new sources of community enrichment.

Ocean County College, one the first community colleges in the state, provides many educational and cultural experiences to both

students and community members. Georgian Court College in Lakewood does the same. The renovated Strand Theater in Lakewood also
provides a whole range of fine arts programs as does the public library
system. Public schools and churches have continued to play a major
role in intellectual and recreational programs along with the growing
county parks system. The Garden State Philharmonic, the Long Beach
Island Foundation of the Arts and Sciences, the Ocean County Artists
Guild, and the Ocean County Cultural and Heritage Commission are
but a few of the organizations active in the county.

Strand Theater.

Today's Natives

It is difficult to realize today that the county of Ocean prior to the
1940's was primarily rural in nature. In that year the total population
of the county was 37,000. Lakewood was the town with the largest
population, 8,500 people. In the 1990 census, Dover, Brick and
Lakewood, in that order, were the three largest in total population. The
population of Dover Township alone today is almost double that of the
total population of the whole county in 1940. The county's population
reached 453,000 in the 1990 census. The population density of this
"rural county" in 1990, even with all of its protected open space, is 543

persons per square mile. New Jersey's density of almost 1000 people per square mile surpasses the density of Belgium and Japan, the two nations with the highest population density in the world.

The "good old days" were not always as attractive as many would like to believe. The county has changed, and today its residents offer a wide variety of talents and a rich multi-cultural heritage. Many physical and intellectual improvements have been made and many opportunities exist to help the county meet the demands of the twenty-first century. These residents, together with its rich history and environment, continue to make Ocean County "a very good land to fall in with a pleasant land to see."

Crestwood Village from the air. This senior village in the Pinelands has over 9,500 homes located in Whiting, Manchester Township.   Courtesy of Miroslav "Mike" Kokes, Builder of Crestwood.)

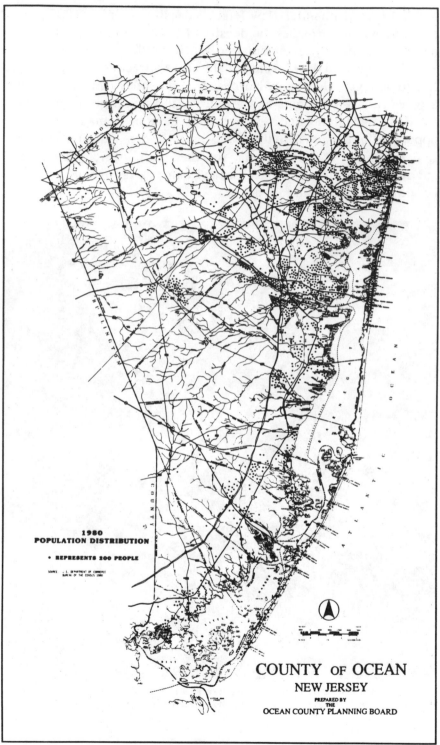

1980
POPULATION DISTRIBUTION

• REPRESENTS 200 PEOPLE

SOURCE U. S. DEPARTMENT OF COMMERCE
BUREAU OF THE CENSUS 1980

COUNTY OF OCEAN
NEW JERSEY
PREPARED BY
THE
OCEAN COUNTY PLANNING BOARD

Population Map.

Characteristics of Ocean County Municipalties – 1990 Census

Municipality	Land Area (sq mi)	Housing Units	POPULATION			Group Quarters
			Total	Under 18	Density	
Barnegat Township	33.62	4,902	12,235	30.0%	364	115
Barnegat Light Borough	0.72	1,187	675	13.2%	938	18
Bay Head Borough	0.59	1,001	1,226	15.1%	2,078	0
Beach Haven Borough	0.98	2,569	1,475	15.9%	1,505	15
Beachwood Borough	2.76	3,244	9,324	29.2%	3,378	0
Berkeley Township	42.89	19,873	37,319	11.6%	870	525
Brick Township	26.28	28,843	66,473	23.6%	2,529	303
Dover Township	41.09	35,653	76,371	24.5%	1,859	1,158
Eagleswood Township	16.37	696	1,476	25.9%	90	0
Harvey Cedars Borough	0.55	1,121	362	11.3%	658	0
Island Heights Borough	0.60	695	1,470	23.1%	2,450	0
Jackson Township	100.03	11,833	33,233	27.1%	332	328
Lacey Township	83.99	9,513	22,141	25.2%	264	154
Lakehurst Borough	0.92	1,087	3,078	32.5%	3,346	0
Lakewood Township	24.82	17,888	45,048	27.9%	1,815	2,163
Lavallette Borough	0.80	3,069	2,299	15.3%	2,874	0
Little Egg Harbor Township	49.10	7,194	13,333	24.7%	272	122
Long Beach Township	5.31	8,836	3,407	11.5%	642	0
Manchester Township	82.59	20,790	35,976	12.1%	436	770
Mantoloking Borough	0.39	467	334	8.4%	856	0
Ocean Township	20.80	2,828	5,416	24.6%	260	53
Ocean Gate Borough	0.44	1,052	2,078	22.8%	4,723	0
Pine Beach Borough	0.62	872	1,954	21.2%	3,152	0
Plumsted Township	40.02	2,200	6,005	26.7%	150	0
Point Pleasant Borough	3.53	8,006	18,177	21.9%	5,149	243
Point Pleasant Beach Borough	1.44	3,235	5,112	18.9%	3,550	179
Seaside Heights Borough	0.48	2,844	2,366	25.2%	4,929	64
Seaside Park Borough	0.65	2,454	1,871	17.9%	2,878	8
Ship Bottom Borough	0.69	2,084	1,352	14.2%	1,959	0
South Toms River Borough	1.15	1,133	3,869	33.3%	3,364	0
Stafford Township	47.57	8,298	13,325	23.8%	280	128
Surf City Borough	0.72	2,482	1,375	13.2%	1,910	0
Tuckerton Borough	3.65	1,914	3,048	22.9%	835	5
OCEAN COUNTY	636.16	219,863	433,203	22.7%	681	6,351

Source: NJ State Data Center, 1990 Census Information (PL94–171).
Prepared by: Ocean County Planning Board, April 1991.

Ocean County Historical Museum.

Epilogue

Ocean County has changed a great deal during my lifetime and, in fact, it has changed in my eyes in the short time I spent preparing this book. As a direct result of gathering information for this text, I now view the area and its people in a new light. I have become more conscious of the things surrounding me and I am also better able to relate these surroundings to this area's past.

One of my last acts in putting the book together was to take pictures of places mentioned in the book as they are today. This activity revealed that many in the county suffered the same short sightedness as I had, not seeing history right before their eyes. While visiting Tuckerton to take pictures of the remains of the Tuckerton Tower and the Indian Shell Mounds, I spent the greater part of the day trying to determine their exact location. Storekeepers, business people, people on the street, and gas station attendants, not only were not of much help, but many had not even heard of these historic spots right in their back yard. People in the municipal buildings of Tuckerton and Little Egg Harbor knew about the sites, but only in a general way. I finally discovered the mounds with the help of a long time resident out walking his dog. I found the foundations of the tower in the middle of a housing development on Mystic Island.

Jackson Historical Museum.

As I viewed each of these sites, I felt an immediate link with the past. Tuckerton was now more than a city that I traveled through on the way to Atlantic City. I felt a part of its history. This same relationship was found in recent visits to the dwarf pine forest, Albert Hall, The Festival of the Atlantic, Reedy Creek, Island Beach, Barnegat Light, Huddy Park, Rockefeller Park, Double Trouble Park, and many other places mentioned in the text.

The book not only made me more conscious of my surroundings, but also made me aware of the vast amount of material that is available about the county. There are still survivors of early families to interview, and there are many written sources, artifacts, structures, and historic and natural sites available for those seeking to know more about the county. To help both amateur and professional historians, there are at least twelve local historical societies, seventeen ethnic cultural societies, twenty-two libraries, twelve museums and the newly expanded Ocean County Museum and Research Center. The Ocean County Cultural and Heritage Commission coordinates all these sources and publishes a directory listing them. No resident in the county should suffer from an absence of information.

The preparation of this book widened my view, not only of the many people who have contributed to the county, but also of the many people now living in the county who know a great deal about its history and are willing to share their knowledge. Pauline Miller, Director of the County Cultural and Heritage Commission, should be recognized, in particular, for her contributions to the knowledge of county history. Her support of this book from the begining kept me at the job and made me feel it was worthwhile. Fellow historians, Joseph Eid, Carolyn Campbell, Kevin Dann, and Marilyn Kralik, not only helped review the material, but made many contributions in their areas of expertise. Proofreaders included many family and friends. Wayne Hartman, a colleague, not only gave me a lesson in grammar, but also urged me to take a careful look at duplication of material. Without a doubt, the most positive reaction to those reading the book has been its readability. My wife, Vilma, must take most of the credit for that plus.

A word of thanks to Dean Haines, County Clerk, Superior Court Judge Bernard Kannen, and Anthony Defrio, Drafting Technician, Ocean County Planning Board, for their help in assembling practical material on Ocean County Government. Special recognition should also be given to the Ocean Historical Museum, to Joseph Eid, and to W.E. Hess for the use of their picture files. Bill Hess, a noted shore historian and good friend, before his death, gave me his picture collection for the students to use in the Social Studies Laboratory of Point Pleasant Beach High School. The illustrations, charts, maps, and art direction of Sheila Kierce not only add to the attractiveness of the book but also are an integral part of the text.

My view of the county has been aided, not only by my work, but by the research of the many authors listed in the bibliography. It is my hope that those who read my book will become interested in learning more about Ocean County and will turn to some of these sources to expand their knowledge.

Annotated Bibliography

Suggested Readings:

*To learn more about the information given in the text,
the following sources are recommended.*

Chapter I - The Setting

1. Robert Jahn's, *Down Barnegat Bay* (Barnegat Bay region),
   Rita Moonsammy, et al. (ed.), *Pinelands Folklore* (Pinelands),
   John Lloyd's, *Six Miles at Sea* (Long Beach Island).

All three books give geographic information and also present a deep feeling for the area that they cover.

2. John Cunningham's, *Jersey Shore*
   Jane Methot's, *Up and Down the Beach*
   Harold Wilson's, *The Story of the Jersey Shore*

These books present general information about the shore area.

3. Materials furnished by the New Jersey and United States Fish and Wildlife Services, the Pinelands Commission, and the New Jersey Department of Environmental Protection are readily available and supply a great deal of information about the geography of the area and about environmental concerns.

4. Hagstrom's, *Ocean County Atlas*, presents a fully indexed display of highways, airports, railroads, intercoastal charts, zip codes, beaches, golf courses, parks and hospitals.

   The New Jersey Intercoastal Waterway Chart, Nautical Chart 12324, presents a detailed map of Ocean County waterways.

   The Ocean County Telephone Book supplies maps of streets in Ocean County communities.

Chapter II - The Native Americans

1. Edwin Salter's *The History of Ocean and Monmouth County* presents many interesting tales about Indians during the early days of this county.

2. C.A. Waslager's book, *The Delawares,* is must reading for his clear picture of the Indians of New Jersey.

3. John and Herbert Kraft's two books, *The Lenapehoking* and *The Lenape,* are the most current books on the Lenape. *The Lenapehoking,* in particular, is a source easily used by the beginning historian.

4. Robert Hamilton - (Greywolf) has written an extremely interesting chapter on the Indians of New Jersey in the book, *The New Jersey Ethnic Experience.* Important to read as an Indian view of the history of the Lenape.

5. Charles Boland's *They All Discovered America* presents some interesting views on the origins of the first Americans

6. Pauline Miller's filmstrip, *Indians of New Jersey,* available in the office of the Cultural and Heritage Commission, presents interesting information on the Indians and the Indian artifacts of this area.

7. The American Heritage book, *Indians,* is an excellent source of general information on this topic.

8. William Hess, a local historian, in *On History's Trail* tells a great deal about Walum Olum.

Chapter III - The Early Settlers

1. Leah Blackman's, *A History of Little Egg Harbor,* originally part of a surveyor's report in the 1880's gives an excellent account of the life of early settlers and of the Quakers in that area. She also presents the family trees of the early families.

2. Charles Boland's, *We All Discovered America,* suggests many of the people that might have reached the New World before Columbus. Although controversial, it does furnish food for thought!

3. Pauline Miller's books on Toms River and Island Beach are must reading for readers wishing to know more about the early settlements in that region.

4. Graham Hodges in his books, *African Americans in Monmouth County, New Jersey, 1784-1860* and *African Americans in Monmouth County During the Age of Revolution,* helps the reader understand the role of Black Americans during the early history of Ocean County.

5. Robert VanBenthusen and Audrey Wilson prepared the book, *Monmouth County.* It contains an excellent view in words and pictures of Old Monmouth County.

Chapter IV - Patriots or Loyalist

1. Edwin Salter's *The History of Ocean and Monmouth County* contains a good picture of the struggle within Old Monmouth County concerning the decision to break from England. This book is also recommended for his description of the role of black Loyalists and other Loyalist groups. He also presents a good view of Huddy's role in the Patriot cause.

2. Tom Fleming, probably one of the most prolific writers on New Jersey's role in the Revolutionary War, should be read when attempting to assess the conflicting concerns of the different groups within the state. His *New Jersey, A Bicentennial History* is of particular interest.

3. Pauline Miller's book, *Early History of Toms River and Dover Township* was a good source of information on the activities of privateers.

4. Graham Hodges, in *African Americans in Monmouth County During the Age of the American Revolution,* describes another struggle for liberty going on during the war in Ocean County.

5. David Fowler's doctoral thesis clearly defines the role of the Pine Robbers in the war. When published, it should be included in your reading.

6. Arthur Pierce in *Smugglers Wood,* Robert Jahn in *Down Barnegat Bay,* and Harold Wilson in *The Story of the Jersey Shore,* give a great deal of information about the war in their area of expertise.

7. The *American Heritage, The Revolution,* is a must for its overall view of the Revolution and the battles in New Jersey.

Chapter V - Wreckers or Lifesavers

1. Leland Downey, a noted Brick Township historian, tells the history of shipwrecks off the New Jersey coast in *Broken Spars.*

2. Robert Jahn's book, *Down Barnegat Bay,* is an excellent source for information about lifesavers and shipwrecks.

3. Pauline Miller in *Three Centuries of Island Beach* talks about lifesavers and, in particular, about Newell and Francis.

4. John Bailey Lloyd's *Six Miles at Sea* is an important source on lifesaving. His stories about the naming of Ship Bottom and on forty-two years of lifesaving are must reading for Long Beach Islanders. His description of the Coast Guard during Prohibition, although not related to this theme, makes interesting reading.

5. Harold Wilson's *The Story of the Jersey Shore* tells about past shipwrecks while Gordon Bishop's *Gems of New Jersey* describes the role of present wrecks.

6. Thomas Gallagher's *Fire At Sea* is an excellent source on the Morro Castle.

Chapter VI - Travelers

1. The books *Jersey Shore*, written by John Cunningham, and *The Story of the New Jersey Shore,* written by Harold Wilson, are must reading for information on travelers to Ocean County.

2. Joseph Eid in *Trolleys Across the Sand Dunes* presents an excellent picture of trolleys at the shore.

3. John Lloyds' *Six Miles at Sea* presents information on the horsecars and trolleys on Long Beach Island.

4. Newspaper articles in *The Ocean County Observer* are extremely helpful in providing information on bridge construction.

5. William Hess's book, *On History's Trail,* and Henry Beck's books are helpful with information on early roads in the county.

6. John Brinkman's book, *Tuckerton Railroad,* gives information on railroads in the southern part of the county.

7. *L Z 129 "Hindenburg"* by Douglas Robinson is recommended not only for information on the Hindenburg, but on other airships as well.

8. Information on airships can also be found in the *American Heritage Magazine.*

Chapter VII - Toilers

1. John McPhee's *Pine Barrens and Pineland Folklore,* edited by Rita Moonsammy, et. al., contain excellent descriptions of the iron industry and other Pineland related industries.

2. Henry Beck's books are good sources for information about early industries in south Jersey.

3. Again John Cunningham's works and Harold Wilson's *The Story of the Jersey Shore* present excellent descriptions of job opportunities in Ocean County over the years.

4. *United States Census Reports* yield valuable information about the economy and people of the county.

5. Chamber of Commerce Bulletins are valuable guides to the economy of today.

6. John Cunningham's pamphlet, *Rich Harvest,* gives a good picture of the history of the poultry industry.

7. Gordon Bishop's *Gems of New Jersey* gives an excellent view of many of the economic factors important to the current history of Ocean County.

Chapter VIII - Tourists

1. Paul Axel-Lute, *Lakewood in the Pines,* contains a good description of the tourist industry in Lakewood.

2. Again both the books by Cunningham and Harold Wilson are excellent sources of information about tourism at the shore.

3. John Bailey Lloyd for tourism on Long Beach Island and Robert Jahn on early tourism along Barnegat Bay are interesting reading.

4. Gordon Bishop's *Gems of New Jersey,* is an attractive and informative view of current tourism.

5. Dorothy Mount's, *A Story of New Egypt and Plumsted Township*, tells about inland tourism.

6. *The Historic Sites Survey*, prepared by the Ocean County Cultural and Heritage Commission, contains most of the buildings that describe the county's past. In addition, each community booklet presents a survey of the town's history and its people. This is a valuable source for a survey of towns in Ocean County.

Chapter IX - Citizens

1. The League of Women Voters has prepared two books that are very helpful. *Meet Ocean County*, describes in detail the functioning of county government while *New Jersey Spotlight on Government* does the same for state government.

2. Leonard Irwin's book, *New Jersey the State and Its Government*, was used extensively in high schools a few years ago for information on local, county and state government.

3. *The Ocean County Government Directory*, contains the most up-to-date information on government in New Jersey.

4. Graham Hodges in his books on *African American History in Monmouth County* relates the progress of Black rights in the county.

5. *The New Jersey Citizen*, by James Hackett, presents information on New Jersey citizenship and especially the history of women's rights.

6. Vivian Zinkin in the book, *Place Names in Ocean County*, not only traces the origin of the names of Ocean County communities, but also reveals information about their history.

Chapter X - The New Natives

1. There are many books I strongly recommend for an understanding of the Piney including Henry Beck books on south Jersey, John McPhee's *Pine Barrens*, Arthur Pierce's, *Smugglers Wood*, and *Pineland Folklore*, edited by Rita Moonsammy et. al.

2. Gordon Bishop has an excellent section in *Gems of New Jersey* on senior developments and other groups in New Jersey today.

3. The books of both John Cunningham and Harold Wilson have been mentioned at the end of almost all chapters. They again deserve to be mentioned here as well.

4. Most communities have published some form of history. Check your local library or historic association.

5. *Chickaree on the Wall,* written by Martha Smith, Carolyn Campbell and M. Peryl King is a must for information on the one room schools and education in the County.

6. Leah Blackman's *History of Little Egg Harbor* traces the family tree for many of the families in the southern part of the county.

7. Vivian Zinkin's *Place Names in Ocean County,* is a guide for many of the labels used in early Ocean County.

Practical Bibliography

List of Works Used

Books

Axel-Lute, Paul. *Lakewood in the Pines*. South Orange: Author, 1986.

Beck, Henry. *Forgotten Towns of South Jersey*. New Brunswick: Rutgers University Press, 1961.

Beck, Henry. *The Roads Home*. New Brunswick: Rutgers University Press, 1983.

Beck, Henry. *The Jersey Midlands*. New Brunswick: Rutgers University Press, 1962.

Bishop, Gordon. *Gems of New Jersey*. Englewood Cliffs, NJ.: Prentice Hall, 1985.

Blackman, Leah. *History of Little Egg Harbor*. Tuckerton, N.J.: Great John Mathis Foundation, 1963.

Boland, Charles. *They All Discovered America*. New York: Doubleday, 1961.

Brescia, Lillis and Louis. *Stafford Township, A Pictorial Review*. Stafford Township: Tercentenary Committee, 1964.

Campbell, Carolyn, King, M. Peryl and Smith, Martha. *Chickaree in The Wall*. Toms River: Ocean County Historical Society, 1987.

Cassidy, Frederic, ed.. *Dictionary of American Regional English*. Cambridge: Bellhop Press of Harvard University Press, 1991

Cunningham, Barbara (Ed.) *New Jersey, Ethnic Experience*. Union, N.J.: Wm. Wise and Co., 1977.

Cunningham, John T. *New Jersey A Mirror on America*. Florham Park: Afton Publisher, 1976.

Cunningham, John T. *The Jersey Shore*. New Brunswick: Rutgers University Press, 1958.

Downey, Antoinette. *Pictorial Album of Point Pleasant Beach*. Ocean County Historical Society, 1971.

Downey, Leland. *Broken Spars*. Brick, N.J.: Brick Township Historical Society, 1983.

Eaton, Charlotte. *Stevenson at Manasquan*. Chicago: Bookfellows, 1921.

Eid, Joseph. *Trolley's Across the Sand Dunes*. Brick: N.J.: Eid, 1977.

Fair, Philip and Rabold, Ted. *New Jersey, Yesterday and Today*. Harrisburg: Penns Valley, 1981.

Fleming, Thomas. *New Jersey, A Bicentennial History.* New York: Norton, 1977.

Gallagher, Thomas G. *Fire at Sea, The Story of the Morro Castle.* N.Y.: Reinhart, 1959.

Grumet, Robert. *The Lenape.* N.Y.: Chelsea House, 1989.

Hackett, James. *The New Jersey Citizen.* New Brunswick: Rutgers University Press, 1957.

Hess, William. *On History's Trail.* Point Pleasant Beach: Barnegat Products, 1973.

Hodges, Graham R.. *African-Americans in Monmouth County New Jersey 1784-1860.* Lincroft, NJ.: Monmouth County Park System, 1992.

Hodges, Graham R.. *African-Americans in Monmouth County During the Age of the American Revolution.* Lincroft, N.J.: Monmouth County Park System, 1990.

Irwin, Leonard. New Jersey. *The State and its Government.* New York: Oxford Books, 1958.

Jahn, Robert. *Down Barnegat Bay.* Mantoloking, N.J.: Beachcomber Press, 1981.

Josephy, Alvin, (ed). *The American Heritage Book of the Indians.* New York: American Heritage, 1961.

Juet, Robert. J. Juet's Journal. *The Voyage of the Half Moon.* Newark: New Jersey Historical Society, 1959.

Kobbe, Gustav. *The Jersey Coast and Pines.* Short Hills: Gateway Press, 1889.

Kraft, Bayard. *Under Barnegat's Beam.* New York: Parson & Company, 1960.

Kraft, Herbert. *The Lenape.* Newark: New Jersey Historical Society, 1986.

Kraft, John and Herbert. *The Indians of Lenapehoking.* South Orange, N.J.: Seton Hall Museum, 1985.

Kross, Peter. *New Jersey History.* Wilmington: Middle Atlantic Press, 1987.

Kushner, Helen (ed.),. *New Jersey Spotlight on Government.* New Brunswick: League of Women Voters, 1978.

League of Women Voters. *Meet Ocean County.* The League, 1978.

Levin, Michael. *Ocean County Tidal Wetlands.* Devan: Environmental Research Assoc., 1973.

Lloyd, John Bailey. *Six Miles at Sea, Long Beach Island, N.J..* Harvey Cedars: Down The Shore Pub., 1986.

Methot, June. *Up and Down the Beach*. Navesink, N.J.: Whip Publisher, 1988.

McPhee, John. *The Pine Barrens*. New York: Farrar, Straus & Giroux, 1968.

Miller, Pauline. *Early History of Toms River and Dover Township*. Toms River, 1967.

Miller, Pauline. *Three Centuries of Island Beach*. Ocean County Historical Society, 1981.

Molloy, Ann. *Wampum*. New York: Hasting House, 1977.

Moonsammy, Rita; Cohen, David and Williams, Lorraine *Pineland Folklore*. New Brunswick: Rutgers University Press, 1987.

Mount, Dorothy. *A Story of New Egypt and Plumsted Township*. New Egypt Historical Society, 1979.

Pierce, Arthur. *Smugglers Wood*. New Brunswick: Rutgers University Press, 1960.

Robinson, Douglas. *LZ 129 Hindenburg*. N.Y.: Arco, 1964.

Salter, Edwin. *A History of Ocean and Monmouth County*. Toms River: Ocean Historical Society, 1890.

Siebold, David and Adams, Charles. *Legends of Long Beach Island*. Wysomissing, Pa: Siebold, 1985.

Smith, Martha (ed.). *Tales of Ocean County*. Ocean County Historical Society, 1988.

Van Benthusen, Robert, and Wilson, Audrey. *Monmouth County*. Norfolk, Va.: Donning Co., 1983.

Voynick, Stephen. *The Mid Atlantic Treasure Coast*. Wilmington: Middle Atlantic Press, 1984.

Weslager, C.A.. *The Delaware Indians, A History*. New Brunswick, N.J.: Rutgers University Press, 1972.

Wilson, Harold. *The Story of the New Jersey Shore*. Princeton: D. Van Nostrand, 1964.

Zezula, Joanne. *Brick Township, Changing Scenes*, Brick Township Historical Society.

Zinkin, Vivian. *Place Names of Ocean County New Jersey 1609-1849*. Toms River, N.J.: Ocean County Historical Society, 1976.

Pamphlets and Journals

Cunningham, John. *New Jersey's Rich Harvest*. Trenton: Agricultural Society, 1981.

The Great March Storm, 1962. Ocean County Sun, 1962.

Historical Sites Survey, Toms River: Ocean Cultural and Heritage Commission, 1980 (Series of Phamplets on the Background and History of many Ocean County Communities).

New Jersey Highway Authority. *Annual Report.* 1989.

New Jersey Highway Authority. *Fact Sheet, Garden State Parkway.* May 1989.

New Jersey State Data Center. *1980 and 1990 Census of Population and Housing.* N.J. Department of Labor, 1991.

Ocean County, *A Guide to Places of Historic and Cultural Interest.* Ocean County Cultural and Heritage Commission, 1988.

Ocean County Cultural Directory. Ocean County Cultural and Heritage Commission. 1991.

Ocean County Office of Information. *Ocean County Government Directory.* 1988.

Ocean County Planning Board. *Ocean County Concept Plan.* November, 1975.

Ocean County 208 Project-Planning Staff. *Ocean County Water Quality Management Planning.* June 1978.

Report on Blue Panel on Ocean County, 1987. March, 1988.

Rigus, Golden, and Halper, Inc.. *Management Recommendations for Barnegat, Final Report*, August 1990.

Tiner, Ralph W.. *Wetlands of New Jersey.* July 1985.

Trust For Public Lands. *Northern Barnegat Bay, Reedy Creek Area and Herring Point Project Summary.*

U.S. of Interior Fish and Wildlife Service. *Proposed Reedy Creek Additions to the Forsythe National Wild Life Refuge.* December, 1990.

Vogler, Jack and Donfrio, Anthony. *Ocean County Census Trends.* Trenton: Department of Labor, 1985.

Unpublished Works

Donnatiello, Eugene. *A Brief Bibliography of Joseph Brick.* Brick Township N.J.: Brick Township Historical Society.

Fowler, David. *Egregious Villains , Wood Rangers, The Pine Robbers Phenomenon in the Revolutionary War.* (Rutgers University Doctoral Thesis).

A History of the Toms River Plant. CIBA Public Relations Office, 1990.

Kole, Edward. *The History of the Ocean County Court House* (Draft Research Report of Ocean County Court System).

Kralik, Marilyn. *The Buying of Barnegat Bay.* (University of Pennsylvania Doctoral Thesis)

Lee, Virginia Curtis. Phebe Doolittle Curtis, 1823-1920. *Remembrances of a Great, Great, Granddaughter*

Van Benthusen. Ocean County, *A Bibliography of Published Works.* (Draft Copy)

Magazines and Periodicals

"Did You Know." *Shore Heritage Newsletter.* Winter, 1990/91.

"The First Petition For a County to be Formed from Monmouth and Burlington Counties." *Shore Heritage Newsletter.* Winter, 1991.

"The Lavallette Boardwalk and Beachfront." *Shore Heritage Newsletter.* Summer 1991.

"The Old Life Savers of the Jersey Coast." *Coast Magazine.* August, 1984.

The Wreck of the Ship John Minturn. *Coast Magazine.* February, 1984.

"Tucker's Beach The Disappearing Island." *Shore Heritage Newsletter.* Winter, 1988/89.

Newspapers

Allen, G.K.. "Doc Cramer, Future Hall of Famer." *The Beachcomber*, July 1, 1976.

Bennett, Donald. "Bumblebees Flew at Island Beach." *Ocean County Observer.* December 15, 1991.

Bennett, Donald. "County Rail lines Led to Future." *Ocean County Observer.* March 24, 1991.

Bennett, Donald. "State Join Celebration of New Bridge." *Ocean County Observer.* March 29, 1991.

Carney, Leo. "Maestro Forms Charity Orchestra." *The New York Times*, May 10, 1991.

Christopher, Sam. "Coming to America. Italian Immigrants, Early Settlers in County." *Ocean County Observer.* August 11, 1991.

Christopher, Sam. "Rooster and Hens." *Ocean County Observer.* September 23, 1990.

Christe, Jack. "Thousands See, Hear Festival Finale." *Asbury Park Press*, September 1990.

Gaise, John. "Ordained by Music, Priest's Stage Days Reveal Alter Ego." *Asbury Park Press*, Manahawkin Bureau.

Grosko, Tom. "Rotary Tours Nuke Plant." *The Review*. November 14, 1991.

"NJN Documentary Profiles Lavallette Boatbuilder." *The Review*, October 24, 1991.

Parry, Wayne. "Lacey Site Among 10 OKed for State Funds." *Asbury Park Press*, October 16, 1991.

Rogers Lois. "Tuckerton Tower - A Mystery." *The Journal*. January 25, 1989.

Whitehouse, Beth. "So Do Your Know Where the Term Benny is From." *Asbury Park Press*, May 1991.

Audio Visual Materials

Hess, William, *Ocean County Picture Collection*. Point Pleasant Beach High School.

Jahn, Robert, (Director). *Ocean County History Lecture Series*. Point Pleasant: Ocean County Library, Multi Media Presentation, 1991.

Johnson, Arthur. *Historical Events and Buildings in Point Pleasant Beach*. Point Pleasant Beach, Video Tape: 1987.

Miller, Pauline. *Indians of Ocean County*. Toms River: Ocean County Cultural and Heritage Commission, filmstrip.

Miller, Pauline. *Disappearing Island*. Toms River: Ocean County Cultural and Heritage Commission, filmstrip.

Ocean County Historical Museum. *Ocean County Picture Collection*, Toms River.

Photograph and Illustration Index

Index

SIXTH EDITION

POETRY

An Introduction

Michael Meyer

University of Connecticut

BEDFORD / ST. MARTIN'S   Boston ◆ New York

For Bedford/St. Martin's

Senior Executive Editor: Stephen A. Scipione
Executive Editor: Ellen Thibault
Developmental Editor: Christina Gerogiannis
Production Editor: Annette Pagliaro Sweeney
Production Supervisor: Jennifer Peterson
Marketing Manager: Adrienne Petsick
Editorial Assistant: Sophia Snyder
Production Assistants: David Ayers, Lidia MacDonald-Carr
Copyeditor: Paula Woolley
Senior Art Director: Anna Palchik
Text Design: Claire Seng-Niemoeller
Cover Art and Design: Sara Gates
Composition: Glyph International
Printing and Binding: Haddon Craftsmen, Inc., an RR Donnelley & Sons Company

President: Joan E. Feinberg
Editorial Director: Denise B. Wydra
Editor in Chief: Karen S. Henry
Director of Marketing: Karen R. Soeltz
Director of Editing, Design, and Production: Marcia Cohen
Assistant Director of Editing, Design, and Production: Elise S. Kaiser
Managing Editor: Elizabeth M. Schaaf

Library of Congress Control Number: 2009924668

Manufactured in the United States of America.

4 3 2 1
f e d c

For information, write: Bedford/St. Martin's
75 Arlington Street, Boston, MA 02116
(617-399-4000)

ISBN-10: 0-312-53919-3
ISBN-13: 978-0-312-53919-1

Acknowledgments

Fleur Adcock. "The Video" from *Poems 1960–2000* by Fleur Adcock (Bloodaxe Books, 2000). Copyright © 2000 by Fleur Adcock. Reprinted by permission of Bloodaxe Books Ltd.

Anna Akhmatova. "Lot's Wife" from Anna Akhmatova, *Selected Poems,* translated by Richard McKane (Bloodaxe Books, 1989). Copyright © 1967 by Richard McKane. Reprinted by permission of Bloodaxe Books Ltd.

Claribel Alegría. "I Am Mirror" from *Sobrevivo* by Claribel Alegría. Reprinted by permission of the author.

Acknowledgments and copyrights are continued at the back of the book on pages 762–70, which constitute an extension of the copyright page. It is a violation of the law to reproduce these selections by any means whatsoever without the written permission of the copyright holder.

For My Wife
Regina Barreca

About Michael Meyer

Michael Meyer has taught writing and literature courses for more than thirty years — since 1981 at the University of Connecticut and before that at the University of North Carolina at Charlotte and the College of William and Mary. In addition to being an experienced teacher, Meyer is a highly regarded literary scholar. His scholarly articles have appeared in distinguished journals such as *American Literature, Studies in the American Renaissance,* and *Virginia Quarterly Review.* An internationally recognized authority on Henry David Thoreau, Meyer is a former president of the Thoreau Society and coauthor (with Walter Harding) of *The New Thoreau Handbook,* a standard reference source. His first book, *Several More Lives to Live: Thoreau's Political Reputation in America,* was awarded the Ralph Henry Gabriel Prize by the American Studies Association. He is also the editor of *Frederick Douglass: The Narrative and Selected Writings.* He has lectured on a variety of American literary topics from Cambridge University to Peking University. His other books for Bedford/St. Martin's include *The Bedford Introduction to Literature,* Eighth Edition, and *Thinking and Writing about Literature,* Second Edition.

Preface for Instructors

Like its predecessors, this sixth edition of *Poetry: An Introduction* assumes that reading and understanding literature offer valuable means of apprehending life in its richness and diversity. This book also reflects the hope that its selections will inspire students to become lifelong readers of imaginative literature as well as more thoughtful and skillful writers.

This text is flexibly organized into four parts that may be taught consecutively or in any order you prefer. Part One — the first eleven chapters — is devoted to the elements of poetry; Part Two consists of eleven chapters that feature a variety of approaches to poetry; Part Three is a collection of poems that includes albums of world and contemporary literature; and Part Four discusses strategies for critical thinking, reading, and writing about literature that can be assigned selectively throughout the course. Sample student papers and more than one thousand assignments appear in the text, offering students the support they need to write about poetry.

Poetry: An Introduction accommodates many teaching styles and addresses the needs of today's poetry classrooms. Among the features of the sixth edition are new sample student papers, new thematic case studies, a new in-depth chapter on the contemporary poet Billy Collins, and a new online resource, *Re: Writing for Literature*, that offers instructors more options for teaching and students even more help for exploring, enjoying, and writing about literature.

FEATURES OF *POETRY: AN INTRODUCTION*, SIXTH EDITION

Following is a description of the features and contents that have long made *Poetry: An Introduction* a favorite of students and teachers. What is new to this edition is described starting on page viii. (For a description of *Re:Writing for Literature*, see p. ix of this preface.)

Teachable poems your students will want to read

Chosen for their appeal to students, *Poetry*'s rich and diverse selections range from the classic to the contemporary and include such gems as Martín Espada's "Latin Night at the Pawnshop," Carl Sandburg's "Chicago," and Kay Ryan's "Hailstorm." The poems represent a variety of periods, nationalities, cultures, styles, and voices — from the serious to the humorous and from the canonical to very recent works. As in previous editions, classic works by John Donne, Robert Frost, Elizabeth Bishop, Langston Hughes, and others are generously represented. In addition, there are many contemporary selections from writers such as Thomas Lux, Cathy Song, Susan Minot, and Tony Hoagland. Recent selections appear throughout the anthology and are also conveniently collected in Chapter 23, "An Album of Contemporary Poems."

Many options for teaching, learning — and enjoying

Over six editions, in its continuing effort to make literature come to life for students and the course a pleasure to teach for instructors, *Poetry: An Introduction* has developed and refined these innovative features:

A CLEAR, LIVELY DISCUSSION OF THE ELEMENTS OF POETRY.   The first eleven chapters are devoted to the elements of poetry — diction, tone, images, figures of speech, symbols, sounds, rhythm, and poetic forms. Each begins with a focused, student-friendly discussion of the element interspersed with lively examples that show students how that element contributes to the meanings of a poem. At the end of each of these chapters is a mini-anthology of poems for further study, each accompanied by questions for critical thinking and writing.

ENRICHING PERSPECTIVES AND VISUALS.   Intriguing documents and images — including personal journals, letters, critical essays, interviews, photographs, and paintings — appear throughout the book to stimulate class discussion and writing. A visual portfolio titled "Encountering Poetry: Images of Poetry in Popular Culture" (p. 8) opens students' eyes to the presence of poetry in their lives.

USEFUL CONNECTIONS BETWEEN POPULAR AND LITERARY CULTURE.   *Poetry* draws carefully on examples from popular culture to explain the elements of poetry, inviting students to relate to literature through what they already know. Writing questions that help students draw connections between popular culture and more canonical works appear after each example. The examples include greeting-card verse and contemporary song lyrics, such as Bruce Springsteen's "Devils & Dust" and S. Pearl Sharp's "It's the Law: A Rap Poem."

POETS — AND POEMS — IN DEPTH AND THEMATIC CASE STUDIES. In-depth c
ters on Emily Dickinson, Robert Frost, Langston Hughes, Julia Alvarez,
now Billy Collins, provide multiple works by each poet along with letters, int.
views, draft manuscript pages, photos, and other contextual materials tha
enhance the study of these authors and their works. A case study chapter on
T. S. Eliot's "The Love Song of J. Alfred Prufrock" invites students to respond
to critical and cultural approaches to poetry; and the book's thematic chapters,
including case studies on love and longing and on life's important milestones,
connect students to literature through universal human experience.

ACCESSIBLE COVERAGE OF LITERARY THEORY. For instructors who wish to incorporate literary theory into their courses, Chapter 26, "Critical Strategies
for Reading," introduces students to a variety of critical strategies, ranging
from formalism to cultural criticism. In brief examples, the approaches are
applied in analyzing Robert Frost's "Mending Wall" and other works so
that students will have a sense of how to use these strategies in their own
reading and writing.

Plenty of help with reading and writing about poetry

SEVEN CHAPTERS ON READING AND WRITING ABOUT POETRY ensure that students get the help they need, beginning — in the book's introduction and
first chapter — with how to approach a poem and think critically about it.
Annotated versions of several poems — William Hathaway's humorous
"Oh, Oh," Elizabeth Bishop's widely taught "Manners," and John Donne's
classic sonnet "Death Be Not Proud" — model for students the kind of critical reading that leads to excellent writing about poetry. Chapters 2 and 11
take students through every step of the writing process, from generating
topics to documenting sources — while sixteen sample papers throughout
the book model the results. (See the "Resources for Reading and Writing
about Poetry" chart at the back of the book on p. 794.) For students who
need help with researched writing, Chapter 28, "The Literary Research
Paper," offers detailed advice for finding, evaluating, and incorporating
print and electronic sources in a paper. It also includes the most current
MLA documentation guidelines.

MORE THAN 1,500 QUESTIONS AND ASSIGNMENTS — First Response prompts,
Considerations for Critical Thinking and Writing questions, Connections
to Other Selections questions, Critical Strategies questions, and Creative
Response questions — give students many opportunities for thinking and
writing. In addition, these helpful checklists offer questions and suggestions for reading and writing about poetry:

- Suggestions for Approaching Poetry (Ch. 1, p. 38)
- Questions for Responsive Reading and Writing (Ch. 2, p. 59)
- Suggestions for Scanning a Poem (Ch. 8, p. 222)

NEW TO THIS EDITION

95 new poems

These new poems represent canonical, multicultural, contemporary, and popular literature. Complementing the addition of several classic works that have long made classroom discussion come alive are numerous works not frequently anthologized, such as Wyn Cooper's "Puritan Impulse" and Allen Braden's "Sweethearts." Featuring many of the most engaging poets of the twenty-first century, *Poetry* includes plenty of humorous poems on daily life and contemporary issues, including:

- Joan Murray's "We Old Dudes" (a funny and instantly recognizable new take on Gwendolyn Brooks' famous "We Real Cool")
- Denise Duhamel's "Language Police Report" (on political correctness and censorship)
- X. J. Kennedy's "On a Young Man's Remaining an Undergraduate for Twelve Years" (a glorious ode to college life)

From Chapter 15: A Study of Billy Collins: The Author Reflects on Five Poems

An exciting new chapter on Billy Collins, created with Billy Collins

Five of Collins' own poems appear in Chapter 15 alongside compelling personal insights—written specifically for Michael Meyer's anthologies—into each work, plus a delightful collection of rare photographs and manuscript pages. Like its sister chapter created with Julia Alvarez (Chapter 16), this new collection shows poetry as a living, changing art form, featuring the observations that contemporary writers offer on their time. Once again, students will enjoy the opportunity to have a major poet speak directly to them, this time in Collins' unique style, about how he writes, why he writes, and the kinds of surprises that occur along the way.

Two new thematic case studies

In Chapter 20, *Poetry*'s new chapter on **formative experiences and coming of-age,** writers such as Charles Simic, Anne Carson, and Yusef Komunyakaa get to the heart of many of life's important milestones with memorable poems that students will relate to. The new Chapter 22, on **our relationship with the environment,** offers literature that is as varied, rich, and often as personal as the subject itself—with such works as Gail White's "Dead Armadillos" (on beauty, scarcity, and what we choose to save) and Edward Hirsch's "First Snowfall: Intimations" (an evocative childhood memory of playing in the snow).

More help with academic writing

Poetry now provides twice as many documented student papers (sixteen total) — all following the most up-to-date MLA guidelines and all useful models for writing. Revised coverage of conducting research online offers clear, practical advice.

ADDITIONAL RESOURCES FOR TEACHING AND LEARNING

Innovative multimedia tools for reading and writing

The sixth edition of *Poetry* offers an unparalleled set of multimedia tools to help students read, enjoy, think about, and write about poetry. The following resources are available to students and instructors:

Re:Writing for Literature

Good writing comes from *Re:Writing for Literature,* the best collection of Web resources for literature and composition classrooms. Free, open, and easy to access at *bedfordstmartins.com/rewritinglit,* students will find tutorials for close reading, links to author biographies, quizzes on literary works, and a glossary of literary terms. Model documents, writing exercises, grammar help, and resources for finding and citing sources provide invaluable writing help. The site features the *VirtuaLit Interactive Poetry Tutorial* offering in-depth readings with coverage of literary elements, cultural contexts, and critical approaches for Elizabeth Bishop's "The Fish," Theodore Roethke's "My Papa's Waltz," and Andrew Marvell's "To His Coy Mistress."

LiterActive CD-ROM

This groundbreaking resource is packed with contextual materials, activities for exploring poetry, and help with research and documentation. In addition to the *VirtuaLit* tutorials described above, *LiterActive* offers:

- A *Multimedia and Documents Gallery* stocked with hundreds of images, audio and video clips, and contextual documents supporting forty-three authors

- A *Research and Documentation Guide* with advice for students on how to find, evaluate, summarize, interpret, and document sources

LiterActive CD-ROM

This CD-ROM, a $10 value, is **available free** when packaged with *Poetry*; to order the two together, use ISBN-13: 978-0-312-59437-4/ISBN-10: 0-312-59437-2.

Re:Writing Plus

Re:Writing Plus gathers our premium digital content into one collection for literature and composition. Explore our newest resource, *Video Central,* a growing collection of over fifty brief videos for the writing classroom. To order *Poetry: An Introduction* with *Re:Writing Plus,* use package ISBN-10: 0-312-61567-1/ISBN-13: 978-0-312-61567-3.

TradeUp Program

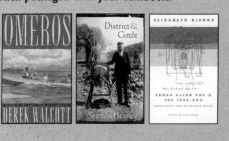

Instructor's Manual: *Resources for Teaching* POETRY: AN INTRODUCTION, SIXTH EDITION
ISBN-10: 0-312-54336-0/ISBN-13: 978-0-312-54336-5

This comprehensive manual supports every selection, offering help resources for new and experienced instructors alike. Resources include commentaries, biographical information, and writing assignments, as well as teaching tips from instructors who have taught with the book, additional suggestions for connections among the selections, and thematic groupings with questions for discussion and writing. The manual is available online at bedfordstmartins.com/meyerpoetry/catalog.

Literature Aloud, two-CD set
(ISBN-10: 0-312-43011-6 / ISBN-13: 978-0-312-43011-5)
These enriching audio recordings feature celebrated writers and actors reading stories, poems, and selected scenes included in Michael Meyer's anthologies. Poetry highlights include E. E. Cummings, T. S. Eliot, Robert Frost, Sylvia Plath, Langston Hughes, and other major authors reading their own works. This resource is free to instructors who adopt the text.

ACKNOWLEDGMENTS

This book has benefited from the ideas, suggestions, and corrections of scores of careful readers who helped transform various stages of an evolving manuscript into a finished book and into subsequent editions. I remain grateful to those I have thanked in prefaces of *The Bedford Introduction to Literature*, particularly to the late Robert Wallace of Case Western Reserve University. I would also like to give special thanks to Ronald Wallace of the University of Wisconsin and William Henry Louis of Mary Washington College. In addition, many instructors who have used *Poetry: An Introduction* responded to a questionnaire on the book. For their valuable comments and advice I am grateful to Steve Abbott, Columbus State Community College; Candace Barrington, Central Connecticut State University; Emily Bobo, Ivy Tech Community College; Heather Bouwman, University of St. Thomas; Michael Chappell, Western Connecticut State University; James Gifford, Mohawk Valley Community College; Marina Gore, Hudson Valley Community College; Erin Goss, Loyola College in Maryland; Leslie J. Henson, Butte-Glenn Community College District; Michael Kaffer, Spring Hill College; Steven G. Kellman, University of Texas at San Antonio; Francia Kissel, Indiana University-Purdue University Indianapolis; Bonnie Lyons, University of Texas at San Antonio; James A. McWard, Johnson County Community College; Gary Pandolfi, Quinnipiac University; Kelly Seufert, Queens College, CUNY; Barbara Foster Tribble, University of St. Thomas; Edward P. Walkiewicz, Oklahoma State University; and Jason Williams, Grossmont College.

I am also indebted to those who cheerfully answered questions and generously provided miscellaneous bits of information. What might have seemed them like inconsequential conversations turned out to be important leads. mong these friends and colleagues are Raymond Anselment, Barbara Campoell, Ann Charters, Irving Cummings, William Curtin, Margaret Higonnet, Patrick Hogan, Lee Jacobus, Greta Little, George Monteiro, Brenda Murphy, Joel Myerson, Rose Quiello, Thomas Recchio, William Sheidley, Milton Stern, Kenneth Wilson, and the dedicated reference librarians at the Homer Babbidge Library, University of Connecticut.

I am particularly happy to acknowledge the tactful help of Roxanne Cody, owner of R. J. Julia Booksellers in Madison, Connecticut, whose passion for books authorizes her as the consummate matchmaker for writers, readers, and titles. It's a wonder that somebody doesn't call the cops.

I continue to be grateful for what I have learned from teaching my students and for the many student papers I have received over the years that I have used in various forms to serve as good and accessible models of student writing. I am particularly indebted to Stefanie Wortman for her excellent work on the sixth edition of *Resources for Teaching POETRY: AN INTRODUCTION*.

At Bedford / St. Martin's, my debts once again require more time to acknowledge than the deadline allows. Charles H. Christensen and Joan Feinberg initiated this project and launched it with their intelligence, energy, and sound advice. Earlier editions of the book were shaped by editors Karen Henry, Kathy Retan, Alanya Harter, Aron Keesbury, and Ellen Thibault; their work was as first-rate as it was essential. As developmental editor for the sixth edition, Christina Gerogiannis expertly kept the book on track and made the journey a pleasure to the end; her valuable contributions richly remind me how fortunate I am to be a Bedford / St. Martin's author. Stephanie Naudin, associate editor, energetically developed the book's instructor's manual, and Sophia Snyder, editorial assistant, gracefully handled a variety of editorial tasks. Permissions were deftly arranged by Arthur Johnson, Martha Friedman, and Susan Doheny. The difficult tasks of production were skillfully managed by Annette Pagliaro Sweeney. Paula Woolley provided careful copyediting, and Janet Cocker and Mary Lou Wilshaw-Watts did more-than-meticulous proofreading. I thank all of the people at Bedford — including Sara Gates, who designed the cover, and Adrienne Petsick and Jenna Bookin Barry, the marketing managers — who helped make this formidable project a manageable one.

Finally, I am grateful to my sons Timothy and Matthew for all kinds of help, but mostly I'm just grateful they're my sons. And for making all the difference, I thank my wife, Regina Barreca.

Brief Contents

AN ANTHOLOGY OF POEMS   585

CRITICAL THINKING AND WRITING ABOUT POETRY   659

Contents

There is no
happiness like
mine. I have
been eating
poetry.

— MARK STRAND

A poet has a duty to words . . . words can do wonderful things.

— GWENDOLYN BROOKS

Contents

Between my
finger and my
thumb / The
squat pen rests. /
I'll dig with it.
— SEAMUS HEANEY

Like a piece of
ice on a hot
stove the poem
must ride on its
own melting.

— ROBERT FROST

Literature is
the apparatus
through which
the world tries to
keep intact its
important ideas
and feelings.

— MARY OLIVER

7. Sounds   186

8. Patterns of Rhythm   217

Some Principles of Meter   218

Poems for Further Study   226

I would define, in brief, the Poetry of words as the Rhythmical Creation of Beauty. Its sole arbiter is Taste.

—EDGAR ALLAN POE

A short poem
need not be
small.
— MARVIN BELL

10. Open Form   272

In poetry you have a form looking for a subject and a subject looking for a form. When they come together successfully you have a poem.
— W. H. AUDEN

APPROACHES TO POETRY 309

My business is circumference.
— EMILY DICKINSON

A cartoon from a letter from Emily Dickinson to William Cowper Dickinson.

13. A Study of Robert Frost   359

A Brief Biography   360

An Introduction to His Work   364

A poem . . . begins as a lump in the throat, a sense of wrong, a homesickness, a love-sickness . . .

— ROBERT FROST

CHRONOLOGY   367

A manuscript page from "Neither Out Far nor In Deep."

PERSPECTIVES ON ROBERT FROST   387

I believe that poetry should be direct, comprehensible, and the epitome of simplicity.

— LANGSTON HUGHES

A couple on West 127th St., New York, during the Harlem Renaissance.

15. A Study of Billy Collins: The Author Reflects on Five Poems 436

When I'm asked what made me into a writer, I point to the watershed experience of coming to this country. Not understanding the language, I had to pay close attention to each word— great training for a writer.

— JULIA ALVAREZ

Genuine poetry can communicate before it is understood.

— T. S. ELIOT

For a man to
become a
poet . . . he must
be in love or
miserable.
— LORD BYRON

22. A Thematic Case Study: The Natural World   571

Poetry has become a kind of tool for knowing the world in a particular way.
— JANE HIRSHFIELD

AN ANTHOLOGY OF POEMS   585

23. An Album of Contemporary Poems   587

24. An Album of World Literature   600

If there were no poetry on any day in the world, poetry would be invented that day. For there would be an intolerable hunger.
— MURIEL RUKEYSER

25. A Collection of Poems   615

– LUCILLE CLIFTON

— WILLIAM
WORDSWORTH

CRITICAL THINKING AND WRITING ABOUT POETRY

26. Critical Strategies for Reading   661

Great literature
is simply
language
charged with
meaning to the
utmost possible
degree.

— EZRA POUND

The answers
you get from
literature depend
upon the ques-
tions you pose.
— MARGARET
  ATWOOD

I can't write five
words but that I
change seven.
— DOROTHY
PARKER

Contents

Thematic Contents

Thematic Contents

Childhood

Friendship

Place

Thematic Contents

Animals

Thematic Contents

Myths and Fairy Tales

Life in America

Popular Culture

Thematic Contents

Health and Sickness

Love and Longing

Sexuality

Humor and Satire

(Note: The following list includes poems from Chapter 19, "A Thematic Case Study: Humor and Satire," as well as other poems in the text that fit within this theme.)

Class

Race and Stereotyping

Thematic Contents

Language and Literature

Science and Technology

Religion

Spirituality and Immortality

Mortality

INTRODUCTION

Reading
Imaginative Literature

Poetry does not need to be defended,
any more than air or food needs to be
defended.
— LANGSTON HUGHES[1]

THE NATURE OF LITERATURE

Literature does not lend itself to a single tidy definition because the making of it over the centuries has been as complex, unwieldy, and natural as life itself. Is literature everything that has been written, from ancient prayers to graffiti? Does it include songs and stories that were not written down until many years after they were recited? Does literature include the television scripts from *The Sopranos* as well as Shakespeare's *King Lear*? Is literature only writing that has permanent value and continues to move people? Must literature be true or beautiful or moral? Should it be socially useful?

Although these kinds of questions are not conclusively answered in this book, they are implicitly raised by the poems included here. No definition

[1] Photograph © copyright of the Estate of Carl Van Vechten; Gravure and Compilation © copyright of the Eakins Press Foundation.

of literature, particularly a brief one, is likely to satisfy everyone because definitions tend to weaken and require qualification when confronted by the uniqueness of individual works. In this context it is worth recalling Herman Melville's humorous use of a definition of a whale in *Moby-Dick* (1851). In the course of the novel Melville presents his imaginative and symbolic whale as inscrutable, but he begins with a quotation from Georges Cuvier, a French naturalist who defines a whale in his nineteenth-century study *The Animal Kingdom* this way: "The whale is a mammiferous animal without hind feet." Cuvier's description is technically correct, of course, but there is little wisdom in it. Melville understood that the reality of the whale (which he describes as the "ungraspable phantom of life") cannot be caught by isolated facts. If the full meaning of the whale is to be understood, it must be sought on the open sea of experience, where the whale itself is, rather than in exclusionary definitions. Although they may be helpful, facts and definitions do not always reveal the whole truth.

Despite Melville's reminder that a definition can be too limiting and even comical, it is useful for our purposes to describe literature as a fiction consisting of carefully arranged words designed to stir the imagination. Stories, poems, and plays are fictional. They are made up — imagined — even when based on actual historic events. Such imaginative writing differs from other kinds of writing because its purpose is not primarily to transmit facts or ideas. Imaginative literature is a source more of pleasure than of information, and we read it for basically the same reasons we listen to music or view a dance: enjoyment, delight, and satisfaction. Like other art forms, imaginative literature offers pleasure and usually attempts to convey a perspective, a mood, a feeling, or an experience. Writers transform the facts the world provides — people, places, and objects — into experiences that suggest meanings.

Consider, for example, the difference between the following factual description of a snake and a poem on the same subject. Here is the *Webster's Eleventh New Collegiate Dictionary* definition:

> any of numerous limbless scaled reptiles (suborder Serpentes or Ophidia) with a long tapering body and with salivary glands often modified to produce venom which is injected through grooved or tubular fangs.

Contrast this matter-of-fact definition with Emily Dickinson's poetic evocation of a snake in "A narrow Fellow in the Grass":

A narrow Fellow in the Grass
Occasionally rides —
You may have met Him — did you not
His notice sudden is —

The Grass divides as with a Comb —   5
A spotted shaft is seen —
And then it closes at your feet
And opens further on —

He likes a Boggy Acre
A floor too cool for Corn —   10
Yet when a Boy, and Barefoot —
I more than once at Noon

Have passed, I thought, a Whip lash
Unbraiding in the Sun
When stooping to secure it   15
It wrinkled, and was gone —

Several of Nature's People
I know, and they know me —
I feel for them a transport
Of cordiality —   20

But never met this Fellow
Attended, or alone
Without a tighter breathing
And Zero at the Bone —

The dictionary provides a succinct, anatomical description of what a snake is, whereas Dickinson's poem suggests what a snake can mean. The definition offers facts; the poem offers an experience. The dictionary description would probably allow someone who had never seen a snake to sketch one with reasonable accuracy. The poem also provides some vivid subjective descriptions — for example, the snake dividing the grass "as with a Comb" — yet it offers more than a picture of serpentine movements. The poem conveys the ambivalence many people have about snakes — the kind of feeling, for example, so evident on the faces of visitors viewing the snakes at a zoo. In the poem there is both a fascination with and a horror of what might be called snakehood; this combination of feelings has been coiled in most of us since Adam and Eve.

That "narrow Fellow" so cordially introduced by way of a riddle (the word *snake* is never used in the poem) is, by the final stanza, revealed as a snake in the grass. In between, Dickinson uses language expressively to convey her meaning. For instance, in the line "His notice sudden is," listen to the *s* sound in each word and note how the verb *is* unexpectedly appears at the end, making the snake's hissing presence all the more "sudden." And anyone who has ever been surprised by a snake knows the "tighter breathing / And Zero at the Bone" that Dickinson evokes so successfully by the rhythm of her word choices and line breaks. Perhaps even more significant, Dickinson's poem allows those who have never encountered a snake to imagine such an experience.

A good deal more could be said about the numbing fear that undercuts the affection for nature at the beginning of this poem, but the point here is that imaginative literature gives us not so much the full, factual proportions of the world as some of its experiences and meanings. Instead of defining the world, literature encourages us to try it out in our imaginations.

THE VALUE OF LITERATURE

Mark Twain once shrewdly observed that a person who chooses not to read has no advantage over a person who is unable to read. In industrialized societies today, however, the question is not who reads, because nearly everyone can and does, but what is read. Why should anyone spend precious time with literature when there is so much reading material available that provides useful information about everything from the daily news to personal computers? Why should a literary artist's imagination compete for attention that could be spent on the firm realities that constitute everyday life? In fact, national best-seller lists include collections of stories, poems, or plays much less often than they do cookbooks and, not surprisingly, diet books. Although such fare may be filling, it doesn't stay with you. Most people have other appetites, too.

Certainly one of the most important values of literature is that it nourishes our emotional lives. An effective literary work may seem to speak directly to us, especially if we are ripe for it. The inner life that good writers reveal in their characters often gives us glimpses of some portion of ourselves. We can be moved to laugh, cry, tremble, dream, ponder, shriek, or rage with a character by simply turning a page instead of turning our lives upside down. Although the experience itself is imagined, the emotion is real. That's why the final chapters of a good adventure novel can make a reader's heart race as much as a 100-yard dash or why the repressed love of Hester Prynne in Nathaniel Hawthorne's *The Scarlet Letter* is painful to a sympathetic reader. Human emotions speak a universal language regardless of when or where a work was written.

In addition to appealing to our emotions, literature broadens our perspectives on the world. Most of the people we meet are pretty much like ourselves, and what we can see of the world even in a lifetime is astonishingly limited. Literature allows us to move beyond the inevitable boundaries of our own lives and culture because it introduces us to people different from ourselves, places remote from our neighborhoods, and times other than our own. Reading makes us more aware of life's possibilities as well as its subtleties and ambiguities. Put simply, people who read literature experience more life and have a keener sense of a common human identity than those who do not. It is true, of course, that many people go through life without reading imaginative literature, but that is a loss rather than a gain. They may find themselves troubled by the same kinds of questions that reveal Daisy Buchanan's restless, vague discontentment in F. Scott Fitzgerald's *The Great Gatsby:* "'What'll we do with ourselves this afternoon?' cried Daisy, 'and the day after that, and the next thirty years?'"

Sometimes students mistakenly associate literature more with school than with life. Accustomed to reading it in order to write a paper or pass an examination, students may perceive such reading as a chore instead of a pleasurable opportunity, something considerably less important than studying for the "practical" courses that prepare them for a career. The study of literature, however, is also practical because it engages you in the kinds of problem solving important in a variety of fields, from philosophy to science and technology. The interpretation of literary texts requires you to deal with uncertainties, value judgments, and emotions; these are unavoidable aspects of life.

People who make the most significant contributions to their professions — whether in business, engineering, teaching, or some other area — tend to be challenged rather than threatened by multiple possibilities. Instead of retreating to the way things have always been done, they bring freshness and creativity to their work. F. Scott Fitzgerald once astutely described the "test of a first-rate intelligence" as "the ability to hold two opposed ideas in the mind at the same time, and still retain the ability to function." People with such intelligence know how to read situations, shape questions, interpret details, and evaluate competing points of view. Equipped with a healthy respect for facts, they also understand the value of pursuing hunches and exercising their imaginations. Reading literature encourages a suppleness of mind that is helpful in any discipline or work.

Once the requirements for your degree are completed, what ultimately matters are not the courses listed on your transcript but the sensibilities and habits of mind that you bring to your work, friends, family, and, indeed, the rest of your life. A healthy economy changes and grows with the times; people do, too, if they are prepared for more than simply filling a job description. The range and variety of life that literature affords can help you to interpret your own experiences and the world in which you live.

To discover the insights that literature reveals requires careful reading and sensitivity. One of the purposes of a college literature class is to cultivate the analytic skills necessary for reading well. Class discussions often help establish a dialogue with a work that perhaps otherwise would not speak to you. Analytic skills can also be developed by writing about what you read. Writing is an effective means of clarifying your responses and ideas because it requires you to account for the author's use of language as well as your own. This book is based on two premises: that reading literature is pleasurable and that reading and understanding a work sensitively by thinking, talking, or writing about it increase the pleasure of the experience of it.

Understanding its basic elements — such as point of view, symbol, theme, tone, and irony — is a prerequisite to an informed appreciation of literature. This kind of understanding allows you to perceive more in a literary work in much the same way that a spectator at a tennis match sees more if he or she understands the rules and conventions of the game. But literature is not simply a spectator sport. The analytic skills that open up literature also have their uses when you watch a television program or film and, more important, when you attempt to sort out the significance of the people, places, and events that constitute your own life. Literature enhances and sharpens your perceptions. What could be more lastingly practical as well as satisfying?

THE CHANGING LITERARY CANON

Perhaps the best reading creates some kind of change in us: we see more clearly; we're alert to nuances; we ask questions that previously didn't occur to us. Henry David Thoreau had that sort of reading in mind when he remarked in *Walden* that the books he valued most were those that caused him to date "a new era in his life from the reading." Readers are sometimes changed by literature, but it is also worth noting that the life of a literary work can also be affected by its readers. Melville's *Moby-Dick,* for example, was not valued as a classic until the 1920s, when critics rescued the novel from the obscurity of being cataloged in many libraries (including Yale's) not under fiction but under cetology, the study of whales. Indeed, many writers contemporary to Melville who were important and popular in the nineteenth century—William Cullen Bryant, Henry Wadsworth Longfellow, and James Russell Lowell, to name a few—are now mostly unread; their names appear more often on elementary schools built early in the twentieth century than in anthologies. Clearly, literary reputations and what is valued as great literature change over time and in the eyes of readers.

Such changes have accelerated during the past forty years as the literary *canon*—those works considered by scholars, critics, and teachers to be the most important to read and study—has undergone a significant series of shifts. Writers who previously were overlooked, undervalued, neglected, or studiously ignored have been brought into focus in an effort to create a more diverse literary canon, one that recognizes the contributions of the many cultures that make up American society. Since the 1960s, for example, some critics have reassessed writings by women who had been left out of the standard literary traditions dominated by male writers. Many more female writers are now read alongside the male writers who traditionally populated literary history. This kind of enlargement of the canon also resulted from another reform movement of the 1960s: the civil rights movement sensitized literary critics to the political, moral, and esthetic necessity of rediscovering African American literature, and more recently Asian and Hispanic writers have been making their way into the canon. Moreover, on a broader scale the canon is being revised and enlarged to include the works of writers from parts of the world other than the West—a development that reflects the changing values, concerns, and complexities of the past several decades or so, when literary landscapes have shifted as dramatically as the political boundaries of Eastern Europe and the former Soviet Union.

. . .

No semester's reading list—or anthology—can adequately or accurately echo all of the new voices competing to be heard as part of the mainstream literary canon, but recent efforts to open up the canon attempt to sensitize readers to the voices of women, minorities, and writers from all over the world. This development has not occurred without its urgent advocates or passionate dissenters. It's no surprise that issues about race, gender, and class often get people off the fence and on their feet (these controversies are discussed further in Chapter 26, "Critical Strategies for Reading"). Although what we regard as literature—whether it's called great, classic, or canonical—continues to generate debate, there is no question that such controversy will continue to reflect readers' values as well as the writers they admire.

ENCOUNTERING POETRY:
IMAGES OF POETRY
IN POPULAR CULTURE

Although poets may find it painful to acknowledge, poetry is not nearly as popular as prose among contemporary readers. A quick prowl through almost any bookstore reveals many more shelves devoted to novels or biographies, for example, than the meager space allotted to poetry. Moreover, few poems are made into films (although there have been some exceptions, such as Alfred, Lord Tennyson's "The Charge of the Light Brigade" [p. 236]), and few collections of poetry have earned their authors extraordinary wealth or celebrity status.

Despite these facts, however, there is plenty of poetry being produced that saturates our culture and suggests just how essential it is to our lives. When in 2001 Billy Collins was named the poet laureate of the United States, he shrewdly observed that "we should notice that there is no *prose* laureate." What Collins implicitly acknowledges here is the importance of poetry. He acknowledges the idea that poetry is central to any literature because it is the art closest to language itself; its emphasis on getting each word just right speaks to us and for us. The audience for poetry may be relatively modest in comparison to the readership of prose, but there is nothing shy about poetry's presence in contemporary life. Indeed, a particularly observant person might find it difficult to reach the end of a day without encountering poetry in some shape or form.

You may, for instance, read yet again that magnetic poem composed on your refrigerator door as you reach for your breakfast juice, or perhaps you'll be surprised by some poetic lines while riding the bus or subway, where you might encounter a Poetry in Motion poster, featuring the work of a local poet or well-known author such as Dorothy Parker. What the poems have in common is the celebration of language as a means of surprising, delighting, provoking, or inspiring their readers. There's no obligation and no quiz. The poems are for the taking: all for pleasure.

The following portfolio of images — including provocative posters, a humorous cartoon, poetry-related art in public spaces, and vibrant photographs from the poetry slam scene — illustrate the significance of poetry in our culture. These images recognize the importance not only of such canonical authors as Carl Sandburg and T. S. Eliot but also of aspiring poets — spoken word performers or Magnetic Poetry authors, for example — whose works reflect the growth of poetry as a popular form of expression.

Perhaps the largest, most recent explosion of poetry can be found on the Internet. As Poetry Portal (poetry-portal.com) indicates, the number of poetry sites is staggering; these include sites that provide poems, audio readings, e-zines, reviews, criticism, festivals, slams, conferences, workshops, and even collaborative poetry writing in real time. This growth in poetry on the Internet is significant because it reflects an energy and vitality about the poetic activity in our daily lives. Poetry may not be rich and famous, but it is certainly alive and well. Consider, for example, the following images of poetry that can be found in contemporary life. What do they suggest to you about the nature of poetry and its audience?

DOROTHY PARKER, *Unfortunate Coincidence*

Begun in New York City in 1992, the Poetry in Motion program has spread from coast to coast on buses and subways. Offering works ranging from ancient Chinese poetry to contemporary poetry, Poetry in Motion posters give riders more to read than their own reflections in the window. In this example, Dorothy Parker, a poet known for her sharp wit, becomes a presence on a New York subway car.

POETRY IN MOTION

UNFORTUNATE COINCIDENCE

By the time you swear you're his,
    Shivering and sighing,
And he vows his passion is
    Infinite, undying —
Lady, make a note of this:
    One of you is lying.

—Dorothy Parker (1893–1967)

CONSIDERATIONS FOR CRITICAL THINKING AND WRITING

1. How does the unromantic nature of this poem seem especially appropriate for New York City subway riders?
2. What kinds of poetry do you find on billboards or public transportation in your own environment? If there is none, what poem would you choose to post on a bus or train in your area?

Carl Sandburg, *Window*

This mural, painted on a station wall of the Chicago El, features the poem "Window," from a collection of poems by Carl Sandburg titled *Chicago*. This work transforms the evening commute into an encounter with a vivid image.

© Jason Reblando. Reprinted by permission of the photographer.

Considerations for Critical Thinking and Writing

1. Discuss the effectiveness of the images in these two lines.
2. **CREATIVE RESPONSE.** Try writing two lines of vivid imagery that capture the movement seen from a quickly moving automobile during daylight.

Roz Chast, *The Love Song of J. Alfred Crew*

This *New Yorker* cartoon by Roz Chast (b. 1954) updates lines from T. S. Eliot's "The Love Song of J. Alfred Prufrock" (page 494, lines 120–24) with the kind of language used in the popular J. Crew clothing catalog. Though published in 1917, Eliot's poem clearly remains fashionable.

CONSIDERATIONS FOR CRITICAL THINKING AND WRITING

1. Read "The Love Song of J. Alfred Prufrock" (p. 494) and compare the speaker's personality to the kind of image associated with the typical J. Crew customer. How does this comparison serve to explain the humor in the cartoon?

2. Explain why you think the J. Crew company would be flattered or annoyed to have its image treated this way in a cartoon.

Tim Taylor, *I shake the delicate apparatus*

Magnetic Poetry™ kits are available in a number of languages, including Yiddish, Norwegian, and sign language, along with a variety of thematic versions such as those dedicated to cats, love, art, rock and roll, college, and Shakespeare. This poem by Tim Taylor (b. 1957) graces his Manhattan apartment refrigerator and is but one example of the creative expression that poetry magnets inspire in kitchens around the world.

Reprinted by permission of Tim Taylor (poem) and Pelle Cass (image).

> I shake the delicate apparatus
> I pound with delirious feet
>
> frantic
> the suit s
> the repulsive shadow power s
> cry and pant and moan
> whispering of diamond s
> of death
>
> but we two
> sweet essential s
> we soar

CONSIDERATIONS FOR CRITICAL THINKING AND WRITING

1. Write a paragraph that describes what you think is the essential meaning of this poem.
2. How do you explain the enormous popularity of Magnetic Poetry?

© Kevin Fleming/Bettmann/CORBIS.

At a poetry slam, poets perform their own work and are judged by the audience — not only on what they say but also on how they say it. As a poet performs, the audience cheers, snaps fingers, stomps feet, and sometimes boos the poet off the stage. Judged on a scale from one to ten, the poet with the most points at the end of the night wins a cash prize. The roots of the poetry slam trace to Chicago in 1984, when construction worker and writer Marc Smith broke format at an "open mike" night by performing his poetry at an event traditionally slated for music. Shown here are a poster advertising an annual event hosted by Poetry Slam, Inc. (poetryslam.com) and an image from a poetry slam held in New York City.

CONSIDERATIONS FOR CRITICAL THINKING AND WRITING

1. What sorts of poetry events occur on your campus or in your community?

2. If possible, attend a slam and comment on the kinds of performances you see. Explain whether you think the performance and audience participation add to or detract from the experience of hearing spoken poetry.

NATIONAL POETRY SLAM

You talkin to me?

A poet vs. poet, in-your-face, smack-talkin' war of words.

MINNEAPOLIS AUGUST 13 - 1

Visit www.nps2002.com for event locations and time

Reprinted by permission of Eric Dunn (designer/copy-writer) and Mike Wigton (copywriter).

Poetry-portal.com

Poetry Portal (poetry-portal.com), offering access to databases of poems and a cornucopia of online resources about poetry, is an excellent site to begin an exploration of poetry on the Internet.

Reprinted by permission of poetry-portal.com and Colin John Holcombe.

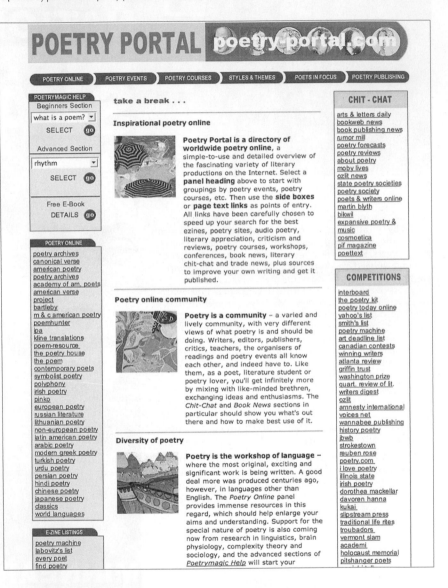

CONSIDERATIONS FOR CRITICAL THINKING AND WRITING

1. Log on to the home page of poetry-portal.com and explore some of the on-line sites listed there. Describe three sites that you found particularly interesting. Any surprises?

2. In what sense does the Poetry Portal demonstrate that poetry is, indeed, a "community"?

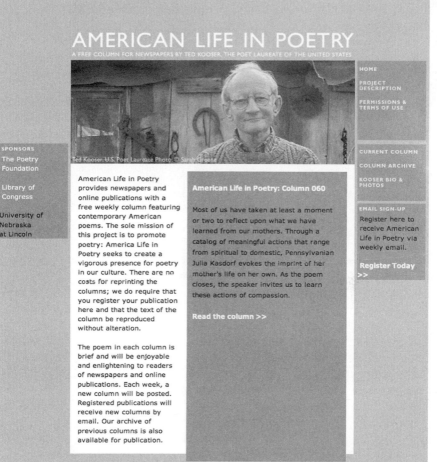

American Life in Poetry (americanlifeinpoetry.org) is a weekly newspaper column featuring a contemporary poem and brief introduction. Initiated by Ted Kooser, a poet laureate of the United States, and supported by the Poetry Foundation in partnership with the Library of Congress, this popular source is distributed free to newspapers and online publications. The site provides countless readers with a wide variety of high-quality, accessible poems. The reprint from the Detroit *Metro Times* (*next page*), featuring a poem by David Allan Evans, offers an engaging example of the weekly column.

DAVID ALLAN EVANS, *Neighbors*

April 6-12, 2005

metrotimes

detroit's weekly alternative   www.metrotimes.com • free

ART BAR

POETRY FOR THE PEOPLE: New Pulitzer-winner Ted Kooser, America's 13th poet laureate, gets us. He's no suit sitting in an office consulting ancient texts. For 35 years, he worked in the insurance business. "I wrote each morning ... and I often took my fresh drafts of poems and showed them to my secretary. ... If she didn't understand them, I went home and worked to make them more clear."

Kooser received funding as poet laureate and founded "American Life In Poetry," a free weekly newspaper column. *Metro Times* readers love to be talked to straight up, so we've signed up. Here's our and Kooser's premiere. If we don't have room in print, find it faithfully on our Web site. Kooser is excited *MT* signed on — "This is wonderful news! ... REALLY a start!"

Reprinted from Train Windows, *Ohio University Press, 1976, by permission of the author, whose most recent book is* The Bull Rider's Advice: New and Selected Poems. *This weekly column is supported by The Poetry Foundation, The Library of Congress, and the department of · English at the University of Nebraska, Lincoln.*

AMERICAN LIFE IN POETRY
by Ted Kooser,
U.S. poet laureate
We all know that the manner in which people behave toward one another can tell us a lot about their private lives. In this amusing poem by David Allan Evans, poet laureate of South Dakota, we learn something about a marriage by being shown a couple as they take on an ordinary household task.

Neighbors

They live alone
together,

she with her wide hind
and bird face,
he with his hung belly
and crewcut.

They never talk
but keep busy.

Today they are
washing windows
(each window together)
she on the inside,
he on the outside.
He squirts Windex
at her face,
she squirts Windex
at his face.

Now they are waving
to each other
with rags,

not smiling.

Courtesy of the Detroit *Metro Times*, the Poetry Foundation, and David Allan Evans.

CONSIDERATIONS FOR CRITICAL THINKING AND WRITING

1. Put together a cluster of images that reflect your encounters with poetry. Where do you find poetry? How is it used? What do these images suggest to you about the state of poetry in contemporary culture?

2. Surely not all manifestations of poetry in popular culture represent good poetry. Does bad poetry undercut good poetry? Does it cheapen its value? At this point in your study of poetry — the beginning — how do you define a good poem or a bad poem?

3. What is your favorite poem? Where did you first encounter it? Why is it important to you? Alternatively, if you can't come up with a favorite poem, why can't you?

The Elements
of Poetry

1

Reading Poetry

Ink runs from the corners of my mouth.
There is no happiness like mine.
I have been eating poetry
— MARK STRAND

© Lilo Raymond.

READING POETRY RESPONSIVELY

Perhaps the best way to begin reading poetry responsively is not to allow yourself to be intimidated by it. Come to it, initially at least, the way you might listen to a song on the radio. You probably listen to a song several times before you hear it all, before you have a sense of how it works, where it's going, and how it gets there. You don't worry about analyzing a song when you listen to it, even though after repeated experiences with it you know and anticipate a favorite part and know, on some level, why it works for you. Give yourself a chance to respond to poetry. The hardest work has already been done by the poet, so all you need to do at the start is listen for the pleasure produced by the poet's arrangement of words.

Try reading the following poem aloud. Read it aloud before you read it silently. You may stumble once or twice, but you'll make sense of it if you pay attention to its punctuation and don't stop at the end of every line where there is no punctuation. The title gives you an initial sense of what the poem is about.

Marge Piercy (b. 1936)

The Secretary Chant

1973

My hips are a desk.
From my ears hang
chains of paper clips.
Rubber bands form my hair.
My breasts are wells of mimeograph ink.   5
My feet bear casters.
Buzz. Click.
My head is a badly organized file.
My head is a switchboard
where crossed lines crackle.   10
Press my fingers
and in my eyes appear
credit and debit.
Zing. Tinkle.
My navel is a reject button.   15
From my mouth issue canceled reams.
Swollen, heavy, rectangular
I am about to be delivered
of a baby
Xerox machine.   20
File me under W
because I wonce
was
a woman.

What is your response to this secretary's chant? The point is simple
enough — she feels dehumanized by her office functions — but the pleasures are manifold. Piercy makes the speaker's voice sound mechanical by
using short bursts of sound and by having her make repetitive, flat, matter-
of-fact statements ("My breasts . . . My feet . . . My head . . . My navel").
"The Secretary Chant" makes a serious statement about how such women
are reduced to functionaries. The point is made, however, with humor, as
we are asked to visualize the misappropriation of the secretary's body — her
identity — as it is transformed into little more than a piece of office equipment, which seems to be breaking down in the final lines, when we learn
that she "wonce / was / a woman." Is there the slightest hint of something
subversive in this misspelling of "once"? Maybe so, but the humor is clear
enough, particularly if you try to make a drawing of what this dehumanized secretary has become.

The next poem creates a different kind of mood. Think about the title,
"Those Winter Sundays," before you begin reading the poem. What associations do you have with winter Sundays? What emotions does the phrase
evoke in you?

ROBERT HAYDEN (1913–1980)

Those Winter Sundays   *1962*

Sundays too my father got up early
and put his clothes on in the blueblack cold,
then with cracked hands that ached
from labor in the weekday weather made
banked fires blaze. No one ever thanked him.   5

I'd wake and hear the cold splintering, breaking.
When the rooms were warm, he'd call,
and slowly I would rise and dress,
fearing the chronic angers of that house,

Speaking indifferently to him,   10
who had driven out the cold
and polished my good shoes as well.
What did I know, what did I know
of love's austere and lonely offices?

Does the poem match the feelings you have about winter Sundays?
Either way, your response can be useful in reading the poem. For most of
us, Sundays are days at home; they might be cozy and pleasant experiences
or they might be dull and depressing. Whatever they are, Sundays are more
evocative than, say, Tuesdays. Hayden uses that response to call forth a
sense of missed opportunity in the poem. The person who reflects on those
winter Sundays didn't know until much later how much he had to thank
his father for "love's austere and lonely offices." This is a poem about a
cold past and a present reverence for his father—elements brought together by the phrase "Winter Sundays." *His* father? You may have noticed
that the poem doesn't use a masculine pronoun; hence the voice could be a
woman's. Does the gender of the voice make any difference to your reading? Would it make any difference about which details are included or
what language is used?

What is most important about your initial readings of a poem is that you
ask questions. If you read responsively, you'll find yourself asking all kinds of
questions about the words, descriptions, sounds, and structure of a poem.
The specifics of those questions will be generated by the particular poem. We
don't, for example, ask how humor is achieved in "Those Winter Sundays"
because there is none, but it is worth asking what kind of tone is established
by the description of "the chronic angers of that house." The remaining
chapters in this part of the book will help you to formulate and answer questions about a variety of specific elements in poetry, such as speaker, image,
metaphor, symbol, rhyme, and rhythm. For the moment, however, read the
following poem several times and note your response at different points in the
poem. Then write down a half-dozen or so questions about what produces

your response to the poem. To answer questions, it's best to know first what the questions are, and that's what the rest of this chapter is about.

JOHN UPDIKE (1932–2009)

Dog's Death   *1969*

She must have been kicked unseen or brushed by a car.
Too young to know much, she was beginning to learn
To use the newspapers spread on the kitchen floor
And to win, wetting there, the words, "Good dog! Good dog!"

We thought her shy malaise was a shot reaction.   5
The autopsy disclosed a rupture in her liver.
As we teased her with play, blood was filling her skin
And her heart was learning to lie down forever.

Monday morning, as the children were noisily fed
And sent to school, she crawled beneath the youngest's bed.   10
We found her twisted and limp but still alive.
In the car to the vet's, on my lap, she tried

To bite my hand and died. I stroked her warm fur
And my wife called in a voice imperious with tears.
Though surrounded by love that would have upheld her,   15
Nevertheless she sank and, stiffening, disappeared.

Back home, we found that in the night her frame,
Drawing near to dissolution, had endured the shame
Of diarrhoea and had dragged across the floor
To a newspaper carelessly left there. *Good dog.*   20

Here's a simple question to get started with your own questions: What would the poem's effect have been if Updike had titled it "Good Dog" instead of "Dog's Death"?

THE PLEASURE OF WORDS

The impulse to create and appreciate poetry is as basic to human experience as language itself. Although no one can point to the precise origins of poetry, it is one of the most ancient of the arts, because it has existed ever since human beings discovered pleasure in language. The tribal ceremonies of peoples without written languages suggest that the earliest primitive cultures incorporated rhythmic patterns of words into their rituals. These chants, very likely accompanied by the music of a simple beat and the dance of a measured step, expressed what people regarded as significant and memorable in their lives. They echoed the concerns of the chanters and the listeners by chronicling acts of bravery, fearsome foes, natural disasters, mysterious events, births, deaths, and whatever else brought people pain or pleasure, bewilderment or revelation. Later cultures, such as the ancient Greeks, made poetry an integral part of religion.

Thus, from its very beginnings, poetry has been associated with what has mattered most to people. These concerns — whether natural or supernatural — can, of course, be expressed without vivid images, rhythmic patterns, and pleasing sounds, but human beings have always sensed a magic in words that goes beyond rational, logical understanding. Poetry is not simply a method of communication; it is a unique experience in itself.

What is special about poetry? What makes it valuable? Why should we read it? How is reading it different from reading prose? To begin with, poetry pervades our world in a variety of forms, ranging from advertising jingles to song lyrics. These may seem to be a long way from the chants heard around a primitive campfire, but they serve some of the same purposes. Like poems printed in a magazine or book, primitive chants, catchy jingles, and popular songs attempt to stir the imagination through the carefully measured use of words.

Although reading poetry usually makes more demands than does the kind of reading we use to skim a magazine or newspaper, the appreciation of poetry comes naturally enough to anyone who enjoys playing with words. Play is an important element of poetry. Consider, for example, how the following words appeal to the children who gleefully chant them in playgrounds:

> I scream, you scream
> We all scream
> For ice cream.

These lines are an exuberant evocation of the joy of ice cream. Indeed, chanting the words turns out to be as pleasurable as eating ice cream. In poetry, the expression of the idea is as important as the idea expressed.

But is "I scream . . ." poetry? Some poets and literary critics would say that it certainly is one kind of poem because the children who chant it experience some of the pleasures of poetry in its measured beat and repeated sounds. However, other poets and critics would define poetry more narrowly and insist, for a variety of reasons, that this isn't true poetry but merely *doggerel,* a term used for lines whose subject matter is trite and whose rhythm and sounds are monotonously heavy-handed.

Although probably no one would argue that "I scream . . ." is a great poem, it does contain some poetic elements that appeal, at the very least, to children. Does that make it poetry? The answer depends on one's definition, but poetry has a way of breaking loose from definitions. Because there are nearly as many definitions of poetry as there are poets, Edwin Arlington Robinson's succinct observations are useful: "poetry has two outstanding characteristics. One is that it is undefinable. The other is that it is eventually unmistakable."

This comment places more emphasis on how a poem affects a reader than on how a poem is defined. By characterizing poetry as "undefinable," Robinson acknowledges that it can include many different purposes, subjects, emotions, styles, and forms. What effect does the following poem have on you?

WILLIAM HATHAWAY (B. 1944)

Oh, Oh   *1982*

© William Hathaway.

My girl and I amble a country lane,
moo cows chomping daisies, our own
sweet saliva green with grass stems.
"Look, look," she says at the crossing,
"the choo-choo's light is on." And sure
enough, right smack dab in the middle
of maple dappled summer sunlight
is the lit headlight — so funny.
An arm waves to us from the black window.
We wave gaily to the arm. "When I hear
trains at night I dream of being president,"
I say dreamily. "And me first lady," she
says loyally. So when the last boxcars,
named after wonderful, faraway places,
and the caboose chuckle by we look
eagerly to the road ahead. And there,
poised and growling, are fifty Hell's Angels.

15

A SAMPLE CLOSE READING

An Annotated Version of "Oh, Oh"

After you've read a poem two or three times, a deeper, closer reading — line by line, word by word, syllable by syllable — will help you discover even more about the poem. Ask yourself: What happens (or does not happen) in the poem? What are the poem's central ideas? How do the poem's words, images, and sounds, for example, contribute to its meaning? What is the poem's overall tone? How is the poem put together?

You can flesh out your close reading by writing your responses in the margins of the page. The following interpretive notes offer but one way to read Hathaway's poem.

WILLIAM HATHAWAY (B. 1944)
Oh, Oh   *1982*

The title offers an interjection expressing strong emotion and foreboding.

The informal language conjures up an idyllic picture of a walk in the country, where the sights, sounds, and tastes are full of pleasure.

My girl and I amble a country lane,
moo cows chomping daisies, our own
sweet saliva green with grass stems.
"Look, look," she says at the crossing,
"the choo-choo's light is on." And sure   5

The carefully orchestrated *d*s, *m*s, *p*s, and *s*s of lines 6–8 create sounds that are meant to be savored.

enough, right smack dab in the middle
of maple dappled summer sunlight
is the lit headlight — so funny.

Filled with confidence and hope, the couple imagines a successful future together in exotic locations. Even the train is happy for them as it "chuckle[s]" in approval of their dreams.

An arm waves to us from the black window.
We wave gaily to the arm. "When I hear   10
trains at night I dream of being president,"
I say dreamily. "And me first lady," she
says loyally. So when the last boxcars,
named after wonderful, faraway places,
and the caboose chuckle by we look   15
eagerly to the road ahead. And there,
poised and growling, are fifty Hell's Angels.

The visual effect of the many *o*s in lines 1–5 (and 15) suggests an innocent, wide-eyed openness to experience while the repetitive *oo* sounds echo a kind of reassuring, satisfied cooing.

"Right smack dab in the middle" of the poem, the "black window" hints that all is not well.

Not until the very last line does "the road ahead" yield a terrifying surprise. The strategically "poised" final line derails the leisurely movement of the couple and brings their happy story to a dead stop. The emotional reversal parked in the last few words awaits the reader as much as it does the couple. The sight and sound of the motorcycle gang signal that what seemed like heaven is, in reality, hell: Oh, oh.

MORE HELP WITH CLOSE READING

Close readings of Andrew Marvell's "To His Coy Mistress," Elizabeth Bishop's "The Fish," and Theodore Roethke's "My Papa's Waltz" are available on *LiterActive* and at bedfordstmartins.com/rewritinglit. As you explore each poem, highlighted sections are annotated with critical interpretations and explanations of literary elements at work.

Hathaway's poem serves as a convenient reminder that poetry can be full of surprises. Full of confidence, this couple, like the reader, is unprepared for the shock to come. When we see those "fifty Hell's Angels," we are confronted with something like a bucket of cold water in the face.

But even though our expectations are abruptly and powerfully reversed, we are finally invited to view the entire episode from a safe distance — the distance provided by the delightful humor in this poem. After all, how seriously can we take a poem that is titled "Oh, Oh"? The poet has his way with us, but we are brought in on the joke, too. The terror takes on comic proportions as the innocent couple is confronted by no fewer than *fifty* Hell's Angels. This is the kind of raucous overkill that informs a short animated film produced some years ago titled *Bambi Meets Godzilla*: you might not have seen it, but you know how it ends. The poem's good humor comes through when we realize how pathetically inadequate the response of "Oh, Oh" is to the circumstances.

As you can see, reading a description of what happens in a poem is not the same as experiencing a poem. The exuberance of "I scream . . ." and the surprise of Hathaway's "Oh, Oh" are in the hearing or reading rather than in the retelling. A *paraphrase* is a prose restatement of the central ideas of a poem in your own language. Consider the difference between the following poem and the paraphrase that follows it. What is missing from the paraphrase?

ROBERT FRANCIS (1901–1987)

Catch   1950

Two boys uncoached are tossing a poem together,
Overhand, underhand, backhand, sleight of hand, every hand,
Teasing with attitudes, latitudes, interludes, altitudes,
High, make him fly off the ground for it, low, make him stoop,
Make him scoop it up, make him as-almost-as-possible miss it,   5
Fast, let him sting from it, now, now fool him slowly,
Anything, everything tricky, risky, nonchalant,
Anything under the sun to outwit the prosy,
Over the tree and the long sweet cadence down,
Over his head, make him scramble to pick up the meaning,   10
And now, like a posy, a pretty one plump in his hands.

Paraphrase: A poet's relationship to a reader is similar to a game of catch. The poem, like a ball, should be pitched in a variety of ways to challenge and create interest. Boredom and predictability must be avoided if the game is to be engaging and satisfying.

. . .

A paraphrase can help us achieve a clearer understanding of a poem, but, unlike a poem, it misses all of the sport and fun. It is the poem that "outwit[s] the prosy" because the poem serves as an example of what it suggests poetry should be. Moreover, the two players—the poet and the reader—are "uncoached." They know how the game is played, but their expectations do not preclude spontaneity and creativity or their ability to surprise and be surprised. The solid pleasure of the workout—of reading poetry—is the satisfaction derived from exercising your imagination and intellect.

That pleasure is worth emphasizing. Poetry uses language to move and delight even when it includes a cast of fifty Hell's Angels. The pleasure is in having the poem work its spell on us. For that to happen, it is best to relax and enjoy poetry rather than worry about definitions of it. Pay attention to what the poet throws you. We read poems for emotional and intellectual discovery—to feel and to experience something about the world and ourselves. The ideas in poetry—what can be paraphrased in prose—are important, but the real value of a poem consists in the words that work their magic by allowing us to feel, see, and be more than we were before. Perhaps the best way to approach a poem is similar to what Francis's "Catch" implies: expect to be surprised, stay on your toes, and concentrate on the delivery.

A SAMPLE STUDENT ANALYSIS

Tossing Metaphors Together in "Catch"

The following sample paper on Robert Francis's "Catch" was written in response to an assignment that asked students to discuss the use of metaphor in the poem. Notice that Chris Leggett's paper is clearly focused and well organized. His discussion of the use of metaphor in the poem stays on track from beginning to end without any detours concerning unrelated topics (for a definition of **metaphor,** see p. 135). His title draws on the central metaphor of the poem, and he organizes the paper around four key words used in the poem: "attitudes, latitudes, interludes, altitudes." These constitute the heart of the paper's four substantive paragraphs, and they are effectively framed by introductory and concluding paragraphs. Moreover, the transitions between paragraphs clearly indicate that the author was not merely tossing a paper together.

Chris Leggett

Professor Lyles

English 203-1

November 9, 2009

Tossing Metaphors Together in "Catch"

Exploration of the meaning of the word catch.

The word "catch" is an attention getter. It usually means something is about to be hurled at someone and that he or she is expected to catch it. "Catch" can also signal a challenge to another player if the toss is purposefully difficult. Robert Francis, in his poem "Catch," uses the extended metaphor of

Thesis statement identifying purpose of poem's metaphors.

two boys playing catch to explore the considerations a poet makes when "tossing a poem together" (line 1). Line 3 of "Catch" enumerates these considerations metaphorically as "attitudes, latitudes, interludes, [and] altitudes."

Reference to specific language in poem, around which the paper is organized.

While regular prose is typically straightforward and easily understood, poetry usually takes great effort to understand and appreciate. To exemplify this, Francis presents the reader not with a normal game of catch with the ball flying back and forth in a repetitive and predictable fashion, but with a physically challenging game in which one must concentrate, scramble, and exert oneself

Introductory analysis of the poem's purpose.

to catch the ball, as one must stretch the intellect to truly grasp a poem.

Analysis of the meaning of attitude in the poem.

The first consideration mentioned by Francis is attitude. Attitude, when applied to the game of catch, indicates the ball's pitch in flight—upward, downward, or straight. It could also describe the players' attitudes toward each other or toward the game in general. Below this literal level lies *attitude's* meaning in relation to poetry. Attitude in this case represents a poem's tone. A poet may "teas[e] with attitude" (3) by experimenting with different tones to achieve the desired mood. The underlying tone of "Catch" is a playful one, set

Discussion of how the attitude metaphor contributes to poem's tone.

and reinforced by the use of a game. This playfulness is further reinforced by such words and phrases as "teasing" (3), "outwit" (8), and "fool him" (6).

Analysis of the meaning of latitude in the poem.

Considered also in the metaphorical game of catch is latitude, which, when applied to the game, suggests the range the object may be thrown— how high, how low, or how far. Poetic latitude, along similar lines, concerns a poem's breadth, or the scope of topic. Taken one level further, latitude suggests freedom from normal restraints or limitations, indicating the ability to

Leggett 2

go outside the norm to find originality of expression. The entire game of catch described in Francis's poem reaches outside the normal expectations of something being merely tossed back and forth in a predictable manner. The ball is thrown in almost every conceivable fashion, "overhand, underhand . . . every hand" (2). Other terms describing the throws—such as "tricky," "risky," "fast," "slowly," and "Anything under the sun"(6-8)—express endless latitude for avoiding predictability in Francis's game of catch and metaphorically in writing poetry.

Discussion of how the latitude metaphor contributes to the poem's scope and message.

During a game of catch the ball may be thrown at different intervals, establishing a steady rhythm or a broken, irregular one. Other intervening features, such as the field being played on or the weather, could also affect the game. These features of the game are alluded to in the poem by the use of the word "interludes." "Interlude" in the poetic sense represents the poem's form, which can similarly establish or diminish rhythm or enhance meaning.

Analysis of the meaning of interlude in the poem.

Lines 6 and 9, respectively, show a broken and a flowing rhythm. Line 6 begins rapidly as a hard toss that stings the catcher's hand is described. The rhythm of the line is immediately slowed, however, by the word "now" followed by a comma, followed by the rest of the line. In contrast, line 9 flows smoothly as the reader visualizes the ball flying over the tree and sailing downward. The words chosen for this line function perfectly. The phrase "the long sweet cadence down" establishes a sweet rhythm that reads smoothly and rolls off the tongue easily. The choice of diction not only affects the poem's rhythmic flow but also establishes through connotative language the various levels at which the poem can be understood, represented in "Catch" as altitude.

Discussion of how the interlude metaphor contributes to the poem's form and rhythm.

While "altitudes" when referring to the game of catch means how high an object is thrown, in poetry it could refer to the level of diction, lofty or down-to-earth, formal or informal. It suggests also the levels at which a poem can be comprehended, the literal as well as the interpretive. In Francis's game of catch, the ball is thrown high to make the player reach, low to "make him stoop" (4), or "over his head [to] make him scramble" (10), implying that the player should have to exert himself to catch it. So too, then, should the reader of poetry put great effort into understanding the full meaning of a poem. Francis exemplifies

Analysis of the meaning of altitudes in the poem.

this consideration in writing poetry by giving "Catch" not only an enjoyable literal meaning concerning the game of catch, but also a rich metaphorical meaning—reflecting the process of writing poetry. Francis uses several phrases and words with multiple meanings. The phrase "tossing a poem to-gether" (1) can be understood as tossing something back and forth or the process of constructing a poem. While "prosy" (8) suggests prose itself, it also means the mundane or the ordinary. In the poem's final line the word "posy" of course represents a flower, while it is also a variant of the word "poesy," meaning poetry, or the practice of composing poetry.

Francis effectively describes several considerations to be taken in writ-ing poetry in order to "outwit the prosy" (8). His use of the extended metaphor in "Catch" shows that a poem must be unique, able to be comprehended on multiple levels, and a challenge to the reader. The various rhythms in the lines of "Catch" exemplify the ideas they express. While achieving an enjoyable poem on the literal level, Francis has also achieved a rich metaphorical mean-ing. The poem offers a good workout both physically and intellectually.

Discussion of how the altitude metaphor contributes to the poem's literal and symbolic meanings, with refer-ences to specific language.

Conclusion summarizing ideas explored in paper.

Work Cited

Francis, Robert. "Catch." *Poetry: An Introduction*. Ed. Michael Meyer. 6th ed. Boston: Bedford/St. Martin's, 2010. 26. Print.

Before beginning your own writing assignment on poetry, you should re-view Chapter 2, "Writing about Poetry: From Inquiry to Final Paper," and Chapter 27, "Reading and the Writing Process," which provides a step-by-step overview of how to choose a topic, develop a thesis, and organize various types of writing assignments. If you are using outside sources in your paper, you should make sure that you are familiar with the conventional documen-tation procedures described in Chapter 28, "The Literary Research Paper."

Poets often remind us that beauty can be found in unexpected places. What is it that Elizabeth Bishop finds so beautiful about the "battered" fish she describes in the following poem?

Web Explore contexts for Elizabeth Bishop and approaches to this poem on *LiterActive* and at bedfordstmartins.com/ rewritinglit.

ELIZABETH BISHOP (1911–1979)
The Fish   *1946*

I caught a tremendous fish
and held him beside the boat
half out of water, with my hook
fast in a corner of his mouth.
He didn't fight.   5
He hadn't fought at all.
He hung a grunting weight,
battered and venerable
and homely. Here and there
his brown skin hung in strips   10
like ancient wall-paper,
and its pattern of darker brown
was like wall-paper:
shapes like full-blown roses
stained and lost through age.   15
He was speckled with barnacles,
fine rosettes of lime,
and infested
with tiny white sea-lice,
and underneath two or three   20
rags of green weed hung down.
While his gills were breathing in
the terrible oxygen
— the frightening gills,
fresh and crisp with blood,   25
that can cut so badly —
I thought of the coarse white flesh
packed in like feathers,
the big bones and the little bones,
the dramatic reds and blacks   30
of his shiny entrails,
and the pink swim-bladder
like a big peony.
I looked into his eyes
which were far larger than mine   35
but shallower, and yellowed,
the irises backed and packed
with tarnished tinfoil
seen through the lenses
of old scratched isinglass.   40
They shifted a little, but not
to return my stare.
— It was more like the tipping
of an object toward the light.
I admired his sullen face,   45
the mechanism of his jaw,
and then I saw

that from his lower lip
— if you could call it a lip —
grim, wet, and weapon-like,   50
hung five old pieces of fish-line,
or four and a wire leader
with the swivel still attached,
with all their five big hooks
grown firmly in his mouth.   55
A green line, frayed at the end
where he broke it, two heavier lines,
and a fine black thread
still crimped from the strain and snap
when it broke and he got away.   60
Like medals with their ribbons
frayed and wavering,
a five-haired beard of wisdom
trailing from his aching jaw.
I stared and stared   65
and victory filled up
the little rented boat,
from the pool of bilge
where oil had spread a rainbow
around the rusted engine   70
to the bailer rusted orange,
the sun-cracked thwarts,
the oarlocks on their strings,
the gunnels — until everything
was rainbow, rainbow, rainbow!   75
And I let the fish go.

Considerations for Critical Thinking and Writing

1. **FIRST RESPONSE.** Which lines in this poem provide especially vivid details of
    the fish? What makes these descriptions effective?

2. How is the fish characterized? Is it simply a weak victim because it "didn't
    fight" (line 5)?

3. Comment on lines 65–76. In what sense has "victory filled up" the boat
    (66), given that the speaker finally lets the fish go?

The speaker in Bishop's "The Fish" ends on a triumphantly joyful
note. The ***speaker*** is the voice used by the author in the poem; like the narrator in a work of fiction, the speaker is often a created identity rather than
the author's actual self. The two should not automatically be equated.
Contrast the attitude toward life of the speaker in "The Fish" with that of
the speaker in the following poem.

PHILIP LARKIN (1922–1985)

A Study of Reading Habits   1964

When getting my nose in a book
Cured most things short of school,
It was worth ruining my eyes
To know I could still keep cool,
And deal out the old right hook   5
To dirty dogs twice my size.

Later, with inch-thick specs,
Evil was just my lark:
Me and my cloak and fangs
Had ripping times in the dark.   10
The women I clubbed with sex!
I broke them up like meringues.

Don't read much now: the dude
Who lets the girl down before
The hero arrives, the chap   15
Who's yellow and keeps the store,
Seem far too familiar. Get stewed:
Books are a load of crap.

What the speaker sees and describes in "The Fish" is close if not identical to Bishop's own vision and voice. The joyful response to the fish is clearly shared by the speaker and the poet, between whom there is little or no distance. In "A Study of Reading Habits," however, Larkin distances himself from a speaker whose sensibilities he does not wholly share. The poet—and many readers—might identify with the reading habits described by the speaker in the first twelve lines, but Larkin uses the last six lines to criticize the speaker's attitude toward life as well as reading. The speaker recalls in lines 1–6 how as a schoolboy he identified with the hero, whose virtuous strength always triumphed over "dirty dogs," and in lines 7–12 he recounts how his schoolboy fantasies were transformed by adolescence into a fascination with violence and sex. This description of early reading habits is pleasantly amusing, because many readers of popular fiction will probably recall having moved through similar stages, but at the end of the poem the speaker provides more information about himself than he intends to.

As an adult the speaker has lost interest in reading because it is no longer an escape from his own disappointed life. Instead of identifying with heroes or villains, he finds himself identifying with minor characters who are irresponsible and cowardly. Reading is now a reminder of his failures, so he turns to alcohol. His solution, to "Get stewed" because "Books are a load of crap," is obviously self-destructive. The speaker is ultimately exposed by Larkin as someone who never grew beyond fantasies. Getting drunk is consistent with the speaker's immature reading habits. Unlike the speaker, the poet understands that life is often distorted by escapist fantasies, whether through a steady diet of popular fiction or through alcohol. The speaker in this poem, then, is not Larkin but a created identity whose voice is filled with disillusionment and delusion.

The problem with Larkin's speaker is that he misreads books as well as his own life. Reading means nothing to him unless it serves as an escape from himself. It is not surprising that Larkin has him read fiction rather than poetry because poetry places an especially heavy emphasis on language. Fiction, indeed any kind of writing, including essays and drama, relies on carefully chosen and arranged words, but poetry does so to an even greater extent. Notice, for example, how Larkin's deft use of trite expressions and slang characterizes the speaker so that his language reveals nearly as much about his dreary life as what he says. Larkin's speaker would have no use for poetry.

What is "unmistakable" in poetry (to use Robinson's term again) is its intense, concentrated use of language — its emphasis on individual words to convey meanings, experiences, emotions, and effects. Poets never simply process words; they savor them. Words in poems frequently create their own tastes, textures, scents, sounds, and shapes. They often seem more sensuous than ordinary language, and readers usually sense that a word has been hefted before making its way into a poem. Although poems are crafted differently from the ways a painting, sculpture, or musical composition is created, in each form of art the creator delights in the medium. Poetry is carefully orchestrated so that the words work together as elements in a structure to sustain close, repeated readings. The words are chosen to interact with one another to create the maximum desired effect, whether the purpose is to capture a mood or feeling, create a vivid experience, express a point of view, narrate a story, or portray a character.

Here is a poem that looks quite different from most *verse*, a term used for lines composed in a measured rhythmical pattern, which are often, but not necessarily, rhymed.

ROBERT MORGAN (B. 1944)

Mountain Graveyard   1979

for the author of "Slow Owls"

Spore Prose

stone	notes
slate	tales
sacred	cedars
heart	earth
asleep	please
hated	death

Though unconventional in its appearance, this is unmistakably poetry because of its concentrated use of language. The poem demonstrates how serious play with words can lead to some remarkable discoveries. At first glance "Mountain Graveyard" may seem intimidating. What, after all, does this list of words add up to? How is it in any sense a poetic use of language? But if the words are examined closely, it is not difficult to see how they work. The wordplay here is literally in the form of a game. Morgan uses a series of **anagrams** (words made from the letters of other words, such as *read* and *dare*) to evoke feelings about death. "Mountain Graveyard" is one of several poems that Morgan has called "Spore Prose" (another anagram) because he finds in individual words the seeds of poetry. He wrote the poem in honor of the fiftieth birthday of another poet, Jonathan Williams, the author of "Slow Owls," whose title is also an anagram.

The title, "Mountain Graveyard," indicates the poem's setting, which is also the context in which the individual words in the poem interact to provide a larger meaning. Morgan's discovery of the words on the stones of a graveyard is more than just clever. The observations he makes among the silent graves go beyond the curious pleasure a reader experiences in finding that the words *sacred cedars*, referring to evergreens common in cemeteries, consist of the same letters. The surprise and delight of realizing the connection between *heart* and *earth* are tempered by the more sober recognition that everyone's story ultimately ends in the ground. The hope that the dead are merely asleep is expressed with a plea that is answered grimly by a hatred of death's finality.

Little is told in this poem. There is no way of knowing who is buried or who is looking at the graves, but the emotions of sadness, hope, and pain are unmistakable — and are conveyed in fewer than half the words of this sentence. Morgan takes words that initially appear to be a dead, prosaic list and energizes their meanings through imaginative juxtapositions.

Explore contexts for E. E. Cummings on *LiterActive*.

The following poem also involves a startling discovery about words. With the peculiar title "l(a," the poem cannot be read aloud, so there is no sound, but is there sense, a **theme** — a central idea or meaning — in the poem?

E. E. CUMMINGS (1894–1962)

l(a   *1958*

l(a

le
af
fa

ll

© Bettmann/CORBIS.

s)
one
l

iness

CONSIDERATIONS FOR CRITICAL THINKING AND WRITING

1. **FIRST RESPONSE.** Discuss the connection between what appears inside and outside the parentheses in this poem.

2. What does Cummings draw attention to by breaking up the words? How do this strategy and the poem's overall shape contribute to its theme?

3. Which seems more important in this poem — what is expressed or the way it is expressed?

Although "Mountain Graveyard" and "l(a" do not resemble the kind of verse that readers might recognize immediately as poetry on a page, both are actually a very common type of poem, called the *lyric,* usually a brief poem that expresses the personal emotions and thoughts of a single speaker. Lyrics are often written in the first person, but sometimes — as in "Mountain Graveyard" and "l(a" — no speaker is specified. Lyrics present a subjective mood, emotion, or idea. Very often they are about love or death, but almost any subject or experience that evokes some intense emotional response can be found in lyrics. In addition to brevity and emotional intensity, lyrics are also frequently characterized by their musical qualities. The word *lyric* derives from the Greek word *lyre,* meaning a musical instrument that originally accompanied the singing of a lyric. Lyric poems can be organized in a variety of ways, such as the sonnet, elegy, and ode (see Chapter 9), but it is enough to point out here that lyrics are an extremely popular kind of poetry with writers and readers.

The following anonymous lyric was found in a sixteenth-century manuscript.

ANONYMOUS

Western Wind

c. 1500

Western wind, when wilt thou blow,
The small rain down can rain?
Christ, if my love were in my arms,
And I in my bed again!

This speaker's intense longing for his lover is characteristic of lyric poetry. He impatiently addresses the western wind that brings spring to England and could make it possible for him to be reunited with the woman he loves. We do not know the details of these lovers' lives because this poem focuses on the speaker's emotion. We do not learn why the lovers are apart or if they will be together again. We don't even know if the speaker is a man. But those issues are not really important. The poem gives us a feeling rather than a story.

A poem that tells a story is called a **narrative poem.** Narrative poetry may be short or very long. An **epic,** for example, is a long narrative poem on a serious subject chronicling heroic deeds and important events. Among the most famous epics are Homer's *Iliad* and *Odyssey,* the Old English *Beowulf,* Dante's *Divine Comedy,* and John Milton's *Paradise Lost.* More typically, however, narrative poems are considerably shorter, as is the case with the following poem, which tells the story of a child's memory of her father.

REGINA BARRECA (B. 1957)

Nighttime Fires   1986

Courtesy of Robert Benson, © 2004.

When I was five in Louisville
we drove to see nighttime fires. Piled seven of us,
all pajamas and running noses, into the Olds,
drove fast toward smoke. It was after my father
lost his job, so not getting up in the morning
gave him time: awake past midnight, he
          read old newspapers
with no news, tried crosswords until he split
          the pencil
between his teeth, mad. When he heard
the wolf whine of the siren, he woke my mother,
and she pushed and shoved   10
us all into waking. Once roused we longed for burnt wood
and a smell of flames high into the pines. My old man liked
driving to rich neighborhoods best, swearing in a good mood
as he followed fire engines that snaked like dragons
and split the silent streets. It was festival, carnival.   15

If there were a Cadillac or any car
in a curved driveway, my father smiled a smile
from a secret, brittle heart.
His face lit up in the heat given off by destruction
like something was being made, or was being set right.   20
I bent my head back to see where sparks
ate up the sky. My father who never held us
would take my hand and point to falling cinders that
covered the ground like snow, or, excited, show us
the swollen collapse of a staircase. My mother   25
watched my father, not the house. She was happy
only when we were ready to go, when it was finally over
and nothing else could burn.
Driving home, she would sleep in the front seat
as we huddled behind. I could see his quiet face in the   30
rearview mirror, eyes like hallways filled with smoke.

This narrative poem could have been a short story if the poet had wanted to say more about the "brittle heart" of this unemployed man whose daughter so vividly remembers the desperate pleasure he took in watching fire consume other people's property. Indeed, a reading of William Faulkner's famous short story "Barn Burning" suggests how such a character can be further developed and how his child responds to him. The similarities between Faulkner's angry character and the poem's father, whose "eyes [are] like hallways filled with smoke," are coincidental, but the characters' sense of "something . . . being set right" by flames is worth comparing. Although we do not know everything about this man and his family, we have a much firmer sense of their story than we do of the story of the couple in "Western Wind."

Although narrative poetry is still written, short stories and novels have largely replaced the long narrative poem. Lyric poems tend to be the predominant type of poetry today. Regardless of whether a poem is a narrative or a lyric, however, the strategies for reading it are somewhat different from those for reading prose. Try these suggestions for approaching poetry.

Suggestions for Approaching Poetry

1. Assume that it will be necessary to read a poem more than once. Give yourself a chance to become familiar with what the poem has to offer. Like a piece of music, a poem becomes more pleasurable with each encounter.

2. Pay attention to the title; it will often provide a helpful context for the poem and serve as an introduction to it. Larkin's "A Study of Reading Habits" is precisely what its title describes.

3. As you read the poem for the first time, avoid becoming entangled in words or lines that you don't understand. Instead, give yourself a chance to take in the entire poem before attempting to resolve problems encountered along the way.

4. On a second reading, identify any words or passages that you don't understand. Look up words you don't know; these might include names, places, historical and mythical references, or anything else that is unfamiliar to you.

5. Read the poem aloud (or perhaps have a friend read it to you). You'll probably discover that some puzzling passages suddenly fall into place when you hear them. You'll find that nothing helps, though, if the poem is read in an artificial, exaggerated manner. Read in as natural a voice as possible, with slight pauses at line breaks. Silent reading is preferable to imposing a te-tumpty-te-tum reading on a good poem.

6. Read the punctuation. Poems use punctuation marks — in addition to the space on the page — as signals for readers. Be especially careful not to assume that the end of a line marks the end of a sentence, unless it is concluded by punctuation. Consider, for example, the opening lines of Hathaway's "Oh, Oh":

> My girl and I amble a country lane,
> moo cows chomping daisies, our own
> sweet saliva green with grass stems.

Line 2 makes little or no sense if a reader stops after "own." Keeping track of the subjects and verbs will help you find your way among the sentences.

7. Paraphrase the poem to determine whether you understand what happens in it. As you work through each line of the poem, a paraphrase will help you to see which words or passages need further attention.

8. Try to get a sense of who is speaking and what the setting or situation is. Don't assume that the speaker is the author; often it is a created character.

9. Assume that each element in the poem has a purpose. Try to explain how the elements of the poem work together.

10. Be generous. Be willing to entertain perspectives, values, experiences, and subjects that you might not agree with or approve of. Even if baseball bores you, you should be able to comprehend its imaginative use in Francis's "Catch."

11. Try developing a coherent approach to the poem that helps you to shape a discussion of the text. See Chapter 26, "Critical Strategies for Reading," to review formalist, biographical, historical, psychological, feminist, and other possible critical approaches.

12. Don't expect to produce a definitive reading. Many poems do not resolve all of the ideas, issues, or tensions in them, and so it is not always possible to drive their meaning into an absolute corner. Your reading will explore rather than define the poem. Poems are not trophies to be stuffed and mounted. They're usually more elusive. And don't be afraid that a close reading will damage the poem. Poems aren't hurt when we analyze them; instead, they come alive as we experience them and put into words what we discover through them.

A list of more specific questions using the literary terms and concepts discussed in the following chapters begins on page 59. That list, like the suggestions just made, raises issues and questions that can help you to read just about any poem closely. These strategies should be a useful means for getting inside poems to understand how they work. Furthermore, because reading poetry inevitably increases sensitivity to language, you're likely to find yourself a better reader of words in any form—whether in a novel, a newspaper editorial, an advertisement, a political speech, or a conversation—after having studied poetry. In short, many of the reading skills that make poetry accessible also open up the world you inhabit.

You'll probably find some poems amusing or sad, some fierce or tender, and some fascinating or dull. You may find, too, some poems that will get inside you. Their kinds of insights—the poet's and yours—are what Emily Dickinson had in mind when she defined poetry this way: "If I read a book and it makes my whole body so cold no fire can ever warm me, I know that it is poetry. If I feel physically as if the top of my head were taken off, I know that it is poetry." Dickinson's response may be more intense than most—poetry was, after all, at the center of her life—but you, too, might find yourself moved by poems in unexpected ways. In any case, as Edwin Arlington Robinson knew, poetry is, to an alert and sensitive reader, "eventually unmistakable."

BILLY COLLINS (B. 1941)

Introduction to Poetry   1988

I ask them to take a poem
and hold it up to the light
like a color slide

or press an ear against its hive.

I say drop a mouse into a poem   5
and watch him probe his way out,

or walk inside the poem's room
and feel the walls for a light switch.

I want them to water-ski
across the surface of a poem   10
waving at the author's name on the shore.

But all they want to do
is tie the poem to a chair with rope
and torture a confession out of it.

They begin beating it with a hose   15
to find out what it really means.

CONSIDERATIONS FOR CRITICAL THINKING AND WRITING

1. **FIRST RESPONSE.** In what sense does this poem offer suggestions for approaching poetry? What kinds of advice does the speaker provide in lines 1–11?
2. How does the mood of the poem change beginning in line 12? What do you make of the shift from "them" to "they"?
3. Paraphrase the poem. How is your paraphrase different from what is included in the poem?

POETRY IN POPULAR FORMS

Before you try out these strategies for reading on a few more poems, it is worth acknowledging that the verse that enjoys the widest readership appears not in collections, magazines, or even anthologies for students, but in greeting cards. A significant amount of the personal daily mail delivered in the United States consists of greeting cards. That represents millions of lines of verse going by us on the street and in planes over our heads. These verses share some similarities with the poetry included in this anthology, but there are also important differences that indicate the need for reading serious poetry closely rather than casually.

The popularity of greeting cards is easy to explain: just as many of us have neither the time nor the talent to make gifts for birthdays, weddings, anniversaries, graduations, Valentine's Day, Mother's Day, and other holidays, we are unlikely to write personal messages when cards conveniently say them for us. Although impersonal, cards are efficient and convey an important message no matter what the occasion for them: I care. These greetings are rarely serious poetry; they are not written to be. Nevertheless, they demonstrate the impulse in our culture to generate and receive poetry.

In a handbook for greeting-card freelancers, a writer and past editor of such verse began with this advice:

> Once you determine what you want to say—and in this regard it is best to stick to one basic idea—you must choose your words to do several things at the same time:
>
> 1. Your idea must be expressed as a complete idea; it must have a beginning, a middle, and an end.
> 2. There must be coherence in your verse. Every line must be linked logically and smoothly with its neighbors.
> 3. Your expressions . . . must be conversational. High-flown language rarely comes off successfully in greeting-card writing.
> 4. You must write with emphasis—and something else: enthusiasm. It's necessary to create interest in that all-important first line. From that point on, writing your verse is a matter of developing your idea and bringing it to a peak of emphasis in the last line. Occasionally you will find that you have shot your wad too early in the verse, and whatever you say after that point sounds like an afterthought.
> 5. You must do all of the above and at the same time make everything come out right in the meter-and-rhyme department.[1]

This advice is followed by a list of approximately fifty of the most frequently used rhyme sounds accompanied by rhyming words, such as *love, of, above* for the sound *uv*. The point of these prescriptions is that the verse must be written so that it is immediately accessible—consumable—by both the buyer and the recipient. Writers of these cards are expected to avoid any complexity.

Compare the following greeting-card verse with the poem that comes after it. "Magic of Love," by Helen Farries, has been a longtime favorite in a major greeting-card company's "wedding line"; with different endings it has been used also in valentines and friendship cards.

---

[1] Chris Fitzgerald, "Conventional Verse: The Sentimental Favorite," *The Greeting Card Writer's Handbook,* ed. H. Joseph Chadwick (Cincinnati: Writer's Digest, 1975), 13, 17.

HELEN FARRIES

Magic of Love

date unknown

There's a wonderful gift that can give you a lift,
It's a blessing from heaven above!
It can comfort and bless, it can bring happiness —
It's the wonderful MAGIC OF LOVE!

Like a star in the night, it can keep your faith bright,   5
Like the sun, it can warm your hearts, too —
It's a gift you can give every day that you live,
And when given, it comes back to you!

When love lights the way, there is joy in the day
And all troubles are lighter to bear,   10
Love is gentle and kind, and through love you will find
There's an answer to your every prayer!

May it never depart from your two loving hearts,
May you treasure this gift from above —
You will find if you do, all your dreams will come true,   15
In the wonderful MAGIC OF LOVE!

JOHN FREDERICK NIMS (1913–1999)

Love Poem

1947

My clumsiest dear, whose hands shipwreck vases,
At whose quick touch all glasses chip and ring,
Whose palms are bulls in china, burs in linen,
And have no cunning with any soft thing

Except all ill-at-ease fidgeting people: 5
The refugee uncertain at the door
You make at home; deftly you steady
The drunk clambering on his undulant floor.

Unpredictable dear, the taxi drivers' terror,
Shrinking from far headlights pale as a dime   10
Yet leaping before red apoplectic streetcars —
Misfit in any space. And never on time.

A wrench in clocks and the solar system. Only
With words and people and love you move at ease.
In traffic of wit expertly maneuver   15
And keep us, all devotion, at your knees.

Forgetting your coffee spreading on our flannel,
Your lipstick grinning on our coat,
So gaily in love's unbreakable heaven
Our souls on glory of spilt bourbon float.   20

Be with me, darling, early and late. Smash glasses —
I will study wry music for your sake.
For should your hands drop white and empty
All the toys of the world would break.

Considerations for Critical Thinking and Writing

1. **FIRST RESPONSE.** Read these two works aloud. How are they different? How the same?

2. To what extent does the advice to would-be greeting-card writers apply to each work?

3. Compare the two speakers. Which do you find more appealing? Why?

4. How does Nims's description of love differ from Farries's?

In contrast to poetry, which transfigures and expresses an emotion or experience through an original use of language, the verse in "Magic of Love" relies on *clichés* — ideas or expressions that have become tired and trite from overuse, such as describing love as "a blessing from heaven above." Clichés anesthetize readers instead of alerting them to the possibility of fresh perceptions. They are used to draw out *stock responses* — predictable, conventional reactions to language, characters, symbols, or situations; God, heaven, the flag, motherhood, hearts, puppies, and peace are some often-used objects of stock responses. Advertisers manufacture careers from this sort of business.

Clichés and stock responses are two of the major ingredients of sentimentality in literature. **Sentimentality** exploits the reader by inducing responses that exceed what the situation warrants. This pejorative term should not be confused with *sentiment,* which is synonymous with *emotion* or *feeling.* Sentimentality cons readers into falling for the mass murderer who is devoted to stray cats, and it requires that we not think twice about what we're feeling because those tears shed for the little old lady, the rage aimed at the vicious enemy soldier, and the longing for the simple virtues of poverty might disappear under the slightest scrutiny. The experience of sentimentality is not unlike biting into a swirl of cotton candy; it's momentarily sweet but wholly insubstantial.

Clichés, stock responses, and sentimentality are generally the hallmarks of weak writing. Poetry — the kind that is unmistakable — achieves freshness, vitality, and genuine emotion that sharpen our perceptions of life.

Although the most widely read verse is found in greeting cards, the most widely *heard* poetry appears in song lyrics. Not all songs are poetic, but a good many share the same effects and qualities as poems. Consider these lyrics by Bruce Springsteen.

Bruce Springsteen (B. 1949)

Devils & Dust   *2005*

I got my finger on the trigger
But I don't know who to trust
When I look into your eyes
There's just devils and dust
We're a long, long way from home, Bobbie   5
Home's a long, long way from us
I feel a dirty wind blowing
Devils and dust

I got God on my side
I'm just trying to survive   10
What if what you do to survive
Kills the things you love
Fear's a powerful thing
It can turn your heart black you can trust
It'll take your God filled soul   15
And fill it with devils and dust

Well I dreamed of you last night
In a field of blood and stone
The blood began to dry
The smell began to rise   20
Well I dreamed of you last night, Bobbie
In a field of mud and bone
Your blood began to dry
The smell began to rise

We've got God on our side   25
We're just trying to survive
What if what you do to survive
Kills the things you love
Fear's a powerful thing, baby
It'll turn your heart black you can trust   30
It'll take your God filled soul
Fill it with devils and dust

Now every woman and every man
They want to take a righteous stand
Find the love that God wills   35
And the faith that He commands
I've got my finger on the trigger
And tonight faith just ain't enough
When I look inside my heart
There's just devils and dust   40

Well I've got God on my side
And I'm just trying to survive
What if what you do to survive
Kills the things you love

Fear's a dangerous thing   45
It can turn your heart black you can trust
It'll take your God filled soul
Fill it with devils and dust

Yeah, it'll take your God filled soul

Fill it with devils and dust   50

CONSIDERATIONS FOR CRITICAL THINKING AND WRITING

1. **FIRST RESPONSE.** How do images of war and the phrases that are repeated evoke a particular mood in this song?

2. Do you think this song can accurately be called a narrative poem? Why or why not? How would you describe its theme?

3. How does your experience of reading "Devils & Dust" compare with listening to Springsteen singing the song (available on *Devils & Dust*)?

S. PEARL SHARP (B. 1942)

It's the Law: A Rap Poem   *1991*

You can learn about the state of the U.S.A.
By the laws we have on the books today.
The rules we break are the laws we make
The things that we fear, we legislate.

We got laws designed to keep folks in line   5
Laws for what happens when you lose your mind
Laws against stealing, laws against feeling,
The laws we have are a definite sign
That our vision of love is going blind.
(They probably got a law against this rhyme.)   10
Unh-hunh . . . . .

We got laws for cool cats & laws for dirty dogs
Laws about where you can park your hog
Laws against your mama and your papa, too
Even got a law to make the laws come true.   15
It's against the law to hurt an ol' lady,
It's against the law to steal a little baby,
The laws we make are what we do to each other
There is no law to make brother love brother
Hmmm   20

Now this respect thang is hard for some folks to do
They don't respect themselves so they can't respect you
This is the word we should get around —
These are the rules: we gonna run 'em on down.
Listen up!:   25

It ain't enough to be cute,
It ain't enough to be tough
You gotta walk tall
You gotta strut your stuff

You gotta learn to read, you gotta learn to write.   30
Get the tools you need to win this fight
Get your common sense down off the shelf
Start in the mirror . . . . Respect your Self!

When you respect yourself you keep your body clean
You walk tall, walk gentle, don't have to be mean   35
You keep your mind well fed, you keep a clear head
And you think 'bout who you let in your bed —
Unh-hunh . . . . . .

When you respect yourself you come to understand
That your body is a temple for a natural plan,   40
It's against that plan to use drugs or dope —
Use your heart and your mind when you need to cope . . .
It's the law!

We got laws that got started in '86
And laws made back when the Indians got kicked   45
If we want these laws to go out of favor
Then we've got to change our behavior

Change what!? you say, well let's take a look
How did the laws get on the books? Yeah.
I said it up front but let's get tougher   50
The laws we make are what we do to each other

If you never shoot at me then I don't need
A law to keep you from shooting at me, do you see?
There's a universal law that's tried and true
Says Don't do to me —   55
What you don't want done to you
Unh-hunh!
Don't do to me —
What you don't want done to you
It's the law!   60

CONSIDERATIONS FOR CRITICAL THINKING AND WRITING

1. **FIRST RESPONSE.** According to this rap poem, what do laws reveal "about
   the state of the U.S.A." (line 1)?

2. How are the "laws" different from the "rules" prescribed in the middle
   stanzas of the poem?

3. What is the theme of this rap poem?

Perspective

ROBERT FRANCIS (1901–1987)

On "Hard" Poetry   *1965*

When Robert Frost said he liked poems hard he could scarcely have meant he liked them difficult. If he had meant difficult he would have said he didn't like them easy. What he said was that he didn't like them soft.

Poems can be soft in several ways. They can be soft in form (invertebrate). They can be soft in thought and feeling (sentimental). They can be soft with excess verbiage. Frost used to advise [writers] to squeeze the water out of a poem. He liked poems dry. What is dry tends to be hard, and what is hard is always dry, except perhaps on the outside.

Yet though hardness here does not mean difficulty, some difficulty naturally goes with hardness. A hard poem may not be hard to read but is hard to write. Not too hard, preferably. Not so hard to write that there is no flow in the writer. But hard enough for the growing poem to meet with some healthy resistance. Frost often found this healthy resistance in a tight rhyme scheme and strict meter. There are other ways of getting good resistance, of course.

And in the reader too, a hard poem will bring some difficulty. Preferably not too much. Not enough difficulty to completely baffle him. Ideally a hard poem should not be too hard to make sense of, but hard to exhaust its meaning and its beauty.

"What I care about is the hardness of the poems. I don't like them soft, I want them to be little pebbles, but placed where they won't dislodge easily. And I'd like them to be little pebbles of precious stone — precious, or semiprecious" ([Robert Frost] interview with John Ciardi, *Saturday Review,* March 21, 1959).

Here is hard prose talking about hard poetry. Frost was never shrewder or more illuminating. Here, as well as in anything else he ever said, is his flavor.

What contemporary of his can you imagine saying this or anything like it?

In 1843 Emerson jotted in his journal: "Hard clouds and hard expressions, and hard manners, I love."

From *The Satirical Rogue on Poetry*

CONSIDERATIONS FOR CRITICAL THINKING AND WRITING

1. What is the distinction between "hard" and "soft" poetry?

2. Explain whether you would characterize Bruce Springsteen's "Devils & Dust" (p. 44) as hard or soft.

3. **CREATIVE RESPONSE.** Given Francis's brief essay and his poem "Catch" (p. 26), write a review of Helen Farries's "Magic of Love" (p. 42) as you think Francis would.

POEMS FOR FURTHER STUDY

PETER PEREIRA (B. 1959)

Anagrammer 2003

If you believe in the magic of language,
then *Elvis* really *Lives*
and *Princess Diana* foretold *I end as car spin.*

If you believe the letters themselves
contain a power within them, 5
then you understand
what makes *outside tedious,*
how *desperation* becomes *a rope ends it.*

The circular logic that allows *senator* to become *treason,*
and *treason* to become *atoners.* 10

That *eleven plus two* is *twelve plus one,*
and an *admirer* is also *married.*

That if you could just re-arrange things the right way
you'd find your true life,
the right path, the answer to your questions: 15
you'd understand how *the Titanic*
turns into *that ice tin,*
and *debit card* becomes *bad credit.*

How *listen* is the same as *silent,*
and not one letter separates *stained* from *sainted.* 20

CONSIDERATIONS FOR CRITICAL THINKING AND WRITING

1. **FIRST RESPONSE.** How is "the magic of language" (line 1) created in the poem?
2. Explain what you think is the poem's theme.
3. **CREATIVE RESPONSE.** Try savoring the letters in your own first and/or last name by writing some anagrams for them.

CONNECTION TO ANOTHER SELECTION

1. Compare Pereira's use of anagrams in this poem with Robert Morgan's in "Mountain Graveyard" (p. 34). How does each poem employ anagrams to achieve its effects?

MARY OLIVER (B. 1935)

The Poet with His Face in His Hands 2005

You want to cry aloud for your
mistakes. But to tell the truth the world
doesn't need any more of that sound.

So if you're going to do it and can't
stop yourself, if your pretty mouth can't   5
hold it in, at least go by yourself across

the forty fields and the forty dark inclines
of rocks and water to the place where
the falls are flinging out their white sheets

like crazy, and there is a cave behind all that   10
jubilation and water fun and you can
stand there, under it, and roar all you

want and nothing will be disturbed; you can
drip with despair all afternoon and still,
on a green branch, its wings just lightly touched   15

by the passing foil of the water, the thrush,
puffing out its spotted breast, will sing
of the perfect, stone-hard beauty of everything.

CONSIDERATIONS FOR CRITICAL THINKING AND WRITING

1. **FIRST RESPONSE.** Describe the kind of poet the speaker characterizes. What is the speaker's attitude toward that sort of poet?

2. Explain which single phrase used by the speaker to describe the poet most reveals for you the speaker's attitude toward the poet.

3. How is nature contrasted with the poet?

CONNECTION TO ANOTHER SELECTION

1. Compare the thematic use of nature in Oliver's poem and in Elizabeth Bishop's "The Fish" (p. 31).

LISA PARKER (B. 1972)

Snapping Beans   *1998*

For Fay Whitt

I snapped beans into the silver bowl
that sat on the splintering slats
of the porchswing between my grandma and me.
I was home for the weekend,
from school, from the North,   5
Grandma hummed "What A Friend We Have In Jesus"
as the sun rose, pushing its pink spikes
through the slant of cornstalks,
through the fly-eyed mesh of the screen.
We didn't speak until the sun overcame   10
the feathered tips of the cornfield
and Grandma stopped humming. I could feel

the soft gray of her stare
against the side of my face
when she asked, *How's school a-goin'?*   15
I wanted to tell her about my classes,
the revelations by book and lecture,
as real as any shout of faith
and potent as a swig of strychnine.
She reached the leather of her hand   20
over the bowl and cupped
my quivering chin; the slick smooth of her palm
held my face the way she held tomatoes
under the spigot, careful not to drop them,
and I wanted to tell her   25
about the nights I cried into the familiar
heartsick panels of the quilt she made me,
wishing myself home on the evening star.
I wanted to tell her
the evening star was a planet,   30
that my friends wore noserings and wrote poetry
about sex, about alcoholism, about Buddha.
I wanted to tell her how my stomach burned
acidic holes at the thought of speaking in class,
speaking in an accent, speaking out of turn,   35
how I was tearing, splitting myself apart
with the slow-simmering guilt of being happy
despite it all.
I said, *School's fine.*
We snapped beans into the silver bowl between us   40
and when a hickory leaf, still summer green,
skidded onto the porchfront,
Grandma said,
It's funny how things blow loose like that.

CONSIDERATIONS FOR CRITICAL THINKING AND WRITING

1. **FIRST RESPONSE.** Describe the speaker's feelings about starting a life at college. How do those feelings compare with your own experiences?

2. How does the grandmother's world differ from the speaker's at school? What details especially reveal those differences?

3. Given that the poem is about how "school['s] a-goin'" (line 15), why do you think the title is "Snapping Beans"?

4. Discuss the significance of the grandmother's response to the hickory leaf in line 44. How do you read the last line?

CONNECTION TO ANOTHER SELECTION

1. Discuss the treatment of the grandmothers in this poem and in "Behind Grandma's House" by Gary Soto (p. 184).

Alberto Ríos (b. 1952)

Seniors   *1985*

William cut a hole in his Levi's pocket
so he could flop himself out in class
behind the girls so the other guys
could see and shit what guts we all said.
All Konga wanted to do over and over   5
was the rubber band trick, but he showed
everyone how, so nobody wanted to see
anymore and one day he cried, just cried
until his parents took him away forever.
Maya had a Hotpoint refrigerator standing   10
in his living room, just for his family to show
anybody who came that they could afford it.

Me, I got a French kiss, finally, in the catholic
darkness, my tongue's farthest half vacationing
loudly in another mouth like a man in Bermudas,   15
and my body jumped against a flagstone wall,
I could feel it through her thin, almost
nonexistent body: I had, at that moment, that moment,
a hot girl on a summer night, the best of all
the things we tried to do. Well, she   20
let me kiss her, anyway, all over.

Or it was just a flagstone wall
with a flaw in the stone, an understanding cavity
for burning young men with smooth dreams —
the true circumstance is gone, the true   25
circumstances about us all then
are gone. But when I kissed her, all water,
she would close her eyes, and they into somewhere
would disappear. Whether she was there
or not, I remember her, clearly, and she moves   30
around the room, sometimes, until I sleep.

I have lain on the desert in watch
low in the back of a pick-up truck
for nothing in particular, for stars, for
the things behind stars, and nothing comes   35
more than the moment: always now, here in a truck,
the moment again to dream of making love and sweat,
this time to a woman, or even to all of them
in some allowable way, to those boys, then,
who couldn't cry, to the girls before they were   40
women, to friends, me on my back, the sky over me
pressing its simple weight into her body
on me, into the bodies of them all, on me.

CONSIDERATIONS FOR CRITICAL THINKING AND WRITING

1. **FIRST RESPONSE.** Comment on the use of slang in the poem. Does it surprise you? How does it characterize the speaker?

2. How does the language of the final stanza differ from that of the first stanza? To what purpose?

3. Write an essay that discusses the speaker's attitudes toward sex and life. How are they related?

CONNECTIONS TO OTHER SELECTIONS

1. Compare the treatment of sex in this poem with that in Sharon Olds's "Sex without Love" (p. 91).

2. Think about "Seniors" as a kind of love poem and compare the speaker's voice here with the one in T. S. Eliot's "The Love Song of J. Alfred Prufrock" (p. 494). How are these two voices used to evoke different cultures? Of what value is love in these cultures?

ALFRED, LORD TENNYSON (1809–1892)

Crossing the Bar   1889

Sunset and evening star,
   And one clear call for me!
And may there be no moaning of the bar,°   *sandbar*
   When I put out to sea,

But such a tide as moving seems asleep,   5
   Too full for sound and foam,
When that which drew from out the boundless deep
   Turns again home.

Twilight and evening bell,
   And after that the dark!   10
And may there be no sadness of farewell,
   When I embark;

For tho' from out our bourne of Time and Place
   The flood may bear me far,
I hope to see my Pilot face to face   15
   When I have crost the bar.

CONSIDERATIONS FOR CRITICAL THINKING AND WRITING

1. **FIRST RESPONSE.** How does Tennyson make clear that this poem is about more than a sea journey?

2. Why do you think Tennyson directed to his publishers to place "Crossing the Bar" as the last poem in all collections of his poetry?

3. Discuss the purpose of the punctuation (or its absence) at the end of each line.

CONNECTION TO ANOTHER SELECTION

I. Compare the speaker's mood in "Crossing the Bar" with that in Dylan Thomas's "Do Not Go Gentle into That Good Night" (p. 253).

LI HO (791–817)

A Beautiful Girl Combs Her Hair

date unknown

TRANSLATED BY DAVID YOUNG

Awake at dawn
she's dreaming
by cool silk curtains

fragrance of spilling hair
half sandalwood, half aloes   5

windlass creaking at the well
singing jade

the lotus blossom wakes, refreshed

her mirror
two phoenixes   10
a pool of autumn light

standing on the ivory bed
loosening her hair
watching the mirror

one long coil, aromatic silk   15
a cloud down to the floor

drop the jade comb — no sound

delicate fingers
pushing the coils into place
color of raven feathers   20

shining blue-black stuff
the jewelled comb will hardly hold it

spring wind makes me restless
her slovenly beauty upsets me

eighteen and her hair's so thick   25
she wears herself out fixing it!

she's finished now
the whole arrangement in place

in a cloud-patterned skirt
she walks with even steps   30
a wild goose on the sand

turns away without a word
where is she off to?

down the steps to break a spray of
    cherry blossoms

    35

CONSIDERATIONS FOR CRITICAL THINKING AND WRITING

1. **FIRST RESPONSE.** Try to paraphrase the poem. What is lost by rewording?
2. How does the speaker use sensuous language to create a vivid picture of the girl?
3. What are the speaker's feelings toward the girl? Do they remain the same throughout the poem?

CONNECTIONS TO OTHER SELECTIONS

1. Compare the description of hair in this poem with that in Cathy Song's "The White Porch" (p. 130). What significant similarities do you find?
2. Write an essay that explores the differing portraits in this poem and in Sylvia Plath's "Mirror" (p. 148). Which portrait is more interesting to you? Explain why.

BILLY COLLINS (B. 1941)

Marginalia

1998

Sometimes the notes are ferocious,
skirmishes against the author
raging along the borders of every page
in tiny black script.
If I could just get my hands on you,   5
Kierkegaard,° or Conor Cruise O'Brien,°
they seem to say,
I would bolt the door and beat some logic into your head.

Other comments are more offhand, dismissive —
"Nonsense." "Please!" "HA!!" —   10
that kind of thing.
I remember once looking up from my reading,
my thumb as a bookmark,
trying to imagine what the person must look like
who wrote "Don't be a ninny"   15
alongside a paragraph in *The Life of Emily Dickinson*.

Students are more modest
needing to leave only their splayed footprints
along the shore of the page.

6 *Kierkegaard:* Søren Aaby Kierkegaard (1813–1855), Danish philosopher and theologian; *Conor Cruise O'Brien* (1917–2008): Irish historian, critic, and statesman.

One scrawls "Metaphor" next to a stanza of Eliot's.°   20
Another notes the presence of "Irony"
fifty times outside the paragraphs of *A Modest Proposal.*°

Or they are fans who cheer from the empty bleachers,
hands cupped around their mouths.
"Absolutely," they shout   25
to Duns Scotus° and James Baldwin.°
"Yes." "Bull's-eye." "My man!"
Check marks, asterisks, and exclamation points
rain down along the sidelines.

And if you have managed to graduate from college   30
without ever having written "Man vs. Nature"
in a margin, perhaps now
is the time to take one step forward.

We have all seized the white perimeter as our own
and reached for a pen if only to show   35
we did not just laze in an armchair turning pages;
we pressed a thought into the wayside,
planted an impression along the verge.

Even Irish monks in their cold scriptoria°
jotted along the borders of the Gospels   40
brief asides about the pains of copying,
a bird singing near their window,
or the sunlight that illuminated their page —
anonymous men catching a ride into the future
on a vessel more lasting than themselves.   45

And you have not read Joshua Reynolds,°
they say, until you have read him
enwreathed with Blake's° furious scribbling.

Yet the one I think of most often,
the one that dangles from me like a locket,   50
was written in the copy of *Catcher in the Rye*°
I borrowed from the local library
one slow, hot summer.
I was just beginning high school then,
reading books on a davenport in my parents' living room,   55
and I cannot tell you
how vastly my loneliness was deepened,

---

20 *Eliot's:* Thomas Stearns Eliot (1888-1965), American-born English poet and critic (see p. 491).   22 *A Modest Proposal:* An essay by English satirist Jonathan Swift (1667-1745). 26 *Duns Scotus* (1265?-1308): Scottish theologian; *James Baldwin* (1924-1987): African American essayist and novelist.   39 *scriptoria:* Rooms in a monastery used for writing and copying. 46 *Joshua Reynolds* (1723-1792): English portrait artist who entertained many of the important writers of his time.   48 *Blake's:* William Blake (1757-1827), English mystic and poet.   51 *Catcher in the Rye:* A novel (1951) about adolescence by American author J. D. Salinger (B. 1919).

how poignant and amplified the world before me seemed,
when I found on one page

a few greasy looking smears   60
and next to them, written in soft pencil—
by a beautiful girl, I could tell,
whom I would never meet—
"Pardon the egg salad stains, but I'm in love."

CONSIDERATIONS FOR CRITICAL THINKING AND WRITING

1. **FIRST RESPONSE.** How does your own experience of finding notations written in the margins of books compare with the speaker's?

2. How does Collins use humor to characterize the speaker?

3. Given the poem's final sixteen lines, consider how the title might go beyond simply announcing the subject matter of the poem.

CONNECTIONS TO OTHER SELECTIONS

1. Discuss the speakers' responses to reading in this poem and in Philip Larkin's "A Study of Reading Habits" (p. 33). How is reading used as a measure of each speaker's character?

2. Describe the speakers' attitudes toward books in this poem and in Anne Bradstreet's "The Author to Her Book" (p. 137).

CHRISTIAN BÖK (B. 1966)

Vowels   *2001*

loveless vessels

we vow
solo love

we see
love solve loss

else we see
love sow woe

selves we woo
we lose

losses we levee
we owe

we sell
loose vows

so we love
less well

© Christian Yde Frostholm

10

15

so low
so level

wolves evolve

Considerations for Critical Thinking and Writing

1. **FIRST RESPONSE.** What do you think Bök is up to in this poem? How is the title related to the lines that follow it?
2. Paraphrase the narrative that the poem tells.
3. **CREATIVE RESPONSE.** Using Bök's strategy and style, choose a single word and try writing your own poem in the same manner.

2

Writing about Poetry: From Inquiry to Final Paper

© Robert Turney.

Poems reveal secrets when they are analyzed. The poet's pleasure in finding ingenious ways to enclose her secrets should be matched by the reader's pleasure in unlocking and revealing secrets.

— DIANE WAKOSKI

FROM READING TO WRITING

Writing about poetry can be a rigorous means of testing the validity of your own reading of a poem. Anyone who has been asked to write several pages about a fourteen-line poem knows how intellectually challenging this exercise is, because it means paying close attention to language. Such scrutiny of words, however, sensitizes you not only to the poet's use of language but also to your own use of language. At first you may feel intimidated by having to compose a paper that is longer than the poem you're writing about, but a careful reading will reveal that there's plenty to write about what the poem says and how it says it. Keep in mind that your job is not to produce a definitive reading of the poem — even Carl Sandburg once confessed that "I've written some poetry I don't understand myself." It is enough to develop an interesting thesis and to present it clearly and persuasively.

An interesting thesis will come to you if you read and reread, take notes, annotate the text, and generate ideas (for a discussion of this process, see Chapter 27, "Reading and the Writing Process"). Although it requires energy to read closely and to write convincingly about the charged language found in poetry, there is nothing mysterious about such reading and writing. This chapter provides a set of questions designed to sharpen your reading and writing about poetry. Following these questions is a sample paper that offers a clear and well-developed thesis concerning Elizabeth Bishop's "Manners."

Questions for Responsive Reading and Writing

The following questions can help you respond to important elements that reveal a poem's effects and meanings. The questions are general, so not all of them will necessarily be relevant to a particular poem. Many, however, should prove useful for thinking, talking, and writing about each poem in this collection. If you are uncertain about the meaning of a term used in a question, consult the Glossary of Literary Terms beginning on page 745.

Before addressing these questions, read the poem you are studying in its entirety. Don't worry about interpretation on a first reading; allow yourself the pleasure of enjoying whatever makes itself apparent to you. Then on subsequent readings, use the questions to understand and appreciate how the poem works.

1. Who is the speaker? Is it possible to determine the speaker's age, sex, sensibilities, level of awareness, and values?
2. Is the speaker addressing anyone in particular?
3. How do you respond to the speaker? Favorably? Negatively? What is the situation? Are there any special circumstances that inform what the speaker says?
4. Is there a specific setting of time and place?
5. Does reading the poem aloud help you to understand it?
6. Does a paraphrase reveal the basic purpose of the poem?
7. What does the title emphasize?
8. Is the theme presented directly or indirectly?
9. Do any allusions enrich the poem's meaning?
10. How does the diction reveal meaning? Are any words repeated? Do any carry evocative connotative meanings? Are there any puns or other forms of verbal wit?
11. Are figures of speech used? How does the figurative language contribute to the poem's vividness and meaning?

(continued)

12. Do any objects, persons, places, events, or actions have allegorical or symbolic meanings? What other details in the poem support your interpretation?

13. Is irony used? Are there any examples of situational irony, verbal irony, or dramatic irony? Is understatement or paradox used?

14. What is the tone of the poem? Is the tone consistent?

15. Does the poem use onomatopoeia, assonance, consonance, or alliteration? How do these sounds affect you?

16. What sounds are repeated? If there are rhymes, what is their effect? Do they seem forced or natural? Is there a rhyme scheme? Do the rhymes contribute to the poem's meaning?

17. Do the lines have a regular meter? What is the predominant meter? Are there significant variations? Does the rhythm seem appropriate for the poem's tone?

18. Does the poem's form — its overall structure — follow an established pattern? Do you think the form is a suitable vehicle for the poem's meaning and effects?

19. Is the language of the poem intense and concentrated? Do you think it warrants more than one or two close readings?

20. Did you enjoy the poem? What, specifically, pleased or displeased you about what was expressed and how it was expressed?

21. Is there a particular critical approach that seems especially appropriate for this poem? (See Chapter 26, "Critical Strategies for Reading.")

22. How might biographical information about the author help to determine the poem's central concerns?

23. How might historical information about the poem provide a useful context for interpretation?

24. To what extent do your own experiences, values, beliefs, and assumptions inform your interpretation?

25. What kinds of evidence from the poem are you focusing on to support your interpretation? Does your interpretation leave out any important elements that might undercut or qualify your interpretation?

26. Given that there are a variety of ways to interpret the poem, which one seems the most useful to you?

ELIZABETH BISHOP (1911–1979)

Manners

1965

for a Child of 1918

 Explore contexts for Elizabeth Bishop and approaches to this poem on *LiterActive* and at bedfordstmartins.com/ rewritinglit.

My grandfather said to me
as we sat on the wagon seat,
"Be sure to remember to always
speak to everyone you meet."

We met a stranger on foot.
My grandfather's whip tapped his hat.
"Good day, sir. Good day. A fine day."
And I said it and bowed where I sat.

Then we overtook a boy we knew
with his big pet crow on his shoulder.
"Always offer everyone a ride;
don't forget that when you get older,"

my grandfather said. So Willy
climbed up with us, but the crow
gave a "Caw!" and flew off. I was worried.
How would he know where to go?

But he flew a little way at a time
from fence post to fence post, ahead;
and when Willy whistled he answered.
"A fine bird," my grandfather said,   20

"and he's well brought up. See, he answers
nicely when he's spoken to.
Man or beast, that's good manners.
Be sure that you both always do."

When automobiles went by,   25
the dust hid the people's faces,
but we shouted "Good day! Good day!
Fine day!" at the top of our voices.

When we came to Hustler Hill,
he said that the mare was tired,   30
so we all got down and walked,
as our good manners required.

© Bettmann/CORBIS.

A SAMPLE CLOSE READING

An Annotated Version of "Manners"

The following annotations represent insights about the relationship of various elements at work in the poem gleaned only after several close readings. Don't expect to be able to produce these kinds of interpretive notes on a first reading because such perceptions will not be apparent until you've read the poem and then gone back to the beginning to discover how each word, line, and stanza contributes to the overall effect. Writing your responses in the margins of the page can be a useful means of recording your impressions as well as discovering new insights as you read the text closely.

ELIZABETH BISHOP (1911–1979)

Manners   *1965*

for a Child of 1918

Title refers to what is socially correct, polite and/or decent behavior.

WWI ended in 1918 and denotes a shift in values and manners that often rapid social changes brought about by war.

My grandfather said to me
as we sat on the wagon seat,
"Be sure to remember to always
speak to everyone you meet."

Wagon seat suggests a simpler past — as does simple language and informal diction of the child speaker.

We met a stranger on foot.   5
My grandfather's whip tapped his hat.
"Good day, sir. Good day. A fine day."
And I said it and bowed where I sat.

Grandfather seems kind, but he also carries a whip that reinforces his authoritative voice.

Idea that values "always" transcend time is emphasized by the grandfather's urging: "don't forget."

Then we overtook a boy we knew
with his big pet crow on his shoulder.   10
"Always offer everyone a ride;
don't forget that when you get older,"

"My grandfather," repeated four times in first five stanzas, reflects the child's affection and a sense of belonging in his world. The crow, however, worries the child and indicates an uncertain future.

my grandfather said. So Willy
climbed up with us, but the crow
gave a "Caw!" and flew off. I was worried.   15
How would he know where to go?

But he flew a little way at a time
from fence post to fence post, ahead;
and when Willy whistled he answered.
"A fine bird," my grandfather said,   20

Predictable quatrains and *abcb* rhyme scheme throughout the poem take the worry out of where they — and the crow — are headed.

"and he's well brought up. See, he answers
nicely when he's spoken to.
Man or beast, that's good manners.
Be sure that you both always do."

Third time the grandfather says "always." This and the inverted syntax of line 24 call attention, again, to idea that good manners are forever important.

When automobiles went by,   25
the dust hid the people's faces,

The modern symbolic automobile races by raising dust that obscures everyone's vision and forces them to shout. Rhymes in lines 26 and 28 are off (unlike all the other rhymes) just enough to suggest the dissonant future that will supersede the calm wagon ride.

but we shouted "Good day! Good day!

Fine day!" at the top of our voices.

When we came to Hustler Hill,

he said that the mare was tired,   30

so we all got down and walked,

as our good manners required.

The horse, like the simple past it symbolizes, is weakened by the hustle of modern life, but even so, "our" good manners prevail, internalized from the grandfather's values.

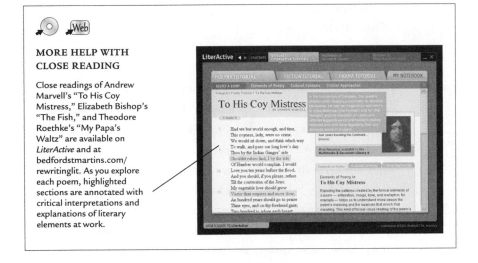

MORE HELP WITH CLOSE READING

Close readings of Andrew Marvell's "To His Coy Mistress," Elizabeth Bishop's "The Fish," and Theodore Roethke's "My Papa's Waltz" are available on *LiterActive* and at bedfordstmartins.com/rewritinglit. As you explore each poem, highlighted sections are annotated with critical interpretations and explanations of literary elements at work.

A SAMPLE STUDENT ANALYSIS

Memory in Elizabeth Bishop's "Manners"

The following sample paper on Elizabeth Bishop's "Manners" was written in response to an assignment that called for a 750-word discussion of the ways in which at least five of the following elements work to develop and reinforce the poem's themes:

diction and tone	irony	form
images	sound and rhyme	speaker
figures of speech	rhythm and meter	setting and situation
symbols		

In her paper, Debra Epstein discusses the ways in which a number of these elements contribute to what she sees as a central theme of "Manners": the loss of a way of life that Bishop associates with the end of World War I. Not all of the elements of poetry are covered equally in Epstein's paper because some, such as the speaker and setting, are more important to her argument than others. Notice how rather than merely listing each of the elements, Epstein mentions them in her discussion as she needs to in order to develop the thesis that she clearly and succinctly expresses in her opening paragraph.

Web Research the poets in this chapter at bedfordstmartins.com/ rewritinglit.

Epstein 1

Debra Epstein

Professor Brown

English 210

May 1, 2009

Memory in Elizabeth Bishop's "Manners"

Thesis providing interpretation of poem.

The subject of Elizabeth Bishop's "Manners" has to do with behaving well, but the theme of the poem has more to do with a way of life than with etiquette. The poem suggests that modern society has lost something important—a friendly openness, a generosity of spirit, a sense of decency and consideration—in its race toward progress. Although the narrative is simply told, Bishop enriches this poem about manners by developing an implicit theme through her subtle use of such elements of poetry as speaker, setting, rhyme, meter, symbol, and images.

Statement of elements in poem to be discussed in paper.

Summary of poem's narrative and introduction to discussion of elements.

The dedication suggests that the speaker is "a Child of 1918" who accompanies his or her grandfather on a wagon ride and who is urged to practice good manners by greeting people, offering everyone a ride, and speaking when spoken to by anyone. During the ride they say hello to a stranger, give a ride to a boy with a pet crow, shout greetings to a passing automobile, and get down from the wagon when they reach a hill because the horse is tired. They walk because "good manners required" (line 32) such consideration, even for a horse. This summary indicates what goes on in the poem but not its significance. That requires a closer look at some of the poem's elements.

Analysis of speaker in poem.

Given the speaker's simple language (there are no metaphors or similes and only a few words out of thirty-two lines are longer than two syllables), it seems likely that he or she is a fairly young child, rather than an adult

Epstein 2

reminiscing. (It is interesting to note that Bishop herself, though not identical with the speaker, would have been seven in 1918.) Because the speaker is
a young child who uses simple diction, Bishop has to show us the ride's
significance indirectly rather than having the speaker explicitly state it.

The setting for the speaker's narrative is important because 1918 was
the year World War I ended, and it marked the beginning of a new era of
technology that was the result of rapid industrialization during the war.
Horses and wagons would soon be put out to pasture. The grandfather's
manners emphasize a time gone by; the child must be told to "remember"
what the grandfather says because he or she will take that advice into a new
and very different world.

Analysis of poem's setting.

The grandfather's world of the horse and wagon is uncomplicated, and
this is reflected in both the simple quatrains that move predictably along in
an *abcb* rhyme scheme and the frequent anapestic meter (ăs wĕ sát ŏn thĕ
wágŏn [2]) that pulls the lines rapidly and lightly. The one moment Bishop
breaks the set rhyme scheme is in the seventh stanza when the automobile
(the single four-syllable word in the poem) rushes by in a cloud of dust so
that people cannot see or hear each other. The only off rhymes in the
poem—"faces" (26) and "voices" (28)—are also in this stanza, which suggests that the automobile and the people in it are somehow off or out of sync
with what goes on in the other stanzas. The automobile is a symbol of a way
of life in which people—their faces hidden—and manners take a back seat
to speed and noise. The people in the car don't wave, don't offer a ride, and
don't speak when spoken to.

Analysis of rhyme scheme and meter.

Analysis of symbols.

Maybe the image of the crow's noisy cawing and flying from post to
post is a foreshadowing that should prepare readers for the automobile. The
speaker feels "worried" about the crow's apparent directionlessness: "How
would he know where to go?" (16). However, neither the child nor the grandfather (nor the reader on a first reading) clearly sees the two worlds that
Bishop contrasts in the final stanza.

Analysis of images.

"Hustler Hill" is the perfect name for what finally tires out the mare.
There is no hurry for the grandfather and child, but there is for those people

Conclusion supporting thesis on poem's theme.

Epstein 3

in the car and the postwar hustle and bustle they represent. The fast-paced
future overtakes the tired symbol of the past in the poem. The pace slows as
the wagon passengers get down to walk, but the reader recognizes that the
grandfather's way has been lost to a world in which good manners are not
required.

Epstein 4

Work Cited

Bishop, Elizabeth. "Manners." *Poetry: An Introduction.* Ed. Michael Meyer.
6th ed. Boston: Bedford/St. Martin's, 2010. 60. Print.

3

Word Choice, Word Order, and Tone

I still feel that a poet has a duty to words, and that words can do wonderful things. And it's too bad to just let them lie there without doing anything with and for them.

— GWENDOLYN BROOKS

By permission of The Granger Collection, New York.

WORD CHOICE

Diction

Like all good writers, poets are keenly aware of ***diction,*** their choice of words. Poets, however, choose words especially carefully because the words in poems call attention to themselves. Characters, actions, settings, and symbols may appear in a poem, but in the foreground, before all else, is the poem's language. Also, poems are usually briefer than other forms of writing. A few inappropriate words in a 200-page novel (which would have about 100,000 words) create fewer problems than they would in a 100-word poem. Functioning in a compressed atmosphere, the words in a poem must convey meanings gracefully and economically. Readers therefore have to be alert to the ways in which those meanings are released.

 Explore the poetic elements in this chapter on *LiterActive* and at bedfordstmartins.com/rewritinglit.

Although poetic language is often more intensely charged than ordinary speech, the words used in poetry are not necessarily different from everyday speech. Inexperienced readers may sometimes assume that language must be high-flown and out of date to be included in a poem: instead of reading about a boy "enjoying a swim," they expect to read about a boy "disporting with pliant arm o'er a glassy wave." During the eighteenth century this kind of *poetic diction* — the use of elevated language rather than ordinary language — was highly valued in English poetry, but since the nineteenth century poets have generally overridden the distinctions that were once made between words used in everyday speech and those used in poetry. Today all levels of diction can be found in poetry.

A poet, like any writer, has several levels of diction from which to choose; they range from formal to middle to informal. *Formal diction* consists of a dignified, impersonal, and elevated use of language. Notice, for example, the formality of Thomas Hardy's description of the sunken luxury liner *Titanic* in this stanza from "The Convergence of the Twain" (the entire poem appears on p. 86):

> In a solitude of the sea
> Deep from human vanity,
> And the Pride of Life that planned her, stilly couches she.

There is nothing casual or relaxed about these lines. Hardy's use of "stilly," meaning "quietly" or "calmly," is purely literary; the word rarely, if ever, turns up in everyday English.

The language used in Sharon Olds's "Last Night" (p. 84) represents a less formal level of diction; the speaker uses a *middle diction* spoken by most educated people. Consider how Olds's speaker struggles the next day to comprehend her passion:

> Love? It was more like dragonflies
> in the sun, 100 degrees at noon,
> the ends of their abdomens stuck together, I
> close my eyes when I remember.

The words used to describe this encounter are common enough, yet it is precisely Olds's use of language that evokes the extraordinary nature of this couple's connection.

Informal diction is evident in Philip Larkin's "A Study of Reading Habits" (p. 33). The speaker's account of his early reading is presented *colloquially,* in a conversational manner that in this instance includes slang expressions not used by the culture at large:

> When getting my nose in a book
> Cured most things short of school,
> It was worth ruining my eyes
> To know I could still keep cool,
> And deal out the old right hook
> To dirty dogs twice my size.

This level of diction is clearly not that of Hardy's or Olds's speakers.

Poets may also draw on another form of informal diction, called **dialect.** Dialects are spoken by definable groups of people from a particular geographic region, economic group, or social class. New England dialects are often heard in Robert Frost's poems, for example. Gwendolyn Brooks uses a black dialect in "We Real Cool" (p. 96) to characterize a group of pool players. Another form of diction related to particular groups is *jargon,* a category of language defined by a trade or profession. Sociologists, photographers, carpenters, baseball players, and dentists, for example, all use words that are specific to their fields. Sally Croft offers an appetizing dish of cookbook jargon in "Home-Baked Bread" (p. 126).

Many levels of diction are available to poets. The variety of diction to be found in poetry is enormous, and that is how it should be. No language is foreign to poetry because it is possible to imagine any human voice as the speaker of a poem. When we say a poem is formal, informal, or somewhere in between, we are making a descriptive statement rather than an evaluative one. What matters in a poem is not only which words are used but how they are used.

Denotations and Connotations

One important way that the meaning of a word is communicated in a poem is through sound: snakes *hiss,* saws *buzz.* This and other matters related to sound are discussed in Chapter 7. Individual words also convey meanings through denotations and connotations. *Denotations* are the literal, dictionary meanings of a word. For example, *bird* denotes a feathered animal with wings (other denotations for the same word include a shuttlecock, an airplane, or an odd person), but in addition to its denotative meanings, *bird* also carries *connotations* — associations and implications that go beyond a word's literal meanings. Connotations derive from how the word has been used and the associations people make with it. Therefore, the connotations of *bird* might include fragility, vulnerability, altitude, the sky, or freedom, depending on the context in which the word is used. Consider also how different the connotations are for the following types of birds: hawk, dove, penguin, pigeon, chicken, peacock, duck, crow, turkey, gull, owl, goose, coot, and vulture. These words have long been used to refer to types of people as well as birds. They are rich in connotative meanings.

Connotations derive their resonance from a person's experiences with a word. Those experiences may not always be the same, especially when the people having them are in different times and places. *Theater,* for instance, was once associated with depravity, disease, and sin, whereas today the word usually evokes some sense of high culture and perhaps visions of elegant opulence. In several ethnic communities in the United States many people would find *squid* appetizing, but elsewhere the word is likely to produce negative connotations. Readers must recognize, then, that words written in other times and places may have unexpected connotations. Annotations usually help in these matters, which is why it makes sense to pay attention to them when they are available.

Ordinarily, though, the language of poetry is accessible, even when the circumstances of the reader and the poet are different. Although connotative language may be used subtly, it mostly draws on associations experienced by many people. Poets rely on widely shared associations rather than the idiosyncratic response that an individual might have to a word. Someone who has received a severe burn from a fireplace accident may associate the word *hearth* with intense pain instead of home and family life, but that reader must not allow a personal experience to undermine the response the poet intends to evoke. Connotative meanings are usually public meanings.

Perhaps this can be seen most clearly in advertising, where language is also used primarily to convey moods and feelings rather than information. For instance, three decades of increasing interest in nutrition and general fitness have created a collective consciousness that advertisers have capitalized on successfully. Knowing that we want to be slender or lean or slim (not *spare* or *scrawny* and certainly not *gaunt*), advertisers have created a new word to describe beers, wines, sodas, cheeses, canned fruits, and other products that tend to overload what used to be called sweatclothes and sneakers. The word is *lite*. The assumed denotative meaning of *lite* is "low in calories," but as close readers of ingredient labels know, some *lites* are heavier than regularly prepared products. There can be no doubt about the connotative meaning of *lite*, however. Whatever is *lite* cannot hurt you; less is more. Even the word is lighter than *light*; there is no unnecessary droopy *g* or plump *h*. *Lite* is a brilliantly manufactured use of connotation.

Connotative meanings are valuable because they allow poets to be economical and suggestive simultaneously. In this way emotions and attitudes are carefully woven into the texture of the poem's language. Read the following poem and pay close attention to the connotative meanings of its words.

RANDALL JARRELL (1914–1965)

The Death of the Ball Turret Gunner   *1945*

From my mother's sleep I fell into the State
And I hunched in its belly till my wet fur froze.
Six miles from earth, loosed from its dream of life,
I woke to black flak and the nightmare fighters.
When I died they washed me out of the turret with a hose.

The title of this poem establishes the setting and the speaker's situation. Like the setting of a short story, the setting of a poem is important when the time and place influence what happens. "The Death of the Ball Turret Gunner" is set in the midst of a war and, more specifically, in a ball turret — a Plexiglas sphere housing machine guns on the underside of a bomber. The speaker's situation obviously places him in extreme danger; indeed, his fate is announced in the title.

Although the poem is written in the first-person singular, its speaker is clearly not the poet. Jarrell uses a **persona,** a speaker created by the poet. In this poem the persona is a disembodied voice that makes the gunner's story all the more powerful. What is his story? A paraphrase might read something like this:

> After I was born, I grew up to find myself at war, cramped into the turret of a bomber's belly some 31,000 feet above the ground. Below me were exploding shells from antiaircraft guns and attacking fighter planes. I was killed, but the bomber returned to base, where my remains were cleaned out of the turret so the next man could take my place.

This paraphrase is accurate, but its language is much less suggestive than the poem's. The first line of the poem has the speaker emerge from his "mother's sleep," the anesthetized sleep of her giving birth. The phrase also suggests the comfort, warmth, and security he knew as a child. This safety was left behind when he "fell," a verb that evokes the danger and involuntary movement associated with his subsequent "State" (*fell* also echoes, perhaps, the fall from innocence to experience related in the Bible).

Several dictionary definitions appear for the noun *state;* it can denote a territorial unit, the power and authority of a government, a person's social status, or a person's emotional or physical condition. The context provided by the rest of the poem makes clear that "State" has several denotative meanings here: because it is capitalized, it certainly refers to the violent world of a government at war, but it also refers to the gunner's vulnerable status as well as his physical and emotional condition. By having "State" carry more than one meaning, Jarrell has created an intentional ambiguity. **Ambiguity** allows for two or more simultaneous interpretations of a word, a phrase, an action, or a situation, all of which can be supported by the context of a work. Through his ambiguous use of "State," Jarrell connects the horrors of war not just to bombers and gunners but to the governments that control them.

Related to this ambiguity is the connotative meaning of "State" in the poem. The context demands that the word be read with a negative charge. The word is not used with patriotic pride but to suggest an anonymous, impersonal "State" that kills rather than nurtures the life in its "belly." The state's "belly" is a bomber, and the gunner is "hunched" like a fetus in the cramped turret, where, in contrast to the warmth of his mother's womb, everything is frozen, even the "wet fur" of his flight jacket (newborn infants have wet fur too). The gunner is not just 31,000 feet from the ground but "Six miles from earth." *Six miles* has roughly the same denotative meaning as 31,000 feet, but Jarrell knew that the connotative meaning of *six miles* makes the speaker's position seem even more remote and frightening.

When the gunner is born into the violent world of war, he finds himself waking up to a "nightmare" that is all too real. The poem's final line is grimly understated, but it hits the reader with the force of an exploding shell: what the State-bomber-turret gives birth to is a gruesome death that is merely one of an endless series. It may be tempting to reduce the theme of this poem to the idea that "war is hell," but Jarrell's target is more specific. He implicates the "State," which routinely executes such violence, and he does so without preaching or hysterical denunciations. Instead, his use of language conveys his theme subtly and powerfully.

WORD ORDER

Meanings in poems are conveyed not only by denotations and connotations but also by the poet's arrangement of words into phrases, clauses, and sentences to achieve particular effects. The ordering of words into meaningful verbal patterns is called **syntax.** A poet can manipulate the syntax of a line to place emphasis on a word; this is especially apparent when a poet varies normal word order. In Emily Dickinson's "A narrow Fellow in the Grass" (p. 2), for example, the speaker says about the snake that "His notice sudden is." Ordinarily, that would be expressed as "his notice is sudden." By placing the verb *is* unexpectedly at the end of the line, Dickinson creates the sense of surprise we feel when we suddenly come upon a snake. Dickinson's inversion of the standard word order also makes the final sound of the line a hissing *is*.

TONE

Tone is the writer's attitude toward the subject, the mood created by all of the elements in the poem. Writing, like speech, can be characterized as serious or light, sad or happy, private or public, angry or affectionate, bitter or nostalgic, or by any other attitudes and feelings that human beings experience. In Jarrell's "The Death of the Ball Turret Gunner," the tone is clearly serious; the voice in the poem even sounds dead. Listen again to the persona's final words: "When I died they washed me out of the turret with a hose." The brutal, restrained matter-of-factness of this line is effective because the reader is called on to supply the appropriate anger and despair — a strategy that makes those emotions all the more convincing.

Consider how tone is used to convey meaning in the next poem, inspired by the poet's contemplation of mortality.

JUDITH ORTIZ COFER (B. 1952)

Common Ground   *1987*

Blood tells the story of your life
in heartbeats as you live it;
bones speak in the language
of death, and flesh thins
with age when up   5
through your pores rises
the stuff of your origin.

    These days,
when I look into the mirror I see
my grandmother's stern lips   10
speaking in parentheses at the corners
of my mouth of pain and deprivation
I have never known. I recognize
my father's brows arching in disdain
over the objects of my vanity, my mother's   15
nervous hands smoothing lines
just appearing on my skin,
like arrows pointing downward
to our common ground.

CONSIDERATIONS FOR CRITICAL THINKING AND WRITING

1. **FIRST RESPONSE.** How do you interpret the title? How did your idea of its meaning change as you read the poem?
2. What is the relationship between the first and second stanzas?
3. How does this poem make you feel? What is its tone? How do the diction and imagery create the tone?

COLETTE INEZ (B. 1931)

Back When All Was Continuous Chuckles   *2004*

after a line by Anselm Hollo°

Doris and I were helpless on the Beeline Bus
laughing at what was it? "What did the moron
who killed his mother and father eat
at the orphan's picnic?" "Crow?" Har-har.

Anselm Hollo: Finnish poet (b. 1934) who teaches creative writing in the United States.

The bus was grinding towards Hempstead,   5
past the cemetery whose stones Doris
and I found hilarious. Freaky ghouls and skeletons.
"What did the dead man say to the ghost?"

"I like the movie better than the book."
Even "I don't get it" was funny.   10
The war was on, rationing, sirens.
Silly billies, we poked each other's arms

with balled fists, held hands and howled
at crabby ladies in funny hats, dusty feathers,
fake fruit. Doris' mom wore this headgear   15
before she got the big C which no one said out loud.

In a shadowy room her skin seemed gray
as moon dust on Smith Street, as Doris' house
where we tiptoed down the hall.
Sometimes we heard moans from the back room   20

and I helped wring out cloths while Doris
brought water in a glass held to her mother's lips.
But soon we were flipping through joke books
and writhing on the floor, war news shut off

back when we pretended all was continuous chuckles,   25
and we rode the bus past Greenfield's rise
where stones, trumpeting angels,
would bear names we later came to recognize.

Considerations for Critical Thinking and Writing

1. **FIRST RESPONSE.** Compare the difference between the title and its slightly revised version as it appears in line 25. How does that difference reveal the theme?

2. At what point does the tone of the poem shift from chuckles to something else?

3. What is the effect of the rhymes in lines 26 and 28? How do the rhymes serve to reinforce the poem's theme?

Connection to Another Selection

1. Discuss the tone of this poem and that of Gwendolyn Brooks's "We Real Cool" (p. 96).

The next work is a ***dramatic monologue,*** a type of poem in which a character — the speaker — addresses a silent audience in such a way as to reveal unintentionally some aspect of his or her temperament or personality. What tone is created by Machan's use of a persona?

Katharyn Howd Machan (b. 1952)

Hazel Tells LaVerne   1976

last night
im cleanin out my
howard johnsons ladies room
when all of a sudden
up pops this frog   5
musta come fiom the sewer
swimmin aroun an tryin ta
climb up the sida the bowl
so i goes ta flushm down
but sohelpmegod he starts talkin   10
bout a golden ball
an how i can be a princess
me a princess
well my mouth drops
all the way to the floor   15
an he says
kiss me just kiss me
once on the nose
well i screams
ya little green pervert   20
an i hitsm with my mop
an has ta flush
the toilet down three times
me
a princess   25

Considerations for Critical Thinking and Writing

1. **FIRST RESPONSE.** What do you imagine the situation and setting are for this poem? Do you like this revision of the fairy tale "The Frog Prince"?

2. What creates the poem's humor? How does Hazel's use of language reveal her personality? Is her treatment of the frog consistent with her character?

3. Although it has no punctuation, this poem is easy to follow. How does the arrangement of the lines organize Hazel's speech for clarity and emphasis?

4. What is the theme? Is it conveyed through denotative or connotative language?

5. **CREATIVE RESPONSE.** Write what you think might be LaVerne's reply to Hazel. First, write LaVerne's response as a series of ordinary sentences, and then try editing and organizing them into poetic lines.

Connection to Another Selection

1. Although Robert Browning's "My Last Duchess" (p. 180) is a more complex poem than Machan's, both use dramatic monologues to reveal character. How are the strategies in each poem similar?

A SAMPLE STUDENT RESPONSE

Alex Georges

Professor Myerov

English 200

October 2, 2009

Tone in Katharyn Howd Machan's "Hazel Tells LaVerne"

"Tone," Michael Meyer writes, "is the writer's attitude toward the subject, the mood created by all of the elements of the poem" (72) and is used to convey meaning and character. In her dramatic monologue, "Hazel Tells LaVerne," the poet Katharyn Howd Machan reveals through the persona of Hazel—a funny, tough-talking, no-nonsense cleaning lady—a satirical revision of "The Frog Prince" fairy tale. Hazel's attitude toward the possibility of a fairy-tale romance is evident in her response to the frog prince. She has no use for him or his offers "bout a golden ball / an how i can be a princess" (lines 11-12). If Hazel is viewed by the reader as a princess, it is clear from her words and tone that she is far from a traditional one.

Machan's word choice and humorous tone also reveal much about Hazel's personality and circumstances. Through the use of slang, alternate spellings, and the omission of punctuation, we learn a great deal about the character:

> well i screams
>
> ya little green pervert
>
> an i hitsm with my mop
>
> an has ta flush
>
> the toilet down three times
>
> me
>
> a princess (19-25)

Listening to her speak, the reader understands that Hazel, a cleaner at Howard Johnson's, does not have an extensive education. She speaks in the colloquial, running words into one another and using phrases like "ya little green pervert" (20) and "i screams" (19). The lack of complete sentences,

Georges 2

capital letters, and punctuation adds to her informal tone. Hazel's speech defines her social status, brings out details of her personality, and gives the reader
her view of herself. She is accustomed to the thankless daily grind of work and
will not allow herself even a moment's fantasy of becoming a princess. It is a
notion that she has to flush away—literally, has "ta flush . . . down three
times." She tells LaVerne that the very idea of such fantasy is absurd to her, as
she states in the final lines: "me / a princess" (24-25).

Georges 3

Works Cited

Machan, Katharyn Howd. "Hazel Tells LaVerne." *Poetry: An Introduction*. Ed.
    Michael Meyer. 6th ed. Boston: Bedford/St. Martin's, 2010. 75. Print.
Meyer, Michael, ed. *Poetry: An Introduction*. 6th ed. Boston: Bedford/St.
    Martin's, 2010. 72. Print.

MARTÍN ESPADA (B. 1957)
Latin Night at the Pawnshop   *1987*

Chelsea, Massachusetts
Christmas, 1987

The apparition of a salsa band
gleaming in the Liberty Loan
pawnshop window:

Golden trumpet,
silver trombone,   5
congas, maracas, tambourine,

all with price tags dangling
like the city morgue ticket
on a dead man's toe.

CONSIDERATIONS FOR CRITICAL THINKING AND WRITING

1. **FIRST RESPONSE.** What is "Latin" about this night at the pawnshop?
2. What kind of tone is created by the poet's word choice and by the poem's rhythm?
3. Does it matter that this apparition occurs on Christmas night? Why or why not?
4. What do you think is the central point of this poem?

How do the speaker's attitude and tone change during the course of this next poem?

PAUL LAURENCE DUNBAR (1872–1906)

To a Captious Critic   *1903*

Dear critic, who my lightness so deplores,
Would I might study to be prince of bores,
Right wisely would I rule that dull estate —
But, sir, I may not; till you abdicate.

CONSIDERATIONS FOR CRITICAL THINKING AND WRITING

1. **FIRST RESPONSE.** How do Dunbar's vocabulary and syntax signal the level of diction used in the poem?
2. Describe the speaker's tone. How does it characterize the speaker as well as the critic?
3. **CREATIVE RESPONSE.** Using "To a Captious Critic" as a model, try writing a four-line witty reply to someone in your own life — perhaps a roommate, coach, teacher, waiter, dentist, or anyone else who provokes a strong response in you.

DICTION AND TONE IN FOUR LOVE POEMS

The first three of these love poems share the same basic situation and theme: a male speaker addresses a female (in the first poem it is a type of female) urging that love should not be delayed because time is short. This theme is as familiar in poetry as it is in life. In Latin this tradition is known as *carpe diem,* "seize the day." Notice how the poets' diction helps create a distinctive tone in each poem, even though the subject matter and central ideas are similar (although not identical) in all three.

ROBERT HERRICK (1591–1674)

To the Virgins, to Make Much of Time   1648

Gather ye rose-buds while ye may,
   Old Time is still a-flying;
And this same flower that smiles today,
   Tomorrow will be dying.

The glorious lamp of heaven, the sun,
   The higher he's a-getting,
The sooner will his race be run,
   And nearer he's to setting.

That age is best which is the first,
   When youth and blood are warmer;
But being spent, the worse, and worst
   Times still succeed the former.

Courtesy of the National Portrait Gallery,
London.

Then be not coy, but use your time,
   And while ye may, go marry;
For having lost but once your prime,   15
   You may for ever tarry.

CONSIDERATIONS FOR CRITICAL THINKING AND WRITING

1. **FIRST RESPONSE.** Would there be any change in meaning if the title of this poem were "To Young Women, to Make Much of Time"? Do you think the poem can apply to young men, too?

2. What do the virgins have in common with the flowers (lines 1–4) and the course of the day (5–8)?

3. How does the speaker develop his argument? What will happen to the virgins if they don't "marry"? Paraphrase the poem.

4. What is the tone of the speaker's advice?

The next poem was also written in the seventeenth century, but it includes some words that have changed in usage and meaning over the past three hundred years. The title of Andrew Marvell's "To His Coy Mistress" requires some explanation. "Mistress" does not refer to a married man's illicit lover but to a woman who is loved and courted — a sweetheart. Marvell uses "coy" to describe a woman who is reserved and shy rather than coquettish or flirtatious. Often such shifts in meanings over time are explained in the notes that accompany reprintings of poems. You should keep in mind, however, that it is helpful to have a reasonably thick dictionary available when you are reading poetry. The most thorough is the *Oxford English Dictionary (OED)*, which provides histories of words. The *OED* is a multivolume leviathan, but there are other useful unabridged dictionaries and desk dictionaries.

Web Explore contexts for Andrew Marvell and approaches to this poem on *LiterActive* and at bedfordstmartins.com/rewritinglit.

Knowing its original meaning can also enrich your understanding of why a contemporary poet chooses a particular word. Elizabeth Bishop begins "The Fish" (p. 31) this way: "I caught a tremendous fish." We know immediately in this context that "tremendous" means very large. In addition, given that the speaker clearly admires the fish in the lines that follow, we might even understand "tremendous" in the colloquial sense of wonderful and extraordinary. But a dictionary gives us some further relevant insights. Because, by the end of the poem, we see the speaker thoroughly moved as a result of the encounter with the fish ("everything / was rainbow, rainbow, rainbow!"), the dictionary's additional information about the history of *tremendous* shows why it is the perfect adjective to introduce the fish. The word comes from the Latin *tremere* (to tremble) and therefore once meant "such as to make one tremble." That is precisely how the speaker is at the end of the poem: deeply affected and trembling. Knowing the origin of *tremendous* gives us the full heft of the poet's word choice.

Although some of the language in "To His Coy Mistress" requires annotations for the modern reader, this poem continues to serve as a powerful reminder that time is a formidable foe, even for lovers.

ANDREW MARVELL (1621–1678)

To His Coy Mistress   *1681*

Had we but world enough, and time,
This coyness, lady, were no crime.
We would sit down, and think which way
To walk, and pass our long love's day.
Thou by the Indian Ganges'° side   5
Shouldst rubies find; I by the tide
Of Humber° would complain.° I would   *write love songs*
Love you ten years before the Flood,
And you should, if you please, refuse
Till the conversion of the Jews.   10
My vegetable love should grow°
Vaster than empires, and more slow;
An hundred years should go to praise
Thine eyes and on thy forehead gaze,
Two hundred to adore each breast,   15
But thirty thousand to the rest:

---

5 *Ganges:* A river in India sacred to the Hindus.   7 *Humber:* A river that flows through Marvell's native town, Hull.   11 *My vegetable love . . . grow:* A slow, unconscious growth.

An age at least to every part,
And the last age should show your heart.
For, lady, you deserve this state,
Nor would I love at lower rate.   20
    But at my back I always hear
Time's wingèd chariot hurrying near;
And yonder all before us lie
Deserts of vast eternity.
Thy beauty shall no more be found,   25
Nor in thy marble vault shall sound
My echoing song; then worms shall try
That long preserved virginity,
And your quaint honor turn to dust,
And into ashes all my lust.   30
The grave's a fine and private place,
But none, I think, do there embrace.
    Now, therefore, while the youthful hue
Sits on thy skin like morning dew,
And while thy willing soul transpires°   *breathes forth*   35
At every pore with instant fires,
Now let us sport us while we may,
And now, like amorous birds of prey,
Rather at once our time devour
Than languish in his slow-chapped° power.   *slow-jawed*   40
Let us roll all our strength and all
Our sweetness up into one ball,
And tear our pleasures with rough strife
Thorough° the iron gates of life.   *through*
Thus, though we cannot make our sun   45
Stand still, yet we will make him run.

Considerations for Critical Thinking and Writing

1. **FIRST RESPONSE.** Do you think this *carpe diem* poem is hopelessly dated, or does it speak to our contemporary concerns?

2. This poem is divided into a three-part argument. Briefly summarize each section: if (lines 1–20), but (21–32), therefore (33–46).

3. What is the speaker's tone in lines 1–20? How much time would he spend adoring his mistress? Is he sincere? How does he expect his mistress to respond to these lines?

4. How does the speaker's tone change beginning with line 21? What is his view of time in lines 21–32? What does this description do to the lush and leisurely sense of time in lines 1–20? How do you think his mistress would react to lines 21–32?

5. In the final lines of Herrick's "To the Virgins, to Make Much of Time" (p. 79), the speaker urges the virgins to "go marry." What does Marvell's speaker urge in lines 33–46? How is the pace of these lines (notice the verbs) different from that of the first twenty lines of the poem?

6. This poem is sometimes read as a vigorous but simple celebration of flesh. Is there more to the theme than that?

The third in this series of *carpe diem* poems is a twenty-first-century work. The language of Ann Lauinger's "Marvell Noir" is more immediately accessible than that of Marvell's "To His Coy Mistress"; an ordinary dictionary will quickly identify any words unfamiliar to a reader. But the title might require a dictionary of biography for the reference to Marvell, as well as a dictionary of allusions to provide a succinct description that explains the reference to film noir. An ***allusion*** is a brief cultural reference to a person, a place, a thing, an event, or an idea in history or literature. Allusive words, like connotative words, are both suggestive and economical; poets use allusions to conjure up biblical authority, scenes from Shakespeare's plays, historic figures, wars, great love stories, and anything else that might serve to deepen and enrich their own work. The title of "Marvell Noir" makes two allusions that an ordinary dictionary may not explain, because it alludes to Marvell's most famous poem, "To His Coy Mistress," and to dark crime films (*noir* is "black" in French) of the 1940s that were often filmed in black and white featuring tough-talking, cynical heroes such as Humphrey Bogart and hardened, cold women like Joan Crawford. Lauinger assumes that her reader will understand the allusions.

Allusions imply reading and cultural experiences shared by the poet and reader. Literate audiences once had more in common than they do today because more people had similar economic, social, and educational backgrounds. But a judicious use of specialized dictionaries, encyclopedias, and other reference tools can help you decipher allusions that grow out of this body of experience. As you read more, you'll be able to make connections based on your own experiences with literature. In a sense, allusions make available what other human beings have deemed worth remembering, and that is certainly an economical way of supplementing and enhancing your own experience.

Lauinger's version of the *carpe diem* theme follows. What strikes you as particularly modern about it?

Ann Lauinger

Marvell Noir   *2005*

Sweetheart, if we had the time,
A week in bed would be no crime.
I'd light your Camels, pour your Jack;
You'd do shiatsu on my back.
When you got up to scramble eggs,   5
I'd write a sonnet to your legs,

And you could watch my stubble grow.
Yes, gorgeous, we'd take it slow.
I'd hear the whole sad tale again:
A roadhouse band; you can't trust men;   10
He set you up; you had to eat,
And bitter with the bittersweet
Was what they dished you; Ginger lied;
You weren't there when Sanchez died;
You didn't know the pearls were fake . . .   15
Aw, can it, sport! Make no mistake,
You're in it, doll, up to your eyeballs!
Tears? Please! You'll dilute our highballs,
And make that angel face a mess
For the nice Lieutenant. I confess   20
I'm nuts for you — but take the rap?
You must think I'm some other sap!
And, precious, I kind of wish I was.
Well, when they spring you, give a buzz;
Guess I'll get back to Archie's wife,   25
And you'll get twenty-five to life.
You'll have time then, more than enough,
To reminisce about the stuff
That dreams are made of, and the men
You suckered. Sadly, in the pen   30
Your kind of talent goes to waste.
But Irish bars are more my taste
Than iron ones: stripes ain't my style.
You're going down; I promise I'll
Come visit every other year.   35
Now kiss me, sweet — the squad car's here.

CONSIDERATIONS FOR CRITICAL THINKING AND WRITING

1. **FIRST RESPONSE.** How does Lauinger's poem evoke Marvell's *carpe diem* poem (p. 80) and the tough-guy tone of a "noir" narrative, a crime story or thriller that is especially dark?

2. Discuss the ways in which time is a central presence in the poem.

3. Explain the allusion to dreams in lines 28–29.

CONNECTION TO ANOTHER SELECTION

1. Compare the speaker's voice in this poem with that of the speaker in "To His Coy Mistress" (p. 80). What significant similarities and differences do you find?

This fourth love poem is a twentieth-century work in which the speaker's voice is a woman's. How does it sound different from the way the men speak in the previous three poems?

SHARON OLDS (B. 1942)

Last Night

1996

The next day, I am almost afraid.
Love? It was more like dragonflies
in the sun, 100 degrees at noon,
the ends of their abdomens stuck together, I
close my eyes when I remember. I hardly   5
knew myself, like something twisting and
twisting out of a chrysalis,
enormous, without language, all
head, all shut eyes, and the humming
like madness, the way they writhe away,   10
and do not leave, back, back,
away, back. Did I know you? No kiss,
no tenderness — more like killing, death-grip
holding to life, genitals
like violent hands clasped tight   15
barely moving, more like being closed
in a great jaw and eaten, and the screaming
I groan to remember it, and when we started
to die, then I refuse to remember,
the way a drunkard forgets. After,   20
you held my hands extremely hard as my
body moved in shudders like the ferry when its
axle is loosed past engagement, you kept me
sealed exactly against you, our hairlines
wet as the arc of a gateway after   25
a cloudburst, you secured me in your arms till I slept —
that was love, and we woke in the morning
clasped, fragrant, buoyant, that was
the morning after love.

CONSIDERATIONS FOR CRITICAL THINKING AND WRITING

1. **FIRST RESPONSE.** How is your response to this poem affected by the fact that the speaker is female? Explain why this is or isn't a *carpe diem* poem.

2. Comment on the descriptive passages of "Last Night." Which images seem especially vivid to you? How do they contribute to the poem's meaning?

3. Explain how the poem's tone changes from beginning to end.

CONNECTIONS TO OTHER SELECTIONS

1. How does the speaker's description of intimacy compare with Herrick's and Marvell's?

2. Compare the speaker's voice in Olds's poem with the voice you imagine for the coy mistress in Marvell's poem.

3. **CRITICAL STRATEGIES.** Read the section on formalist criticism (pp. 666–68) in Chapter 26, "Critical Strategies for Reading," and compare the themes in Olds's poem and Philip Larkin's "A Study of Reading Habits" (p. 33) the way you think a feminist critic might analyze them.

POEMS FOR FURTHER STUDY

BARBARA HAMBY (B. 1929)

Ode to American English   *2004*

I was sitting in Paris one day missing English, American, really,
    with its pill-popping Hungarian goulash of everything
from Anglo-Saxon to Zulu, because British English
    is not the same, if the paperback dictionary I bought
at Brentano's on the Avenue de l'Opéra is any indication,   5
    too cultured by half. Oh, the English know their delphiniums,
but what about doowop, donuts, Dick Tracy, Tricky Dick?
    With their elegant Oxfordian accents, how could they
understand my yearning for the hotrod, hotdog, hot flash
    vocabulary of the U.S. of A., the fragmented fandango   10
of Dagwood's everyday flattening of Mr. Beasley on the sidewalk,
    fetuses floating on billboards, drive-by monster
hip-hop stereos shaking the windows of my dining room
    like a 7.5 earthquake, Ebonics, Spanglish, "you know"
used as a comma and period, the inability of 90% of the population   15
    to get the past perfect. *I have went, I have saw,*
I have tooken Jesus into my heart, the battle cry of the Bible Belt,
    but no one uses the King James anymore, only plain-speak
versions, in which Jesus, raising Lazarus from the dead, says,
    "Dude, wake up," and the L-man bolts up like a B-movie   20
mummy. "Whoa, I was toasted." Yes, ma'am, I miss the mongrel
    plenitude of American English, its fall-guy, rat-terrier,
dog-pound neologisms, the bomb of it all, the rushing River Jordan
    backwoods mutability of it, the low-rider, boom-box cruise of it,
from New Joisey to Ha-wah-ya with its sly dog, malasada-scarfing   25
    beach blanket lingo to the ubiquitous Valley Girl's
like-like stuttering, shopaholic rant. I miss its quotidian beauty,
    its querulous back-biting righteous indignation, its preening
rotgut flag-waving cowardice. *Suffering Succotash,* sputters
    Sylvester the Cat; *sine die,*° say the pork-bellied legislators   30
of the swamps and plains. I miss all those guys, their Tweety-bird
    resilience, their Doris Day optimism, the candid unguent
of utter unhappiness on every channel, the midnight televangelist
    euphoric stew, the junk mail-voice mail vernacular.

30 *sine die:* Latin for "without a day"; indefinitely.

On every *boulevard* and *rue* I miss the Tarzan cry of Johnny   35
    Weismueller, Johnny Cash, Johnny B. Goode,
and all the smart-talking, gum-snapping hard-girl dialogue,
    finger-popping x-rated street talk, sports babble,
Cheetoes, Cheerios, chili-dog diatribes. Yeah, I miss 'em all,
    sitting here on my sidewalk throne sipping champagne,   40
verses lined up like hearses, metaphors juking, nouns zipping
    in my head like Corvettes on dexedrine, French verbs
slitting my throat, yearning for James Dean to jump my curb.

CONSIDERATIONS FOR CRITICAL THINKING AND WRITING

1. **FIRST RESPONSE.** Consult the Glossary of Literary Terms (p. 745) for the definition of *ode*. How does this poem constitute an ode to American English?

2. Explain how the diction of this poem is vital to its meaning. What is it about American English that causes the speaker to admire it so much?

3. What kind of characterization of American life is presented by the varieties of English cataloged in the poem?

CONNECTIONS TO OTHER SELECTIONS

1. Discuss the strategic use of American phrasing in this poem and in Florence Cassen Mayers's "All-American Sestina" (p. 256), and compare the tone of each poem.

2. Write an essay comparing the themes of Hamby's poem and Lydia Huntley Sigourney's "Indian Names" (p. 645). Compare how the diction of each poem controls its tone.

THOMAS HARDY (1840–1928)

The Convergence of the Twain   1912

Lines on the Loss of the "Titanic" °

I

In a solitude of the sea
Deep from human vanity,
And the Pride of Life that planned her, stilly couches she.

II

Steel chambers, late the pyres
Of her salamandrine fires, °   5
Cold currents thrid, ° and turn to rhythmic tidal lyres.   *thread*

"Titanic": A luxurious ocean liner, reputed to be unsinkable, which sank after hitting an iceberg on its maiden voyage in 1912. Only a third of the 2,200 passengers survived. 5 *salamandrine fires:* Salamanders were, according to legend, able to survive fire; hence the ship's fires burned even though under water.

III

Over the mirrors meant
To glass the opulent
The sea-worm crawls — grotesque, slimed, dumb, indifferent.

IV

Jewels in joy designed 10
To ravish the sensuous mind
Lie lightless, all their sparkles bleared and black and blind.

V

Dim moon-eyed fishes near
Gaze at the gilded gear
And query: "What does this vaingloriousness down here?" 15

VI

Well: while was fashioning
This creature of cleaving wing,
The Immanent Will that stirs and urges everything

VII

Prepared a sinister mate
For her — so gaily great — 20
A Shape of Ice, for the time far and dissociate.

VIII

And as the smart ship grew
In stature, grace, and hue,
In shadowy silent distance grew the Iceberg too.

IX

Alien they seemed to be: 25
No mortal eye could see
The intimate welding of their later history,

X

Or sign that they were bent
By paths coincident
On being anon twin halves of one august event, 30

XI

Till the Spinner of the Years
Said "Now!" And each one hears,
And consummation comes, and jars two hemispheres.

CONSIDERATIONS FOR CRITICAL THINKING AND WRITING

1. **FIRST RESPONSE.** Describe a contemporary disaster comparable to the sinking of the *Titanic*. How was your response to it similar to or different from the speaker's response to the fate of the *Titanic*?

2. How do the words used to describe the ship in this poem reveal the speaker's attitude toward the *Titanic*?

3. The diction of the poem suggests that the *Titanic* and the iceberg participate in something like an arranged marriage. What specific words imply this?

4. Who or what causes the disaster? Does the speaker assign responsibility?

DAVID R. SLAVITT (B. 1935)

Titanic   *1983*

Who does not love the *Titanic*?
If they sold passage tomorrow for that same crossing,
who would not buy?

To go down . . . We all go down, mostly
alone. But with crowds of people, friends, servants,   5
well fed, with music, with lights! Ah!

And the world, shocked, mourns, as it ought to do
and almost never does. There will be the books and movies
to remind our grandchildren who we were
and how we died, and give them a good cry.   10

Not so bad, after all. The cold
water is anesthetic and very quick.
The cries on all sides must be a comfort.

We all go: only a few, first-class.

CONSIDERATIONS FOR CRITICAL THINKING AND WRITING

1. **FIRST RESPONSE.** What, according to the speaker in this poem, is so compelling about the *Titanic*? Do you agree?

2. Discuss the speaker's tone. Is "Titanic" merely a sarcastic poem?

3. What is the effect of the poem's final line? What emotions does it elicit?

1. How does "Titanic" differ in its attitude toward opulence from "The Convergence of the Twain" (p. 86)?

2. Which poem, "Titanic" or "The Convergence of the Twain," is more emotionally satisfying to you? Explain why.

3. Compare the speakers' tones in "Titanic" and "The Convergence of the Twain."

4. CRITICAL STRATEGIES. Read the section on Marxist criticism (pp. 673–74) in Chapter 26, "Critical Strategies for Reading," and analyze the attitudes toward opulence that are manifested in the two poems.

PETER MEINKE (B. 1932)

(Untitled)   *1991*

this is a poem to my son Peter
whom I have hurt a thousand times
whose large and vulnerable eyes
have glazed in pain at my ragings
thin wrists and fingers hung   5
boneless in despair, pale freckled back
bent in defeat, pillow soaked
by my failure to understand.
I have scarred through weakness
and impatience your frail confidence forever   10
because when I needed to strike
you were there to be hurt and because
I thought you knew
you were beautiful and fair
your bright eyes and hair   15
but now I see that no one knows that
about himself, but must be told
and retold until it takes hold
because I think anything can be killed
after a while, especially beauty   20
so I write this for life, for love, for
you, my oldest son Peter, age 10,
going on 11.

CONSIDERATIONS FOR CRITICAL THINKING AND WRITING

1. FIRST RESPONSE. How would you characterize the speaker? The son is described physically but not the father. What sort of physical description do you think would reveal the father?

2. Why do you think the poem ends with "going on 11"? Would it have made any difference to the tone or meaning if the poem ended at line 22?

3. CREATIVE RESPONSE. Provide at least two titles for this untitled work and explain your rationale for each.

JOANNE DIAZ (B. 1972)

On My Father's Loss of Hearing   2006

Courtesy of Jason Reblando.

> *I'd like to see more poems treat the deaf*
> *as being abled differently, not lost*
> *or missing something, weakened, deficient.*
> *   —from a listserv for the deaf*

Abled differently—so vague compared
with deaf, obtuse but true to history,
from deave: to deafen, stun, amaze with noise.
Perhaps that's what we've done—amazed
         him with
our sorrows and complaints, the stupid jabs,
the loneliness of boredom in the house,

our wants so foreign to his own. What else
is there but loss? He's lost the humor of
sarcastic jokes, the snarky dialogue
of British films eludes him, phone calls   10
cast him adrift in that cochlear maze
that thrums and bristles even now, when
it doesn't have to: an unnecessary kind
of elegance, the vestige of a sense

no longer obligated to transmit   15
the crack of thawing ice that fills the yard's
wide dip in winter, or the scrape of his
dull rake in spring, its prongs' vibration thrilled
by grass and peat moss. Imagine his desires
released like saffron pistils in the wind;   20
mark their trace against the cords of wood

he spent the summer splitting. See his quiet
flicker like a film, a Super-8
projected on the wall, and all of us
there, laughing on the porch without a sound.   25
No noisome cruelty, no baffled rage,
no aging children sullen in their lack.
Love hurts much less in this serenity.

CONSIDERATIONS FOR CRITICAL THINKING AND WRITING

1. **FIRST RESPONSE.** Why does the speaker prefer the word *deaf* to the phrase "abled differently" as a means of describing her father? Which description do you prefer? Why?

2. Explain how sound and silence move through the poem from beginning to end.

3. Choose a single word from each stanza that strikes you as particularly effective, and explain why you think Diaz chose it over other possibilities.

4. What do you make of the poem's final line? How does it relate to the tone of the rest of the poem?

CONNECTION TO ANOTHER SELECTION

1. Discuss the relationship between love and pain in "On My Father's Loss of Hearing" and in the Meinke poem that precedes it.

SHARON OLDS (B. 1942)

Sex without Love   *1984*

How do they do it, the ones who make love
without love? Beautiful as dancers,
gliding over each other like ice skaters
over the ice, fingers hooked
inside each other's bodies, faces   5
red as steak, wine, wet as the
children at birth whose mothers are going to
give them away. How do they come to the
come to the   come to the   God   come to the
still waters, and not love   10
the one who came there with them, light
rising slowly as steam off their joined
skin? These are the true religious,
the purists, the pros, the ones who will not
accept a false Messiah, love the   15
priest instead of the God. They do not
mistake the lover for their own pleasure,
they are like great runners: they know they are alone
with the road surface, the cold, the wind,
the fit of their shoes, their over-all cardio-   20
vascular health — just factors, like the partner
in the bed, and not the truth, which is the
single body alone in the universe
against its own best time.

CONSIDERATIONS FOR CRITICAL THINKING AND WRITING

1. **FIRST RESPONSE.** What is the nature of the question asked by the speaker in the poem's first two lines? What is being asked here?
2. What is the effect of describing the lovers as athletes? How do these descriptions and phrases reveal the speaker's tone toward the lovers?
3. To what extent does the title suggest the central meaning of this poem? Try to compose some alternative titles that are equally descriptive.

CONNECTION TO ANOTHER SELECTION

1. How does the treatment of sex and love in this poem compare with that in Olds's "Last Night" (p. 84)?

MARY OLIVER (B. 1935)

Oxygen

2005

Everything needs it: bone, muscles, and even,
while it calls the earth its home, the soul.
So the merciful, noisy machine

stands in our house working away in its
lung-like voice. I hear it as I kneel   5
before the fire, stirring with a

stick of iron, letting the logs
lie more loosely. You, in the upstairs room,
are in your usual position, leaning on your

right shoulder which aches   10
all day. You are breathing
patiently; it is a

beautiful sound. It is
your life, which is so close
to my own that I would not know   15

where to drop the knife of
separation. And what does this have to do
with love, except

everything? Now the fire rises
and offers a dozen, singing, deep-red   20
roses of flame. Then it settles

to quietude, or maybe gratitude, as it feeds
as we all do, as we must, upon the invisible gift:
our purest, sweet necessity: the air.

CONSIDERATIONS FOR CRITICAL THINKING AND WRITING

1. **FIRST RESPONSE.** Though this is a poem about someone who is seriously ill,
   its tone isn't sad. Why not?
2. What is the connection between the loved one's breathing and the fire?
   How does the speaker's choice of words to describe each connect them?
3. In what sense might this celebration of oxygen be considered a love poem?

CATHY SONG (B. 1955)

The Youngest Daughter

1983

The sky has been dark
for many years.
My skin has become as damp
and pale as rice paper

and feels the way   5
mother's used to before the drying sun
parched it out there in the fields.

    Lately, when I touch myself,
my hands react as if
I had just touched something   10
hot enough to burn.
My skin, aspirin-colored,
tingles with migraine. Mother
has been massaging the left side of my face
especially in the evenings   15
when it flares up.

This morning
her breathing was graveled,
her voice gruff with affection
when I took her into the bath.   20
She was in good humor,
making jokes about her great breasts,
floating in the milky water
like two walruses,
flaccid and whiskered around the nipples.   25
I scrubbed them with a sour taste
in my mouth, thinking:
six children and an old man
have sucked from these brown nipples.

I was almost tender   30
when I came to the blue bruises
that freckle her body,
places where she has been injecting insulin
for thirty years, ever since
I can remember. I soaped her slowly,   35
she sighed deeply, her eyes closed.

In the afternoons
when she has rested,
she prepares our ritual of tea and rice,
garnished with a shred of gingered fish,   40
a slice of pickled turnip
a token for my white body.
We eat in the familiar silence.
She knows I am not to be trusted,
even now planning my escape.   45
As I toast to her health
with the tea she has poured,
a thousand cranes curtain the window,
fly up in a sudden breeze.

CONSIDERATIONS FOR CRITICAL THINKING AND WRITING

1. **FIRST RESPONSE.** Though the speaker is the youngest daughter in the family, how old do you think she is based on the description of her in the poem? What, specifically, makes you think so?

2. How would you characterize the relationship between mother and daughter? How are lines 44–45 ("She knows I am not to be trusted, / even now planning my escape") particularly revealing of the nature of the relationship?

3. Interpret the final four lines of the poem. Why do you think it ends with this image?

JOHN KEATS (1795–1821)

Ode on a Grecian Urn

1819

I

Thou still unravished bride of quietness,
   Thou foster-child of silence and slow time,
Sylvan° historian, who canst thus express
   A flowery tale more sweetly than our rhyme:
What leaf-fringed legend haunts about thy shape   5
   Of deities or mortals, or of both,
      In Tempe or the dales of Arcady?°
What men or gods are these? What maidens loath?
   What mad pursuit? What struggle to escape?
      What pipes and timbrels? What wild ecstasy?   10

II

Heard melodies are sweet, but those unheard
   Are sweeter; therefore, ye soft pipes, play on;
Not to the sensual ear, but, more endeared,
   Pipe to the spirit ditties of no tone:
Fair youth, beneath the trees, thou canst not leave   15
   Thy song, nor ever can those trees be bare;
      Bold Lover, never, never canst thou kiss,
Though winning near the goal — yet, do not grieve;
   She cannot fade, though thou hast not thy bliss,
      For ever wilt thou love, and she be fair!   20

III

Ah, happy, happy boughs! that cannot shed
   Your leaves, nor ever bid the Spring adieu;

Explore contexts for John Keats on *LiterActive*.

---

3 *Sylvan:* Rustic. The urn is decorated with a forest scene.   7 *Tempe, Arcady:* Beautiful rural valleys in Greece.

And, happy melodist, unwearièd,
    For ever piping songs for ever new;
More happy love! more happy, happy love!   25
    For ever warm and still to be enjoyed,
        For ever panting, and for ever young;
All breathing human passion far above,
    That leaves a heart high-sorrowful and cloyed,
        A burning forehead, and a parching tongue.   30

IV

Who are these coming to the sacrifice?
    To what green altar, O mysterious priest,
Lead'st thou that heifer lowing at the skies,
    And all her silken flanks with garlands drest?
What little town by river or sea shore,   35
    Or mountain-built with peaceful citadel,
        Is emptied of this folk, this pious morn?
And, little town, thy streets for evermore
    Will silent be; and not a soul to tell
        Why thou art desolate, can e'er return.   40

V

O Attic° shape! Fair attitude! with brede°
    Of marble men and maidens overwrought,
With forest branches and the trodden weed;
    Thou, silent form, dost tease us out of thought
As doth eternity: Cold Pastoral!   45
    When old age shall this generation waste,
        Thou shalt remain, in midst of other woe
Than ours, a friend to man, to whom thou say'st,
    Beauty is truth, truth beauty — that is all
        Ye know on earth, and all ye need to know.   50

41 *Attic:* Possessing classic Athenian simplicity; *brede:* Design.

Considerations for Critical Thinking and Writing

1. **FIRST RESPONSE.** What does the speaker's diction reveal about his attitude toward the urn in this ode? Does his view develop or change?

2. How is the happiness in stanza 3 related to the assertion in lines 11–12 that "Heard melodies are sweet, but those unheard / Are sweeter"?

3. What is the difference between the world depicted on the urn and the speaker's world?

4. What do lines 49 and 50 suggest about the relation of art to life? Why is the urn described as a "Cold Pastoral" (line 45)?

5. Which world does the speaker seem to prefer, the urn's or his own?

6. Describe the overall tone of the poem.

CONNECTIONS TO OTHER SELECTIONS

1. Write an essay comparing the view of time in this ode with that in Marvell's "To His Coy Mistress" (p. 80). Pay particular attention to the connotative language in each poem.

2. Compare the tone and attitude toward life in this ode with those in John Keats's "To Autumn" (p. 127).

GWENDOLYN BROOKS (1917–2000)

We Real Cool

1960

The Pool Players.
Seven at the Golden Shovel.

Explore contexts
for Gwendolyn Brooks
on *LiterActive*.

We real cool. We
Left school. We

Lurk late. We
Strike straight. We

Sing sin. We
Thin gin. We

Jazz June. We
Die soon.

CONSIDERATIONS FOR CRITICAL THINKING AND WRITING

1. **FIRST RESPONSE.** How does the speech of the pool players in this poem help to characterize them? What is the effect of the pronouns coming at the ends of the lines? How would the poem sound if the pronouns came at the beginnings of lines?

2. What is the author's attitude toward the players? Is there a change in tone in the last line?

3. How is the pool hall's name related to the rest of the poem and its theme?

JOAN MURRAY (B. 1945)

We Old Dudes

2006

We old dudes. We
White shoes. We

Golf ball. We
Eat mall. We

Soak teeth. We
Palm Beach; We

Vote red. We
Soon dead.

CONSIDERATIONS FOR CRITICAL THINKING AND WRITING

1. **FIRST RESPONSE.** Consider the poem's humor. To what extent does it make a serious point?

2. What does the reference to Palm Beach tell you about these "old dudes"?

3. **CREATIVE RESPONSE.** Write a poem similar in style that characterizes your life as a student.

CONNECTION TO ANOTHER SELECTION

1. Compare the themes of "We Old Dudes" and Brooks's "We Real Cool." How do the two poems speak to each other?

ALICE JONES (B. 1949)

The Larynx   *1993*

Under the epiglottic flap
the long-ringed tube sinks
its shaft down to the bronchial
fork, divides from two
to four then infinite branches,   5
each ending finally in a clump
of transparent sacs knit
with small vessels into a mesh
that sponge-like soaks up breath
and gives it off with a push   10
from the diaphragm's muscular wall,
forces wind out of the lungs'
wide tree, up through this organ's
single pipe, through the puzzle
box of gristle, where resonant   15
plates of cartilage fold
into shield, horns, bows,
bound by odd half-spirals
of muscles that modulate air
as it rises through this empty place   20
at our core, where lip-like
folds stretch across the vestibule,
small and tough, they flutter,
bend like birds' wings finding
just the right angle to stay   25
airborne; here the cords arch
in the hollow of this ancient instrument,
curve and vibrate to make a song.

CONSIDERATIONS FOR CRITICAL THINKING AND WRITING

1. **FIRST RESPONSE.** What is the effect of having this poem written as one long sentence? How does the length of the sentence contribute to the poem's meaning?

2. Make a list of words and phrases from the poem that strike you as scientific, and compare those with a list of words that seem poetic. How do they compete or complement each other in terms of how they affect your reading?

3. Comment on the final three lines. How would your interpretation of this poem change if it ended before the semicolon in line 26?

CONNECTION TO ANOTHER SELECTION

1. Compare the diction and the ending in "The Larynx" with those of "The Foot" (p. 226), another poem by Jones.

LOUIS SIMPSON (B. 1923)

In the Suburbs   *1963*

There's no way out.
You were born to waste your life.
You were born to this middleclass life

As others before you
Were born to walk in procession
To the temple, singing.

CONSIDERATIONS FOR CRITICAL THINKING AND WRITING

1. **FIRST RESPONSE.** Is the title of this poem especially significant? What images does it conjure up for you?

2. What does the repetition in lines 2–3 suggest?

3. Discuss the possible connotative meanings of lines 5 and 6. Who are the "others before you"?

CONNECTION TO ANOTHER SELECTION

1. Write an essay on suburban life based on this poem and John Ciardi's "Suburban" (p. 525).

HERBERT LOMAS (B. 1924)

The Fly's Poem about Emily°   *2008*

Beelzebub° sent me.
I ate their meat.
I was the fly on
the dead poet's feet.

The Fly's Poem about Emily: See Emily Dickinson's poem "I heard a Fly buzz — when I died —"
(p. 335).   1 *Beelzebub:* An ancient name for a devil or demon; also called "Lord of the Flies."

I've a good tube   5
for the scents of food.
I love life
and find death good.

My little head
is as black as my tube,   10
but when she died
I buzzed and survived.

Later I ate her.
My buzz is no bell,
but I'm remembered on earth   15
as well as in hell,

and I was eating her sweat
when God received her.

CONSIDERATIONS FOR CRITICAL THINKING AND WRITING

1. **FIRST RESPONSE.** Explain why you think it is essential (or not) to read Dickinson's poem in order to appreciate this poem.
2. Characterize the fly by the tone of its language. What kinds of emotions does the language produce in you?
3. Consider whether there is any humor in the poem. Or is it all grim?

CONNECTION TO ANOTHER SELECTION

1. How does this poem, read alongside Emily Dickinson's "I heard a Fly buzz — when I died —" (p. 335), create a kind of dialogue about the nature of death?

A NOTE ON READING TRANSLATIONS

Sometimes translation can inadvertently be a comic business. Consider, for example, the discovery made by John Steinbeck's wife, Elaine, when in a Yokohama bookstore she asked for a copy of her husband's famous novel *The Grapes of Wrath* and learned that it had been translated into Japanese as *Angry Raisins.* Close but no cigar (perhaps translated as: Nearby, yet no smoke). As amusing as that *Angry Raisins* title is, it teaches an important lesson about the significance of a poet's or a translator's choices when crafting a poem: a powerful piece moves us through diction and tone, both built word by careful word. Translations are frequently regarded as merely vehicular, a way to arrive at the original work. It is, of course, the original work — its spirit, style, and meaning — that most readers expect to find in a translation. Even so, it is important to understand that a translation is *by nature* different from the original — and that despite that difference, a fine translation can be an important part of the journey and become part of the literary landscape itself.

Reading a translation of a poem is not the same as reading the original, but neither is watching two different performances of *Hamlet*. The translator provides a reading of the poem in much the same way that a director shapes the play. Each interprets the text from a unique perspective.

Basically, there are two distinct approaches to translation: literal translations and adaptations. A literal translation sets out to create a word-for-word equivalent that is absolutely faithful to the original. As simple and direct as this method may sound, literal translations are nearly impossible over extended passages because of the structural differences between languages. Moreover, the meaning of a single word in one language may not exist in another language, or it may require a phrase, clause, or entire sentence to capture its implications. Adaptations of works offer broader, more open-ended approaches to translation. Unlike a literal translation, an adaptation moves beyond denotative meanings in an attempt to capture the spirit of a work so that its idioms, dialects, slang, and other conventions are re-created in the language of the translation.

The question we ask of an adaptation should not be "Is this exactly how the original reads?" Instead, we ask, "Is this an insightful, graceful rendering worth reading?" To translate poetry it is not enough to know the language of the original; it is also necessary that the translator be a poet. A translated poem is more than a collation of decisions based on dictionaries and grammars; it must also be poetry. However undefinable poetry may be, it is unmistakable in its intense use of language. Poems are not merely translated; they are savored.

Three Translations of a Poem by Sappho

Sappho, born about 630 B.C. and a native of the Greek island of Lesbos, is the author of a hymn to Aphrodite, the goddess of love and beauty in Greek myth. The three translations that follow suggest how widely translations can differ from one another. The first, by Henry T. Wharton, is intended to be a literal prose translation of the original Greek.

SAPPHO (CA. 630 B.C.–CA. 570 B.C.)

Immortal Aphrodite of the broidered throne *date unknown*

TRANSLATED BY HENRY T. WHARTON (1885)

Immortal Aphrodite of the broidered throne, daughter of Zeus, weaver of wiles, I pray thee break not my spirit with anguish and distress, O Queen. But come hither, if ever before thou

© Bettmann/CORBIS.

didst hear my voice afar, and listen, and leaving thy father's golden house camest with chariot yoked, and fair fleet sparrows drew thee, flapping fast their wings around the dark earth, from heaven through mid sky. Quickly arrived they; and thou, blessed one, smiling with immortal countenance, didst ask What now is befallen me, and Why now I call, and What I in my mad heart most desire to see. "What Beauty now wouldst thou draw to love thee? Who wrongs thee, Sappho? For even if she flies she shall soon follow, and if she rejects gifts shall yet give, and if she loves not shall soon love, however loth." Come, I pray thee, now too, and release me from cruel cares; and all that my heart desires to accomplish, accomplish thou, and be thyself my ally.

Beautiful-throned, immortal Aphrodite

TRANSLATED BY THOMAS WENTWORTH HIGGINSON (1871)

Beautiful-throned, immortal Aphrodite,
Daughter of Zeus, beguiler, I implore thee,
Weigh me not down with weariness and anguish
    O Thou most holy!

Come to me now, if ever thou in kindness   5
Hearkenedst my words, — and often hast thou hearkened —
Heeding, and coming from the mansions golden
    Of thy great Father,

Yoking thy chariot, borne by the most lovely
Consecrated birds, with dusky-tinted pinions,   10
Waving swift wings from utmost heights of heaven
    Through the mid-ether;

Swiftly they vanished, leaving thee, O goddess,
Smiling, with face immortal in its beauty,
Asking why I grieved, and why in utter longing   15
    I had dared call thee;

Asking what I sought, thus hopeless in desiring,
Wildered in brain, and spreading nets of passion —
Alas, for whom? and saidst thou, "Who has harmed thee?
    "O my poor Sappho!   20

"Though now he flies, ere long he shall pursue thee;
"Fearing thy gifts, he too in turn shall bring them;
"Loveless to-day, to-morrow he shall woo thee,
    "Though thou shouldst spurn him."

Thus seek me now, O holy Aphrodite!   25
Save me from anguish; give me all I ask for,
Gifts at thy hand; and thine shall be the glory,
    Sacred protector!

Prayer to my lady of Paphos

TRANSLATED BY MARY BARNARD (1958)

Dapple-throned Aphrodite,
eternal daughter of God,
snare-knitter! Don't, I beg you,

cow my heart with grief! Come,
as once when you heard my far-   5
off cry and, listening, stepped

from your father's house to your
gold car, to yoke the pair whose
beautiful thick-feathered wings

oaring down mid-air from heaven   10
carried you to light swiftly
on dark earth; then, blissful one,

smiling your immortal smile
you asked, What ailed me now that
made me call you again? What   15

was it that my distracted
heart most wanted? "Whom has
Persuasion to bring round now

"to your love? Who, Sappho, is
unfair to you? For, let her   20
run, she will soon run after;

"if she won't accept gifts, she
will one day give them; and if
she won't love you — she soon will

"love, although unwillingly . . . "   25
If ever — come now! Relieve
this intolerable pain!

What my heart most hopes will
happen, make happen; you your-
self join forces on my side!   30

CONSIDERATIONS FOR CRITICAL THINKING AND WRITING

1. **FIRST RESPONSE.** Try rewriting Wharton's prose version in contemporary language. How does your prose version differ in tone from Wharton's?

2. Explain which translation seems closest to Wharton's prose version.

3. Discuss the images and metaphors in Higginson's and Barnard's versions. Which version is more appealing to you? Explain why.

4. Explain which version seems to you to be the most contemporary in its use of language.

Two Translations of a Poem by Pablo Neruda

The following poem by the Chilean Nobel Prize–winner Pablo Neruda is in its original Spanish. By using a substantial Spanish/English dictionary, you might be able to translate it into English even if you are unfamiliar with Spanish. Following the poem are two translations that offer some subtle and intriguing differences in their approaches to the poem.

© Luis Poirot.

PABLO NERUDA (1904–1973)

Verbo   1968

Voy a arrugar esta palabra,
voy a torcerla,
sí,
es demasiado lisa,
es como si un gran perro o un gran río   5
le hubíera repasado lengua o agua
durante muchos años.

Quiero que en la palabra
se vea la aspereza,
la sal ferruginosa,   10
la fuerza desdentada
de la tierra,
la sangre
de los que hablaron y de los que no hablaron.

Quiero ver la sed   15
adentro de las sílabas:
quiero tocar el fuego
en el sonido:
quiero sentir la oscuridad
del grito. Quiero   20
palabras ásperas
como piedras vírgenes.

Word

TRANSLATED BY BEN BELITT (1974)

I'm going to crumple this word,
to twist it,
yes,
it's too slick
like a big dog or a river   5
had been lapping it down with its tongue, or water
had worn it away with the years.

I want gravel
to show in the word,
the ferruginous salt,   10
the gap-toothed power
of the soil.
There must be a blood-letting
for talker and non-talker alike.

I want to see thirst   15
in the syllables,
touch fire
in the sound;
feel through the dark
for the scream. Let   20
my words be acrid
as virginal stone.

Word

TRANSLATED BY KRISTIN LINKLATER (1992)

I'm going to crumple this word,
I'm going to twist it,
yes,
it's too smooth,
it's as though a big dog or a big river   5
had been licking it over and over with tongue or water
for many years.

I want the word
to reveal the roughness,
the ferruginous salt,   10
the toothless strength
of the earth,
the blood
of those who talked and of those who did not talk.

I want to see the thirst   15
inside the syllables,

I want to touch the fire
in the sound:
I want to feel the darkness
of the scream. I want   20
rough words,
like virgin rocks.

CONSIDERATIONS FOR CRITICAL THINKING AND WRITING

1. **FIRST RESPONSE.** Discuss whether or not the two translations convey the same essential themes.

2. What are the major differences that you see in diction, syntax, and tone between the translations?

3. Which translation do you think is the most effective? Explain why you prefer one translation over another.

Web Research the poets in this chapter on LitLinks at bedfordstmartins.com/ rewritinglit.

4

Images

© Daniel J. Harper.

Between my finger and my thumb
The squat pen rests.
I'll dig with it.
— SEAMUS HEANEY

POETRY'S APPEAL TO THE SENSES

A poet, to borrow a phrase from Henry James, is one on whom nothing is lost. Poets take in the world and give us impressions of what they experience through images. An *image* is language that addresses the senses. The most common images in poetry are visual; they provide verbal pictures of the poets' encounters — real or imagined — with the world. But poets also create images that appeal to our other senses. Li Ho arouses several senses in "A Beautiful Girl Combs Her Hair" (p. 53):

Awake at dawn
she's dreaming
by cool silk curtains

fragrance of spilling hair
half sandalwood, half aloes

windlass creaking at the well
singing jade

5

These vivid images deftly blend textures, fragrances, and sounds that tease out the sensuousness of the moment. Images give us the physical world to experience in our imaginations. Some poems, like the following one, are written to do just that; they make no comment about what they describe.

 Explore the poetic element in this chapter on *LiterActive* or at bedfordstmartins.com/ rewritinglit.

WILLIAM CARLOS WILLIAMS (1883–1963)

Poem   *1934*

As the cat
climbed over
the top of

the jamcloset
first the right   5
forefoot

carefully
then the hind
stepped down

into the pit of   10
the empty
flowerpot

This poem defies paraphrase because it is all an image of agile movement. No statement is made about the movement; the title, "Poem" — really no title — signals Williams's refusal to comment on the movements. To impose a meaning on the poem, we'd probably have to knock over the flowerpot.

We experience the image in Williams's "Poem" more clearly because of how the sentence is organized into lines and groups of lines, or stanzas. Consider how differently the sentence is read if it is arranged as prose:

> As the cat climbed over the top of the jamcloset, first the right forefoot carefully then the hind stepped down into the pit of the empty flowerpot.

The poem's line and stanza division transforms what is essentially an awkward prose sentence into a rhythmic verbal picture. Especially when the poem is read aloud, this line and stanza division allows us to feel the image we see. Even the lack of a period at the end suggests that the cat is only pausing.

Images frequently do more than offer only sensory impressions, however. They also convey emotions and moods, as in the following poem.

Jeannette Barnes (b. 1956)

Battle-Piece   *1999*

Confederate monument, Ocean Pond, Olustee, Florida, 1864

Picknickers sojourn here an hour,
get their fill, get gone.
Seldom, they quickstep as far downhill
as this bivouac; they miss sting, snap,

grit in clenched teeth, carbine, cartridge,   5
cap, *hurrah boys.* Cannon-cracks
the peal, the clap of doom.

Into the billows, white, filthy,
choked by smoke, Clem, Eustace, Willy —
it would be useless to name names or call them all.   10

Anyway, that's done already. Every fall
sons of sons and reverent veterans' wives
lay wreaths, a prize of plastic daisies,

everlasting. Nobody calls this lazy.
It's August, and it's late, it's afternoon,   15
heat-mist glistens on slick granite, sun

fingers through sleek pines, their edges cropped
like the clipped elegant grass. It is a shock
to see a caisson blown

to flinders; a horse shrieks,   20
the mortar-shell zooms, spiral-
ripping tender belly. Oh, yes, here

are raked paths, cindered, sweet trees
and cool water. That whimper
you do not hear now was the doves,   25
spooning. Evening calls you all, eager

as spruce-gum-chewing, apple-filching boys
to pull one long last gulp of switchel
as if, now, somebody's sons had almost done

haying. Keen to victual, nearly home, feature the sharp   30
surprise when, smooth as oiled stone
stroking the clean edge of a scythe, these boys achieved
each his marble pillow, astonished by the sky.

Considerations for Critical Thinking and Writing

1. **FIRST RESPONSE.** Contrast the images used to describe the present moment
    at the battle site with the images used to describe the actual battle.
2. Describe the speaker's tone. What do the images reveal about the speaker's
    emotions?
3. Analyze the diction and images of the final stanza. What makes it so powerful?

What mood is established in this next poem's view of Civil War troops moving across a river?

Explore contexts for Walt Whitman on *LiterActive*.

WALT WHITMAN (1819–1892)

Cavalry Crossing a Ford   1865

A line in long array where they wind betwixt green islands,
They take a serpentine course, their arms flash in the sun — hark to the
    musical clank,
Behold the silvery river, in it the splashing horses loitering stop to drink,
Behold the brown-faced men, each group, each person, a picture, the
    negligent rest on the saddles,
Some emerge on the opposite bank, others are just entering the ford — while,
Scarlet and blue and snowy white,
The guidon flags flutter gaily in the wind.

CONSIDERATIONS FOR CRITICAL THINKING AND WRITING

1. **FIRST RESPONSE.** Do the colors and sounds establish the mood of this poem? What *is* the mood?
2. How would the poem's mood have been changed if Whitman had used "look" or "see" instead of "behold" (lines 3–4)?
3. Where is the speaker as he observes this troop movement?
4. Does "serpentine" in line 2 have an evil connotation in this poem? Explain your answer.

Whitman seems to capture momentarily all of the troop's actions, and through carefully chosen, suggestive details — really very few — he succeeds in making "each group, each person, a picture." Specific details, even when few are provided, give us the impression that we see the entire picture; it is as if those are the details we would remember if we had viewed the scene ourselves. Notice, too, that the movement of the "line in long array" is emphasized by the continuous winding syntax of the poem's lengthy lines.

Movement is also central to the next poem, in which action and motion are created through carefully chosen verbs.

DAVID SOLWAY (B. 1941)

Windsurfing   1993

It rides upon the wrinkled hide
of water, like the upturned hull
of a small canoe or kayak
waiting to be righted — yet its law

is opposite to that of boats,   5
it floats upon its breastbone and
brings whatever spine there is to light.
A thin shaft is slotted into place.
Then a puffed right-angle of wind
pushes it forward, out into the bay,   10
where suddenly it glitters into speed,
tilts, knifes up, and for the moment's
nothing but a slim projectile
of cambered fiberglass,
peeling the crests.   15

                The man's
clamped to the mast, taut as a guywire.
Part of the sleek apparatus
he controls, immaculate nerve
of balance, plunge and curvet,   20
he clinches all component movements
into single motion.
It bucks, stalls, shudders, yaws, and dips
its hissing sides beneath the surface
that sustains it, tensing   25
into muscle that nude ellipse
of lunging appetite and power.

And now the mechanism's wholly
dolphin, springing toward its prey
of spume and beaded sunlight,   30
tossing spray, and hits the vertex
of the wide, salt glare of distance,
and reverses.

                Back it comes through
a screen of particles,   35
scalloped out of water, shimmer
and reflection, the wind snapping
and lashing it homeward,
shearing the curve of the wave,
breaking the spell of the caught breath   40
and articulate play of sinew, to enter
the haven of the breakwater
and settle in a rush of silence.

Now the crossing drifts
in the husk of its wake   45
and nothing's the same again
as, gliding elegantly on a film of water,
the man guides
his brash, obedient legend
into shore.   50

CONSIDERATIONS FOR CRITICAL THINKING AND WRITING

1. **FIRST RESPONSE.** Draw a circle around the verbs that seem especially effective in conveying a strong sense of motion, and explain why they are effective.

2. How is the man made to seem to be one with his board and sail?

3. How does the rhythm of the poem change beginning with line 45?

CONNECTIONS TO OTHER SELECTIONS

1. Consider the effects of the images in "Windsurfing" and Li Ho's "A Beautiful Girl Combs Her Hair" (p. 53). In an essay, explain how these images elicit the emotional responses they do.

2. Compare the descriptions in "Windsurfing" and Elizabeth Bishop's "The Fish" (p. 31). How does each poet appeal to your senses to describe windsurfing and fishing?

"Windsurfing" is awash with images of speed, fluidity, and power. Even the calming aftermath of the breakwater is described as a "rush of silence," adding to the sense of motion that is detailed and expanded throughout the poem.

Poets choose details the way they choose the words to present those details: only telling ones will do. Consider the images Theodore Roethke uses in "Root Cellar."

 Explore contexts for Theodore Roethke on *LiterActive*.

THEODORE ROETHKE (1908–1963)

Root Cellar   1948

Nothing would sleep in that cellar, dank as a ditch,
Bulbs broke out of boxes hunting for chinks in the dark,
Shoots dangled and drooped,
Lolling obscenely from mildewed crates,
Hung down long yellow evil necks, like tropical snakes.   5
And what a congress of stinks!
Roots ripe as old bait,
Pulpy stems, rank, silo-rich,
Leaf-mold, manure, lime, piled against slippery planks.
Nothing would give up life: 10
Even the dirt kept breathing a small breath.

CONSIDERATIONS FOR CRITICAL THINKING AND WRITING

1. **FIRST RESPONSE.** Explain why you think this is a positive or negative rendition of a root cellar.

2. What senses are engaged by the images in this poem? Is the poem simply a series of sensations, or do the detailed images make some kind of point about the root cellar?

3. What controls the choice of details in the poem? Why isn't there, for example, a rusty shovel leaning against a dirt wall or a worn gardener's glove atop one of the crates?

4. Look up *congress* in a dictionary for its denotative meanings. Explain why "congress of stinks" (line 6) is especially appropriate given the nature of the rest of the poem's imagery.

5. What single line in the poem suggests a theme?

6. **CREATIVE RESPONSE**. Try writing a poem of ten lines or so that consists of a series of evocative images that creates a strong impression about something you know well.

The tone of the images and mood of the speaker are consistent in Roethke's "Root Cellar." In Matthew Arnold's "Dover Beach," however, they shift as the theme is developed.

MATTHEW ARNOLD (1822–1888)

Dover Beach   *1867*

The sea is calm tonight.
The tide is full, the moon lies fair
Upon the straits; — on the French coast the light
Gleams and is gone; the cliffs of England stand,
Glimmering and vast, out in the tranquil bay.   5
Come to the window, sweet is the night-air!
Only, from the long line of spray
Where the sea meets the moon-blanched land,
Listen! you hear the grating roar
Of pebbles which the waves draw back, and fling,   10
At their return, up the high strand,
Begin, and cease, and then again begin,
With tremulous cadence slow, and bring
The eternal note of sadness in.

Sophocles long ago   15
Heard it on the Aegean, and it brought
Into his mind the turbid ebb and flow
Of human misery;° we
Find also in the sound a thought,
Hearing it by this distant northern sea.   20

The Sea of Faith
Was once, too, at the full, and round earth's shore

15-18 *Sophocles . . . misery:* In *Antigone* (lines 656–77), Sophocles likens the disasters that beset the house of Oedipus to a "mounting tide."

Lay like the folds of a bright girdle furled.
But now I only hear
Its melancholy, long, withdrawing roar,   25
Retreating, to the breath
Of the night-wind, down the vast edges drear
And naked shingles° of the world.   *pebble beaches*

Ah, love, let us be true
To one another! for the world, which seems   30
To lie before us like a land of dreams,
So various, so beautiful, so new,
Hath really neither joy, nor love, nor light,
Nor certitude, nor peace, nor help for pain;
And we are here as on a darkling plain   35
Swept with confused alarms of struggle and flight,
Where ignorant armies clash by night.

Considerations for Critical Thinking and Writing

1. **FIRST RESPONSE.** Discuss what you consider to be this poem's central point. How do the speaker's descriptions of the ocean work toward making that point?

2. Contrast the images in lines 4–8 and 9–13. How do they reveal the speaker's mood? To whom is he speaking?

3. What is the cause of the "sadness" in line 14? What is the speaker's response to the ebbing "Sea of Faith"? Is there anything to replace his sense of loss?

4. What details of the beach seem related to the ideas in the poem? How is the sea used differently in lines 1–14 and 21–28?

5. Describe the differences in tone between lines 1–8 and 35–37. What has caused the change?

6. **CRITICAL STRATEGIES.** Read the section on mythological strategies (pp. 677–80) in Chapter 26, "Critical Strategies for Reading," and discuss how you think a mythological critic might make use of the allusion to Sophocles in this poem.

Connections to Other Selections

1. Explain how the images in Wilfred Owen's "Dulce et Decorum Est" (p. 121) develop further the ideas and sentiments suggested by Arnold's final line concerning "ignorant armies clash[ing] by night."

2. Contrast Arnold's images with those of Anthony Hecht in his parody "The Dover Bitch" (p. 538). How do Hecht's images create a very different mood from that of "Dover Beach"?

Consider the poetic appetite for images displayed in the celebration of chile peppers in the following passionate poem.

Jimmy Santiago Baca (b. 1952)

Green Chile

I prefer red chile over my eggs
and potatoes for breakfast.
Red chile *ristras*° decorate my door,   *a braided string of peppers*
dry on my roof, and hang from eaves.
They lend open-air vegetable stands   5
historical grandeur, and gently swing
with an air of festive welcome.
I can hear them talking in the wind,
haggard, yellowing, crisp, rasping
tongues of old men, licking the breeze.   10

   But grandmother loves green chile.
When I visit her,
she holds the green chile pepper
in her wrinkled hands.
Ah, voluptuous, masculine,   15
an air of authority and youth simmers
from its swan-neck stem, tapering to a flowery
collar, fermenting resinous spice.
A well-dressed gentleman at the door
my grandmother takes sensuously in her hand,   20
rubbing its firm glossed sides,
caressing the oily rubbery serpent,
with mouth-watering fulfillment,
fondling its curves with gentle fingers.
Its bearing magnificent and taut   25
as flanks of a tiger in mid-leap,
she thrusts her blade into
and cuts it open, with lust
on her hot mouth, sweating over the stove,
bandanna round her forehead,   30
mysterious passion on her face
and she serves me green chile con carne
between soft warm leaves of corn tortillas,
with beans and rice — her sacrifice
to her little prince.   35
I slurp from my plate
with last bit of tortilla, my mouth burns
and I hiss and drink a tall glass of cold water.

All over New Mexico, sunburned men and women
drive rickety trucks stuffed with gunny-sacks   40
of green chile, from Belen, Veguita, Willard, Estancia,
San Antonio y Socorro, from fields
to roadside stands, you see them roasting green chile
in screen-sided homemade barrels, and for a dollar a bag,
we relive this old, beautiful ritual again and again.   45

CONSIDERATIONS FOR CRITICAL THINKING AND WRITING

1. **FIRST RESPONSE.** What's the difference between red and green chiles in this poem? Find the different images the speaker uses to distinguish between the two.

2. What kinds of images are used to describe the grandmother's preparation of green chile? What is the effect of those images?

3. **CREATIVE RESPONSE.** Try writing a description — in poetry or prose — that uses vivid images to evoke a powerful response (either positive or negative) to a particular food.

POEMS FOR FURTHER STUDY

AMY LOWELL (1874–1925)

The Pond
1919

Cold, wet leaves
Floating on moss-colored water,
And the croaking of frogs —
Cracked bell-notes in the twilight.

CONSIDERATIONS FOR CRITICAL THINKING AND WRITING

1. **FIRST RESPONSE.** This poem is not a complete sentence. What is missing? Does it matter in terms of understanding what is described by the images?

2. What senses are stimulated by the images? Which sense seems to be the most dominant in the poem? Why?

3. **CREATIVE RESPONSE.** Is the title of the poem necessary to convey its meaning? Choose an appropriate alternate title and explain how it subtly suggests something different from "The Pond."

H. D. (HILDA DOOLITTLE/1886–1961)

Heat
1916

O wind, rend open the heat,
cut apart the heat,
rend it to tatters.

Fruit cannot drop
through this thick air —   5
fruit cannot fall into heat
that presses up and blunts
the points of pears
and rounds the grapes.

Cut the heat— 10
plough through it,
turning it on either side
of your path.

CONSIDERATIONS FOR CRITICAL THINKING AND WRITING

1. **FIRST RESPONSE.** Is this poem more about heat or fruit? Explain your answer.
2. What physical properties are associated with heat in this poem?
3. Explain the effect of the description of fruit in lines 4–9.
4. Why is the image of the cutting plow especially effective in lines 10–13?

LINDA PASTAN (B. 1932)

Pass/Fail   *1975*

Examination dreams are reported to persist even into old age . . .
                                    —Time *magazine*

You will never graduate
from this dream
of blue books.
No matter how
you succeed awake,   5
asleep there is a test
waiting to be failed.
The dream beckons
with two dull pencils,
but you haven't even   10
taken the course;
when you reach for a book—
it closes its door
in your face; when
you conjugate a verb—   15
it is in the wrong
language.
Now the pillow becomes
a blank page. Turn it
to the cool side;   20
you will still smother
in all of the feathers
that have to be learned
by heart.

CONSIDERATIONS FOR CRITICAL THINKING AND WRITING

1. **FIRST RESPONSE.** How well do the images in this poem capture for you the anxieties about taking exams?

2. Instead of a first-person point of view, Pastan uses the second person. Does her strategy make any difference to your reading of "Pass/Fail"?

3. **CREATIVE RESPONSE.** Write a poem in Pastan's style that expresses your experience taking examinations.

CONNECTION TO ANOTHER SELECTION

1. Discuss the significance of being graded in this poem and in Pastan's "Marks" (p. 152).

RUTH FAINLIGHT (B. 1931)

Crocuses   2006

Pale, bare, tender stems rising
from the muddy winter-faded grass,

shivering petals the almost luminous
blue and mauve of bruises on the naked

bodies of men, women, children
herded into a forest clearing

before the shouted order, crack of gunfire,
final screams and prayers and moans.

CONSIDERATIONS FOR CRITICAL THINKING AND WRITING

1. **FIRST RESPONSE.** Comment on Fainlight's choice of title. What effect does it have on your reading of the poem?

2. Trace your response to each image in the poem and describe the poem's tone as it moves from line to line.

3. **CREATIVE RESPONSE.** Try writing an eight-line poem in the style of Fainlight's based on images that gradually but radically shift in tone.

MARY ROBINSON (1758–1800)

London's Summer Morning   1806

Who has not wak'd to list° the busy sounds   listen to
Of summer's morning, in the sultry smoke
Of noisy London? On the pavement hot
The sooty chimney-boy, with dingy face
And tatter'd covering, shrilly bawls his trade,   5
Rousing the sleepy housemaid. At the door
The milk-pail rattles, and the tinkling bell
Proclaims the dustman's office; while the street

Is lost in clouds impervious. Now begins
The din of hackney-coaches, waggons, carts;   10
While tinmen's shops, and noisy trunk-makers,
Knife-grinders, coopers, squeaking cork-cutters,
Fruit-barrows, and the hunger-giving cries
Of vegetable venders, fill the air.
Now ev'ry shop displays its varied trade,   15
And the fresh-sprinkled pavement cools the feet
Of early walkers. At the private door
The ruddy housemaid twirls the busy mop,
Annoying the smart 'prentice, or neat girl,
Tripping with band-box° lightly. Now the sun   *hat box*   20
Darts burning splendour on the glitt'ring pane,
Save where the canvas awning throws a shade
On the gay merchandize. Now, spruce and trim,
In shops (where beauty smiles with industry),
Sits the smart damsel; while the passenger   25
Peeps thro' the window, watching ev'ry charm.
Now pastry dainties catch the eye minute
Of humming insects, while the limy snare
Waits to enthral them. Now the lamp-lighter
Mounts the tall ladder, nimbly vent'rous,   30
To trim the half-fill'd lamp; while at his feet
The pot-boy° yells discordant! All along   *drink server*
The sultry pavement, the old-clothes-man cries
In tones monotonous, and side-long views
The area for his traffic: now the bag   35
Is slily open'd, and the half-worn suit
(Sometimes the pilfer'd treasure of the base
Domestic spoiler), for one half its worth,
Sinks in the green abyss. The porter now
Bears his huge load along the burning way;   40
And the poor poet wakes from busy dreams,
To paint the summer morning.

CONSIDERATIONS FOR CRITICAL THINKING AND WRITING

1. **FIRST RESPONSE.** How effective is this picture of a London summer morning in 1806? Which images do you find particularly effective?

2. How does the end of the poem bring us full circle to its beginning? What
   effect does this structure have on your understanding of the poem?

3. **CREATIVE RESPONSE.** Try writing about the start of your own day — in the
   dormitory, at home, the start of a class — using a series of images that provide a vivid sense of what happens and how you experience it.

CONNECTION TO ANOTHER SELECTION

1. How does Robinson's description of London differ from William Blake's
   "London," the next poem? What would you say is the essential difference in
   purpose between the two poems?

WILLIAM BLAKE (1757–1827)

London   *1794*

I wander through each chartered° street,   *defined by law*
Near where the chartered Thames does flow,
And mark in every face I meet
Marks of weakness, marks of woe.

In every cry of every man,   5
In every Infant's cry of fear,
In every voice, in every ban,
The mind-forged manacles I hear.

How the Chimney-sweeper's cry
Every black'ning Church appalls;   10
And the hapless Soldier's sigh
Runs in blood down Palace walls.

But most through midnight streets I hear
How the youthful Harlot's curse
Blasts the new-born Infant's tear,   15
And blights with plagues the Marriage hearse.

Explore contexts
for William Blake
on *LiterActive*.

CONSIDERATIONS FOR CRITICAL THINKING AND WRITING

1. **FIRST RESPONSE.** What feelings do the visual images in this poem suggest to you?

2. What is the predominant sound heard in the poem?

3. What is the meaning of line 8? What is the cause of the problems that the speaker sees and hears in London? Does the speaker suggest additional causes?

4. The image in lines 11 and 12 cannot be read literally. Comment on its effectiveness.

5. How does Blake's use of denotative and connotative language enrich this poem's meaning?

6. An earlier version of Blake's last stanza appeared this way:

    But most the midnight harlot's curse
    From every dismal street I hear,
    Weaves around the marriage hearse
    And blasts the new-born infant's tear.

Examine carefully the differences between the two versions. How do Blake's revisions affect his picture of London life? Which version do you think is more effective? Why?

A SAMPLE STUDENT RESPONSE

Anna Tamara

Professor Burton

English 211

September 30, 2009

Imagery in William Blake's "London" and Mary Robinson's

"London's Summer Morning"

Both William Blake and Mary Robinson use strong imagery to examine and bring to life the city of London, yet each writer paints a very different picture. The images in both poems "[address] the senses," as Meyer writes (106). But while Blake's images depict a city weighed down by oppression and poverty, Robinson's images are lighter, happier, and, arguably, idealized. Both poems use powerful imagery in very different ways to establish theme.

In Blake's poem, oppression and social discontent are defined by the speaker, who sees "weakness" and "woe" (line 4) in the faces he meets; he hears cries of men and children and "mind-forged manacles" (8). And, through imagery, the poem makes a political statement:

> How the Chimney-sweeper's cry
>
> Every black'ning Church appalls;
>
> And the hapless Soldier's sigh
>
> Runs in blood down Palace walls. (9-12)

These images indicate the speaker's dark view of the religious and governmental institutions that he believes cause the city's suffering. The "black'ning Church" and bloody "Palace walls" can be seen to represent misused power and corruption, while the "manacles" are the rules and physical and psychological burdens that lead to societal ills. In Blake's view of London, children are sold into servitude (as chimney sweeps) and soldiers pay in blood.

Robinson's poem, on the other hand, offers the reader a pleasant view of a sunny London morning through a different series of images. The reader hears "the tinkling bell" (7) and sees a bright moment in which "the sun / Darts burning splendour on the glitt'ring pane" (20-21). Even the chimney-boy is shown in a rosy glow. Though he is described as having a "dingy face / and

Tamara 2

tatter'd covering," he wakes the "sleepy" house servant when he "shrilly bawls
his trade" (4-6). In contrast to the chimney-sweep of Blake's "London,"
Robinson's boy is painted as a charming character who announces the morning
amid a backdrop of happy workers. Also unlike Blake's London, Robinson's is a
city of contentment in which a "ruddy housemaid twirls the busy mop" (18) . . .

Tamara 4

Works Cited

Blake, William. "London." *Poetry: An Introduction*. Ed. Michael Meyer. 6th ed.
    Boston: Bedford/St. Martin's, 2010. 119. Print.

Meyer, Michael, ed. *Poetry: An Introduction*. 6th ed. Boston: Bedford/St.
    Martin's, 2010. 106. Print.

Robinson, Mary. "London's Summer Morning." *Poetry: An Introduction*. Ed.
    Michael Meyer. 6th ed. Boston: Bedford/St. Martin's, 2010. 117-18. Print.

WILFRED OWEN (1893–1918)

Dulce et Decorum Est   *1920*

Bent double, like old beggars under sacks,
Knock-kneed, coughing like hags, we cursed through
    sludge,
Till on the haunting flares we turned our backs,
And towards our distant rest began to trudge.

Men marched asleep. Many had lost their boots,   5
But limped on, blood-shod. All went lame, all blind;
Drunk with fatigue; deaf even to the hoots
Of gas-shells dropping softly behind.

Gas! GAS! Quick, boys! — An ecstasy of fumbling,
Fitting the clumsy helmets just in time,   10
But someone still was yelling out and stumbling

Explore contexts
for Wilfred Owen
on *LiterActive*.

And flound'ring like a man in fire or lime. —
Dim through the misty panes and thick green light,
As under a green sea, I saw him drowning.

In all my dreams before my helpless sight   15
He plunges at me, guttering, choking, drowning.

If in some smothering dreams, you too could pace
Behind the wagon that we flung him in,
And watch the white eyes writhing in his face,
His hanging face, like a devil's sick of sin,   20
If you could hear, at every jolt, the blood
Come gargling from the froth-corrupted lungs
Bitter as the cud
Obscene as cancer,
Of vile, incurable sores on innocent tongues, —   25
My friend, you would not tell with such high zest
To children ardent for some desperate glory,
The old lie: *Dulce et decorum est*
Pro patria mori.

CONSIDERATIONS FOR CRITICAL THINKING AND WRITING

1. **FIRST RESPONSE.** The Latin quotation in lines 28 and 29 is from Horace: "It is sweet and fitting to die for one's country." Owen served as a British soldier during World War I and was killed. Is this poem unpatriotic? What is its purpose?

2. Which images in the poem are most vivid? To which senses do they speak?

3. Describe the speaker's tone. What is his relationship to his audience?

4. How are the images of the soldiers in this poem different from the images that typically appear in recruiting posters?

MARVIN BELL (B. 1937)

The Uniform   1994

Of the sleeves, I remember their weight, like wet wool,
on my arms, and the empty ends which hung past my hands.
Of the body of the shirt, I remember the large buttons
and larger buttonholes, which made a rack of wheels
down my chest and could not be quickly unbuttoned.   5
Of the collar, I remember its thickness without starch,
by which it lay against my clavicle without moving.
Of my trousers, the same — heavy, bulky, slow to give
for a leg, a crowded feeling, a molasses to walk in.
Of my boots, I remember the brittle soles, of a material   10
that had not been made love to by any natural substance,
and the laces: ropes to make prisoners of my feet.
Of the helmet, I remember the webbed, inner liner,

a brittle plastic underwear on which wobbled
the crushing steel pot then strapped at the chin. 15
Of the mortar, I remember the mortar plate,
heavy enough to kill by weight, which I carried by rope.
Of the machine gun, I remember the way it fit
behind my head and across my shoulder blades
as I carried it, or, to be precise, as it rode me. 20
Of tactics, I remember the likelihood of shooting
the wrong man, the weight of the rifle bolt, the difficulty
of loading while prone, the shock of noise.
For earplugs, some used cigarette filters or toilet paper.
I don't hear well now, for a man of my age, 25
and the doctor says my ears were damaged and asks
if I was in the Army, and of course I was but then
a wounded eardrum wasn't much in the scheme.

CONSIDERATIONS FOR CRITICAL THINKING AND WRITING

1. **FIRST RESPONSE.** What overall impression do the speaker's images convey about his uniform?

2. Write a description of the speaker's uniform using adjectives that are not in the poem.

3. Which lines seem especially revealing to you of the speaker's attitude toward his time in the army?

CONNECTION TO ANOTHER SELECTION

1. Compare the vision of war expressed in "Uniform" with that in Wilfred Owen's "Dulce et Decorum Est" (p. 121).

PATRICIA SMITH (B. 1955)

What It's Like to Be a Black Girl (for Those of You Who Aren't)

1991

First of all, it's being 9 years old and
feeling like you're not finished, like your
edges are wild, like there's something,
everything, wrong. it's dropping food coloring
in your eyes to make them blue and suffering 5
their burn in silence. it's popping a bleached
white mophead over the kinks of your hair and
primping in front of the mirrors that deny your
reflection. it's finding a space between your
legs, a disturbance at your chest, and not knowing 10
what to do with the whistles. it's jumping
double dutch until your legs pop, it's sweat
and vaseline and bullets, it's growing tall and
wearing a lot of white, it's smelling blood in

your breakfast, it's learning to say fuck with   15
grace but learning to fuck without it, it's
flame and fists and life according to motown,
it's finally having a man reach out for you
then caving in
around his fingers.   20

CONSIDERATIONS FOR CRITICAL THINKING AND WRITING

1. **FIRST RESPONSE.** Describe the speaker's tone. What images in particular contribute to it? How do you account for the selected tone?

2. How does the speaker characterize her life? On which elements of it does she focus?

3. Discuss the poem's final image. What sort of emotions does it elicit in you?

RAINER MARIA RILKE (1875–1926)

The Panther   *1927*

TRANSLATED BY STEPHEN MITCHELL

His vision, from the constantly passing bars,
has grown so weary that it cannot hold
anything else. It seems to him there are
a thousand bars; and behind the bars, no world.

As he paces in cramped circles, over and over,   5
the movement of his powerful soft strides
is like a ritual dance around a center
in which a mighty will stands paralyzed.

Only at times, the curtain of the pupils
lifts, quietly — . An image enters in,   10
rushes down through the tensed, arrested muscles,
plunges into the heart and is gone.

CONSIDERATIONS FOR CRITICAL THINKING AND WRITING

1. **FIRST RESPONSE.** Why do you think Rilke chooses a panther rather than, say, a lion as the subject of the poem's images?

2. What kind of "image enters in" the heart of the panther in the final stanza?

3. How are images of confinement achieved in the poem? Why doesn't Rilke describe the final image in lines 10–12?

CONNECTION TO ANOTHER SELECTION

1. Write an essay explaining how a sense of movement is achieved by the images and rhythms in this poem and in Emily Dickinson's "A Bird came down the Walk —" (p. 190).

JANE KENYON (1947–1995)

The Blue Bowl   *1990*

Like primitives we buried the cat
with his bowl. Bare-handed
we scraped sand and gravel
back into the hole.
         They fell with a hiss   5

and thud on his side,
on his long red fur, the white feathers
between his toes, and his
long, not to say aquiline, nose.

We stood and brushed each other off.   10
There are sorrows keener than these.

Silent the rest of the day, we worked,
ate, stared, and slept. It stormed
all night; now it clears, and a robin
burbles from a dripping bush   15
like the neighbor who means well
but always says the wrong thing.

CONSIDERATIONS FOR CRITICAL THINKING AND WRITING

1. **FIRST RESPONSE.** How do the descriptions of the cat—for example, "the white feathers / between his toes"—affect your reading of the poem?
2. Why do you think Kenyon titles the poem "The Blue Bowl" rather than, perhaps, "The Cat's Bowl"?
3. What is the effect of being reminded that "There are sorrows keener than these"?
4. Why is the robin's song "the wrong thing"?

CONNECTION TO ANOTHER SELECTION

1. Write an essay comparing the death of this cat with the death of the dog in John Updike's "Dog's Death" (p. 22). Which poem draws a more powerful response from you? Explain why.

DONNA MASINI (B. 1954)

Slowly   *2004*

I watched a snake once, swallow a rabbit.
Fourth grade, the reptile zoo
the rabbit stiff, nose in, bits of litter stuck to its fur,

its head clenched in the wide
jaws of the snake, the snake   5
sucking it down its long throat.

All throat that snake—I couldn't tell
where the throat ended, the body
began. I remember the glass

case, the way that snake   10
took its time (all the girls, groaning, shrieking
but weren't we amazed, fascinated,

saying we couldn't look, but looking, weren't we
held there, weren't we
imagining—what were we imagining?).   15

Mrs. Peterson urged us to *move on girls,*
but we couldn't move. It was like
watching a fern unfurl, a minute

hand move across a clock. I didn't know why
the snake didn't choke, the rabbit never   20
moved, how the jaws kept opening

wider, sucking it down, just so
I am taking this in, slowly,
taking it into my body:

this grief. How slow   25
the body is to realize.
You are never coming back.

Considerations for Critical Thinking and Writing

1. **First Response.** What, ultimately, is this poem about?
2. Comment on the effectiveness of the short, quick images in the first stanza in establishing the setting and plot.
3. Explain how time is depicted through the poem's images.

Connection to Another Selection

1. Compare the treatment of grief in "Slowly" and in Jane Kenyon's "The Blue Bowl" (p. 125).

Sally Croft (b. 1935)

Home-Baked Bread   *1981*

Nothing gives a household a greater sense of stability and common comfort than the aroma of cooling bread. Begin, if you like, with a loaf of whole wheat, which requires neither sifting nor kneading, and go on from there to more cunning triumphs.
                                                  —The Joy of Cooking

What is it she is not saying?
Cunning triumphs. It rings
of insinuation. Step into my kitchen,

I have prepared a cunning triumph
for you. Spices and herbs   5
sealed in this porcelain jar,

a treasure of my great-aunt
who sat up past midnight
in her Massachusetts bedroom
when the moon was dark. Come,   10
rest your feet. I'll make
you tea with honey and slices

of warm bread spread with peach butter.
I picked the fruit this morning
still fresh with dew. The fragrance   15
is seductive? I hoped you would say that.
See how the heat rises
when the bread opens. Come,

we'll eat together, the small flakes
have scarcely any flavor. What cunning   20
triumphs we can discover in my upstairs room
where peach trees breathe their sweetness
beside the open window and
sun lies like honey on the floor.

CONSIDERATIONS FOR CRITICAL THINKING AND WRITING

1. **FIRST RESPONSE.** Why does the speaker in this poem seize on the phrase "cunning triumphs" from the *Joy of Cooking* excerpt?

2. Distinguish between the voice we hear in lines 1–3 and the second voice in lines 3–24. Who is the "you" in the poem?

3. Why is the word "insinuation" an especially appropriate choice in line 3?

4. How do the images in lines 20–24 bring together all of the senses evoked in the preceding lines?

5. **CREATIVE RESPONSE.** Write a paragraph — or stanza — that describes the sensuous (and perhaps sensual) qualities of a food you enjoy.

JOHN KEATS (1795–1821)

To Autumn   *1819*

I

Season of mists and mellow fruitfulness,
    Close bosom-friend of the maturing sun;
Conspiring with him how to load and bless
    With fruit the vines that round the thatch-eves run;
To bend with apples the mossed cottage-trees,   5
    And fill all fruit with ripeness to the core;
        To swell the gourd, and plump the hazel shells
    With a sweet kernel; to set budding more,

Explore contexts
for John Keats
on *LiterActive*.

And still more, later flowers for the bees,
Until they think warm days will never cease,   10
    For summer has o'er-brimmed their clammy cells.

II

Who hath not seen thee oft amid thy store?
  Sometimes whoever seeks abroad may find
Thee sitting careless on a granary floor,
    Thy hair soft-lifted by the winnowing wind;   15
Or on a half-reaped furrow sound asleep,
  Drowsed with the fume of poppies, while thy hook°   *scythe*
    Spares the next swath and all its twinèd flowers:
And sometimes like a gleaner thou dost keep
  Steady thy laden head across a brook;   20
  Or by a cider-press, with patient look,
    Thou watchest the last oozings hours by hours.

III

Where are the songs of spring? Ay, where are they?
  Think not of them, thou hast thy music too —
While barred clouds bloom the soft-dying day,   25
  And touch the stubble-plains with rosy hue;
Then in a wailful choir the small gnats mourn
  Among the river swallows,° borne aloft   *willows*
    Or sinking as the light wind lives or dies;
And full-grown lambs loud bleat from hilly bourn;°   *territory*   30
  Hedge-crickets sing; and now with treble soft
  The redbreast whistles from a garden-croft,
    And gathering swallows twitter in the skies.

CONSIDERATIONS FOR CRITICAL THINKING AND WRITING

1. **FIRST RESPONSE.** How is autumn made to seem like a person in each stanza of this ode?

2. Which senses are most emphasized in each stanza?

3. How is the progression of time expressed in the ode?

4. How does the imagery convey tone? Which words have especially strong connotative values?

5. What is the speaker's view of death?

CONNECTIONS TO OTHER SELECTIONS

1. Compare this poem's tone and perspective on death with those of Robert Frost's "After Apple-Picking" (p. 376).

2. Write an essay comparing the significance of this poem's images of "mellow fruitfulness" (line 1) with that of the images of ripeness in Theodore Roethke's "Root Cellar" (p. 111). Explain how the images in each poem lead to very different feelings about the same phenomenon.

C. K. WILLIAMS (B. 1936)

Shock   *1999*

Furiously a crane
in the scrap yard out of whose grasp
a car it meant to pick up slipped,
lifts and lets fall, lifts and lets fall
the steel ton of its clenched pincers
onto the shuddering carcass
which spurts fragments of anguished glass
until it's sufficiently crushed
to be hauled up and flung onto
the heap from which one imagines
it'll move on to the shredding
or melting down that awaits it.

© Christopher Felver/CORBIS.

Also somewhere a crow
with less evident emotion
punches its beak through the dead   15
breast of a dove or albino
sparrow until it arrives at
a coil of gut it can extract,
then undo with a dexterous twist
an oily stretch just the right length   20
to be devoured, the only
suggestion of violation
the carrion jerked to one side
in involuntary dismay.

Splayed on the soiled pavement   25
the dove or sparrow; dismembered
in the tangled remnants of itself
the wreck, the crane slamming once more
for good measure into the all
but dematerialized hulk,   30
then luxuriously swaying
away, as, gorged, glutted, the crow
with savage care unfurls the full,
luminous glitter of its wings,
so we can preen, too, for so much   35
so well accomplished, so well seen.

CONSIDERATIONS FOR CRITICAL THINKING AND WRITING

1. **FIRST RESPONSE.** What do you think is the significance of the poem's title?
2. What connections can you make between the images in stanzas 1 and 2?
3. Explain how the third stanza develops a theme from the images provided in the first two stanzas.

EZRA POUND (1885–1972)

In a Station of the Metro°

1913

The apparition of these faces in the crowd;
Petals on a wet, black bough.

Metro: Underground railroad in Paris.

CONSIDERATIONS FOR CRITICAL THINKING AND WRITING

1. **FIRST RESPONSE.** Why is the title essential for this poem?
2. What kind of mood does the image in the second line convey?
3. Why is "apparition" (line 1) a better word choice than, say, "appearance" or "sight"?
4. **CREATIVE RESPONSE.** Write a two-line vivid image for a poem titled "At a Desk in the Library."

CATHY SONG (B. 1955)

The White Porch

1983

I wrap the blue towel
after washing,
around the damp
weight of hair, bulky
as a sleeping cat,   5
and sit out on the porch.
Still dripping water,
it'll be dry by supper,
by the time the dust
settles off your shoes,   10
though it's only five
past noon. Think
of the luxury: how to use
the afternoon like the stretch
of lawn spread before me.   15
There's the laundry,
sun-warm clothes at twilight,
and the mountain of beans
in my lap. Each one,
I'll break and snap   20
thoughtfully in half.

But there is this slow arousal.
The small buttons
of my cotton blouse
are pulling away from my body.   25
I feel the strain of threads,
the swollen magnolias

heavy as a flock of birds
in the tree. Already,
the orange sponge cake   30
is rising in the oven.
I know you'll say it makes
your mouth dry
and I'll watch you
drench your slice of it   35
in canned peaches
and lick the plate clean.

So much hair, my mother
used to say, grabbing
the thick braided rope   40
in her hands while we washed
the breakfast dishes, discussing
dresses and pastries.
My mind often elsewhere
as we did the morning chores together.   45
Sometimes, a few strands
would catch in her gold ring.
I worked hard then,
anticipating the hour
when I would let the rope down   50
at night, strips of sheets,
knotted and tied,
while she slept in tight blankets.
My hair, freshly washed
like a measure of wealth,   55
like a bridal veil.
Crouching in the grass,
you would wait for the signal,
for the movement of curtains
before releasing yourself   60
from the shadow of moths.
Cloth, hair and hands,
smuggling you in.

CONSIDERATIONS FOR CRITICAL THINKING AND WRITING

1. **FIRST RESPONSE.** How is hair made erotic in this poem? Discuss the images
   that you deem especially effective.

2. Who is the "you" to whom the speaker refers in each stanza?

3. What role does the mother play in this poem about desire?

4. Why do you think the poem is titled "The White Porch"?

CONNECTIONS TO OTHER SELECTIONS

1. Compare the images used to describe the speaker's "slow arousal" (line 22)
   in this poem with Sally Croft's images in "Home-Baked Bread" (p. 126).
   What similarities do you see? What makes each description so effective?

2. Write an essay comparing the images of sensuality in this poem with those in Li Ho's "A Beautiful Girl Combs Her Hair" (p. 53). Which poem seems more erotic to you? Why?

Perspective

T. E. HULME (1883–1917)
On the Differences between Poetry and Prose   1924

In prose as in algebra concrete things are embodied in signs or counters which are moved about according to rules, without being visualized at all in the process. There are in prose certain type situations and arrangements of words, which move as automatically into certain other arrangements as do functions in algebra. One only changes the *X*'s and the *Y*'s back into physical things at the end of the process. Poetry, in one aspect at any rate, may be considered as an effort to avoid this characteristic of prose. It is not a counter language, but a visual concrete one. It is a compromise for a language of intuition which would hand over sensations bodily. It always endeavors to arrest you, and to make you continuously see a physical thing, to prevent you gliding through an abstract process. It chooses fresh epithets and fresh metaphors, not so much because they are new, and we are tired of the old, but because the old cease to convey a physical thing and become abstract counters. A poet says a ship "coursed the seas" to get a physical image, instead of the counter word "sailed." Visual meanings can only be transferred by the new bowl of metaphor; prose is an old pot that lets them leak out. Images in verse are not mere decoration, but the very essence of an intuitive language. Verse is a pedestrian taking you over the ground, prose — a train which delivers you at a destination.

From "Romanticism and Classicism," in *Speculations*,
edited by Herbert Read

CONSIDERATIONS FOR CRITICAL THINKING AND WRITING

1. What distinctions does Hulme make between poetry and prose? Which seems to be the most important difference?

2. Write an essay that discusses Hulme's claim that poetry "is a compromise for a language of intuition which would hand over sensations bodily."

Web Research the poets in this chapter at bedfordstmartins.com/ rewritinglit.

5

Figures of Speech

Like a piece of ice on a hot stove the
poem must ride on its own melting.
— ROBERT FROST

Figures of speech are broadly defined as a way of saying one thing in terms of something else. An overeager funeral director might, for example, be described as a vulture. Although figures of speech are indirect, they are designed to clarify, not obscure, our understanding of what they describe. Poets frequently use them because, as Emily Dickinson said, the poet's work is to "tell all the Truth but tell it slant" to capture the reader's interest and imagination. But figures of speech are not limited to poetry. Hearing them, reading them, or using them is as natural as using language itself.

Suppose that in the middle of a class discussion concerning the economic causes of World War II your history instructor introduces a series of statistics by saying, "Let's get down to brass tacks." Would anyone be likely to expect a display of brass tacks for students to examine? Of course not. To interpret the statement literally would be to wholly misunderstand the instructor's point that the time has come for a close look at the economic circumstances leading to the war. A literal response transforms the statement into the sort of hilariously bizarre material often found in a sketch by Woody Allen.

The class does not look for brass tacks because, in a nutshell, they understand that the instructor is speaking figuratively. They would understand, too, that in the preceding sentence "in a nutshell" refers to brevity and conciseness rather than to the covering of a kernel of a nut. Figurative language makes its way into our everyday speech and writing as well as into literature because it is a means of achieving color, vividness, and intensity.

Consider the difference, for example, between these two statements:

Literal: The diner strongly expressed anger at the waiter.
Figurative: The diner leaped from his table and roared at the waiter.

The second statement is more vivid because it creates a picture of ferocious anger by likening the diner to some kind of wild animal, such as a lion or tiger. By comparison, "strongly expressed anger" is neither especially strong nor especially expressive; it is flat. Not all figurative language avoids this kind of flatness, however. Figures of speech such as "getting down to brass tacks" and "in a nutshell" are clichés because they lack originality and freshness. Still, they suggest how these devices are commonly used to give language some color, even if that color is sometimes a bit faded.

There is nothing weak about William Shakespeare's use of figurative language in the following passage from *Macbeth*. Macbeth has just learned that his wife is dead, and he laments her loss as well as the course of his own life.

WILLIAM SHAKESPEARE (1564–1616)

From Macbeth *(Act V, Scene v)*   *1605–1606*

Tomorrow, and tomorrow, and tomorrow
Creeps in this petty pace from day to day
To the last syllable of recorded time;
And all our yesterdays have lighted fools
The way to dusty death. Out, out, brief candle!   5
Life's but a walking shadow, a poor player,
That struts and frets his hour upon the stage,
And then is heard no more. It is a tale
Told by an idiot, full of sound and fury,
Signifying nothing.   10

This passage might be summarized as "life has no meaning," but such a brief paraphrase does not take into account the figurative language that reveals the depth of Macbeth's despair and his view of the absolute meaninglessness of life. By comparing life to a "brief candle," Macbeth emphasizes the darkness and death that surround human beings. The light of life is too brief and unpredictable to be of any comfort. Indeed, life for Macbeth is a "walking shadow," futilely playing a role that is more farcical than dramatic, because life is, ultimately, a desperate story filled with pain and devoid of significance. What the figurative language provides, then, is the emotional force of Macbeth's assertion; his comparisons are disturbing because they are so apt.

The remainder of this chapter discusses some of the most important figures of speech used in poetry. A familiarity with them will help you to understand how poetry achieves its effects.

SIMILE AND METAPHOR

The two most common figures of speech are simile and metaphor. Both compare things that are ordinarily considered unlike each other. A **simile** makes an explicit comparison between two things by using words such as *like, as, than, appears,* or *seems:* "A sip of Mrs. Cook's coffee is like a punch in the stomach." The force of the simile is created by the differences between the two things compared. There would be no simile if the comparison were stated this way: "Mrs. Cook's coffee is as strong as the cafeteria's coffee." This is a literal comparison because Mrs. Cook's coffee is compared with something like it, another kind of coffee. Consider how simile is used in this poem.

 Explore the poetic elements in this chapter on *LiterActive* or at bedfordstmartins.com/ rewritinglit.

MARGARET ATWOOD (B. 1939)

you fit into me   1971

you fit into me
like a hook into an eye

a fish hook
an open eye

© Sophie Bassouls/CORBIS SYGMA.

If you blinked on a second reading, you got the point of this poem because you recognized that the simile "like a hook into an eye" gives way to a play on words in the final two lines. There the hook and eye, no longer a pleasant domestic image of a clothing fastener or door latch that fits closely together, become a literal, sharp fishhook and a human eye. The wordplay qualifies the simile and drastically alters the tone of this poem by creating a strong and unpleasant surprise.

A **metaphor,** like a simile, makes a comparison between two unlike things, but it does so implicitly, without words such as *like* or *as:* "Mrs. Cook's coffee is a punch in the stomach." Metaphor asserts the identity of dissimilar things. Macbeth tells us that life *is* a "brief candle," life *is* "a walking shadow," life *is* "a poor player," life *is* "a tale / Told by an idiot." Metaphor transforms people, places, objects, and ideas into whatever the poet imagines them to be, and if metaphors are effective, the reader's experience, understanding, and appreciation of what is described are enhanced. Metaphors are frequently more demanding than similes because they are not signaled by particular words. They are both subtle and powerful.

Here is a poem about presentiment, a foreboding that something terrible is about to happen.

EMILY DICKINSON (1830–1886)

Presentiment — is that long Shadow — on the lawn —   *ca. 1863*

Presentiment — is that long Shadow — on the lawn —
Indicative that Suns go down —

The notice to the startled Grass
That Darkness — is about to pass —

The metaphors in this poem define the abstraction "Presentiment." The sense of foreboding that Dickinson expresses is identified with a particular moment — the moment when darkness is just about to envelop an otherwise tranquil, ordinary scene. The speaker projects that fear onto the "startled Grass" so that it seems any life must be frightened by the approaching "Shadow" and "Darkness" — two richly connotative words associated with death. The metaphors obliquely tell us ("tell it slant" was Dickinson's motto, remember) that presentiment is related to a fear of death, and, more important, the metaphors convey the feelings that attend that idea.

Some metaphors are more subtle than others because their comparison of terms is less explicit. Notice the difference between the following two metaphors, both of which describe a shaggy derelict refusing to leave the warmth of a hotel lobby: "He was a mule standing his ground" is a quite explicit comparison. The man is a mule; X is Y. But this metaphor is much more covert: "He brayed his refusal to leave." This second version is an ***implied metaphor*** because it does not explicitly identify the man with a mule. Instead it hints at or alludes to the mule. Braying is associated with mules and is especially appropriate in this context because of the mule's reputation for stubbornness. Implied metaphors can slip by readers, but they offer the alert reader the energy and resonance of carefully chosen, highly concentrated language.

Some poets write extended comparisons in which part or all of the poem consists of a series of related metaphors or similes. Extended metaphors are more common than extended similes. In "Catch" (p. 26), Robert Francis creates an **extended metaphor** that compares poetry to a game of catch. The entire poem is organized around this comparison. Because these comparisons are at work throughout the entire poem, they are called **controlling metaphors.** Extended comparisons can serve as a poem's organizing principle; they are also a reminder that in good poems metaphor and simile are not merely decorative but inseparable from what is expressed.

Notice the controlling metaphor in this poem, published posthumously by a woman whose contemporaries identified her more as a wife and mother than as a poet. Bradstreet's first volume of poetry, *The Tenth Muse,* was published by her brother-in-law in 1650 without her prior knowledge.

ANNE BRADSTREET (CA. 1612–1672)

The Author to Her Book   1678

Thou ill-formed offspring of my feeble brain,
Who after birth did'st by my side remain,
Till snatched from thence by friends, less wise than true,
Who thee abroad exposed to public view;
Made thee in rags, halting, to the press to trudge,   5
Where errors were not lessened, all may judge.
At thy return my blushing was not small,
My rambling brat (in print) should mother call;
I cast thee by as one unfit for light,
Thy visage was so irksome in my sight;   10
Yet being mine own, at length affection would
Thy blemishes amend, if so I could:
I washed thy face, but more defects I saw,
And rubbing off a spot, still made a flaw.
I stretched thy joints to make thee even feet,   15
Yet still thou run'st more hobbling than is meet;
In better dress to trim thee was my mind,
But nought save homespun cloth in the house I find.
In this array, 'mongst vulgars may'st thou roam;
In critics' hands beware thou dost not come;   20
And take thy way where yet thou are not known.
If for thy Father asked, say thou had'st none;
And for thy Mother, she alas is poor,
Which caused her thus to send thee out of door.

The extended metaphor likening her book to a child came naturally to Bradstreet and allowed her to regard her work both critically and affectionately. Her conception of the book as her child creates just the right tone of amusement, self-deprecation, and concern.

The controlling metaphor in the following poem is identified by the title.

JAY ROGOFF (B. 1954)

Death's Theater   2006

It's not all tragedy; he's not averse
to melodrama if everyone gets shot,
or musical comedy if the plot
is big and earthy, with a crop of chorus
girls good enough to eat. He loves a farce,   5
that nervous frenzy, those doors slamming shut
in your face. He's Mr. Opening Night,
top hat and cape, arriving in a hearse,
knocking them dead, each show a limited run:
one performance, curtain up, curtain down.   10
He'll undertake conning supporting roles,
rebuild the sets, rewrite your lines. He peddles
tickets, and pens reviews in which you shine.
He sends flowers. He coughs through your big scene.

CONSIDERATIONS FOR CRITICAL THINKING AND WRITING

1. **FIRST RESPONSE.** How is the somber topic of this poem lightened in tone by Rogoff's use of the controlling metaphor?
2. Which words or phrases seem especially carefully chosen to evoke Death's presence throughout the poem?
3. Consider the possible meanings of the title and their relevance to the poem's themes.

OTHER FIGURES

Perhaps the humblest figure of speech — if not one of the most familiar — is the pun. A *pun* is a play on words that relies on a word having more than one meaning or sounding like another word. For example, "A fad is in one era and out the other" is the sort of pun that produces obligatory groans. But most of us find pleasant and interesting surprises in puns. Here's one that has a slight edge to its humor.

EDMUND CONTI (B. 1929)

Pragmatist   *1985*

Apocalypse soon
Coming our way
Ground zero at noon
Halve a nice day.

Grimly practical under the circumstances, the pragmatist divides the familiar cheerful cliché by half. As simple as this poem is, its tone is mixed because it makes us laugh and wince at the same time.

Puns can be used to achieve serious effects as well as humorous ones. Although we may have learned to underrate puns as figures of speech, it is a mistake to underestimate their power and the frequency with which they appear in poetry. A close examination, for example, of Henry Reed's "Naming of Parts" (p. 177), Robert Frost's "Design" (p. 386), or almost any lengthy passage from a Shakespeare play will confirm the value of puns.

Synecdoche is a figure of speech in which part of something is used to signify the whole: a neighbor is a "wagging tongue" (a gossip); a criminal is placed "behind bars" (in prison). Less typically, synecdoche refers to the whole used to signify the part: "Germany invaded Poland"; "Princeton won the fencing match." Clearly, certain individuals participated in these activities, not all of Germany or Princeton. Another related figure of speech is **metonymy,** in which something closely associated with a subject is substituted for it: "She preferred the silver screen [motion pictures] to reading." "At precisely ten o'clock the paper shufflers [office workers] stopped for coffee."

Synecdoche and metonymy may overlap and are therefore sometimes difficult to distinguish. Consider this description of a disapproving minister entering a noisy tavern: "As those pursed lips came through the swinging door, the atmosphere was suddenly soured." The pursed lips signal the presence of the minister and are therefore a synecdoche, but they additionally suggest an inhibiting sense of sin and guilt that makes the bar patrons feel uncomfortable. Hence the pursed lips are also a metonymy, as they are in this context so closely connected with religion. Although the distinction between synecdoche and metonymy can be useful, a figure of speech is usually labeled a metonymy when it overlaps categories.

Knowing the precise term for a figure of speech is, finally, less important than responding to its use in a poem. Consider how metonymy and synecdoche convey the tone and meaning of the following poem.

DYLAN THOMAS (1914–1953)

The Hand That Signed the Paper   *1936*

The hand that signed the paper felled a city;
Five sovereign fingers taxed the breath,
Doubled the globe of dead and halved a
    country;
These five kings did a king to death.

The mighty hand leads to a sloping shoulder,
The finger joints are cramped with chalk;
A goose's quill has put an end to murder
That put an end to talk.

The hand that signed the treaty bred a fever,
And famine grew, and locusts came;
Great is the hand that holds dominion over
Man by a scribbled name.

© Hulton-Deutsch Collection/CORBIS.

10

   Explore contexts
for Dylan Thomas
on *LiterActive*.

The five kings count the dead but do not soften
The crusted wound nor stroke the brow;
A hand rules pity as a hand rules heaven;
Hands have no tears to flow.

15

    The "hand" in this poem is a synecdoche for a powerful ruler because it is a part of someone used to signify the entire person. The "goose's quill" is a metonymy that also refers to the power associated with the ruler's hand. By using these figures of speech, Thomas depersonalizes and ultimately dehumanizes the ruler. The final synecdoche tells us that "Hands have no tears to flow." It makes us see the political power behind the hand as remote and inhuman. How is the meaning of the poem enlarged when the speaker says, "A hand rules pity as a hand rules heaven"?

    One of the ways writers energize the abstractions, ideas, objects, and animals that constitute their created worlds is through ***personification,*** the attribution of human characteristics to nonhuman things: temptation pursues the innocent; trees scream in the raging wind; mice conspire in the cupboard. We are not explicitly told that these things are people; instead, we are invited to see that they behave like people. Perhaps it is human vanity that makes personification a frequently used figure of speech. Whatever the reason, personification, a form of metaphor that connects the nonhuman with the human, makes the world understandable in human terms. Consider this concise example from William Blake's *The Marriage of Heaven and Hell,* a long poem that takes delight in attacking conventional morality: "Prudence is a rich ugly old maid courted by Incapacity." By personifying prudence, Blake transforms what is usually considered a virtue into a comic figure hardly worth emulating.

Often related to personification is another rhetorical figure called
apostrophe, an address either to someone who is absent and therefore cannot hear the speaker or to something nonhuman that cannot comprehend. Apostrophe provides an opportunity for the speaker of a poem to
think aloud, and often the thoughts expressed are in a formal tone. John
Keats, for example, begins "Ode on a Grecian Urn" (p. 94) this way: "Thou
still unravished bride of quietness." Apostrophe is frequently accompanied by intense emotion that is signaled by phrasing such as "O Life." In
the right hands — such as Keats's — apostrophe can provide an intense and
immediate voice in a poem, but when it is overdone or extravagant it can
be ludicrous. Modern poets are more wary of apostrophe than their predecessors because apostrophizing strikes many self-conscious twenty-first-
century sensibilities as too theatrical. Thus modern poets tend to avoid
exaggerated situations in favor of less charged though equally meditative
moments, as in this next poem, with its amusing, half-serious cosmic
twist.

JANICE TOWNLEY MOORE (B. 1939)

To a Wasp   1984

You must have chortled
finding that tiny hole
in the kitchen screen. Right
into my cheese cake batter
you dived,   5
no chance to swim ashore,
no saving spoon,
the mixer whirring
your legs, wings, stinger,
churning you into such   10
delicious death.
Never mind the bright April day.
Did you not see
rising out of cumulus clouds
That fist aimed at both of us?   15

Moore's apostrophe "To a Wasp" is based on the simplest of domestic
circumstances; there is almost nothing theatrical or exaggerated in the
poem's tone until "That fist" in the last line, when exaggeration takes center stage. As a figure of speech, exaggeration is known as **overstatement**
or **hyperbole** and adds emphasis without intending to be literally true:
"The teenage boy ate everything in the house." Notice how the speaker of
Andrew Marvell's "To His Coy Mistress" (p. 80) exaggerates his devotion in
the following overstatement:

> An hundred years should go to praise
> Thine eyes and on thy forehead gaze,
> Two hundred to adore each breast,
> But thirty thousand to the rest:

That comes to 30,500 years. What is expressed here is heightened emotion, not deception.

The speaker also uses the opposite figure of speech, **understatement,** which says less than is intended. In the next section he sums up why he cannot take 30,500 years to express his love:

> The grave's a fine and private place,
> But none, I think, do there embrace.

The speaker is correct, of course, but by deliberately understating — saying "I think" when he is actually certain — he makes his point, that death will overtake their love, all the more emphatic. Another powerful example of understatement appears in the final line of Randall Jarrell's "The Death of the Ball Turret Gunner" (p. 70), when the disembodied voice of the machine-gunner describes his death in a bomber: "When I died they washed me out of the turret with a hose."

Paradox is a statement that initially appears to be self-contradictory but that, on closer inspection, turns out to make sense: "The pen is mightier than the sword." In a fencing match, anyone would prefer the sword, but if the goal is to win the hearts and minds of people, the art of persuasion can be more compelling than swordplay. To resolve the paradox, it is necessary to discover the sense that underlies the statement. If we see that "pen" and "sword" are used as metonymies for writing and violence, then the paradox rings true. **Oxymoron** is a condensed form of paradox in which two contradictory words are used together. Combinations such as "sweet sorrow," "silent scream," "sad joy," and "cold fire" indicate the kinds of startling effects that oxymorons can produce. Paradox is useful in poetry because it arrests a reader's attention by its seemingly stubborn refusal to make sense, and once a reader has penetrated the paradox, it is difficult to resist a perception so well earned. Good paradoxes are knotty pleasures. Here is a simple but effective one.

J. Patrick Lewis (B. 1942)
The Unkindest Cut 1993

Knives can harm you, heaven forbid;
Axes may disarm you, kid;
Guillotines are painful, but
There's nothing like a paper cut!

We all know how bloody paper cuts can be, but this quatrain is also a humorous version of "the pen is mightier than the sword." The wounds escalate to the paper cut, which paradoxically is more damaging than even the broad blade of a guillotine. "The unkindest cut" of all (an allusion to Shakespeare's *Julius Caesar,* III.ii.188) is produced by chilling words on a page rather than cold steel, but it is more painfully fatal nonetheless.

The following poems are rich in figurative language. As you read and study them, notice how their figures of speech vivify situations, clarify ideas, intensify emotions, and engage your imagination. Although the terms for the various figures discussed in this chapter are useful for labeling the particular devices used in poetry, they should not be allowed to get in the way of your response to a poem. Don't worry about rounding up examples of figurative language. First relax and let the figures work their effects on you. Use the terms as a means of taking you further into poetry, and they will serve your reading well.

POEMS FOR FURTHER STUDY

GARY SNYDER (B. 1930)

How Poetry Comes to Me

1992

It comes blundering over the
Boulders at night, it stays
Frightened outside the
Range of my campfire
I go to meet it at the
Edge of the light

CONSIDERATIONS FOR CRITICAL THINKING AND WRITING

1. **FIRST RESPONSE.** How does personification in this poem depict the creative process?

2. Why do you suppose Snyder makes each successive line shorter?

3. **CREATIVE RESPONSE.** How would eliminating the title change your understanding of the poem? Substitute another title that causes you to reinterpret it.

A SAMPLE STUDENT RESPONSE

Jennifer Jackson

Professor Kahane

English 215

October 16, 2009

Metaphor in Gary Snyder's "How Poetry Comes to Me"

"A metaphor," Michael Meyer writes, "makes a comparison between two unlike things . . . implicitly, without words such as *like* or *as*" (135). In his poem "How Poetry Comes to Me," Gary Snyder uses metaphor to compare poetic inspiration and creativity with a kind of wild creature.

In this work, poetry itself is both an ungraceful beast and a timid animal. It is something big and unwieldy, that "comes blundering over the / Boulders at night" (lines 1-2). The word "blunder" suggests that poetic inspiration moves clumsily, blindly—not knowing where it will go next—and somewhat dangerously. Yet it is hesitant and "stays / Frightened outside the / Range of [the] campfire" (2-4). According to Snyder's poem, the creature poetry comes only part way to meet the poet; the poet has to go to meet it on its terms, "at the / Edge of the light" (5-6). The metaphor of the poem as wild animal tells the reader that poetic inspiration is elusive and unpredictable. It must be sought out carefully or it will run back over the boulders, by the way it came. . . .

Works Cited

Meyer, Michael, ed. *Poetry: An Introduction*. 6th ed. Boston: Bedford/St. Martin's, 2010. 135. Print.

Snyder, Gary. "How Poetry Comes to Me." *Poetry: An Introduction*. Ed. Michael Meyer. 6th ed. Boston: Bedford/St. Martin's, 2010. 143. Print.

MARGARET ATWOOD (B. 1939)

February 1995

Winter. Time to eat fat
and watch hockey. In the pewter mornings, the cat,
a black fur sausage with yellow
Houdini eyes, jumps up on the bed and tries
to get onto my head. It's his   5
way of telling whether or not I'm dead.
If I'm not, he wants to be scratched; if I am
he'll think of something. He settles
on my chest, breathing his breath
of burped-up meat and musty sofas,   10
purring like a washboard. Some other tomcat,
not yet a capon, has been spraying our front door,
declaring war. It's all about sex and territory,
which are what will finish us off
in the long run. Some cat owners around here   15
should snip a few testicles. If we wise
hominids were sensible, we'd do that too,
or eat our young, like sharks.
But it's love that does us in. Over and over
again, *He shoots, he scores!* and famine   20
crouches in the bedsheets, ambushing the pulsing
eiderdown, and the windchill factor hits
thirty below, and pollution pours
out of our chimneys to keep us warm.
February, month of despair,   25
with a skewered heart in the centre.
I think dire thoughts, and lust for French fries
with a splash of vinegar.
Cat, enough of your greedy whining
and your small pink bumhole.   30
Off my face! You're the life principle,
more or less, so get going
on a little optimism around here.
Get rid of death. Celebrate increase. Make it be spring.

CONSIDERATIONS FOR CRITICAL THINKING AND WRITING

1. **FIRST RESPONSE.** How do your own associations with February compare with the speaker's?

2. Explain how the poem is organized around an extended metaphor that defines winter as a "Time to eat fat / and watch hockey" (lines 1–2).

3. Explain the paradox in "it's love that does us in" (line 19).

4. What theme(s) do you find in the poem? How is the cat central to them?

WILLIAM CARLOS WILLIAMS (1883–1963)

To Waken an Old Lady

1921

Old age is
a flight of small
cheeping birds
skimming
bare trees   5
above a snow glaze.
Gaining and failing
they are buffeted
by a dark wind—
But what?   10
On harsh weedstalks
the flock has rested,
the snow
is covered with broken
seedhusks   15
and the wind tempered
by a shrill
piping of plenty.

CONSIDERATIONS FOR CRITICAL THINKING AND WRITING

1. **FIRST RESPONSE.** Consider the images and figures of speech in this poem
   and explain why you think it is a positive or negative assessment of old
   age.
2. How does the title relate to the rest of the poem?

CONNECTION TO ANOTHER SELECTION

1. Discuss the shift in tone in "To Waken an Old Lady" and in Colette Inez's
   "Back When All Was Continuous Chuckles" (p. 73).

ERNEST SLYMAN (B. 1946)

Lightning Bugs

1988

In my backyard,
They burn peepholes in the night
And take snapshots of my house.

CONSIDERATIONS FOR CRITICAL THINKING AND WRITING

1. **FIRST RESPONSE.** Explain why the title is essential to this poem.
2. What makes the description of the lightning bugs effective? How do the
   second and third lines complement each other?
3. **CREATIVE RESPONSE.** As Slyman has done, take a simple, common fact of
   nature and make it vivid by using a figure of speech to describe it.

PETER MEINKE (B. 1932)

Unnatural Light   1996

After the break-in
we hung spotlights on the garage outside
Light-sensitive they flare on at dusk
fade out at dawn night-blooming suns
on crime watch   5

Through the dense dark
light pulses under oak and laurel
pulling the stems of periwinkle and begonia
the crimson bougainvillea on the trellis
the calamondin with its bitter fruit   10
When the wind blows in their shadows
slide like burglars along the wall
beyond our barred windows
around the shaky birdhouse
spilling crumbs   15

And the white azaleas confused
by so much light confess their startling secrets
three months early   The others farther out
huddle in natural darkness playing it safe
keeping mum   20

CONSIDERATIONS FOR CRITICAL THINKING AND WRITING

1. **FIRST RESPONSE.** Why do you suppose Meinke substitutes spacing for punctuation in this poem?
2. Describe the controlling metaphor. In which lines does it appear?
3. Discuss whether the tone of this poem is light or dark.

CONNECTION TO ANOTHER SELECTION

1. Compare "Unnatural Light" and Emily Dickinson's "Presentiment — is that long Shadow — on the lawn —" (p. 136) as meditations on being "Light-sensitive," as Meinke puts it.

JUDY PAGE HEITZMAN (B. 1952)

The Schoolroom on the Second Floor
of the Knitting Mill   1991

While most of us copied letters out of books,
Mrs. Lawrence carved and cleaned her nails.
Now the red and buff cardinals at my back-room window
make me miss her, her room, her hallway,
even the chimney outside   5
that broke up the sky.

In my memory it is afternoon.
Sun streams in through the door
next to the fire escape where we are lined up
getting our coats on to go out to the playground,   10
the tether ball, its towering height, the swings.
She tells me to make sure the line
does not move up over the threshold.
That would be dangerous.
So I stand guard at the door.   15
Somehow it happens
the way things seem to happen when we're not really looking,
or we are looking, just not the right way.
Kids crush up like cattle, pushing me over the line.

Judy is not a good leader is all Mrs. Lawrence says.   20
She says it quietly. Still, everybody hears.
Her arms hang down like sausages.
I hear her every time I fail.

CONSIDERATIONS FOR CRITICAL THINKING AND WRITING

1. **FIRST RESPONSE.** Does your impression of Mrs. Lawrence change from the beginning to the end of the poem? How so?

2. How can line 2 be read as an implied metaphor?

3. Discuss the use of similes in the poem. How do they contribute to the poem's meaning?

SYLVIA PLATH (1932–1963)

Mirror   *1963*

I am silver and exact. I have no
    preconceptions.
Whatever I see I swallow immediately
Just as it is, unmisted by love or dislike.
I am not cruel, only truthful —
The eye of a little god, four-cornered.
Most of the time I meditate on the
    opposite wall.
It is pink, with speckles. I have looked
    at it so long

© Bettmann/CORBIS.

I think it is a part of my heart. But it flickers.
Faces and darkness separate us over and over.

Now I am a lake. A woman bends over me,   10
Searching my reaches for what she really is.
Then she turns to those liars, the candles or the moon.
I see her back, and reflect it faithfully.
She rewards me with tears and an agitation of hands.
I am important to her. She comes and goes.   15

Each morning it is her face that replaces the darkness.
In me she has drowned a young girl, and in me an old woman
Rises toward her day after day, like a terrible fish.

CONSIDERATIONS FOR CRITICAL THINKING AND WRITING

1. **FIRST RESPONSE.** What is the effect of the personification in this poem? How would our view of the aging woman be different if she, rather than the mirror, told her story?

2. What is the mythical allusion in "Now I am a lake" (line 10)?

3. In what sense can "candles or the moon" be regarded as "liars" (line 12)? Explain this metaphor.

4. Discuss the effectiveness of the simile in the poem's final line.

WILLIAM WORDSWORTH (1770–1850)

London, 1802   *1802*

Milton!° thou should'st be living at this hour:
England hath need of thee: she is a fen
Of stagnant waters: altar, sword, and pen,
Fireside, the heroic wealth of hall and bower,
Have forfeited their ancient English dower   5
Of inward happiness. We are selfish men;
Oh! raise us up, return to us again;
And give us manners, virtue, freedom, power.
Thy soul was like a star, and dwelt apart:
Thou hadst a voice whose sound was like the sea: 10
Pure as the naked heavens, majestic, free,
So didst thou travel on life's common way,
In cheerful godliness; and yet thy heart
The lowliest duties on herself did lay.

1 *Milton:* John Milton (1608–1674), poet, famous especially for his religious epic *Paradise Lost* and his defense of political freedom.

CONSIDERATIONS FOR CRITICAL THINKING AND WRITING

1. **FIRST RESPONSE.** Describe the poem's tone. Is it nostalgic, angry, or something else?

2. Explain the metonymies in lines 3–6 of this poem. What is the speaker's assessment of England?

3. How would the effect of the poem be different if it were in the form of an address to Wordsworth's contemporaries rather than an apostrophe to Milton? What qualities does Wordsworth attribute to Milton by the use of figurative language?

4. **CRITICAL STRATEGIES.** Read the section on literary history criticism (pp. 672–73) in Chapter 26, "Critical Strategies for Reading," and use the library to find out about the state of London in 1802. How does the poem reflect or refute the social values of its time?

JIM STEVENS (B. 1922)

Schizophrenia   *1992*

It was the house that suffered most.

It had begun with slamming doors, angry feet scuffing the carpets,
dishes slammed onto the table,
greasy stains spreading on the cloth.

Certain doors were locked at night,   5
feet stood for hours outside them,
dishes were left unwashed, the cloth
disappeared under a hardened crust.

The house came to miss the shouting voices,
the threats, the half-apologies, noisy   10
reconciliations, the sobbing that followed.

Then lines were drawn, borders established,
some rooms declared their loyalties,
keeping to themselves, keeping out the other.
The house divided against itself.   15

Seeing cracking paint, broken windows,
the front door banging in the wind,
the roof tiles flying off, one by one,
the neighbors said it was a madhouse.

It was the house that suffered most.   20

CONSIDERATIONS FOR CRITICAL THINKING AND WRITING

1. **FIRST RESPONSE.** What is the effect of personifying the house in this poem?
2. How are the people who live in the house characterized? What does their behavior reveal about them? How does the house respond to them?
3. Comment on the title. If the title were missing, what, if anything, would be missing from the poem? Explain your answer.

WALT WHITMAN (1819–1892)

A Noiseless Patient Spider   *1868*

A noiseless patient spider,
I mark'd where on a little promontory it stood isolated,
Mark'd how to explore the vacant vast surrounding,
It launch'd forth filament, filament, filament, out of itself,
Ever unreeling them, ever tirelessly speeding them.   5

And you O my soul where you stand,
Surrounded, detached, in measureless oceans of space,

Ceaselessly musing, venturing, throwing, seeking
    the spheres to connect them,
Till the bridge you will need be form'd, till the ductile anchor hold,
Till the gossamer thread you fling catch somewhere, O my soul.   10

CONSIDERATIONS FOR CRITICAL THINKING AND WRITING

1. **FIRST RESPONSE.** Spiders are not usually regarded as pleasant creatures. Why does the speaker in this poem liken his soul to one? What similarities are there in the poem between spider and soul? Are there any significant differences?

2. How do the images of space relate to the connections made between the speaker's soul and the spider?

JOHN DONNE (1572–1631)

A Valediction: Forbidding Mourning   *1611*

As virtuous men pass mildly away,
    And whisper to their souls to go,
While some of their sad friends do say,
    The breath goes now, and some say, no:

So let us melt, and make no noise,   5
    No tear-floods, nor sigh-tempests move;
'Twere profanation of our joys
    To tell the laity our love.

Moving of th' earth° brings harms and fears,   *earthquakes*
    Men reckon what it did and meant,   10
But trepidation of the spheres,°
    Though greater far, is innocent.

Dull sublunary° lovers' love
    (Whose soul is sense) cannot admit
Absence, because it doth remove   15
    Those things which elemented° it.   *composed*

But we by a love so much refined,
    That ourselves know not what it is,
Inter-assured of the mind,
    Care less, eyes, lips, and hands to miss.   20

Our two souls therefore, which are one,
    Though I must go, endure not yet
A breach, but an expansion,
    Like gold to airy thinness beat.

11 *trepidation of the spheres:* According to Ptolemaic astronomy, the planets sometimes moved violently, like earthquakes, but these movements were not felt by people on earth.
13 *sublunary:* Under the moon; hence, mortal and subject to change.

> If they be two, they are two so 25
> As stiff twin compasses are two;
> Thy soul the fixed foot, makes no show
> To move, but doth, if th' other do.
>
> And though it in the center sit,
> Yet when the other far doth roam, 30
> It leans, and hearkens after it,
> And grows erect, as that comes home.
>
> Such wilt thou be to me, who must
> Like th' other foot, obliquely run;
> Thy firmness makes my circle just,° 35
> And makes me end, where I begun.

35 *circle just:* The circle is a traditional symbol of perfection.

CONSIDERATIONS FOR CRITICAL THINKING AND WRITING

1. **FIRST RESPONSE.** A valediction is a farewell. Donne wrote this poem for his wife before leaving on a trip to France. What kind of "mourning" is the speaker forbidding?
2. Explain how the simile in lines 1–4 is related to the couple in lines 5–8. Who is described as dying?
3. How does the speaker contrast the couple's love to "sublunary lovers' love" (line 13)?
4. Explain the similes in lines 24 and 25–36.

LINDA PASTAN (B. 1932)

Marks   1978

My husband gives me an A
for last night's supper,
an incomplete for my ironing,
a B plus in bed.
My son says I am average, 5
an average mother, but if
I put my mind to it
I could improve.
My daughter believes
in Pass/Fail and tells me 10
I pass. Wait 'til they learn
I'm dropping out.

CONSIDERATIONS FOR CRITICAL THINKING AND WRITING

1. **FIRST RESPONSE.** Explain the appropriateness of the controlling metaphor in this poem. How does it reveal the woman's relationship to her family?
2. Discuss the meaning of the title.
3. How does the last line serve as both the climax of the woman's story and the poem's controlling metaphor?

KAY RYAN (B. 1945)

Hailstorm   *2005*

Like a storm
of hornets, the
little white planets
layer and relayer
as they whip around
in their high orbits,
getting more and
more dense before
they crash against
our crust. A maelstrom
of ferocious little
fists and punches,
so hard to believe
once it's past.

© Christopher Felver/CORBIS.

CONSIDERATIONS FOR CRITICAL THINKING AND WRITING

1. **FIRST RESPONSE.** Describe the progression in violence from the simile to the metaphor as the hailstorm develops.

2. Why is "maelstrom" just the right word in line 10?

3. **CREATIVE RESPONSE.** Try writing a poem in a similar style using one or two striking similes or metaphors to describe a thunderstorm, snowstorm, or windstorm.

RONALD WALLACE (B. 1945)

Building an Outhouse   *1991*

Is not unlike building a poem: the pure
mathematics of shape; the music of hammer
and tenpenny nail, of floor joist, stud wall,
and sill; the cut wood's sweet smell.

If the Skil saw rear up in your unpracticed hand,   5
cussing, hawking its chaw of dust,
and you're lost in the pounding particulars
of fly rafters, siding, hypotenuse, and load,
until nothing seems level or true
but the scorn of the tape's clucked tongue,   10

let the nub of your plainspoken pencil prevail
and it's up! Functional. Tight as a sonnet.
It will last forever (or at least for awhile)
though the critics come sit on it, and sit on it.

CONSIDERATIONS FOR CRITICAL THINKING AND WRITING

1. **FIRST RESPONSE.** Explain how the poem's diction contributes to the extended simile. Why is the language of building especially appropriate here?

2. What is the effect of the repetition and sounds in the final line? How does that affect the poem's tone?

3. Consult the Glossary of Literary Terms (p. 745) for the definition of a sonnet. To what extent does "Building an Outhouse" conform to a sonnet's structure?

ELAINE MAGARRELL (B. 1928)

The Joy of Cooking

1988

I have prepared my sister's tongue,
scrubbed and skinned it,
trimmed the roots, small bones, and gristle.
Carved through the hump it slices thin and neat.
Best with horseradish   5
and economical — it probably will grow back.
Next time perhaps a creole sauce
or mold of aspic?

I will have my brother's heart,
which is firm and rather dry,   10
slow cooked. It resembles muscle
more than organ meat
and needs an apple-onion stuffing
to make it interesting at all.
Although beef heart serves six   15
my brother's heart barely feeds two.
I could also have it braised
and served in sour sauce.

CONSIDERATIONS FOR CRITICAL THINKING AND WRITING

1. **FIRST RESPONSE.** Describe the poem's tone. Do you find it amusing, bitter, or something else?

2. How are the tongue and heart used to characterize the sister and brother in this poem?

3. How is the speaker's personality revealed in the poem's language?

CONNECTION TO ANOTHER SELECTION

1. Write an essay that explains how cooking becomes a way of talking about something else in this poem and in Sally Croft's "Home-Baked Bread" (p. 126).

RUTH FAINLIGHT (B. 1931)

The Clarinettist

2002

Pale round arms raising her clarinet
at the exact angle, she sways, then halts,
poised for the music

like a horse that gathers itself up before the leap
with the awkward, perfect, only   5
possible movement

an alto in a quattrocento chorus, blond head
lifted from the score, open-mouthed
for hallelujah

a cherub on a ceiling cornice leaning out   10
from heaped-up clouds of opalescent pink,
translucent blue

a swimmer breasting frothy surf like ripping through
lace curtains, a dancer centred as a spinning top,
an August moon   15

alone, in front of the orchestra, the conductor's
other, and unacknowledged opposite,
she starts the tune.

CONSIDERATIONS FOR CRITICAL THINKING AND WRITING

1. **FIRST RESPONSE.** This poem is structured as one long sentence. How does this structure create a kind of suspense as the clarinettist is "poised for the music" (line 3)?

2. How do the similes and metaphors capture the moment that the clarinettist "starts the tune" (line 18)? What sort of description of her emerges from them?

3. **CREATIVE RESPONSE.** Create a similar three-line stanza that adds to Fainlight's description and maintains the poem's tone.

Perspective

JOHN R. SEARLE (B. 1932)

Figuring Out Metaphors

1979

If you hear somebody say, "Sally is a block of ice," or, "Sam is a pig," you are likely to assume that the speaker does not mean what he says literally, but that he is speaking metaphorically. Furthermore, you are not likely to have very much trouble figuring out what he means. If he says, "Sally is a prime number between 17 and 23," or "Bill is a barn door," you might still assume he is speaking metaphorically, but it is much harder to figure out what he means. The existence of such utterances — utterances in which the speaker means metaphorically something different from what the sentence means literally — poses a series of questions for any theory of language and communication: What is metaphor, and how does it differ from both literal and other forms of figurative utterances? Why do we use expressions metaphorically instead of saying exactly and literally what we mean? How do metaphorical utterances work, that is, how is it possible for speakers to communicate to hearers when speaking metaphorically inasmuch as they do not say what they mean? And why do some metaphors work and others do not?

From *Expression and Meaning*

CONSIDERATIONS FOR CRITICAL THINKING AND WRITING

1. Searle poses a series of important questions. Write an essay that explores one of these questions, basing your discussion on the poems in this chapter.

2. **CREATIVE RESPONSE.** Try writing a brief poem that provides a context for the line "Sally is a prime number between 17 and 23" or the line "Bill is a barn door." Your task is to create a context so that either one of these metaphoric statements is as readily understandable as "Sally is a block of ice" or "Sam is a pig." Share your poem with your classmates and explain how the line generated the poem you built around it.

Web Research the poets in this chapter at bedfordstmartins.com/ rewritinglit.

6

Symbol, Allegory, and Irony

© Barbara Savage Cheresh.

> Poetry is serious business; literature is the apparatus through which the world tries to keep intact its important ideas and feelings.
> — MARY OLIVER

SYMBOL

A **symbol** is something that represents something else. An object, a person, a place, an event, or an action can suggest more than its literal meaning. A handshake between two world leaders might be simply a greeting, but if it is done ceremoniously before cameras, it could be a symbolic gesture signifying unity, issues resolved, and joint policies that will be followed. We live surrounded by symbols. When a $100,000 Mercedes-Benz comes roaring by in the fast lane, we get a quick glimpse of not only an expensive car but an entire lifestyle that suggests opulence, broad lawns, executive offices, and power. One of the reasons some buyers are willing to spend roughly the cost of five Chevrolets for a single Mercedes-Benz is that they are aware of the car's symbolic value. A symbol is a vehicle

Explore the poetic elements in this chapter on *LiterActive* or at bedfordstmartins.com/ rewritinglit.

for two things at once: it functions as itself, and it implies meanings beyond itself.

The meanings suggested by a symbol are determined by the context in which it appears. The Mercedes could symbolize very different things depending on where it was parked. Would an American political candidate be likely to appear in a Detroit blue-collar neighborhood with such a car? Probably not. Although a candidate might be able to afford the car, it would be an inappropriate symbol for someone seeking votes from all of the people. As a symbol, the German-built Mercedes would backfire if voters perceived it as representing an entity partially responsible for layoffs of automobile workers or, worse, as a sign of decadence and corruption. Similarly, a huge portrait of Mao Tse-tung conveys different meanings to residents of Beijing than it would to farmers in Prairie Center, Illinois. Because symbols depend on contexts for their meaning, literary artists provide those contexts so that the reader has enough information to determine the probable range of meanings suggested by a symbol.

In the following poem, the speaker describes walking at night. How is the night used symbolically?

ROBERT FROST (1874–1963)

Acquainted with the Night   *1928*

I have been one acquainted with the night.
I have walked out in rain — and back in rain.
I have outwalked the furthest city light.

I have looked down the saddest city lane.
I have passed by the watchman on his beat   5
And dropped my eyes, unwilling to explain.

I have stood still and stopped the sound of feet
When far away an interrupted cry
Came over houses from another street,

But not to call me back or say good-by;   10
And further still at an unearthly height
One luminary clock against the sky

Proclaimed the time was neither wrong nor right.
I have been one acquainted with the night.

In approaching this or any poem, you should read for literal meanings first and then allow the elements of the poem to invite you to symbolic readings, if they are appropriate. Here the somber tone suggests that the lines have symbolic meaning, too. The flat matter-of-factness created by the repetition of "I have" (lines 1–5, 7, 14) understates the symbolic subject matter of the poem, which is, finally, more about the "night" located in the speaker's mind or soul than it is about walking away from a city and back again. The speaker is "acquainted with the night." The importance of this phrase is emphasized by Frost's title and by the fact that he begins and ends the poem with it. Poets frequently use this kind of repetition to alert readers to details that carry more than literal meanings.

The speaker in this poem has personal knowledge of the night but does not indicate specifically what the night means. To arrive at the potential meanings of the night in this context, it is necessary to look closely at its connotations, along with the images provided in the poem. The connotative meanings of night suggest, for example, darkness, death, and grief. By drawing on these connotations, Frost uses a ***conventional symbol*** — something that is recognized by many people to represent certain ideas. Roses conventionally symbolize love or beauty; laurels, fame; spring, growth; the moon, romance. Poets often use conventional symbols to convey tone and meaning.

Frost uses the night as a conventional symbol, but he also develops it into a ***literary*** or ***contextual symbol*** that goes beyond traditional, public meanings. A literary symbol cannot be summarized in a word or two. It tends to be as elusive as experience itself. The night cannot be reduced to or equated with darkness or death or grief, but it evokes those associations and more. Frost took what perhaps initially appears to be an overworked, conventional symbol and prevented it from becoming a cliché by deepening and extending its meaning.

The images in "Acquainted with the Night" lead to the poem's symbolic meaning. Unwilling, and perhaps unable, to explain explicitly to the watchman (and to the reader) what the night means, the speaker nevertheless conveys feelings about it. The brief images of darkness, rain, sad city lanes, the necessity for guards, the eerie sound of a distressing cry coming over rooftops, and the "luminary clock against the sky" proclaiming "the time was neither wrong nor right" all help to create a sense of anxiety in this tight-lipped speaker. Although we cannot know what unnamed personal experiences have acquainted the speaker with the night, the images suggest that whatever the night means, it is somehow associated with insomnia, loneliness, isolation, coldness, darkness, death, fear, and a sense of alienation from humanity and even time. Daylight — ordinary daytime thoughts and life itself — seems remote and unavailable in this poem. The night is literally the period from sunset to sunrise, but, more important, it is an internal state of being felt by the speaker and revealed through the images.

Frost used symbols rather than an expository essay that would explain the conditions that cause these feelings because most readers can provide their own list of sorrows and terrors that evoke similar emotions. Through symbol, the speaker's experience is compressed and simultaneously expanded by the personal darkness that each reader brings to the poem. The suggestive nature of symbols makes them valuable for poets and evocative for readers.

ALLEGORY

Unlike expansive, suggestive symbols, **allegory** is a narration or description usually restricted to a single meaning because its events, actions, characters, settings, and objects represent specific abstractions or ideas. Although the elements in an allegory may be interesting in themselves, the emphasis tends to be on what they ultimately mean. Characters may be given names such as Hope, Pride, Youth, and Charity; they have few, if any, personal qualities beyond their abstract meanings. These personifications are a form of extended metaphor, but their meanings are severely restricted. They are not symbols because, for instance, the meaning of a character named Charity is precisely that virtue.

There is little or no room for broad speculation and exploration in allegories. If Frost had written "Acquainted with the Night" as an allegory, he might have named his speaker Loneliness and had him leave the City of Despair to walk the Streets of Emptiness, where Crime, Poverty, Fear, and other characters would define the nature of city life. The literal elements in an allegory tend to be de-emphasized in favor of the message. Symbols, however, function both literally and symbolically, so that "Acquainted with the Night" is about both a walk and a sense that something is terribly wrong.

Allegory especially lends itself to **didactic poetry,** which is designed to teach an ethical, moral, or religious lesson. Many stories, poems, and plays are concerned with values, but didactic literature is specifically created to convey a message. "Acquainted with the Night" does not impart advice or offer guidance. If the poem argued that city life is self-destructive or sinful, it would be didactic; instead, it is a lyric poem that expresses the emotions and thoughts of a single speaker.

Although allegory is often enlisted in didactic causes because it can so readily communicate abstract ideas through physical representations, not all allegories teach a lesson. Here is a poem describing a haunted palace while also establishing a consistent pattern that reveals another meaning.

EDGAR ALLAN POE (1809–1849)

The Haunted Palace

1839

I

In the greenest of our valleys,
  By good angels tenanted,
Once a fair and stately palace —
  Radiant palace — reared its head.

In the monarch Thought's dominion —   5
   It stood there!
Never seraph spread a pinion
   Over fabric half so fair.

II

Banners yellow, glorious, golden,
   On its roof did float and flow;   10
(This — all this — was in the olden
   Time long ago)
And every gentle air that dallied,
   In that sweet day,
Along the ramparts plumed and pallid,   15
   A wingèd odor went away.

III

Wanderers in that happy valley
   Through two luminous windows saw
Spirits moving musically
   To a lute's well-tunèd law,   20
Round about a throne, where sitting
   (Porphyrogene!)°   *born to purple, royal*
In state his glory well befitting,
   The ruler of the realm was seen.

IV

And all with pearl and ruby glowing   25
   Was the fair palace door,
Through which came flowing, flowing, flowing
   And sparkling evermore,
A troop of Echoes whose sweet duty
   Was but to sing,   30
In voices of surpassing beauty,
   The wit and wisdom of their king.

V

But evil things, in robes of sorrow,
   Assailed the monarch's high estate;
(Ah, let us mourn, for never morrow   35
   Shall dawn upon him, desolate!)
And, round about his home, the glory
   That blushed and bloomed
Is but a dim-remembered story
   Of the old time entombed.   40

VI

And travelers now within that valley,
    Through the red-litten windows see
Vast forms that move fantastically
    To a discordant melody;
While, like a rapid ghastly river,   45
    Through the pale door,
A hideous throng rush out forever,
    And laugh — but smile no more.

     On one level this poem describes how a once happy palace is desolated by "evil things" (line 33). If the reader pays close attention to the diction, however, an allegorical meaning becomes apparent on a second reading. A systematic pattern develops in the choice of words used to describe the palace, so that it comes to stand for a human mind. The palace, banners, windows, door, echoes, and throng are equated with a person's head, hair, eyes, mouth, voice, and laughter. That mind, once harmoniously ordered, is overthrown by evil, haunting thoughts that lead to the mad laughter in the poem's final lines. Once the general pattern is seen, the rest of the details fall neatly into place to strengthen the parallels between the surface description of a palace and the allegorical representation of a disordered mind.

     Modern writers generally prefer symbol over allegory because they tend to be more interested in opening up the potential meanings of an experience instead of transforming it into a closed pattern of meaning. Perhaps the major difference is that while allegory may delight a reader's imagination, symbol challenges and enriches it.

IRONY

Another important resource writers use to take readers beyond literal meanings is *irony,* a technique that reveals a discrepancy between what appears to be and what is actually true. Here is a classic example in which appearances give way to the underlying reality.

EDWIN ARLINGTON ROBINSON *(1869–1935)*

Richard Cory   *1897*

Whenever Richard Cory went down town,
We people on the pavement looked at him:
He was a gentleman from sole to crown,
Clean favored, and imperially slim.

And he was always quietly arrayed,   5
And he was always human when he talked;
But still he fluttered pulses when he said,
"Good-morning," and he glittered when he walked.

And he was rich — yes, richer than a king —
And admirably schooled in every grace: 10
In fine, we thought that he was everything
To make us wish that we were in his place.

So on we worked, and waited for the light,
And went without the meat, and cursed the bread;
And Richard Cory, one calm summer night,   15
Went home and put a bullet through his head.

Richard Cory seems to have it all. Those less fortunate, the "people on the pavement," regard him as well-bred, handsome, tasteful, and richly endowed with both money and grace. Until the final line of the poem, the reader, like the speaker, is charmed by Cory's good fortune, so quietly expressed in his decent, easy manner. That final, shocking line, however, shatters the appearances of Cory's life and reveals him to have been a desperately unhappy man. While everyone else assumes that Cory represented "everything" to which they aspire, the reality is that he could escape his miserable life only as a suicide. This discrepancy between what appears to be true and what actually exists is known as ***situational irony:*** what happens is entirely different from what is expected. We are not told why Cory shoots himself; instead, the irony in the poem shocks us into the recognition that appearances do not always reflect realities.

Words are also sometimes intended to be taken at other than face value. **Verbal irony** is saying something different from what is meant. If after reading "Richard Cory," you said, "That rich gentleman sure was happy," your statement would be ironic. Your tone of voice would indicate that just the opposite was meant; hence verbal irony is usually easy to detect in spoken language. In literature, however, a reader can sometimes take literally what a writer intends ironically. The remedy for this kind of misreading is to pay close attention to the poem's context. There is no formula that can detect verbal irony, but contradictory actions and statements as well as the use of understatement and overstatement can often be signals that verbal irony is present.

A SAMPLE STUDENT RESPONSE

Cipriano Diaz

Professor Young

English 200

September 16, 2009

Irony in Edwin Arlington Robinson's "Richard Cory"

In Edwin Arlington Robinson's poem "Richard Cory," appearances are not reality. The character Richard Cory, viewed by the townspeople as "richer than a king" (line 9) and "a gentleman from sole to crown" (3), is someone who inspires envy. The poem's speaker says, "we thought that he was everything / To make us wish that we were in his place" (11-12). However, the final shocking line of the poem creates a situational irony that emphasizes the difference between what seems—and what really is.

In lines 1 through 14, the speaker sets up a shining, princely image of Cory, associating him with such regal words as "imperially" (4), "crown" (3), and "king" (9). Cory is viewed by the townspeople from the "pavement" as if he is on a pedestal (2); far below him, those who must work and "[go] without meat" stand in stark contrast (14). Further, not only is Cory a gentleman, he is so good-looking that he "flutter[s] the pulses" (7) of those around him when he speaks. He's a rich man who "glitter[s] when he walk[s]" (8). He is also a decent man who is "always human when he talk[s]" (6). However, this noble image of Cory is unexpectedly shattered "one calm summer night" in the final couplet (15). What the speaker and townspeople believed Cory to be and aspired to imitate was merely an illusion. The irony is that what Cory seemed to be—a happy, satisfied man—is exactly what he was not. . . .

Work Cited

Robinson, Edwin Arlington. "Richard Cory." *Poetry: An Introduction.* Ed. Michael Meyer. 6th ed. Boston: Bedford/St. Martin's, 2010. 162. Print.

Consider how verbal irony is used in this poem.

KENNETH FEARING (1902–1961)

AD   *1938*

Wanted: Men;
Millions of men are *wanted at once* in a big new field;
New, tremendous, thrilling, great.
If you've ever been a figure in the chamber of horrors,
If you've ever escaped from a psychiatric ward,   5
If you thrill at the thought of throwing poison into wells, have heavenly
    visions of people, by the thousands, dying in flames —

You are the very man we want
We mean business and our business is *you*
Wanted: A race of brand-new men.   10

Apply: Middle Europe;
No skill needed;
No ambition required; no brains wanted and no character allowed;

Take a permanent job in the coming profession
Wages: *Death.*   15

This poem was written as Nazi troops stormed across Europe at the start of World War II. The advertisement suggests on the surface that killing is just an ordinary job, but the speaker indicates through understatement that there is nothing ordinary about the "business" of this "*coming profession.*" Fearing uses verbal irony to indicate how casually and mindlessly people are prepared to accept the horrors of war.

"AD" is a ***satire,*** an example of the literary art of ridiculing a folly or vice in an effort to expose or correct it. The object of satire is usually some human frailty; people, institutions, ideas, and things are all fair game for satirists. Fearing satirizes the insanity of a world mobilizing itself for war: his irony reveals the speaker's knowledge that there is nothing "*New, tremendous, thrilling,* [or] *great*" about going off to kill and be killed. The implication of the poem is that no one should respond to advertisements for war. The poem serves as a satiric corrective to those who would troop off armed with unrealistic expectations: wage war, and the wages consist of death.

Dramatic irony is used when a writer allows a reader to know more about a situation than a character does. This creates a discrepancy between what a character says or thinks and what the reader knows to be true. Dramatic irony is often used to reveal character. In the following poem the speaker delivers a public address that ironically tells us more about him than it does about the patriotic holiday he is commemorating.

E. E. CUMMINGS (1894–1962)

next to of course god america i   1926

"next to of course god america i
love you land of the pilgrims' and so forth oh
say can you see by the dawn's early my
country 'tis of centuries come and go
and are no more what of it we should worry   5
in every language even deafanddumb
thy sons acclaim your glorious name by gorry
by jingo by gee by gosh by gum
why talk of beauty what could be more beautiful than these heroic happy dead   10
who rushed like lions to the roaring slaughter
they did not stop to think they died instead
then shall the voice of liberty be mute?"

He spoke. And drank rapidly a glass of water

This verbal debauch of chauvinistic clichés (notice the run-on phrases and lines) reveals that the speaker's relationship to God and country is not, as he claims, one of love. His public address suggests a hearty mindlessness that leads to "roaring slaughter" rather than to reverence or patriotism. Cummings allows the reader to see through the speaker's words to their dangerous emptiness. What the speaker means and what Cummings means are entirely different. Like Fearing's "AD," this poem is a satire that invites the reader's laughter and contempt in order to deflate the benighted attitudes expressed in it.

When a writer uses God, destiny, or fate to dash the hopes and expectations of a character or humankind in general, it is called **cosmic irony.** In "The Convergence of the Twain" (p. 86), for example, Thomas Hardy describes how "The Immanent Will" brought together the *Titanic* and a deadly iceberg. Technology and pride are no match for "the Spinner of the Years." Here's a painfully terse version of cosmic irony.

STEPHEN CRANE (1871–1900)

A Man Said to the Universe   1899

A man said to the universe:
"Sir, I exist!"
"However," replied the universe,
"The fact has not created in me
A sense of obligation."

Unlike in "The Convergence of the Twain," there is the slightest bit of humor in Crane's poem, but the joke is on us.

Irony is an important technique that allows a writer to distinguish between appearances and realities. In situational irony a discrepancy exists between what we expect to happen and what actually happens; in verbal irony a discrepancy exists between what is said and what is meant; in dramatic irony a discrepancy exists between what a character believes and what the reader knows to be true; and in cosmic irony a discrepancy exists between what a character aspires to and what universal forces provide. With each form of irony, we are invited to move beyond surface appearances and sentimental assumptions to see the complexity of experience. Irony is often used in literature to reveal a writer's perspective on matters that previously seemed settled.

POEMS FOR FURTHER STUDY

Bob Hicok (b. 1960)

Making it in poetry   2004

The young teller
at the credit union
asked why so many
small checks
from universities?   5
Because I write
poems I said. Why
haven't I heard
of you? Because
I write poems   10
I said.

Considerations for Critical Thinking and Writing

1. **FIRST RESPONSE.** Explain how the speaker's verbal irony is central to the poem's humor.
2. What sort of portrait of the poet-speaker emerges from this very brief poem?

Connection to Another Selection

1. Compare the lives of the poets in Hicok's poem and in Richard Wakefield's "In a Poetry Workshop" (p. 649).

JANE KENYON (1947–1995)

Surprise   *1996*

He suggests pancakes at the local diner,
followed by a walk in search of mayflowers,
while friends convene at the house
bearing casseroles and a cake, their cars
pulled close along the sandy shoulders
of the road, where tender ferns unfurl
in the ditches, and this year's budding leaves
push last year's spectral leaves from the tips
of the twigs of the ash trees. The gathering
itself is not what astounds her, but the casual   10
accomplishment with which he has lied.

Courtesy of Donald Hall.

CONSIDERATIONS FOR CRITICAL THINKING AND WRITING

1. **FIRST RESPONSE.** Does it matter that this poem is set in the spring?
2. Consider the connotative meaning of "ash trees" in line 9. Why are they particularly appropriate?
3. Why do you suppose Kenyon uses "astounds" rather than "surprises" in line 10? Use a dictionary to help you determine the possible reasons for this choice.
4. Discuss the irony in the poem.

CONNECTIONS TO OTHER SELECTIONS

1. Write an essay on the nature of the surprises in Kenyon's poem and in Hathaway's "Oh, Oh" (p. 24). Include in your discussion a comparison of the tone and irony in each poem.
2. Compare and contrast in an essay the irony associated with the birthday parties in this poem and in Sharon Olds's "Rite of Passage" (p. 546).

MARTÍN ESPADA (B. 1957)

Bully   *1990*

Boston, Massachusetts, 1987

In the school auditorium
the Theodore Roosevelt statue
is nostalgic
for the Spanish-American War,
each fist lonely for a saber   5
or the reins of anguish-eyed horses,
or a podium to clatter with speeches
glorying in the malaria of conquest.

But now the Roosevelt school
is pronounced *Hernández*.   10
Puerto Rico has invaded Roosevelt
with its army of Spanish-singing children
in the hallways,
brown children devouring
the stockpiles of the cafeteria,   15
children painting *Taíno* ancestors°
that leap naked across murals.

Roosevelt is surrounded
by all the faces
he ever shoved in eugenic spite   20
and cursed as mongrels, skin of one race,
hair and cheekbones of another.

Once Marines tramped
from the newsreel of his imagination;
now children plot to spray graffiti   25
in parrot-brilliant colors
across the Victorian mustache
and monocle.

16 Taíno *ancestors:* The most culturally developed Indian tribe in the Caribbean when
Columbus arrived in Hispaniola in 1492.

CONSIDERATIONS FOR CRITICAL THINKING AND WRITING

1. **FIRST RESPONSE.** Describe the speaker's sense of the past as well as the pres-
    ent. In what sense do two very different cultures collide in this poem?

2. What do you think is the poem's central theme? How do the images and
    symbols work together to contribute to the theme?

3. **CRITICAL STRATEGIES.** Read the section on new historicist and cultural crit-
    icism (pp. 675–76) in Chapter 26, "Critical Strategies for Reading," and then do
    some research on Theodore Roosevelt's role in the Spanish-American War
    and on what was happening in the Boston public school system in the late
    1980s. How does this information affect your reading of the poem?

KEVIN PIERCE (B. 1958)

Proof of Origin   2005

*NEWSWIRE — A U.S. judge ordered a Georgia school district to remove from textbooks
stickers challenging the theory of evolution.*

Though close to their hearts is the version that starts
With Adam and Eve and no clothes,
What enables their grip as the stickers they strip
Is Darwinian thumbs that oppose.

CONSIDERATIONS FOR CRITICAL THINKING AND WRITING

1. **FIRST RESPONSE.** How do the rhymes contribute to the humorous tone?
2. Discuss the levels of irony in the poem.
3. How do you read the title? Can it be explained in more than one way?

CARL SANDBURG (1878–1967)

Buttons   *1905*

I have been watching the war map slammed up for advertising in front
     of the newspaper office.
Buttons — red and yellow buttons — blue and black buttons — are shoved
     back and forth across the map.

A laughing young man, sunny with freckles,
Climbs a ladder, yells a joke to somebody in the crowd,
And then fixes a yellow button one inch west
And follows the yellow button with a black button one inch west.

(Ten thousand men and boys twist on their bodies in a red soak along a
     river edge,
Gasping of wounds, calling for water, some rattling death in their
     throats.)
Who would guess what it cost to move two buttons one inch on the war
     map here in front of the newspaper office where the freckle-faced
     young man is laughing to us?

CONSIDERATIONS FOR CRITICAL THINKING AND WRITING

1. **FIRST RESPONSE.** Why is the date of this poem significant?
2. Discuss the symbolic meaning of the buttons and whether you think the
   symbolism is too spelled out or not.
3. What purpose does the "laughing young man, sunny with freckles" (line 3)
   serve in the poem?

CONNECTION TO ANOTHER SELECTION

1. Discuss the symbolic treatment of war in this poem, Kenneth Fearing's
   "AD" (p. 165), and Henry Reed's "Naming of Parts" (p. 177).

WALLACE STEVENS (1879–1955)

Anecdote of the Jar   *1923*

I placed a jar in Tennessee,
And round it was, upon a hill.
It made the slovenly wilderness
Surround that hill.

The wilderness rose up to it,   5
And sprawled around, no longer wild.
The jar was round upon the ground
And tall and of a port in air.

It took dominion everywhere.
The jar was gray and bare.   10
It did not give of bird or bush,
Like nothing else in Tennessee.

CONSIDERATIONS FOR CRITICAL THINKING AND WRITING

1. **FIRST RESPONSE.** How is the jar different from its surroundings? What effect does the jar's placement have upon the "slovenly wilderness" (line 3)?

2. What do you make of all the "round" sounds in lines 2, 4, 6, and 7? How do they echo the relationship between the jar and the wilderness?

3. In what sense might this poem be regarded as an anecdote about the power and limitations of art and nature?

CONNECTION TO ANOTHER SELECTION

1. Compare the thematic function of the jar in Stevens's poem with that of the urn in John Keats's "Ode on a Grecian Urn" (p. 94). What important similarities and differences do you see in the meanings of each? Discuss why you think Stevens and Keats have similar or different ideas about art.

MAY SWENSON (1919–1989)

All That Time   *1991*

I saw two trees embracing.
One leaned on the other
as if to throw her down.
But she was the upright one.
Since their twin youth, maybe she
had been pulling him toward her
all that time,

and finally almost uprooted him.
He was the thin, dry, insecure one,

the most wind-warped, you could see.   10
And where their tops tangled
it looked like he was crying
on her shoulder.
On the other hand, maybe he

had been trying to weaken her,   15
break her, or at least
make her bend
over backwards for him
just a little bit.
And all that time   20
she was standing up to him

the best she could.
She was the most stubborn,
the straightest one, that's a fact.
But he had been willing   25
to change himself—
even if it was for the worse—
all that time.

At the top they looked like one
tree, where they were embracing.   30
It was plain they'd be
always together.

Too late now to part.
When the wind blew, you could hear
them rubbing on each other.   35

CONSIDERATIONS FOR CRITICAL THINKING AND WRITING

1. **FIRST RESPONSE.** Paraphrase the allegory in the poem.
2. Explain why you think the narrative does or doesn't have a happy ending.
3. Discuss the title's significance. How might the theme of the poem shift for you if the title were instead "Too late now to part" (line 33)?

WILLIAM STAFFORD (1914–1993)

Traveling through the Dark   *1962*

Traveling through the dark I found a deer
dead on the edge of the Wilson River road.
It is usually best to roll them into the canyon:
that road is narrow; to swerve might make more dead.

By glow of the tail-light I stumbled back of the car   5
and stood by the heap, a doe, a recent killing;

she had stiffened already, almost cold.
I dragged her off; she was large in the belly.

My fingers touching her side brought me the reason —
her side was warm; her fawn lay there waiting,   10
alive, still, never to be born.
Beside that mountain road I hesitated.

The car aimed ahead its lowered parking lights;
under the hood purred the steady engine.
I stood in the glare of the warm exhaust turning red;   15
around our group I could hear the wilderness listen.

I thought hard for us all — my only swerving —
then pushed her over the edge into the river.

CONSIDERATIONS FOR CRITICAL THINKING AND WRITING

1. **FIRST RESPONSE.** Notice the description of the car in this poem: the "glow of the tail-light" (line 5), the "lowered parking lights" (13), and how the engine "purred" (14). How do these and other details suggest symbolic meanings for the car and the "recent killing" (line 6)?

2. Discuss the speaker's tone. Does the speaker seem, for example, tough, callous, kind, sentimental, confused, or confident?

3. What is the effect of the last stanza's having only two lines rather than the established four lines of the previous stanzas?

4. Discuss the appropriateness of this poem's title. In what sense has the speaker "thought hard for us all" (line 17) ? What are those thoughts?

5. Is this a didactic poem?

JULIO MARZÁN (B. 1946)

Ethnic Poetry   *1994*

The ethnic poet said: "The earth is maybe
a huge maraca / and the sun a trombone /
and life / is to move your ass / to slow beats."
The ethnic audience roasted a suckling pig.

The ethnic poet said: "Oh thank Goddy, Goddy /   5
I be me, my toenails curled downward /
deep, deep, deep into Mama earth."
The ethnic audience shook strands of sea shells.

The ethnic poet said: "The sun was created black /
so we should imagine light / and also dream /   10
a walrus emerging from the broken ice."
The ethnic audience beat on sealskin drums.

The ethnic poet said: "Reproductive organs /
Eagles nesting California redwoods /

Shut up and listen to my ancestors."   15
The ethnic audience ate fried bread and honey.

The ethnic poet said: "Something there is that
doesn't love a wall / That sends
the frozen-ground-swell under it."
The ethnic audience deeply understood humanity.   20

CONSIDERATIONS FOR CRITICAL THINKING AND WRITING

1. **FIRST RESPONSE.** What is the implicit definition of ethnic poetry in this
   poem?
2. The final stanza quotes lines from Robert Frost's "Mending Wall" (p. 370).
   Read the entire poem. Why do you think Marzán chooses these lines and
   this particular poem as one kind of ethnic poetry?
3. What is the poem's central irony? Pay particular attention to the final line.
   What is being satirized here?
4. **CRITICAL STRATEGIES.** Read the section on the literary canon (pp. 664–65)
   in Chapter 26, "Critical Strategies for Reading," and discuss how the formation of the literary canon is related to the theme of "Ethnic Poetry."

CONNECTION TO ANOTHER SELECTION

1. Write an essay that discusses the speakers' ideas about what poetry should
   be in "Ethnic Poetry" and in Langston Hughes's "Formula" (p. 414).

MARK HALLIDAY (B. 1949)

Graded Paper   *1991*

On the whole this is quite successful work:
your main argument about the poet's ambivalence —
how he loves the very things he attacks —
is mostly persuasive and always engaging.

At the same time,   5
                there are spots
where your thinking becomes, for me,
alarmingly opaque, and your syntax seems to jump
backwards through unnecessary hoops,
as on p. 2 where you speak of "precognitive awareness   10
not yet disestablished by the shell that encrusts
each thing that a person actually says"
or at the top of p. 5 where your discussion of
"subverbal undertow miming the subversion of self-belief
woven counter to desire's outreach"   15
leaves me groping for firmer footholds.

(I'd have said it differently,
or rather, said something else.)
And when you say that women "could not fulfill themselves" (p. 6)
"in that era" (only forty years ago, after all!)   20
are you so sure that the situation is so different today?
Also, how does Whitman bluff his way into
your penultimate paragraph? He is the *last* poet
I would have quoted in this context!
What plausible way of behaving   25
does the passage you quote represent? Don't you think
literature should ultimately reveal possibilities for *action*?

Please notice how I've repaired your use of semicolons.

And yet, despite what may seem my cranky response,
I do admire the freshness of   30
your thinking and your style; there is
a vitality here; your sentences thrust themselves forward
with a confidence as impressive as it is cheeky. . . .
You are not
                    me, finally,   35
and though this is an awkward problem, involving
the inescapable fact that you are so young, so young
it is also a delightful provocation.

CONSIDERATIONS FOR CRITICAL THINKING AND WRITING

1. **FIRST RESPONSE.** How do you characterize the grader of this paper based on the comments about the paper?

2. Is the speaker a man or a woman? What makes you think so? Does the gender of the speaker affect your reading of the poem? How?

3. Explain whether or not you think the teacher's comments on the paper are consistent with the grade awarded it. How do you account for the grade?

CONNECTION TO ANOTHER SELECTION

1. Compare the ways in which Halliday reveals the speaker's character in this poem with the strategies used by Robert Browning in "My Last Duchess" (p. 180).

CHARLES SIMIC (B. 1938)

The Storm   2008

I'm going over to see what those weeds
By the stone wall are worried about.
Perhaps, they don't care for the way
The shadows creep across the lawn
In the silence of the afternoon.   5

The sky keeps being blue,
Though we hear no birds,
See no butterflies among the flowers
Or ants running over our feet.

Trees, you bend your branches ever so slightly 10
In deference to something
About to make its entrance
Of which we know nothing,
Spellbound as we are by the deepening quiet,
The light just beginning to dim. 15

CONSIDERATIONS FOR CRITICAL THINKING AND WRITING

1. **FIRST RESPONSE.** How does the diction of this poem invite more than just a literal reading about a storm?
2. How does Simic manipulate sound in the poem to help create its tone?
3. Describe how the images in each stanza advance the sense of the storm's progression.

CONNECTION TO ANOTHER SELECTION

1. Write a comparative analysis of the themes of "The Storm" and Emily Dickinson's "Presentiment — is that long Shadow — on the lawn —" (p. 136).

JAMES MERRILL (1926–1995)

Casual Wear 1984

Your average tourist: Fifty. 2.3
Times married. Dressed, this year, in Ferdi Plinthbower
Originals. Odds 1 to 9
Against her strolling past the Embassy

Today at noon. Your average terrorist: 5
Twenty-five. Celibate. No use for trends,
At least in clothing. Mark, though, where it ends.
People have come forth made of colored mist

Unsmiling on one hundred million screens
To tell of his prompt phone call to the station, 10
"Claiming responsibility" — devastation
Signed with a flourish, like the dead wife's jeans.

CONSIDERATIONS FOR CRITICAL THINKING AND WRITING

1. **FIRST RESPONSE.** What is the effect of the statistics in this poem?
2. Describe the speaker's tone. Is it appropriate for the subject matter? Explain why or why not.

3. Comment on the ironies that emerge from the final two lines. How are the tourist and terrorist linked by the speaker's description? Explain why you think the speaker sympathizes more with the tourist or the terrorist — or with neither.

CONNECTION TO ANOTHER SELECTION

1. Compare the satire in this poem with that in Peter Meinke's "The ABC of Aerobics" (p. 295). What is satirized in each poem? Which satire do you think is more pointed?

HENRY REED (1914–1986)

Naming of Parts

Today we have naming of parts. Yesterday,
We had daily cleaning. And tomorrow morning,
We shall have what to do after firing. But today,
Today we have naming of parts. Japonica
Glistens like coral in all of the neighboring gardens,   5
          And today we have naming of parts.

This is the lower sling swivel. And this
Is the upper sling swivel, whose use you will see,
When you are given your slings. And this is the piling swivel,
Which in your case you have not got. The branches   10
Hold in the gardens their silent, eloquent gestures,
          Which in our case we have not got.

This is the safety-catch, which is always released
With an easy flick of the thumb. And please do not let me
See anyone using his finger. You can do it quite easy   15
If you have any strength in your thumb. The blossoms
Are fragile and motionless, never letting anyone see
          Any of them using their finger.

And this you can see is the bolt. The purpose of this
Is to open the breech, as you see. We can slide it   20
Rapidly backwards and forwards: we call this
Easing the spring. And rapidly backwards and forwards
The early bees are assaulting and fumbling the flowers:
          They call it easing the Spring.

They call it easing the Spring: it is perfectly easy   25
If you have any strength in your thumb: like the bolt,
And the breech, and the cocking-piece, and the point of balance,
Which in our case we have not got; and the almond-blossom
Silent in all of the gardens and the bees going backwards and forwards,
          For today we have naming of parts.   30

CONSIDERATIONS FOR CRITICAL THINKING AND WRITING

1. **FIRST RESPONSE.** Characterize the two speakers in this poem. Identify the lines spoken by each. How do their respective lines differ in tone?
2. What is the effect of the last line of each stanza?
3. How do ambiguities and puns contribute to the poem's meaning?
4. What symbolic contrast is made between the rifle instruction and the gardens? How is this contrast ironic?

RACHEL HADAS (B. 1948)

The Compact

2003

The short steep ride in the red bus uphill
from the Girls' School to the Boys' School left
time to whip our compacts out and powder
cheeks, noses. What for? For the boys? Well, yes,
we might have answered if we had been asked.   5
No one asked. Good thing. We didn't know.
Those uphill rides were forty years ago.

If every gesture halves a hidden whole,
if every moment twins a hidden half,
then my thumb clicking that pink plastic catch   10
(sweet whiff of powder; flash of a tiny mirror)
opens not only the compact but also
the first half of a parenthesis
stretching its arms out, longing to be closed.

CONSIDERATIONS FOR CRITICAL THINKING AND WRITING

1. **FIRST RESPONSE.** Discuss the denotative meanings of the "compact" as well as its potential symbolic meanings.
2. Why is it appropriate that the bus is red (rather than a yellow school bus) and that the trip is an uphill ride?
3. How do the final lines create an effective ending for the poem?

BRUCE WEIGL (B. 1949)

Snowy Egret

1985

My neighbor's boy has lifted his father's shotgun and stolen
down to the backwaters of the Elizabeth
and in the moon he's blasted a snowy egret
from the shallows it stalked for small fish.

Midnight. My wife wakes me. He's in the backyard   5
with a shovel, so I go down half drunk with pills
that let me sleep to see what I can see and if it's safe.
The boy doesn't hear me come across the dewy grass.
He says through tears he has to bury it.
He says his father will kill him   10
and he digs until the hole is deep enough and gathers
the egret carefully into his arms
as if not to harm the blood-splattered wings
gleaming in the flashlight beam.

His man's muscled shoulders   15
shake with the weight of what he can't set right no matter what,
but one last time he tries to stay a child, sobbing,
Please don't tell.
He says he only meant to flush it from the shadows,
he only meant to watch it fly   20
but the shot spread too far
ripping into the white wings
spanned awkwardly for a moment
until it glided into brackish death.

I want to grab his shoulders,   25
shake the lies loose from his lips, but he hurts enough;
he burns with shame for what he's done,
with fear for his hard father's
fists I've seen crash down on him for so much less.
I don't know what to do but hold him.   30
If I let go he'll fly to pieces before me.
What a time we share, that can make a good boy steal away,
wiping out from the blue face of the pond
what he hadn't even known he loved, blasting
such beauty into nothing.   35

CONSIDERATIONS FOR CRITICAL THINKING AND WRITING

1. **FIRST RESPONSE.** Describe the boy's relationship with his father. Why is that important in the speaker's account of the boy's actions?

2. Describe how Weigl's use of both the past and present affects your reading of the narrative.

3. Read line 19, "He says he only meant to flush it from the shadows," symbolically. What significance does it take on as the narrative develops?

ROBERT BROWNING (1812–1889)

My Last Duchess   *1842*

Courtesy of the National Portrait Gallery, London.

Ferrara°

That's my last Duchess painted on the wall,
Looking as if she were alive. I call
That piece a wonder, now: Frà Pandolf's°
    hands
Worked busily a day, and there she stands.
Will't please you sit and look at her? I said
"Frà Pandolf" by design, for never read
Strangers like you that pictured countenance,
The depth and passion of its earnest glance,
But to myself they turned (since none puts by
The curtain I have drawn for you, but I)   10
And seemed as they would ask me, if they durst,
How such a glance came there; so, not the first
Are you to turn and ask thus. Sir, 'twas not
Her husband's presence only, called that spot
Of joy into the Duchess' cheek: perhaps   15
Frà Pandolf chanced to say "Her mantle laps
Over my lady's wrist too much," or "Paint
Must never hope to reproduce the faint
Half-flush that dies along her throat": such stuff
Was courtesy, she thought, and cause enough   20
For calling up that spot of joy. She had
A heart — how shall I say? — too soon made glad,
Too easily impressed; she liked whate'er
She looked on, and her looks went everywhere.
Sir, 'twas all one! My favor at her breast,   25
The dropping of the daylight in the West,
The bough of cherries some officious fool
Broke in the orchard for her, the white mule
She rode with round the terrace — all and each
Would draw from her alike the approving speech,   30
Or blush, at least. She thanked men, — good! but thanked
Somehow — I know not how — as if she ranked
My gift of a nine-hundred-years-old name
With anybody's gift. Who'd stoop to blame
This sort of trifling? Even had you skill   35
In speech — which I have not — to make your will
Quite clear to such an one, and say, "Just this
Or that in you disgusts me; here you miss,

> Explore contexts
> for Robert Browning
> on *LiterActive*.

Ferrara: In the sixteenth century, the duke of this Italian city arranged to marry a second time after the mysterious death of his very young first wife.   3 *Frà Pandolf:* A fictitious artist.

Or there exceed the mark" — and if she let
Herself be lessoned so, nor plainly set   40
Her wits to yours, forsooth, and made excuse,
— E'en then would be some stooping; and I choose
Never to stoop. Oh sir, she smiled, no doubt,
Whene'er I passed her; but who passed without
Much the same smile? This grew; I gave commands;   45
Then all smiles stopped together. There she stands
As if alive. Will't please you rise? We'll meet
The company below, then. I repeat,
The Count your master's known munificence
Is ample warrant that no just pretense   50
Of mine for dowry will be disallowed;
Though his fair daughter's self, as I avowed
At starting, is my object. Nay, we'll go
Together down, sir. Notice Neptune, though,
Taming a sea-horse, thought a rarity,   55
Which Claus of Innsbruck° cast in bronze for me!

56 *Claus of Innsbruck:* Also a fictitious artist.

Considerations for Critical Thinking and Writing

1. **FIRST RESPONSE.** What do you think happened to the duchess?

2. To whom is the duke addressing his remarks about the duchess in this poem? What is ironic about the situation?

3. Why was the duke unhappy with his first wife? What does this reveal about him? What does the poem's title suggest about his attitude toward women in general?

4. What seems to be the visitor's response (lines 53–54) to the duke's account of his first wife?

Connection to Another Selection

1. Write an essay describing the ways in which the speakers of "My Last Duchess" and Katharyn Howd Machan's "Hazel Tells LaVerne" (p. 75) inadvertently reveal themselves.

William Blake (1757–1827)

The Chimney Sweeper   *1789*

When my mother died I was very young,
And my father sold me while yet my tongue
Could scarcely cry " 'weep! 'weep! 'weep! 'weep!"
So your chimneys I sweep, and in soot I sleep.

There's little Tom Dacre, who cried when his head, 5
That curled like a lamb's back, was shaved: so I said
"Hush, Tom! never mind it, for when your head's bare
You know that the soot cannot spoil your white hair."

And so he was quiet, and that very night,
As Tom was a-sleeping, he had such a sight! 10
That thousands of sweepers, Dick, Joe, Ned, and Jack,
Were all of them locked up in coffins of black.

And by came an Angel who had a bright key,
And he opened the coffins and set them all free;
Then down a green plain leaping, laughing, they run, 15
And wash in a river, and shine in the sun.

Then naked and white, all their bags left behind,
They rise upon clouds and sport in the wind;
And the Angel told Tom, if he'd be a good boy,
He'd have God for his father, and never want joy. 20

And so Tom awoke; and we rose in the dark,
And got with our bags and our brushes to work.
Though the morning was cold, Tom was happy and warm;
So if all do their duty they need not fear harm.

CONSIDERATIONS FOR CRITICAL THINKING AND WRITING

1. **FIRST RESPONSE.** Discuss the validity of this statement: "'The Chimney Sweeper' is a sentimental poem about a shameful eighteenth-century social problem; such a treatment of child abuse cannot be taken seriously."

2. Characterize the speaker in this poem and describe his tone. Is his tone the same as the poet's? Consider especially lines 7, 8, and 24.

3. What is the symbolic value of the dream in lines 11 to 20?

4. Why is irony central to the meaning of this poem?

WALT WHITMAN (1819–1892)

From Song of Myself   *1881*

6

A child said *What is the grass?* fetching it to me with full hands;
How could I answer the child? I do not know what it is any more than he.

I guess it must be the flag of my disposition, out of hopeful green stuff
    woven.

Or I guess it is the handkerchief of the Lord,
A scented gift and remembrancer designedly dropt, 5
Bearing the owner's name someway in the corners, that we may see and
    remark, and say *Whose?*

Or I guess the grass is itself a child, the produced babe of the vegetation.

Or I guess it is a uniform hieroglyphic,
And it means, Sprouting alike in broad zones and narrow zones,
Growing among black folks as among white,   10
Kanuck, Tuckahoe, Congressman, Cuff,° I give them the same, I receive
    them the same.

And now it seems to me the beautiful uncut hair of graves.

Tenderly will I use you curling grass,
It may be you transpire from the breasts of young men,
It may be if I had known them I would have loved them,   15
It may be you are from old people, or from offspring taken soon out of
    their mothers' laps,
And here you are the mothers' laps.

This grass is very dark to be from the white heads of old mothers,
Darker than the colorless beards of old men,
Dark to come from under the faint red roofs of mouths.   20

O I perceive after all so many uttering tongues,
And I perceive they do not come from the roofs of mouths for nothing.

I wish I could translate the hints about the dead young men and women,
And the hints about old men and mothers, and the offspring taken soon
    out of their laps.

What do you think has become of the young and old men?   25
And what do you think has become of the women and children?

They are alive and well somewhere,
The smallest sprout shows there is really no death,
And if ever there was it led forward life, and does not wait at the end to
    arrest it,
And ceas'd the moment life appear'd.   30

All goes onward and outward . . . and nothing collapses,
And to die is different from what any one supposed, and luckier.

---

11 *Kanuck . . . Cuff:* Kanuck, a French Canadian; Tuckahoe, a Virginian; Cuff, an African American.

CONSIDERATIONS FOR CRITICAL THINKING AND WRITING

1. **FIRST RESPONSE.** What does the grass mean to the speaker? Describe the various symbolic possibilities offered in lines 1–11. What seems to be the most important symbolic meaning?

2. Describe the tone of lines 12–26. Explain why these lines are or aren't representative of the poem's entire tone.

3. How does the final line compare with your own view of death?

CONNECTION TO ANOTHER SELECTION

1. Compare attitudes toward death in Whitman's poem and in Emily Dickinson's "I heard a Fly buzz — when I died —" (p. 335).

Gary Soto (b. 1952)

Behind Grandma's House   1985

Courtesy of Gary Soto.

At ten I wanted fame. I had a comb
And two Coke bottles, a tube of Bryl-creem.
I borrowed a dog, one with
Mismatched eyes and a happy tongue,
And wanted to prove I was tough
In the alley, kicking over trash cans,
A dull chime of tuna cans falling.
I hurled light bulbs like grenades
And men teachers held their heads,
Fingers of blood lengthening
On the ground. I flicked rocks at cats,
Their goofy faces spurred with foxtails.
I kicked fences. I shooed pigeons.
I broke a branch from a flowering peach
And frightened ants with a stream of spit.   15
I said "*Chale,*" "In your face," and "No way
Daddy-O" to an imaginary priest
Until grandma came into the alley,
Her apron flapping in a breeze,
Her hair mussed, and said, "Let me help you,"   20
And punched me between the eyes.

Explore contexts
for Gary Soto
on *LiterActive.*

Considerations for Critical Thinking and Writing

1. **First Response.** What is the central irony of this poem?
2. How does the speaker characterize himself at ten?
3. Though the "grandma" appears only briefly, she seems, in a sense, fully characterized. How would you describe her? Why do you think she says, "Let me help you"?

Connection to Another Selection

1. Write an essay comparing the themes of "Behind Grandma's House" and Sharon Olds's "Rite of Passage" (p. 546).

Perspective

Ezra Pound (1885–1972)

On Symbols   1912

I believe that the proper and perfect symbol is the natural object, that if a man uses "symbols" he must so use them that their symbolic function does not obtrude; so that *a* sense, and the poetic quality of the passage, is not lost to those who do not understand the symbol as such, to whom, for instance, a hawk is a hawk.

From "Prolegomena," *Poetry Review*, February 1912

CONSIDERATIONS FOR CRITICAL THINKING AND WRITING

1. Discuss whether you agree with Pound that the "perfect symbol" is a "natural object" that does not insist on being read as a symbol.

2. Write an essay in which you discuss Bruce Weigl's "Snowy Egret" (p. 178) as an example of the "perfect symbol" Pound proposes.

Web Research the poets in this chapter at bedfordstmartins.com/ rewritinglit.

7

Sounds

In a poem the words should be as pleasing to the ear as the meaning is to the mind.

—MARIANNE MOORE

Bettmann/CORBIS.

LISTENING TO POETRY

Poems yearn to be read aloud. Much of their energy, charm, and beauty come to life only when they are heard. Poets choose and arrange words for their sounds as well as for their meanings. Most poetry is best read with your lips, teeth, and tongue because they serve to artic-ulate the effects that sound may have in a poem. When a voice is breathed into a good poem, there is pleasure in the reading, the saying, and the hearing.

 Explore the poetic elements in this chapter on *LiterActive* or at bedfordstmartins.com/ rewritinglit.

The earliest poetry—before writing and painting—was chanted or sung. The rhythmic quality of such oral performances served two purposes: it helped the chanting bard remember the lines and it entertained audiences with patterned sounds of language, which were sometimes accompanied by musical instruments. Poetry has always been closely related to music. Indeed, as the word suggests, lyric poetry evolved from songs. "Western Wind" (p. 36), an anonymous Middle English lyric, survived as song long before it was written down. Had Robert Frost lived in a nonliterate society, he probably would have sung some version—a very different version to be sure—of "Acquainted with the Night" (p. 158) instead of writing it down. Even though Frost creates a speaking rather than a singing voice, the speaker's anxious tone is distinctly heard in any careful reading of the poem.

Like lyrics, early narrative poems were originally part of an anonymous oral folk tradition. A *ballad* such as "Bonny Barbara Allan" (p. 615) told a story that was sung from one generation to the next until it was finally transcribed. Since the eighteenth century, this narrative form has sometimes been imitated by poets who write *literary ballads.* John Keats's "La Belle Dame sans Merci" (p. 635) is, for example, a more complex and sophisticated nineteenth-century reflection of the original ballad traditions that developed in the fifteenth century and earlier. In considering poetry as sound, we should not forget that poetry traces its beginnings to song.

These next lines exemplify poetry's continuing relation to song. What poetic elements can you find in this ballad, which was adapted by Paul Simon and Art Garfunkel and became a popular antiwar song in the 1960s?

Anonymous

Scarborough Fair

date unknown

Where are you going? To Scarborough Fair?
Parsley, sage, rosemary, and thyme,
Remember me to a bonny lass there,
For once she was a true lover of mine.

Tell her to make me a cambric shirt,   5
Parsley, sage, rosemary, and thyme,
Without any needle or thread work'd in it,
And she shall be a true lover of mine.

Tell her to wash it in yonder well,
Parsley, sage, rosemary, and thyme,   10
Where water ne'er sprung nor a drop of rain fell,
And she shall be a true lover of mine.

Tell her to plough me an acre of land,
Parsley, sage, rosemary, and thyme,
Between the sea and the salt sea strand,   15
And she shall be a true lover of mine.

Tell her to plough it with one ram's horn,
Parsley, sage, rosemary, and thyme,
And sow it all over with one peppercorn,
And she shall be a true lover of mine.   20

Tell her to reap it with a sickle of leather,
Parsley, sage, rosemary, and thyme,
And tie it all up with a tom tit's feather,
And she shall be a true lover of mine.

Tell her to gather it all in a sack,   25
Parsley, sage, rosemary, and thyme,
And carry it home on a butterfly's back,
And then she shall be a true lover of mine.

CONSIDERATIONS FOR CRITICAL THINKING AND WRITING

1. **FIRST RESPONSE.** What do you associate with "Parsley, sage, rosemary, and thyme"? What images does this poem evoke? How so?

2. What kinds of demands does the speaker make on his former lover? What do these demands have in common?

3. What is the tone of this ballad?

4. Choose a contemporary song that you especially like and examine the lyrics. Write an essay explaining whether or not you consider the lyrics poetic.

Of course, reading "Scarborough Fair" is not the same as hearing it. Like the lyrics of a song, many poems must be heard — or at least read with listening eyes — before they can be fully understood and enjoyed. The sounds of words are a universal source of music for human beings. This has been so from ancient tribes to bards to the two-year-old child in a bakery gleefully chanting "Cuppitycake, cuppitycake!"

Listen to the sound of this poem as you read it aloud. How do the words provide, in a sense, their own musical accompaniment?

JOHN UPDIKE (1932–2009)

Player Piano   *1958*

My stick fingers click with a snicker
And, chuckling, they knuckle the keys;
Light-footed, my steel feelers flicker
And pluck from these keys melodies.

My paper can caper; abandon   5
Is broadcast by dint of my din,
And no man or band has a hand in
The tones I turn on from within.

At times I'm a jumble of rumbles,
At others I'm light like the moon,   10
But never my numb plunker fumbles,
Misstrums me, or tries a new tune.

The speaker in this poem is a piano that can play automatically by means of a mechanism that depresses keys in response to signals on a perforated roll. Notice how the speaker's voice approximates the sounds of a piano. In each stanza a predominant sound emerges from the carefully chosen words. How is the sound of each stanza tuned to its sense?

Like Updike's "Player Piano," this next poem is also primarily about sounds.

MAY SWENSON (1919–1989)

A Nosty Fright   *1984*

The roldengod and the soneyhuckle,
the sack eyed blusan and the wistle rheed
are all tangled with the oison pivy,
the fallen nine peedles and the wumbleteed.

A mipchunk caught in a wobceb tried   5
to hip and skide in a dandy sune
but a stobler put up a EEP KOFF sign.
Then the unfucky lellow met a phytoon

and was sept out to swea. He difted for drays
till a hassgropper flying happened to spot   10
the boolish feast all debraggled and wet,
covered with snears and tot.

Loonmight shone through the winey poods
where rushmooms grew among risted twoots.
Back blats flew betreen the twees   15
and orned howls hounded their soots.

A kumkpin stood with tooked creeth
on the sindow will of a house
where a icked wold itch lived all alone
except for her stoombrick, a mitten and a kouse.   20

"Here we part," said hassgropper.
"Pere we hart," said mipchunk, too.
They purried away on opposite haths,
both scared of some "Bat!" or "Scoo!"

October was ending on a nosty fright   25
with scroans and greeches and chanking clains,
with oblins and gelfs, coaths and urses,
skinning grulls and stoodblains.

Will it ever be morning, Nofember virst,
skue bly and the sappy hun, our friend?   30
With light breaves of wall by the fayside?
I sope ho, so that this oem can pend.

At just the right moments Swenson transposes letters to create amusing sound effects and wild wordplays. Although there is a story lurking in "A Nosty Fright," any serious attempt to interpret its meaning is confronted with "a EEP KOFF sign." Instead, we are invited to enjoy the delicious sounds the poet has cooked up.

Few poems revel in sound so completely. More typically, the sounds of a poem contribute to its meaning rather than become its meaning. Consider how sound is used in the next poem.

EMILY DICKINSON (1830–1886)

A Bird came down the Walk —

c. 1862

A Bird came down the Walk —
He did not know I saw —
He bit an Angleworm in halves
And ate the fellow, raw,

And then he drank a Dew   5
From a convenient Grass —
And then hopped sidewise to the Wall
To let a Beetle pass —

He glanced with rapid eyes
That hurried all around —   10
They looked like frightened Beads, I thought —
He stirred his Velvet Head

Like one in danger, Cautious,
I offered him a Crumb
And he unrolled his feathers   15
And rowed him softer home —

Than Oars divide the Ocean,
Too silver for a seam —
Or Butterflies, off Banks of Noon
Leap, plashless as they swim.   20

This description of a bird offers a close look at how differently a bird moves when it hops on the ground than when it flies in the air. On the ground the bird moves quickly, awkwardly, and irregularly as it plucks up a worm, washes it down with dew, and then hops aside to avoid a passing beetle. The speaker recounts the bird's rapid, abrupt actions from a somewhat superior, amused perspective. By describing the bird in human terms (as if, for example, it chose to eat the worm "raw"), the speaker is almost condescending. But when the attempt to offer a crumb fails and the frightened bird flies off, the speaker is left looking up instead of down at the bird.

With that shift in perspective the tone shifts from amusement to awe in response to the bird's graceful flight. The jerky movements of lines 1 to 13 give way to the smooth motion of lines 15 to 20. The pace of the first three stanzas is fast and discontinuous. We tend to pause at the end of each line, and this reinforces a sense of disconnected movements. In contrast, the final six lines are to be read as a single sentence in one flowing movement, lubricated by various sounds.

Read again the description of the bird flying away. Several *o*-sounds contribute to the image of the serene, expansive, confident flight, just as the *s*-sounds serve as smooth transitions from one line to the next. Notice how these sounds are grouped in the following vertical columns:

unrolled	softer	too	his	Ocean	Banks
rowed	Oars	Noon	feathers	silver	plashless
home	Or		softer	seam	as
Ocean	off		Oars	Butterflies	swim

This blending of sounds (notice how "Leap, plashless" brings together the *p*- and *l*-sounds without a ripple) helps convey the bird's smooth grace in the air. Like a feathered oar, the bird moves seamlessly in its element.

The repetition of sounds in poetry is similar to the function of the tones and melodies that are repeated, with variations, in music. Just as the patterned sounds in music unify a work, so do the words in poems, which have been carefully chosen for the combinations of sounds they create. These sounds are produced in a number of ways.

The most direct way in which the sound of a word suggests its meaning is through **onomatopoeia,** which is the use of a word that resembles the sound it denotes: *quack, buzz, rattle, bang, squeak, bowwow, burp, choo-choo, ding-a-ling, sizzle.* The sound and sense of these words are closely related, but such words represent a very small percentage of the words available to us. Poets usually employ more subtle means for echoing meanings.

Onomatopoeia can consist of more than just single words. In its broadest meaning the term refers to lines or passages in which sounds help to convey meanings, as in these lines from Updike's "Player Piano":

My stick fingers click with a snicker
And, chuckling, they knuckle the keys.

The sharp, crisp sounds of these two lines approximate the sounds of a piano; the syllables seem to "click" against one another. Contrast Updike's rendition with the following lines:

My long fingers play with abandon
And, laughing, they cover the keys.

The original version is more interesting and alive because the sounds of the words are pleasurable and reinforce the meaning through a careful blending of consonants and vowels.

Alliteration is the repetition of the same consonant sounds at the beginnings of nearby words: "*descending dewdrops*," "*luscious lemons*." Sometimes the term is also used to describe the consonant sounds within words: "*trespasser's reproach*," "*wedded lady*." Alliteration is based on sound rather than spelling. "*Keen*" and "*car*" alliterate, but "*car*" does not alliterate with "*cite*." Rarely is heavy-handed alliteration effective. Used too self-consciously, it can be distracting instead of strengthening meaning or emphasizing a relation between words. Consider the relentless *h*'s in this line: "Horrendous horrors haunted Helen's happiness." Those *h*'s certainly suggest that Helen is being pursued, but they have a more comic than serious effect because they are overdone.

Assonance is the repetition of the same vowel sound in nearby words: "*asleep* under a *tree*," "*time* and *tide*," "*haunt*" and "*awesome*," "*each evening*." Both alliteration and assonance help to establish relations among words in a line or a series of lines. Whether the effect is **euphony** (lines that are musically pleasant to the ear and smooth, like the final lines of Dickinson's "A Bird came down the Walk—") or **cacophony** (lines that are discordant and difficult to pronounce, like the claim that "never my numb plunker fumbles" in Updike's "Player Piano"), the sounds of words in poetry can be as significant as the words' denotative or connotative meanings.

A SAMPLE STUDENT RESPONSE

Ryan Lee

Professor McDonough

English 211

December 1, 2009

Sound in Emily Dickinson's "A Bird came down the Walk—"

In her poem "A Bird came down the Walk—" Emily Dickinson uses the sound and rhythm of each line to reflect the motion of a bird walking awkwardly—and then flying gracefully. Particularly when read aloud, the staccato phrases and stilted breaks in lines 1 through 14 create a sense of the bird's movement on land, quick and off-balanced, which helps bring the scene to life.

The first three stanzas are structured to make the bird's movement consistent. The bird hops around, eating worms while keeping guard for any threats. Vulnerable on the ground, the bird is intensely aware of danger:

> He glanced with rapid eyes
>
> That hurried all around—
>
> They looked like frightened Beads, I thought—
>
> He stirred his Velvet Head (9-12)

In addition to choosing words that portray the bird as cautious—it "glanced with rapid eyes" (9) that resemble "frightened Beads" (11)—Dickinson chooses to end each line abruptly. This abrupt halting of sound allows the reader to experience the bird's fear more immediately, and the effect is similar to the missing of a beat or a breath.

These halting lines stand in contrast to the smoothness of the last six lines, during which the bird takes flight. The sounds in these lines are pleasingly soft, and rich in the "s" sound. The bird

> unrolled his feathers
>
> And rowed him softer home—
>
>
>
> Than Oars
>
> divide the Ocean,
>
> Too silver for a seam—(15-18). . . .

Work Cited

Dickinson, Emily. "A Bird came down the Walk—." *Poetry: An Introduction*. Ed. Michael Meyer. 6th ed. Boston: Bedford/St. Martin's, 2010. 190. Print.

This next poem provides a feast of sounds. Read the poem aloud and try to determine the effects of its sounds.

GALWAY KINNELL (B. 1927)

Blackberry Eating   *1980*

Photo by Charlie Nye.

I love to go out in late September
among the fat, overripe, icy, black
        blackberries
to eat blackberries for breakfast,
the stalks very prickly, a penalty
they earn for knowing the black art
of blackberry-making; and as I stand among
        them
lifting the stalks to my mouth, the ripest
        berries
fall almost unbidden to my tongue,
as words sometimes do, certain peculiar words
like *strengths* or *squinched*,
many-lettered, one-syllabled lumps,
which I squeeze, squinch open, and splurge well
in the silent, startled, icy, black language
of blackberry-eating in late September.

        10

CONSIDERATIONS FOR CRITICAL THINKING AND WRITING

1. **FIRST RESPONSE.** What types of sounds does Kinnell use throughout this poem? What categories can you place them in? What is the effect of these sounds?

2. How do lines 4–6 fit into the poem? What does this prickly image add to the poem?

3. Explain what you think the poem's theme is.

4. Write an essay that considers the speaker's love of blackberry eating along with the speaker's appetite for words. How are the two blended in the poem?

RHYME

Like alliteration and assonance, **rhyme** is a way of creating sound patterns. Rhyme, broadly defined, consists of two or more words or phrases that repeat the same sounds: *happy* and *snappy*. Rhyme words often have similar spellings, but that is not a requirement of rhyme; what matters is that the words sound alike: *vain* rhymes with *reign* as well as *rain*. Moreover, words may look alike but not rhyme at all. In **eye rhyme** the spellings are similar, but the pronunciations are not, as with *bough* and *cough*, or *brow* and *blow*.

Not all poems use rhyme. Many great poems have no rhymes, and many weak verses use rhyme as a substitute for poetry. These are especially apparent in commercial messages and greeting-card lines. At its worst, rhyme is merely a distracting decoration that can lead to dullness and predictability. But used skillfully, rhyme creates lines that are memorable and musical.

Here is a poem using rhyme that you might remember the next time you are in a restaurant.

RICHARD ARMOUR (1906–1989)

Going to Extremes   1954

Shake and shake
  The catsup bottle
None'll come —
  And then a lot'll.

The experience recounted in Armour's poem is common enough, but the rhyme's humor is special. The final line clicks the poem shut — an effect that is often achieved by the use of rhyme. That click provides a sense of a satisfying and fulfilled form. Rhymes have a number of uses: They can emphasize words, direct a reader's attention to relations between words, and provide an overall structure for a poem.

Rhyme is used in the following poem to imitate the sound of cascading water.

ROBERT SOUTHEY (1774–1843)

From "The Cataract of Lodore"   1820

     "How does the water

   Come down at Lodore?"
. . . .
From its sources which well
   In the tarn on the fell;
      From its fountains   5
      In the mountains,
   Its rills and its gills;
Through moss and through brake,
      It runs and it creeps
   For awhile, till it sleeps   10
      In its own little lake.
   And thence at departing,
   Awakening and starting,
   It runs through the reeds
      And away it proceeds,   15

Through meadow and glade,
    In sun and in shade,
And through the wood-shelter,
    Among crags in its flurry,
      Helter-skelter,   20
      Hurry-scurry.
Here it comes sparkling,
And there it lies darkling;
Now smoking and frothing
    Its tumult and wrath in,   25
      Till in this rapid race
        On which it is bent,
        It reaches the place
        Of its steep descent.

    The cataract strong   30
    Then plunges along,
    Striking and raging
      As if a war waging
Its caverns and rocks among:
    Rising and leaping,   35
    Sinking and creeping,
    Swelling and sweeping,
Showering and springing,
      Flying and flinging,
    Writhing and ringing,   40
Eddying and whisking,
Spouting and frisking,
Turning and twisting,
    Around and around
    With endless rebound!   45
    Smiting and fighting,
    A sight to delight in;
    Confounding, astounding,
Dizzying and deafening the ear with its sound.
. . . .
Dividing and gliding and sliding,   50
And falling and brawling and spawling,
And driving and riving and striving,
And sprinkling and twinkling and wrinkling,
And sounding and bounding and rounding,
And bubbling and troubling and doubling,   55
And grumbling and rumbling and tumbling,
And clattering and battering and shattering;
Retreating and beating and meeting and sheeting,
Delaying and straying and playing and spraying,
Advancing and prancing and glancing and dancing,   60
Recoiling, turmoiling and toiling and boiling,
And gleaming and streaming and steaming and beaming,
And rushing and flushing and brushing and gushing,
And flapping and rapping and clapping and slapping,

And curling and whirling and purling and twirling,   65
And thumping and plumping and bumping and jumping,
And dashing and flashing and splashing and clashing;
And so never ending, but always descending,
Sounds and motions forever and ever are blending,
All at once and all o'er, with a mighty uproar;   70
And this way the water comes down at Lodore.

This deluge of rhymes consists of "Sounds and motions forever and ever . . . blending" (line 69). The pace quickens as the water creeps from its mountain source and then descends in rushing cataracts. As the speed of the water increases, so do the number of rhymes, until they run in fours: "dashing and flashing and splashing and clashing" (line 67). Most rhymes meander through poems instead of flooding them; nevertheless, Southey's use of rhyme suggests how sounds can flow with meanings. "The Cataract of Lodore" has been criticized, however, for overusing onomatopoeia. Some readers find the poem silly; others regard it as a brilliant example of sound effects. What do you think?

A variety of types of rhyme is available to poets. The most common form, **end rhyme,** comes at the ends of lines (lines 14–17).

> It runs through the reeds
>   And away it proceeds,
> Through meadow and glade,
>   In sun and in shade.

Internal rhyme places at least one of the rhymed words within the line, as in "Dividing and gliding and sliding" (line 50) or, more subtly, in the fourth and final words of "In mist or cloud, on mast or shroud."

The rhyming of single-syllable words such as *glade* and *shade* is known as **masculine rhyme,** as we see in these lines from A. E. Housman:

> Loveliest of trees, the cherry now
> Is hung with bloom along the bough.

Rhymes using words of more than one syllable are also called masculine when the same sound occurs in a final stressed syllable, as in *defend, contend; betray, away.* A **feminine rhyme** consists of a rhymed stressed syllable followed by one or more rhymed unstressed syllables, as in *butter, clutter; gratitude, attitude; quivering, shivering.* This rhyme is evident in John Millington Synge's verse:

> Lord confound this surly sister,
> Blight her brow and blotch and blister.

All of the examples so far have been **exact rhymes** because they share the same stressed vowel sounds as well as any sounds that follow the vowel. In **near rhyme** (also called **off rhyme, slant rhyme,** and **approximate rhyme**), the sounds are almost but not exactly alike. There are several kinds of near rhyme. One of the most common is **consonance,** an identical consonant sound preceded by a different vowel sound: *home, same; worth, breath; trophy, daffy.* Near rhyme can also be achieved by using different vowel sounds with identical consonant sounds: *sound, sand; kind, conned; fellow, fallow.* The dissonance of *blade* and *blood* in the following lines from Wilfred Owen helps to reinforce their grim tone:

> Let the boy try along this bayonet-blade
> How cold steel is, and keen with hunger of blood.

Near rhymes greatly broaden the possibility for musical effects in English, a language that, compared with Spanish or Italian, contains few exact rhymes. Do not assume, however, that a near rhyme represents a failed attempt at exact rhyme. Near rhymes allow a musical subtlety and variety and can avoid the sometimes overpowering jingling effects that exact rhymes may create.

These basic terms hardly exhaust the ways in which the sounds in poems can be labeled and discussed, but the terms can help you to describe how poets manipulate sounds for effect. Read "God's Grandeur" (p. 199) aloud and try to determine how the sounds of the lines contribute to their sense.

Perspective

David Lenson (b. 1945)

On the Contemporary Use of Rhyme   1988

One impediment to a respectable return to rhyme is the popular survival of "functional" verse: greeting cards, pedagogical and mnemonic devices ("Thirty days hath September"), nursery rhymes, advertising jingles, and of course song lyrics. Pentameters, irregular rhymes, and free verse aren't much use in songwriting, where the meter has to be governed by the time signature of the music.

Far from universities, there has been a revival of rhymed couplets in rap music, in which, to the accompaniment of synthesizers, vocalists deliver lengthy first-person narratives in tetrameter. While most writing teachers would dismiss such lyrics as doggerel, the aim of the songs is really not so far from that of Alexander Pope: to use rhyme to sharpen social insight, in the hope that the world may be reordered.

From *The Chronicle of Higher Education,* February 24, 1988

Considerations for Critical Thinking and Writing

1. Read some contemporary song lyrics from a wide range of groups or vocalists. Is Lenson correct in his assessment that irregular rhyme is not much use in songwriting?

2. Examine the rhymed couplets of some rap music. Discuss whether they are used "to sharpen social insight." What is the effect of using rhymes in rap music?

3. What is your own response to rhymed poetry? Do you like yours with or without? What do you think informs your preference?

SOUND AND MEANING

GERARD MANLEY HOPKINS (1844–1889)

God's Grandeur   *1877*

The world is charged with the grandeur of God.
   It will flame out, like shining from shook foil;°   *shaken gold foil*
   It gathers to a greatness, like the ooze of oil
Crushed.° Why do men then now not reck his rod?°
Generations have trod, have trod, have trod;   5
   And all is seared with trade; bleared, smeared with toil;
   And wears man's smudge and shares man's smell: the soil
Is bare now, nor can foot feel, being shod.

And for all this, nature is never spent;
   There lives the dearest freshness deep down things;   10
And though the last lights off the black West went
   Oh, morning, at the brown brink eastward, springs —
Because the Holy Ghost over the bent
   World broods with warm breast and with ah! bright wings.

---

4 *Crushed:* Olives crushed in their oil; *reck his rod:* Obey God.

    The subject of this poem is announced in the title and the first line: "The world is charged with the grandeur of God." The poem is a celebration of the power and greatness of God's presence in the world, but the speaker is also perplexed and dismayed by people who refuse to recognize God's authority and grandeur as they are manifested in the creation. Instead of glorifying God, "men" have degraded the earth through meaningless toil and cut themselves off from the spiritual renewal inherent in the beauty of nature. The relentless demands of commerce and industry have blinded people to the earth's natural and spiritual resources. Despite this abuse and insensitivity to God's grandeur, however, "nature is never spent"; the morning light that "springs" in the east redeems the "black West" of the night and is a sign that the spirit of the Holy Ghost is ever present in the world. This summary of the poem sketches some of the thematic significance of the lines, but it does not do justice to how they are organized around the use of sound. Hopkins's poem, unlike Southey's "The Cataract of Lodore," uses sounds in a subtle and complex way.

    In the opening line Hopkins uses alliteration — a device apparent in almost every line of the poem — to connect "Go*d*" to the "wor*ld*," which is "charged" with his "grandeur." These consonants unify the line as well. The alliteration in lines 2 and 3 suggests a harmony in the creation: the *f*'s in "*f*lame" and "*f*oil," the *sh*'s in "*sh*ining" and "*sh*ook," the *g*'s in "*g*athers" and "*g*reatness," and the visual (not alliterative) similarities of "*ooze* of *oil*" emphasize a world that is held together by God's will.

That harmony is abruptly interrupted by the speaker's angry question in line 4: "Why do men then now not reck his rod?" The question is as painful to the speaker as it is difficult to pronounce. The arrangement of the alliteration ("*now*," "*not*"; "*reck*," "*rod*"), the assonance ("n*o*t," "r*o*d"; "m*e*n," "th*e*n," "r*e*ck"), and the internal rhyme ("m*en*," "th*en*") contribute to the difficulty in saying the line—a difficulty associated with human behavior. That behavior is introduced in line 5 by the repetition of "have trod" to emphasize the repeated mistakes—sins—committed by human beings. The tone is dirgelike because humanity persists in its mistaken path rather than progressing. The speaker's horror at humanity is evident in the cacophonous sounds of lines 6 to 8. Here the alliteration of "*sm*eared," "*sm*udge," and "*sm*ell" along with the internal rhymes of "s*eared*," "bl*eared*," and "sm*eared*" echo the disgust with which the speaker views humanity's "toil" with the "s*oil*," an end rhyme that calls attention to our mistaken equation of nature with production rather than with spirituality.

In contrast to this cacophony, the final six lines build toward the joyful recognition of the new possibilities that accompany the rising sun. This recognition leads to the euphonic description of the "H*o*ly Ghost *o*ver" (notice the reassuring consistency of the assonance) the world. Traditionally represented as a dove, the Holy Ghost brings love and peace to the "*w*orld," and "*b*roods *w*ith *w*arm *b*reast and *w*ith ah! *b*right *w*ings." The effect of this alliteration is mellifluous: the sound bespeaks the harmony that prevails at the end of the poem resulting from the speaker's recognition that "nature is never spent" because God loves and protects the world.

The sounds of "God's Grandeur" enhance the poem's theme; more can be said about its sounds, but it is enough to point out here that for this poem the sound strongly echoes the theme in nearly every line. Here are some more poems in which sound plays a significant role.

POEMS FOR FURTHER STUDY

THOMAS LUX (B. 1946)

Onomatopoeia

1994

The word sounds like the thing.
The sound of the word next to
the sound of another word
sounds like the thing feels
or you desire it to feel. You want

5

this alive
from its insides
and the mind, the denotative, the dictionary
means naught: what you want
to be known must be known   10
cellularly, belly-wise,
or on the tongue: *cerulean blue,*
for example, or *punch drunk.*
Those who live elsewhere
than their bodies don't buy it, don't like it,   15
this in-the-body; the science
and the math tests on it
are yet inconclusive.
There's always this little humming
beneath the surface   20
of the painting, the dance, the play
(the good ones) that tells your heart
that it — the painting, the dance, the play — tells
a truth: *dewlap, dewlap,*
it's dawn's time, it says — the sound   25
provides the thing its lungs, mouth,
and blood-beat. The sound, the noise of the sound, is
the thing — the deaf can hear it,
the blind see it, this tuning fork
beneath the breastbone, sweetly   30
accompanying its song.

CONSIDERATIONS FOR CRITICAL THINKING AND WRITING

1. **FIRST RESPONSE.** Compare Lux's poetic definition of *onomatopoeia* with the textbook definition on page 191. What does Lux's treatment of *onomatopoeia* add to the standard definition?

2. Which lines contain images that particularly emphasize the physical sensation that sounds evoke for those who live "in-the-body" (line 16)?

3. **CREATIVE RESPONSE.** Write a sentence — or a short poem — that consists almost exclusively of onomatopoetic words.

CONNECTION TO ANOTHER SELECTION

1. Choose a poem from this chapter and write an essay that explains how its "sound, the noise of the sound, is / the thing" (lines 27–28).

MOLLY PEACOCK (B. 1947)

Of Night   2008

A city mouse darts from the paws of night.
A body drops from the jaws of night.
A woman denies the laws of night,
awake and trapped in the *was* of night.

A young man turns in the gauze of night,   5
unraveling the cause of night:
that days extend their claws at night
to reenact old wars at night,
though dreams can heal old sores at night
and spring begins its thaw at night,   10
while worry bones are gnawed at night.
He sips her through a straw at night.
Verbs whisper in the clause of night.
A finger to her lips
               the pause of night.

CONSIDERATIONS FOR CRITICAL THINKING AND WRITING

1. **FIRST RESPONSE.** Describe the overall tone created by the images through line 8. Discuss the relationship between those images and the ones in the final six lines in terms of what you think the poem's theme might be.

2. What is the effect of the line-end repetitions? Comment also on Peacock's use of internal near rhymes.

3. Why do you think Peacock chose to space line 14 the way she did?

LEWIS CARROLL (CHARLES LUTWIDGE DODGSON/1832–1898)

Jabberwocky   *1871*

'Twas brillig, and the slithy toves
   Did gyre and gimble in the wabe:
All mimsy were the borogoves,
   And the mome raths outgrabe.

"Beware the Jabberwock, my son!   5
   The jaws that bite, the claws that catch!
Beware the Jubjub bird, and shun
   The frumious Bandersnatch!"

He took his vorpal sword in hand;
   Long time the manxome foe he sought—   10
So rested he by the Tumtum tree,
   And stood awhile in thought.

And, as in uffish thought he stood,
   The Jabberwock, with eyes of flame,
Came whiffling through the tulgey wood,   15
   And burbled as it came!

One, two! One, two! And through and through
   The vorpal blade went snicker-snack!
He left it dead, and with its head
   He went galumphing back.   20

"And hast thou slain the Jabberwock?
   Come to my arms, my beamish boy!

O frabjous day! Callooh, Callay!"
  He chortled in his joy.

'Twas brillig, and the slithy toves   25
  Did gyre and gimble in the wabe:
All mimsy were the borogoves,
  And the mome raths outgrabe.

CONSIDERATIONS FOR CRITICAL THINKING AND WRITING

1. **FIRST RESPONSE.** What happens in this poem? Does it have any meaning?

2. Not all of the words used in this poem appear in dictionaries. In *Through the Looking Glass,* Humpty Dumpty explains to Alice that "'slithy' means 'lithe and slimy.' 'Lithe' is the same as 'active.' You see it's like a portmanteau — there are two meanings packed up into one word." Are there any other portmanteau words in the poem?

3. Which words in the poem sound especially meaningful, even if they are devoid of any denotative meanings?

CONNECTION TO ANOTHER SELECTION

1. Compare Carroll's strategies for creating sound and meaning with those used by Swenson in "A Nosty Fright" (p. 189).

HARRYETTE MULLEN (B. 1953)

Blah-Blah   2002

Ack-ack, aye-aye.
Baa baa, Baba, Bambam, Bebe, Berber, Bibi, blah-blah, Bobo,
      bonbon,
booboo, Bora Bora, Boutros Boutros, bye-bye.
Caca, cancan, Cece, cha-cha, chichi, choo-choo, chop chop,   5
      chow chow, Coco, cocoa,
come come, cuckoo.
Dada, Dee Dee, Didi, dindin, dodo, doodoo, dumdum,
      Duran Duran.
Fifi, fifty-fifty, foofoo, froufrou.   10
Gaga, Gigi, glug-glug, go-go, goody-goody, googoo, grisgris.
Haha, harhar, hear hear, heehee, hey hey, hip-hip, hoho,
      Hsing-Hsing, hubba-hubba, humhum.
is is, It'sIts.
JarJar, Jo Jo, juju.   15
Kiki, knock knock, Koko, Kumkum.
Lala, Lili, Ling-Ling looky-looky, Lulu.
Mahi mahi, mama, Mau Mau, Mei-Mei, Mimi, Momo, murmur,
      my my.
Na Na, No-no, now now.   20
Oh-oh, oink oink.

Pago Pago, Palau Palau, papa, pawpaw, peepee, Phen Fen,
        pooh-pooh, poopoo, pupu, putt-putt.
Rah-rah, ReRe.
Shih-Shih, Sing Sing, Sirhan Sirhan, Sen Sen, Sisi, so-so.   25
Tata, taki-taki, talky-talky, Tam Tam, Tartar, teetee, Tintin,
Tingi Tingi, tom-tom, toot toot, tsetse, tsk tsk, tutu,
        tumtum, tut tut.
Van Van, veve, vroom-vroom.
Wahwah, Walla Walla, weewee, win-win.   30
Yadda yadda Yari Yari, yaya, ylang ylang, yo-yo, yuk-yuk,
        yum-yum.
Zizi, ZsaZsa, Zouzou, Zuzu.

CONSIDERATIONS FOR CRITICAL THINKING AND WRITING

1. **FIRST RESPONSE.** The title probably makes sense to you, but does the rest of the poem? Why or why not?
2. Read the poem aloud, and describe the poem's sound effects.
3. **CREATIVE RESPONSE.** Write ten lines of your own alliterative string of words and read it aloud to hear what it sounds like.

CONNECTION TO ANOTHER SELECTION

1. Compare Mullen's strategies for emphasizing sound in her poem with those of May Swenson in "A Nosty Fright" (p. 189) and Lewis Carroll in "Jabberwocky" (p. 202).

WILLIAM HEYEN (B. 1940)

The Trains   1984

Signed by Franz Paul Stangl, Commandant,
there is in Berlin a document,
an order of transmittal from Treblinka:

248 freight cars of clothing,
400,000 gold watches,   5
25 freight cars of women's hair.

Some clothing was kept, some pulped for paper.
The finest watches were never melted down.
All the women's hair was used for mattresses, or dolls.

Would these words like to use some of that same paper?   10
One of those watches may pulse in your own wrist.
Does someone you know collect dolls, or sleep on human hair?

He is dead at last, Commandant Stangl of Treblinka,
but the camp's three syllables still sound like freight cars
straining around a curve, Treblinka,   15

Treblinka. Clothing, time in gold watches,
women's hair for mattresses and dolls' heads.
Treblinka. The trains from Treblinka.

CONSIDERATIONS FOR CRITICAL THINKING AND WRITING

1. **FIRST RESPONSE.** How does the sound of the word *Treblinka* inform your understanding of the poem?

2. Why does the place name of Treblinka continue to resonate over time? To learn more about Treblinka, search the Web, perhaps starting at ushm.org, the site of the United States Holocaust Memorial Museum.

3. Why do you suppose Heyen uses the word *in* instead of *on* in line 11?

4. Why is sound so important for establishing the tone of this poem? In what sense do "the camp's three syllables still sound like freight cars" (line 14)?

5. **CRITICAL STRATEGIES.** Read the section on reader-response strategies (pp. 680–82) in Chapter 26, "Critical Strategies for Reading." How does this poem make you feel? Why?

JOHN DONNE (1572–1631)

Song   *1633*

Go and catch a falling star,
   Get with child a mandrake root,°
Tell me where all past years are,
   Or who cleft the Devil's foot,
Teach me to hear mermaids singing,   5
   Or to keep off envy's stinging,
         And find
         What wind
Serves to advance an honest mind.

If thou be'st borne to strange sights,   10
   Things invisible to see,
Ride ten thousand days and nights,
   Till age snow white hairs on thee,
Thou, when thou return'st, wilt tell me
   All strange wonders that befell thee,   15
         And swear
         Nowhere
Lives a woman true, and fair.

If thou findst one, let me know,
   Such a pilgrimage were sweet —   20
Yet do not, I would not go,
   Though at next door we might meet;

2 *mandrake root:* This V-shaped root resembles the lower half of the human body.

Though she were true, when you met her,
  And last, till you write your letter,
      Yet she   25
      Will be
False, ere I come, to two or three.

CONSIDERATIONS FOR CRITICAL THINKING AND WRITING

1. **FIRST RESPONSE.** What is the speaker's tone in this poem? What is his view of a woman's love? What does the speaker's use of hyperbole reveal about his emotional state?

2. Do you think Donne wants the speaker's argument to be taken seriously? Is there any humor in the poem?

3. Most of these lines end with masculine rhymes. What other kinds of rhymes are used for end rhymes?

ALEXANDER POPE (1688–1774)

From An Essay on Criticism   *1711*

But most by numbers° judge a poet's song;   *versification*
And smooth or rough, with them, is right or wrong;
In the bright muse though thousand charms conspire,
Her voice is all these tuneful fools admire;
Who haunt Parnassus° but to please their ear,   5
Not mend their minds; as some to church repair,
Not for the doctrine, but the music there.
These equal syllables alone require,
Though oft the ear the open vowels tire;
While expletives° their feeble aid do join;   10
And ten low words oft creep in one dull line;
While they ring round the same unvaried chimes,
With sure returns of still expected rhymes;
Where'er you find "the cooling western breeze,"
In the next line, it "whispers through the trees":   15
If crystal streams "with pleasing murmurs creep,"
The reader's threatened (not in vain) with "sleep":
Then, at the last and only couplet fraught
With some unmeaning thing they call a thought,
A needless Alexandrine° ends the song,   20
That, like a wounded snake, drags its slow length along.
Leave such to tune their own dull rhymes, and know
What's roundly smooth, or languishingly slow;
And praise the easy vigor of a line,

---

5 *Parnassus:* A Greek mountain sacred to the Muses.   10 *expletives:* Unnecessary words used to fill a line, as the *do* in this line.   20 *Alexandrine:* A twelve-syllable line, as line 21.

Where Denham's strength, and Waller's° sweetness join.   25
True ease in writing comes from art, not chance,
As those move easiest who have learned to dance.
'Tis not enough no harshness gives offense,
The sound must seem an echo to the sense:
Soft is the strain when Zephyr° gently blows,   *the west wind* 30
And the smooth stream in smoother numbers flows;
But when loud surges lash the sounding shore,
The hoarse, rough verse should like the torrent roar:
When Ajax° strives some rock's vast weight to throw,
The line too labors, and the words move slow;   35
Not so, when swift Camilla° scours the plain,
Flies o'er th' unbending corn, and skims along the main.

25 *Denham's . . . Waller's:* Sir John Denham (1615–1669) and Edmund Waller (1606–1687) were
poets who used heroic couplets.   34 *Ajax:* A Greek warrior famous for his strength in the
Trojan War.   36 *Camilla:* A goddess famous for her delicate speed.

Considerations for Critical Thinking and Writing

1. **FIRST RESPONSE.** In these lines Pope describes some faults he finds in
   poems and illustrates those faults within the lines that describe them. How
   do the sounds in lines 4, 9, 10, 11, and 21 illustrate what they describe?

2. What is the objection to the "expected rhymes" in lines 12–17? How do they
   differ from Pope's end rhymes?

3. Some lines discuss how to write successful poetry. How do lines 23, 24,
   32–33, 35, 36, and 37 illustrate what they describe?

4. Do you agree that in a good poem "The sound must seem an echo to
   the sense" (line 29)?

Haki R. Madhubuti (b. 1942)

The B Network   *1998*

brothers bop & pop and be-bop in cities locked up
and chained insane by crack and other acts
of desperation computerized in pentagon cellars producing
boppin brothers boastin of being better, best & beautiful.

if the boppin brothers are beautiful where are the sisters   5
who seek brotherman with a drugless head unbossed or beaten
by the bodacious West?

in a time of big wind being blown by boastful brothers,
will other brothers beat back backwardness to better & best
without braggart bosses beatin butts,   10
takin names and diggin graves?

beatin badness into bad may be urban but is it beautiful & serious?
or is it betrayal in an era of prepared easy death hangin on
corners trappin young brothers before they know the
difference between big death and big life?   15

brothers bop & pop and be-bop in cities locked up
and chained insane by crack and other acts
of desperation computerized in pentagon cellars producing
boppin brothers boastin of being better, best, beautiful
and definitely not *Black*.   20

the critical best is that
brothers better be the best if they are to avoid backwardness
brothers better be the best if they are to conquer beautiful bigness
Comprehend that bad is only *bad* if it's big, Black and better
than boastful braggarts belittling our best and brightest   25
with bosses seeking inches when miles are better.

brothers need to bop to being Black & bright & above board
the black train of beautiful wisdom that is bending this bind
toward a new & knowledgeable beginning that is
bountiful & bountiful & beautiful   30
While be-boppin to be
better than the test,
brotherman.

better yet write the exam.

CONSIDERATIONS FOR CRITICAL THINKING AND WRITING

1. **FIRST RESPONSE.** Read this poem aloud. How is that a different experience from reading it silently?

2. Why has the poet included all those words beginning with *b*? How do you explain the title?

3. What is the speaker's assessment of the status of African Americans in the United States? What sort of advice, if any, is offered to them?

4. Comment on the possible interpretations of the final line.

CONNECTION TO ANOTHER SELECTION

1. Compare the style and themes of "The B Network" with those of Langston Hughes's "Dream Boogie" (p. 421).

MAXINE HONG KINGSTON (B. 1940)

Restaurant   *1981*

for Lilah Kan

The main cook lies sick on a banquette, and
        his assistant
has cut his thumb. So the quiche cook takes
their places at the eight-burner range, and
        you and I
get to roll out twenty-three rounds of pie

Courtesy of Gail K. Evenari.

dough and break a hundred eggs, four at a crack,   5
and sift out shell with a China cap, pack
spinach in the steel sink, squish and squeeze
the water out, and grate a full moon of cheese.
Pam, the pastry chef, who is baking Choco-
late Globs (once called Mulattos) complains about the disco,   10
which Lewis, the salad man, turns up louder out of spite.
"Black so-called musician," "Broads. Whites."
The porters, who speak French, from the Ivory Coast,
sweep up droppings and wash the pans without soap.
We won't be out of here until three A.M. In this basement,   15
I lose my size. I am a bent-over
child, Gretel or Jill, and I can
lift a pot as big as a tub with both hands.
Using a pitchfork, you stoke the broccoli and bacon.
Then I find you in the freezer, taking   20
a nibble of a slab of chocolate as big as a table.
We put the quiches in the oven, then we are able
to stick our heads up out of the sidewalk into the night
and wonder at the clean diners behind glass in candlelight.

CONSIDERATIONS FOR CRITICAL THINKING AND WRITING

1. **FIRST RESPONSE.** How do the sounds of this poem contribute to the descriptions of what goes on in the restaurant kitchen? How do they contribute to the description of the diners?

2. In what sense does the speaker "lose [her] size" in the kitchen (line 16)? How would you describe her?

3. Examine the poem's rhymes. What effect do they have on your reading?

4. Describe the tone of the final line. How does it differ from that of the rest of the poem?

CONNECTION TO ANOTHER SELECTION

1. Write an essay analyzing how the kitchen activities described in this poem and in Elaine Magarrell's "The Joy of Cooking" (p. 154) are used to convey the themes of these poems.

ANDREW HUDGINS (B. 1951)

The Cow   2006

I love the red cow
with all of my heart.
She's gentle when pulling
my cherry-red cart.

We take her rich milk   5
and swallow it down.

With nothing, it's white,
with chocolate brown.

When she grows too feeble
to give us fresh cream,   10
we'll slit her red throat,
hang her from a beam,

and pull out her insides
to throw to the dogs,
just as we do   15
when we slaughter the hogs.

We've now owned six cows
that I can remember.
We drain them and gut them,
skin and dismember,   20

package and label them,
and stock up the freezer.
We all love beefsteak —
from baby to geezer!

Tossed on the grill,   25
the bloody steaks sputter.
As a last, grateful tribute,
so humble we stutter,

we offer up thanks
with a reverent mutter —   30
then slather her chops
with her own creamy butter.

Considerations for Critical Thinking and Writing

1. **FIRST RESPONSE.** Describe the tone of each stanza. How do the rhymes serve to establish the tone?

2. Characterize the speaker. How do you reconcile what is said in the first stanza with the description in the final stanza?

3. This poem appeared in the July/August 2006 humor issue of *Poetry*. How does that context affect your reading of it?

4. **CREATIVE RESPONSE.** Bring something to the table yourself: add a four-line stanza in Hudgins's style that rhymes and concludes the meal.

Paul Humphrey (b. 1915)

Blow   1983

Her skirt was lofted by the gale;
When I, with gesture deft,
Essayed to stay her frisky sail
She luffed, and laughed, and left.

CONSIDERATIONS FOR CRITICAL THINKING AND WRITING

1. **FIRST RESPONSE.** How do alliteration and assonance contribute to the euphonic effects in this poem?
2. What is the poem's controlling metaphor? Why is it especially appropriate?
3. Explain the ambiguity of the title.

ROBERT FRANCIS (1901–1987)

The Pitcher
1953

His art is eccentricity, his aim
How not to hit the mark he seems to aim at,

His passion how to avoid the obvious,
His technique how to vary the avoidance.

The others throw to be comprehended. He   5
Throws to be a moment misunderstood.

Yet not too much. Not errant, arrant, wild,
But every seeming aberration willed.

Not to, yet still, still to communicate
Making the batter understand too late.   10

CONSIDERATIONS FOR CRITICAL THINKING AND WRITING

1. **FIRST RESPONSE.** Explain how each pair of lines in this poem works together to describe the pitcher's art.
2. Consider how the poem itself works the way a good pitcher does. Which lines illustrate what they describe?
3. Comment on the effects of the poem's rhymes. How are the final two lines different in their rhyme from the previous lines? How does sound echo sense in lines 9–10?
4. Write an essay that examines "The Pitcher" as an extended metaphor for talking about poetry. How well does the poem characterize strategies for writing poetry as well as pitching?
5. Write an essay that develops an extended comparison between writing or reading poetry and playing or watching another sport.

CONNECTION TO ANOTHER SELECTION

1. Write an essay comparing "The Pitcher" with another work by Francis, "Catch" (p. 26). One poem defines poetry implicitly, the other defines it explicitly. Which poem do you prefer? Why?

HELEN CHASIN (B. 1938)

The Word Plum

1968

The word *plum* is delicious

pout and push, luxury of
self-love, and savoring murmur
full in the mouth and falling
like fruit   5

taut skin
pierced, bitten, provoked into
juice, and tart flesh

question
and reply, lip and tongue   10
of pleasure.

CONSIDERATIONS FOR CRITICAL THINKING AND WRITING

1. **FIRST RESPONSE.** What is the effect of the repetitions of the alliteration and assonance throughout the poem? How does it contribute to the poem's meaning?
2. Which sounds in the poem are like the sounds one makes while eating a
   plum?
3. Discuss the title. Explain whether you think this poem is more about the
   word *plum* or about the plum itself. Can the two be separated in the poem?

CONNECTION TO ANOTHER SELECTION

1. How is Galway Kinnell's "Blackberry Eating" (p. 194) similar in technique
   to Chasin's poem? Try writing such a poem yourself: Choose a food to
   describe that allows you to evoke its sensuousness in sounds.

RICHARD WAKEFIELD (B. 1952)

The Bell Rope

2005

In Sunday school the boy who learned a psalm
by heart would get to sound the steeple bell
and send its tolling through the sabbath calm
to call the saved and not-so-saved as well.
For lack of practice all the lines are lost—   5
something about how angels' hands would bear
me up to God—but on one Pentecost
they won me passage up the steeple stair.
I leapt and grabbed the rope up high to ride
it down, I touched the floor, the rope went slack,   10
the bell was silent. Then, beatified,

I rose, uplifted as the rope pulled back.
I leapt and fell again; again it took
me up, but still the bell withheld its word—
until at last the church foundation shook   15
in bass approval, felt as much as heard,
and after I let go the bell tolled long
and loud as if repaying me for each
unanswered pull with heaven-rending song
a year of Sunday school could never teach   20
and that these forty years can not obscure.
Some nights when sleep won't come I think of how
just once there came an answer, clear and sure.
If I could find that rope I'd grasp it now.

CONSIDERATIONS FOR CRITICAL THINKING AND WRITING

1. **FIRST RESPONSE.** Describe the rhyme scheme and then read the poem
   aloud. How does Wakefield manage to avoid making this heavily rhymed
   poem sound clichéd or sing-songy?

2. Comment on the appropriateness of Wakefield's choice of diction and how
   it relates to the poem's images.

3. Explain how sound becomes, in a sense, the theme of the poem.

CONNECTION TO ANOTHER SELECTION

1. Compare the images and themes of "The Bell Rope" with those in Robert
   Frost's "Birches" (p. 377).

JOHN KEATS (1795–1821)

Ode to a Nightingale   *1819*

I

My heart aches, and a drowsy numbness pains
    My sense, as though of hemlock° I had drunk,   *a poison*
Or emptied some dull opiate to the drains
    One minute past, and Lethe-wards° had sunk:
'Tis not through envy of thy happy lot,   5
    But being too happy in thine happiness—
        That thou, light-wingèd Dryad° of the trees,   *wood nymph*
            In some melodious plot
Of beechen green, and shadows numberless,
    Singest of summer in full-throated ease.   10

4 *Lethe-wards:* Toward Lethe, the river of forgetfulness in the Hades of Greek mythology.

II

O, for a draught of vintage! that hath been
    Cooled a long age in the deep-delved earth,
Tasting of Flora° and the country green,   *goddess of flowers*
    Dance, and Provençal song,° and sunburnt mirth!
O for a beaker full of the warm South,   15
    Full of the true, the blushful Hippocrene,°
        With beaded bubbles winking at the brim,
            And purple-stainèd mouth;
    That I might drink, and leave the world unseen,
        And with thee fade away into the forest dim.   20

III

Fade far away, dissolve, and quite forget
    What thou among the leaves hast never known,
The weariness, the fever, and the fret
    Here, where men sit and hear each other groan;
Where palsy shakes a few, sad, last gray hairs,   25
    Where youth grows pale, and specter-thin, and dies,
        Where but to think is to be full of sorrow
            And leaden-eyed despairs,
    Where Beauty cannot keep her lustrous eyes;
        Or new Love pine at them beyond tomorrow.   30

IV

Away! away! for I will fly to thee,
    Not charioted by Bacchus and his pards,°
But on the viewless wings of Poesy,
    Though the dull brain perplexes and retards:
Already with thee! tender is the night,   35
    And haply the Queen-Moon is on her throne,
        Clustered around by all her starry Fays;
            But here there is no light,
    Save what from heaven is with the breezes blown
        Through verdurous glooms and winding mossy ways.   40

V

I cannot see what flowers are at my feet,
    Nor what soft incense hangs upon the boughs,
But, in embalmèd° darkness, guess each sweet   *perfumed*
    Wherewith the seasonable month endows

---

14 *Provençal song:* The medieval troubadours of Provence, France, were known for their singing.   16 *Hippocrene:* The fountain of the Muses in Greek mythology.   32 *Bacchus and his pards:* The Greek god of wine traveled in a chariot drawn by leopards.

The grass, the thicket, and the fruit-tree wild;   45
  What hawthorn, and the pastoral eglantine;
    Fast fading violets covered up in leaves;
      And mid-May's eldest child,
  The coming musk-rose, full of dewy wine,
    The murmurous haunt of flies on summer eves.   50

VI

Darkling° I listen; and for many a time   *in the dark*
  I have been half in love with easeful Death,
Called him soft names in many a musèd rhyme,
  To take into the air my quiet breath;
Now more than ever seems it rich to die,   55
  To cease upon the midnight with no pain,
    While thou art pouring forth thy soul abroad
      In such an ecstasy!
  Still wouldst thou sing, and I have ears in vain —
    To thy high requiem become a sod.   60

VII

Thou wast not born for death, immortal Bird!
  No hungry generations tread thee down;
The voice I hear this passing night was heard
  In ancient days by emperor and clown:
Perhaps the selfsame song that found a path   65
  Through the sad heart of Ruth,° when, sick for home,
    She stood in tears amid the alien corn:
      The same that oft-times hath
  Charmed magic casements, opening on the foam
    Of perilous seas, in faery lands forlorn.   70

VIII

Forlorn! the very word is like a bell
  To toll me back from thee to my sole self!
Adieu! the fancy cannot cheat so well
  As she is famed to do, deceiving elf.
Adieu! adieu! thy plaintive anthem fades   75
  Past the near meadows, over the still stream,
    Up the hill side; and now 'tis buried deep
      In the next valley-glades:
  Was it a vision, or a waking dream?
    Fled is that music: — Do I wake or sleep?   80

66 *Ruth:* A young widow in the Bible (see the book of Ruth).

CONSIDERATIONS FOR CRITICAL THINKING AND WRITING

1. **FIRST RESPONSE.** Why does the speaker in this ode want to leave his world for the nightingale's? What might the nightingale symbolize?

2. How does the speaker attempt to escape his world? Is he successful?

3. What changes the speaker's view of death at the end of stanza VI?

4. What does the allusion to Ruth (line 66) contribute to the ode's meaning?

5. In which lines is the imagery especially sensuous? How does this effect add to the conflict presented?

6. What calls the speaker back to himself at the end of stanza VII and the beginning of stanza VIII?

7. Choose a stanza and explain how sound is related to its meaning.

8. How regular is the stanza form of this ode?

HOWARD NEMEROV (B. 1920)

Because You Asked about the Line between Prose and Poetry

1980

Sparrows were feeding in a freezing drizzle
That while you watched turned into pieces of snow
Riding a gradient invisible
From silver aslant to random, white, and slow.

There came a moment that you couldn't tell.
And then they clearly flew instead of fell.

CONSIDERATIONS FOR CRITICAL THINKING AND WRITING

1. **FIRST RESPONSE.** Describe the distinction that this poem makes between prose and poetry. How does the poem itself become an example of that distinction?

2. Identify the kinds of rhymes Nemerov employs. How do the rhymes in the first and second stanzas differ from each other?

3. Comment on the poem's punctuation. How is it related to theme?

8

Patterns of Rhythm

I would define, in brief, the Poetry of words as the Rhythmical Creation of Beauty. Its sole arbiter is Taste.

— EDGAR ALLAN POE[1]

The rhythms of everyday life surround us in regularly recurring movements and sounds. As you read these words, your heart pulsates while somewhere else a clock ticks, a cradle rocks, a drum beats, a dancer sways, a foghorn blasts, a wave recedes, or a child skips. We may tend to overlook rhythm because it is so tightly woven into the fabric of our experience, but it is there nonetheless, one of the conditions of life. Rhythm is also one of the conditions of speech because the voice alternately rises and falls as words are stressed or unstressed and as the pace quickens or slackens. In poetry *rhythm* refers to the recurrence of stressed and unstressed sounds. Depending on how the sounds are arranged, this can result in a pace that is fast or slow, choppy or smooth.

Explore the poetic element in this chapter on *LiterActive* or at bedfordstmartins.com/rewritinglit.

[1] Photograph by W. S. Hartshorn. 1848. Prints and Photographs Division, Library of Congress.

SOME PRINCIPLES OF METER

Poets use rhythm to create pleasurable sound patterns and to reinforce meanings. "Rhythm," Edith Sitwell once observed, "might be described as, to the world of sound, what light is to the world of sight. It shapes and gives new meaning." Prose can use rhythm effectively too, but prose that does so tends to be an exception. The following exceptional lines are from a speech by Winston Churchill to the House of Commons after Allied forces lost a great battle to German forces at Dunkirk during World War II:

> We shall not flag or fail. We shall go on to the end. We shall fight in France, we shall fight on the seas and oceans, we shall fight with growing confidence and growing strength in the air, we shall defend our island, whatever the cost may be, we shall fight on the beaches, we shall fight on the landing grounds, we shall fight in the fields and in the streets, we shall fight in the hills; we shall never surrender.

The stressed repetition of "we shall" bespeaks the resolute singleness of purpose that Churchill had to convey to the British people if they were to win the war. Repetition is also one of the devices used in poetry to create rhythmic effects. In the following excerpt from "Song of the Open Road," Walt Whitman urges the pleasures of limitless freedom on his reader:

> Allons!° the road is before us!   *Let's go!*
> It is safe — I have tried it — my own feet have tried it well — be not detain'd!
> Let the paper remain on the desk unwritten, and the book on the
>   shelf unopen'd!
> Let the tools remain in the workshop! Let the money remain unearn'd!
> Let the school stand! mind not the cry of the teacher!   5
> Let the preacher preach in his pulpit! Let the lawyer plead in the
>   court, and the judge expound the law.
>
> Camerado,° I give you my hand!   *friend*
> I give you my love more precious than money,
> I give you myself before preaching or law;
> Will you give me yourself? will you come travel with me?   10
> Shall we stick by each other as long as we live?

These rhythmic lines quickly move away from conventional values to the open road of shared experiences. Their recurring sounds are created not by rhyme or alliteration and assonance (see Chapter 7) but by the repetition of words and phrases.

Although the repetition of words and phrases can be an effective means of creating rhythm in poetry, the more typical method consists of patterns of accented or unaccented syllables. Words contain syllables that are either stressed or unstressed. A **stress** (or **accent**) places more emphasis on one syllable than on another. We say "*syl*lable" not "syl*la*ble," "*em*phasis" not "em*pha*sis." We routinely stress syllables when we speak: "*Is* she con*tent* with the *con*tents of the *yel*low *pack*age?" To distinguish between two people we might say "Is *she* con*tent*. . . ?" In this way stress can be used to emphasize a particular word in a sentence. Poets often arrange words so that the desired meaning is suggested by the rhythm; hence emphasis is controlled by the poet rather than left entirely to the reader.

When a rhythmic pattern of stresses recurs in a poem, the result is **meter.** Taken together, all the metrical elements in a poem make up what is called the poem's **prosody. Scansion** consists of measuring the stresses in a line to determine its metrical pattern. Several methods can be used to mark lines. One widely used system uses ' for a stressed syllable and ˘ for an unstressed syllable. In a sense, the stress mark represents the equivalent of tapping one's foot to a beat:

> Hickory, dickory, dock,
> The mouse ran up the clock.
> The clock struck one,
> And down he run,
> Hickory, dickory, dock.

In the first two lines and the final line of this familiar nursery rhyme we hear three stressed syllables. In lines 3 and 4, where the meter changes for variety, we hear just two stressed syllables. The combination of stresses provides the pleasure of the rhythm we hear.

To hear the rhythms of "Hickory, dickory, dock" does not require a formal study of meter. Nevertheless, an awareness of the basic kinds of meter that appear in English poetry can enhance your understanding of how a poem achieves its effects. Understanding the sound effects of a poem and having a vocabulary with which to discuss those effects can intensify your pleasure in poetry. Although the study of meter can be extremely technical, the terms used to describe the basic meters of English poetry are relatively easy to comprehend.

The **foot** is the metrical unit by which a line of poetry is measured. A foot usually consists of one stressed and one or two unstressed syllables. A vertical line is used to separate the feet: "The clock | struck one" consists of two feet. A foot of poetry can be arranged in a variety of patterns; here are five of the chief ones:

Foot	*Pattern*	*Example*
iamb	˘ ´	away
trochee	´ ˘	Lovely
anapest	˘ ˘ ´	understand
dactyl	´ ˘ ˘	desperate
spondee	´ ´	dead set

The most common lines in English poetry contain meters based on iambic feet. However, even lines that are predominantly iambic will often include variations to create particular effects. Other important patterns include trochaic, anapestic, and dactylic feet. The spondee is not a sustained meter but occurs for variety or emphasis.

Iambic
        Whăt képt | hĭs eyés | frŏm gív | ĭng báck | thĕ gáze
Trochaic
        Hé wăs | loúdĕr | thán thĕ | préachĕr
Anapestic
        Ĭ ăm cálled | tŏ thĕ frónt | ŏf thĕ roóm
Dactylic
        Síng ĭt ăll | mérrĭlў

These meters have different rhythms and can create different effects. Iambic and anapestic are known as ***rising meters*** because they move from unstressed to stressed sounds, while trochaic and dactylic are known as ***falling meters.*** Anapests and dactyls tend to move more lightly and rapidly than iambs or trochees. Although no single kind of meter can be considered always better than another for a given subject, it is possible to determine whether the meter of a specific poem is appropriate for its subject. A serious poem about a tragic death would most likely not be well served by lilting rhythms. Keep in mind, too, that though one or another of these four basic meters might constitute the predominant rhythm of a poem, variations can occur within lines to change the pace or call attention to a particular word.

A ***line*** is measured by the number of feet it contains. Here, for example, is an iambic line with three feet: "Ĭf she | shŏuld wríte | ă nóte." These are the names for line lengths:

monometer: one foot	pentameter: five feet
dimeter: two feet	hexameter: six feet
trimeter: three feet	heptameter: seven feet
tetrameter: four feet	octameter: eight feet

By combining the name of a line length with the name of a foot, we can describe the metrical qualities of a line concisely. Consider, for example, the pattern of feet and length of this line:

I didn't want the boy to hit the dog.

The iambic rhythm of this line falls into five feet; hence it is called ***iambic pentameter.*** Iambic is the most common pattern in English poetry because its rhythm appears so naturally in English speech and writing. Unrhymed iambic pentameter is called ***blank verse;*** Shakespeare's plays are built on such lines.

Less common than the iamb, trochee, anapest, or dactyl is the ***spondee,*** a two-syllable foot in which both syllables are stressed (´ ´). Note the effect of the spondaic foot at the beginning of this line:

Dĕad sét | ăgaínst | thĕ plán | hĕ wént | ăwáy.

Spondees can slow a rhythm and provide variety and emphasis, particularly in iambic and trochaic lines. A line that ends with a stressed syllable is said to have a *masculine ending,* whereas a line that ends with an extra unstressed syllable is said to have a *feminine ending.* Consider, for example, these two lines from Timothy Steele's "Waiting for the Storm" (the entire poem appears on p. 223):

feminine: Thĕ sánd | ăt mý feet | grŏw cóld | ĕr,
masculine: Thĕ dámp | aĭr chíll | ănd spréad.

The effects of English meters are easily seen in the following lines by Samuel Taylor Coleridge, in which the rhythm of each line illustrates the meter described in it:

Trochee trips from long to short;
From long to long in solemn sort
Slow Spondee stalks; strong foot yet ill able
Ever to come up with Dactylic trisyllable.
Iambics march from short to long—
With a leap and a bound the swift Anapests throng.

The speed of a line is also affected by the number of pauses in it. A pause within a line is called a *caesura* and is indicated by a double vertical line (‖). A caesura can occur anywhere within a line and need not be indicated by punctuation:

Camerado, ‖ I give you my hand!
I give you my love ‖ more precious than money.

A slight pause occurs within each of these lines and at its end. Both kinds of pauses contribute to the lines' rhythm.

When a line has a pause at its end, it is called an *end-stopped line.* Such pauses reflect normal speech patterns and are often marked by punctuation. A line that ends without a pause and continues into the next line for its meaning is called a *run-on line.* Running over from one line to another is also called *enjambment.* The first and eighth lines of the following poem are run-on lines; the rest are end-stopped.

WILLIAM WORDSWORTH (1770–1850)

My Heart Leaps Up

1807

My heart leaps up when I behold
    A rainbow in the sky:
So was it when my life began;
So is it now I am a man;

So be it when I shall grow old,
    Or let me die!
The child is father of the Man;
And I could wish my days to be
Bound each to each by natural piety.

Run-on lines have a different rhythm from end-stopped lines. Lines 3 and 4 and lines 8 and 9 are iambic, but the effect of their two rhythms is very different when we read these lines aloud. The enjambment of lines 8 and 9 reinforces their meaning; just as the "days" are bound together, so are the lines.

The rhythm of a poem can be affected by several devices: the kind and number of stresses within lines, the length of lines, and the kinds of pauses that appear within lines or at their ends. In addition, as we saw in Chapter 7, the sound of a poem is affected by alliteration, assonance, rhyme, and consonance. These sounds help to create rhythms by controlling our pronunciations, as in the following lines by Alexander Pope (the entire poem appears on p. 206):

Soft is the strain when Zephyr gently blows,
And the smooth stream in smoother numbers flows;
But when loud surges lash the sounding shore,
The hoarse, rough verse should like the torrent roar.

These lines are effective because their rhythm and sound work with their meaning.

Suggestions for Scanning a Poem

These suggestions should help you in talking about a poem's meter.

1. After reading the poem through, read it aloud and mark the stressed syllables in each line. Then mark the unstressed syllables.

2. From your markings, identify what kind of foot is dominant (iambic, trochaic, dactylic, or anapestic) and divide the lines into feet, keeping in mind that the vertical line marking a foot may come in the middle of a word as well as at its beginning or end.

3. Determine the number of feet in each line. Remember that there may be variations; some lines may be shorter or longer than the predominant meter. What is important is the overall pattern. Do not assume that variations represent the poet's inability to fulfill the overall pattern. Notice the effects of variations and whether they emphasize words and phrases or disrupt your expectation for some other purpose.

4. Listen for pauses within lines and mark the caesuras; many times there will be no punctuation to indicate them.

5. Recognize that scansion does not always yield a definitive measurement of a line. Even experienced readers may differ over the scansion of a given line. What is important is not a precise description of the line but an awareness of how a poem's rhythms contribute to its effects.

The following poem demonstrates how you can use an understanding of meter and rhythm to gain a greater appreciation for what a poem is saying.

TIMOTHY STEELE (B. 1948)

Waiting for the Storm   *1986*

Breeze sent | a wrink | ling dark | ness
Across | the bay. ‖ I knelt
Beneath | an up | turned boat,
And, mo | ment by mo | ment, felt

The sand | at my feet | grow cold | er,
The damp | air chill | and spread.
Then the | first rain | drops sound | ed
On the hull | above | my head.

The predominant meter of this poem is iambic trimeter, but there is plenty of variation as the storm rapidly approaches and finally begins to pelt the sheltered speaker. The emphatic spondee ("Breeze sent") pushes the darkness quickly across the bay while the caesura at the end of the sentence in line 2 creates a pause that sets up a feeling of suspense and expectation that is measured in the ticking rhythm of line 4, a run-on line that brings us into the chilly sand and air of the second stanza. Perhaps the most impressive sound effect used in the poem appears in the second syllable of "sounded" in line 7. That "ed" precedes the sound of the poem's final word, "head," just as if it were the first drop of rain hitting the hull above the speaker. The visual, tactile, and auditory images make "Waiting for the Storm" an intense sensory experience.

A SAMPLE STUDENT RESPONSE

Marco Pacini

Professor Fierstein

English 201

November 2, 2009

The Rhythm of Anticipation in Timothy Steele's "Waiting for the Storm"

In his poem "Waiting for the Storm," Timothy Steele uses run-on lines, or enjambment, to create a feeling of anticipation. Every line ends unfinished or is a continuation of the previous line, so we must read on to gain completion. This open-ended rhythm mirrors the waiting experienced by the speaker of the poem.

Nearly every line of the poem leaves the reader in suspense:

> I knelt
> Beneath an upturned boat,
> And moment by moment, felt
>
> The sand at my feet grow colder,
> The damp air chill and spread. (2-6)

Action is interrupted at every line break. We have to wait to find out where the speaker knelt and what was felt, since information is given in small increments. So, like the speaker, we must take in the details of the storm little by little, "moment by moment" (4). Even when the first drops of rain hit the hull, the poem ends before we can see or feel the storm's full force, and we are left waiting, in a continuous state of anticipation. . . .

Work Cited

Steele, Timothy. "Waiting for the Storm." *Poetry: An Introduction*. Ed. Michael Meyer. 6th ed. Boston: Bedford/St. Martin's, 2010. 223. Print.

This next poem also reinforces meanings through its use of meter and rhythm.

WILLIAM BUTLER YEATS (1865–1939)

That the Night Come   1912

She lived | in storm | and strife,
Her soul | had such | desire
For what | proud death | may bring
That it | could not | endure
The com | mon good | of life,   5
But lived | as 'twere | a king
That packed | his mar | riage day
With ban | neret | and pen | non,
Trumpet | and ket | tledrum,
And the | outrag | eous can | non,   10
To bun | dle time | away
That the | night come.

Scansion reveals that the predominant meter here is iambic trimeter: Each line contains three stressed and unstressed syllables that form a regular, predictable rhythm through line 7. That rhythm is disrupted, however, when the speaker compares the woman's longing for what death brings to a king's eager anticipation of his wedding night. The king packs the day with noisy fanfares and celebrations to fill up time and distract himself. Unable to accept "The common good of life," the woman fills her days with "storm and strife." In a determined effort "To bundle time away," she, like the king, impatiently awaits the night.

Lines 8–10 break the regular pattern established in the first seven lines. The extra unstressed syllable in lines 8 and 10 along with the trochaic feet in lines 9 ("trumpet") and 10 ("And the") interrupt the basic iambic trimeter and parallel the woman's and the king's frenetic activity. These lines thus echo the inability of the woman and king to "endure" regular or normal time. The last line is the most irregular in the poem. The final two accented syllables sound like the deep resonant beats of a kettledrum or a cannon firing. The words "night come" dramatically remind us that what the woman anticipates is not a lover but the mysterious finality of death. The meter serves, then, in both its regularity and variations to reinforce the poem's meaning and tone.

The following poems are especially rich in their rhythms and sounds. As you read and study them, notice how patterns of rhythm and the sounds of words reinforce meanings and contribute to the poems' effects. And, perhaps most important, read the poems aloud so that you can hear them.

POEMS FOR FURTHER STUDY

ALFRED, LORD TENNYSON (1809–1892)

Break, Break, Break   *1842*

Break, break, break,
    On thy cold gray stones, O Sea!
And I would that my tongue could utter
    The thoughts that arise in me.

O, well for the fisherman's boy,   5
    That he shouts with his sister at play!
O, well for the sailor lad,
    That he sings in his boat on the bay!

And the stately ships go on
    To their haven under the hill;   10
But O for the touch of a vanished hand,
    And the sound of a voice that is still!

Break, break, break
    At the foot of thy crags, O Sea!
But the tender grace of a day that is dead   15
    Will never come back to me.

CONSIDERATIONS FOR CRITICAL THINKING AND WRITING

1. **FIRST RESPONSE.** Paraphrase the poem and describe its tone.
2. How do lines 1 and 13 differ from the predominant meter of the rest of the lines? How do these lines control the poem's tone?
3. What is the effect of the repetition? What does "break" refer to in addition to the waves?

ALICE JONES (B. 1949)

The Foot   *1993*

Our improbable support, erected
on the osseous architecture
of the calcaneus, talus, cuboid,
navicular, cuneiforms, metatarsals,
phalanges, a plethora of hinges,   5

all strung together by gliding
tendons, covered by the pearly
plantar fascia, then fat-padded
to form the sole, humble surface
of our contact with earth.   10

Here the body's broadest tendon
anchors the heel's fleshy base,

the finely wrinkled skin stretches
forward across the capillaried arch,
to the ball, a balance point.   15

A wide web of flexor tendons
and branched veins maps the dorsum,
fades into the stub-laden bone
splay, the stuffed sausage sacks
of toes, each with a tuft   20

of proximal hairs to introduce
the distal nail, whose useless
curve remembers an ancestor,
the vanished creature's wild
and necessary claw.   25

CONSIDERATIONS FOR CRITICAL THINKING AND WRITING

1. **FIRST RESPONSE.** What is the effect of the diction? What sort of tone is established by the use of anatomical terms? How do the terms affect the rhythm?

2. Jones has described the form of "The Foot" as "five stubby stanzas." Explain why the lines of this poem may or may not warrant this description of the stanzas.

3. **CRITICAL STRATEGIES.** Read the section on formalist strategies (pp. 666–68) in Chapter 26, "Critical Strategies for Reading." Describe the effect of the final stanza. How would your reading be affected if the poem ended after the comma in the middle of line 22?

A. E. HOUSMAN (1859–1936)

When I was one-and-twenty   *1896*

When I was one-and-twenty
  I heard a wise man say,
"Give crowns and pounds and guineas
  But not your heart away;
Give pearls away and rubies   5
  But keep your fancy free."
But I was one-and-twenty,
  No use to talk to me.

When I was one-and-twenty
  I heard him say again,   10
"The heart out of the bosom
  Was never given in vain;
'Tis paid with sighs a plenty
  And sold for endless rue."
And I am two-and-twenty,   15
  And oh, 'tis true, 'tis true.

CONSIDERATIONS FOR CRITICAL THINKING AND WRITING

1. **FIRST RESPONSE.** How does the basic metrical pattern affect your understanding of the speaker?

2. How do lines 1–8 parallel lines 9–16 in their use of rhyme and metaphor? Are there any significant differences between the stanzas?

3. What do you think has happened to change the speaker's attitude toward love?

4. Explain why you agree or disagree with the advice given by the "wise man."

5. What is the effect of the repetition in line 16?

RITA DOVE (B. 1952)

Fox Trot Fridays   *2001*

Thank the stars there's a day
each week to tuck in

the grief, lift your pearls, and
stride brush stride

quick-quick with a   5
heel-ball-toe. Smooth

as Nat King Cole's
slow satin smile,

easy as taking
one day at a time: 10

one man and
one woman,

rib to rib,
with no heartbreak in sight —

just the sweep of Paradise   15
and the space of a song

to count all the wonders in it.

CONSIDERATIONS FOR CRITICAL THINKING AND WRITING

1. **FIRST RESPONSE.** Explain how the rhythm of the lines is aptly partnered with the fox trot.

2. Do some background research so that you can discuss why Dove chooses Nat King Cole as the right kind of singer for this poem.

3. The fox trot is more than a dance step for Dove. What is its appeal in this poem?

RACHEL HADAS (B. 1948)

The Red Hat

1995

It started before Christmas. Now our son
officially walks to school alone.
Semi-alone, it's accurate to say:
I or his father track him on the way.
He walks up on the east side of West End,   5
we on the west side. Glances can extend
(and do) across the street; not eye contact.
Already ties are feeling and not fact.
Straus Park is where these parallel paths part;
he goes alone from there. The watcher's heart   10
stretches, elastic in its love and fear,
toward him as we see him disappear,
striding briskly. Where two weeks ago,
holding a hand, he'd dawdle, dreamy, slow,
he now is hustled forward by the pull   15
of something far more powerful than school.

The mornings we turn back to are no more
than forty minutes longer than before,
but they feel vastly different — flimsy, strange,
wavering in the eddies of this change,   20
empty, unanchored, perilously light
since the red hat vanished from our sight.

CONSIDERATIONS FOR CRITICAL THINKING AND WRITING

1. **FIRST RESPONSE.** What emotions do the parents experience throughout the poem? How do you think the boy feels? Does the metrical pattern affect your understanding of the parents or the boy?

2. What prevents the rhymed couplets in this poem from sounding sing-songy? What is the predominant meter?

3. What is it that "pull[s]" the boy along in lines 15 16?

4. Why do you think Hadas titled the poem "The Red Hat" rather than, for example, "Paths Part" (line 9)?

5. **CRITICAL STRATEGIES.** Read the section on psychological strategies (pp. 670–72) in Chapter 26, "Critical Strategies for Reading." How does the speaker reveal her personal psychology in this poem?

ROBERT HERRICK (1591–1674)

Delight in Disorder

1648

A sweet disorder in the dress
Kindles in clothes a wantonness.
A lawn° about the shoulders thrown   *linen scarf*
Into a fine distraction;

An erring lace, which here and there   5
Enthralls the crimson stomacher,
A cuff neglectful, and thereby
Ribbons to flow confusedly;
A winning wave, deserving note,
In the tempestuous petticoat;   10
A careless shoestring, in whose tie
I see a wild civility;
Do more bewitch me than when art
Is too precise in every part.

CONSIDERATIONS FOR CRITICAL THINKING AND WRITING

1. **FIRST RESPONSE.** Why does the speaker in this poem value "disorder" so highly? How do the poem's organization and rhythmic order relate to its theme? Are they "precise in every part" (line 14)?

2. Which words in the poem indicate disorder? Which words indicate the speaker's response to that disorder? What are the connotative meanings of each set of words? Why are they appropriate? What do they suggest about the woman and the speaker?

3. Write a short essay in which you agree or disagree with the speaker's views on dress.

BEN JONSON (1573–1637)

Still to Be Neat   *1609*

Still° to be neat, still to be dressed,   *continually*
As you were going to a feast;
Still to be powdered, still perfumed;
Lady, it is to be presumed,
Though art's hid causes are not found,   5
All is not sweet, all is not sound.

Give me a look, give me a face
That makes simplicity a grace;
Robes loosely flowing, hair as free;
Such sweet neglect more taketh me   10
Then all th' adulteries of art.
They strike mine eyes, but not my heart.

CONSIDERATIONS FOR CRITICAL THINKING AND WRITING

1. **FIRST RESPONSE.** What are the speaker's reservations about the lady in the first stanza? What do you think "sweet" means in line 6?

2. What does the speaker want from the lady in the second stanza? How has the meaning of "sweet" shifted from line 6 to line 10? What other words in the poem are especially charged with connotative meanings?

3. How do the rhythms of Jonson's lines help to reinforce meanings? Pay particular attention to lines 6 and 12.

CONNECTION TO ANOTHER SELECTION

1. Write an essay comparing the themes of "Still to Be Neat" and Herrick's preceding poem, "Delight in Disorder." How do the speakers make similar points but from different perspectives?

2. How does the rhythm of "Still to Be Neat" compare with that of "Delight in Disorder"? Which do you find more effective? Explain why.

SONIA SANCHEZ (B. 1934)

Summer Words of a Sistuh Addict   *1969*

the first day i shot dope
was on a sunday.
         i had just come
home from church
         got mad at my motha
cuz she got mad at me. u dig?
         went out. shot up
behind a feelen against her.
         it felt good.
gooder than dooing it. yeah.   © Christopher Felver/CORBIS.   10
         it was nice.
i did it. uh huh. i did it.   uh. huh.
i want to do it again. it felt so gooooood.
         and as the sistuh
         sits in her silent/   15
         remembered/high
         someone leans for
         ward gently asks her:
           sistuh.
           did u   20
           finally
         learn how to hold yo/mother?
and the music of the day
         drifts in the room
to mingle with the sistuh's young tears.   25
   and we all sing.

CONSIDERATIONS FOR CRITICAL THINKING AND WRITING

1. **FIRST RESPONSE.** Comment on the effect of the spelling and grammar in the poem.

2. Describe the difference in the rhythm and tone in lines 1 to 13 in contrast with those in lines 14 to 26. How do you account for the difference?

3. In what sense does the "sistuh's" speech consist of those "Summer Words" referred to in the title?

WILLIAM BLAKE (1757–1827)

The Lamb   *1789*

      Little Lamb, who made thee?
      Dost thou know who made thee?
Gave thee life, and bid thee feed
By the stream and o'er the mead;
Gave thee clothing of delight,
Softest clothing, wooly, bright;
Gave thee such a tender voice,
Making all the vales rejoice?
      Little Lamb, who made thee?
      Dost thou know who made thee?

      Little Lamb, I'll tell thee,
      Little Lamb, I'll tell thee:
He is callèd by thy name,
For he calls himself a Lamb.
He is meek, and he is mild;
He became a little child.
I a child, and thou a lamb,
We are callèd by his name.
      Little Lamb, God bless thee!
      Little Lamb, God bless thee!

Courtesy of the National Portrait Gallery, London.

15

Explore contexts
for William Blake
on *LiterActive.*

20

CONSIDERATIONS FOR CRITICAL THINKING AND WRITING

1. **FIRST RESPONSE.** This poem is from Blake's *Songs of Innocence.* Describe its tone. How do the meter, rhyme, and repetition help to characterize the speaker's voice?

2. Why is it significant that the animal addressed by the speaker is a lamb? What symbolic value would be lost if the animal were, for example, a doe?

3. How does the second stanza answer the question raised in the first? What is the speaker's view of the creation?

WILLIAM BLAKE (1757–1827)

The Tyger   *1794*

Tyger! Tyger! burning bright
In the forests of the night,
What immortal hand or eye
Could frame thy fearful symmetry?

In what distant deeps or skies   5
Burnt the fire of thine eyes?
On what wings dare he aspire?
What the hand dare seize the fire?

And what shoulder, and what art,
Could twist the sinews of thy heart?   10
And when thy heart began to beat,
What dread hand? and what dread feet?

What the hammer? what the chain?
In what furnace was thy brain?
What the anvil? what dread grasp   15
Dare its deadly terrors clasp?

When the stars threw down their spears,
And watered heaven with their tears,
Did he smile his work to see?
Did he who made the Lamb make thee?   20

Tyger! Tyger! burning bright
In the forests of the night,
What immortal hand or eye
Dare frame thy fearful symmetry?

CONSIDERATIONS FOR CRITICAL THINKING AND WRITING

1. **FIRST RESPONSE.** This poem from Blake's *Songs of Experience* is often paired with "The Lamb." Describe the poem's tone. Is the speaker's voice the same here as in "The Lamb"? Which words are repeated, and how do they contribute to the tone?

2. What is revealed about the nature of the tiger by the words used to describe its creation? What do you think the tiger symbolizes?

3. Unlike in "The Lamb," more than one question is raised in "The Tyger." What are these questions? Are they answered?

4. Compare the rhythms in "The Lamb" and "The Tyger." Each basically uses a seven-syllable line, but the effects are very different. Why?

5. Using these two poems as the basis of your discussion, describe what distinguishes innocence from experience.

CARL SANDBURG (1878–1967)

Chicago   *1916*

Hog Butcher for the World,
Tool Maker, Stacker of Wheat,
Player with Railroads and the Nation's Freight Handler;
Stormy, husky, brawling,
City of the Big Shoulders: 5

They tell me you are wicked and I believe them, for I have seen your painted
        women under the gas lamps luring the farm boys.
And they tell me you are crooked and I answer: Yes, it is true I have seen the
        gunman kill and go free to kill again.

And they tell me you are brutal and my reply is: On the faces of women and
    children I have seen the marks of wanton hunger.
And having answered so I turn once more to those who sneer at this my city,
    and I give them back the sneer and say to them:
Come and show me another city with lifted head singing so proud to be alive
    and coarse and strong and cunning.   10
Flinging magnetic curses amid the toil of piling job on job, here is a tall bold
    slugger set vivid against the little soft cities;
Fierce as a dog with tongue lapping for action, cunning as a savage pitted
    against the wilderness,
    Bareheaded,
    Shoveling,
    Wrecking,   15
    Planning,
    Building, breaking, rebuilding,
Under the smoke, dust all over his mouth, laughing with white teeth,
Under the terrible burden of destiny laughing as a young man laughs,
Laughing even as an ignorant fighter laughs who has never lost a battle,   20
Bragging and laughing that under his wrist is the pulse, and under his ribs
    the heart of the people,
    Laughing!
Laughing the stormy, husky, brawling laughter of Youth, half-naked,
    sweating, proud to be Hog Butcher, Tool Maker, Stacker of Wheat,
    Player with Railroads and Freight Handler to the Nation.

CONSIDERATIONS FOR CRITICAL THINKING AND WRITING

1. **FIRST RESPONSE.** Sandburg's personification of Chicago creates a strong
   identity for the city. Explain why you find the city attractive or not.

2. How do the length and rhythm of lines 1 to 5 compare with those of the
   final lines?

3. **CREATIVE RESPONSE.** Using "Chicago" as a model for style, try writing a
   tribute or condemnation about a place that you know well. Make an effort
   to use vivid images and stylistic techniques that capture its rhythms.

CONNECTION TO ANOTHER SELECTION

1. Compare "Chicago" with William Blake's "London" (p. 119) in style and theme.

MARK DOTY (B. 1953)

Tunnel Music   *1995*

Times Square, the shuttle's quick chrome
flies open and the whole car floods with
—what is it? Infernal industry, the tunnels
under Manhattan broken into hell at last?

Guttural churr and whistle and grind   5
of the engines that spin the poles?

Enormous racket, ungodly. What it is
is percussion: nine black guys

with nine lovely and previously unimagined
constructions of metal ripped and mauled,   10
welded and oiled: scoured chemical drums,
torched rims, unnamable disks of chrome.

Artifacts of wreck? The end of industry?
A century's failures reworked, bent,
hammered out, struck till their shimmying   15
tumbles and ricochets from tile walls:

anything dinged, busted or dumped
can be beaten till it sings.
A kind of ghostly joy in it, though
this music's almost unrecognizable,   20

so utterly of the coming world it is.

CONSIDERATIONS FOR CRITICAL THINKING AND WRITING

1. **FIRST RESPONSE.** How do these lines capture the rhythms and sounds of
   both the subway and the metal drums?

2. Why do you suppose Doty chooses Times Square as his stop rather than,
   say, Penn Station or 125th Street?

3. Discuss the significance of the last line. To what extent would you read the
   poem differently if it ended at line 20?

CONNECTION TO ANOTHER SELECTION

1. Compare the themes in Doty's poem with those in Carl Sandburg's
   "Chicago."

MARK TURPIN (B. 1953)

Sledgehammer's Song   *2003*

The way you hold the haft,
The way it climbs a curve,
A manswung curve,
The way it undoes what was done.
The way a stake sinks,   5
Cement splits or a stud
Spins off its nails.

The way shoulders shrug.
The way the breezes waft
And wake and tease a cheek,   10
The way it undoes what was done.
The way a cabinet cracks

And rakes and bares
The nail-scarred wall beneath.

The way a stance is spread,   15
The way the steel head pings
And thrums and thuds,
The way it undoes what was done.
The way a bathtub breaks:
Pieces barrowed, porcelain   20
Left in a bin.

The way sight is stark.
The way the weight wills the arms,
The back and heart,
The way it undoes what was done.   25
The way the weight is weighed,
Stalling the swing,
The sorrow mid-arc.

CONSIDERATIONS FOR CRITICAL THINKING AND WRITING

1. **FIRST RESPONSE.** Explain how the meter of these lines gets into the swing of a sledgehammer's work.

2. Why is the repetition at the beginning of many lines particularly appropriate for this poem?

3. Is this hammer work depicted as simply mindlessly destructive or as something else? Explain your response with reference to the poem's diction and images.

ALFRED, LORD TENNYSON (1809–1892)

The Charge of the Light Brigade   *1855*

1

Half a league, half a league,
    Half a league onward,
All in the valley of Death
    Rode the six hundred.
"Forward, the Light Brigade!   5
Charge for the guns!" he said:
Into the valley of Death
    Rode the six hundred.

2

"Forward, the Light Brigade!"
Was there a man dismayed?   10

Not though the soldier knew
  Some one had blundered:
Their's not to make reply,
Their's not to reason why,
Their's but to do and die: 15
Into the valley of Death
  Rode the six hundred.

3

Cannon to right of them,
Cannon to left of them,
Cannon in front of them   20
  Volleyed and thundered;
Stormed at with shot and shell,
Boldly they rode and well,
Into the jaws of Death,
Into the mouth of Hell   25
  Rode the six hundred.

4

Flashed all their sabers bare,
Flashed as they turned in air
Sabring the gunners there,
Charging an army, while   30
  All the world wondered:
Plunged in the battery-smoke
Right through the line they broke;
Cossack and Russian
Reeled from the saber-stroke   35
  Shattered and sundered.
Then they rode back, but not
  Not the six hundred.

5

Cannon to right of them,
Cannon to left of them,   40
Cannon behind them
  Volleyed and thundered;
Stormed at with shot and shell,
While horse and hero fell,
They that had fought so well   45
Came through the jaws of Death,
Back from the mouth of Hell,
All that was left of them,
  Left of six hundred.

6

When can their glory fade?   50
O the wild charge they made!
    All the world wondered.
Honor the charge they made!
Honor the Light Brigade,
    Noble six hundred!   55

CONSIDERATIONS FOR CRITICAL THINKING AND WRITING

1. **FIRST RESPONSE.** How do the meter and rhyme contribute to the meaning of this poem's lines?

2. What is the speaker's attitude toward war?

3. Describe the tone, paying particular attention to stanza 2.

CONNECTION TO ANOTHER SELECTION

1. Compare the theme of "The Charge of the Light Brigade" with that of Wilfred Owen's "Dulce et Decorum Est" (p. 121).

THEODORE ROETHKE (1908–1963)

My Papa's Waltz   *1948*

Explore contexts for Theodore Roethke and approaches to this poem on *LiterActive* or at bedfordstmartins.com/rewritinglit.

The whiskey on your breath
Could make a small boy dizzy;
But I hung on like death:
Such waltzing was not easy.

We romped until the pans   5
Slid from the kitchen shelf;
My mother's countenance
Could not unfrown itself.

The hand that held my wrist
Was battered on one knuckle;   10
At every step you missed
My right ear scraped a buckle.

You beat time on my head
With a palm caked hard by dirt,
Then waltzed me off to bed   15
Still clinging to your shirt.

CONSIDERATIONS FOR CRITICAL THINKING AND WRITING

1. **FIRST RESPONSE.** What details characterize the father in this poem? How does the speaker's choice of words reveal his feeling about his father? Is the remembering speaker still a boy?

2. Characterize the rhythm of the poem. Does it move "like death" (line 3), or is it more like a waltz? Is the rhythm regular throughout the poem? What is its effect?

3. Comment on the appropriateness of the title. Why do you suppose Roethke didn't use "My Father's Waltz"?

THYLIAS MOSS (B. 1954)

Tornados   *1991*

Truth is, I envy them
not because they dance; I out jitterbug them
as I'm shuttled through and through legs
strong as looms, weaving time. They
do black more justice than I, frenzy   5
of conductor of philharmonic and electricity, hair
on end, result of the charge when horns and strings release
the pent up Beethoven and Mozart. Ions played

instead of notes. The movement
is not wrath, not hormone swarm because   10
I saw my first forming above the church a surrogate
steeple. The morning of my first baptism and
salvation already tangible, funnel for the spirit
coming into me without losing a drop, my black
guardian angel come to rescue me before all the words   15

get out, *I looked over Jordan and what did I see coming for*
to carry me home. Regardez, it all comes back, even the first
grade French, when the tornado stirs up the past, bewitched spoon
lost in its own spin, like a roulette wheel that won't
be steered, like the world. They drove me underground,   20
tornado watches and warnings, atomic bomb drills. Adult
storms so I had to leave the room. Truth is

the tornado is a perfect nappy curl, tightly wound,
spinning wildly when I try to tamper with its nature, shunning
the hot comb and pressing oil even though if absolutely straight   25
I'd have the longest hair in the world. Bouffant tornadic
crown taking the royal path on a trip to town, stroll down
Tornado Alley where it intersects Memory Lane. Smoky spirit-
clouds, shadows searching for what cast them.

CONSIDERATIONS FOR CRITICAL THINKING AND WRITING

1. **FIRST RESPONSE.** What connections does the speaker make between herself and the tornado? Explain why you think they are primarily positive or negative.

2. Describe the poem's rhythm. Do you find any moments where the lines' rhythm reflects their meaning?

3. Could the title of this poem just as effectively have been "Bouffant Tornadic Crown" (lines 26–27)? Explain why or why not.

FLOYD SKLOOT (B. 1947)

Winter Solstice   2005

I wake in darkness and fog to the hoofbeat of deer
racing across the hill's frosted crest from east to west.
As in a dream, within the rise and fall of wind I hear
the rise and fall of the deer pack's breath
as it becomes the beat of my heart within my chest.   5
I am fitted so close to my wife's body her breath
seems to be my breath as we curl together, awake
but not awake, her back rising against my rising chest
in the lingering pre-dawn dark.
Now, in the space between our breath, silence comes to rest.   10

CONSIDERATIONS FOR CRITICAL THINKING AND WRITING

1. FIRST RESPONSE. What emotions do these images produce in you?
2. Explain how the meter and rhyme contribute to the poem's tone.
3. Comment on the significance of the title. How is it related to the images in the poem?

Perspective

LOUISE BOGAN (1897–1970)

On Formal Poetry   1953

What is formal poetry? It is poetry written in form. And what is *form*? The elements of form, so far as poetry is concerned, are meter and rhyme. Are these elements merely mold and ornaments that have been impressed upon poetry from without? Are they indeed restrictions which bind and fetter language and the thought and emotion behind, under, within language in a repressive way? Are they arbitrary rules which have lost all validity since they have been broken to good purpose by "experimental poets," ancient and modern? Does the breaking up of form, or its total elimination, always result in an increase of power and of effect; and is any return to form a sort of relinquishment of freedom, or retreat to old fogeyism?

From *A Poet's Alphabet*

CONSIDERATIONS FOR CRITICAL THINKING AND WRITING

1. Choose one of the questions Bogan raises and write an essay in response to it using two or three poems from this chapter to illustrate your answer.

2. **CREATIVE RESPONSE.** Try writing a poem in meter and rhyme. Does the experience make your writing feel limited or not?

Web | Research the poets in this chapter at bedfordstmartins.com/ rewritinglit.

9

Poetic Forms

© Tom Jorgensen/ The University of Iowa.

A short poem need not be small.
— MARVIN BELL

Poems come in a variety of shapes. Although the best poems always have their own unique qualities, many of them also conform to traditional patterns. Frequently the *form* of a poem — its overall structure or shape — follows an already established design. A poem that can be categorized by the patterns of its lines, meter, rhymes, and stanzas is considered a *fixed form* because it follows a prescribed model such as a sonnet. However, poems written in a fixed form do not always fit models precisely; writers sometimes work variations on traditional forms to create innovative effects.

Not all poets are content with variations on traditional forms. Some prefer to create their own structures and shapes. Poems that do not conform to established patterns of meter, rhyme, and stanza are called *free verse* or *open form* poetry. (See Chapter 10 for further discussion of open forms.) This kind of poetry creates its own ordering principles through the careful arrangement of words and phrases in line lengths that embody rhythms appropriate to the meaning. Modern and contemporary poets in particular have learned to use the blank space on the page as a significant functional element (for a striking example, see Cummings's "in Just-," p. 272). Good poetry of this kind is structured in ways that can be as demanding, interesting, and satisfying as fixed forms. Open and fixed forms represent different poetic styles, but they are identical in the sense that both use language in concentrated ways to convey meanings, experiences, emotions, and effects.

SOME COMMON POETIC FORMS

A familiarity with some of the most frequently used fixed forms of poetry is useful because it allows for a better understanding of how a poem works. Classifying patterns allows us to talk about the effects of established rhythm and rhyme and to recognize how significant variations from them affect the pace and meaning of the lines. An awareness of form also allows us to anticipate how a poem is likely to proceed. As we shall see, a sonnet creates a different set of expectations in a reader from those of, say, a limerick. A reader isn't likely to find in limericks the kind of serious themes that often make their way into sonnets. The discussion that follows identifies some of the important poetic forms frequently encountered in English poetry.

The shape of a fixed-form poem is often determined by the way in which the lines are organized into stanzas. A **stanza** consists of a grouping of lines, set off by a space, that usually has a set pattern of meter and rhyme. This pattern is ordinarily repeated in other stanzas throughout the poem. What is usual is not obligatory, however; some poems may use a different pattern for each stanza, somewhat like paragraphs in prose.

Traditionally, though, stanzas do share a common **rhyme scheme,** the pattern of end rhymes. We can map out rhyme schemes by noting patterns of rhyme with lowercase letters: the first rhyme sound is designated *a,* the second becomes *b,* the third *c,* and so on. Using this system, we can describe the rhyme scheme in the following poem this way: *aabb, ccdd, eeff.*

A. E. HOUSMAN (1859–1936)

Loveliest of trees, the cherry now   *1896*

Loveliest of trees, the cherry now	*a*
Is hung with bloom along the bough,	*a*
And stands about the woodland ride	*b*
Wearing white for Eastertide.	*b*
Now, of my threescore years and ten,	*c* 5
Twenty will not come again,	*c*
And take from seventy springs a score,	*d*
It only leaves me fifty more.	*d*
And since to look at things in bloom	*e*
Fifty springs are little room,	*e* 10

About the woodlands I will go   *f*
To see the cherry hung with snow.   *f*

CONSIDERATIONS FOR CRITICAL THINKING AND WRITING

1. FIRST RESPONSE. What is the speaker's attitude in this poem toward time and life?

2. Why is spring an appropriate season for the setting rather than, say, winter?

3. Paraphrase each stanza. How do the images in each reinforce the poem's themes?

4. Lines 1 and 12 are not intended to rhyme, but they are close. What is the effect of the near rhyme of "now" and "snow"? How does the rhyme enhance the theme?

Poets often create their own stanzaic patterns; hence there is an infinite number of kinds of stanzas. One way of talking about stanzaic forms is to describe a given stanza by how many lines it contains.

A *couplet* consists of two lines that usually rhyme and have the same meter; couplets are frequently not separated from each other by space on the page. A *heroic couplet* consists of rhymed iambic pentameter. Here is an example from Alexander Pope's "Essay on Criticism":

One science only will one genius fit;   *a*
So vast is art, so narrow human wit: *a*
Not only bounded to peculiar arts,   *b*
But oft in those confined to single parts. *b*

A *tercet* is a three-line stanza. When all three lines rhyme, they are called a *triplet.* Two triplets make up this captivating poem.

ROBERT HERRICK (1591–1674)

Upon Julia's Clothes   *1648*

Whenas in silks my Julia goes,   *a*
Then, then, methinks, how sweetly flows   *a*
That liquefaction of her clothes.   *a*

Next, when I cast mine eyes, and see   *b*
That brave vibration, each way free,   *b*
O, how that glittering taketh me!   *b*

CONSIDERATIONS FOR CRITICAL THINKING AND WRITING

1. FIRST RESPONSE. What purpose does alliteration serve in this poem?

2. Comment on the effect of the meter. How is it related to the speaker's description of Julia's clothes?

3. Look up the word *brave* in the *Oxford English Dictionary*. Which of its meanings is appropriate to describe Julia's movement? Some readers interpret lines 4–6 to mean that Julia has no clothes on. What do you think?

CONNECTION TO ANOTHER SELECTION

1. Compare the tone of this poem with that of Paul Humphrey's "Blow" (p. 210). Are the situations and speakers similar? Is there any difference in tone between these two poems?

Terza rima consists of an interlocking three-line rhyme scheme: *aba, bcb, cdc, ded,* and so on. Dante's *Divine Comedy* uses this pattern, as does Robert Frost's "Acquainted with the Night" (p. 158) and Percy Bysshe Shelley's "Ode to the West Wind" (p. 265).

A *quatrain,* or four-line stanza, is the most common stanzaic form in the English language and can have various meters and rhyme schemes (if any). The most common rhyme schemes are *aabb, abba, aaba,* and *abcb.* This last pattern is especially characteristic of the popular **ballad stanza,** which consists of alternating eight- and six-syllable lines. Samuel Taylor Coleridge adopted this pattern in "The Rime of the Ancient Mariner"; here is one representative stanza:

> All in a hot and copper sky
> The bloody Sun, at noon,
> Right up above the mast did stand,
> No bigger than the Moon.

There are a number of longer stanzaic forms, and the list of types of stanzas could be extended considerably, but knowing these three most basic patterns should prove helpful to you in talking about the form of a great many poems. In addition to stanzaic forms, there are fixed forms that characterize entire poems. Lyric poems can be, for example, sonnets, villanelles, sestinas, or epigrams.

Sonnet

The **sonnet** has been a popular literary form in English since the sixteenth century, when it was adopted from the Italian *sonnetto,* meaning "little song." A sonnet consists of fourteen lines, usually written in iambic pentameter. Because the sonnet has been such a favorite form, writers have experimented with many variations on its essential structure. Nevertheless, there are two basic types of sonnets: the Italian and the English.

The **Italian sonnet** (also known as the **Petrarchan sonnet,** from the fourteenth-century Italian poet Petrarch) divides into two parts. The first eight lines (the **octave**) typically rhyme *abbaabba.* The final six lines (the **sestet**) may vary; common patterns are *cdecde, cdcdcd,* and *cdccdc.* Very often the octave presents a situation, an attitude, or a problem that the sestet comments upon or resolves, as in John Keats's "On First Looking into Chapman's Homer."

JOHN KEATS (1795–1821)

On First Looking into Chapman's Homer°

1816

Much have I traveled in the realms of gold,
    And many goodly states and kingdoms
        seen;
Round many western islands have I been
Which bards in fealty to Apollo° hold.
Oft of one wide expanse had I been told
    That deep-browed Homer ruled as his
        demesne;
    Yet did I never breathe its pure serene°
Till I heard Chapman speak out loud and bold:
Then felt I like some watcher of the skies
    When a new planet swims into his ken;
Or like stout Cortez° when with eagle eyes
    He stared at the Pacific — and all his men
Looked at each other with a wild surmise —
    Silent, upon a peak in Darien.

Courtesy of the National Portrait Gallery, London.

atmosphere

10

Explore contexts for John Keats on *LiterActive*.

Chapman's Homer: Before reading George Chapman's (ca. 1560-1634) poetic Elizabethan translations of Homer's *Iliad* and *Odyssey,* Keats had known only stilted and pedestrian eighteenth-century translations.   4 *Apollo:* Greek god of poetry.   11 *Cortez:* Vasco Núñez de Balboa, not Hernando Cortés, was the first European to sight the Pacific from Darien, a peak in Panama.

CONSIDERATIONS FOR CRITICAL THINKING AND WRITING

1. **FIRST RESPONSE.** How do the images shift from the octave to the sestet? How does the tone change? Does the meaning change as well?

2. What is the controlling metaphor of this poem?

3. What is it that the speaker discovers?

4. How does the rhythm of the lines change between the octave and the sestet? How does that change reflect the tones of both the octave and the sestet?

5. Does Keats's mistake concerning Cortés and Balboa affect your reading of the poem? Explain why or why not.

The Italian sonnet pattern is also used in the next sonnet, but notice that the thematic break between octave and sestet comes within line 9 rather than between lines 8 and 9. This unconventional break helps to reinforce the speaker's impatience with the conventional attitudes he describes.

WILLIAM WORDSWORTH (1770–1850)

The World Is Too Much with Us   *1807*

The world is too much with us; late and soon,
Getting and spending, we lay waste our powers;
Little we see in Nature that is ours;
We have given our hearts away, a sordid boon!
This Sea that bares her bosom to the moon;   5
The winds that will be howling at all hours,
And are up-gathered now like sleeping flowers;
For this, for everything, we are out of tune;
It moves us not. — Great God! I'd rather be
A Pagan suckled in a creed outworn;   10
So might I, standing on this pleasant lea,
Have glimpses that would make me less forlorn;
Have sight of Proteus rising from the sea;
Or hear old Triton blow his wreathèd horn.

CONSIDERATIONS FOR CRITICAL THINKING AND WRITING

1. **FIRST RESPONSE.** What is the speaker's complaint in this sonnet? How do the conditions described affect him?
2. Look up "Proteus" and "Triton." What do these mythological allusions contribute to the sonnet's tone?
3. What is the effect of the personification of the sea and wind in the octave?

CONNECTION TO ANOTHER SELECTION

1. Compare the theme of this sonnet with that of Gerard Manley Hopkins's "God's Grandeur" (p. 199).

The **English sonnet,** more commonly known as the **Shakespearean sonnet,** is organized into three quatrains and a couplet, which typically rhyme *abab cdcd efef gg.* This rhyme scheme is more suited to English poetry because English has fewer rhyming words than Italian. English sonnets, because of their four-part organization, also have more flexibility about where thematic breaks can occur. Frequently, however, the most pronounced break or turn comes with the concluding couplet.

In the following Shakespearean sonnet, the three quatrains compare the speaker's loved one to a summer's day and explain why the loved one is even more lovely. The couplet bestows eternal beauty and love upon both the loved one and the sonnet.

WILLIAM SHAKESPEARE (1564–1616)

Shall I compare thee to a summer's day?   *1609*

Shall I compare thee to a summer's day?
Thou art more lovely and more temperate:
Rough winds do shake the darling buds of May,
And summer's lease hath all too short a date.
Sometime too hot the eye of heaven shines,   5
And often is his gold complexion dimmed;
And every fair from fair sometime declines,
By chance, or nature's changing course, untrimmed.
But thy eternal summer shall not fade,
Nor lose possession of that fair thou ow'st°   *possess*   10
Nor shall death brag thou wand'rest in his shade,
When in eternal lines to time thou grow'st.
    So long as men can breathe or eyes can see,
    So long lives this, and this gives life to thee.

CONSIDERATIONS FOR CRITICAL THINKING AND WRITING

1. **FIRST RESPONSE.** Describe the shift in tone and subject matter that begins in line 9.
2. Why is the speaker's loved one more lovely than a summer's day? What qualities does he admire in the loved one?
3. What does the couplet say about the relation between art and love?
4. Which syllables are stressed in the final line? How do these syllables relate to the line's meaning?

Sonnets have been the vehicles for all kinds of subjects, including love, death, politics, and cosmic questions. Although most sonnets tend to treat their subjects seriously, this fixed form does not mean a fixed expression; humor is also possible in it. Compare this next Shakespearean sonnet with "Shall I compare thee to a summer's day?" They are, finally, both love poems, but their tones are markedly different.

WILLIAM SHAKESPEARE (1564–1616)

My mistress' eyes are nothing like the sun   *1609*

My mistress' eyes are nothing like the sun;
Coral is far more red than her lips' red;
If snow be white, why then her breasts are dun;
If hairs be wires, black wires grow on her head.
I have seen roses damasked red and white,   5
But no such roses see I in her cheeks;
And in some perfumes is there more delight
Than in the breath that from my mistress reeks.

I love to hear her speak, yet well I know
That music hath a far more pleasing sound;   10
I grant I never saw a goddess go:
My mistress, when she walks, treads on the ground.
    And yet, by heaven, I think my love as rare
    As any she,° belied with false compare.   *lady*

CONSIDERATIONS FOR CRITICAL THINKING AND WRITING

1. **FIRST RESPONSE.** What does "mistress" mean in this sonnet? Write a description of this particular mistress based on the images used in the sonnet.

2. What sort of person is the speaker? Does he truly love the woman he describes?

3. In what sense are this sonnet and "Shall I compare thee to a summer's day?" about poetry as well as love?

EDNA ST. VINCENT MILLAY (1892–1950)

I will put Chaos into fourteen lines   *1954*

© CORBIS.

I will put Chaos into fourteen lines
And keep him there; and let him thence escape
If he be lucky; let him twist, and ape
Flood, fire, and demon — his adroit designs
Will strain to nothing in the strict confines
Of this sweet Order, where, in pious rape,
I hold his essence and amorphous shape,
Till he with Order mingles and combines.
Past are the hours, the years, of our duress,
His arrogance, our awful servitude: 10
I have him. He is nothing more nor less
Than something simple not yet understood;
I shall not even force him to confess;
Or answer. I will only make him good.

CONSIDERATIONS FOR CRITICAL THINKING AND WRITING

1. **FIRST RESPONSE.** Does the poem contain "Chaos"? If so, how? If not, why not?

2. What properties of a sonnet does this poem possess?

3. What do you think is meant by the phrase "pious rape" in line 6?

4. What is the effect of the personification in the poem?

CONNECTION TO ANOTHER SELECTION

1. Compare the theme of this poem with that of Robert Frost's "Design" (p. 386).

A SAMPLE STUDENT RESPONSE

Alexia Sykes

Professor Jones

English 211

December 1, 2009

The Fixed Form in Edna St. Vincent Millay's

"I will put Chaos into fourteen lines"

In her poem "I will put Chaos into fourteen lines," Edna St. Vincent Millay does exactly what her title promises. Though the poem is of a fixed form, using patterns in meter, rhyme, line, and stanza, a sense of chaos is created through a complex structure, only to be calmed in the last six lines by a simpler rhyme scheme.

The first octave of the poem is structured *abbaabba,* a structure commonly found in sonnets. Although this is a fixed structure, the rhyme scheme is so complex that a chaotic tone is established:

> Flood, Fire, and demon—his adroit designs
>
> Will strain to nothing in the strict confines
>
> Of this sweet Order, where, in pious rape,
>
> I hold his essence and amorphous shape,
>
> Till he with Order mingles and combines. (lines 4-8)

Rhyming couplets are fired at the reader and the seemingly haphazard pattern gives the impression that there is little or no structure at all, particularly on a first reading. It is difficult to determine the framework of the poem, and the absence of a decipherable structure creates in the reader a feeling of randomness, the same disorder mentioned by the speaker. It is not until the end of the poem that relief is provided. The final six lines contain a much simpler, more repetitive structure: *cdcdcd*. This rhyme scheme provides stability and consistency. The pattern is simple and predictable; order is restored. Chaos has been tamed and made "good" (14) by the poem's form. . . .

Sykes 3

Work Cited

Millay, Edna St. Vincent. "I will put Chaos into fourteen lines." *Poetry: An*
    Introduction. Ed. Michael Meyer. 6th ed. Boston: Bedford/St. Martin's,
    2010. 249. Print.

MOLLY PEACOCK (B. 1947)

Desire   *1984*

It doesn't speak and it isn't schooled,
like a small foetal animal with wettened fur.
It is the blind instinct for life unruled,
visceral frankincense and animal myrrh.
It is what babies bring to kings,   5
an eyes-shut, ears-shut medicine of the heart
that smells and touches endings and beginnings
without the details of time's experienced *part-*
fit-into-part-fit-into-part. Like a paw,
it is blunt; like a pet who knows you   10
and nudges your knee with its snout — but more raw
and blinder and younger and more divine, too,
than the tamed wild — it's the drive for what is real,
deeper than the brain's detail: the drive to feel.

CONSIDERATIONS FOR CRITICAL THINKING AND WRITING

1. **FIRST RESPONSE.** Taken together, what do all of the metaphors that appear
   in this poem reveal about the speaker's conception of desire?
2. What is the "it" being described in lines 3–5? How do the allusions to the
   three wise men relate to the other metaphors used to define desire?
3. How is this English sonnet structured? What is the effect of its irregular
   meter?

CONNECTION TO ANOTHER SELECTION

1. Compare the treatment of desire in this poem with that of Sharon Olds's
   "Last Night" (p. 84). In an essay, identify the theme of each poem and compare their conceptions of desire. How alike are these two poems?

MARK JARMAN (B. 1952)

Unholy Sonnet

1993

After the praying, after the hymn-singing,
After the sermon's trenchant commentary
On the world's ills, which make ours secondary,
After communion, after the hand-wringing,
And after peace descends upon us, bringing   5
Our eyes up to regard the sanctuary
And how the light swords through it, and how, scary
In their sheer numbers, motes of dust ride, clinging —
There is, as doctors say about some pain,
Discomfort knowing that despite your prayers,   10
Your listening and rejoicing, your small part
In this communal stab at coming clean,
There is one stubborn remnant of your cares
Intact. There is still murder in your heart.

CONSIDERATIONS FOR CRITICAL THINKING AND WRITING

1. **FIRST RESPONSE.** Describe the rhyme scheme and structure of this sonnet. Explain why it is an English or Italian sonnet.

2. What are the effects of the use of "after" in lines 1, 2, 4, and 5 and "there" in lines 9, 13, and 14?

3. In what sense might this poem be summed up as a "communal stab" (line 12)? Discuss the accuracy of this assessment.

4. **CREATIVE RESPONSE.** Try writing a reply to the theme of Jarman's poem using the same sonnet form that he uses.

CONNECTION TO ANOTHER SELECTION

1. Jarman has said that his "Unholy Sonnets" (there are about twenty of them) are modeled after John Donne's *Holy Sonnets* but that he does not share the same Christian assumptions about faith and mercy that inform Donne's sonnets. Instead, Jarman says, he "work[s] against any assumption or shared expression of faith, to write a devotional poetry against the grain." Keeping this statement in mind, write an essay comparing and contrasting the tone and theme of Jarman's sonnet with those of John Donne's "Death Be Not Proud" (p. 300).

X. J. KENNEDY (B. 1929)

"The Purpose of Time Is to Prevent Everything from Happening at Once"

2002

Suppose your life a folded telescope
Durationless, collapsed in just a flash
As from your mother's womb you, bawling, drop
Into a nursing home. Suppose you crash

Your car, your marriage — toddler laying waste   5
A field of daisies, schoolkid, zit-faced teen
With lover zipping up your pants in haste
Hearing your parents' tread downstairs — all one.

Einstein was right. That would be too intense.
You need a chance to preen, to give a dull   10
Recital before an indifferent audience
Equally slow in jeering you and clapping.
Time takes its time unraveling. But, still,
You'll wonder when your life ends: Huh? What happened?

CONSIDERATIONS FOR CRITICAL THINKING AND WRITING

1. **FIRST RESPONSE.** Comment on how the images in the octave manage to sum up a human life.

2. How serious a reflection on the passage of time is this poem?

3. What kind of sonnet is it? Why might a fixed form be a more appropriate ordering principle for the theme of this poem than an open form?

Villanelle

The **villanelle** is a fixed form consisting of nineteen lines of any length divided into six stanzas: five tercets and a concluding quatrain. The first and third lines of the initial tercet rhyme; these rhymes are repeated in each subsequent tercet (*aba*) and in the final two lines of the quatrain (*abaa*). Moreover, line 1 appears in its entirety as lines 6, 12, and 18, while line 3 appears as lines 9, 15, and 19. This form may seem to risk monotony, but in competent hands a villanelle can create haunting echoes, as in Dylan Thomas's "Do Not Go Gentle into That Good Night."

DYLAN THOMAS (1914–1953)

Do Not Go Gentle into That Good Night   *1952*

Do not go gentle into that good night,
Old age should burn and rave at close of day;
Rage, rage against the dying of the light.

Though wise men at their end know dark is right,
Because their words had forked no lightning they   5
Do not go gentle into that good night.

Good men, the last wave by, crying how bright
Their frail deeds might have danced in a green bay,
Rage, rage against the dying of the light.

Wild men who caught and sang the sun in flight,   10
And learn, too late, they grieved it on its way,
Do not go gentle into that good night.

Grave men, near death, who see with blinding sight
Blind eyes could blaze like meteors and be gay,
Rage, rage against the dying of the light.   15

And you, my father, there on the sad height,
Curse, bless, me now with your fierce tears, I pray.
Do not go gentle into that good night.
Rage, rage against the dying of the light.

CONSIDERATIONS FOR CRITICAL THINKING AND WRITING

1. **FIRST RESPONSE.** How does Thomas vary the meanings of the poem's two
   refrains: "Do not go gentle into that good night" and "Rage, rage against
   the dying of the light"?

2. Thomas's father was close to death when this poem was written. How does
   the tone contribute to the poem's theme?

3. How is "good" used in line 1?

4. Characterize the men who are "wise" (line 4), "Good" (7), "Wild" (10), and
   "Grave" (13).

5. What do figures of speech contribute to this poem?

6. Discuss this villanelle's sound effects.

WENDY COPE (B. 1945)

Lonely Hearts   *1986*

Can someone make my simple wish come true?
Male biker seeks female for touring fun.
Do you live in North London? Is it you?

Gay vegetarian whose friends are few,
I'm into music, Shakespeare and the sun.   5
Can someone make my simple wish come true?

Executive in search of something new —
Perhaps bisexual woman, arty, young.
Do you live in North London? Is it you?

Successful, straight and solvent? I am too —   10
Attractive Jewish lady with a son.
Can someone make my simple wish come true?

I'm Libran, inexperienced and blue —
Need slim non-smoker, under twenty-one.
Do you live in North London? Is it you?   15

Please write (with photo) to Box 152
Who knows where it may lead once we've begun?
Can someone make my simple wish come true?
Do you live in North London? Is it you?

CONSIDERATIONS FOR CRITICAL THINKING AND WRITING

1. **FIRST RESPONSE.** Why does the repetitive form of the villanelle seem particularly appropriate for the subject matter of "Lonely Hearts"?

2. How closely does "Lonely Hearts" conform to the conventional form of the villanelle? Are there any significant variations that produce interesting effects?

3. How are the several speakers' voices in the poem unified by tone?

Sestina

Although the **sestina** usually does not rhyme, it is perhaps an even more demanding fixed form than the villanelle. A sestina consists of thirty-nine lines of any length divided into six six-line stanzas and a three-line concluding stanza called an **envoy.** The difficulty lies in repeating the six words at the ends of the first stanza's lines at the ends of the lines in the other five six-line stanzas as well. Those words must also appear in the final three lines, where they often resonate important themes. The sestina originated in the Middle Ages, but contemporary poets continue to find it a fascinating and challenging form.

ALGERNON CHARLES SWINBURNE (1837–1909)

Sestina   1872

I saw my soul at rest upon a day
As a bird sleeping in the nest of night,
Among soft leaves that give the starlight way
To touch its wings but not its eyes with light;
So that it knew as one in visions may,   5
And knew not as men waking, of delight.

This was the measure of my soul's delight;
It had no power of joy to fly by day,
Nor part in the large lordship of the light;
But in a secret moon-beholden way   10
Had all its will of dreams and pleasant night,
And all the love and life that sleepers may.

But such life's triumph as men waking may
It might not have to feed its faint delight
Between the stars by night and sun by day,   15
Shut up with green leaves and a little light;
Because its way was as a lost star's way,
A world's not wholly known of day or night.

All loves and dreams and sounds and gleams of night
Made it all music that such minstrels may,   20
And all they had they gave it of delight;
But in the full face of the fire of day
What place shall be for any starry light,
What part of heaven in all the wide sun's way?

Yet the soul woke not, sleeping by the way,   25
Watched as a nursling of the large-eyed night,
And sought no strength nor knowledge of the day,
Nor closer touch conclusive of delight,
Nor mightier joy nor truer than dreamers may,
Nor more of song than they, nor more of light.   30

For who sleeps once and sees the secret light
Whereby sleep shows the soul a fairer way
Between the rise and rest of day and night,
Shall care no more to fare as all men may,
But be his place of pain or of delight,   35
There shall he dwell, beholding night as day.

Song, have thy day and take thy fill of light
Before the night be fallen across thy way;
Sing while he may, man hath no long delight.

CONSIDERATIONS FOR CRITICAL THINKING AND WRITING

1. **FIRST RESPONSE.** How are the six end words — "day," "night," "way," "light," "may," and "delight" — central to the sestina's meaning?

2. Number the end words of the first stanza 1, 2, 3, 4, 5, and 6, and then use those numbers for the corresponding end words in the remaining five stanzas to see how the pattern of the line-end words is worked out in this sestina. Also locate the six end words in the envoy.

3. Underline the images that seem especially vivid to you. What effects do they create? What is the tone of the sestina?

4. **CRITICAL STRATEGIES.** Read the section on psychological strategies (pp. 670–72) in Chapter 26, "Critical Strategies for Reading." Write a brief essay explaining why you think a poet might derive pleasure from writing in a fixed form such as a villanelle or sestina. Can you think of similar activities outside the field of writing in which discipline and restraint give pleasure? How might this reflect an author's personal psychology?

FLORENCE CASSEN MAYERS (B. 1940)

All-American Sestina   *1996*

One nation, indivisible
two-car garage
three strikes you're out
four-minute mile

five-cent cigar   5
six-string guitar

six-pack Bud
one-day sale
five-year warranty
two-way street   10
fourscore and seven years ago
three cheers

three-star restaurant
sixty-
four-dollar question   15
one-night stand
two-pound lobster
five-star general

five-course meal
three sheets to the wind   20
two bits
six-shooter
one-armed bandit
four-poster

four-wheel drive   25
five-and-dime
hole in one
three-alarm fire
sweet sixteen
two-wheeler   30

two-tone Chevy
four rms, hi flr, w/vu
six-footer
high five
three-ring circus   35
one-room schoolhouse

two thumbs up, five-karat diamond
Fourth of July, three-piece suit
six feet under, one-horse town

Considerations for Critical Thinking and Writing

1. **FIRST RESPONSE.** Discuss the significance of the title; what is "All-American" about this sestina?

2. How is the structure of this poem different from that of a conventional sestina? (What structural requirement does Mayers add for this sestina?)

3. Do you think important themes are raised by this poem, as is traditional for a sestina? If so, what are they? If not, what is being played with by using this convention?

CONNECTION TO ANOTHER SELECTION

1. Describe and compare the strategy used to create meaning in "All-American Sestina" with that used by E. E. Cummings in "next to of course god america i" (p. 166).

Epigram

An *epigram* is a brief, pointed, and witty poem. Although most rhyme and often are written in couplets, epigrams take no prescribed form. Instead, they are typically polished bits of compressed irony, satire, or paradox. Here is an epigram that defines itself.

SAMUEL TAYLOR COLERIDGE (1772–1834)

What Is an Epigram?

1802

What is an epigram? A dwarfish whole;
Its body brevity, and wit its soul.

These additional examples by A. R. Ammons, David McCord, and Paul Laurence Dunbar satisfy Coleridge's definition.

A. R. AMMONS (B. 1926)

Coward

1975

Bravery runs in my family.

DAVID MCCORD (1897–1997)

Epitaph on a Waiter

By and by
God caught his eye.

PAUL LAURENCE DUNBAR (1872–1906)

Theology

1896

There is a heaven, for ever, day by day,
The upward longing of my soul doth tell
    me so.
There is a hell, I'm quite as sure; for pray,
If there were not, where would my
        neighbors go?

Courtesy of the Ohio Historical Society.

CONSIDERATIONS FOR CRITICAL THINKING AND WRITING

1. **FIRST RESPONSE.** In what sense is each of these epigrams, as Coleridge puts it, a "dwarfish whole"?
2. Explain which of these epigrams, in addition to being witty, makes a serious point.
3. **CREATIVE RESPONSE.** Try writing a few epigrams that say something memorable about whatever you choose to focus on.

Limerick

The **limerick** is always light and humorous. Its usual form consists of five predominantly anapestic lines rhyming *aabba;* lines 1, 2, and 5 contain three feet, while lines 3 and 4 contain two. Limericks have delighted everyone from schoolchildren to sophisticated adults, and they range in subject matter from the simply innocent and silly to the satiric or obscene. The sexual humor helps to explain why so many limericks are written anonymously. Here is one that is anonymous but more concerned with physics than physiology.

ANONYMOUS
There was a young lady named Bright

There was a young lady named Bright,
Who traveled much faster than light,
    She started one day
    In a relative way,
And returned on the previous night.

This next one is a particularly clever definition of a limerick.

LAURENCE PERRINE (1915–1995)
The limerick's never averse   1982

The limerick's never averse
To expressing itself in a terse
    Economical style,
    And yet, all the while,
The limerick's *always* a verse.

CONSIDERATIONS FOR CRITICAL THINKING AND WRITING

1. **FIRST RESPONSE.** How does this limerick differ from others you know? How is it similar?

2. Scan Perrine's limerick. How do the lines measure up to the traditional fixed metrical pattern?

3. **CREATIVE RESPONSE.** Try writing a limerick. Use the following basic pattern.

   ⌣ ⌣ ´   ⌣ ⌣ ´   ⌣ ⌣ ´
   ⌣ ⌣ ´   ⌣ ⌣ ´   ⌣ ⌣ ´
              ⌣ ⌣ ´   ⌣ ⌣ ´
              ⌣ ⌣ ´   ⌣ ⌣ ´
   ⌣ ⌣ ´   ⌣ ⌣ ´   ⌣ ⌣ ´

You might begin with a friend's name or the name of your school or town. Your instructor is, of course, fair game, too, provided your tact matches your wit.

The next selection is a real tongue twister.

KEITH CASTO
She Don't Bop 1987

A nervous young woman named Trudy
Was at odds with a horn player, Rudy.
His horn so annoyed her
The neighbors would loiter
To watch Rudy toot Trudy fruity.

Haiku

Another brief fixed poetic form, borrowed from the Japanese, is the **haiku.** A haiku is usually described as consisting of seventeen syllables organized into three unrhymed lines of five, seven, and five syllables. Owing to language difference, however, English translations of haiku are often only approximated, because a Japanese haiku exists in time (Japanese syllables have duration). The number of syllables in our sense is not as significant as the duration in Japanese. These poems typically present an intense emotion or vivid image of nature, which, in the Japanese, are also designed to lead to a spiritual insight.

MATSUO BASHŌ (1644–1694)
Under cherry trees *date unknown*

Under cherry trees
Soup, the salad, fish and all . . .
Seasoned with petals.

CAROLYN KIZER (B. 1925)

After Bashō   1984

Tentatively, you
slip onstage this evening,
pallid, famous moon.

SONIA SANCHEZ (B. 1935)

c'mon man hold me   1998

c'mon man hold me
touch me before time love me
from behind your eyes.

> ### CONSIDERATIONS FOR CRITICAL THINKING AND WRITING
>
> 1. FIRST RESPONSE. What different emotions do these three haiku evoke?
> 2. What differences and similarities are there between the effects of a haiku and those of an epigram?
> 3. CREATIVE RESPONSE. Compose a haiku. Try to make it as allusive and suggestive as possible.

Elegy

An elegy in classical Greek and Roman literature was written in alternating hexameter and pentameter lines. Since the seventeenth century, however, the term *elegy* has been used to describe a lyric poem written to commemorate someone who is dead. The word is also used to refer to a serious meditative poem produced to express the speaker's melancholy thoughts. Elegies no longer conform to a fixed pattern of lines and stanzas, but their characteristic subject is related to death and their tone is mournfully contemplative.

THEODORE ROETHKE (1908–1963)

Elegy for Jane   1953
My Student, Thrown by a Horse

I remember the neckcurls, limp and damp as tendrils;
And her quick look, a sidelong pickerel smile;
And how, once startled into talk, the light syllables leaped for her,
And she balanced in the delight of her thought,

A wren, happy, tail into the wind,   5
Her song trembling the twigs and small branches.
The shade sang with her;
The leaves, their whispers turned to kissing;
And the mold sang in the bleached valleys under the rose.

Oh, when she was sad, she cast herself down into such a pure depth,   10
Even a father could not find her:
Scraping her cheek against straw;
Stirring the clearest water.

My sparrow, you are not here,
Waiting like a fern, making a spiny shadow.   15
The sides of wet stones cannot console me,
Nor the moss, wound with the last light.

If only I could nudge you from this sleep,
My maimed darling, my skittery pigeon.
Over this damp grave I speak the words of my love: 20
I, with no rights in this matter,
Neither father nor lover.

CONSIDERATIONS FOR CRITICAL THINKING AND WRITING

1. **FIRST RESPONSE.** Does this elegy use any kind of formal pattern for its
   structure? What holds it together?

2. List the images that compare Jane to nature. How is she depicted by these
   images?

3. Describe the shift in tone that begins in line 14. How do the speaker's feelings change in lines 14–22?

4. What is the significance of Jane's having been the speaker's student? How
   does that affect your reading of lines 21–22?

CONNECTION TO ANOTHER SELECTION

1. Compare "Elegy for Jane" with A. E. Housman's "To an Athlete Dying
   Young" (p. 631). How does each poem avoid sentimentality in its description of a young person who had died?

ANDREW HUDGINS (B. 1951)

Elegy for My Father, Who Is Not Dead   *1991*

One day I'll lift the telephone
and be told my father's dead. He's ready.
In the sureness of his faith, he talks
about the world beyond this world
as though his reservations have   5

been made. I think he wants to go,
a little bit — a new desire
to travel building up, an itch
to see fresh worlds. Or older ones.
He thinks that when I follow him   10
he'll wrap me in his arms and laugh,
the way he did when I arrived
on earth. I do not think he's right.
He's ready. I am not. I can't
just say good-bye as cheerfully   15
as if he were embarking on a trip
to make my later trip go well.
I see myself on deck, convinced
his ship's gone down, while he's convinced
I'll see him standing on the dock   20
and waving, shouting, Welcome back.

CONSIDERATIONS FOR CRITICAL THINKING AND WRITING

1. **FIRST RESPONSE.** Why does this speaker elegize his father if the father "is
   not dead"?

2. How does the speaker's view of immortality differ from his father's?

3. Explain why you think this is an optimistic or a pessimistic poem — or explain why these two categories fail to describe the poem.

4. In what sense can this poem be regarded as an elegy?

CONNECTION TO ANOTHER SELECTION

1. Write an essay comparing attitudes toward death in this poem and in
   Dylan Thomas's "Do Not Go Gentle into That Good Night" (p. 253). Both
   speakers invoke their fathers, nearer to death than they are; what impact
   does this invocation have?

BRENDAN GALVIN (B. 1938)

An Evel Knievel° Elegy   2008

We have all felt our parachutes
malfunctioning at a job interview
or cocktail party, with bystanders
reading the freefall on our faces,
and some of us have imagined   5

Evel Knievel (1938–2007): American motorcycle stunt performer whose daredevil jumps
over lines of vehicles, canyons, and rivers were nationally televised in the 1960s and 70s.

how it must have felt for you
above the Snake River Canyon
or the fountains outside Caesar's
Palace, though a mental bungee
reversed our flops before we were   10
converted to sacks of poker chips and spent
a month or more in a coma. You were
our star-spangled Icarus,° Evel,
while we dressed off the rack
for working lives among the common   15
asps and vipers, never jumping
the rattlers in what you and
the networks considered a sport.
Stunts, Evel. We loved their heights
and distances from our gray quotidian   20
so much we bought the kids three
hundred million dollars' worth
of your wheels and getups. You were
our airborne Elvis, and rode
your rocket-powered bike through fire.   25
Which we admired, though some,
annealing or annulled, knew that
they stand in fire all their lives,
and turned away, and didn't applaud,
and would not suffer the loss   30
of your departure.

Icarus: In Greek mythology, a character who fell to the earth and died after refusing to heed
his father's advice about not flying too close to the sun on manufactured wings of wax and
feathers that melted from the heat.

CONSIDERATIONS FOR CRITICAL THINKING AND WRITING

1. **FIRST RESPONSE.** To what extent is this poem a meditation upon popular
   culture as well as an elegy for Evel Knievel?

2. Discuss Galvin's use of metaphor to characterize Knievel. Choose three
   metaphors that seem especially vivid to you and explain why.

3. Discuss the thematic significance of lines 26 to 31. How would you read the
   poem differently if it ended in the middle of line 26?

Ode

An *ode* is characterized by a serious topic and formal tone, but no prescribed formal pattern describes all odes. In some odes the pattern of each
stanza is repeated throughout, while in others each stanza introduces a
new pattern. Odes are lengthy lyrics that often include lofty emotions conveyed by a dignified style. Typical topics include truth, art, freedom, justice,
and the meaning of life. Frequently such lyrics tend to be more public than
private, and their speakers often use apostrophe.

Percy Bysshe Shelley (1792–1822)

Ode to the West Wind   *1820*

I

O wild West Wind, thou breath of Autumn's being,
Thou, from whose unseen presence the leaves dead
Are driven, like ghosts from an enchanter fleeing,

Yellow, and black, and pale, and hectic red,
Pestilence-stricken multitudes: O thou,   5
Who chariotest to their dark wintry bed

The wingèd seeds, where they lie cold and low,
Each like a corpse within its grave, until
Thine azure sister of the Spring shall blow

Her clarion o'er the dreaming earth, and fill   10
(Driving sweet buds like flocks to feed in air)
With living hues and odors plain and hill:

Wild Spirit, which art moving everywhere;
Destroyer and preserver; hear, oh, hear!

II

Thou on whose stream, mid the steep sky's commotion,   15
Loose clouds like earth's decaying leaves are shed,
Shook from the tangled boughs of Heaven and Ocean,

Angels° of rain and lightning: there are spread   *messengers*
On the blue surface of thine airy surge,
Like the bright hair uplifted from the head   20

Of some fierce Maenad,° even from the dim verge
Of the horizon to the zenith's height,
The locks of the approaching storm. Thou dirge

Of the dying year, to which this closing night
Will be the dome of a vast sepulcher,   25
Vaulted with all thy congregated might

Of vapors, from whose solid atmosphere
Black rain, and fire, and hail will burst: oh, hear!

III

Thou who didst waken from his summer dreams
The blue Mediterranean, where he lay,   30
Lulled by the coil of his crystálline streams,

---

21 *Maenad:* In Greek mythology, a frenzied worshipper of Dionysus, god of wine and fertility.

Beside a pumice isle in Baiae's bay,°
And saw in sleep old palaces and towers
Quivering within the wave's intenser day,

All overgrown with azure moss and flowers   35
So sweet, the sense faints picturing them! Thou
For whose path the Atlantic's level powers

Cleave themselves into chasms, while far below
The sea-blooms and the oozy woods which wear
The sapless foliage of the ocean, know   40

Thy voice, and suddenly grow gray with fear,
And tremble and despoil themselves: oh, hear!

IV

If I were a dead leaf thou mightest bear;
If I were a swift cloud to fly with thee;
A wave to pant beneath thy power, and share   45

The impulse of thy strength, only less free
Than thou, O uncontrollable! If even
I were as in my boyhood, and could be

The comrade by thy wanderings over Heaven,
As then, when to outstrip thy skyey speed   50
Scarce seemed a vision; I would ne'er have striven

As thus with thee in prayer in my sore need.
Oh, lift me as a wave, a leaf, a cloud!
I fall upon the thorns of life! I bleed!

A heavy weight of hours has chained and bowed   55
One too like thee: tameless, and swift, and proud.

V

Make me thy lyre,° even as the forest is:
What if my leaves are falling like its own!
The tumult of thy mighty harmonies

Will take from both a deep, autumnal tone,   60
Sweet though in sadness. Be thou, Spirit fierce,
My spirit! Be thou me, impetuous one!

Drive my dead thoughts over the universe
Like withered leaves to quicken a new birth!
And, by the incantation of this verse,   65

---

32 *Baiae's bay:* A bay in the Mediterranean Sea.   57 *Make me thy lyre:* Sound is produced
on an Aeolian lyre, or wind harp, by wind blowing across its strings.

Scatter, as from an unextinguished hearth
Ashes and sparks, my words among mankind!
Be through my lips to unawakened earth

The trumpet of a prophecy! O Wind,
If Winter comes, can Spring be far behind?   70

CONSIDERATIONS FOR CRITICAL THINKING AND WRITING

1. **FIRST RESPONSE.** Write a summary of each of this ode's five sections.
2. What is the speaker's situation? What is his "sore need" (line 52)? What does the speaker ask of the wind in lines 57–70?
3. What does the wind signify in this ode? How is it used symbolically?
4. Determine the meter and rhyme of the first five stanzas. How do these elements contribute to the ode's movement? Is this pattern continued in the other four sections?

BARON WORMSER (B. 1948)

Labor   *2008*

I spent a couple of years during my undestined
Twenties on a north woods acreage
That grew, as the locals poetically phrased it,
"Stones and rocks." I loved it.

No real insulation in the old farmhouse,   5
Which meant ten cords of hardwood,
Which meant a muscled mantra of cutting,
Yarding, splitting, stacking and burning.

I was the maul coming down *kerchunk*
On the round of maple; I was the hellacious   10
Screeching saw; I was the fire.
I was fiber and grew imperceptibly.

I lost interest in everything except for trees.
Career, ambition and politics bored me.
I loved putting on my steel-toe, lace-up   15
Work boots in the morning. I loved the feel

Of my feet on grass slick with dew or frost
Or ice-skimmed mud or crisp snow crust.
I loved the moment after I felled a tree
When it was still again and I felt the awe   20

Of what I had done and awe for the tree that had
Stretched toward the sky for silent decades.
On Saturday night the regulars who had worked
In the woods forever mocked me as I limped into

The bar out on the state highway. "Workin' hard 25
There, sonny, or more like hardly workin'?"
I cradled my bottle between stiff raw hands,
Felt a pinching tension in the small of my back,

Inhaled ripe sweat, damp flannel,
Cheap whiskey then nodded — a happy fool. 30
They grinned back. Through their proper
Scorn I could feel it. They loved it too.

for Hayden Carruth

CONSIDERATIONS FOR CRITICAL THINKING AND WRITING

1. **FIRST RESPONSE.** To what extent does the poem conform to the definitions of an ode?
2. What is it about tree cutting that so enthralls the speaker?
3. Do you think this poem is sentimental? Why or why not?
4. **CREATIVE RESPONSE.** Write an ode concerning an activity that you know well and can express strong feelings about, using vivid images and metaphors.

CONNECTION TO ANOTHER SELECTION

1. Compare the themes in "Labor" and in Mark Turpin's "Sledgehammer's Song" (p. 235).

Parody

A *parody* is a humorous imitation of another, usually serious, work. It can take any fixed or open form because parodists imitate the tone, language, and shape of the original. While a parody may be teasingly close to a work's style, it typically deflates the subject matter to make the original seem absurd. Parody can be used as a kind of literary criticism to expose the defects in a work, but it is also very often an affectionate acknowledgment that a well-known work has become both institutionalized in our culture and fair game for some fun. Read Robert Frost's "The Road Not Taken" (p. 365) and then study this parody.

BLANCHE FARLEY (B. 1937)

The Lover Not Taken   *1984*

Committed to one, she wanted both
And, mulling it over, long she stood,
Alone on the road, loath
To leave, wanting to hide in the undergrowth.
This new guy, smooth as a yellow wood 5

Really turned her on. She liked his hair,
His smile. But the other, Jack, had a claim
On her already and she had to admit, he did wear
Well. In fact, to be perfectly fair,
He understood her. His long, lithe frame   10

Beside hers in the evening tenderly lay.
Still, if this blond guy dropped by someday,
Couldn't way just lead on to way?
No. For if way led on and Jack
Found out, she doubted if he would ever come back.   15

Oh, she turned with a sigh.
Somewhere ages and ages hence,
She might be telling this. "And I —"
She would say, "stood faithfully by."
But by then who would know the difference?   20

With that in mind, she took the fast way home,
The road by the pond, and phoned the blond.

CONSIDERATIONS FOR CRITICAL THINKING AND WRITING

1. **FIRST RESPONSE.** To what degree does this poem duplicate Frost's style? How does it differ?

2. Does this parody seem successful to you? Explain what you think makes a successful parody.

3. **CREATIVE RESPONSE.** Choose a poet whose work you know reasonably well or would like to know better and determine what is characteristic about his or her style. Then choose a poem to parody. It's probably best to attempt a short poem or a section of a long work. If you have difficulty selecting an author, you might consider Herrick, Blake, Keats, Dickinson, Whitman, Hughes, or Frost, as a number of their works are included in this book.

Picture Poem

By arranging lines into particular shapes, poets can sometimes organize typography into *picture poems* of what they describe. Words have been arranged into all kinds of shapes, from apples to light bulbs. Notice how the shape of this next poem embodies its meaning.

MICHAEL MCFEE (B. 1954)

In Medias Res°   *1985*

His waist
like the plot
thickens, wedding
pants now breathtaking,

In Medias Res: A Latin term for a story that begins "in the middle of things."

belt no longer the cinch   5
it once was, belly's cambium
expanding to match each birthday,
his body a wad of anonymous tissue
swung in the same centrifuge of years
that separates a house from its foundation,   10
undermining sidewalks grim with joggers
and loose-filled graves and families
and stars collapsing on themselves,
no preservation society capable
of plugging entropy's dike,   15
under his zipper's sneer
a belly hibernation-
soft, ready for
the kill.

Considerations for Critical Thinking and Writing

1. **First response.** Explain how the title is related to this poem's shape and
   meaning.
2. Identify the puns. How do they work in the poem?
3. What is "cambium" (line 6)? Why is the phrase "belly's cambium" especially
   appropriate?
4. What is the tone of this poem? Is it consistent throughout?

Perspective

Elaine Mitchell (b. 1924)

Form   *1994*

Is it a corset
or primal wave?
Don't try to force it.

Even endorse it
to shape and deceive.   5
Ouch, too tight a corset.

Take it off. No remorse. It
's an ace up your sleeve.
No need to force it.

Can you make a horse knit?   10
Who would believe?
Consider. Of course, it

might be a resource. Wit,
your grateful slave.
Form. Sometimes you force it,   15

sometimes divorce it
to make it behave.
So don't try to force it.
Respect a good corset.

CONSIDERATIONS FOR CRITICAL THINKING AND WRITING

1. **FIRST RESPONSE.** What is the speaker's attitude toward form?
2. Explain why you think the form of this poem does or does not conform to the speaker's advice.
3. Why is the metaphor of a corset an especially apt image for this poem?

Web Research the poets in this chapter at bedfordstmartins.com/rewritinglit.

10

Open Form

I believe every space and comma is a living part of the poem and has its function, just as every muscle and pore of the body has its function. And the way the lines are broken is a functioning part essential to the poem's life.
— DENISE LEVERTOV

By permission of David Geier and New Directions.

Many poems, especially those written in the past century, are composed of lines that cannot be scanned for a fixed or predominant meter. Moreover, very often these poems do not rhyme. Known as *free verse* (from the French, *vers libre*), such lines can derive their rhythmic qualities from the repetition of words, phrases, or grammatical structures; the arrangement of words on the printed page; or some other means. In recent years the term *open form* has been used in place of *free verse* to avoid the erroneous suggestion that this kind of poetry lacks all discipline and shape.

Although the following two poems do not use measurable meters, they do have rhythm.

E. E. CUMMINGS (1894–1962)

in Just-   *1923*

in Just-
spring   when the world is mud-
luscious the little
lame balloonman

whistles   far   and wee   5

and eddieandbill come
running from marbles and
piracies and it's
spring

when the world is puddle-wonderful   10

the queer
old balloonman whistles
far   and   wee
and bettyandisbel come dancing

from hop-scotch and jump-rope and   15

it's
spring
and

   the

      goat-footed   20

balloonMan   whistles
far
and
wee

Explore contexts
for E. E. Cummings
on *LiterActive*.

CONSIDERATIONS FOR CRITICAL THINKING AND WRITING

1. **FIRST RESPONSE.** What is the effect of this poem's arrangement of words and use of space on the page? How would the effect differ if the text were written out in prose?

2. What is the effect of Cummings's combining the names "eddieandbill" (line 6) and "bettyandisbel" (line 14)?

3. The allusion in line 20 refers to Pan, a Greek god associated with nature. How does this allusion add to the meaning of the poem?

WALT WHITMAN (1819–1892)

From "I Sing the Body Electric"   *1855*

O my body! I dare not desert the likes of you in other men and women,
    nor the likes of the parts of you,
I believe the likes of you are to stand or fall with the likes of the soul, (and
    that they are the soul,)
I believe the likes of you shall stand or fall with my poems, and that they
    are my poems.
Man's, woman's, child's, youth's, wife's, husband's, mother's, father's,
    young man's, young woman's poems.

Head, neck, hair, ears, drop and tympan of the
    ears.
Eyes, eye-fringes, iris of the eye, eyebrows, and
    the waking or sleeping of the lids,
Mouth, tongue, lips, teeth, roof of the mouth,
    jaws, and the jaw-hinges,
Nose, nostrils of the nose, and the partition,
Cheeks, temples, forehead, chin, throat, back
    of the neck, neck-slue,
Strong shoulders, manly beard, scapula, hind-
    shoulders, and the ample
    side-round of the chest,
Upper-arm, armpit, elbow-socket, lower-arm,
    arm-sinews, arm-bones,
Wrist and wrist-joints, hand, palm, knuckles,
    thumb, forefinger, finger-joints, finger-
    nails,

Courtesy of the Bayley-Whitman Collection
of Ohio Wesleyan University of Delaware,
Ohio.

Broad breast-front, curling hair of the breast,
    breast-bone, breast-side,
Ribs, belly, backbone, joints of the backbone,
Hips, hip-sockets, hip-strength, inward and outward round, man-balls,
    man-root,   15
Strong set of thighs, well carrying the trunk above,
Leg-fibers, knee, knee-pan, upper-leg, under-leg,
Ankles, instep, foot-ball, toes, toe-joints, the heel;
All attitudes, all the shapeliness, all the belongings of my or your body or
    of any one's body, male or female,
The lung-sponges, the stomach-sac, the bowels sweet and clean,   20
The brain in its folds inside the skull-frame,
Sympathies, heart-valves, palate-valves, sexuality, maternity,
Womanhood, and all that is a woman, and the man that comes from
    woman,
The womb, the teats, nipples, breast-milk, tears, laughter, weeping, love-
    looks, love-perturbations and risings,
The voice, articulation, language, whispering, shouting aloud,   25
Food, drink, pulse, digestion, sweat, sleep, walking, swimming,
Poise on the hips, leaping, reclining, embracing, arm-curving and
    tightening,
The continual changes of the flex of the mouth, and around the eyes,
The skin, the sunburnt shade, freckles, hair,
The curious sympathy one feels when feeling with the hand the naked
    meat of the body,   30
The circling rivers the breath, and breathing it in and out,
The beauty of the waist, and thence of the hips, and thence downward
    toward the knees,
The thin red jellies within you or within me, the bones and the marrow
    in the bones,
The exquisite realization of health;
O I say these are not the parts and poems of the body only, but of the soul, 35
O I say now these are the soul!

CONSIDERATIONS FOR CRITICAL THINKING AND WRITING

1. **FIRST RESPONSE.** What informs this speaker's attitude toward the human body?

2. Read the poem aloud. Is it simply a tedious enumeration of body parts, or do the lines achieve some kind of rhythmic cadence?

Perspective

WALT WHITMAN (1819–1892)

On Rhyme and Meter   *1855*

The poetic quality is not marshaled in rhyme or uniformity or abstract addresses to things nor in melancholy complaints or good precepts, but is the life of these and much else and is in the soul. The profit of rhyme is that it drops seeds of a sweeter and more luxuriant rhyme, and of uniformity that it conveys itself into its own roots in the ground out of sight. The rhyme and uniformity of perfect poems show the free growth of metrical laws and bud from them as unerringly and loosely as lilacs or roses on a bush, and take shapes as compact as the shapes of chestnuts and oranges and melons and pears, and shed the perfume impalpable to form. The fluency and ornaments of the finest poems or music or orations or recitations are not independent but dependent. All beauty comes from beautiful blood and a beautiful brain. If the greatnesses are in conjunction in a man or woman it is enough . . . the fact will prevail through the universe . . . but the gaggery and gilt of a million years will not prevail. Who troubles himself about his ornaments or fluency is lost.

From the preface to the 1855 edition of *Leaves of Grass*

CONSIDERATIONS FOR CRITICAL THINKING AND WRITING

1. According to Whitman, what determines the shape of a poem?

2. Why does Whitman prefer open forms over fixed forms such as the sonnet?

3. Is Whitman's poetry devoid of any structure or shape? Choose one of his poems (listed in the index) to illustrate your answer.

A SAMPLE STUDENT RESPONSE

Avery Bloom

Professor Rios

English 212

October 7, 2009

The Power of Walt Whitman's Open Form Poem

"I Sing the Body Electric"

Walt Whitman's "I Sing the Body Electric" is an ode to the human body. The poem is open form, without rhymes or consistent meter, and instead relies almost entirely on the use of language and the structure of lists to affect the reader. The result is a thorough inventory of parts of the body that illustrates the beauty of the human form and its intimate connection to the soul.

At times, Whitman lists the parts of the body with almost complete objectivity, making it difficult to understand the poem's purpose. The poem initially appears to do little more than recite the names of body parts: "Head, neck, hair, ears, drop and tympan of the ears" (line 5); "Mouth, tongue, lips, teeth, roof of the mouth, jaws, and the jaw-hinges" (7). There are no end rhymes, but the exhaustive and detailed list of body parts—from the brain to "the thin red jellies . . . , the bones and the marrow in the bones" (33)—offers language that has a certain rhythm. The language and rhythm of the list creates a visual image full of energy and momentum that builds, emphasizing the body's functions and movements. As Michael Meyer writes, open form poems "rely on an intense use of language to establish rhythms and relations between meaning and form. [They] use the arrangement of words and phrases . . . to create unique forms" (page 277). No doubt Whitman chose the open form for this work—relying on his "intense use of language" and the rhythm of the list—because it allowed a basic structure that held together but did not restrain, and a full freedom and range of motion to create a poem that is alive with movement and electricity. . . .

Bloom 4

Works Cited

Meyer, Michael, ed. *Poetry: An Introduction*. 6th ed. Boston: Bedford/St.
    Martin's, 2010. 277. Print.

Whitman, Walt. "From 'I Sing the Body Electric.'" *Poetry: An Introduction*.
    Ed. Michael Meyer. 6th ed. Boston: Bedford/St. Martin's, 2010. 273-74.
    Print.

Open form poetry is sometimes regarded as formless because it is unlike the strict fixed forms of a sonnet, villanelle, or sestina. But even though open form poems may not employ traditional meters and rhymes, they still rely on an intense use of language to establish rhythms and relations between meaning and form. Open form poems use the arrangement of words and phrases on the printed page, pauses, line lengths, and other means to create unique forms that express their particular meaning and tone.

Cummings's "in Just-" and the excerpt from Whitman's "I Sing the Body Electric" demonstrate how the white space on a page and rhythmic cadences can be aligned with meaning, but there is one kind of open form poetry that doesn't even look like poetry on a page. A ***prose poem*** is printed as prose and represents, perhaps, the most clear opposite of fixed forms. Here is a brief example.

ROBERT HASS (B. 1941)

A Story about the Body   *1989*

The young composer, working that summer at an artists' colony, had watched her for a week. She was Japanese, a painter, almost sixty, and he thought he was in love with her. He loved her work, and her work was like the way she moved her body, used her hands, looked at him directly when she made amused and considered answers to his questions. One night, walking back from a concert, they came to her door and she turned to him and said, "I think you would like to have me. I would like that too, but I must tell you that I have had a double mastectomy," and when he didn't understand, "I've lost both my breasts." The radiance that he had carried around in his belly and chest cavity — like music — withered very quickly, and he made himself look at her when he said, "I'm sorry. I don't think I could." He walked back to his own cabin through the pines, and in the morning he found a small blue bowl on the porch outside his door. It looked to be full of rose petals, but he found when he picked it up that the rose petals were on top; the rest of the bowl — she must have swept them from the corners of her studio — was full of dead bees.

CONSIDERATIONS FOR CRITICAL THINKING AND WRITING

1. **FIRST RESPONSE.** Why this title? What other potential titles can you come up with that evoke your reading of the poem?
2. What impression about the "young composer" do you derive from the poem?
3. Why are bees very appropriate in the final line rather than, for example, moths?

CONNECTIONS TO OTHER SELECTIONS

1. Discuss the treatments of love in this poem and in John Frederick Nims's "Love Poem" (p. 42).
2. Read T. E. Hulme's "On the Differences between Poetry and Prose" (p. 132) and write an essay on what you think Hulme would have to say about "A Story about the Body."

RICHARD HAGUE (B. 1947)

Directions for Resisting the SAT 1996

Do not believe in October or May
or in any Saturday morning with pencils.
Do not observe the rules of gravity,
commas, history.
Lie about numbers. 5
Blame your successes,
every one of them,
on rotten luck.
Resign all clubs and committees.
Go down with the ship — any ship. 10
Speak nothing like English.
Desire to live whole,
like an oyster or snail,
and follow no directions.
Listen to no one. 15

Make your marks on everything.

CONSIDERATIONS FOR CRITICAL THINKING AND WRITING

1. **FIRST RESPONSE.** What is the speaker's subversive message? What do you think of the advice offered?

2. What kinds of assumptions do you suppose Hague makes about readers' attitudes toward the SAT? To what extent do you share those attitudes?

3. Discuss Hague's use of spacing and line breaks. What is the effect of the space between lines 15 and 16?

CONNECTION TO ANOTHER SELECTION

1. Compare the treatment of tests in this poem and in Linda Pastan's "Pass / Fail" (p. 116).

Much of the poetry published today is written in open form; however, many poets continue to take pleasure in the requirements imposed by fixed forms. Some write both fixed form and open form poetry. Each kind offers rewards to careful readers as well. Here are several more open form poems that establish their own unique patterns.

GALWAY KINNELL (B. 1927)

After Making Love We Hear Footsteps   *1980*

For I can snore like a bullhorn
or play loud music
or sit up talking with any reasonably sober Irishman
and Fergus will only sink deeper
into his dreamless sleep, which goes by all in one flash,   5
but let there be that heavy breathing
or a stifled come-cry anywhere in the house
and he will wrench himself awake
and make for it on the run — as now, we lie together,
after making love, quiet, touching along the length of our bodies,   10
familiar touch of the long-married,
and he appears — in his baseball pajamas, it happens,
the neck opening so small
he has to screw them on, which one day may make him wonder
about the mental capacity of baseball players —   15
and says, "Are you loving and snuggling? May I join?"
He flops down between us and hugs us and snuggles himself to sleep,
his face gleaming with satisfaction at being this very child.

In the half darkness we look at each other
and smile   20
and touch arms across his little, startlingly muscled body —
this one whom habit of memory propels to the ground of his making,
sleeper only the mortal sounds can sing awake,
this blessing love gives again into our arms.

CONSIDERATIONS FOR CRITICAL THINKING AND WRITING

1. **FIRST RESPONSE.** Explore Kinnell's line endings. Why does he break the lines where he does?
2. How does the speaker's language reveal his character?
3. Describe the shift in tone between lines 18 and 19 with the shift in focus from child to adults. How does the use of space here emphasize this shift?
4. Do you think this poem is sentimental? Explain why or why not.

CONNECTION TO ANOTHER SELECTION

1. Discuss how this poem helps to bring into focus the sense of loss Robert Frost evokes in "Home Burial" (p. 372).

KELLY CHERRY (B. 1940)

Alzheimer's   1990

He stands at the door, a crazy old man
Back from the hospital, his mind rattling
Like the suitcase, swinging from his hand,
That contains shaving cream, a piggy bank,
A book he sometimes pretends to read,   5
His clothes. On the brick wall beside him
Roses and columbine slug it out for space, claw the mortar.
The sun is shining, as it does late in the afternoon
In England, after rain.
Sun hardens the house, reifies it,   10
Strikes the iron grillwork like a smithy
And sparks fly off, burning in the bushes —
The rosebushes —
While the white wood trim defines solidity in space.
This is his house. He remembers it as his,   15
Remembers the walkway he built between the front room
And the garage, the rhododendron he planted in back,
The car he used to drive. He remembers himself,
A younger man, in a tweed hat, a man who loved
Music. There is no time for that now. No time for music,   20
The peculiar screeching of strings, the luxurious
Fiddling with emotion.
Other things have become more urgent.
Other matters are now of greater import, have more
Consequence, must be attended to. The first   25
Thing he must do, now that he is home, is decide who
This woman is, this old, white-haired woman
Standing here in the doorway,
Welcoming him in.

CONSIDERATIONS FOR CRITICAL THINKING AND WRITING

1. **FIRST RESPONSE.** Why is it impossible to dismiss the character in this poem as merely "a crazy old man" (line 1)?

2. Discuss the effect of the line breaks in lines 1–6 of the poem's first complete sentence. How do the line breaks contribute to the meaning of these lines?

3. What do the images in lines 6–20 indicate about the nature of the man's memory?

4. Why is the final image of the "white-haired woman" especially effective? How does the final line serve as the poem's emotional climax?

WILLIAM CARLOS WILLIAMS (1883–1963)

The Red Wheelbarrow   1923

so much depends
upon

a red wheel
barrow

glazed with rain
water

beside the white
chickens.

CONSIDERATIONS FOR CRITICAL THINKING AND WRITING

1. **FIRST RESPONSE.** What "depends upon" the things mentioned in the poem? What is the effect of these images? Do they have a particular meaning?

2. Do these lines have any kind of rhythm?

3. How does this poem resemble a haiku? How is it different?

NATASHA TRETHEWEY (B. 1966)

On Captivity   2007

Being all Stripped as Naked as We were Born, and endeavoring to hide our Nakedness,
these Cannaballs took [our] Books, and tearing out the Leaves would give each of us a
Leaf to cover us . . .

> — *Jonathan Dickinson, 1699*

At the hands now
        of their captors, those
                they've named *savages,*
        do they say the word itself
savagely — hissing   5

that first letter,
          the serpent's image,
                    releasing
          thought into speech?
For them now,   10

everything is flesh
          as if their thoughts, made
                    suddenly corporeal,
          reveal even more
their nakedness—   15

the shame of it:
          their bodies rendered
                    plain as the natives'—
          homely and pale,
their ordinary sex,   20

the secret illicit hairs
          that do not (cannot)
                    cover enough.
          This is how they are brought,
naked as newborns,   25

to knowledge. Adam and Eve
          in the New World,
                    they have only the Bible
          to cover them. Think of it:
a woman holding before her   30

the torn leaves of *Genesis,*
          and a man covering himself
                    with the Good Book's
          frontispiece—his own name
inscribed on the page.   35

Considerations for Critical Thinking and Writing

1. **FIRST RESPONSE.** Trethewey has written about the sources of her epigraph:
    "Because the conquerors made use of the written word to claim land
    [in North America] inhabited by native people, I found the detail of settlers
    forced to cover themselves with torn pages from books a compelling irony"
    (*The Best American Poetry 2008,* p. 182). How does this comment contribute to
    the central irony in the poem?

2. Discuss Trethewey's use of alliteration in lines 1 to 9.

3. In what sense are the captors "brought, / naked as newborns, / to knowledge"
    (lines 24–26)?

GARY GILDNER (B. 1938)

First Practice   *1984*

After the doctor checked to see
we weren't ruptured,
the man with the short cigar took us
under the grade school,
where we went in case of attack   5
or storm, and said
he was Clifford Hill, he was
a man who believed dogs
ate dogs, he had once killed
for his country, and if   10
there were any girls present
for them to leave now.
                    No one
left. OK, he said, he said I take
that to mean you are hungry   15
men who hate to lose as much
as I do. OK. Then
he made two lines of us
facing each other,
and across the way, he said,   20
is the man you hate most
in the world,
and if we are to win
that title I want to see how.
But I don't want to see   25
any marks when you're dressed,
he said. He said, *Now.*

CONSIDERATIONS FOR CRITICAL THINKING AND WRITING

1. **FIRST RESPONSE.** Do you recognize this coach? How does he compare with sports coaches you have known?

2. Comment on the significance of Clifford Hill's name.

3. Locate examples of irony in the poem and explain how they contribute to the theme.

4. Discuss the effect of line spacing in line 13.

CONNECTION TO ANOTHER SELECTION

1. Write an essay comparing the coach in this poem and the teacher in Judy Page Heitzman's "The Schoolroom on the Second Floor of the Knitting Mill" (p. 147).

Marilyn Nelson Waniek (b. 1946)

Emily Dickinson's Defunct   1978

She used to
pack poems
in her hip pocket.
Under all the
gray old lady   5
clothes she was
dressed for action.
She had hair,
imagine,
in certain places, and   10
believe me
she smelled human
on a hot summer day.
Stalking snakes
or counting   15
the thousand motes
in sunlight
she walked just
like an Indian.
She was New England's   20
favorite daughter,
she could pray
like the devil.
She was a
two-fisted woman,   25
this babe.
All the flies
just stood around
and buzzed
when she died.   30

Considerations for Critical Thinking and Writing

1. **FIRST RESPONSE.** How does the speaker characterize Dickinson? Explain
   why this characterization is different from the popular view of Dickinson.

2. How does the diction of the poem serve to characterize the speaker?

3. Discuss the function of the poem's title.

Connections to Other Selections

1. Waniek alludes to at least two other poems in "Emily Dickinson's Defunct."
   The title refers to E. E. Cummings's "Buffalo Bill 's" (p. 623), and the final
   lines (27–30) refer to Dickinson's "I heard a Fly buzz—when I died—"
   (p. 335). Read those poems and write an essay discussing how they affect
   your reading of Waniek's poem.

JEFFREY HARRISON (B. 1957)

The Names of Things   *2006*

Just after breakfast and still
waking up, I take the path cut
through the meadow, my mind caught
in some rudimentary stage,
the stems of timothy bending   5
inward with the weight of a single
drop of condensed fog clinging
to each of their fuzzy heads
that brush wetly against my jeans.
Out on a rise, the lupines stand   10
like a choir singing their purples,
pinks and whites to the buttercups
spread thickly through the grasses—
and to the sparser daisies, orange
hawkweed, pink and white clover,   15
purple vetch, butter-and-eggs.
It's a pleasure to name things
as long as one doesn't get
hung up about it. A pleasure, too,
to pick up the dirt road and listen   20
to my sneakers soaked with dew
scrunching on the damp pinkish sand—
that must be feldspar, an element
of granite, I remember from
fifth grade. I don't know what   25
this black salamander with yellow spots
is called—I want to say yellow-
spotted salamander, as if names
innocently sprang from things
themselves. Purple columbines   30
nod in a ditch, escapees
from someone's garden. It isn't
until I'm on my way back
that they remind me of the school
shootings in Colorado,   35
the association clinging to the spurs
of their delicate, complex blooms.
And I remember the hawk
in hawkweed, and that it's also
called devil's paintbrush, and how   40
lupines are named after wolves . . .
how like second thoughts the darker
world encroaches even on these
fields protected as a sanctuary,
something ulterior always   45

creeping in like seeds carried
in the excrement of these buoyant
goldfinches, whose yellow bodies
are as bright as joy itself,
but whose species name in Latin   50
means "sorrowful."

CONSIDERATIONS FOR CRITICAL THINKING AND WRITING

1. **FIRST RESPONSE.** "It's a pleasure to name things / as long as one doesn't get/ hung up about it" (lines 17–19). Do you think these lines adequately sum up the theme of this poem?

2. Locate and describe the shift in tone as this meditation on names progresses.

3. Discuss the effect of the images and their meanings in lines 42 to 51.

CONNECTION TO ANOTHER SELECTION

1. Compare the themes in this poem and in Robert Frost's "Nothing Gold Can Stay" (p. 383).

JULIO MARZÁN (B. 1946)
The Translator at the Reception for Latin American Writers   *1997*

Air-conditioned introductions,
then breezy Spanish conversation
fan his curiosity to know
what country I come from.
"Puerto Rico and the Bronx."   5

Spectacled downward eyes
translate disappointment
like a poison mushroom
puffed in his thoughts as if,
after investing a sizable   10
intellectual budget, transporting
a huge cast and camera crew
to film on location
Mayan pyramid grandeur,
indigenes whose ancient gods   15
and comet-tail plumage
inspire a glorious epic
of revolution across a continent,
he received a lurid script
for a social documentary   20
rife with dreary streets

and pathetic human interest,
meager in the profits of high culture.

Understandably he turns,
catches up with the hostess,   25
praising the uncommon quality
of her offerings of cheese.

CONSIDERATIONS FOR CRITICAL THINKING AND WRITING

1. **FIRST RESPONSE.** What is the speaker's attitude toward the person he meets
   at the reception? What lines in particular lead you to that conclusion?
2. Why is that person so disappointed about the answer, "Puerto Rico and the
   Bronx" (line 5)?
3. Explain lines 6 to 23. How do they reveal both the speaker and the person
   encountered at the reception?
4. Why is the setting of this poem significant?

TODD BOSS (B. 1968)

Advance   2008

With a squeal, the already
otherworldly broadcast
stuttered,
      scattered,
            leaving   5
only a tattered hiss.
          At first
my father's fingers
        fussed
the dial of our radio,   10
          signals
fritzed as a flintless lighter,

then he leaned in closer,
intent on
      teasing   15
         the news
we needed
      out of that box.
I never saw him touch more
slightly anything or anyone,   20
all his
      fingertips navigating
in and out of
         nonsense for
the lifeline of our lives,   25

before
            swiping it off.
                        Now
no more news was ours but
the storm's dark musings   30
on the matter.

                Even last
fall's fruit, jarred in the root
cellar just around the corner,
sucked   35
            its cupped lids
                        tighter.

CONSIDERATIONS FOR CRITICAL THINKING AND WRITING

1. **FIRST RESPONSE.** Explain which words evoke the sounds of tuning the radio, and how.

2. Describe the ways in which Boss creates tension and suspense in the poem.

3. Type out the poem as a prose paragraph. How is the experience of reading the paragraph different from that of reading the poem? What do the line breaks of the poem contribute to your reading experience?

ROBERT MORGAN (B. 1944)

Overalls   *1990*

Even the biggest man will look
babylike in overalls, bib
up to his neck holding the trousers
high on his belly, with no chafing
at the waist, no bulging over   5
the belt. But it's the pockets on
the chest that are most interesting,
buttons and snaps like medals, badges,
flaps open with careless ease, thin
sheath for the pencil, little pockets   10
and pouches and the main zipper
compartment like a wallet over
the heart and the slit where the watch
goes, an eye where the chain is caught.
Every bit of surface is taken   15
up with patches, denim mesas
and envelopes, a many-level
cloth topography. And below,
the loops for hammers and pliers
like holsters for going armed   20
and armored yet free-handed
into the field another day
for labor's playful war with time.

CONSIDERATIONS FOR CRITICAL THINKING AND WRITING

1. **FIRST RESPONSE.** How does the poem's last line announce its theme?

2. Why is it that the "pockets on / the chest . . . are most interesting" (lines 6–7) to the speaker?

3. Describe the way images of childhood and adulthood, along with work and war, are interwoven in Morgan's treatment of overalls.

LOUISE GLÜCK (B. 1943)

March 2008

The light stays longer in the sky,
    but it's a cold light,
it brings no relief from winter.

My neighbor stares out the window,
talking to her dog. He's sniffing the garden,
trying to reach a decision about the
    dead flowers.   5

It's a little early for all this.
Everything's still very bare —
nevertheless, something's different today
    from yesterday.

Photo © Sigrid Estrada.

We can see the mountain: the peak's glittering where the ice
    catches the light.
But on the sides the snow's melted, exposing bare rock.   10

My neighbor's calling the dog, making
    her unconvincing doglike sounds.
The dog's polite; he raises his head when she calls,
but he doesn't move. So she goes on calling,
her failed bark slowly deteriorating into a human voice.

All her life she dreamed of living by the sea   15
but fate didn't put her there.
It laughed at her dreams;
it locked her up in the hills, where no one escapes.

The sun beats down on the earth, the earth flourishes.
And every winter, it's as though the rock underneath the earth rises   20
higher and higher and the earth becomes rock, cold and rejecting.

She says hope killed her parents, it killed her grandparents.
It rose up each spring with the wheat
and died between the heat of summer and the raw cold.
In the end, they told her to live near the sea,   25
as though that would make a difference.

By late spring she'll be garrulous, but now she's down to two words,
never and *only*, to express this sense that life's cheated her.

Never the cries of the gulls, only, in summer, the crickets, cicadas.
Only the smell of the field, when all she wanted   30
was the smell of the sea, of disappearance.

The sky above the fields has turned a sort of grayish pink
as the sun sinks. The clouds are silk yarn, magenta and crimson.

And everywhere the earth is rustling, not lying still.
And the dog senses this stirring; his ears twitch.   35

He walks back and forth, vaguely remembering
from other years this elation. The season of discoveries
is beginning. Always the same discoveries, but to the dog
intoxicating and new, not duplicitous.

I tell my neighbor we'll be like this   40
when we lose our memories. I ask her if she's ever seen the sea
and she says, once, in a movie.
It was a sad story, nothing worked out at all.

The lovers part. The sea hammers the shore, the mark each wave leaves
wiped out by the wave that follows.   45
Never accumulation, never one wave trying to build on another,
never the promise of shelter —

The sea doesn't change as the earth changes;
it doesn't lie.
You ask the sea, what can you promise me   50
and it speaks the truth; it says *erasure*.

Finally the dog goes in.
We watch the crescent moon,
very faint at first, then clearer and clearer
as the night grows dark.   55
Soon it will be the sky of early spring, stretching
        above the stubborn ferns and violets.

Nothing can be forced to live.
The earth is like a drug now, like a voice from far away,
a lover or master. In the end, you do what the voice tells you.
It says forget, you forget.   60
It says begin again, you begin again.

CONSIDERATIONS FOR CRITICAL THINKING AND WRITING

1. **FIRST RESPONSE.** Consider whether or not this is "a sad story, [in which] nothing worked out at all" (line 43).

2. What distinctions between living inland and by the sea does the speaker make through the use of imagery?

3. Comment on the significance of the personification in lines 48 to 51.

4. Discuss the meaning and tone of the final stanza.

CONNECTION TO ANOTHER SELECTION

1. Compare Glück's seasonal description in "March" with Margaret Atwood's in "February" (p. 145). Which poem do you find more evocative in capturing the particular qualities of the month? Why?

LINDA PASTAN (B. 1932)

To a Daughter Leaving Home   *1988*

When I taught you
at eight to ride
a bicycle, loping along
beside you
as you wobbled away   5
on two round wheels,
my own mouth rounding
in surprise when you pulled
ahead down the curved
path of the park,   10
I kept waiting
for the thud
of your crash as I
sprinted to catch up,
while you grew   15
smaller, more breakable
with distance,
pumping, pumping
for your life, screaming
with laughter,   20
the hair flapping
behind you like a
handkerchief waving
goodbye.

CONSIDERATIONS FOR CRITICAL THINKING AND WRITING

1. **FIRST RESPONSE.** Comment on the appropriateness of the extended metaphor as a means of creating the theme for this poem. What other extended metaphors do you think would work just as well to convey the same theme?

2. Replace Pastan's title with your own so that the poem's tone is slightly shifted but the theme is still consistent with the body of the poem.

3. **CREATIVE RESPONSE.** Write an open form poem using an extended metaphor for some aspect of your life at school.

CONNECTION TO ANOTHER SELECTION

1. Compare the themes in Pastan's poem and in Rachel Hadas's "The Red Hat" (p. 229).

ANONYMOUS

The Frog   *date unknown*

What a wonderful bird the frog are!
When he stand he sit almost;
When he hop he fly almost.
He ain't got no sense hardly;
He ain't got no tail hardly either.
When he sit, he sit on what he ain't got almost.

CONSIDERATIONS FOR CRITICAL THINKING AND WRITING

1. **FIRST RESPONSE.** How is the poem a description of the speaker as well as of a frog?
2. Though this poem is ungrammatical, it does have a patterned structure. How does the pattern of sentences create a formal structure?

TATO LAVIERA (B. 1951)

AmeRícan   *1985*

we gave birth to a new generation,
AmeRícan, broader than lost gold
never touched, hidden inside the
puerto rican mountains.

we gave birth to a new generation,   5
AmeRícan, it includes everything
imaginable you-name-it-we-got-it
society.

we gave birth to a new generation,
AmeRícan salutes all folklores,   10
european, indian, black, spanish,
and anything else compatible:

AmeRícan,   singing to composer pedro flores'° palm
             trees high up in the universal sky!

AmeRícan,   sweet soft spanish danzas gypsies   15
             moving lyrics la *española*° cascabelling   *Spanish*
             presence always singing at our side!

AmeRícan,   beating jíbaro° modern troubadours
             crying guitars romantic continental
             bolero love songs!   20

AmeRícan,   across forth and across back
             back across and forth back

---

13 *pedro flores:* Puerto Rican composer of popular romantic songs.   18 *jíbaro:* A particular style of music played by Puerto Rican mountain farmers.

    forth across and back and forth
our trips are walking bridges!

    it all dissolved into itself, the attempt   25
was truly made, the attempt was truly
absorbed, digested, we spit out
the poison, we spit out the malice,
we stand, affirmative in action,
to reproduce a broader answer to the   30
marginality that gobbled us up abruptly!

AmeRícan,   walking plena-rhythms° in new york,
strutting beautifully alert, alive,
many turning eyes wondering,
admiring!   35

AmeRícan,   defining myself my own way any way many
ways Am e Rícan, with the big R and the
accent on the í!

AmeRícan,   like the soul gliding talk of gospel
boogie music!   40

AmeRícan,   speaking new words in spanglish tenements,
fast tongue moving street corner *"que
corta"*° talk being invented at the insistence   *that cuts*
of a smile!

AmeRícan,   abounding inside so many ethnic english   45
people, and out of humanity, we blend
and mix all that is good!

AmeRícan,   integrating in new york and defining our
own *destino,*° our own way of life,   *destiny*

AmeRícan,   defining the new america, humane america,   50
admired america, loved america, harmonious
america, the world in peace, our energies
collectively invested to find other civili-
zations, to touch God, further and further,
to dwell in the spirit of divinity!   55

AmeRícan,   yes, for now, for i love this, my second
land, and i dream to take the accent from
the altercation, and be proud to call
myself american, in the u.s. sense of the
word, AmeRícan, America!   60

32 *plena-rhythms:* African–Puerto Rican folklore, music, and dance.

Considerations for Critical Thinking and Writing

1. **FIRST RESPONSE.** How does the arrangement of lines communicate a sense of energy and vitality?
2. How does the speaker portray Puerto Ricans living in the United States?
3. How does the poet describe the United States?

CONNECTION TO ANOTHER SELECTION

1. In an essay compare the themes, styles, and tones of "AmeRícan" and Barbara Hamby's "Ode to American English" (p. 85).

SANDRA M. GILBERT (B. 1936)

Chairlift 2005

What does it allegorize, such unseemly
haste at the beginning
and the end —

the swift attendants gripping, heaving
each of us   5
into a steady place,

and then the long slow silent
journey over
and up the mountain, swaying

in sunshine or buffeted   10
by churning
winds, the sea beyond, with its tiny

sails and lonesome
cloudscapes, and all along,
under the bob of the shadow   15

that hangs below every chair,
a real live human
world of vines and gardens

boiling and blooming and getting
sparser as the humming   20
cables clamber

higher, steeper, until
soon there are only empty
meadows, knots of forest, channels

of frigid   25
granite or ice,
though just before someone suddenly

drags you off
at the summit,
just before the circling seats   30

descend for another
round, you notice
lying in the last deep

weedy cutbank,
all by itself,   35
one mateless leather clog. . . .

CONSIDERATIONS FOR CRITICAL THINKING AND WRITING

1. **FIRST RESPONSE.** Explain why you consider the chairlift to function as an allegory or as a symbol in the poem.

2. How does the end punctuation of the first and last stanzas contribute to the tone of the poem?

3. **CRITICAL STRATEGIES.** Read the section on mythological strategies (pp. 677–80) in Chapter 26, "Critical Strategies for Reading." How might this poem be read as a literary archetype?

PETER MEINKE (B. 1932)

The ABC of Aerobics   *1983*

Air seeps through alleys and our diaphragms
balloon blackly with this mix of
carbon monoxide and the thousand corrosives a city
doles out free to its constituents;
everyone's jogging through Edgemont Park,   5
frightened by death and fatty tissue,
gasping at the maximal heart rate,
hoping to outlive all the others streaming
in the lanes like lemmings lurching toward their last
jump. I join in despair   10
knowing my arteries jammed with
lint and tobacco, lard and bourbon — my
medical history a noxious marsh:
newts and moles slink through the sodden veins,
owls hoot in the lungs' dark branches;   15
probably I shall keel off the john like
queer Uncle George and lie on the bathroom floor
raging about Shirley Clark, my true love in
seventh grade, God bless her wherever she lives
tied to that turkey who hugely   20
undervalues the beauty of her tiny earlobes, one
view of which (either one: they are both perfect)
would add years to my life and I could skip these
x-rays, turn in my insurance card, and trade
yoga and treadmills and jogging and zen and   25
zucchini for drinking and dreaming of her, breathing hard.

CONSIDERATIONS FOR CRITICAL THINKING AND WRITING

1. **FIRST RESPONSE.** How does the title help to establish a pattern throughout the poem? How does the pattern contribute to the poem's meaning?

2. How does the speaker feel about exercise? How do his descriptions of his physical condition serve to characterize him?

3. A primer is a book that teaches children to read or introduces them, in an elementary way, to the basics of a subject. The title "The ABC of Aerobics" indicates that this poem is meant to be a primer. What is it trying to teach us? Is its final lesson serious or ironic?

4. Discuss Meinke's use of humor. Is it effective?

CONNECTIONS TO OTHER SELECTIONS

1. Write an essay comparing the way Sharon Olds connects sex and exercise in "Sex without Love" (p. 91) with Meinke's treatment here.

2. Compare the voice in this poem with that in Galway Kinnell's "After Making Love We Hear Footsteps" (p. 279). Which do you find more appealing? Why?

MARY STEWART HAMMOND (B. 1953)

The Big Fish Story   2006

Late fall and not a soul around for miles.
Just me and my man. And those scallopers
trolling a few hundred feet offshore I'm pointing to
saying *no, non, nein, nyet, nej,*
in every language including body English,   5
to his idea that we take off all our clothes
smack in the middle of the lawn
in broad daylight and go swimming!
This is the line he throws me: "But, sweetheart,
the young have given up scalloping. Those   10
are all old men out there. Their eyesight
is terrible." Which explains why
I'm naked in the water off the coast
of Massachusetts on the fourteenth of October
and loving it, the water still summer warm,   15
feeling like silk, like the feel of his flesh
drawing over my skin when we're landed
on a bed, so I swim off out of his reach
lolling and rolling, diving and surfacing,
floating on my back for his still good eyes.   20
I know what he has in mind and what
I have in mind is to play him for a while
for that line I swallowed, delay the moment
I'll do a slow crawl over to him,
wrap my legs around his waist, and   25
reel him in — just the fish he was after.

CONSIDERATIONS FOR CRITICAL THINKING AND WRITING

1. **FIRST RESPONSE.** How does the speaker's language serve to characterize her?

2. How does Hammond make this narrative both playful and erotic?

Found Poem

This next selection is a ***found poem,*** unintentional verse discovered in a nonpoetic context, such as a conversation, news story, or an advertisement. Found poems are playful reminders that the words in poems are very often the language we use every day. Whether such found language should be regarded as a poem is an issue left for you to consider.

DONALD JUSTICE   (1925–2004)

Order in the Streets   *1969*

(*From instructions printed on a child's toy, Christmas 1968, as reported in the* New York Times)

1. 2. 3.
Switch on.

Jeep rushes
to the scene
of riot   5

Jeep goes
in all directions
by mystery action.

Jeep stops periodically
to turn hood over   10

machine gun appears
with realistic
shooting noise.

After putting down riot,
jeep goes   15
back to the headquarters.

CONSIDERATIONS FOR CRITICAL THINKING AND WRITING

1. **FIRST RESPONSE.** What is the effect of arranging these instructions in discrete lines? How are the language and meaning enhanced by this arrangement?

2. **CREATIVE RESPONSE.** Look for phrases or sentences in ads, textbooks, labels, or directions — in anything that might inadvertently contain provocative material that would be revealed by arranging the words in verse lines. You may even discover some patterns of rhyme and rhythm. After arranging the lines, explain why you organized them as you did.

Web) Research the poets in this chapter at bedfordstmartins.com/ rewritinglit.

11

Combining the Elements of Poetry: A Writing Process

© Bettmann/CORBIS.

In poetry you have a form looking for a subject and a subject looking for a form. When they come together successfully you have a poem.
— W. H. AUDEN

THE ELEMENTS TOGETHER

The elements of poetry that you have studied in the first ten chapters of this book offer a vocabulary and a series of perspectives that open up avenues of inquiry into a poem. As you have learned, there are many potential routes that you can take. By asking questions about the speaker, diction, figurative language, sounds, rhythm, tone, or theme, you clarify your understanding while simultaneously sensitizing yourself to elements and issues especially relevant to the poem under consideration. This process of careful, informed reading allows you to see how the various elements of the poem reinforce its meanings.

A poem's elements do not exist in isolation, however. They work together to create a complete experience for the reader. Knowing how the elements combine helps you to understand the poem's structure and to appreciate it as a whole. Robert Herrick's "Delight in Disorder" (p. 229), for example, is more easily understood (and the humor of the poem is better appreciated) when meter and rhyme are considered together with the poem's meaning. Musing about how he is more charmed by a naturally disheveled appearance than by those that seem contrived, the speaker lists several attributes of dishevelment and concludes that they

> Do more bewitch me than when art
> Is too precise in every part.

Noticing how the couplet's precise and sing-songy rhythm combines with the solid, obvious, and final rhyme of *art* / *part* helps in understanding what the speaker means by "too precise," as the lines are a little too precise themselves. Noticing this, you may even want to chart how rhythm and rhyme work together throughout the early (more disheveled) lines of the poem. Finding a pattern in the ways the elements work together throughout the poem will help you understand how the poem works.

MAPPING THE POEM

When you write about a poem, you are, in some ways, providing a guide for a place that might otherwise seem unfamiliar and remote. Put simply, writing enables you to chart a work so that you can comfortably move around in it to discuss or write about what interests you. Your paper represents a record and a map of your intellectual journey through the poem, pointing out the things worth noting and your impressions about them. Your role as writer is to offer insights into the challenges, pleasures, and discoveries that the poem harbors. These insights are a kind of sightseeing, as you navigate the various elements of the poem to make some overall point about it.

This chapter shows you how one student, Rose Bostwick, moves through the stages of writing about how a poem's elements combine for a final effect. Included here are Rose's annotated version of the poem, her first response, her informal outline, and the final draft of an explication of John Donne's "Death Be Not Proud." A detailed explanation of what is implicit in a poem, an **explication** requires a line-by-line examination of the poem. (For more on explication, see page 702 in Chapter 27, "Reading and the Writing Process.") After reviewing the elements of poetry covered in the preceding chapters, Rose read the poem (which follows) several times, paying careful attention to diction, figurative language, irony, symbol, rhythm, sound, and so on. Her final paper is more concerned with the overall effect of the combination of elements than with a line-by-line breakdown, and her annotated version of the poem details her attention to that task. As you read and reread "Death Be Not Proud," keep notes on how *you* think the elements of this poem work together and to what overall effect.

JOHN DONNE (1572–1631)

John Donne, now regarded as a major poet of the early seventeenth century, wrote love poems at the beginning of his career but shifted to religious themes after converting from Catholicism to Anglicanism in the early 1590s. Although trained in law, he was also ordained a priest and became dean of St. Paul's Cathedral in London in 1621. The following poem, from "Holy Sonnets," reflects both his religious faith and his ability to create elegant arguments in verse.

Courtesy of the National Portrait Gallery, London.

Death Be Not Proud   *1611*

Death be not proud, though some have callèd thee
Mighty and dreadful, for thou art not so;
For those whom thou think'st thou dost overthrow
Die not, poor Death, nor yet canst thou kill me.
From rest and sleep, which but thy pictures° be,   *images*   5
Much pleasure; then from thee much more must flow,
And soonest our best men with thee do go,
Rest of their bones, and soul's delivery.°   *deliverance*
Thou art slave to Fate, Chance, kings, and desperate men,
And dost with Poison, War, and Sickness dwell;   10
And poppy or charms can make us sleep as well,
And better than thy stroke; why swell'st° thou then?   *swell with pride*
One short sleep past, we wake eternally
And death shall be no more; Death, thou shalt die.

CONSIDERATIONS FOR CRITICAL THINKING AND WRITING

1. **FIRST RESPONSE.** Why doesn't the speaker fear death? Explain why you find the argument convincing or not.

2. How does the speaker compare death with rest and sleep in lines 5 to 8? What is the point of this comparison?

3. Discuss the poem's rhythm by examining the breaks and end-stopped lines. How does the poem's rhythm contribute to its meaning?

4. What are the signs that this poem is structured as a sonnet?

ASKING QUESTIONS ABOUT THE ELEMENTS

After reading a poem, use the Questions for Responsive Reading and Writing (p. 59) to help you think, talk, and write about any poem. Before you do, though, be sure that you have read the poem several times without worrying actively about interpretation. With poetry, as with all literature, it's important to allow yourself the pleasure of enjoying whatever makes itself apparent to you. On subsequent readings, use the questions to understand and appreciate how the poem works; remember to keep in mind that not all questions will necessarily be relevant to a particular poem. A good starting point is to ask yourself what elements are exemplified in the parts of the poem that especially interest you. Then ask the Questions for Responsive Reading and Writing that relate to those elements. Finally, as you begin to get a sense of what elements are important to the poem and how those elements fit together, it often helps to put your impressions on paper.

A SAMPLE CLOSE READING

An Annotated Version of "Death Be Not Proud"

As she read the poem closely several times, Rose annotated it with impressions and ideas that would lead to insights on which her analysis would be built. Her close examination of the poem's elements allowed her to understand how its parts contribute to its overall effect; her annotations provide a useful map of her thinking.

Speaker scolds Death.

In formal diction, speaker personifies and rebukes Death for undeserved pride.

Most lines are iambic pentameter, but first two begin with stressed syllables for emphasis.

Death Be Not Proud   *1611*

Death be not proud, though some have callèd
    thee
Mighty and dreadful, for thou art not so;
For those whom thou think'st thou dost
    overthrow
Die not, poor Death, nor yet canst thou
    kill me.
From rest and sleep, which but thy
    pictures° be,   *images*   5
Much pleasure; then from thee much more
    must flow,

Death cannot kill speaker, who even taunts Death.

Death is only like sleep rather than something eternal.

And soonest our best men with thee do go,

Rest of their bones, and soul's

    delivery.°   *deliverance*

Thou art slave to Fate, Chance, kings, and

    desperate men,

And dost with Poison, War, and Sickness

    dwell;   10

And poppy or charms can make us sleep

    as well,

And better than thy stroke; why

    swell'st° thou then?   *swell with pride*

One short sleep past, we wake eternally

And death shall be no more; Death, thou

    shalt die.

Margin note (top right): Each quatrain (4-line stanza) develops the argument that Death is ultimately weak and cannot be justly proud or rightly feared, building toward the conclusion of final two lines.

Margin note (right): Rather than a power, Death is a slave to other forces.

Margin note (left): Argument in the couplet climaxes with allusion to humanity's resurrection and death of Death itself. In addition to Christianity, does sonnet form finally control Death too?

A SAMPLE FIRST RESPONSE

After Rose carefully read "Death Be Not Proud" and had a sense of how the elements work, she took the first step toward a formal explication by writing informally about the relevant elements and addressing the question *Why doesn't the speaker fear death? Explain why you find the argument convincing or not.* Note that at this point, she was not as concerned with textual evidence and detail as she would need to be in her final paper.

I've read the poem "Death Be Not Proud" by John Donne a few times now, and I have a sense of how it works. The poem is a sonnet, and each of the three quatrains presents a piece of the argument that Death should not be proud, because it is not really all-powerful, and may even be a source of pleasure. As a reader, I resist this seeming paradox at first, but I know it must be a trick, a riddle of some sort that the poem will proceed to untangle. I think one of the reasons the poem comes off as such a powerful statement is that Donne at first seems to be playful and paradoxical in his characterizations of Death. He's almost teasing Death. But beneath the teasing tone you feel the strong foundation of the real reason Death should not be proud—Donne's faith in the immortality of the soul. The poem begins to feel more solemn as it progresses, as the hints at the idea of immortality become more clearly articulated.

Donne utilizes two literary conventions to increase the effect of this poem: he uses the convention of personifying death, so that he can address it directly, and he uses the metaphor of death as a kind of sleep. These two things determine the tone and the progression from playful to solemn in the poem.

The last clause of the poem (line 14) plays with the paradoxical-seeming character of what he's been declaring. Ironically, it seems the only thing susceptible to death is death itself. Or, when death becomes powerless is when it only has power over itself.

ORGANIZING YOUR THOUGHTS

Showing in a paper how different elements of a particular poem work together is often quite challenging. While you may have a clear intuitive sense of what elements are important to the poem and how they complement one another, it is important to organize your thoughts in such a way as to make the relationships clear to your audience. The simplest way is to go line by line, but that can quickly become rote for writer and reader. Because you will want to organize your paper in the way that best serves your thesis, it may help to write an informal outline that charts how you think the argument moves. You may find, for example, that the argument is not persuasive if you start with the final lines and go back to the beginning of the poem or passage. However you decide to organize your argument, keep in mind that a single idea, or thesis, will have to run throughout the entire paper.

A SAMPLE INFORMAL OUTLINE

In her informal outline (following), Rose discovers that her argument works best if she begins at the beginning. Note that, though her later paper concerns itself with how several elements of poetry contribute to the poem's theme and message, her informal outline concerns itself much more with what that message is and how it develops as the poem progresses. She will fill in the details later.

Thesis: *From the very first word, addressing "Death" directly, Donne uses the literary conventions of personifying death and comparing it to sleep to begin an argument that Death should not be proud of its might or dreadfulness. But these two elements of his argument come to be seen as the superficial points when the true reason for death's powerlessness becomes clear. The Christian belief in the immortality of the soul is the reason for death's powerlessness and likeness to sleep.*

Body of essay: *Show how argument proceeds by quatrains from playful address to Death, and statement that Death is much like sleep, its "picture," to statement that Death is "slave" to other forces (and so should not be proud of being the mightiest), to the couplet, which articulates clearly the idea of immortality and gives the final paradox, "Death, thou shalt die."*

Conclusion: *Donne's faith in the immortality of the soul enables him to "prove" in this argument that Death is truly like its metaphorical representation, sleep. Faith allows him to derive a source for this conventional trope, and it allows him to state his truth in paradoxes. He relies on the conventional idea that death is an end, and a conqueror, and the only all-powerful force, to make the paradoxes that lend his argument the force of mystery — the mystery of faith.*

THE ELEMENTS AND THEME

As you create an informal outline, your understanding of the poem will grow, change, and finally, solidify. You will develop a much clearer sense of what the poem's elements combine to create, and you will have chosen a scheme for organizing your argument. The next step before drafting is to determine the paper's thesis, which will not only keep your paper focused but will also help you center your thoughts. For papers that discuss how the elements of poetry come together, the thesis is a single and concise statement of what the elements combine to create — the idea around which all the elements revolve. In the earlier discussion of Robert Herrick's "Delight in Disorder," for example, the two elements, rhythm and rhyme, work together to create the speaker's self-directed irony. To state this as a thesis, we might say that by making his own rhythm and rhyme "too precise," Herrick's speaker is making fun of himself while complimenting a certain type of woman. (You may ask yourself if he's doing a little flirting.)

Once you understand how all of the elements of the poem fit together and have articulated your understanding in the thesis statement, the next step is to flesh out your argument. By including quotations from the poem to illustrate the points you will be making, you will better explain exactly how each element relates to the others and, more specifically, to your thesis, and you will have created a finished paper that helps readers navigate the poem's geography.

A SAMPLE EXPLICATION

The Use of Conventional Metaphors for Death in John Donne's "Death Be Not Proud"

In Rose's final draft, she focuses on the use of metaphor in "Death Be Not Proud." Her essay provides a coherent reading that relates each line of the poem to the speaker's intense awareness of death. Although the essay discusses each stanza in order, the introductory paragraph provides a brief overview explaining how the poem's metaphor and arguments contribute to its total meaning. In addition, Rose does not hesitate to discuss a line out of sequence when it can be usefully connected to another phrase. She also works quotations into her sentences to support her points. When she adds something to a quotation to clarify it, she encloses her words in brackets so that they will not be mistaken for the poet's, and she uses a slash to indicate line divisions: "soonest . . . with thee do go, / [for] Rest of their bones, and soul's delivery." Finally, Rose is sure to cite the line numbers for any direct quotations from the poem. As you read through her final draft, remember that the word *explication* comes from the Latin *explicare,* "to unfold." How successful do you think Rose is at unfolding this poem to reveal how its elements — here ranging from metaphor, structure, meter, personification, paradox, and irony to theme — contribute to its meaning?

Bostwick 1

Rose Bostwick

English 101

Professor Hart

February 24, 2009

The Use of Conventional Metaphors for Death

in John Donne's "Death Be Not Proud"

In the sonnet that begins "Death be not proud . . ." John Donne argues that death is not "mighty and dreadful" but is more like its metaphorical representation, sleep. Death, Donne puts forth, is even a source of pleasure and rest. The poet builds this argument on two foundations. One is made up of the metaphors and literary conventions for death: death is compared with sleep and is often personified so that it can be addressed directly. The poem is an address to death that at first seems paradoxical and somewhat playful, but which then rises in all the emotion of faith as it reveals the second foundation of the argument—the Christian belief in the immortality of the soul. Seen against the backdrop of this belief, death loses its powerful threat and is seen as only a metaphorical sleep, or rest.

[margin note] Thesis providing interpretation of the poem's use of metaphor and how it contributes to the poem's central argument.

Discussion of how form and meter contribute to the poem's central argument.

    The poem is an ironic argument that proceeds according to the structure of the sonnet form. Each quatrain contains a new development or aspect of the argument, and the final couplet serves as a conclusion. The metrical scheme is mainly iambic pentameter, but in several places in the poem, the stress pattern is altered for emphasis. For example, the first foot of the poem is inverted, so that "Death," the first word, receives the stress. This announces to us right away that Death is being personified and addressed. This inversion also serves to begin the poem energetically and forcefully. The second line behaves in the same way. The first syllable of "Mighty" receives the stress, emphasizing the meaning of the word and its assumed relation to Death.

Discussion of how personification contributes to the poem's central argument.

    This first quatrain offers the first paradox and sets up the argument that death has been conventionally personified with the wrong attributes, might and dreadfulness. The poet tells death not to be proud, "though some have called thee / Mighty and dreadful," because, he says, death is "not so" (lines 1–2). Donne will turn this conventional characterization of death on its head with the paradox of the third and fourth lines: he says the people overthrown by death (as if by a conqueror) "Die not, poor death, nor yet canst thou kill me." These lines establish the paradox of death not being able to cause death.

Discussion of how metaphor of sleep and idea of immortality support the poem's central argument.

    The next quatrain will not begin to answer the question of why this paradox is so, but will posit another slight paradox—the idea of death as pleasurable. In lines 5–8, Donne uses the literary convention of describing death as a metaphorical sleep, or rest, to construct the argument that death must give pleasure: "From rest and sleep, which but thy pictures be, / Much pleasure; then from thee much more must flow" (5–6). At this point, the argument seems almost playful, but is carefully hinting at the solemnity of the deeper foundation of the belief in immortality. The metaphor of sleep for death includes the idea of waking; one doesn't sleep forever. The next two lines put forth the idea that death is pleasurable enough to be desired by "our best men" who "soonest . . . with thee do go, / [for] Rest of their bones, and soul's delivery" (7–8). This last line comes closer to announcing the true reason for death's powerlessness and pleasure: it is the way to the "soul's delivery" from the body and life on earth, and implicitly, into another, better realm.

A new reason for death's powerlessness arises in the next four lines. The poet says to death:

> Thou art slave to Fate, Chance, kings, and desperate men,
>
> And dost with Poison, War, and Sickness dwell;
>
> And poppy or charms can make us sleep as well,
>
> And better than thy stroke; why swell'st thou then? (9–12)

Donne argues here that there are forces more powerful than death that actually control it. Fate and chance determine when death occurs, and to whom it comes. Kings, with the powers of law and war, can summon death and throw it on whom they wish. And desperate men, murderers or suicides, can also summon death with the strength of their emotions. In lines 11 and 12, Donne again uses the metaphor of death as a kind of sleep, but says that drugs or "charms" give one a better sleep than death. And he asks playfully why death should be so proud, after all these illustrations of its weakness have been given: "why swell'st thou then?" (12).

Finally, with the last couplet, Donne reveals the true, deeper reason behind his argument that death should not be proud of its power. These lines also offer an explanation of the metaphor for death of sleep, or rest: "One short sleep past, we wake eternally / And death shall be no more; Death, thou shalt die" (13–14). After death, the soul lives on, according to Christian theology and belief. In the Christian heaven, where the soul is immortal, death will no longer exist, and so this last paradox, "Death, thou shalt die," becomes true. Again in this line, a significant inversion of metrical stress occurs. "Death," in the second clause, receives the stress, recalling the first line, emphasizing that it is an address and giving the clause a forceful sense of finality. His belief in the immortality of the soul enables Donne to "prove" in this argument that death is in actuality like its metaphorical representation, sleep. His faith allows him to derive a source for this conventional metaphor and to "disprove" the metaphor of death as an all-powerful conqueror. His Christian beliefs also allow him to state his truth in paradoxes, the mysteries that are justified by the mystery of faith.

Discussion of how language and tone contribute to the poem's central argument.

Discussion of function of religious faith in the poem and how word order and meter create emphasis.

Conclusion supporting thesis in context of poet's beliefs.

Bostwick 4

Work Cited

Donne, John. "Death Be Not Proud." *Poetry: An Introduction.* Ed. Michael
Meyer. 6th ed. Boston: Bedford/St. Martin's, 2010. 300. Print.

Before you begin writing your own paper on poetry, review the Suggestions for Approaching Poetry (pp. 38–39) and Chapter 2, "Writing about
Poetry," particularly the Questions for Responsive Reading and Writing
(pp. 59–60). These suggestions and questions will help you to focus
and sharpen your critical thinking and writing. You'll also find help in
Chapter 27, "Reading and the Writing Process," which offers a systematic
overview of choosing a topic, developing a thesis, and organizing various
types of assignments. If you use outside sources for the paper, be sure to
acknowledge them adequately by using the conventional documentation
procedures detailed in Chapter 28, "The Literary Research Paper."

Web Research
John Donne at
bedfordstmartins.com/
rewritinglit.

Approaches
to Poetry

12

A Study of Emily Dickinson

My business is circumference.

— EMILY DICKINSON

In this chapter you'll find a variety of poems by Emily Dickinson so that you can study her work in some depth. While this collection is not wholly representative of her work, it does offer enough poems to suggest some of the techniques and concerns that characterize her writings. The poems speak not only to readers but also to one another. That's natural enough: the more familiar you are with a writer's work, the easier it is to perceive and enjoy the strategies and themes the poet uses. If you are asked to write about a number of poems by the same author, you may find useful the Questions for Writing about an Author in Depth (p. 352) and the sample paper on Dickinson's attitudes toward religious faith in four of her poems (pp. 355-58).

Explore contexts
for Emily Dickinson
on *LiterActive*.

Emily E. Dickinson.

This daguerreotype of Emily Dickinson, taken shortly after her sixteenth birthday, and the silhouette (*opposite page*), created when she was fourteen years old, are the only authenticated mechanically produced images of the poet.

A BRIEF BIOGRAPHY

Emily Dickinson (1830–1886) grew up in a prominent and prosperous household in Amherst, Massachusetts. Along with her younger sister, Lavinia, and older brother, Austin, she experienced a quiet and reserved family life headed by her father, Edward Dickinson. In a letter to Austin at law school, she once described the atmosphere in her father's house as

(*Below*) This recently discovered print of a mid-1850s daguerreotype, acquired by the scholar Philip F. Gura in 2000, may represent the poet in her twenties.
By permission of the Collection of Philip and Leslie Gura.
(*Right*) The silhouette shows Dickinson at age fourteen.
Amherst College Archives and Special Collections. Used by permission of the Trustees of Amherst College.

Edward Dickinson.
By permission of the Houghton Library, Harvard University.

Letter from Emily Dickinson to cousin William Cowper Dickinson.
Courtesy of the Todd-Bingham Picture Collection, Manuscripts and Archives, Yale University Library. © The President and Fellows of Yale University.

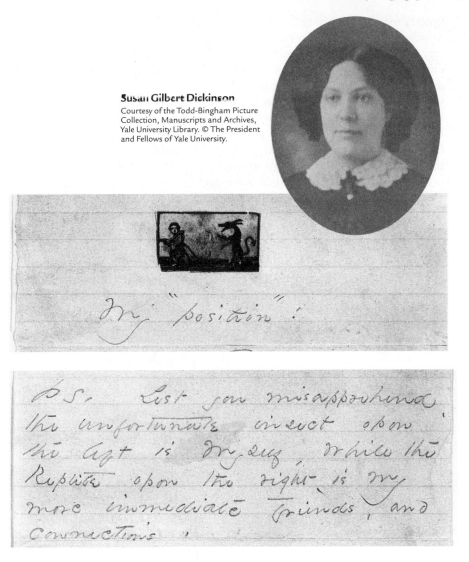

Susan Gilbert Dickinson
Courtesy of the Todd-Bingham Picture
Collection, Manuscripts and Archives,
Yale University Library. © The President
and Fellows of Yale University.

Letter from Emily Dickinson to Susan Gilbert Dickinson.
By permission of the Houghton Library, Harvard University MS Am 1118.5 (B114). © The President and Fellows of Harvard
College.

(*Opposite page*) Shown here are the poet's father, Edward Dickinson, a prominent public
figure in Amherst, and a page from a letter sent to her cousin William Cowper Dickinson.
Emily Dickinson sometimes included in her correspondence images cut from books and
magazines. This illustrated letter reads, "Life is but a Strife — / T'is a bubble — / T'is a dream — /
And man is but a little *boat* / Which paddles down the stream —"

(*This page*) Following a party held next door at the home of Dickinson's brother, Austin, and
sister-in-law Susan (*top*), the poet was reprimanded by her father for staying out too late. The
next day, Dickinson wrote a playful note to Susan that included a cartoon poking fun at her
father. The note reads, "My 'position'" and features an image of a young person pursued by
a dragonlike creature, cut from the Dickinsons' copy of the *New England Primer*, a book of
moral lessons. The note concludes: "P.S. — Lest you misapprehend, the unfortunate insect
upon the *left* is Myself, while the Reptile upon the *right*, is my more immediate friends, and
connections [*sic*]."

"pretty much all sobriety." Her mother, Emily Norcross Dickinson, was not as powerful a presence in her life; she seems not to have been as emotionally accessible as Dickinson would have liked. Her daughter is said to have characterized her as not the sort of mother "to whom you hurry when you are troubled." Both parents raised Dickinson to be a cultured Christian woman who would one day be responsible for a family of her own. Her father attempted to protect her from reading books that might "joggle" her mind, particularly her religious faith, but Dickinson's individualistic instincts and irreverent sensibilities created conflicts that did not allow her to fall into step with the conventional piety, domesticity, and social duty prescribed by her father and the orthodox Congregationalism of Amherst.

The Dickinsons were well known in Massachusetts. Her father was a lawyer and served as the treasurer of Amherst College (a position Austin eventually took up as well), and her grandfather was one of the college's founders. Although nineteenth-century politics, economics, and social issues do not appear in the foreground of her poetry, Dickinson lived in a family environment that was steeped in them: her father was an active town official and served in the General Court of Massachusetts, the state senate, and the U.S. House of Representatives.

Dickinson, however, withdrew not only from her father's public world but also from almost all social life in Amherst. She refused to see most people, and aside from a single year at South Hadley Female Seminary (now Mount Holyoke College), one excursion to Philadelphia and Washington, and several brief trips to Boston to see a doctor about eye problems, she lived all her life in her father's house. She dressed only in white and developed a reputation as a reclusive eccentric. Dickinson selected her own society carefully and frugally. Like her poetry, her relationship to the world was intensely reticent. Indeed, during the last twenty years of her life she rarely left the house.

Though Dickinson never married, she had significant relationships with several men who were friends, confidants, and mentors. She also enjoyed an intimate relationship with her friend Susan Huntington Gilbert, who became her sister-in-law by marrying Austin. Susan and her husband lived next door and were extremely close with Dickinson. Biographers have attempted to find in a number of her relationships the source for the passion of some of her love poems and letters. Several possibilities have been put forward as the person she addressed in three letters as "Dear Master": Benjamin Newton, a clerk in her father's office who talked about books with her; Samuel Bowles, editor of the *Springfield Republican* and friend of the family; the Reverend Charles Wadsworth, a Presbyterian preacher with a reputation for powerful sermons; and an old friend and widower, Judge Otis P. Lord. Despite these speculations, no biographer has been able to identify definitively the object of Dickinson's love. What matters, of course, is not with whom she was in love — if, in fact, there was any single person — but that she wrote about such passions so intensely and convincingly in her poetry.

Choosing to live life internally within the confines of her home, Dickinson brought her life into sharp focus, for she also chose to live within the limitless expanses of her imagination—a choice she was keenly aware of and which she described in one of her poems this way: "I dwell in Possibility—" (p. 332). Her small circle of domestic life did not impinge on her creative sensibilities. Like Henry David Thoreau, she simplified her life so that doing without was a means of being within. In a sense she redefined the meaning of deprivation because being denied something—whether faith, love, literary recognition, or some other desire—provided a sharper, more intense understanding than she would have experienced had she achieved what she wanted: "'Heaven,'" she wrote, "is what I cannot reach!" This poem (p. 326)—along with many others, such as "Water, is taught by thirst" (p. 323) and "Success is counted sweetest / By those who ne'er succeed" (p. 322)—suggests just how persistently she saw deprivation as a way of sensitizing herself to the value of what she was missing. For Dickinson, hopeful expectation was always more satisfying than achieving a golden moment. Perhaps that's one reason she was so attracted to John Keats's poetry (see, for example, his "Ode on a Grecian Urn," p. 94).

Dickinson enjoyed reading Keats as well as Emily and Charlotte Brontë; Robert and Elizabeth Barrett Browning; Alfred, Lord Tennyson; and George Eliot. Even so, these writers had little or no effect on the style of her writing. In her own work she was original and innovative, but she did draw on her knowledge of the Bible, classical myths, and Shakespeare for allusions and references in her poetry. She also used contemporary popular church hymns, transforming their standard rhythms into free-form hymn meters. Among American writers she appreciated Ralph Waldo Emerson and Thoreau, but she apparently felt Walt Whitman was better left unread. She once mentioned to Thomas Wentworth Higginson, a leading critic with whom she corresponded about her poetry, that as for Whitman "I never read his Book—but was told that he was disgraceful" (for the kind of Whitman poetry she had been warned against, see his "I Sing the Body Electric," p. 273). Nathaniel Hawthorne, however, intrigued her with his faith in the imagination and his dark themes: "Hawthorne appals—entices," a remark that might be used to describe her own themes and techniques.

AN INTRODUCTION TO HER WORK

Today, Dickinson is regarded as one of America's greatest poets, but when she died at the age of fifty-six after devoting most of her life to writing poetry, her nearly two thousand poems—only a dozen of which were published, anonymously, during her lifetime—were unknown except to a small number of friends and relatives. Dickinson was not recognized as a major poet until the twentieth century, when modern readers ranked her as a major new voice whose literary innovations were unmatched by any other nineteenth-century poet in the United States.

Dickinson neither completed many poems nor prepared them for publication. She wrote her drafts on scraps of paper, grocery lists, and the backs of recipes and used envelopes. Early editors of her poems took the liberty of making them more accessible to nineteenth-century readers when several volumes of selected poems were published in the 1890s. The poems were made to appear like traditional nineteenth-century verse by assigning them titles, rearranging their syntax, normalizing their grammar, and regularizing their capitalizations. Instead of dashes, editors used standard punctuation; instead of the highly elliptical telegraphic lines so characteristic of her poems, editors added articles, conjunctions, and prepositions to make them more readable and in line with conventional expectations. In addition, the poems were made more predictable by organizing them into categories such as friendship, nature, love, and death. Not until 1955, when Thomas Johnson published Dickinson's complete works in a form that attempted to be true to her manuscript versions, did readers have the opportunity to see the full range of her style and themes.

Like that of Robert Frost, Dickinson's popular reputation has sometimes relegated her to the role of a New England regionalist who writes quaint uplifting verses that touch the heart. In 1971 that image was mailed first class all over the country by the U.S. Postal Service. In addition to issuing a commemorative stamp featuring a portrait of Dickinson, the Postal Service affixed the stamp to a first-day-of-issue envelope that included an engraved rose and one of her poems. Here's the poem chosen from among the nearly two thousand she wrote:

If I can stop one Heart from breaking   *c. 1864*

If I can stop one Heart from breaking
I shall not live in vain
If I can ease one Life the Aching
or cool one Pain

Or help one fainting Robin
Unto his Nest again
I shall not live in Vain.

This is typical not only of many nineteenth-century popular poems but also of the kind of verse that can be found in contemporary greeting cards. The speaker tells us what we imagine we should think about and makes the point simply with a sentimental image of a "fainting Robin." To point out that robins don't faint or that altruism isn't necessarily the only rule of conduct by which one should live one's life is to make trouble for this poem. Moreover, its use of language is unexceptional; the metaphors used, like that robin, are a bit weary. If this poem were characteristic of Dickinson's poetry, the U.S. Postal Service probably would not have been urged to issue a stamp in her honor, nor would you be reading her poems in this anthology or many others. Here's a poem by Dickinson that is more typical of her writing:

If I shouldn't be alive

c. 1860

If I shouldn't be alive
When the Robins come,
Give the one in Red Cravat,
A Memorial crumb.

If I couldn't thank you,
Being fast asleep,
You will know I'm trying
With my Granite lip!

This poem is more representative of Dickinson's sensibilities and techniques. Although the first stanza sets up a rather mild concern that the speaker might not survive the winter (a not uncommon fear for those who fell prey to pneumonia, for example, during Dickinson's time), the concern can't be taken too seriously — a gentle humor lightens the poem when we realize that all robins have red cravats and are therefore the speaker's favorite. Furthermore, the euphemism that describes the speaker "Being fast asleep" in line 6 makes death seem not so threatening after all. But the sentimental expectations of the first six lines — lines that could have been written by any number of popular nineteenth-century writers — are dashed by the penultimate word of the last line. *Granite* is the perfect word here because it forces us to reread the poem and to recognize that it's not about feeding robins or offering a cosmetic treatment of death; rather, it's a bone-chilling description of a corpse's lip that evokes the cold, hard texture and grayish color of tombstones. These lips will never say "thank you" or anything else.

Instead of the predictable rhymes and sentiments of "If I can stop one Heart from breaking," this poem is unnervingly precise in its use of language and tidily points out how much emphasis Dickinson places on an individual word. Her use of near rhyme with "asleep" and "lip" brilliantly mocks a euphemistic approach to death by its jarring dissonance. This is a better poem, not because it's grim or about death, but because it demonstrates Dickinson's skillful use of language to produce a shocking irony.

Dickinson found irony, ambiguity, and paradox lurking in the simplest and commonest experiences. The materials and subject matter of her poetry are quite conventional. Her poems are filled with robins, bees, winter light, household items, and domestic duties. These materials represent the range of what she experienced in and around her father's house. She used them because they constituted so much of her life and, more important, because she found meanings latent in them. Though her world was simple, it was also complex in its beauties and its terrors. Her lyric poems capture impressions of particular moments, scenes, or moods, and she characteristically focuses on topics such as nature, love, immortality, death, faith, doubt, pain, and the self.

Though her materials were conventional, her treatment of them was innovative because she was willing to break whatever poetic conventions stood in the way of the intensity of her thought and images. Her conciseness, brevity, and wit are tightly packed. Typically she offers her observations via one or two images that reveal her thought in a powerful manner. She once characterized her literary art by writing, "My business is circumference." Her method is to reveal the inadequacy of declarative statements by evoking qualifications and questions with images that complicate firm assertions and affirmations. In one of her poems she describes her strategies this way: "Tell all the Truth but tell it slant—/ Success in Circuit lies" (p. 340). This might well stand as a working definition of Dickinson's aesthetics and is embodied in the following poem:

The Thought beneath so slight a film —   c. 1860

The Thought beneath so slight a film —
Is more distinctly seen —
As laces just reveal the surge —
Or Mists — the Apennine°

Italian mountain range

Paradoxically, "Thought" is more clearly understood precisely because a slight "film"—in this case language—covers it. Language, like lace, enhances what it covers and reveals it all the more—just as a mountain range is more engaging to the imagination if it is covered in mists rather than starkly presenting itself. Poetry for Dickinson intensifies, clarifies, and organizes experience.

Dickinson's poetry is challenging because it is radical and original in its rejection of most traditional nineteenth-century themes and techniques. Her poems require active engagement from the reader because she seems to leave out so much with her elliptical style and remarkable contracting metaphors. But these apparent gaps are filled with meaning if we are sensitive to her use of devices such as personification, allusion, symbolism, and startling syntax and grammar. Because her use of dashes is sometimes puzzling, it helps to read her poems aloud to hear how carefully the words are arranged. What might initially seem intimidating on a silent page can surprise the reader with meaning when heard. It's also worth keeping in mind that Dickinson was not always consistent in her views and that they can change from poem to poem, depending on how she felt at a given moment. For example, her definition of religious belief in " 'Faith' is a fine invention" (p. 354) reflects an ironically detached wariness in contrast to the faith embraced in "I never saw a Moor —" (p. 355). Dickinson was less interested in absolute answers to questions than she was in examining and exploring their "circumference."

Because Dickinson's poems are all relatively brief (none is longer than fifty lines), they invite browsing and sampling, but perhaps a useful way into their highly metaphoric and witty world is this "how to" poem that reads almost like a recipe:

To make a prairie it takes a clover and one bee   *date unknown*

To make a prairie it takes a clover and one bee,
One clover, and a bee,
And revery.
The revery alone will do,
If bees are few.

This quiet but infinite claim for a writer's imagination brings together the range of ingredients in Dickinson's world of domestic and ordinary natural details. Not surprisingly, she deletes rather than adds to the recipe, because the one essential ingredient is the writer's creative imagination. *Bon appétit.*

Chronology

1830	Born December 10 in Amherst, Massachusetts.
1840	Starts her first year at Amherst Academy.
1847–48	Graduates from Amherst Academy and attends South Hadley Female Seminary (now Mount Holyoke College).
1855	Visits Philadelphia and Washington, D.C.
1857	Ralph Waldo Emerson lectures in Amherst.
1862	Starts corresponding with Thomas Wentworth Higginson, asking for advice about her poems.
1864	Visits Boston for eye treatments.
1870	Higginson visits her in Amherst.
1873	Higginson visits her for a second and final time.
1874	Her father dies in Boston.
1875	Her mother suffers from paralysis.
1882	Her mother dies.

1886   Dies on May 15 in Amherst, Massachusetts.

1890   First edition of her poetry, edited by Mabel Loomis Todd and Thomas Wentworth Higginson, is published.

1955   Thomas H. Johnson publishes *The Poems of Emily Dickinson* in three volumes, thereby making available her poetry known to that date.

Success is counted sweetest   *c. 1859*

Success is counted sweetest
By those who ne'er succeed.
To comprehend a nectar
Requires sorest need.

Not one of all the purple Host   5
Who took the Flag today
Can tell the definition
So clear of Victory

As he defeated — dying —
On whose forbidden ear   10
The distant strains of triumph
Burst agonized and clear!

CONSIDERATIONS FOR CRITICAL THINKING AND WRITING

1. **FIRST RESPONSE.** How is "success" defined in this poem? To what extent does that definition agree with your own understanding of the word?
2. What do you think is meant by the use of "comprehend" in line 3? How can a nectar be comprehended?
3. Why do the defeated understand victory better than the victorious?
4. Discuss the effect of the poem's final line.

CONNECTION TO ANOTHER SELECTION

1. In an essay compare the themes of this poem with those of John Keats's "Ode on a Grecian Urn" (p. 94).

Some things that fly there be —   *c. 1859*

Some things that fly there be —
Birds — Hours — the Bumblebee —
Of these no Elegy.

Some things that stay there be —
Grief — Hills — Eternity —
Nor this behooveth me.

There are that resting, rise.
Can I expound the skies?
How still the Riddle lies!

CONSIDERATIONS FOR CRITICAL THINKING AND WRITING

1. **FIRST RESPONSE.** Given the question the speaker raises in line 8, what do you suppose is the nature of the "Riddle" (line 9) in this poem?

2. What distinction is made between the "things that fly" in the first stanza and the "things that stay" in the second stanza?

3. Discuss the connotative value of the diction in line 7. How might this suggest some possible themes for the poem?

Water, is taught by thirst   *c. 1859*

Water, is taught by thirst.
Land — by the Oceans passed.
Transport — by throe —
Peace — by its battles told —
Love, by Memorial Mold —
Birds, by the Snow.

CONSIDERATIONS FOR CRITICAL THINKING AND WRITING

1. **FIRST RESPONSE.** Which image in the poem do you find most powerful? Explain why.

2. How is the paradox of each line of the poem resolved? How is the first word of each line "taught" by the phrase that follows it?

3. **CREATIVE RESPONSE.** Try your hand at writing similar lines in which something is "taught."

CONNECTIONS TO OTHER SELECTIONS

1. What does this poem have in common with "Success is counted sweetest" (p. 322)? Which poem do you think is more effective? Explain why.

2. How is the crucial point of this poem related to "I like a look of Agony" (p. 328)?

Safe in their Alabaster Chambers —   *1859 version*

Safe in their Alabaster Chambers —
Untouched by Morning
And untouched by Noon —
Sleep the meek members of the Resurrection —
Rafter of satin,   5
And Roof of stone.

Light laughs the breeze
In her Castle above them —
Babbles the Bee in a stolid Ear,
Pipe the Sweet Birds in ignorant cadence —   10
Ah, what sagacity perished here!

Safe in their Alabaster Chambers —   *1861 version*

Safe in their Alabaster Chambers —
Untouched by Morning —
And untouched by Noon —
Lie the meek members of the Resurrection —
Rafter of Satin — and Roof of Stone!   5

Grand go the Years — in the Crescent — above them —
Worlds scoop their arcs —
And Firmaments — row —
Diadems — drop — and Doges° — surrender —
Soundless as dots — on a Disc of Snow —   10

9 *Doges:* Chief magistrates of Venice from the twelfth to the sixteenth centuries.

CONSIDERATIONS FOR CRITICAL THINKING AND WRITING

1. **FIRST RESPONSE.** Dickinson permitted the 1859 version of this poem, entitled "The Sleeping," to be printed in the *Springfield Republican*. The second version she sent privately to Thomas Wentworth Higginson. Why do you suppose she would agree to publish the first but not the second version?

2. Are there any significant changes in the first stanzas of the two versions? If you answered yes, explain the significance of the changes.

3. Describe the different kinds of images used in the two second stanzas. How do those images affect the tones and meanings of those stanzas?

4. Discuss why you prefer one version of the poem to the other.

CONNECTIONS TO OTHER SELECTIONS

1. Compare the theme in the 1861 version with the theme of Robert Frost's "Design" (p. 386).

2. In an essay discuss the attitude toward death in the 1859 version and in "Apparently with no surprise" (p. 355).

Portraits are to daily faces   *c. 1860*

Portraits are to daily faces
As an Evening West,
To a fine, pedantic sunshine —
In a satin Vest!

CONSIDERATIONS FOR CRITICAL THINKING AND WRITING

1. **FIRST RESPONSE.** Dickinson once described her literary art this way: "My business is circumference." Does this poem fit her characterization of her poetry?

2. How is the basic strategy of this poem similar to the following statement: "Doorknob is to door as button is to sweater"?

3. Identify the four metonymies in the poem. Pay close attention to their connotative meanings.

4. If you don't know the meaning of "pedantic" (line 3), look it up in a dictionary. How does its meaning affect your reading of "fine" (line 3)?

CONNECTIONS TO OTHER SELECTIONS

1. Compare Dickinson's view of poetry in this poem with Robert Francis's perspective in "Catch" (p. 26). What important similarities and differences do you find?

2. Write an essay describing Robert Frost's strategy in "Mending Wall" (p. 370) or "Birches" (p. 377) as the "business of circumference."

3. How is the theme of this poem related to the central idea in "The Thought beneath so slight a film —" (p. 320)?

4. Compare the use of the word "fine" here with its use in "'Faith' is a fine invention" (p. 354).

Some keep the Sabbath going to Church —   *c. 1860*

Some keep the Sabbath going to Church —
I keep it, staying at Home —
With a Bobolink for a Chorister —
And an Orchard, for a Dome —

Some keep the Sabbath in Surplice°   *holy robes*   5
I just wear my Wings —
And instead of tolling the Bell, for Church,
Our little Sexton — sings.

God preaches, a noted Clergyman —
And the sermon is never long,   10
So instead of getting to Heaven, at last —
I'm going, all along.

CONSIDERATIONS FOR CRITICAL THINKING AND WRITING

1. **FIRST RESPONSE.** What is the effect of referring to "Some" people (line 1)?

2. Characterize the speaker's tone.

3. How does the speaker distinguish himself or herself from those who go to church?

4. How might "Surplice" (line 5) be read as a pun?

5. According to the speaker, how should the Sabbath be observed?

CONNECTION TO ANOTHER SELECTION

1. Write an essay that discusses nature in this poem and in Walt Whitman's "When I Heard the Learn'd Astronomer" (p. 650).

"Heaven" — is what I cannot reach!   c. 1861

"Heaven" — is what I cannot reach!
The Apple on the Tree —
Provided it do hopeless — hang —
That — "Heaven" is — to Me!

The Color, on the Cruising Cloud —   5
The interdicted Land —
Behind the Hill — the House behind —
There — Paradise — is found!

Her teasing Purples — Afternoons —
The credulous — decoy —   10
Enamored — of the Conjuror —
That spurned us — Yesterday!

CONSIDERATIONS FOR CRITICAL THINKING AND WRITING

1. **FIRST RESPONSE.** How does the speaker define heaven? How does that definition compare with conventional views of heaven?

2. Look up the myth of Tantalus and explain the allusion in line 3.

3. Given the speaker's definition of heaven, how do you think he or she would describe hell?

CONNECTIONS TO OTHER SELECTIONS

1. Write an essay that discusses desire in this poem and in "Water, is taught by thirst" (p. 323).

2. Discuss the speakers' attitudes toward pleasure in this poem and in Sharon Olds's "Last Night" (p. 84).

"Hope" is the thing with feathers —   c. 1861

"Hope" is the thing with feathers —
That perches in the soul —
And sings the tune without the words —
And never stops — at all —

And sweetest — in the Gale — is heard —   5
And sore must be the storm —
That could abash the little Bird
That kept so many warm —

I've heard it in the chillest land —
And on the strangest Sea —   10
Yet, never, in Extremity,
It asked a crumb — of Me.

CONSIDERATIONS FOR CRITICAL THINKING AND WRITING

1. **FIRST RESPONSE.** Why do you think the speaker defines hope in terms of a bird? Why is this metaphor more appropriate than, say, a dog?

2. Discuss the effects of the rhymes in each stanza.

3. What is the central point of the poem?

CONNECTIONS TO OTHER SELECTIONS

1. Compare the tone of this definition of hope with that of "'Faith' is a fine invention" (p. 354). How is "Extremity" (line 11) handled differently than the "Emergency" (4) in the latter poem?

2. Compare the strategies used to define hope in this poem and heaven in the preceding poem, "'Heaven' — is what I cannot reach!" Which poem, in your opinion, creates a more successful definition? In an essay explain why.

The Robin's my Criterion for Tune—   c. 1861

The Robin's my Criterion for Tune —
Because I grow — where Robins do —
But, were I Cuckoo born —
I'd swear by him —
The ode familiar — rules the Noon —   5
The Buttercup's, my Whim for Bloom —
Because, we're Orchard sprung —
But, were I Britain born,
I'd Daisies spurn —
None but the Nut — October fit —   10
Because, through dropping it,
The Seasons flit — I'm taught —
Without the Snow's Tableau
Winter, were lie — to me —
Because I see — New Englandly—   15
The Queen, discerns like me —
Provincially —

CONSIDERATIONS FOR CRITICAL THINKING AND WRITING

1. **FIRST RESPONSE.** What does this poem suggest about the importance Dickinson invests in the sense of place in her poetry?

2. How does the dictionary define *provincial*? How does the speaker define *provincial* in the poem?

3. Choose another Dickinson poem from the collection in this anthology and explain how the poet sees "New Englandly" (line 15) in it.

I like a look of Agony   c. 1861

I like a look of Agony,
Because I know it's true —
Men do not sham Convulsion,
Nor simulate, a Throe —

The Eyes glaze once — and that is Death —
Impossible to feign
The Beads upon the Forehead
By homely Anguish strung.

CONSIDERATIONS FOR CRITICAL THINKING AND WRITING

1. **FIRST RESPONSE.** Why does the speaker "like a look of Agony"? How do you respond to her appreciation of "Convulsion" (line 3)?

2. Discuss the image of "The Eyes glaze once —" (line 5). Why is that a particularly effective metaphor for death?

3. Characterize the speaker. One critic described the voice in this poem as "almost a hysterical shriek." Explain why you agree or disagree.

CONNECTION TO ANOTHER SELECTION

1. Write an essay on Dickinson's attitudes toward pain and deprivation, using this poem and " 'Heaven' — is what I cannot reach!" (p. 326).

Wild Nights — Wild Nights!   c. 1861

Wild Nights — Wild Nights!
Were I with thee
Wild Nights should be
Our luxury!

Futile — the Winds —   5
To a Heart in port —
Done with the Compass —
Done with the Chart!

Rowing in Eden —
Ah, the Sea!   10
Might I but moor — Tonight —
In Thee!

CONSIDERATIONS FOR CRITICAL THINKING AND WRITING

1. **FIRST RESPONSE.** Thomas Wentworth Higginson, Dickinson's mentor, once said he was afraid that some "malignant" readers might "read into [a poem like this] more than that virgin recluse ever dreamed of putting there." What do you think?

2. Look up the meaning of *luxury* in a dictionary. Why does this word work especially well here?

3. Given the imagery of the final stanza, do you think the speaker is a man or a woman? Explain why.

4. **CRITICAL STRATEGIES.** Read the section on psychological strategies (pp. 670–72) in Chapter 26, "Critical Strategies for Reading." What do you think this poem reveals about the author's personal psychology?

CONNECTION TO ANOTHER SELECTION

1. Write an essay that compares the voice, figures of speech, and theme of this poem with those of Margaret Atwood's "you fit into me" (p. 135).

What Soft — Cherubic Creatures —   *1862*

What Soft — Cherubic Creatures —
These Gentlewomen are —
One would as soon assault a Plush —
Or violate a Star —

Such Dimity° Convictions —   *sheer cotton fabric* 5
A Horror so refined
Of freckled Human Nature —
Of Deity — ashamed —

It's such a common — Glory —
A Fisherman's — Degree —   10
Redemption — Brittle Lady —
Be so — ashamed of Thee —

CONSIDERATIONS FOR CRITICAL THINKING AND WRITING

1. **FIRST RESPONSE.** Characterize the "Gentlewomen" in this poem.

2. How do the sounds produced in the first line help to reinforce meaning?

3. What are "Dimity Convictions" (line 5), and what do they make "Of freckled Human Nature" (line 7)?

4. Discuss the irony in the final stanza.

CONNECTION TO ANOTHER SELECTION

1. How are the "Gentlewomen" in this poem similar to the "Gentlemen" in "'Faith' is a fine invention" (p. 354)?

The Soul selects her own Society —   *c. 1862*

The Soul selects her own Society —
Then — shuts the Door —
To her divine Majority —
Present no more —

Manuscript page for "What Soft—Cherubic Creatures—" (p. 329), taken from one of Dickinson's forty fascicles—small booklets hand-sewn with white string that contained her poetry as well as other miscellaneous writings. These fascicles are important for Dickinson scholars, as this manuscript page makes clear: her style to some extent resists translation into the conventions of print.

Unmoved — she notes the Chariots — pausing —   5
At her low Gate —
Unmoved — an Emperor be kneeling
Upon her Mat —

I've known her — from an ample nation —
Choose One —   10
Then — close the Valves of her attention —
Like Stone —

CONSIDERATIONS FOR CRITICAL THINKING AND WRITING

1. **FIRST RESPONSE.** Characterize the speaker. Is she self-reliant and self-sufficient? cold? angry?

2. Why do you suppose the "Soul" in this poem is female? Would it make any difference if it were male?

3. Discuss the effect of the images in the final two lines. Pay particular attention to the meanings of "Valves" in line 11.

Much Madness is divinest Sense —   *c. 1862*

Much Madness is divinest Sense —
To a discerning Eye —
Much Sense — the starkest Madness —
'Tis the Majority
In this, as All, prevail —
Assent — and you are sane —
Demur — you're straightway dangerous —
And handled with a Chain —

CONSIDERATIONS FOR CRITICAL THINKING AND WRITING

1. **FIRST RESPONSE.** Thomas Wentworth Higginson's wife once referred to Dickinson as the "partially cracked poetess of Amherst." Assuming that Dickinson had some idea of how she was regarded by "the Majority" (line 4), how might this poem be seen as an insight into her life?

2. Discuss the conflict between the individual and society in this poem. Which images are used to describe each? How do these images affect your attitudes about them?

3. Comment on the effectiveness of the poem's final line.

CONNECTION TO ANOTHER SELECTION

1. Discuss the theme of self-reliance in this poem and in the preceding poem, "The Soul selects her own Society —."

I dwell in Possibility —   *c. 1862*

I dwell in Possibility —
A fairer House than Prose —
More numerous of Windows —
Superior — for Doors —

Of Chambers as the Cedars —   5
Impregnable of Eye —
And for an Everlasting Roof
The Gambrels° of the Sky —   *angled roofs*

Of Visitors — the fairest —
For Occupation — This —   10
The spreading wide my narrow Hands
To gather Paradise —

CONSIDERATIONS FOR CRITICAL THINKING AND WRITING

1. **FIRST RESPONSE.** What distinction is made between poetry and prose in this poem? Explain why you agree or disagree with the speaker's distinctions.

2. What is the poem's central metaphor in the second and third stanzas?

3. How does the use of metaphor in this poem become a means for the speaker to envision and create a world beyond the circumstances of his or her actual life?

CONNECTIONS TO OTHER SELECTIONS

1. Compare what this poem says about poetry and prose with T. E. Hulme's comments in "On the Differences between Poetry and Prose" (p. 132).

2. How can the speaker's sense of expansiveness in this poem be reconciled with the speaker's insistence on contraction in "The Soul selects her own Society —" (p. 329)? Are these poems contradictory? Explain why or why not.

They dropped like Flakes —   *1862*

They dropped like Flakes —
They dropped like Stars —
Like Petals from a Rose —
When suddenly across the June
A wind with fingers — goes —

They perished in the Seamless Grass —
No eye could find the place —
But God can summon every face
On his Repealless — List.

CONSIDERATIONS FOR CRITICAL THINKING AND WRITING

1. **FIRST RESPONSE.** How are the similes in the first three lines related to one another?

2. What do you think is happening in lines 4–5?

3. Explain why you find the final two lines either alarming or comforting.

CONNECTION TO ANOTHER SELECTION

1. Compare the tone and themes of this poem with those in "Apparently with no surprise" (p. 355).

After great pain, a formal feeling comes —   *c. 1862*

After great pain, a formal feeling comes —
The Nerves sit ceremonious, like Tombs —
The stiff Heart questions was it He, that bore,
And Yesterday, or Centuries before?

The Feet, mechanical, go round —   5
Of Ground, or Air, or Ought —
A Wooden way
Regardless grown,
A Quartz contentment, like a stone —

This is the Hour of Lead —   10
Remembered, if outlived,
As Freezing persons, recollect the Snow —
First — Chill — then Stupor — then the letting go —

CONSIDERATIONS FOR CRITICAL THINKING AND WRITING

1. **FIRST RESPONSE.** What do you think has caused the speaker's pain?

2. How does the rhythm of the lines create a slow, somber pace?

3. Discuss why "the Hour of Lead" (line 10) could serve as a useful title for this poem.

CONNECTIONS TO OTHER SELECTIONS

1. How might this poem be read as a kind of sequel to "The Bustle in a House" (p. 339)?

2. Write an essay that discusses this poem in relation to Robert Frost's "Home Burial" (p. 372).

Pain — has an Element of Blank —   *c. 1862*

Pain — has an Element of Blank —
It cannot recollect
When it begun — or if there were
A time when it was not —

It has no Future — but itself —
Its Infinite contain
Its Past — enlightened to perceive
New Periods — of Pain.

CONSIDERATIONS FOR CRITICAL THINKING AND WRITING

1. **FIRST RESPONSE.** What does the speaker say is the relationship between pain and time?
2. Explain why you think this poem refers primarily to physical or emotional pain — or both.
3. Comment on Dickinson's choice of "enlightened" in line 7. Why do you suppose she didn't choose a word like *fated* or *doomed*?

CONNECTION TO ANOTHER SELECTION

1. Consider the significance of pain in this poem and in Dickinson's "I like a look of Agony" (p. 328).

The Morning after Wo —   *c. 1862*

The Morning after Wo —
'Tis frequently the Way —
Surpasses all that rose before —
For utter Jubilee —

As Nature did not care —   5
And piled her Blossoms on —
And further to parade a Joy
Her Victim stared upon —

The Birds declaim their Tunes —
Pronouncing every word   10
Like Hammers — Did they know they fell
Like Litanies of Lead —

On here and there — a creature —
They'd modify the Glee
To fit some Crucifixel Clef —   15
Some Key of Calvary —

CONSIDERATIONS FOR CRITICAL THINKING AND WRITING

1. **FIRST RESPONSE.** How does the diction of this poem serve to identify the nature of the "Wo" in line 1?

2. Paraphrase the disjuncture the speaker describes between what the "Victim" (line 8) experiences and how "Nature" (5) responds to wo.

3. Examine carefully Dickinson's use of sound and rhythm and explain how that affects tone.

CONNECTION TO ANOTHER SELECTION

1. Compare the themes of "The Morning after Wo—" and "The Bustle in a House" (p. 339).

I heard a Fly buzz—when I died—   *c. 1862*

I heard a Fly buzz—when I died—
The Stillness in the Room
Was like the Stillness in the Air—
Between the Heaves of Storm—

The Eyes around—had wrung them dry—   5
And Breaths were gathering firm
For that last Onset—when the King
Be witnessed—in the Room—

I willed my Keepsakes—Signed away
What portion of me be   10
Assignable—and then it was
There interposed a Fly—

With Blue—uncertain stumbling Buzz—
Between the light—and me—
And then the Windows failed—and then   15
I could not see to see—

CONSIDERATIONS FOR CRITICAL THINKING AND WRITING

1. **FIRST RESPONSE.** What was expected to happen "when the King" was "witnessed" (lines 7–8)? What happened instead?

2. Why do you think Dickinson chooses a fly rather than perhaps a bee or gnat?

3. What is the effect of the last line? Why not end the poem with "I could not see" instead of the additional "to see"?

4. Discuss the sounds in the poem. Are there any instances of onomatopoeia?

CONNECTIONS TO OTHER SELECTIONS

1. Contrast the symbolic significance of the fly with that of the spider in Walt Whitman's "A Noiseless Patient Spider" (p. 150).

2. Consider the meaning of "light" (line 14) in this poem and in "There's a certain Slant of light" (p. 703).

3. Compare the themes in Dickinson's poem and in Herbert Lomas's "The Fly's Poem about Emily" (p. 98).

One need not be a Chamber — to be Haunted —

c. 1863

One need not be a Chamber — to be Haunted —
One need not be a House —
The Brain has Corridors — surpassing
Material Place —

Far safer, of a Midnight Meeting   5
External Ghost
Than its interior Confronting —
That Cooler Host.

Far safer, through an Abbey gallop,
The Stones a'chase —   10
Than Unarmed, one's a'self encounter —
In lonesome Place —

Ourself behind ourself, concealed —
Should startle most —
Assassin hid in our Apartment   15
Be Horror's least.

The Body — borrows a Revolver —
He bolts the Door —
O'erlooking a superior spectre —
Or More —   20

CONSIDERATIONS FOR CRITICAL THINKING AND WRITING

1. **FIRST RESPONSE.** Paraphrase the poem. Which stanza is most difficult to paraphrase? Why?
2. What is the poem's controlling metaphor? Explain why you think it is effective or not.
3. What is the "superior spectre" in line 19?

CONNECTIONS TO OTHER SELECTIONS

1. Compare and contrast this poem with Edgar Allan Poe's "The Haunted Palace" (p. 160) and Jim Stevens's "Schizophrenia" (p. 150). In an essay explain which poem you find the most frightening.

Because I could not stop for Death —

c. 1863

Because I could not stop for Death —
He kindly stopped for me —
The Carriage held but just Ourselves —
And Immortality.

We slowly drove — He knew no haste   5
And I had put away
My labor and my leisure too,
For His Civility —

We passed the School, where Children strove
At Recess — in the Ring —
We passed the Fields of Gazing Grain —
We passed the Setting Sun —

Or rather — He passed Us —
The Dews drew quivering and chill —
For only Gossamer, my Gown —
My Tippet° — only Tulle —

    10

    15
    shawl

We paused before a House that seemed
A Swelling of the Ground —
The Roof was scarcely visible —
The Cornice — in the Ground —

    20

Since then — 'tis Centuries — and yet
Feels shorter than the Day
I first surmised the Horses' Heads
Were toward Eternity —

CONSIDERATIONS FOR CRITICAL THINKING AND WRITING

1. **FIRST RESPONSE.** Why couldn't the speaker "stop for Death"?
2. How is death personified in this poem? How does the speaker respond to him? Why are they accompanied by Immortality?
3. What is the significance of the things they "passed" in the third stanza?
4. What is the "House" in lines 17–20?
5. Discuss the rhythm of the lines. How, for example, is the rhythm of line 14 related to its meaning?

CONNECTIONS TO OTHER SELECTIONS

1. Compare the tone of this poem with that of Dickinson's "Apparently with no surprise" (p. 355).
2. Write an essay comparing Dickinson's view of death in this poem and in "If I shouldn't be alive" (p. 319). Which poem is more powerful for you? Explain why.

I felt a Cleaving in my Mind —

    c. 1864

I felt a Cleaving in my Mind —
As if my Brain had split —
I tried to match it — Seam by Seam —
But could not make them fit.

The thought behind, I strove to join
Unto the thought before —
But Sequence ravelled out of Sound
Like Balls — upon a Floor.

CONSIDERATIONS FOR CRITICAL THINKING AND WRITING

1. **FIRST RESPONSE.** What is going on in the speaker's mind?
2. What is the poem's controlling metaphor? Describe the simile in lines 7 and 8. How does it clarify the first stanza?
3. Discuss the rhymes. How do they reinforce meaning?

CONNECTION TO ANOTHER SELECTION

1. Compare the power of the speaker's mind described here with the power of imagination described in "To make a prairie it takes a clover and one bee" (p. 321).

A Light exists in Spring   *c. 1864*

A Light exists in Spring
Not present on the Year
At any other period —
When March is scarcely here

A Color stands abroad   5
On Solitary Fields
That Science cannot overtake
But Human Nature feels.

It waits upon the Lawn,
It shows the furthest Tree   10
Upon the furthest Slope you know
It almost speaks to you.

Then as Horizons step
Or Noons report away
Without the Formula of sound   15
It passes and we stay —

A quality of loss
Affecting our Content
As Trade had suddenly encroached
Upon a Sacrament.   20

CONSIDERATIONS FOR CRITICAL THINKING AND WRITING

1. **FIRST RESPONSE.** Based on Dickinson's description, how would you characterize the nature of the light on a New England March day? How is that light different from that of a summer's day?
2. What kinds of feelings are evoked in the speaker by the light?
3. How are "Science" and "Trade" (lines 7, 19) depicted in contrast to what "Human Nature feels" (8)?

CONNECTION TO ANOTHER SELECTION

1. Compare Dickinson's thematic use of light in this poem and in "There's a certain Slant of light" (p. 703).

Oh Sumptuous moment   *c. 1868*

Oh Sumptuous moment
Slower go
That I may gloat on thee —
'Twill never be the same to starve
Now I abundance see —

Which was to famish, then or now —
The difference of Day
Ask him unto the Gallows led —
With morning in the sky

CONSIDERATIONS FOR CRITICAL THINKING AND WRITING

1. **FIRST RESPONSE.** How do the sounds of the first stanza contribute to its meaning?
2. What kind of experience do you imagine the speaker is describing?
3. How do the final three lines shed light on the meaning of lines 1 to 6?

CONNECTIONS TO OTHER SELECTIONS

1. Compare and contrast the themes of this poem, "Water, is taught by thirst" (p. 323), and "'Heaven' — is what I cannot reach!" (p. 326).

The Bustle in a House   *c. 1866*

The Bustle in a House
The Morning after Death
Is solemnest of industries
Enacted upon Earth —

The Sweeping up the Heart
And putting Love away
We shall not want to use again
Until Eternity.

CONSIDERATIONS FOR CRITICAL THINKING AND WRITING

1. **FIRST RESPONSE.** What is the relationship between love and death in this poem?
2. Why do you think mourning (notice the pun in line 2) is described as industry?

3. Discuss the tone of the poem's ending. Consider whether you think it is hopeful, sad, resigned, or some other mood.

CONNECTIONS TO OTHER SELECTIONS

1. Compare this poem with "After great pain, a formal feeling comes—" (p. 333). Which poem is, for you, a more powerful treatment of mourning?
2. How does this poem qualify "I like a look of Agony" (p. 328)? Does it contradict the latter poem? Explain why or why not.

Tell all the Truth but tell it slant—   *c. 1868*

Tell all the Truth but tell it slant—
Success in Circuit lies
Too bright for our infirm Delight
The Truth's superb surprise

As Lightning to the Children eased
With explanation kind
The Truth must dazzle gradually
Or every man be blind—

CONSIDERATIONS FOR CRITICAL THINKING AND WRITING

1. **FIRST RESPONSE.** What do you think the first line means? Why should truth be told "slant" and circuitously?
2. How does the second stanza explain the first?
3. How is this poem an example of its own theme?

CONNECTIONS TO OTHER SELECTIONS

1. How does the first stanza of "I know that He exists" (p. 354) suggest an idea similar to this poem's? Why do you think the last eight lines of the former aren't similar in theme to this poem?
2. Write an essay on Dickinson's attitudes about the purpose and strategies of poetry by considering this poem as well as "The Thought beneath so slight a film—" (p. 320) and "Portraits are to daily faces" (p. 324).

There is no Frigate like a Book   *c. 1873*

There is no Frigate like a Book
To take us Lands away
Nor any Coursers like a Page
Of prancing Poetry—

This Traverse may the poorest take
Without oppress of Toll—
How frugal is the Chariot
That bears the Human soul.

CONSIDERATIONS FOR CRITICAL THINKING AND WRITING

1. **FIRST RESPONSE.** Which lines present reading as a mode of transportation? Why do you think that is an effective controlling metaphor in a poem about the value of books?

2. How does the poem's rhythm suggest a kind of "prancing Poetry" (line 4)?

CONNECTION TO ANOTHER SELECTION

1. Compare the use of extended metaphor in this poem with that in "I dwell in Possibility—" (p. 332). How consistent is the use of extended metaphor in each poem, and what is the effect?

Fame is the one that does not stay —   c. 1879

Fame is the one that does not stay—
Its occupant must die
Or out of sight of estimate
Ascend incessantly—
Or be that most insolvent thing
A Lightning in the Germ—
Electrical the embryo
But we demand the Flame

CONSIDERATIONS FOR CRITICAL THINKING AND WRITING

1. **FIRST RESPONSE.** How is "fame" defined in this poem? Does the definition seem to correspond with what you know of Dickinson's relationship to fame?

2. Check a dictionary for definitions of "Germ" (line 6). How is Dickinson using the word?

3. Discuss the possible meanings of the final two lines.

CONNECTION TO ANOTHER SELECTION

1. To what extent might Dickinson's "Success is counted sweetest" (p. 322) serve as a commentary on this poem?

Perspectives on Emily Dickinson

EMILY DICKINSON

A Description of Herself   1862

Mr Higginson,
    Your kindness claimed earlier gratitude – but I was ill – and write today, from my pillow.
    Thank you for the surgery – it was not so painful as I supposed. I bring you others° – as you ask – though they might not differ –
    While my thought is undressed – I can make the distinction, but when I put them in the Gown – they look alike, and numb.
    You asked how old I was? I made no verse — but one or two° — until this winter – Sir –
    I had a terror – since September – I could tell to none – and so I sing, as the Boy does by the Burying Ground – because I am afraid – You inquire my Books – For Poets – I have Keats – and Mr and Mrs Browning. For Prose – Mr Ruskin – Sir Thomas Browne – and the Revelations. I went to school – but in your manner of the phrase – had no education. When a little Girl, I had a friend, who taught me Immortality – but venturing too near, himself – he never returned – Soon after, my Tutor, died – and for several years, my Lexicon – was my only companion – Then I found one more – but he was not contented I be his scholar – so he left the Land.
    You ask of my Companions Hills – Sir – and the Sundown – and a Dog – large as myself, that my Father bought me – They are better than Beings – because they know – but do not tell – and the noise in the Pool, at Noon – excels my Piano. I have a Brother and Sister – My Mother does not care for thought – and Father, too busy with his Briefs – to notice what we do – He buys me many Books – but begs me not to read them – because he fears they joggle the Mind. They are religious – except me – and address an Eclipse, every morning – whom they call their "Father." But I fear my story fatigues you – I would like to learn – Could you tell me how to grow – or is it unconveyed – like Melody – or Witchcraft?

From a letter to Thomas Wentworth Higginson, April 25, 1862

others: Dickinson had sent poems to Higginson for his opinions and enclosed more with this letter.   *one or two:* Actually she had written almost 300 poems.

CONSIDERATIONS FOR CRITICAL THINKING AND WRITING

1. What impression does this letter give you of Dickinson?
2. What kinds of thoughts are there in the foreground of her thinking?
3. To what extent is the style of her letter writing like that of her poetry?

Thomas Wentworth Higginson (1823–1911)

On Meeting Dickinson for the First Time   1870

A large county lawyer's house, brown brick, with great trees & a garden — I sent up my card. A parlor dark & cool & stiffish, a few books & engravings & an open piano. . . .

A step like a pattering child's in entry & in glided a little plain woman with two smooth bands of reddish hair & a face a little like Belle Dove's; not plainer — with no good feature — in a very plain & exquisitely clean white pique & a blue net worsted shawl. She came to me with two day lilies which she put in a sort of childlike way into my hand & said "These are my introduction" in a soft frightened breathless childlike voice — & added under her breath Forgive me if I am frightened; I never see strangers & hardly know what I say — but she talked soon & thenceforward continuously — & deferentially — sometimes stopping to ask me to talk instead of her — but readily recommencing . . . thoroughly ingenuous & simple . . . & saying many things which you would have thought foolish & I wise — & some things you wd. hv. liked. I add a few over the page. . . .

> "Women talk; men are silent; that is why I dread women."
> "My father only reads on Sunday — he reads *lonely* & *rigorous* books."
> "If I read a book [and] it makes my whole body so cold no fire ever can warm me I know *that* is poetry. If I feel physically as if the top of my head were taken off, I know *that* is poetry. These are the only ways I know it. Is there any other way."
> "How do most people live without any thoughts. There are many people in the world (you must have noticed them in the street) How do they live. How do they get strength to put on their clothes in the morning"
> "When I lost the use of my Eyes it was a comfort to think there were so few real *books* that I could easily find some one to read me all of them"
> "Truth is such a *rare* thing it is delightful to tell it."
> "I find ecstasy in living — the mere sense of living is joy enough"
> I asked if she never felt want of employment, never going off the place & never seeing any visitor "I never thought of conceiving that I could ever have the slightest approach to such a want in all future time" (& added) "I feel that I have not expressed myself strongly enough."

From a letter to his wife, August 16, 1870

Considerations for Critical Thinking and Writing

1. How old is Dickinson when Higginson meets her? Does this description seem commensurate with her age? Explain why or why not.

2. Choose one of the quotations from Dickinson that Higginson includes and write an essay about what it reveals about her.

MABEL LOOMIS TODD (1856–1932)

The Character *of Amherst*   *1881*

I must tell you about the *character* of Amherst. It is a lady whom the people call the *Myth*. She is a sister of Mr. Dickinson, & seems to be the climax of all the family oddity. She has not been outside of her own house in fifteen years, except once to see a new church, when she crept out at night, & viewed it by moonlight. No one who calls upon her mother & sister ever see her, but she allows little children once in a great while, & one at a time, to come in, when she gives them cake or candy, or some nicety, for she is very fond of little ones. But more often she lets down the sweetmeat by a string, out of a window, to them. She dresses wholly in white, & her mind is said to be perfectly wonderful. She writes finely, but no one *ever* sees her. Her sister, who was at Mrs. Dickinson's party, invited me to come & sing to her mother sometime. . . . People tell me the *myth* will hear every note — she will be near, but unseen. . . . Isn't that like a book? So interesting.

                                        From a letter to her parents, November 6, 1881

CONSIDERATIONS FOR CRITICAL THINKING AND WRITING

1. Todd, who in the 1890s would edit Dickinson's poems and letters, had known her for only two months when she wrote this letter. How does Todd characterize Dickinson?

2. Does this description seem positive or negative to you? Explain your answer.

3. A few of Dickinson's poems, such as "Much Madness is divinest Sense —" (p. 331), suggest that she was aware of this perception of her. Refer to her poems in discussing Dickinson's response to this perception.

RICHARD WILBUR (B. 1921)

On Dickinson's Sense of Privation   *1960*

What did Emily Dickinson do, as a poet, with her sense of privation? One thing she quite often did was to pose as the laureate and attorney of the empty-handed, and question God about the economy of His creation. Why, she asked, is a fatherly God so sparing of His presence? Why is there never a sign that prayers are heard? Why does Nature tell us no comforting news of its Maker? Why do some receive a whole loaf, while others must starve on a crumb? Where is the benevolence in shipwreck and earthquake? By asking such questions as these, she turned complaint into critique, and used her own sufferings as experiential evidence about the nature of the deity. The God who emerges from these poems is a God who does not answer, an unrevealed God whom one cannot confidently approach through Nature or through doctrine.

But there was another way in which Emily Dickinson dealt with her sentiment of lack — another emotional strategy which was both more frequent and more fruitful. I refer to her repeated assertion of the paradox that privation is more plentiful than plenty; that to renounce is to possess the more; that "The

Banquet of abstemiousness / Defaces that of wine." We all know how the poet illustrated this ascetic paradox in her behavior—how in her latter years she chose to live in relative retirement, keeping the world, even in its dearest aspects, at a physical remove. She would write her friends, telling them how she missed them, then flee upstairs when they came to see her; afterward, she might send a note of apology, offering the odd explanation that "We shun because we prize." Any reader of Dickinson biographies can furnish other examples, dramatic or homely, of this prizing and shunning, this yearning and renouncing: in my own mind's eye is a picture of Emily Dickinson watching a gay circus caravan from the distance of her chamber window.

> From "Sumptuous Destitution" in *Emily Dickinson: Three Views,*
> by Richard Wilbur, Louise Bogan, and Archibald MacLeish

Considerations for Critical Thinking and Writing

1. Which poems by Dickinson reprinted in this anthology suggest that she was "the laureate and attorney of the empty-handed"?
2. Which poems suggest that "privation is more plentiful than plenty"?
3. Of these two types of poems, which do you prefer? Write an essay that explains your preference.

Sandra M. Gilbert (b. 1936) and
Susan Gubar (b. 1944)

On Dickinson's White Dress   *1979*

Today a dress that the Amherst Historical Society assures us is *the* white dress Dickinson wore—or at least one of her "Uniforms of Snow"—hangs in a drycleaner's plastic bag in the closet of the Dickinson homestead. Perfectly preserved, beautifully flounced and tucked, it is larger than most readers would have expected this self-consciously small poet's dress to be, and thus reminds visiting scholars of the enduring enigma of Dickinson's central metaphor, even while it draws gasps from more practical visitors, who reflect with awe upon the difficulties of maintaining such a costume. But what exactly did the literal and figurative whiteness of this costume represent? What rewards did it offer that would cause an intelligent woman to overlook those practical difficulties? Comparing Dickinson's obsession with whiteness to [Herman] Melville's, William R. Sherwood suggests that "it reflected in her case the Christian mystery and not a Christian enigma . . . a decision to announce . . . the assumption of a worldly death that paradoxically involved regeneration." This, he adds, her gown—"a typically slant demonstration of truth"—should have revealed "to anyone with the wit to catch on."[1]

We might reasonably wonder, however, if Dickinson herself consciously intended her wardrobe to convey any one message. The range of associations

[1] *Circumference and Circumstance: Stages in the Mind and Art of Emily Dickinson* (New York: Columbia UP, 1968) 152, 231.

her white poems imply suggests, on the contrary, that for her, as for Melville, white is the ultimate symbol of enigma, paradox, and irony, "not so much a color as the visible absence of color, and at the same time the concrete of all colors." Melville's question [in *Moby-Dick*] might, therefore, also be hers: "is it for these reasons that there is such a dumb blankness, full of meaning, in a wide landscape of snows—a colorless, all-color of atheism from which we shrink?" And his concluding speculation might be hers too, his remark "that the mystical cosmetic which produces every one of [Nature's] hues, the great principle of light, for ever remains white or colorless in itself, and if operating without medium upon matter, would touch all objects . . . with its own blank tinge." For white, in Dickinson's poetry, frequently represents both the energy (the white heat) of Romantic creativity, and the loneliness (the polar cold) of the renunciation or tribulation Romantic creativity may demand, both the white radiance of eternity—or Revelation—and the white terror of a shroud.

> From *The Madwoman in the Attic: The Woman Writer*
> *and the Nineteenth-Century Literary Imagination*

CONSIDERATIONS FOR CRITICAL THINKING AND WRITING

1. What meanings do Gilbert and Gubar attribute to Dickinson's white dress?

2. Discuss the meaning of the implicit whiteness in "Safe in their Alabaster Chambers—" (p. 323) and "After great pain, a formal feeling comes—" (p. 333). To what extent do these poems incorporate the meanings of whiteness that Gilbert and Gubar suggest?

3. What other reasons can you think of that might account for Dickinson's wearing only white?

CYNTHIA GRIFFIN WOLFF (B. 1935)

On the Many Voices in Dickinson's Poetry   *1986*

There were many "Voices." This fact has sometimes puzzled Dickinson's readers. One poem may be delivered in a child's Voice; another in the Voice of a young woman scrutinizing nature and the society in which she makes her place. Sometimes the Voice is that of a woman self-confidently addressing her lover in a language of passion and sexual desire. At still other times, the Voice of the verse seems so precariously balanced at the edge of hysteria that even its calmest observations grate like the shriek of dementia. There is the Voice of the housewife and the Voice that has recourse to the occasionally agonizing, occasionally regal language of the conversion experience of latter-day New England Puritanism. In some poems the Voice is distinctive principally because it speaks in the aftermath of wounding and can comprehend extremities of pain. Moreover, these Voices are not always entirely distinct from one another: the child's Voice that opens a poem may yield to the Voice of a young woman speaking the idiom of ardent love; in a different poem, the speaker may fall into a mood of almost religious contemplation in an attempt to analyze or define such abstract entities as loneliness or madness or eternity; the diction of the housewife may be conflated with the sovereign language of the New Jerusalem, and taken together, they may render some aspect of the word-smith's labor. No manageable set of discrete categories suffices to capture the diversity of discourse, and any attempt to simplify Dickinson's methods does violence to the verse.

Yet there is a paradox here. This is, by no stretch of the imagination, a body of poetry that might be construed as a series of lyrics spoken by many different people. Disparate as these many Voices are, somehow they all appear to issue from the same "self." . . . It is the enigmatic "Emily Dickinson" readers suppose themselves to have found in this poetry, even in the extreme case when Dickinson's supposed speaker is male. One explanation for this sense of intrinsic unity in the midst of diversity is the persistence with which Dickinson addresses the same set of problems, using a remarkably durable repertoire of linguistic modes. Evocations of injury and wounding—threats to the coherence of the self—appear in the earliest poems and continue until the end; ways of rendering face-to-face encounters change, but this preoccupation with "interview" is sustained by metaphors of "confrontation" that weave throughout. The summoning of one or another Voice in a given poem, then, is not an unself-conscious emotive reflection of Emily Dickinson's mood at the moment of creation. Rather, each different Voice is a calculated tactic, an attempt to touch her readers and engage them intimately with the poetry. Each Voice had its unique advantages; each its limitations. A poet self-conscious in her craft, she calculated this element as carefully as every other.

From *Emily Dickinson*

Considerations for Critical Thinking and Writing

1. From the poems in this anthology, try adding to the list of voices Wolff cites.
2. Despite the many voices in Dickinson's poetry, why, according to Wolff, is there still a "sense of intrinsic unity" in her poetry?
3. Choose a Dickinson poem and describe how the choice of voice is a "calculated tactic."

Paula Bennett (b. 1936)

On "I heard a Fly buzz—when I died —" 1990

Dickinson's rage against death, a rage that led her at times to hate both life and death, might have been alleviated, had she been able to gather hard evidence about an afterlife. But, of course, she could not. "The *Bareheaded life*— under the grass—," she wrote to Samuel Bowles in c. 1860, "worries one like a Wasp." If death was the gate to a better life in "the childhood of the kingdom of Heaven," as the sentimentalists—and Christ—claimed, then, perhaps, there was compensation and healing for life's woes. . . . But how do we know? What can we know? In "I heard a Fly buzz—when I died," Dickinson concludes that we do not know much. . . .

Like many people in her period, Dickinson was fascinated by death-bed scenes. How, she asked various correspondents, did this or that person die? In particular, she wanted to know if their deaths revealed any information about the nature of the afterlife. In this poem, however, she imagines her own death-bed scene, and the answer she provides is grim, as grim (and, at the same time, as ironically mocking) as anything she ever wrote.

In the narrowing focus of death, the fly's insignificant buzz, magnified tenfold by the stillness in the room, is all that the speaker hears. This kind of distortion in scale is common. It is one of the "illusions" of perception. But here it is horrifying because it defeats every expectation we have. Death is supposed to be an experience of awe. It is the moment when the soul, departing the body, is taken up by God. Hence the watchers at the bedside wait for the moment when the "King" (whether God or death) "be witnessed" in the room. And hence the speaker assigns away everything but that which she expects God (her soul) or death (her body) to take.

What arrives instead, however, is neither God nor death but a fly, "[w]ith Blue — uncertain — stumbling Buzz," a fly, that is, no more secure, no more sure, than we are. Dickinson had associated flies with death once before in the exquisite lament, "How many times these low feet / staggered." In this poem, they buzz "on the / chamber window," and speckle it with dirt, reminding us that the housewife, who once protected us from such intrusions, will protect us no longer. Their presence is threatening but only in a minor way, "dull" like themselves. They are a background noise we do not have to deal with yet.

In "I heard a Fly buzz," on the other hand, there is only one fly and its buzz is not only foregrounded. Before the poem is over, the buzz takes up the entire field of perception, coming between the speaker and the "light" (of day, of life, of knowledge). It is then that the "Windows" (the eyes that are the windows of the soul as well as, metonymically, the light that passes through the panes of glass) "fail" and the speaker is left in darkness — in death, in ignorance. She cannot "see" to "see" (understand).

Given that the only sure thing we know about "life after death" is that flies — in their adult form and more particularly, as maggots — devour us, the poem is at the very least a grim joke. In projecting her death-bed scene, Dickinson confronts her ignorance and gives back the only answer human knowledge can with any certainty give. While we may hope for an afterlife, no one, not even the dying, can prove it exists.

From *Emily Dickinson: Woman Poet*

CONSIDERATIONS FOR CRITICAL THINKING AND WRITING

1. According to Bennett, what is the symbolic value of the fly?

2. Does Bennett leave out any significant elements of the poem in her analysis? Explain why you think she did or did not.

3. Choose a Dickinson poem and write a detailed analysis that attempts to account for all of its major elements.

MARTHA NELL SMITH (B. 1953)

On "Because I could not stop for Death—"   1993

That this poem begins and ends with humanity's ultimate dream of self-importance — Immortality and Eternity — could well be the joke central to its meaning, for Dickinson carefully surrounds the fantasy of living ever after with the dirty facts of life — dusty carriage rides, schoolyards, and farmers' fields. Many may contend that, like the Puritans and metaphysicals before her, Dickinson pulls the sublime down to the ridiculous but unavoidable facts of existence, thus imbues life on earth with its real import. On the other hand, Dickinson may have argued otherwise. Very late in her life, she wrote, "When Jesus tells us about his Father, we distrust him. When he shows us his Home, we turn away, but when he confides to us that he is 'acquainted with Grief,' we listen, for that is also an Acquaintance of our own." Instead of sharing their faith, Dickinson may be showing the community around her, most of whom were singing "When we all get to Heaven what a day of rejoicing that will be," how selfishly selective is their belief in a system that bolsters egocentrism by assuring believers not only that their individual identities will survive death, but also that they are one of the exclusive club of the saved. Waiting for the return of Eden or Paradise, which "is always eligible" and which she "never believed . . . to be a superhuman site," those believers may simply find themselves gathering dust. Surrounded by the faithful, Dickinson struggled with trust and doubt in Christian promises herself, but whether she believed in salvation or even in immortality is endlessly debatable. Readers can select poems and letters and construct compelling arguments to prove that she did or did not. But for every declaration evincing belief, there is one like that to Elizabeth Holland:

> The Fiction of "Santa Claus" always reminds me of the reply to my early question of "Who made the Bible" — "Holy Men moved by the Holy Ghost," and though I have now ceased my investigations, the Solution is insufficient —

What "Because I could not stop for Death —" will not allow is any hard and fast conclusion to be drawn about the matter. Once again . . . by mixing tropes and tones Dickinson underscores the importance of refusing any single-minded response to a subject and implicitly attests to the power in continually opening possibilities by repeatedly posing questions.

From *Comic Power in Emily Dickinson,* by Suzanne Juhasz,
Cristanne Miller, and Martha Nell Smith

CONSIDERATIONS FOR CRITICAL THINKING AND WRITING

1. In what sense, according to Smith, could a joke be central to the meaning of "Because I could not stop for Death —"?

2. Compare the potential joke in this poem and in "I know that He exists" (p. 354). How is your reading of each poem influenced by considering them together?

3. Read the sample paper on "Religious Faith in Four Poems by Emily Dickinson" (pp. 355–58) and write an analysis of "Because I could not stop for Death —" that supports or refutes the paper's thesis.

RONALD WALLACE (B. 1945)

Miss Goff   *1994*

When Zack Pulanski brought the plastic vomit
and slid it slickly to the vinyl floor
and raised his hand, and her tired eyes fell on it
with horror, the heartless classroom lost in laughter
as the custodian slyly tossed his saw dust on it   5
and pushed it, grinning, through the door,
she reached into her ancient corner closet
and found some Emily Dickinson mimeos there

which she passed out. And then, herself
passed out on the cold circumference of her desk.   10
And everybody went their merry ways
but me, who, chancing on one unexpected phrase
after another, sat transfixed until dusk.
Me and Miss Goff, the top of our heads taken off.

CONSIDERATIONS FOR CRITICAL THINKING AND WRITING

1. How does the joke played on Miss Goff in the first stanza give way to something more serious in the second stanza? Explain the shift in tone.

2. Characterize Miss Goff. How does the poem's diction reveal some of her personality?

3. Dickinson once described her own poetry by writing that "my business is circumference," and she made an attempt to define poetry with this comment: "If I read a book [and] it makes my whole body so cold no fire ever can warm me, I know *that* is poetry. If I feel physically as if the top of my head were taken off, I know *that* is poetry." How are these statements relevant to your understanding of Wallace's poem?

4. Discuss the use of irony in "Miss Goff."

Two Complementary Critical Readings

CHARLES R. ANDERSON (1902–1999)

Eroticism in "Wild Nights — Wild Nights!"   *1960*

The frank eroticism of this poem might puzzle the biographer of a spinster, but the critic can only be concerned with its effectiveness as a poem. Unless one insists on taking the "I" to mean Emily Dickinson, there is not even any reversal of the lovers' roles (which has been charged, curiously enough, as a fault in this poem). The opening declaration — "Wild Nights should be / Our luxury!" — sets the key of her song, for *luxuria* included the meaning of lust as well as lavishness of sensuous enjoyment, as she was Latinist enough to know. This is echoed at the end in "Eden," her recurring image, in letters and poems, for the paradise of earthly love. The theme here is that of sexual passion which is lawless, outside the rule of "Chart" and "Compass." But it lives by a law of its own, the law of Eden, which protects it from mundane wind and wave.

This is what gives the magic to her climactic vision, "Rowing in Eden," sheltered luxuriously in those paradisiac waters while the wild storms of this world break about them. Such love was only possible before the Fall. Since then the bower of bliss is frugal of her leases, limiting each occupant to "an instant" she says in another poem, for "Adam taught her Thrift / Bankrupt once through his excesses." In the present poem she limits her yearning to the mortal term, just "Tonight." But this echoes the surge of ecstasy that initiated her song and gives the reiterated "Wild Nights!" a double reference, to the passionate experience in Eden as well as to the tumult of the world shut out by it. So she avoids the chief pitfall of the love lyric, the tendency to exploit emotion for its own sake. Instead she generates out of the conflicting aspects of love, its ecstasy and its brevity, the symbol that contains the poem's meaning.

From Emily Dickinson's Poetry: Stairway of Surprise

Considerations for Critical Thinking and Writing

1. According to Anderson, what is the theme of "Wild Nights — Wild Nights!"?
2. How does Anderson discuss the poem's "frank eroticism"? How detailed is his discussion?
3. If there is a "reversal of the lovers' roles" in this poem, do you think it represents, as some critics have charged, "a fault in this poem"? Explain why or why not.
4. Compare Anderson's treatment of this poem with David S. Reynolds's reading that follows. Discuss which one you find more useful and explain why.

David S. Reynolds (b. 1949)
Popular Literature and "Wild Nights — Wild Nights!"   1988

It is not known whether Dickinson had read any of the erotic literature of the day or if she knew of the stereotype of the sensual woman. Given her fascination with sensational journalism and with popular literature in general, it is hard to believe she would not have had at least some exposure to erotic literature. At any rate, her treatment of the daring theme of woman's sexual fantasy in this deservedly famous poem bears comparison with erotic themes as they appeared in popular sensational writings. The first stanza of the poem provides an uplifting or purification of sexual fantasy not distant from the effect of [Walt] Whitman's cleansing rhetoric, which, as we have seen, was consciously designed to counteract the prurience of the popular "love plot." Dickinson's repeated phrase "Wild Nights" is a simple but dazzling metaphor that communicates wild passion — even lust — but simultaneously lifts sexual desire out of the scabrous by fusing it with the natural image of the night. The second verse introduces a second nature image, the turbulent sea and the contrasting quiet port, which at once universalizes the passion and purifies it further by distancing it through a more abstract metaphor. Also, the second verse makes clear that this is not a poem of sexual consummation but rather of pure fantasy and sexual impossibility. Unlike popular erotic literature, the poem portrays neither a consummated seduction nor the heartless deception that it involves. There is instead a pure, fervent fantasy whose frustration is figured forth in the contrasting images of the ocean (the longed-for-but-never-achieved consummation) and the port (the reality of the poet's isolation). The third verse begins with an image, "Rowing in Eden," that further uplifts sexual passion by yoking it with a religious archetype. Here as elsewhere, Dickinson capitalizes nicely on the new religious style, which made possible such fusions of the divine and the earthly. The persona's concluding wish to "moor" in the sea expresses the sustained intense sexual longing and the simultaneous frustration of that longing. In the course of the poem, Dickinson has communicated great erotic passion, and yet, by effectively projecting this passion through unusual nature and religious images, has rid it of even the tiniest residue of sensationalism.

> From *Beneath the American Renaissance: The Subversive Imagination*
> *in the Age of Emerson and Melville*

CONSIDERATIONS FOR CRITICAL THINKING AND WRITING

1. According to Reynolds, how do Dickinson's images provide a "cleansing" effect in the poem?

2. Explain whether you agree that the poem portrays a "pure, fervent fantasy" or something else.

3. Does Reynolds's reading of the poem compete with Anderson's or complement it? Explain your answer.

4. Given the types of critical strategies described in Chapter 26, how would you characterize Anderson's and Reynolds's approaches?

Questions for Writing about an Author in Depth

As you read multiple works by the same author, you're likely to be struck by the similarities and differences in those selections. You'll begin to recognize situations, events, characters, issues, perspectives, styles, and strategies — even recurring words or phrases — that provide a kind of signature, making the poems in some way identifiable with that particular writer.

The following questions can help you to respond to multiple works by the same author. They should help you to listen to how a writer's works can speak to one another and to you. Additional useful questions can be found in other chapters of this book. See Chapter 2, "Writing about Poetry," and Arguing about Literature (p. 692) in Chapter 27, "Reading and the Writing Process."

1. What topics reappear in the writer's work? What seem to be the major concerns of the author?

2. Does the author have a definable worldview that can be discerned from work to work? Is, for example, the writer liberal, conservative, apolitical, or religious?

3. What social values come through in the author's work? Does he or she seem to identify with a particular group or social class?

4. Is there a consistent voice or point of view from work to work? Is it a persona or the author's actual self?

5. How much of the author's own life experiences and historical moment make their way into the works?

6. Does the author experiment with style from work to work, or are the works mostly consistent with one another?

7. Can the author's work be identified with a literary tradition, such as *carpe diem* poetry, that aligns his or her work with that of other writers?

8. What is distinctive about the author's writing? Is the language innovative? Are the themes challenging? Are the voices conventional? Is the tone characteristic?

9. Could you identify another work by the same author without a name being attached to it? What are the distinctive features that allow you to do so?

10. Do any of the writer's works seem *not* to be by that writer? Why?

11. What other writers are most like this author in style and content? Why?

12. Has the writer's work evolved over time? Are there significant changes or developments? Are there new ideas and styles, or do the works remain largely the same?

13. How would you characterize the author's writing habits? Is it possible to anticipate what goes on in different works, or are you surprised by their content or style?

14. Can difficult or ambiguous passages in a work be resolved by referring to a similar passage in another work?

15. What does the writer say about his or her own work? Do you trust the teller or the tale? Which do you think is more reliable?

A SAMPLE IN-DEPTH STUDY

The following paper was written for an assignment that called for an analysis (about 750 words) on any topic that could be traced in three or four poems by Dickinson. The student, Michael Weitz, chose "'Faith' is a fine invention," "I know that He exists," "I never saw a Moor—," and "Apparently with no surprise."

Previous knowledge of a writer's work can set up useful expectations in a reader. In the case of the four Dickinson poems included in this section, religion emerges as a central topic linked to a number of issues, including faith, immortality, skepticism, and the nature of God. The student selected these poems because he noticed Dickinson's intense interest in religious faith owing to the many poems that explore a variety of religious attitudes in her work. He chose these four because they were closely related, but he might have found equally useful clusters of poems about love, nature, domestic life, or writing. What especially intrigued him was some of the information he read about Dickinson's sternly religious father and the orthodox nature of the religious values of her hometown of Amherst, Massachusetts. Because this paper was not a research paper, he did not pursue these issues beyond the level of the general remarks provided in an introduction to her poetry (though he might have). He did, however, use this biographical and historical information as a means of framing his search for poems that were related to one another. In doing so he discovered consistent concerns along with contradictory themes that became the basis of his paper.

"Faith" is a fine invention

c. 1860

"Faith" is a fine invention
When Gentlemen can *see*—
But *Microscopes* are prudent
In an Emergency.

I know that He exists

c. 1862

I know that He exists.
Somewhere — in Silence —
He has hid his rare life
From our gross eyes.

'Tis an instant's play.   5
'Tis a fond Ambush —
Just to make Bliss
Earn her own surprise!

But — should the play
Prove piercing earnest —   10
Should the glee-glaze —
In Death's — stiff — stare —

Would not the fun
Look too expensive!
Would not the jest —   15
Have crawled too far!

I never saw a Moor —

c. 1865

I never saw a Moor —
I never saw the Sea —
Yet know I how the Heather looks
And what a Billow be.

I never spoke with God
Nor visited in Heaven —
Yet certain am I of the spot
As if the Checks were given —

Apparently with no surprise

c. 1884

Apparently with no surprise
To any happy Flower
The Frost beheads it at its play —
In accidental power —
The blond Assassin passes on —
The Sun proceeds unmoved
To measure off another Day
For an Approving God.

A SAMPLE STUDENT PAPER

Religious Faith in Four Poems by Emily Dickinson

Weitz 1

Michael Weitz

Professor Pearl

English 270

May 5, 2009

Religious Faith in Four Poems by Emily Dickinson

Throughout much of her poetry, Emily Dickinson wrestles with complex
notions of God, faith, and religious devotion. She adheres to no consistent
view of religion; rather, her poetry reveals a vision of God and faith that is
constantly evolving. Dickinson's gods range from the strict and powerful Old

Introduction providing overview of faith in Dickinson's work.

Testament father to a loving spiritual guide to an irrational and ridiculous imaginary figure. Through these varying images of God, Dickinson portrays contrasting images of the meaning and validity of religious faith. Her work reveals competing attitudes toward religious devotion as conventional religious piety struggles with a more cynical perception of God and religious worship.

Dickinson's "I never saw a Moor—" reveals a vision of traditional religious sensibilities. Although the speaker readily admits that "I never spoke with God / Nor visited in Heaven" (lines 5-6), her devout faith in a supreme being does not waver. The poem appears to be a straightforward profession of true faith stemming from the argument that the proof of God's existence is the universe's existence. Dickinson's imagery therefore evolves from the natural to the supernatural, first establishing her convictions that moors and seas exist, in spite of her lack of personal contact with either. This leads to the foundation of her religious faith, again based not on physical experience but on intellectual convictions. The speaker professes that she believes in the existence of Heaven even without conclusive evidence: "Yet certain am I of the spot / As if the Checks were given—" (7-8). But the appearance of such idealistic views of God and faith in "I never saw a Moor—" are transformed in Dickinson's other poems into a much more skeptical vision of the validity of religious piety.

While faith is portrayed as an authentic and deeply important quality in "I never saw a Moor—," Dickinson's "'Faith' is a fine invention" portrays faith as much less essential. Faith is defined in the poem as "a fine invention" (1), suggesting that it is created by man for man and therefore is not a crucial aspect of the natural universe. Thus the strong idealistic faith of "I never saw a Moor—" becomes discredited in the face of scientific rationalism. The speaker compares religious faith with actual microscopes, both of which are meant to enhance one's vision in some way. But "Faith" is useful only "When Gentlemen can *see*—" already (2); "In an Emergency," when one ostensibly cannot see, "*Microscopes* are prudent" (4, 3). Dickinson pits religion against science, suggesting that science, with its tangible evidence and rational attitude, is a more reliable lens through which to view the world. Faith is irreverently reduced to a mere "invention" and one that is ultimately less useful than microscopes or other scientific instruments.

Thesis analyzing poet's attitudes toward God and religion.

Analysis of religious piety in "I never saw a Moor—" supported with textual evidence.

Contrast between attitudes in "Moor" and other poems.

Analysis of scientific rationalism in "'Faith' is a fine invention" supported with textual evidence.

Weitz 3

Rational, scientific observations are not the only contributing factor to the portrayal of religious skepticism in Dickinson's poems; nature itself is seen to be incompatible in some ways with conventional religious ideology. In "Apparently with no surprise," the speaker recognizes the inexorable cycle of natural life and death as a morning frost kills a flower. But the tension in this poem stems not from the "happy Flower" (2) struck down by the frost's "accidental power" (4) but from the apparent indifference of the "Approving God" (8) who condones this seemingly cruel and unnecessary death. God is seen as remote and uncompromising, and it is this perceived distance between the speaker and God that reveals the increasing absurdity of traditional religious faith. The speaker understands that praying to God or believing in religion cannot change the course of nature, and as a result feels so helplessly distanced from God that religious faith becomes virtually meaningless.

> Analysis of God and nature in "Apparently with no surprise" supported with textual evidence.

Dickinson's religious skepticism becomes even more explicit in "I know that He exists," in which the speaker attempts to understand the connection between seeing God and facing death. In this poem Dickinson characterizes God as a remote and mysterious figure; the speaker mockingly asserts, "I know that He exists" (1), even though "He has hid his rare life / From our gross eyes" (3-4). The skepticism toward religious faith revealed in this poem stems from the speaker's recognition of the paradoxical quest that people undertake to know and to see God. A successful attempt to see God, to win the game of hide-and-seek that He apparently is orchestrating, results inevitably in death. With this recognition the speaker comes to view religion as an absurd and reckless game in which the prize may be "Bliss" (7) but more likely is "Death's—stiff—stare—" (12). For, to see God and to meet one's death as a result certainly suggests that the game of trying to see God (the so-called "fun" of line 13) is much "too expensive" and that religion itself is a "jest" that, like the serpent in Genesis, has "crawled too far" (14–16).

> Analysis of characteri- zation of God in "I know that He exists" supported with textual evidence.

Ultimately, the vision of religious faith that Dickinson describes in her poems is one of suspicion and cynicism. She cannot reconcile the physical world to the spiritual existence that Christian doctrine teaches, and as a result the traditional perception of God becomes ludicrous. "I never saw a Moor—" does attempt to sustain a conventional vision of religious devotion, but Dickinson's poems overall are far more likely to suggest that God is elusive, indifferent, and

Weitz 4

Conclusion
providing
well-
supported
final analysis
of poet's
views on God
and faith.

often cruel, thus undermining the traditional vision of God as a loving father
worthy of devout worship. Thus, not only religious faith but also those who are
religiously faithful become targets for Dickinson's irreverent criticism of conventional belief.

Weitz 5

Works Cited

Dickinson, Emily. "Apparently with no surprise." *Poetry: An Introduction*. Ed.
Michael Meyer. 6th ed. Boston. Bedford/St. Martin's, 2010. 355. Print.

---. " 'Faith' is a fine invention." *Poetry: An Introduction*. Ed. Michael Meyer.
6th ed. Boston. Bedford/St. Martin's, 2010. 354. Print.

---. "I know that He exists." *Poetry: An Introduction*. Ed. Michael Meyer. 6th
ed. Boston. Bedford/St. Martin's, 2010. 354. Print.

---. "I never saw a Moor--." *Poetry: An Introduction*. Ed. Michael Meyer. 6th
ed. Boston. Bedford/St. Martin's, 2010. 355. Print.

SUGGESTED TOPICS FOR LONGER PAPERS

1. Irony is abundant in Dickinson's poetry. Choose five poems from this
   chapter that strike you as especially ironic and discuss her use of irony in
   each. Taken individually and collectively, what do these poems suggest to
   you about the poet's sensibilities and her ways of looking at the world?

2. Readers have sometimes noted that Dickinson's poetry does not reflect
   very much of the social, political, economic, religious, and historical events
   of her lifetime. Using the poems in this chapter as the basis of your discussion, what can you say about the contexts in which Dickinson wrote? What
   kind of world do you think she inhabited, and how did she respond to it?

Web Research
Emily Dickinson at
bedfordstmartins.com/
rewritinglit.

13

A Study of Robert Frost

A poem . . . begins as a lump in the throat, a sense of wrong, a home-sickness, a love-sickness. . . . It finds the thought and the thought finds the words.

— ROBERT FROST

Every poem is doubtlessly affected by the personal history of its composer, but Robert Frost's poems are especially known for their reflection of New England life. Although the poems included in this chapter evoke the land-scapes of Frost's life and work, the depth and range of those landscapes are far more complicated than his pop-ular reputation typically acknowledges. He was an enor-mously private man and a much more subtle poet than many of his readers have expected him to be. His poems warrant careful, close readings. As you explore his poetry, you may find useful the Questions

Explore contexts for Robert Frost on *LiterActive*.

Robert Frost

for Writing about an Author in Depth (p. 352) as a means of stimulating your thinking about his life and work.

A BRIEF BIOGRAPHY

Few poets have enjoyed the popular success that Robert Frost (1874–1963) achieved during his lifetime, and no twentieth-century American poet has had his or her work as widely read and honored. Frost is as much associated with New England as the stone walls that help define its landscape; his reputation, however, transcends regional boundaries. Although he was named poet laureate of Vermont only two years before his death, he was for many years the nation's unofficial poet laureate. Frost collected honors the way some people pick up burrs on country walks. Among his awards were four Pulitzer Prizes, the Bollingen Prize, a Congressional Medal, and dozens of honorary degrees. Perhaps his most moving appearance was his

Robert Frost at age eighteen (1892), the year he graduated from high school. "Education," Frost once said, "is the ability to listen to almost anything without losing your temper or your self-confidence."

Courtesy of Rauner Special Collections Library, Dartmouth College.

Robert Frost at age forty-seven (1921) at Stone Cottage in Shaftsbury, Vermont. Frost wrote,
"I would have written of me on my stone: / I had a lover's quarrel with the world."
Courtesy of Rauner Special Collections Library, Dartmouth College.

Robert Frost at his writing desk in Franconia, New Hampshire, 1915. "I have never started a poem whose end I knew," Frost said, "writing a poem is discovering."

recitation of "The Gift Outright" for millions of Americans at the inauguration of John F. Kennedy in 1961.

Frost's recognition as a poet is especially remarkable because his career as a writer did not attract any significant attention until he was nearly forty years old. He taught himself to write while he labored at odd jobs, taught school, or farmed.

Frost's early identity seems very remote from the New England soil. Although his parents were descended from generations of New Englanders, he was born in San Francisco and was named Robert Lee Frost after the Confederate general. After his father died in 1885, his mother moved the family back to Massachusetts to live with relatives. Frost graduated from high school sharing valedictorian honors with the classmate who would become his wife three years later. Between high school and marriage, he attended Dartmouth College for a few months and then taught. His teaching prompted him to enroll at Harvard in 1897, but after less than two years he withdrew without a degree (though Harvard would eventually award him an honorary doctorate in 1937, four years after Dartmouth conferred its honorary degree on him). For the next decade, Frost read and wrote poems when he was not chicken farming or teaching. In 1912, he sold his farm and moved his family to England, where he hoped to find the audience that his poetry did not have in America.

Three years in England made it possible for Frost to return home as a poet. His first two volumes of poetry, *A Boy's Will* (1913) and *North of Boston* (1914), were published in England. During the next twenty years, honors and awards were conferred on collections such as *Mountain Interval* (1916), *New Hampshire* (1923), *West-Running Brook* (1928), and *A Further Range* (1936). These are the volumes on which most of Frost's popular and critical reputation rests. Later collections include *A Witness Tree* (1942), *A Masque of Reason* (1945), *Steeple Bush* (1947), *A Masque of Mercy* (1947), *Complete Poems* (1949), and *In the Clearing* (1962). In addition to publishing his works, Frost endeared himself to audiences throughout the country by presenting his poetry almost as conversations. He also taught at a number of schools, including Amherst College, the University of Michigan, Harvard University, Dartmouth College, and Middlebury College.

Frost's countless poetry readings generated wide audiences eager to claim him as their poet. The image he cultivated resembled closely what the public likes to think a poet should be. Frost was seen as a lovable, wise old man; his simple wisdom and cracker-barrel sayings appeared comforting and homey. From this Yankee rustic, audiences learned that "There's a lot yet that isn't understood" or "We love the things we love for what they are" or "Good fences make good neighbors."

In a sense, Frost packaged himself for public consumption. "I am . . . my own salesman," he said. When asked direct questions about the meanings of his poems, he often winked or scratched his head to give the impression that the customer was always right. To be sure, there is a simplicity in Frost's language, but that simplicity does not fully reflect the depth of the man, the complexity of his themes, or the richness of his art.

The folksy optimist behind the public lectern did not reveal his private troubles to his audiences, although he did address those problems at his writing desk. Frost suffered from professional jealousies, anger, and depression. His family life was especially painful. Three of his four children died: a son at the age of four, a daughter in her late twenties from tuberculosis, and another son by suicide. His marriage was filled with tension. Although Frost's work is landscaped with sunlight, snow, birches, birds, blueberries, and squirrels, it is important to recognize that he was also intimately "acquainted with the night," a phrase that serves as the haunting title of one of his poems (see p. 158).

As a corrective to Frost's popular reputation, one critic, Lionel Trilling, described the world Frost creates in his poems as a "terrifying universe," characterized by loneliness, anguish, frustration, doubts, disappointment, and despair. To point this out is not to annihilate the pleasantness and even good-natured cheerfulness that can be enjoyed in Frost's poetry, but it is to say that Frost is not so one-dimensional as he is sometimes assumed to be. Frost's poetry requires readers who are alert and willing to penetrate the simplicity of its language to see the elusive and ambiguous meanings that lie below the surface.

AN INTRODUCTION TO HIS WORK

Frost's treatment of nature helps to explain the various levels of meaning in his poetry. The familiar natural world his poems evoke is sharply detailed. We hear icy branches clicking against themselves, we see the snow-white trunks of birches, we feel the smarting pain of a twig lashing across a face. The aspects of the natural world Frost describes are designated to give pleasure, but they are also frequently calculated to provoke thought. His use of nature tends to be symbolic. Complex meanings are derived from simple facts, such as a spider killing a moth or the difference between fire and ice (see "Design," p. 386, and "Fire and Ice," p. 382). Although Frost's strategy is to talk about particular events and individual experiences, his poems evoke universal issues.

Frost's poetry has strong regional roots and is "versed in country things," but it flourishes in any receptive imagination because, in the final analysis, it is concerned with human beings. Frost's New England landscapes are the occasion rather than the ultimate focus of his poems. Like the rural voices he creates in his poems, Frost typically approaches his themes indirectly. He explained the reason for this in a talk titled "Education by Poetry":

> Poetry provides the one permissible way of saying one thing and meaning another. People say, "Why don't you say what you mean?" We never do that, do we, being all of us too much poets. We like to talk in parables and in hints and in indirections — whether from diffidence or some other instinct.

The result is that the settings, characters, and situations that make up the subject matter of Frost's poems are vehicles for his perceptions about life.

In "Stopping by Woods on a Snowy Evening" (p. 382), for example, Frost uses the kind of familiar New England details that constitute his poetry for more than descriptive purposes. He shapes them into a meditation on the tension we sometimes feel between life's responsibilities and the "lovely, dark, and deep" attraction that death offers. When the speaker's horse "gives his harness bells a shake," we are reminded that we are confronting a universal theme as well as a quiet moment of natural beauty.

Among the major concerns that appear in Frost's poetry are the fragility of life, the consequences of rejecting or accepting the conditions of one's life, the passion of inconsolable grief, the difficulty of sustaining intimacy, the fear of loneliness and isolation, the inevitability of change, the tensions between the individual and society, and the place of tradition and custom.

Whatever theme is encountered in a poem by Frost, a reader is likely to agree with him that "the initial delight is in the surprise of remembering something I didn't know." To achieve that fresh sense of discovery, Frost allowed himself to follow his instincts; his poetry

> inclines to the impulse, it assumes direction with the first line laid down, it runs a course of lucky events, and ends in a clarification of life — not necessarily a great clarification, such as sects and cults are founded on, but in a momentary stay against confusion.

This description from "On the Figure a Poem Makes" (see p. 388 for the complete essay), Frost's brief introduction to *Complete Poems,* may sound as if his poetry is formless and merely "lucky," but his poems tend to be more conventional than experimental: "The artist in me," as he put the matter in one of his poems, "cries out for design."

From Frost's perspective, "free verse is like playing tennis with the net down." He exercised his own freedom in meeting the challenges of rhyme and meter. His use of fixed forms such as couplets, tercets, quatrains, blank verse, and sonnets was not slavish because he enjoyed working them into the natural English speech patterns — especially the rhythms, idioms, and tones of speakers living north of Boston — that give voice to his themes. Frost often liked to use "Stopping by Woods on a Snowy Evening" as an example of his graceful way of making conventions appear natural and inevitable. He explored "the old ways to be new."

Frost's eye for strong, telling details was matched by his ear for natural speech rhythms. His flexible use of what he called "iambic and loose iambic" enabled him to create moving lyric poems that reveal the personal thoughts of a speaker and dramatic poems that convincingly characterize people caught in intense emotional situations. The language in his poems appears to be little more than a transcription of casual and even rambling speech, but it is in actuality Frost's poetic creation, carefully crafted to reveal the joys and sorrows that are woven into people's daily lives. What is missing from Frost's poems is artificiality, not art. Consider this poem.

The Road Not Taken

1916

Two roads diverged in a yellow wood,
And sorry I could not travel both
And be one traveler, long I stood
And looked down one as far as I could
To where it bent in the undergrowth;   5

Then took the other, as just as fair,
And having perhaps the better claim,
Because it was grassy and wanted wear;
Though as for that the passing there
Had worn them really about the same,   10

And both that morning equally lay
In leaves no step had trodden black.
Oh, I kept the first for another day!
Yet knowing how way leads on to way,
I doubted if I should ever come back.   15

I shall be telling this with a sigh
Somewhere ages and ages hence:
Two roads diverged in a wood, and I—
I took the one less traveled by,
And that has made all the difference.   20

This poem intrigues readers because it is at once so simple and so deeply resonant. Recalling a walk in the woods, the speaker describes how he came to a fork in the road, which forced him to choose one path over another. Though "sorry" that he "could not travel both," he made a choice after carefully weighing his two options. This, essentially, is what happens in the poem; there is no other action. However, the incident is charged with symbolic significance by the speaker's reflections on the necessity and consequences of his decision.

The final stanza indicates that the choice concerns more than simply walking down a road, for the speaker says that choosing the "less traveled" path has affected his entire life—that "that has made all the difference." Frost draws on a familiar enough metaphor when he compares life to a journey, but he is also calling attention to a less commonly noted problem: despite our expectations, aspirations, appetites, hopes, and desires, we can't have it all. Making one choice precludes another. It is impossible to determine what particular decision the speaker refers to: perhaps he had to choose a college, a career, a spouse; perhaps he was confronted with mutually exclusive ideas, beliefs, or values. There is no way to know because Frost wisely creates a symbolic choice and implicitly invites us to supply our own circumstances.

The speaker's reflections about his choice are as central to an understanding of the poem as the choice itself; indeed, they may be more central. He describes the road taken as "having perhaps the better claim, / Because it was grassy and wanted wear"; he prefers the "less traveled" path. This seems to be an expression of individualism, which would account for "the difference" his choice made in his life. But Frost complicates matters by having the speaker also acknowledge that there was no significant difference between the two roads; one was "just as fair" as the other; each was "worn . . . really about the same"; and "both that morning equally lay / In leaves no step had trodden black."

The speaker imagines that in the future, "ages and ages hence," he will recount his choice with "a sigh" that will satisfactorily explain the course of his life, but Frost seems to be having a little fun here by showing us how the speaker will embellish his past decision to make it appear more dramatic. What we hear is someone trying to convince himself that the choice he made significantly changed his life. When he recalls what happened in the "yellow wood," a color that gives a glow to that irretrievable moment when his life seemed to be on verge of a momentous change, he appears more concerned with the path he did not choose than with the one he took. Frost shrewdly titles the poem to suggest the speaker's sense of loss at not being able to "travel both" roads. When the speaker's reflections about his choice are examined, the poem reveals his nostalgia instead of affirming his decision to travel a self-reliant path in life.

The rhymed stanzas of "The Road Not Taken" follow a pattern established in the first five lines (*abaab*). This rhyme scheme reflects, perhaps, the speaker's efforts to shape his life into a pleasing and coherent form. The natural speech rhythms Frost uses allow him to integrate the rhymes unobtrusively, but there is a slight shift in lines 19 and 20, when the speaker asserts self-consciously that the "less traveled" road — which we already know to be basically the same as the other road — "made all the difference." Unlike all of the other rhymes in the poem, "difference" does not rhyme precisely with "hence." The emphasis that must be placed on "differ*ence*" to make it rhyme perfectly with "hence" may suggest that the speaker is trying just a little too hard to pattern his life on his earlier choice in the woods.

Perhaps the best way to begin reading Frost's poetry is to accept the invitation he placed at the beginning of many volumes of his poems. "The Pasture" means what it says, of course; it is about taking care of some farm chores, but it is also a means of "saying one thing in terms of another."

The Pasture   *1913*

I'm going out to clean the pasture spring;
I'll only stop to rake the leaves away
(And wait to watch the water clear, I may):
I shan't be gone long. — You come too.

I'm going out to fetch the little calf
That's standing by the mother. It's so young
It totters when she licks it with her tongue.
I sha'n't be gone long. — You come too.

"The Pasture" is a simple but irresistible songlike invitation to the pleasure of looking at the world through the eyes of a poet.

Chronology

1874	Born on March 26 in San Francisco.
1885	Father dies and family moves to Lawrence, Massachusetts.
1892	Graduates from Lawrence High School.
1893–94	Studies at Dartmouth College.
1895	Marries his high school sweetheart, Elinor White.
1897–99	Studies at Harvard College.

1900	Moves to a farm in West Derry, New Hampshire.
1912	Moves to England, where he farms and writes.
1913	*A Boy's Will* is published in London.
1914	*North of Boston* is published in London.
1915	Moves to a farm near Franconia, New Hampshire.
1916	Elected to National Institute of Letters.
1917–20	Teaches at Amherst College.
1919	Moves to South Shaftsbury, Vermont.
1921–23	Teaches at the University of Michigan.
1923	*Selected Poems* and *New Hampshire* are published; the latter is awarded a Pulitzer Prize.
1928	*West-Running Brook* is published.
1930	*Collected Poems* is published.
1936	*A Further Range* is published; teaches at Harvard.
1938	Wife dies.
1939–42	Teaches at Harvard.
1942	*A Witness Tree,* which is awarded a Pulitzer Prize, is published.
1943–49	Teaches at Dartmouth.
1945	*A Masque of Reason* is published.
1947	*Steeple Bush* and *A Masque of Mercy* are published.
1949	*Complete Poems* (enlarged) is published.
1961	Reads "The Gift Outright" at President John F. Kennedy's inauguration.
1963	Dies on January 29 in Boston.

Mowing   *1913*

There was never a sound beside the wood but one,
And that was my long scythe whispering to the ground.
What was it it whispered? I knew not well myself;
Perhaps it was something about the heat of the sun,
Something, perhaps, about the lack of sound —   5
And that was why it whispered and did not speak.
It was no dream of the gift of idle hours,
Or easy gold at the hand of fay or elf:
Anything more than the truth would have seemed too weak
To the earnest love that laid the swale in rows,   10
Not without feeble-pointed spikes of flowers
(Pale orchises), and scared a bright green snake.

The fact is the sweetest dream that labour knows.
My long scythe whispered and left the hay to make.

CONSIDERATIONS FOR CRITICAL THINKING AND WRITING

1. **FIRST RESPONSE**. Describe the tone of "Mowing." How does reading the poem aloud affect your understanding of it?
2. Discuss the image of the scythe. Do you think it has any symbolic value? Explain why or why not.
3. Paraphrase the poem. What do you think its theme is?
4. Describe the type of sonnet Frost uses in "Mowing."

My November Guest — *1913*

My Sorrow, when she's here with me,
   Thinks these dark days of autumn rain
Are beautiful as days can be;
She loves the bare, the withered tree;
   She walks the sodden pasture lane.   5

Her pleasure will not let me stay.
   She talks and I am fain to list:
She's glad the birds are gone away,
She's glad her simple worsted grey
   Is silver now with clinging mist.   10

The desolate, deserted trees,
   The faded earth, the heavy sky,
The beauties she so truly sees,
She thinks I have no eye for these,
   And vexes me for reason why.   15

Not yesterday I learned to know
   The love of bare November days
Before the coming of the snow,
But it were vain to tell her so,
   And they are better for her praise.   20

CONSIDERATIONS FOR CRITICAL THINKING AND WRITING

1. **FIRST RESPONSE**. How is "Sorrow" personified? What sort of relationship does the speaker have with her?
2. What kind of tone do the poem's images create?
3. What do you think is this poem's theme?

CONNECTION TO ANOTHER SELECTION

1. Compare Frost's treatment of November with Margaret Atwood's evocation of "February" (p. 145). Explain why you prefer one poem over the other.

Storm Fear

1913

When the wind works against us in the dark,
And pelts with snow
The lower chamber window on the east,
And whispers with a sort of stifled bark,
The beast,   5
"Come out! Come out!" —
It costs no inward struggle not to go,
Ah, no!
I count our strength,
Two and a child,   10
Those of us not asleep subdued to mark
How the cold creeps as the fire dies at length, —
How drifts are piled,
Dooryard and road ungraded,
Till even the comforting barn grows far away,   15
And my heart owns a doubt
Whether 'tis in us to arise with day
And save ourselves unaided.

Considerations for Critical Thinking and Writing

1. **FIRST RESPONSE.** What is the "inward struggle" (line 7) in this poem?

2. How is winter depicted by the speaker? What emotions does winter produce in the speaker?

3. Describe the rhyme scheme and its effects on your reading the poem aloud.

Connection to Another Selection

1. Compare the perspectives on nature in "Storm Fear" and in Emily Dickinson's "Presentiment — is that long Shadow — on the lawn —" (p. 136). How are they both poems about fear?

Mending Wall

1914

Something there is that doesn't love a wall,
That sends the frozen-ground-swell under it,
And spills the upper boulders in the sun;
And makes gaps even two can pass abreast.
The work of hunters is another thing: 5
I have come after them and made repair
Where they have left not one stone on a stone,
But they would have the rabbit out of hiding,
To please the yelping dogs. The gaps I mean,
No one has seen them made or heard them made,   10

But at spring mending-time we find them there.
I let my neighbor know beyond the hill;
And on a day we meet to walk the line
And set the wall between us once again.
We keep the wall between us as we go.   15
To each the boulders that have fallen to each.
And some are loaves and some so nearly balls
We have to use a spell to make them balance:
"Stay where you are until our backs are turned!"
We wear our fingers rough with handling them.   20
Oh, just another kind of outdoor game,
One on a side. It comes to little more:
There where it is we do not need the wall:
He is all pine and I am apple orchard.
My apple trees will never get across   25
And eat the cones under his pines, I tell him.
He only says, "Good fences make good neighbors."
Spring is the mischief in me, and I wonder
If I could put a notion in his head:
"*Why* do they make good neighbors? Isn't it   30
Where there are cows? But here there are no cows.
Before I built a wall I'd ask to know
What I was walling in or walling out,
And to whom I was like to give offense.
Something there is that doesn't love a wall,   35
That wants it down." I could say "Elves" to him,
But it's not elves exactly, and I'd rather
He said it for himself. I see him there
Bringing a stone grasped firmly by the top
In each hand, like an old-stone savage armed.   40
He moves in darkness as it seems to me,
Not of woods only and the shade of trees.
He will not go behind his father's saying,
And he likes having thought of it so well
He says again, "Good fences make good neighbors."   45

Considerations for Critical Thinking and Writing

1. **FIRST RESPONSE.** What might the "Something" be that "doesn't love a wall"
   (line 1)? Why does the speaker remind his neighbor each spring that the
   wall needs to be repaired? Is it ironic that the *speaker* initiates the mending?
   Is there anything good about the wall?

2. How do the speaker and his neighbor differ in sensibilities? What is suggested
   about the neighbor in lines 41 and 42?

3. The neighbor likes the saying "Good fences make good neighbors" so well
   that he repeats it (lines 27, 45). Does the speaker also say something twice?
   What else suggests that the speaker's attitude toward the wall is not necessarily Frost's?

4. Although the speaker's language is colloquial, what is poetic about the sounds and rhythms he uses?

5. This poem was first published in 1914; Frost read it to an audience when he visited Russia in 1962. What do these facts suggest about the symbolic value of "Mending Wall"?

CONNECTIONS TO OTHER SELECTIONS

1. How do you think the neighbor in this poem would respond to Dickinson's idea of imagination in "To make a prairie it takes a clover and one bee" (p. 321)?

2. What similarities and differences does the neighbor have with the people Frost describes in "Neither Out Far nor In Deep" (p. 384)?

Home Burial   1914

He saw her from the bottom of the stairs
Before she saw him. She was starting down,
Looking back over her shoulder at some fear.
She took a doubtful step and then undid it
To raise herself and look again. He spoke   5
Advancing toward her: "What is it you see
From up there always — for I want to know."
She turned and sank upon her skirts at that,
And her face changed from terrified to dull.
He said to gain time: "What is it you see,"   10
Mounting until she cowered under him.
"I will find out now — you must tell me, dear."
She, in her place, refused him any help
With the least stiffening of her neck and silence.
She let him look, sure that he wouldn't see,   15
Blind creature; and awhile he didn't see.
But at last he murmured, "Oh," and again, "Oh."

"What is it — what?" she said.

                "Just that I see."

"You don't," she challenged. "Tell me what it is."   20

"The wonder is I didn't see at once.
I never noticed it from here before.
I must be wonted° to it — that's the reason.   *accustomed*
The little graveyard where my people are!
So small the window frames the whole of it.   25
Not so much larger than a bedroom, is it?
There are three stones of slate and one of marble,
Broad-shouldered little slabs there in the sunlight
On the sidehill. We haven't to mind *those*.

But I understand: it is not the stones,   30
But the child's mound —"

                        "Don't, don't, don't, don't," she cried.

She withdrew, shrinking from beneath his arm
That rested on the banister, and slid downstairs;
And turned on him with such a daunting look,   35
He said twice over before he knew himself:
"Can't a man speak of his own child he's lost?"

"Not you! — Oh, where's my hat? Oh, I don't need it!
I must get out of here. I must get air.
I don't know rightly whether any man can."   40

"Amy! Don't go to someone else this time.
Listen to me. I won't come down the stairs."
He sat and fixed his chin between his fists.
"There's something I should like to ask you, dear."

"You don't know how to ask it."   45

                        "Help me, then."
Her fingers moved the latch for all reply.

"My words are nearly always an offense.
I don't know how to speak of anything
So as to please you. But I might be taught,   50
I should suppose. I can't say I see how.
A man must partly give up being a man
With women-folk. We could have some arrangement
By which I'd bind myself to keep hands off
Anything special you're a-mind to name.   55
Though I don't like such things 'twixt those that love.
Two that don't love can't live together without them.
But two that do can't live together with them."
She moved the latch a little. "Don't — don't go.
Don't carry it to someone else this time.   60
Tell me about it if it's something human.
Let me into your grief. I'm not so much
Unlike other folks as your standing there
Apart would make me out. Give me my chance.
I do think, though, you overdo it a little.   65
What was it brought you up to think it the thing
To take your mother-loss of a first child
So inconsolably — in the face of love.
You'd think his memory might be satisfied —"

"There you go sneering now!"   70

                        "I'm not, I'm not!

You make me angry. I'll come down to you.
God, what a woman! And it's come to this,
A man can't speak of his own child that's dead."

"You can't because you don't know how to speak.   75
If you had any feelings, you that dug
With your own hand — how could you? — his little grave;
I saw you from that very window there,
Making the gravel leap and leap in air,
Leap up, like that, like that, and land so lightly   80
And roll back down the mound beside the hole.
I thought, Who is that man? I didn't know you.
And I crept down the stairs and up the stairs
To look again, and still your spade kept lifting.
Then you came in. I heard your rumbling voice   85
Out in the kitchen, and I don't know why,
But I went near to see with my own eyes.
You could sit there with the stains on your shoes
Of the fresh earth from your own baby's grave
And talk about your everyday concerns.   90
You had stood the spade up against the wall
Outside there in the entry, for I saw it."

"I shall laugh the worst laugh I ever laughed.
I'm cursed. God, if I don't believe I'm cursed."

"I can repeat the very words you were saying.   95
'Three foggy mornings and one rainy day
Will rot the best birch fence a man can build.'
Think of it, talk like that at such a time!
What had how long it takes a birch to rot
To do with what was in the darkened parlor   100
You *couldn't* care! The nearest friends can go
With anyone to death, comes so far short
They might as well not try to go at all.
No, from the time when one is sick to death,
One is alone, and he dies more alone.   105
Friends make pretense of following to the grave.
But before one is in it, their minds are turned
And making the best of their way back to life
And living people, and things they understand.
But the world's evil. I won't have grief so   110
If I can change it. Oh, I won't, I won't!"

"There, you have said it all and you feel better.
You won't go now. You're crying. Close the door.
The heart's gone out of it: why keep it up.
Amy! There's someone coming down the road!"   115

"*You* — oh, you think the talk is all. I must go —
Somewhere out of this house. How can I make you —"

"If — you — do!" She was opening the door wider.
"Where do you mean to go? First tell me that.
I'll follow and bring you back by force. I *will!* —"   120

CONSIDERATIONS FOR CRITICAL THINKING AND WRITING

1. **FIRST RESPONSE.** This poem tells a story of a relationship. Is the husband insensitive and indifferent to his wife's grief? Characterize the wife. Has Frost invited us to sympathize with one character more than with the other?

2. How has the burial of the child within sight of the stairway window affected the relationship of the couple in this poem? Is the child's grave a symptom or a cause of the conflict between them?

3. What is the effect of splitting the iambic pentameter pattern in lines 18 and 19, 31 and 32, 45 and 46, and 70 and 71?

4. Is the conflict resolved at the conclusion of the poem? Do you think the husband and wife will overcome their differences?

The Wood-Pile   *1914*

Out walking in the frozen swamp one gray day,
I paused and said, "I will turn back from here.
No, I will go on farther — and we shall see."
The hard snow held me, save where now and then
One foot went through. The view was all in lines   5
Straight up and down of tall slim trees
Too much alike to mark or name a place by
So as to say for certain I was here
Or somewhere else: I was just far from home.
A small bird flew before me. He was careful   10
To put a tree between us when he lighted,
And say no word to tell me who he was
Who was so foolish as to think what *he* thought.
He thought that I was after him for a feather —
The white one in his tail; like one who takes   15
Everything said as personal to himself.
One flight out sideways would have undeceived him.
And then there was a pile of wood for which
I forgot him and let his little fear
Carry him off the way I might have gone,   20
Without so much as wishing him good-night.
He went behind it to make his last stand.
It was a cord of maple, cut and split
And piled — and measured, four by four by eight.
And not another like it could I see.   25
No runner tracks in this year's snow looped near it.
And it was older sure than this year's cutting,
Or even last year's or the year's before.
The wood was gray and the bark warping off it
And the pile somewhat sunken. Clematis   30
Had wound strings round and round it like a bundle.
What held it though on one side was a tree
Still growing, and on one a stake and prop,

These latter about to fall. I thought that only
Someone who lived in turning to fresh tasks   35
Could so forget his handiwork on which
He spent himself, the labor of his ax,
And leave it there far from a useful fireplace
To warm the frozen swamp as best it could
With the slow smokeless burning of decay.   40

CONSIDERATIONS FOR CRITICAL THINKING AND WRITING

1. **FIRST RESPONSE.** What symbolic value can you find in the speaker's account of his discovery of the woodpile?

2. Write a paraphrase of the poem.

3. How does the "small bird" (line 10) figure in the poem? Why do you think it's there? How is it related to the woodpile?

4. Characterize the speaker's tone. How does the rhythm of the poem's lines help to create the tone?

CONNECTIONS TO OTHER SELECTIONS

1. Write an essay comparing the speaker in this poem to the speaker in "Stopping by Woods on a Snowy Evening" (p. 382). How, in each poem, do simple activities reveal something important about the speaker?

2. Discuss the speakers' sense of time in "The Wood-Pile" and in "Nothing Gold Can Stay" (p. 383).

After Apple-Picking   *1914*

My long two-pointed ladder's sticking through a tree
Toward heaven still,
And there's a barrel that I didn't fill
Beside it, and there may be two or three
Apples I didn't pick upon some bough.   5
But I am done with apple-picking now.
Essence of winter sleep is on the night,
The scent of apples: I am drowsing off.
I cannot rub the strangeness from my sight
I got from looking through a pane of glass   10
I skimmed this morning from the drinking trough
And held against the world of hoary grass.
It melted, and I let it fall and break.
But I was well
Upon my way to sleep before it fell,   15
And I could tell
What form my dreaming was about to take.
Magnified apples appear and disappear,
Stem end and blossom end,
And every fleck of russet showing clear.   20
My instep arch not only keeps the ache,

It keeps the pressure of a ladder-round.
I feel the ladder sway as the boughs bend.
And I keep hearing from the cellar bin
The rumbling sound   25
Of load on load of apples coming in.
For I have had too much
Of apple-picking: I am overtired
Of the great harvest I myself desired.
There were ten thousand thousand fruit to touch,   30
Cherish in hand, lift down, and not let fall.
For all
That struck the earth,
No matter if not bruised or spiked with stubble,
Went surely to the cider-apple heap   35
As of no worth.
One can see what will trouble
This sleep of mine, whatever sleep it is.
Were he not gone,
The woodchuck could say whether it's like his   40
Long sleep, as I describe its coming on,
Or just some human sleep.

CONSIDERATIONS FOR CRITICAL THINKING AND WRITING

1. **FIRST RESPONSE.** How does this poem illustrate Frost's view that "Poetry provides the one permissible way of saying one thing and meaning another"? When do you first sense that the detailed description of apple picking is being used that way?

2. What comes after apple picking? What does the speaker worry about in the dream beginning in line 18?

3. Why do you suppose Frost uses apples rather than, say, pears or squash?

Birches   *1916*

When I see birches bend to left and right
Across the lines of straighter darker trees,
I like to think some boy's been swinging them.
But swinging doesn't bend them down to stay
As ice-storms do. Often you must have seen them   5
Loaded with ice a sunny winter morning
After a rain. They click upon themselves
As the breeze rises, and turn many-colored
As the stir cracks and crazes their enamel.
Soon the sun's warmth makes them shed crystal shells   10
Shattering and avalanching on the snow-crust—
Such heaps of broken glass to sweep away
You'd think the inner dome of heaven had fallen.
They are dragged to the withered bracken by the load,

And they seem not to break; though once they are bowed   15
So low for long, they never right themselves:
You may see their trunks arching in the woods
Years afterwards, trailing their leaves on the ground
Like girls on hands and knees that throw their hair
Before them over their heads to dry in the sun.   20
But I was going to say when Truth broke in
With all her matter-of-fact about the ice-storm,
I should prefer to have some boy bend them
As he went out and in to fetch the cows —
Some boy too far from town to learn baseball,   25
Whose only play was what he found himself,
Summer or winter, and could play alone.
One by one he subdued his father's trees
By riding them down over and over again
Until he took the stiffness out of them,   30
And not one but hung limp, not one was left
For him to conquer. He learned all there was
To learn about not launching out too soon
And so not carrying the tree away
Clear to the ground. He always kept his poise   35
To the top branches, climbing carefully
With the same pains you use to fill a cup
Up to the brim, and even above the brim.
Then he flung outward, feet first, with a swish,
Kicking his way down through the air to the ground.   40
So was I once myself a swinger of birches.
And so I dream of going back to be.
It's when I'm weary of considerations,
And life is too much like a pathless wood
Where your face burns and tickles with the cobwebs   45
Broken across it, and one eye is weeping
From a twig's having lashed across it open.
I'd like to get away from earth awhile
And then come back to it and begin over.
May no fate willfully misunderstand me   50
And half grant what I wish and snatch me away
Not to return. Earth's the right place for love:
I don't know where it's likely to go better.
I'd like to go by climbing a birch tree,
And climb black branches up a snow-white trunk,   55
Toward heaven, till the tree could bear no more,
But dipped its top and set me down again.
That would be good both going and coming back.
One could do worse than be a swinger of birches.

CONSIDERATIONS FOR CRITICAL THINKING AND WRITING

1. **FIRST RESPONSE.** What do you think the swinging of birches symbolizes?
2. Why does the speaker in this poem prefer the birches to have been bent by boys instead of ice storms?

3. How is "earth" (line 52) described in the poem? Why does the speaker choose it over "heaven" (line 56)?

4. How might the effect of this poem be changed if it were written in heroic couplets instead of blank verse?

5. CRITICAL STRATEGIES. Read the section on reader-response strategies (pp. 680–82) in Chapter 26, "Critical Strategies for Reading." Trace your response to this poem over three successive careful readings. How does your understanding of the poem change or develop?

An Old Man's Winter Night   *1916*

All out-of-doors looked darkly in at him
Through the thin frost, almost in separate stars,
That gathers on the pane in empty rooms.
What kept his eyes from giving back the gaze
Was the lamp tilted near them in his hand.   5
What kept him from remembering what it was
That brought him to that creaking room was age.
He stood with barrels round him — at a loss.
And having scared the cellar under him
In clomping here, he scared it once again   10
In clomping off — and scared the outer night,
Which has its sounds, familiar, like the roar
Of trees and crack of branches, common things,
But nothing so like beating on a box.
A light he was to no one but himself   15
Where now he sat, concerned with he knew what,
A quiet light, and then not even that.
He consigned to the moon, such as she was,
So late-arising, to the broken moon
As better than the sun in any case   20
For such a charge, his snow upon the roof,
His icicles along the wall to keep;
And slept. The log that shifted with a jolt
Once in the stove, disturbed him and he shifted,
And eased his heavy breathing, but still slept.   25
One aged man — one man — can't keep a house,
A farm, a countryside, or if he can,
It's thus he does it of a winter night.

CONSIDERATIONS FOR CRITICAL THINKING AND WRITING

1. FIRST RESPONSE. Describe the tone of this poem. Which images are especially effective in evoking the old man, the winter, and night?

2. What emotions do you feel for the old man? Is this a sentimental poem?

3. Comment on the sounds described in the poem. What effects do they create?

CONNECTIONS TO OTHER SELECTIONS

1. Compare the speaker in "The Road Not Taken" (p. 365) with the old man in this poem. Are they essentially similar or different? Explain your response in an essay.

2. Discuss images of winter and night in "An Old Man's Winter Night" and "Stopping by Woods on a Snowy Evening" (p. 382).

"Out, Out —" °   1916

The buzz-saw snarled and rattled in the yard
And made dust and dropped stove-length sticks of wood,
Sweet-scented stuff when the breeze drew across it.
And from there those that lifted eyes could count
Five mountain ranges one behind the other   5
Under the sunset far into Vermont.
And the saw snarled and rattled, snarled and rattled,
As it ran light, or had to bear a load.
And nothing happened: day was all but done.
Call it a day, I wish they might have said   10
To please the boy by giving him the half hour
That a boy counts so much when saved from work.
His sister stood beside them in her apron
To tell them "Supper." At the word, the saw,
As if to prove saws knew what supper meant,   15
Leaped out at the boy's hand, or seemed to leap —
He must have given the hand. However it was,
Neither refused the meeting. But the hand!
The boy's first outcry was a rueful laugh,
As he swung toward them holding up the hand   20
Half in appeal, but half as if to keep
The life from spilling. Then the boy saw all —
Since he was old enough to know, big boy
Doing a man's work, though a child at heart —
He saw all spoiled. "Don't let him cut my hand off —   25
The doctor, when he comes. Don't let him, sister!"
So. But the hand was gone already.
The doctor put him in the dark of ether.
He lay and puffed his lips out with his breath.
And then — the watcher at his pulse took fright.   30
No one believed. They listened at his heart.
Little — less — nothing! — and that ended it.
No more to build on there. And they, since they
Were not the one dead, turned to their affairs.

"*Out, Out —*": From Act V, Scene v, of Shakespeare's *Macbeth*.

CONSIDERATIONS FOR CRITICAL THINKING AND WRITING

1. **FIRST RESPONSE.** This narrative poem is about the accidental death of a Vermont boy. What is the purpose of the story? Some readers have argued that the final lines reveal the speaker's callousness and indifference. What do you think?

2. How does Frost's allusion to *Macbeth* contribute to the meaning of this poem? Does the speaker seem to agree with the view of life expressed in Macbeth's lines?

3. **CRITICAL STRATEGIES.** Read the section on Marxist criticism (pp. 673–74) in Chapter 26, "Critical Strategies for Reading." How do you think a Marxist critic would interpret the family and events described in this poem?

CONNECTIONS TO OTHER SELECTIONS

1. What are the similarities and differences in theme between this poem and Frost's "Nothing Gold Can Stay" (p. 383)?

2. Write an essay comparing how grief is handled by the boy's family in this poem and by the couple in "Home Burial" (p. 372).

3. Compare the tone and theme of "'Out, Out—'" with those of Stephen Crane's "A Man Said to the Universe" (p. 166).

The Oven Bird

1916

There is a singer everyone has heard,
Loud, a mid-summer and a mid-wood bird,
Who makes the solid tree trunks sound again.
He says that leaves are old and that for flowers
Mid-summer is to spring as one to ten.   5
He says the early petal-fall is past
When pear and cherry bloom went down in showers
On sunny days a moment overcast;
And comes that other fall we name the fall.
He says the highway dust is over all.   10
The bird would cease and be as other birds
But that he knows in singing not to sing.
The question that he frames in all but words
Is what to make of a diminished thing.

CONSIDERATIONS FOR CRITICAL THINKING AND WRITING

1. **FIRST RESPONSE.** What kind of sonnet is this poem? What is the relationship between the octave and the sestet?

2. The ovenbird is a warbler that makes its domed nest on the ground. What kinds of observations does the speaker have it make about spring, summer, and fall?

3. The final two lines invite symbolic readings. What do you make of them?

4. **CRITICAL STRATEGIES.** Read the section on critical thinking (pp. 661–64) in Chapter 26, "Critical Strategies for Reading," and then research critical commentary on this poem. Write an essay describing the range of interpretations that you find. Which interpretation do you think is the most convincing? Why?

Fire and Ice   *1923*

Some say the world will end in fire,
Some say in ice.
From what I've tasted of desire
I hold with those who favor fire.
But if it had to perish twice,
I think I know enough of hate
To say that for destruction ice
Is also great
And would suffice.

CONSIDERATIONS FOR CRITICAL THINKING AND WRITING

1. **FIRST RESPONSE.** What characteristics of human behavior does the speaker associate with fire and ice?

2. What theories about the end of the world are alluded to in lines 1 and 2?

3. How does the speaker's use of understatement and rhyme affect the tone of this poem?

Stopping by Woods on a Snowy Evening   *1923*

Whose woods these are I think I know.
His house is in the village, though;
He will not see me stopping here
To watch his woods fill up with snow.

My little horse must think it queer   5
To stop without a farmhouse near
Between the woods and frozen lake
The darkest evening of the year.

He gives his harness bells a shake
To ask if there is some mistake.   10
The only other sound's the sweep
Of easy wind and downy flake.

The woods are lovely, dark and deep,
But I have promises to keep,
And miles to go before I sleep,   15
And miles to go before I sleep.

CONSIDERATIONS FOR CRITICAL THINKING AND WRITING

1. **FIRST RESPONSE.** What is the significance of the setting in this poem? How is tone conveyed by the images?

2. What does the speaker find appealing about the woods? What is the purpose of the horse in the poem?

3. Although the last two lines are identical, they are not read at the same speed. Why the difference? What is achieved by the repetition?

4. What is the poem's rhyme scheme? What is the effect of the rhyme in the final stanza?

CONNECTION TO ANOTHER SELECTION

1. What do you think Frost might have to say about "A Parodic Interpretation of 'Stopping by Woods on a Snowy Evening'" by Herbert R. Coursen Jr. (p. 391)?

Nothing Gold Can Stay   *1923*

Nature's first green is gold,
Her hardest hue to hold.
Her early leaf's a flower;
But only so an hour.
The leaf subsides to leaf.
So Eden sank to grief,
So dawn goes down to day.
Nothing gold can stay.

CONSIDERATIONS FOR CRITICAL THINKING AND WRITING

1. **FIRST RESPONSE.** What is meant by "gold" in the poem? Why can't it "stay"?

2. What do the leaf, humanity, and a day have in common?

CONNECTION TO ANOTHER SELECTION

1. Write an essay comparing the tone and theme of "Nothing Gold Can Stay" with those of Robert Herrick's "To the Virgins, to Make Much of Time" (p. 79).

Unharvested   *1936*

A scent of ripeness from over a wall.
And come to leave the routine road
And look for what had made me stall,
There sure enough was an apple tree
That had eased itself of its summer load,   5
And of all but its trivial foliage free,
Now breathed as light as a lady's fan.

For there there had been an apple fall
As complete as the apple had given man.
The ground was one circle of solid red.   10

May something go always unharvested!
May much stay out of our stated plan,
Apples or something forgotten and left,
So smelling their sweetness would be no theft.

CONSIDERATIONS FOR CRITICAL THINKING AND WRITING

1. **FIRST RESPONSE.** Why does the speaker like the idea of some things going unharvested?

2. Explain why this poem is about more than just apples. What lines especially invite deeper readings?

3. What kind of sonnet is this poem? Discuss the effects created by Frost's use of meter and rhyme.

4. **CRITICAL STRATEGIES.** Read the section on mythological criticism (pp. 677–80) in Chapter 26, "Critical Strategies for Reading." How do you think a mythological critic would interpret "Unharvested"?

CONNECTION TO ANOTHER SELECTION

1. Compare the themes in this poem and in "After Apple-Picking" (p. 376).

Neither Out Far nor In Deep   1936

The people along the sand
All turn and look one way.
They turn their back on the land.
They look at the sea all day.

As long as it takes to pass   5
A ship keeps raising its hull;
The wetter ground like glass
Reflects a standing gull.

The land may vary more;
But wherever the truth may be —   10
The water comes ashore,
And the people look at the sea.

They cannot look out far.
They cannot look in deep.
But when was that ever a bar   15
To any watch they keep?

Neither Out Far nor In Deep

The people along the sand
All turn and look one way.
They turn their backs on the land;
They look at the sea all day.

As long as it takes to pass
A ship keeps raising its hull.
The wetter ground like glass
Reflects a standing gull.

The land may vary more,
But wherever the truth may be —
The water comes ashore
And the people look at the sea.

They cannot look out far;
They cannot look in deep;
But when was that ever a bar
To any watch they keep.

Robert Frost

With the permission of The Yale Review.

Manuscript page for Robert Frost's "Neither Out Far nor In Deep" (*opposite*), which was first published in *The Yale Review* in 1934 and later, with a few punctuation changes, in *A Further Range* in 1936.

CONSIDERATIONS FOR CRITICAL THINKING AND WRITING

1. **FIRST RESPONSE.** Frost built this poem around a simple observation that raises some questions. Why do people at the beach almost always face the ocean? What feelings and thoughts are evoked by looking at the ocean?

2. Notice how the verb *look* takes on added meaning as the poem progresses. What are the people looking for?

    3. How does the final stanza extend the poem's significance?

    4. Does the speaker identify with the people described, or does he ironically distance himself from them?

Design   1936

I found a dimpled spider, fat and white,
On a white heal-all,° holding up a moth
Like a white piece of rigid satin cloth —
Assorted characters of death and blight
Mixed ready to begin the morning right,   5
Like the ingredients of a witches' broth —
A snow-drop spider, a flower like a froth,
And dead wings carried like a paper kite.

What had the flower to do with being white,
The wayside blue and innocent heal-all?   10
What brought the kindred spider to that height,
Then steered the white moth thither in the night?
What but design of darkness to appall? —
If design govern in a thing so small.

2 *heal-all:* A common flower, usually blue, once used for medicinal purposes.

CONSIDERATIONS FOR CRITICAL THINKING AND WRITING

    1. **FIRST RESPONSE.** What kinds of speculations are raised in the poem's final two lines? Consider the meaning of the title. Is there more than one way to read it?

    2. How does the division of the octave and sestet in this sonnet serve to organize the speaker's thoughts and feelings? What is the predominant rhyme? How does that rhyme relate to the poem's meaning?

    3. Which words seem especially rich in connotative meanings? Explain how they function in the sonnet.

CONNECTIONS TO OTHER SELECTIONS

    1. Compare the ironic tone of "Design" with the tone of William Hathaway's "Oh, Oh" (p. 24). What would you have to change in Hathaway's poem to make it more like Frost's?

    2. In an essay discuss Frost's view of God in this poem and Dickinson's perspective in "I know that He exists" (p. 354).

    3. Compare "Design" with "In White," Frost's early version of it (following).

Perspectives on Robert Frost

ROBERT FROST

"In White": An Early Version of "Design"   1912

A dented spider like a snow drop white
On a white Heal-all, holding up a moth
Like a white piece of lifeless satin cloth —
Saw ever curious eye so strange a sight? —
Portent in little, assorted death and blight   5
Like the ingredients of a witches' broth? —
The beady spider, the flower like a froth,
And the moth carried like a paper kite.

What had that flower to do with being white,
The blue prunella every child's delight.   10
What brought the kindred spider to that height?
(Make we no thesis of the miller's° plight.)   *miller moth*
What but design of darkness and of night?
Design, design! Do I use the word aright?

CONSIDERATIONS FOR CRITICAL THINKING AND WRITING

1. Read "In White" and "Design" (p. 386) aloud. Which version sounds better to you? Why?

2. Compare these versions line for line, paying particular attention to word choice. List the differences and try to explain why you think Frost revised the lines.

3. How does the change in titles reflect a shift in emphasis in the poem?

ROBERT FROST

On the Living Part of a Poem   1914

The living part of a poem is the intonation entangled somehow in the syntax, idiom, and meaning of a sentence. It is only there for those who have heard it previously in conversation. . . . It is the most volatile and at the same time important part of poetry. It goes and the language becomes dead language, the poetry dead poetry. With it go the accents, the stresses, the delays that are not the property of vowels and syllables but that are shifted at will with the sense. Vowels have length there is no denying. But the accent of sense supersedes all other accent, overrides it and sweeps it away. I will find you the word *come* variously used in various passages, a whole, half, third, fourth, fifth, and sixth note. It is as long as the sense makes it. When men no longer know the intonations on which we string our words they will fall back on what I may call the absolute length of our syllables, which is the length we would give them in passages that meant nothing. . . . I say you can't read a single good sentence with the salt in it unless you have previously heard it spoken. Neither can you with the help of all the characters and diacritical marks pronounce a single word unless you have previously heard it actually pronounced. Words exist in the mouth not books.

From a letter to Sidney Cox in *A Swinger of Birches: A Portrait of Robert Frost*

CONSIDERATIONS FOR CRITICAL THINKING AND WRITING

1. Why does Frost place so much emphasis on hearing poetry spoken?
2. Choose a passage from "Home Burial" (p. 372) or "After Apple-Picking" (p. 376) and read it aloud. How does Frost's description of his emphasis on intonation help explain the effects he achieves in the passage you have selected?
3. Do you think it is true that all poetry must be heard? Do "words exist in the mouth not books"?

AMY LOWELL (1874–1925)
On Frost's Realistic Technique   *1915*

I have said that Mr. Frost's work is almost photographic. The qualification was unnecessary, it is photographic. The pictures, the characters, are reproduced directly from life, they are burnt into his mind as though it were a sensitive plate. He gives out what has been put in unchanged by any personal mental process. His imagination is bounded by what he has seen, he is confined within the limits of his experience (or at least what might have been his experience) and bent all one way like the windblown trees of New England hillsides.

From a review of *North of Boston, The New Republic,* February 20, 1915

CONSIDERATIONS FOR CRITICAL THINKING AND WRITING

1. Consider the "photographic" qualities of Frost's poetry by discussing particular passages that strike you as having been "reproduced directly from life."
2. Write an essay that supports or refutes Lowell's assertion that "He gives out what has been put in unchanged by any personal mental process."

ROBERT FROST
On the Figure a Poem Makes   *1939*

Abstraction is an old story with the philosophers, but it has been like a new toy in the hands of the artists of our day. Why can't we have any one quality of poetry we choose by itself? We can have in thought. Then it will go hard if we can't in practice. Our lives for it.

Granted no one but a humanist much cares how sound a poem is if it is only *a* sound. The sound is the gold in the ore. Then we will have the sound out alone and dispense with the inessential. We do till we make the discovery that the object in writing poetry is to make all poems sound as different as possible from each other, and the resources for that of vowels, consonants, punctuation, syntax, words, sentences, meter are not enough. We need the help of context—meaning—subject matter. That is the greatest help towards variety. All that can be done with words is soon told. So also with meters—particularly in our language where there are virtually but two, strict iambic and loose iambic. The ancients with many were still poor if they depended on meters for all tune. It is painful to watch our sprung-rhythmists straining at the point of omitting one short from a foot for relief from monotony. The possibilities for tune from the dramatic tones of meaning struck across the rigidity of a limited meter are endless. And we are back in poetry as merely one more art of having something to say, sound or unsound. Probably better if sound, because deeper and from wider experience.

Then there is this wildness whereof it is spoken. Granted again that it has an equal claim with sound to being a poem's better half. If it is a wild tune, it is a poem. Our problem then is, as modern abstractionists, to have the wildness pure; to be wild with nothing to be wild about. We bring up as aberrationists, giving way to undirected associations and kicking ourselves from one chance suggestion to another in all directions as of a hot afternoon in the life of a grasshopper. Theme alone can steady us down. Just as the first mystery was how a poem could have a tune in such a straightness as meter, so the second mystery is how a poem can have wildness and at the same time a subject that shall be fulfilled.

It should be of the pleasure of a poem itself to tell how it can. The figure a poem makes. It begins in delight and ends in wisdom. The figure is the same as for love. No one can really hold that the ecstasy should be static and stand still in one place. It begins in delight, it inclines to the impulse, it assumes direction with the first line laid down, it runs a course of lucky events, and ends in a clarification of life—not necessarily a great clarification, such as sects and cults are founded on, but in a momentary stay against confusion. It has denouement. It has an outcome that though unforeseen was predestined from the first image of the original mood—and indeed from the very mood. It is but a trick poem and no poem at all if the best of it was thought of first and saved for the last. It finds its own name as it goes and discovers the best waiting for it in some final phrase at once wise and sad—the happy-sad blend of the drinking song.

No tears in the writer, no tears in the reader. No surprise for the writer, no surprise for the reader. For me the initial delight is in the surprise of remembering something I didn't know I knew. I am in a place, in a situation, as if I had materialized from cloud or risen out of the ground. There is a glad recognition of the long lost and the rest follows. Step by step the wonder of unexpected supply keeps going. The impressions most useful to my purpose seem always those I was unaware of and so made no note of at the time when taken, and the conclusion is come to that like giants we are always hurling experience ahead of us to pave the future with against the day when we may want to strike a line of purpose across it for somewhere. The line will have the more charm for not being mechanically straight. We enjoy the straight crookedness of a good walking stick. Modern instruments of precision are being used to make things crooked as if by eye and hand in the old days.

I tell how there may be a better wildness of logic than of inconsequence. But the logic is backward, in retrospect, after the act. It must be more felt than seen ahead like prophecy. It must be a revelation, or a series of revelations, as much for the poet as for the reader. For it to be that there must have been the greatest freedom of the material to move about in it and to establish relations in it regardless of time and space, previous relation, and everything but affinity. We prate of freedom. We call our schools free because we are not free to stay away from them till we are sixteen years of age. I have given up my democratic prejudices and now willingly set the lower classes free to be completely taken care of by the upper classes. Political freedom is nothing to me. I bestow it right and left. All I would keep for myself is the freedom of my material — the condition of body and mind now and then to summons aptly from the vast chaos of all I have lived through.

Scholars and artists thrown together are often annoyed at the puzzle of where they differ. Both work for knowledge; but I suspect they differ most importantly in the way their knowledge is come by. Scholars get theirs with conscientious thoroughness along projected lines of logic; poets theirs cavalierly and as it happens in and out of books. They stick to nothing deliberately, but let what will stick to them like burrs where they walk in the fields. No acquirement is on assignment, or even self-assignment. Knowledge of the second kind is much more available in the wild free ways of wit and art. A school boy may be defined as one who can tell you what he knows in the order in which he learned it. The artist must value himself as he snatches a thing from some previous order in time and space into a new order with not so much as a ligature clinging to it of the old place where it was organic.

More than once I should have lost my soul to radicalism if it had been the originality it was mistaken for by its young converts. Originality and initiative are what I ask for my country. For myself the originality need be no more than the freshness of a poem run in the way I have described: from delight to wisdom. The figure is the same as for love. Like a piece of ice on a hot stove the poem must ride on its own melting. A poem may be worked over once it is in being, but may not be worried into being. Its most precious quality will remain its having run itself and carried away the poet with it. Read it a hundred times: it will forever keep its freshness as a metal keeps its fragrance. It can never lose its sense of a meaning that once unfolded by surprise as it went.

From *Complete Poems of Robert Frost*

CONSIDERATIONS FOR CRITICAL THINKING AND WRITING

1. Frost places a high premium on sound in his poetry because it "is the gold in the ore." Choose one of Frost's poems in this book and explain the effects of its sounds and how they contribute to its meaning.

2. Discuss Frost's explanation of how his poems are written. In what sense is the process both spontaneous and "predestined"?

3. What do you think Frost means when he says he's given up his "democratic prejudices"? Why is "political freedom" nothing to him?

4. Write an essay that examines in more detail the ways scholars and artists "come by" knowledge.

5. Explain what you think Frost means when he writes, "Like a piece of ice on a hot stove the poem must ride on its own melting."

ROBERT FROST

On the Way to Read a Poem 1951

The way to read a poem in prose or verse is in the light of all the other poems ever written. We may begin anywhere. We *duff* into our first. We read that imperfectly (thoroughness with it would be fatal), but the better to read the second. We read the second the better to read the third, the third the better to read the fourth, the fourth better to read the fifth, the fifth the better to read the first again, or the second if it so happens. For poems are not meant to be read in course any more than they are to be made a study of. I once made a resolve never to put any book to any use it wasn't intended for by its author. Improvement will not be a progression but a widening circulation. Our instinct is to settle down like a revolving dog and make ourselves at home among the poems, completely at our ease as to how they should be taken. The same people will be apt to take poems right as know how to take a hint when there is one and not to take a hint when none is intended. Theirs is the ultimate refinement.

From "Poetry and School," *Atlantic Monthly,* June 1951

CONSIDERATIONS FOR CRITICAL THINKING AND WRITING

1. Given your own experience, how good is Frost's advice about reading in general and his poems in particular?

2. In what sense is a good reader like a "revolving dog" and a person who knows "how to take a hint"?

3. Frost elsewhere in this piece writes, "One of the dangers of college to anyone who wants to stay a human reader (that is to say a humanist) is that he will become a specialist and lose his sensitive fear of landing on the lovely too hard. (With beak and talon.)" Write an essay in response to this concern. Do you agree with Frost's distinction between a "human reader" and a "specialist"?

HERBERT R. COURSEN JR. (B. 1932)

A Parodic Interpretation of "Stopping by Woods on a Snowy Evening" 1962

Much ink has spilled on many pages in exegesis of this little poem. Actually, critical jottings have only obscured what has lain beneath critical noses all these years. To say that the poem means merely that a man stops one night to observe a snowfall, or that the poem contrasts the mundane desire for creature comfort with the sweep of aesthetic appreciation, or that it renders worldly responsibilities paramount, or that it reveals the speaker's latent death-wish is to miss the point rather badly. Lacking has been that mind simple enough to see what is *really* there. . . .

The "darkest evening of the year" in New England is December 21st, a date near that on which the western world celebrates Christmas. It may be that December 21st *is* the date of the poem, or (and with poets this seems more likely) that this is the closest the poet can come to Christmas without giving it all away. Who has "promises to keep" at or near this date, and who must traverse much territory to fulfill these promises? Yes, and who but St. Nick would know the location of *each* home? Only he would know who had "just settled down for a long winter's nap" (the poem's third line — "He will not see me stopping here" — is clearly a veiled allusion) and would not be out inspecting his acreage this night. The unusual phrase "fill up with snow," in the poem's fourth line, is a transfer of Santa's occupational preoccupation to the countryside; he is mulling the filling of countless stockings hung above countless fireplaces by countless careful children. "Harness bells," of course, allude to "Sleighing Song," a popular Christmas tune of the time the poem was written in which the refrain "Jingle Bells! Jingle Bells!" appears; thus again are we put on the Christmas track. The "little horse," like the date, is another attempt at poetic obfuscation. Although the "rein-reindeer" ambiguity has been eliminated from the poem's final version,[1] probably because too obvious, we may speculate that the animal is really a reindeer disguised as a horse by the poet's desire for obscurity, a desire which we must concede has been fulfilled up to now.

The animal is clearly concerned, like the faithful Rudolph — another possible allusion (post facto, hence unconscious) — lest his master fail to complete his mission. Seeing no farmhouse in the second quatrain, but pulling a load of presents, no wonder the little beast wonders! It takes him a full two quatrains to rouse his driver to remember all the empty stockings which hang ahead. And Santa does so reluctantly at that, poor soul, as he ponders the myriad farmhouses and villages which spread between him and his own "winter's nap." The modern St. Nick, lonely and overworked, tosses no "Happy Christmas to all and to all a good night!" into the precipitation. He merely shrugs his shoulders and resignedly plods away.

From "The Ghost of Christmas Past: 'Stopping by Woods on a Snowy Evening,'" *College English,* December 1962

[1] The original draft contained the following line: "That bid me give the reins a shake" (Stageberg-Anderson, *Poetry as Experience* [New York, 1952], p. 457). [Coursen's note.]

CONSIDERATIONS FOR CRITICAL THINKING AND WRITING

1. Is this critical spoof at all credible? Does the interpretation hold any water? Is the evidence reasonable? Why or why not? Which of the poem's details are accounted for and which are ignored?

2. Choose a Frost poem and try writing a parodic interpretation of it.

3. What criteria do you use to distinguish between a sensible interpretation of a poem and an absurd one?

PETER D. POLAND

On "Neither Out Far nor In Deep"   1994

Robert Frost's cryptic little lyric "Neither Out Far nor In Deep" remains as elusive as "the truth" that is so relentlessly pursued in the poem itself. The poem is very much "about" this search for truth, and scholars, for the most part, persistently maintain that such effort is both necessary and noble, adding slowly but inexorably to the storehouse of human knowledge. Suggestive though such an interpretation might be, it distorts Frost's intentions—as a close examination of the curious image of "a standing gull," located strategically at the very heart of this enigmatic work (lines 7–8, its literal and thematic center), will reveal.

As "the people" stare vacantly seaward in search of "the truth," mesmerized by the mysterious, limitless sea, they closely resemble standing (as opposed to flying) gulls. Never directly stated, this comparison, so crucial to the poem's meaning, is clearly implied, and it works very much to the people's disadvantage. For the gull is doing what comes naturally, staring into the teeming sea that is its source of life (that is, of food), and it is merely resting from its life-sustaining labors. "The people," implies Frost, in literally and symbolically turning their backs on their domain, the land, to stare incessantly seaward, are unnatural. Their efforts are life-denying in the extreme.

Frost underscores the life-denying nature of their mindless staring by introducing not a flock of standing gulls, but a single gull only—surprising in that standing gulls (or, more accurately, terns, which typically station themselves en masse by the water's edge) are rarely found alone. The solitary gull points up just what "the people" are doing and how isolating and dehumanizing such activity is. So absorbed are they in their quest for "truth" that they have become oblivious of all else but their own solipsistic pursuit. They have cut themselves off from the land world and all that it represents (struggles and suffering, commitments, obligations, responsibilities) and from one another as well. They have become isolates, like the solitary gull that they resemble. Furthermore, Frost emphasizes not the bird itself but only its reflected image in the glassy surface of the shore; it is the reflected image that is the object of our concern, for it bears significantly on "the people" themselves. In an ironic version of Plato's Parable of the Cave, these relentless pursuers of truth have willfully turned their backs on the only "reality" they can ever know—the land world and all that it represents—and in so doing have been reduced to insubstantial images, shadowy reflections of true human beings engaged in genuinely fruitful human endeavor. Nameless, faceless, mindless, they have become pale copies of the real thing.

All of this adds up to one inescapable conclusion: "The people" are indeed "gulls"—that is, "dupes." In their search for ultimate reality they have been tricked, cheated, conned. It is all a fraud, insists Frost (for all that they do see is the occasional passing ship mentioned in lines 5 and 6), and he clearly holds their vain efforts in contempt. As the final stanzas make dramatically clear, they are wasting away their lives in a meaningless quest, for whatever it is and wherever it might be, "the truth" is surely not here. In short, they can look "Neither Out Far nor In Deep." So why bother?

The poem cries out for comparison with Frost's most famous work, his personal favorite, "Stopping by Woods on a Snowy Evening," wherein the seductive woods — "lovely, dark and deep" — recall the mysterious sea of "Neither Out Far nor In Deep." But the narrator of "Stopping by Woods" realizes how dangerously alluring the woods are. He realizes that he has "promises to keep," that he cannot "sleep" in the face of his societal obligations, and so he shortly turns homeward. "The people" of the present poem, however, continue to "look at the sea all day," seduced by its deep, dark, mysterious depths. Turning their backs on the land world, their world, they have violated their promises; they are asleep to their human responsibilities, as their comparison to the reflected image of a solitary gull suggests. For "gulls" they surely are.

From *The Explicator* 52.2 (Winter 1994)

CONSIDERATIONS FOR CRITICAL THINKING AND WRITING

1. Do you agree with Poland's interpretation of this poem or do you agree with the other readers he mentions who argue that the people on the shore are engaged in a "necessary and noble" pursuit of the truth?

2. How does Poland use "Stopping by Woods on a Snowy Evening" (p. 382) to further his argument?

3. Explain whether or not you think Poland's reading of "Neither Out Far nor In Deep" is consistent with your understanding of Frost's attitudes toward human aspiration in "Birches" (p. 377).

DEREK WALCOTT (B. 1930)

The Road Taken   *1996*

Robert Frost: the icon of Yankee values, the smell of wood smoke, the sparkle of dew, the reality of farmhouse dung, the jocular honesty of an uncle.

Why is the favorite figure of American patriotism not paternal but avuncular? Because uncles are wiser than fathers. They have humor, they keep their distance, they are bachelors, they can't be fooled by rhetoric. Frost loved playing the uncle, relishing the dry enchantment of his own voice, the homely gravel in the throat, the keep-your-distance pseudo-rusticity that suspected every stranger, meaning every reader. The voice is like its weather. It tells you to stay away until you are invited. Its first lines, in the epigraph to Frost's 1949 *Complete Poems,* are not so much invitations as warnings.

> I'm going out to clean the pasture spring;
> I'll only stop to rake the leaves away
> (And wait to watch the water clear, I may):
> I sha'n't be gone long. — You come too.

From the very epigraph, then, the surly ambiguities slide in. Why "I may"? Not for the rhyme, the desperation of doggerel, but because of this truth: that it would take too long to watch the agitated clouded water settle, that is, for as long as patience allows the poet to proceed to the next line. (Note that the parentheses function as a kind of container, or bank, or vessel, of the churned spring.) The refrain, "You come too." An invitation? An order? And how sincere is either? That is the point of Frost's tone, the authoritative but ambiguous distance of a master ironist.

Frost is an autocratic poet rather than a democratic poet. His invitations are close-lipped, wry, quiet; neither the voice nor the metrical line has the open-armed municipal mural expansion of the other democratic poet, Whitman. The people in Frost's dramas occupy a tight and taciturn locale. They are not part of Whitman's parade of blacksmiths, wheelwrights made communal by work. Besieged and threatened, their virtues are as cautious and measured as the scansion by which they are portrayed.

From Joseph Brodsky, Seamus Heaney, and Derek Walcott,
Homage to Robert Frost

CONSIDERATIONS FOR CRITICAL THINKING AND WRITING

1. Why does Walcott characterize Frost as more of an uncle than a father? Explain why you agree or disagree.

2. Choose one of Frost's poems in this anthology and use it to demonstrate that he is a "master ironist."

3. Write an essay that fleshes out Walcott's observation that the people in Frost's poems are "Besieged and threatened, their virtues . . . as cautious and measured as the scansion by which they are portrayed."

Two Complementary Critical Readings

RICHARD POIRIER (B. 1925)

On Emotional Suffocation in "Home Burial"   1977

Frost's poetry recurrently dramatizes the discovery that the sharing of a "home" can produce imaginations of uncontrollable threat inside or outside. "Home" can become the source of those fears from which it is supposed to protect us; it can become the habitation of that death whose anguish it is supposed to ameliorate. And this brings us to one of Frost's greatest poetic dramatizations of the theme, "Home Burial." [T]he pressure is shared by a husband and wife, but . . . the role of the husband is ambiguous. Though he does his best to comprehend the wife's difficulties, he is only partly able to do so. The very title of the poem means something about the couple as well as about the dead child buried in back of the house. It is as if "home" were a burial plot for all of them.

The opening lines of Frost's dramatic narratives are usually wonderfully deft in suggesting the metaphoric nature of "home," the human opportunities or imperatives which certain details represent for a husband or a wife. . . . [I]n "Home Burial," the couple are trapped inside the house, which is described as a kind of prison, or perhaps more aptly, a mental hospital. Even the wife's glance out the window can suggest to the husband the desperation she feels within the confines of what has always been his family's "home"; it looks directly on the family graveyard which now holds the body of their recently dead child: [lines 1–30 of "Home Burial" are quoted here].

The remarkable achievement here is that the husband and wife have become so nearly inarticulate in their animosities that the feelings have been transferred to a vision of household arrangements and to their own bodily movements. They and the house conspire together to create an aura of suffocation. . . . Frost's special genius is in the placement of words. The first line poses the husband as a kind of spy; the opening of the second line suggests a habituated wariness on her part, but from that point to line 5 we are shifted back to his glimpse of her as she moves obsessively again, as yet unaware of being watched, to the window. Suggestions of alienation, secretiveness, male intimidation ("advancing toward her") within a situation of mutual distrust, a miasmic fear inside as well as outside the house — we are made to sense this before anyone speaks. Initially the fault seems to lie mostly with the husband. But as soon as she catches him watching her, and as soon as he begins to talk, it is the grim mutuality of their dilemma and the shared responsibilities for it that sustain the dramatic intelligence and power of the poem.

From Robert Frost: The Work of Knowing

CONSIDERATIONS FOR CRITICAL THINKING AND WRITING

1. According to Poirier, how can the couple's home be regarded as a kind of "mental hospital"? Compare Poirier's view with Kearns's description in the following perspective on the house as a "marital asylum."

2. Explain why you agree or disagree that the husband's behavior is a form of "male intimidation."

3. Write an essay that discusses the "grim mutuality" of the couple's "dilemma."

KATHERINE KEARNS (B. 1949)

On the Symbolic Setting of "Home Burial"   *1987*

"Home Burial" may be used to clarify Frost's intimate relationships between sex, death, and madness. The physical iconography is familiar — a stairwell, a window, a doorway, and a grave — elements which Frost reiterates throughout his poetry. The marriage in "Home Burial" has been destroyed by the death of a first and only son. The wife is in the process of leaving the house, crossing the threshold from marital asylum into freedom. The house is suffocating her. Her window view of the graveyard is not enough and is, in fact, a maddening reminder that she could not enter the earth with her son. With its transparent barrier, the window is a mockery of a widened vision throughout Frost's poetry and seems to incite escape rather than quelling it; in "Home Burial" the woman can "see" through the window and into the grave in a way her husband cannot, and the fear is driving her down the steps toward the door — "She was starting down — / Looking back over her shoulder at some fear" — even before she sees her husband. He threatens to follow his wife and bring her back by force, as if he is the cause of her leaving, but his gesture will be futile because it is based on the mistaken assumption that she is escaping him. Pathetically, he is merely an obstacle toward which she reacts at first dully and then with angry impatience. He is an inanimate part of the embattled household, her real impetus for movement comes from the grave.

The house itself, reduced symbolically and literally to a womblike passageway between the bedroom and the threshold, is a correlative for the sexual tension generated by the man's insistence on his marital rights. He offers to "give up being a man" by binding himself "to keep hands off," but their marriage is already sexually damaged and empty. The man and woman move in an intricate dance, she coming downward and then retracing a step, he "Mounting until she cower[s] under him," she "shrinking from beneath his arm" to slide downstairs. Randall Jarrell examines the image of the woman sinking into "a modest, compact, feminine bundle" upon her skirts;[1] it might be further observed that this childlike posture is also very much a gesture of sexual denial, body bent, knees drawn up protectively against the breasts, all encompassed by voluminous skirts. The two are in profound imbalance, and Frost makes the wife's speech and movements the poetic equivalent of stumbling and resistance; her lines are frequently eleven syllables, and often are punctuated by spondees whose forceful but awkward slowness embodies the woman's vacillations "from terrified to dull," and from frozen and silent immobility to anger. Her egress from the house will be symbolic verification of her husband's impotence, and if she leaves it and does not come back, the house will rot as the best birch fence will rot. Unfilled, without a woman with child, it will fall into itself, an image that recurs throughout Frost's poetry. Thus the child's grave predicts the dissolution of household, . . . almost a literal "home burial."

From "'The Place Is the Asylum': Women and Nature in Robert Frost's Poetry," *American Literature*, May 1987

[1] "Robert Frost's 'Home Burial,'" in *The Moment of Poetry*, ed. Don Cameron Allen (Baltimore: Johns Hopkins UP, 1962), p. 104.

Considerations for Critical Thinking and Writing

1. How does Kearns's discussion of the stairwell, window, doorway, and grave shed light on your reading of "Home Burial"?

2. Discuss whether Kearns sympathizes more with the wife or the husband. Which character do you feel more sympathetic toward? Do you think Frost sides with one or the other? Explain your response.

3. Write an essay in which you agree or disagree with Kearns's assessment that "the wife is in the process of . . . crossing the threshold from marital asylum into freedom."

Suggested Topics for Longer Papers

1. Research Frost's popular reputation and compare that with recent biographical accounts of his personal life. How does knowledge of his personal life affect your reading of his poetry?

2. Frost has been described as a cheerful poet of New England who creates pleasant images of the region as well as a poet who creates a troubling, frightening world bordered by anxiety, anguish, doubts, and darkness. How do the poems in this chapter support both of these readings of Frost's poetry?

Web Research
Robert Frost at
bedfordstmartins.com/
rewritinglit.

14

A Study of Langston Hughes

I believe that poetry should be
direct, comprehensible, and the
epitome of simplicity.
— LANGSTON HUGHES

The poetry of Langston Hughes represents a significant chapter in twentieth-century American literature. The poetry included here both chronicles and evokes African American life during the middle decades of the last century. Moreover, it celebrates the culture and heritage of what is called the "Harlem Renaissance" of the 1920s, which has continued to be a vital tradition and presence in American life. As you introduce yourself to Hughes's innovative techniques and the cultural life embedded in his poetry, keep in mind the Questions for Writing about an Author in Depth (p. 352), which can serve as a guide in your explorations.

Explore contexts
for Langston Hughes
on *LiterActive*.

(*Left*) The publication of *The Weary Blues* in 1926 established Hughes as an important figure in the Harlem Renaissance, a cultural movement characterized by an explosion of black literature, theater, music, painting, and political and racial consciousness that began after the First World War. A stamp commemorating the centennial of Hughes's birth (2002) is but one illustration of his lasting impact on American poetry and culture.

(*Below*) Langston Hughes claimed that Walt Whitman, Carl Sandburg, and Paul Laurence Dunbar were his greatest influences as a poet. However, the experience of black America from the 1920s through the 1960s, the life and language of Harlem, and a love of jazz and the blues clearly shaped the narrative and lyrical experimentation of his poetry. This image of a couple dancing in a Harlem night club is a snapshot of the life that influenced Hughes's work.

In this 1932 image taken by African American photographer James VanDerZee, a Harlem couple in raccoon coats poses with a Cadillac on West 127th Street. VanDerZee once commented, "I tried to pose each person in such a way as to tell a story." His work offered America a dazzling view of black middle-class life in the 1920s and 1930s.
© Donna M. VanDerZee.

A BRIEF BIOGRAPHY

Even as a child, Langston Hughes (1902–1967) was wrapped in an important African American legacy. He was raised by his maternal grandmother, who was the widow of Lewis Sheridan Leary, one of the band of men who participated in John Brown's raid on the federal arsenal at Harpers Ferry in 1859. The raid was a desperate attempt to ignite an insurrection that would ultimately liberate slaves in the South. It was a failure. Leary was killed, but the shawl he wore, which was returned to his wife bloodstained and riddled with bullet holes, was proudly worn by Hughes's grandmother fifty years after the raid, and she used it to cover her grandson at night when he was a young boy.

Throughout his long career as a professional writer, Hughes remained true to the African American heritage he celebrated in his writings, which were frankly "racial in theme and treatment, derived from the life I know." In an influential essay published in *The Nation,* "The Negro Artist and the

The famous Lafayette Theatre, located near 132nd street on 7th Avenue, known during the Harlem Renaissance as the "Boulevard of Dreams," was one of New York's first theaters to desegregate (c. 1912). The theater (now a church) seated 2,000 people and, beginning in 1916, employed its own Lafayette Players, who performed popular and classical plays for almost exclusively black audiences. Known as the "House Beautiful" to many of its patrons, the Lafayette also showcased the blues singer Bessie Smith, the jazz composer Duke Ellington, and other prominent African American performers. Shown here is the vibrant opening night of Shakespeare's *Macbeth*, staged by Orson Welles, featuring leading actors Canada Lee and Rose McLendon, with a musical score by James P. Johnson (1936).
The Granger Collection, New York.

Racial Mountain" (1926), he insisted on the need for black artists to draw on their heritage rather than "to run away spiritually from . . . race":

> We younger Negro artists who create now intend to express our individual dark-skinned selves without fear or shame. If white people are pleased, we are glad. If they are not, it doesn't matter. We know we are beautiful. And ugly too. The tom-tom cries and the tom-tom laughs. If colored people are pleased we are glad. If they are not, their displeasure doesn't matter either. We build our temples for tomorrow, strong as we know how, and we stand on top of the mountain, free within ourselves.

That freedom was hard won for Hughes. His father, James Nathaniel Hughes, could not accommodate the racial prejudice and economic frustration that were the result of James's black and white racial ancestry. James abandoned his wife, Carrie Langston Hughes, only one year after their son was born in Joplin, Missouri, and went to find work in Mexico,

Langston Hughes testifying before the Senate Investigations Subcommittee — Senator Joseph McCarthy's subcommittee on subversive activities — on March 27, 1953. Hughes testified: "From my point [of view] it doesn't matter what the form of government is if the rights of the minorities and the poor people are respected, and if they have a chance to advance equally." (See "Un-American Investigators," p. 423.)
© Bettmann/CORBIS.

where he hoped the color of his skin would be less of an issue than in the United States. During the periods when Hughes's mother shuttled from city to city in the Midwest looking for work, she sent her son to live with his grandmother.

Hughes's spotty relationship with his father — a connection he developed in his late teens and maintained only sporadically thereafter — consisted mostly of arguments about his becoming a writer rather than an engineer and businessman as his father wished. Hughes's father could not appreciate or even tolerate his son's ambition to write about the black experience, and Hughes (whose given name was also James but who refused to be identified by it) could not abide his father's contempt for blacks. Consequently, his determination, as he put it in "The Negro Artist," "to express our individual dark-skinned selves without fear or shame" was not only a profound response to African American culture but also an intensely personal commitment that made a relationship with his own father impossible. Though Hughes had been abandoned by his father, he nevertheless felt an early and deep connection to his ancestors, as he reveals in the following poem, written while crossing the Mississippi River by train as he traveled to visit his father in Mexico, just a month after his high school graduation.

The Negro Speaks of Rivers   1921

I've known rivers:
I've known rivers ancient as the world and older than the
    flow of human blood in human veins.

My soul has grown deep like the rivers.

I bathed in the Euphrates when dawns were young.   5
I built my hut near the Congo and it lulled me to sleep.
I looked upon the Nile and raised the pyramids above it.
I heard the singing of the Mississippi when Abe Lincoln
    went down to New Orleans, and I've seen its muddy
    bosom turn all golden in the sunset.   10

I've known rivers:
Ancient, dusky rivers.

My soul has grown deep like the rivers.

This poem appeared in *The Crisis,* the official publication of the National Association for the Advancement of Colored People, which eventually published more of Hughes's poems than any other magazine or journal. This famous poem's simple and direct free verse makes clear that Africa's "dusky rivers" run concurrently with the poet's soul as he draws spiritual strength as well as individual identity from the collective experience of his ancestors. The themes of racial pride and personal dignity work their way through some forty books that Hughes wrote, edited, or compiled during his forty-five years of writing.

AN INTRODUCTION TO HIS WORK

Hughes's works include volumes of poetry, novels, short stories, essays, plays, opera librettos, histories, documentaries, autobiographies, biographies, anthologies, children's books, and translations, as well as radio and television scripts. This impressive body of work makes him an important literary artist and a leading African American voice of the twentieth century. First and foremost, he considered himself a poet. He set out to be a poet who could address himself to the concerns of his people in poems that could be read with no formal training or extensive literary background. He wanted his poetry to be "direct, comprehensible, and the epitome of simplicity."

Hughes's poetry echoes the voices of ordinary African Americans and the rhythms of their music. He drew on an oral tradition of working-class folk poetry that embraced black vernacular language at a time when some middle-class blacks of the 1920s felt that the use of the vernacular was an embarrassing handicap and an impediment to social progress. Hughes's response to such concerns was unequivocal; at his readings, some of which were accompanied by jazz musicians or singers, his innovative voice found an appreciative audience. As Hughes very well knew, much of the pleasure associated with his poetry comes from reading it aloud; his many recorded readings give testimony to that pleasure.

The blues can be heard moving through Hughes's poetry as well as in the works of many of his contemporaries associated with the Harlem Renaissance, a movement of African American writers, painters, sculptors, actors, and musicians who were active in New York City's Harlem of the 1920s. Hughes's introduction to the "laughter and pain, hunger and heartache" of blues music began the year he spent at Columbia University. He dropped out after only two semesters because he preferred the night life and culture of Harlem to academic life. The sweet, sad blues songs captured for Hughes the intense pain and yearning that he saw around him and that he incorporated into poems such as "The Weary Blues" (p. 412). He also reveled in the jazz music of Harlem and discovered in its open forms and improvisations an energy and freedom that significantly influenced the style of his poetry.

Hughes's life, like the jazz music that influenced his work, was characterized by improvisation and openness. After leaving Columbia, he worked a series of odd jobs and then traveled as a merchant seaman to Africa and Europe from 1923 to 1924. He jumped ship to work for several months in the kitchen of a Paris nightclub. As he broadened his experience through travel, he continued to write poetry. After his return to the United States in 1925 he published poems in two black magazines, *The Crisis* and *Opportunity*, and met the critic Carl Van Vechten, who sent his poems to the publisher Alfred A. Knopf. He also — as a busboy in a Washington, D.C., hotel — met the poet Vachel Lindsay, who was instrumental in advancing Hughes's reputation as a poet. In 1926 Hughes published his first volume of poems,

The Weary Blues, and enrolled in Lincoln University in Pennsylvania, his education funded by a generous patron. His second volume of verse, *Fine Clothes to the Jew,* appeared in 1927, and by the time he graduated from Lincoln in 1929 he was reading his poems publicly on a book tour of the South. Hughes ended the decade as more than a promising poet; as Countee Cullen pronounced in a mixed review of *The Weary Blues* (mixed because Cullen believed that African American poets should embrace universal themes rather than racial themes), Hughes had "arrived."

Hughes wrote more prose than poetry during the 1930s, publishing his first novel, *Not without Laughter* (1930), and a collection of stories, *The Ways of White Folks* (1934). In addition to writing a variety of magazine articles, he also worked on a number of plays and screenplays. Many of his poems from this period reflect proletarian issues. During this decade Hughes's travels took him to all points of the compass — Cuba, Haiti, the Soviet Union, China, Japan, Mexico, France, and Spain — but his general intellectual movement was decidedly toward the left. Hughes was attracted to the American Communist Party, owing to its insistence on equality for all working-class people regardless of race. Like many other Americans of the thirties, he turned his attention away from the exotic twenties and focused on the economic and political issues attending the Great Depression that challenged the freedom and dignity of common humanity.

During World War II, Hughes helped the war effort by writing jingles and catchy verses to sell war bonds and to bolster morale. His protest poems of the thirties were largely replaced by poems that returned to earlier themes centered on the everyday lives of African Americans. In 1942 Hughes described his new collection of poems, *Shakespeare in Harlem,* as "light verse. Afro-American in the blues mood . . . to be read aloud, crooned, shouted, recited, and sung. Some with gestures, some not — as you like." Soon after this collection appeared, the character of Jesse B. Simple emerged from Hughes's 1943 newspaper column for the Chicago *Defender.* Hughes developed this popular urban African American character in five humorous books published over a fifteen-year period: *Simple Speaks His Mind* (1950), *Simple Takes a Wife* (1953), *Simple Stakes a Claim* (1957), *The Best of Simple* (1961), and *Simple's Uncle Sam* (1965). Two more poetry collections appeared in the forties: *Fields of Wonder* (1947) and *One-Way Ticket* (1949).

In the 1950s and 1960s Hughes's poetry again revealed the strong influence of black music, especially in the rhythms of *Montage of a Dream Deferred* (1951) and *Ask Your Mama: 12 Moods for Jazz* (1961). From the poem "Harlem" (p. 422) in *Montage of a Dream Deferred,* Lorraine Hansberry derived the title of her 1959 play *A Raisin in the Sun.* This is only a small measure of Hughes's influence on his fellow African American writers, but it is suggestive nonetheless. For some in the 1950s, however, Hughes and his influence occasioned suspicion. He was watched closely by the FBI and the Special Committee on Un-American Activities of the House of Representatives because of his alleged communist activities in the 1930s. Hughes denied that he was ever a member of the Communist party, but he and others, including Albert Einstein and Paul Robeson, were characterized as "dupes and fellow travelers" by *Life* magazine in 1949. Hughes was subpoenaed to appear before Senator Joseph McCarthy's subcommittee on subversive activities in 1953 and listed by the FBI as a security risk until 1959. His anger and indignation over these attacks from the right can be seen in his poem "Un-American Investigators" (p. 423), published posthumously in *The Panther and the Lash* (1967).

Despite the tremendous amount that Hughes published, including two autobiographies, *The Big Sea* (1940) and *I Wonder as I Wander* (1956), he remains somewhat elusive. He never married or had friends who can lay claim to truly knowing him beyond what he wanted them to know (even though several biographies have been published). And yet Hughes is well known — not for his personal life but for his treatment of the possibilities of African American experiences and identities. Like Walt Whitman, one of his favorite writers, Hughes created a persona that spoke for more than himself. Consider Hughes's voice in the following poem.

I, Too   1925

I, too, sing America.

I am the darker brother.
They send me to eat in the kitchen
When company comes,
But I laugh,   5
And eat well,
And grow strong.

Tomorrow,
I'll be at the table
When company comes.   10
Nobody'll dare
Say to me,
"Eat in the kitchen,"
Then.

Besides,   15
They'll see how beautiful I am
And be ashamed —

I, too, am America.

The "darker brother" who celebrates America is certain of a better future when he will no longer be shunted aside by "company." The poem is characteristic of Hughes's faith in the racial consciousness of African Americans, a consciousness that reflects their integrity and beauty while simultaneously demanding respect and acceptance from others: "Nobody'll dare / Say to me, / 'Eat in the kitchen,' / Then."

Hughes's poetry reveals his hearty appetite for all humanity, his insistence on justice for all, and his faith in the transcendent possibilities of joy and hope that make room for everyone at America's table.

Chronology

1902	Born on February 1, in Joplin, Missouri.
1903–14	Lives primarily with his grandmother in Lawrence, Kansas.
1920	Graduates from high school in Cleveland.
1921–22	Attends Columbia University for one year but then drops out to work odd jobs and discover Harlem.
1923–24	Travels to Africa and Europe while working on a merchant ship.
1926	Publishes his first collection of poems, *The Weary Blues*, and enters Lincoln University in Pennsylvania.
1929	Graduates from Lincoln University.
1930	Publishes his first novel, *Not without Laughter*.
1932	Travels to the Soviet Union.
1934	Publishes his first collection of short stories, *The Ways of White Folks*.
1935	His play *Mulatto* is produced on Broadway.
1937	Covers the Spanish Civil War for the Baltimore *Afro-American*.
1938–39	Founds African American theaters in Harlem and Los Angeles.
1940	Publishes his first autobiography, *The Big Sea*.
1943	Creates the character of Simple in columns for the Chicago *Defender*.
1947	Is poet-in-residence at Atlanta University.
1949	Teaches at University of Chicago's Laboratory School.
1950	Publishes his first volume of Simple sketches, *Simple Speaks His Mind*.
1951	Publishes a translation of Federico García Lorca's *Gypsy Ballads*.
1953	Is subpoenaed to appear before Senator Joseph McCarthy's subcommittee on subversive activities in Washington, D.C.
1954–55	Publishes a number of books for young readers, including *The First Book of Jazz* and *Famous American Negroes*.
1956	Publishes his second autobiography, *I Wonder as I Wander*.
1958	Publishes *The Langston Hughes Reader*.
1960	Publishes *An African Treasury: Articles, Essays, Stories, Poems by Black Africans*.
1961	Is inducted into the National Institute of Arts and Letters.
1962	Publishes *Fight for Freedom: The Story of the NAACP*.

1963	Publishes *Five Plays by Langston Hughes.*
1964	Publishes *New Negro Poets: U.S.A.*
1965	Defends Martin Luther King Jr. from attacks by militant blacks.
1966	Is appointed by President Lyndon B. Johnson to lead the American delegation to the First World Festival of Negro Arts in Dakar.
1967	Dies on May 22 in New York City; his last volume of poems, *The Panther and the Lash,* is published posthumously.
1994	*The Collected Poems of Langston Hughes,* edited by Arnold Rampersad and David Roessel, is published.

Negro   1922

I am a Negro:
    Black as the night is black,
    Black like the depths of my Africa.

I've been a slave:
    Caesar told me to keep his door-steps clean.   5
    I brushed the boots of Washington.

I've been a worker:
    Under my hand the pyramids arose.
    I made mortar for the Woolworth Building.

I've been a singer: 10
    All the way from Africa to Georgia
    I carried my sorrow songs.
    I made ragtime.

I've been a victim:
    The Belgians cut off my hands in the Congo.   15
    They lynch me still in Mississippi.

I am a Negro:
    Black as the night is black,
    Black like the depths of my Africa.

CONSIDERATIONS FOR CRITICAL THINKING AND WRITING

1. **FIRST RESPONSE.** What sort of identity does the speaker claim for the "Negro"? What is the effect of the litany of roles?
2. What is the effect of the repetition of the first and last stanzas?
3. What kind of history of black people does the speaker describe?

CONNECTIONS TO OTHER SELECTIONS

1. How does Hughes's use of night and blackness in "Negro" help to explain their meaning in the poem "Dream Variations" (p. 411)?

2. Write an essay comparing the treatment of oppression in "Negro" with that in William Blake's "The Chimney Sweeper" (p. 181).

Danse Africaine 1922

The low beating of the tom-toms,
The slow beating of the tom-toms,
    Low . . . slow
    Slow . . . low—
    Stirs your blood.
        Dance! 5
A night-veiled girl
    Whirls softly into a
    Circle of light.
    Whirls softly . . . slowly, 10
Like a wisp of smoke around the fire—
    And the tom-toms beat,
    And the tom-toms beat,
And the low beating of the tom-toms
    Stirs your blood. 15

CONSIDERATIONS FOR CRITICAL THINKING AND WRITING

1. **FIRST RESPONSE.** How do the sounds of this poem build its meaning? (What *is* its meaning?)

2. What effect do the repeated rhythms have? You may need to read the poem aloud to answer.

CONNECTION TO ANOTHER SELECTION

1. **CREATIVE RESPONSE.** Try rewriting this poem based on the prescription for poetry in Hughes's "Formula" (p. 414).

Jazzonia 1923

Oh, silver tree!
Oh, shining rivers of the soul!

In a Harlem cabaret
Six long-headed jazzers play.
A dancing girl whose eyes are bold 5
Lifts high a dress of silken gold.

Oh, singing tree!
Oh, shining rivers of the soul!

Were Eve's eyes
In the first garden 10

Just a bit too bold?
Was Cleopatra gorgeous
In a gown of gold?

Oh, shining tree!
Oh, silver rivers of the soul!   15

In a whirling cabaret
Six long-headed jazzers play.

CONSIDERATIONS FOR CRITICAL THINKING AND WRITING

1. **FIRST RESPONSE.** Does "Jazzonia" capture what you imagine a Harlem cabaret to have been like? Discuss the importance of the setting.
2. What is the effect of the variations in lines 1–2, 7–8, and 14–15?
3. What do the allusions to Eve and Cleopatra add to the poem's meaning? Are the questions raised about them answered?

CONNECTION TO ANOTHER SELECTION

1. Compare in an essay the rhythms of "Jazzonia" and "Danse Africaine" (p. 410).

Dream Variations   *1924*

To fling my arms wide
In some place of the sun,
To whirl and to dance
Till the white day is done.
Then rest at cool evening   5
Beneath a tall tree
While night comes on gently,
    Dark like me —
That is my dream!

To fling my arms wide   10
In the face of the sun,
Dance! Whirl! Whirl!
Till the quick day is done.
Rest at pale evening . . .
A tall, slim tree . . .   15
Night coming tenderly
    Black like me.

CONSIDERATIONS FOR CRITICAL THINKING AND WRITING

1. **FIRST RESPONSE.** What distinctions are made in the poem between night and day? Which is the dream?
2. Describe the speaker's "Dream." How might the dream be understood metaphorically?
3. How do the rhythms of the lines contribute to the poem's effects?

CONNECTIONS TO OTHER SELECTIONS

1. In an essay compare and contrast the meanings of darkness and the night in this poem and in William Stafford's "Traveling through the Dark" (p. 172).
2. Discuss the significance of the dream in this poem and in "Dream Boogie" (p. 421).

The Weary Blues   *1925*

Droning a drowsy syncopated tune,
Rocking back and forth to a mellow croon,
    I heard a Negro play.
Down on Lenox Avenue° the other night   *street in Harlem*
By the pale dull pallor of an old gas light   5
        He did a lazy sway. . . .
        He did a lazy sway. . . .
To the tune o' those Weary Blues.
With his ebony hands on each ivory key
He made that poor piano moan with melody.   10
        O Blues!
Swaying to and fro on his rickety stool
He played that sad raggy tune like a musical fool.
        Sweet Blues!
Coming from a black man's soul.   15
        O Blues!
In a deep song voice with a melancholy tone
I heard that Negro sing, that old piano moan —
    "Ain't got nobody in all this world,
        Ain't got nobody but ma self.   20
        I's gwine to quit ma frownin'
        And put ma troubles on the shelf."

Thump, thump, thump, went his foot on the floor.
He played a few chords then he sang some more —
    "I got the Weary Blues   25
        And I can't be satisfied.
        Got the Weary Blues
        And can't be satisfied —
        I ain't happy no mo'
        And I wish that I had died."   30
And far into the night he crooned that tune.
The stars went out and so did the moon.
The singer stopped playing and went to bed
While the Weary Blues echoed through his head.
He slept like a rock or a man that's dead.   35

CONSIDERATIONS FOR CRITICAL THINKING AND WRITING

1. **FIRST RESPONSE.** Write a one-paragraph description of the blues based on how the poem presents this kind of music.

2. How does the speaker's voice compare with the singer's?

3. Comment on the effects of the rhymes.

4. **CRITICAL STRATEGIES.** Read the section on formalist strategies (pp. 666–68) in Chapter 26, "Critical Strategies for Reading," and explain how the rhythm of the lines reflects their meaning.

CONNECTION TO ANOTHER SELECTION

1. Discuss "The Weary Blues" and "Lenox Avenue: Midnight" (p. 415) as vignettes of urban life in America. Do you think that these poems, written more than eighty years ago, are still credible descriptions of city life? Explain why or why not.

Cross   *1925*

My old man's a white old man
And my old mother's black.
If ever I cursed my white old man
I take my curses back.

If ever I cursed my black old mother   5
And wished she were in hell,
I'm sorry for that evil wish
And now I wish her well.

My old man died in a fine big house.
My ma died in a shack.   10
I wonder where I'm gonna die,
Being neither white nor black?

CONSIDERATIONS FOR CRITICAL THINKING AND WRITING

1. **FIRST RESPONSE.** What do you think has caused the speaker to retract his or her hard feelings about his or her parents?

2. Discuss the possible meaning of the title.

3. Why do you think the speaker regrets having "cursed" his or her father and mother? Is it possible to determine if the speaker is male or female? Why or why not?

4. What informs the speaker's attitude toward life?

CONNECTION TO ANOTHER SELECTION

1. Read the perspective by Robert Francis, "On 'Hard' Poetry" (p. 47), and write an essay explaining why you would characterize "Cross" as "hard" or "soft" poetry.

Formula

1926

Poetry should treat
    Of lofty things
Soaring thoughts
    And birds with wings.

The Muse of Poetry
    Should not know   5
That roses
    In manure grow.

The Muse of Poetry
    Should not care   10
That earthly pain
    Is everywhere.

Poetry!
    Treats of lofty things:
Soaring thoughts
    And birds with wings.   15

CONSIDERATIONS FOR CRITICAL THINKING AND WRITING

1. **FIRST RESPONSE.** What makes this poem a parody? What assumptions about poetry are being made fun of?

2. How does "Formula" fit the prescriptions offered in the advice to greeting-card freelancers (p. 41)?

CONNECTIONS TO OTHER SELECTIONS

1. Choose any two poems by Hughes in this collection and explain why they do not fit the "Formula."

2. Write an essay that explains how Helen Farries's "Magic of Love" (p. 42) conforms to the ideas about poetry presented in "Formula."

Esthete in Harlem

1926

Strange,
That in this nigger place
I should meet life face to face;
When, for years, I had been seeking
Life in places gentler-speaking,
Until I came to this vile street
And found Life stepping on my feet!

CONSIDERATIONS FOR CRITICAL THINKING AND WRITING

1. **FIRST RESPONSE.** Why might an esthete find Harlem strange? What changes the speaker's mind?

2. Discuss the effect of the enjambment in lines 6–7.

Lenox Avenue: Midnight   *1926*

The rhythm of life
Is a jazz rhythm,
Honey.
The gods are laughing at us.

The broken heart of love,   5
The weary, weary heart of pain, —
    Overtones,
    Undertones,
To the rumble of street cars,
To the swish of rain.   10

Lenox Avenue,
Honey.
Midnight,
And the gods are laughing at us.

CONSIDERATIONS FOR CRITICAL THINKING AND WRITING

1. **FIRST RESPONSE.** What, in your own experience, is the equivalent of what
   Lenox Avenue is for the speaker?
2. For so brief a poem there are many sounds in these fourteen lines. What are
   they? How do they reinforce the poem's meanings?
3. What do you think is the poem's theme?

CONNECTIONS TO OTHER SELECTIONS

1. In an essay compare the theme of this poem with that of Emily Dickinson's
   "I know that He exists" (p. 354).
2. Compare and contrast the speaker's tone in this poem with that of the
   speaker in Thomas Hardy's "Hap" (p. 626).

Song for a Dark Girl   *1927*

Way Down South in Dixie
    (Break the heart of me)
They hung my black young lover
    To a cross roads tree.

Way Down South in Dixie   5
    (Bruised body high in air)
I asked the white Lord Jesus
    What was the use of prayer.

Way down South in Dixie
    (Break the heart of me)   10
Love is a naked shadow
    On a gnarled and naked tree.

CONSIDERATIONS FOR CRITICAL THINKING AND WRITING

1. **FIRST RESPONSE.** What allusion is made in the first line of each stanza? How is that allusion ironic?

2. What *is* "the use of prayer" (line 8) in this poem? Is the question answered? What, in particular, leads you to your conclusion?

3. Discuss the relationship between love and hatred in the poem.

CONNECTION TO ANOTHER SELECTION

1. Compare the speakers' sensibilities in this poem and in Emily Dickinson's "If I can stop one Heart from breaking" (p. 318). What kinds of cultural assumptions are implicit in each speaker's voice?

Red Silk Stockings

1927

Put on yo' red silk stockings,
Black gal.
Go out an' let de white boys
Look at yo' legs.

Ain't nothin' to do for you, nohow,   5
Round this town, —
You's too pretty.

Put on yo' red silk stockings, gal,
An' tomorrow's chile'll
Be a high yaller.   10

Go out an' let de white boys
Look at yo' legs.

CONSIDERATIONS FOR CRITICAL THINKING AND WRITING

1. **FIRST RESPONSE.** Whom do you think is speaking? Describe his or her tone.

2. Discuss the racial dimensions of this poem.

3. Write a response from the girl—does she put on the red silk stockings? Explain why you imagine her reacting in a certain way.

CONNECTION TO ANOTHER SELECTION

1. Write an essay that compares relations between whites and blacks in this poem and in "Dinner Guest: Me" (p. 426).

Rent-Party° Shout: For a Lady Dancer   1930

Whip it to a jelly!
Too bad Jim!
Mamie's got ma man —
An' I can't find him.
Shake that thing! O!   5
Shake it slow!
That man I love is
Mean an' low.
Pistol an' razor!
Razor an' gun!   10
If I sees ma man he'd
Better run —
For I'll shoot him in de shoulder,
Else I'll cut him down,
Cause I knows I can find him   15
When he's in de ground —
Then can't no other women
Have him layin' round.
So play it, Mr. Nappy!
Yo' music's fine!   20
I'm gonna kill that
Man o' mine!

Rent-Party: In Harlem during the 1920s, parties were given that charged admission to raise money for rent.

CONSIDERATIONS FOR CRITICAL THINKING AND WRITING

1. **FIRST RESPONSE.** Describe the type of music you think might be played at this party today.
2. In what sense is this poem a kind of "Shout"?
3. How is the speaker's personality characterized by her use of language?
4. How does Hughes's use of short lines affect your reading of the poem?

Ballad of the Landlord   1940

Landlord, landlord,
My roof has sprung a leak.
Don't you 'member I told you about it
Way last week?

Landlord, landlord,   5
These steps is broken down.
When you come up yourself
It's a wonder you don't fall down.

Ten Bucks you say I owe you?
Ten Bucks you say is due?   10
Well, that's Ten Bucks more'n I'll pay you
Till you fix this house up new.

What? You gonna get eviction orders?
You gonna cut off my heat?
You gonna take my furniture and   15
Throw it in the street?

Um-huh! You talking high and mighty.
Talk on — till you get through.
You ain't gonna be able to say a word
If I land my fist on you.   20

Police! Police!
Come and get this man!
He's trying to ruin the government
And overturn the land!

Copper's whistle!   25
Patrol bell!
Arrest.

Precinct Station.
Iron cell.
Headlines in press: 30

MAN THREATENS LANDLORD
TENANT HELD NO BAIL
JUDGE GIVES NEGRO 90 DAYS IN COUNTY JAIL

CONSIDERATIONS FOR CRITICAL THINKING AND WRITING

1. **FIRST RESPONSE.** The poem incorporates both humor and serious social commentary. Which do you think is dominant? Explain.
2. Why is the literary ballad an especially appropriate form for the content of this poem?
3. How does the speaker's language simultaneously characterize him and the landlord?

Ku Klux   *1942*

They took me out
To some lonesome place.
They said, "Do you believe
In the great white race?"

I said, "Mister,   5
To tell you the truth,

I'd believe in anything
If you'd just turn me loose."

The white man said, "Boy,
Can it be   10
You're a-standin' there
A-sassin' me?"

They hit me in the head
and knocked me down.
And then they kicked me   15
On the ground.

A klansman said, "Nigger,
Look me in the face —
And tell me you believe in
The great white race."   20

Considerations for Critical Thinking and Writing

1. **FIRST RESPONSE.** Explain how irony is central to "Ku Klux."
2. Is the speaker, in fact, "A-sassin'" the white man (line 12)? How is humor mixed with terror in this poem?

50-50   *1942*

I'm all alone in this world, she said,
Ain't got nobody to share my bed,
Ain't got nobody to hold my hand —
The truth of the matter's
I ain't got no man.   5

Big Boy opened his mouth and said,
Trouble with you is
You ain't got no head!
If you had a head and used your mind
You could have *me* with you   10
All the time.

She answered, Babe, what must I do?

He said, Share your bed—
And your money, too.

Considerations for Critical Thinking and Writing

1. **FIRST RESPONSE.** What do you think is the speaker's attitude toward Big Boy? What's yours?
2. Discuss the significance of the title.
3. **CREATIVE RESPONSE.** Write an additional stanza giving the woman's reply to Big Boy.

Harlem Sweeties

1942

Have you dug the spill
Of Sugar Hill?°
Cast your gims°   *eyes*
On this sepia° thrill: *brown*
Brown sugar lassie,   5
Caramel treat,
Honey-gold baby
Sweet enough to eat.
Peach-skinned girlie,
Coffee and cream,   10
Chocolate darling
Out of a dream.
Walnut tinted
Or cocoa brown,
Pomegranate-lipped   15
Pride of the town.
Rich cream-colored
To plum-tinted black,
Feminine sweetness
In Harlem's no lack.   20
Glow of the quince
To blush of the rose.
Persimmon bronze
To cinnamon toes.
Blackberry cordial,   25
Virginia Dare wine —
All those sweet colors
Flavor Harlem of mine!
Walnut or cocoa,
Let me repeat: 30
Caramel, brown sugar,
A chocolate treat.
Molasses taffy,
Coffee and cream,
Licorice, clove, cinnamon   35
To a honey-brown dream.
Ginger, wine-gold,
Persimmon, blackberry,
All through the spectrum
Harlem girls vary —   40
So if you want to know beauty's
Rainbow-sweet thrill,
Stroll down luscious,
Delicious, *fine* Sugar Hill.

2 *Sugar Hill*: A name for a wealthy section of row houses in Harlem known for the "sweet life"
during the Harlem Renaissance.

1. **FIRST RESPONSE.** Explain how the poem's images serve as a tribute to the Harlem women.

2. Discuss the musical qualities of the poem.

3. Virginia Dare (line 26) is a brand of wine. Research the name on the Internet. Why do you suppose Hughes chose that particular label to include in his tribute?

125th Street °

1950

Face like a chocolate bar
full of nuts and sweet.

Face like a jack-o'-lantern,
candle inside.

Face like a slice of melon,
grin that wide.

125th Street: The main street in Harlem.

1. **FIRST RESPONSE.** How do these three similes create a vivid picture of 125th Street?

2. How does this poem confirm the poet Marvin Bell's observation that "a short poem need not be small"?

Dream Boogie

1951

Good morning, daddy!
Ain't you heard
The boogie-woogie rumble
Of a dream deferred?
Listen closely: 5
You'll hear their feet
Beating out and beating out a—

> *You think*
> *It's a happy beat?*

Listen to it closely: 10
Ain't you heard
something underneath
like a—

What did I say?

Sure,   15
I'm happy!
Take it away!

    Hey, pop!
    Re-bop!
    Mop!   20

    Y-e-a-h!

CONSIDERATIONS FOR CRITICAL THINKING AND WRITING

1. **FIRST RESPONSE.** Answer the question, *"You think / It's a happy beat?"* (lines 8–9).

2. Discuss the poem's musical qualities. Which lines are most musical?

3. Describe the competing tones in the poem. Which do you think is predominant?

CONNECTIONS TO OTHER SELECTIONS

1. In an essay compare and contrast the thematic tensions in this poem and in "Harlem" (below).

2. How are the "dreams" different in "Dream Boogie" and "Dream Variations" (p. 411)?

Harlem   *1951*

What happens to a dream deferred?

    Does it dry up
    like a raisin in the sun?
    Or fester like a sore —
    And then run?   5
    Does it stink like rotten meat?
    Or crust and sugar over —
    like a syrupy sweet?

    Maybe it just sags
    like a heavy load.   10

Or does it explode?

CONSIDERATIONS FOR CRITICAL THINKING AND WRITING

1. **FIRST RESPONSE.** Could the question asked in this poem be raised by any individual or group whose dreams and aspirations are thwarted? Why or why not?

2. In some editions of Hughes's poetry the title of this poem is "Dream Deferred." How would this change affect your reading of the poem's symbolic significance?

3. How might the final line be completed as a simile? What is the effect of the speaker not completing the simile? Why is this an especially useful strategy?

CONNECTION TO ANOTHER SELECTION

1. Write an essay on the themes of "Harlem" and James Merrill's "Casual Wear" (p. 176).

Motto   *1951*

I play it cool
And dig all jive
That's the reason
I stay alive.

My motto,
As I lived and learn,
   is:
Dig And Be Dug
In Return.

CONSIDERATIONS FOR CRITICAL THINKING AND WRITING

1. **FIRST RESPONSE.** Write a paraphrase of the poem. How useful do you think this principle is to live by?
2. Discuss Hughes's use of line spacing in the second stanza.

CONNECTION TO ANOTHER SELECTION

1. Compare the themes of "Motto" and Gwendolyn Brooks's "We Real Cool" (p. 96).

Un-American Investigators   *1953*

The committee's fat,
Smug, almost secure
Co-religionists
Shiver with delight
In warm manure   5
As those investigated —
Too brave to name a name —
Have pseudonyms revealed
In Gentile game
    Of who,   10
    Born Jew,
    Is who?
Is not your name Lipshitz?
    Yes.
Did you not change it   15

For subversive purposes?
　No.
For nefarious gain?
　Not so.
Are you sure?　　　　　　　　　　　　　　　　　　　　　　20
The committee shivers
With delight in
Its manure.

CONSIDERATIONS FOR CRITICAL THINKING AND WRITING

1. **FIRST RESPONSE.** What do you think is the political bent of the speaker? What in the poem suggests this?
2. Research in the library or online the hearings and investigations of the House of Representatives' Special Committee on Un-American Activities. How is this background information relevant to an understanding of this poem?
3. How does the speaker characterize the investigators?
4. Given the images in the poem, what might serve as a substitute for its ironic title?

CONNECTION TO ANOTHER SELECTION

1. Write an essay that connects the committee described in this poem with the speaker in E. E. Cummings's "next to of course god america i" (p. 166). What do they have in common?

Old Walt　　　　　　　　　　　　　　　　　　　　　　*1954*

Old Walt Whitman
Went finding and seeking,
Finding less than sought
Seeking more than found,
Every detail minding　　　　　　　　　　　　　　　　　　5
Of the seeking or the finding.

Pleasured equally
In seeking as in finding,
Each detail minding,
Old Walt went seeking　　　　　　　　　　　　　　　　　10
And finding.

CONSIDERATIONS FOR CRITICAL THINKING AND WRITING

1. **FIRST RESPONSE.** Read any poem by Whitman in this book. Do you agree with the speaker's take on Whitman's poetry?
2. Write an explication of "Old Walt." (For a discussion of how to explicate a poem, see the sample explication on p. 304.)

OLD WALT WHITMAN

WENT BINDING AND SEEKING,

FINDMING LESS THAN SOUGHT,

SEEKING MORE THAN FOUND

PLEABURED EQUALLY IN SEEKING

AS IN FOUND.

1st draft
may 4,
1954

finding,
every detail minding
of the seeking
and the finding.

Manuscript page for "Old Walt" (1954) showing an earlier stage of the poem with Hughes's revisions.

Reprinted by permission of Harold Ober Associates, Incorporated.

3. What is the effect of the poem's repeated sounds?
4. To what extent do you think lines 3 and 4 could be used to describe Hughes's poetry as well as Whitman's?

CONNECTION TO ANOTHER SELECTION

1. How does Hughes's tribute to Whitman compare with his tribute to Frederick Douglass (p. 427)?

High to Low   *1949*

God knows
We have our troubles, too —
One trouble is you:
you talk too loud,
cuss too loud,   5
look too black,
don't get anywhere,
and sometimes it seems
you don't even care.

The way you send your kids to school   10
stockings down,
(not Ethical Culture)
the way you shout out loud in church,
(not St. Phillips)
and the way you lounge on doorsteps   15
just as if you were down South,
(not at 409)
the way you clown —
the way, in other words,
you let me down —   20
me, trying to uphold the race
and you —
well, you can see,
we have our problems,
too, with you.   25

CONSIDERATIONS FOR CRITICAL THINKING AND WRITING

1. **FIRST RESPONSE.** Characterize the speaker. How does the speaker characterize the "you" in the poem?

2. Do you think Hughes empathizes with the speaker or with those being spoken to? Which one do you find more appealing? Why?

3. To what extent are racial matters complicated by class issues in the poem?

CONNECTION TO ANOTHER SELECTION

1. Compare the speaker in "High to Low" with the central character in M. Carl Holman's "Mr. Z" (p. 532) in terms of their racial attitudes.

Dinner Guest: Me   1965

I know I am
The Negro Problem
Being wined and dined,
Answering the usual questions
That come to white mind   5
Which seeks demurely
To probe in polite way
The why and wherewithal
Of darkness U.S.A. —
Wondering how things got this way   10
In current democratic night,
Murmuring gently
Over *fraises du bois,*
"I'm so ashamed of being white."

The lobster is delicious,   15
The wine divine,

And center of attention
At the damask table, mine.
To be a Problem on
Park Avenue at eight   20
Is not so bad.
Solutions to the Problem,
Of course, wait.

CONSIDERATIONS FOR CRITICAL THINKING AND WRITING

1. **FIRST RESPONSE.** What does the speaker satirize in this description of a dinner party? Do you think this "Problem" (line 2) exists today?
2. Why is line 9, "Of darkness U.S.A. —," especially resonant?
3. What effects are created by the speaker's diction?
4. Discuss the effects of the rhymes in lines 15–23.

Frederick Douglass: 1817–1895 °   *1966*

Douglass was someone who,
Had he walked with wary foot
And frightened tread,
From very indecision
Might be dead,   5
Might have lost his soul,
But instead decided to be bold
And capture every street
On which he set his feet,
To route each path   10
Toward freedom's goal,
To make each highway
Choose *his* compass' choice,
To all the world cried,
Hear my voice! . . .   15
Oh, to be a beast, a bird,
Anything but a slave! he said.

Who would be free
Themselves must strike
The first blow, he said.   20

He died in 1895.

He is not dead.

1817–1895: Douglass was actually born in 1818; as a slave, he did not know his true birth date.

CONSIDERATIONS FOR CRITICAL THINKING AND WRITING

1. **FIRST RESPONSE.** This poem was published when the civil rights movement was very active in America. Does that information affect your reading of it?

2. What does Hughes celebrate about the life of Douglass, author of *Narrative of the Life of Frederick Douglass, an American Slave, Written by Himself* (1845)?

CONNECTION TO ANOTHER SELECTION

1. How is the speaker's attitude toward violence in this poem similar to that of the speaker in "Harlem" (p. 422)?

Perspectives on Langston Hughes

LANGSTON HUGHES

On Harlem Rent Parties   1940

Then [in the late twenties and early thirties] it was that house-rent parties began to flourish—and not always to raise the rent either. But, as often as not, to have a get-together of one's own, where you could do the black-bottom with no stranger behind you trying to do it, too. Non-theatrical, non-intellectual Harlem was an unwilling victim of its own vogue. It didn't like to be stared at by white folks. But perhaps the downtowners never knew this—for the cabaret owners, the entertainers, and the speakeasy proprietors treated them fine—as long as they paid.

The Saturday night rent parties that I attended were often more amusing than any night club, in small apartments where God knows who lived—because the guests seldom did—but where the piano would often be augmented by a guitar, or an odd cornet, or somebody with a pair of drums walking in off the street. And where awful bootleg whiskey and good fried fish or steaming chitterling were sold at very low prices. And the dancing and singing and impromptu entertaining went on until dawn came in at the windows.

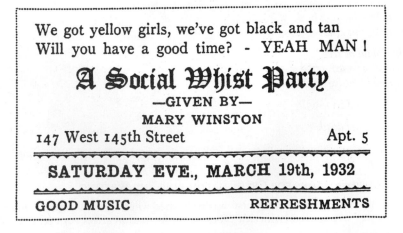

We got yellow girls, we've got black and tan
Will you have a good time? - YEAH MAN !

A Social Whist Party
—GIVEN BY—
MARY WINSTON
147 West 145th Street   Apt. 5

SATURDAY EVE., MARCH 19th, 1932

GOOD MUSIC   REFRESHMENTS

These parties, often termed whist parties or dances, were usually announced by brightly colored cards stuck in the grille of apartment house elevators. Some of the cards were highly entertaining in themselves. [See invitation on opposite page.]

Almost every Saturday night when I was in Harlem I went to a house-rent party. I wrote lots of poems about house-rent parties, and ate there at many a fried fish and pig's foot — with liquid refreshments on the side. I met ladies' maids and truck drivers, laundry workers and shoe shine boys, seamstresses and porters. I can still hear their laughter in my ears, hear the soft slow music, and feel the floor shaking as the dancers danced.

From "When the Negro Was in Vogue," in *The Big Sea*

CONSIDERATIONS FOR CRITICAL THINKING AND WRITING

1. What, according to Hughes, was the appeal of the rent parties in contrast to the nightclubs?
2. Describe the tone in which Hughes recounts his memory of these parties.

JAMES A. EMANUEL (B. 1921)

Hughes's Attitudes toward Religion
1973

Religion, because of its historical importance during and after slavery, is an undeniably useful theme in the work of any major black writer. In a writer whose special province for almost forty-five years was more recent black experience, the theme is doubly vital. Hughes's personal religious orientation is pertinent. Asked about it by the Reverend Dana F. Kennedy of the "Viewpoint" radio and television show (on December 10, 1960), the poet responded:

> I grew up in a not very religious family, but I had a foster aunt who saw that I went to church and Sunday school . . . and I was very much moved, always, by the, shall I say, the rhythms of the Negro church . . . of the spirituals, . . . of those wonderful old-time sermons. . . . There's great beauty in the mysticism of much religious writing, and great help there — but I also think that we live in a world . . . of solid earth and vegetables and a need for jobs and a need for housing. . . .

Two years earlier, the poet had told John Kirkwood of British Columbia's *Vancouver Sun* (December 3, 1958): "I'm not anti-Christian. I'm not against anyone's religion. Religion is one of the innate needs of mankind. What I am against is the misuse of religion. But I won't ridicule it. . . . Whatever part of God is in anybody is not to be played with, and everybody has got a part of God in them."

These typical public protestations by Hughes boil down to his insistence that religion is naturally sacred and beautiful, and that its needed sustenance must not be exploited.

From "Christ in Alabama: Religion in the Poetry of Langston Hughes," in *Modern Black Poets*, edited by Donald B. Gibson

CONSIDERATIONS FOR CRITICAL THINKING AND WRITING

1. Why do you think Emanuel asserts that, owing to slavery, religion "is an undeniably useful theme in the work of any major black writer"?

2. How does Hughes's concern for the "solid earth and vegetables and a need for jobs and a need for housing" qualify his attitudes toward religion?

RICHARD K. BARKSDALE (B. 1915)

On Censoring "Ballad of the Landlord"   1977

In 1940, ["Ballad of the Landlord"] was a rather innocuous rendering of an imaginary dialogue between a disgruntled tenant and a tight-fisted landlord. In creating a poem about two such social archetypes, the poet was by no means taking any new steps in dramatic poetry. The literature of most capitalist and noncapitalist societies often pits the haves against the have-nots, and not infrequently the haves are wealthy men of property who "lord" it over improvident men who own nothing. So the confrontation between tenant and landlord was in 1940 just another instance of the social malevolence of a system that punished the powerless and excused the powerful. In fact, Hughes's tone of dry irony throughout the poem leads one to suspect that the poet deliberately overstated a situation and that some sardonic humor was supposed to be squeezed out of the incident. . . .

Ironically, this poem, which in 1940 depicted a highly probable incident in American urban life and was certainly not written to incite an economic revolt or promote social unrest, became, by the mid-1960s, a verboten assignment in a literature class in a Boston high school. In his Langston Hughes headnote in *Black Voices* (1967), Abraham Chapman reported that a Boston high school English teacher named Jonathan Kozol was fired for assigning it to his students. By the mid-sixties, Boston and many other American cities had become riot-torn, racial tinderboxes, and their ghettos seethed with tenant anger and discontent. So the poem gathered new meanings reflecting the times, and the word of its tenant persona bespoke the collective anger of thousands of black have-nots.

From *Langston Hughes: The Poet and His Critics*

CONSIDERATIONS FOR CRITICAL THINKING AND WRITING

1. Why do you think the Boston School Committee believed that the "Ballad of the Landlord" (p. 417) should be censored?

2. Do you agree with Barksdale that the poem is a "rather innocuous rendering" of economic and social issues? Explain your answer.

3. How did the poem acquire "new meanings reflecting the times" between the 1940s and 1960s? What new meanings might it have for readers today?

KAREN JACKSON FORD
Hughes's Aesthetics of Simplicity 1992

The repression of the great bulk of Hughes's poems is the result of chronic critical scorn for their simplicity. Throughout his long career, but especially after his first two volumes of poetry (readers were at first willing to assume that a youthful poet might grow to be more complex), his books received their harshest reviews for a variety of "flaws" that all originate in an aesthetics of simplicity. From his first book, *The Weary Blues* (1926), to his last one, *The Panther and the Lash* (1967), the reviews invoke a litany of faults: the poems are superficial, infantile, silly, small, unpoetic, common, jejune, iterative, and, of course, simple.[1] Even his admirers reluctantly conclude that Hughes's poetics failed. Saunders Redding flatly opposes simplicity and artfulness. "While Hughes's rejection of his own growth shows an admirable loyalty to his self-commitment as the poet of the 'simple, Negro commonfolk' . . . it does a disservice to his art."[2] James Baldwin, who recognizes the potential of simplicity as an artistic principle, faults the poems for "tak[ing] refuge . . . in a fake simplicity in order to avoid the very difficult simplicity of the experience."[3]

Despite a lifetime of critical disappointments, then, Hughes remained loyal to the aesthetic program he had outlined in 1926 in his decisive poetic treatise, "The Negro Artist and the Racial Mountain." There he had predicted that the common people would "give to this world its truly great Negro artist, the one who is not afraid to be himself," a poet who would explore the "great field of unused [folk] material ready for his art" and recognize that this source would provide "sufficient matter to furnish a black artist with a lifetime of creative work."[4] This is clearly a portrait of the poet Hughes would become, and he maintained his fidelity to this ideal at great cost to his literary reputation.

From "Do Right to Write Right: Langston Hughes's Aesthetics of Simplicity,"
Twentieth Century Literature 38.4 (1992)

[1] Reviews in which these epithets appear are collected in Edward J. Mullen, *Critical Essays on Langston Hughes* (Boston. G. K. Hall, 1986). [Ford's note.]
[2] Redding's comments appear in Mullen 74. [Ford's note.]
[3] Baldwin's comments appear in Mullen 85. [Ford's note.]
[4] *The Nation* 122 (1926): 692. [Ford's note.]

CONSIDERATIONS FOR CRITICAL THINKING AND WRITING

1. What was Hughes's rationale for the value of simplicity in his poetry?
2. Explain whether or not you think there is any justification for regarding Hughes's poetry as "superficial" and too "simple."

DAVID CHINITZ (B. 1962)

The Romanticization of Africa in the 1920s 1997

In Europe black culture was an exotic import; in America it was domestic and increasingly mass-produced. If postwar [World War I] disillusionment judged the majority culture mannered, neurotic, and repressive, Americans had an easily accessible alternative. The need for such an Other produced a discourse in which black Americans figured as barely civilized exiles from the jungle, with — so the clichés ran — tom-toms beating in their blood and dark laughter in their souls. The African American became a model of "natural" human behavior to contrast with the falsified, constrained and impotent modes of the "civilized."

Far from being immune to the lure of this discourse, for the better part of the 1920s Hughes asserted an open pride in the supposed primitive qualities of his race, the atavistic legacy of the African motherland. Unlike most of those who romanticized Africa, Hughes had at least some firsthand experience of the continent; yet he processed what he saw there in images conditioned by European primitivism, rendering "[the land] wild and lovely, the people dark and beautiful, the palm trees tall, the sun bright, and the rivers deep."[1] His short story "Luani of the Jungle," in attempting to glorify aboriginal African vigor as against European anemia, shows how predictable and unextraordinary even Hughes's primitivism could be. To discover in the descendants of idealized Africans the same qualities of innate health, spontaneity, and naturalness requires no great leap; one has only to identify the African American as a displaced primitive, as Hughes does repeatedly in his first book, *The Weary Blues:*

> They drove me out of the forest.
> They took me away from the jungles.
> I lost my trees.
> I lost my silver moons.
>
> Now they've caged me
> In the circus of civilization.[2]

Hughes depicts black atavism vividly and often gracefully, yet in a way that is entirely consistent with the popular iconography of the time. His African Americans retain "among the skyscrapers" the primal fears and instincts of their ancestors "among the palms in Africa."[3] The scion of Africa is still more than half primitive: "All the tom-toms of the jungles beat in my blood, / And all the wild hot moons of the jungles shine in my soul."[4]

From "Rejuvenation through Joy: Langston Hughes, Primitivism and Jazz,"
in *American Literary History,* Spring 1997

[1] *The Big Sea.* 1940. N.Y.: Thunder's Mouth, 1986, 11. [Chinitz's note.]
[2] *The Weary Blues.* N.Y.: Knopf, 1926, 100. [Chinitz's note.]
[3] Ibid. 101.
[4] Ibid. 102.

CONSIDERATIONS FOR CRITICAL THINKING AND WRITING

1. According to Chinitz, why did Europeans and Americans romanticize African culture?

2. Consider the poems published by Hughes in the 1920s reprinted in this anthology. Explain whether you find any "primitivism" in these poems.

3. Later in this essay, Chinitz points out that Hughes eventually rejected the "reductive mischaracterizations of black culture, the commercialism, the sham sociology, and the downright silliness of the primitivist fad." Choose and discuss a poem from this anthology that you think reflects Hughes's later views of primitivism.

Two Complementary Critical Readings

ARNOLD RAMPERSAD (B. 1941)

On the Persona in "The Negro Speaks of Rivers"   1985

Here, the persona moves steadily from dimly starred personal memory ("I've known rivers") toward a rendezvous with modern history (Lincoln going down the Mississippi and seeing the horror of slavery that, according to legend, would make him one day free the slaves). The death wish, benign but suffusing, of its images of rivers older than human blood, of souls grown as deep as these rivers, gives way steadily to an altering, ennobling vision whose final effect gleams in the evocation of the Mississippi's "muddy bosom" turning at last "all golden in the sunset." Personal anguish has been alchemized by the poet into a gracious meditation on his race, whose despised ("muddy") culture and history, irradiated by the poet's vision, changes within the poem from mud into gold. This is a classic example of the essential process of creativity in Hughes.

The poem came to him, according to Hughes (accurately, it seems clear) about ten months after his Mexican illness, when he was riding a train from Cleveland to Mexico to rejoin his father. The time was sundown, the place the Mississippi outside St. Louis. "All day on the train I had been thinking of my father," he would write in *The Big Sea*. "Now it was just sunset and we crossed the Mississippi, slowly, over a long bridge. I looked out of the window of the Pullman at the great muddy river flowing down toward the heart of the South, and I began to think what that river, the old Mississippi, had meant to Negroes in the past — how to be sold down the river was the worst fate that could overtake a slave in bondage. Then I remembered reading how Abraham Lincoln had made a trip down the Mississippi on a raft, and how he had seen slavery at its worst, and had decided within himself that it should be removed from American life. Then I began to think of other rivers in our past — the Congo, and the Niger, and the Nile in Africa — and the thought came to me: 'I've known rivers,' and I put it down on the back of an envelope I had in my pocket, and within the space of ten or fifteen minutes, as the train gathered speed in the dusk, I had written this poem."

From "The Origins of Poetry in Langston Hughes,"
Southern Review 21.3 (1985)

CONSIDERATIONS FOR CRITICAL THINKING AND WRITING

1. How does the biographical information that Rampersad provides affect your reading of "The Negro Speaks of Rivers" (p. 404)?

2. Describe how the poem's images support Rampersad's assertion that Hughes's personal experience is "alchemized" into a reflection on the history of his race.

ADRIAN OKTENBERG (B. 1947)

Memory in "The Negro Speaks of Rivers" 1987

"The Negro Speaks of Rivers" . . . is only the beginning of a long chain of poems by Hughes which confront, distill, extend, and transform the historical experience of black people into an art both limpid and programmatic. . . . The "I" of the poem is not that of "a" Negro but "the" Negro, suggesting the whole of the people and their history. Most of the consonants — *d*'s, *n*'s, *l*'s, *s*'s — are soft, and of the vowels, long *o*'s reoccur, contributing by sound the effect of an ancient voice. The tone of the repeated declarative sentences is muted, lulling. Every element of the poem combines to suggest that when the Negro speaks of rivers it is with the accumulated wisdom of a sage. The function of a sage is to impart the sometimes secret but long accumulated history of a people to its younger members so that they might make the lessons of the past active in the future. This impartation occurs in the central stanza of the poem:

> I bathed in the Euphrates when dawns were young.
> I built my hut near the Congo and it lulled me to sleep.
> I looked upon the Nile and raised the pyramids above it.
> I heard the singing of the Mississippi when Abe Lincoln
>   went down to New Orleans, and I've seen its muddy
>   bosom turn all golden in the sunset.

Moving by suggestion, by naming particular rivers and particular activities performed nearby, the poem implicates the whole history of African and American slavery without ever articulating the word. "I bathed in the Euphrates" and "I built my hut near the Congo" are the normal activities of natural man performed in his natural habitat. That may be an unnecessarily anthropological way of putting it, but the lines are the equivalent of the speaker having said, "I made my life undisturbed in the place where I lived." The shift — and the lesson — occurs in the next two lines. Raising the pyramids above the Nile was the act of slaves, and if ever "Abe Lincoln went down to New Orleans," it would have been in the context of American slavery and the Civil War. Implicit in the history of a people who had first been free and then enslaved is the vision of freedom regained, and therein lies the program. The final line of the poem, "My soul has grown deep like the rivers," suggests wisdom in the word *deep*. The wisdom imparted by the poem, beyond the memory of the suffering of slavery, includes a more deeply embedded memory of freedom. This is perhaps the more powerful memory, or the more sustaining one, and even if deferred, will reemerge in one form or another.

From "From the Bottom Up: Three Radicals of the Thirties" in
A Gift of Tongues: Critical Challenges in Contemporary American Poetry,
edited by Marie Harris and Kathleen Aguero

CONSIDERATIONS FOR CRITICAL THINKING AND WRITING

1. Oktenberg characterizes the speaker of the poem as having "the accumulated wisdom of a sage." Does the knowledge that Hughes was only nineteen years old when he wrote this poem affect your response to Oktenberg's characterization? Explain why or why not.

2. Discuss whether you think Oktenberg's reading competes with or complements Rampersad's interpretation.

SUGGESTED TOPICS FOR LONGER PAPERS

1. Discuss Hughes's use of rhyme, meter, and sounds in five poems of your choice. How do these elements contribute to the poems' meanings?

2. Taken together, how do Hughes's poems provide a critique of relations between blacks and whites in America?

A Study of Billy Collins:
The Author Reflects on Five Poems

© Juliet van Otteren.

More interesting to me than what a poem means is how it travels. In the classroom, I like to substitute for the question, "What is the meaning of the poem?" other questions: "How does this poem go?" or "How does this poem travel through itself in search of its own ending?"
—BILLY COLLINS

Billy Collins selected the five poems presented in this chapter and provided commentaries for each so that readers of this anthology might gain a sense of how he, a former poet laureate and teacher, writes and thinks about poetry. In his perspectives on the poems, Collins explores a variety of literary elements ranging from the poems' origins, allusions, images, metaphors, symbols, and tone to his strategies for maintaining his integrity and sensitivity to both language and the reader. Be advised, however, that these discussions do not constitute CliffsNotes to the poems; Collins does not interpret a single one of them for us. Instead of "beating it with a hose / to find out what it really means," as he writes in his poem "Introduction to Poetry" (p. 40), he "hold[s] it up to the light" so that we can see more clearly how each poem works. He explains that the purpose of his discussions is to have students "see how a poem gets written from the opening lines, through the shifts and maneuvers of the body to whatever closure the poem manages to achieve . . . to make the process of writing a poem less mysterious without taking away the mystery that is at the heart of every good poem."

Along with Collins's illuminating and friendly tutorial, the chapter also provides some additional contexts, such as photos from the poet's personal collection; screen shots that offer a look at his unique — and dynamic — Web presence, including a collection of short animated films set to his work; a collection of draft manuscript pages; and an interview with Michael Meyer.

B.) Collins

A BRIEF BIOGRAPHY AND AN INTRODUCTION TO HIS WORK

Born in New York City in 1941, Billy Collins grew up in Queens, the only child of a nurse and an electrician. His father had hoped that he might go to the Harvard Business School, but following his own lights, he earned a Ph.D. at the University of California, Riverside, in Romantic poetry, and

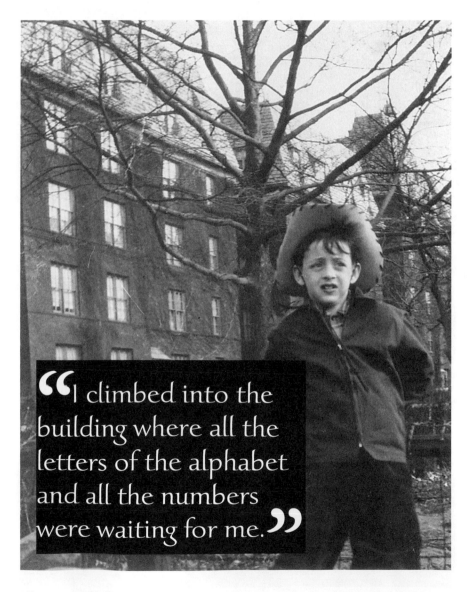

❝I climbed into the building where all the letters of the alphabet and all the numbers were waiting for me.❞

Billy Collins on his first day as a student at St. Joan of Arc School, Jackson Heights, N.Y., 1948.
© Courtesy of Billy Collins.

then began a career in the English department at Lehman College, City University of New York, where he taught writing and literature for more than thirty years. He has also tutored writers at the National University of Ireland at Galway, Sarah Lawrence University, Arizona State University, Columbia University, and Rollins College. Along the way, he wrote poems that eventually earned him a reputation among many people as the most popular living poet in America.

Billy Collins on his first day at Holy Cross College, 1959.
© Courtesy of Billy Collins.

(Left) Billy Collins, senior photo, Holy Cross College, 1963.
© Courtesy of Billy Collins.
(Below) Of this photo, Collins remarks, "The striped pants must be blamed on the '70s. I might add that quitting smoking was about the coolest thing I have ever done."
Courtesy of Billy Collins.

Among his ten collections of poetry are *Ballistics* (2008), *The Trouble with Poetry* (2005), *Nine Horses* (2002), *Sailing Alone Around the Room* (2001), *Picnic, Lightning* (1998), *The Art of Drowning* (1995), *Questions About Angels* (1991), and *The Apple That Astonished Paris* (1988). Collins also edited two anthologies of contemporary poetry designed to entice high school students: *Poetry 180: A Turning Back to Poetry* (2003) and *180 More: Extraordinary Poems for Everyday* (2005). His many honors include fellowships from the New York Foundation for the Arts, the National Endowment for the Arts, and the Guggenheim Foundation. *Poetry* magazine has awarded him the Oscar Blumenthal Prize, the Bess Hokin Prize, the Frederick Bock Prize, and the Levinson Prize.

Collins characterizes himself as someone who was once a professor who wrote poems but who is now a poet who occasionally teaches. This transformation was hard earned because he didn't publish his first complete book of poems until he was in his early forties, with no expectation that twenty years later he would be named United States Poet Laureate (a gift of hope to writers everywhere). Just as writing poetry has been good for Billy Collins, he has been good for poetry. Both their reputations have risen simultaneously owing to his appeal to audiences that pack high school auditoriums, college halls, and public theaters all over the country. His many popular readings — including broadcasts on National Public Radio — have helped to make him a best-selling poet, a phrase that is ordinarily an oxymoron in America.

Unlike many poetry readings, Collins's are attended by readers and fans who come to whoop, holler, and cheer after nearly every poem, as well as to laugh out loud. His audiences are clearly relieved to be in the presence of a poet who speaks to them (not down) without a trace of pretension, superiority, or presumption. His work is welcoming and readable because he weaves observations about the commonplace materials of our lives — the notes we write in the margins of our books, the food we eat, the way we speak, even the way we think of death — into startling, evocative insights that open our eyes wider than they were before.

To understand Collins's attraction to audiences is to better understand his appeal on the page. He wins the affection of audiences with his warmth and genial charm, an affability that makes him appear unreserved and approachable but never intrusive or over the top. He is a quieter, suburban version of Walt Whitman — with a dash of Emily Dickinson's reserve. He gives just enough and lets the poems do the talking so that he remains as mysteriously appealing as his poems. His persona is well crafted and serves to engage readers in the world of his art rather than in his personal life. In a parallel manner, he has often described the openings of his poems as "hospitable" — an invitation to the reader to move further into the poem without having to worry about getting lost in the kind of self-referential obscurity and opacity that sometimes characterize modern poetry.

(Above) The poet
with his dog, Luke.
Scarsdale, N.Y., 1970s.
Courtesy of Billy Collins.
(Left) Billy Collins, in
his office at Lehman
College, 1984.
Courtesy of Billy Collins.

Perhaps not surprisingly, some critics and fellow poets have objected that Collins's poems may sometimes bear up to little more than the pleasures of one reading. Collins, however, believes immediate pleasure can be a primary motivation for reading poetry, and he argues that a poem using simple language should not be considered simpleminded. In his work the ordinary, the everyday, and the familiar often become curious, unusual, and surprising the more closely the poems are read. In interviews, he has compared a first reading of his poems to a reading of the large *E* at the top of an eye chart in an optometrist's office. What starts out clear and unambiguous gradually becomes more complicated and demanding as we squint to make our way to the end. That big *E*—it might be read as "enter"—welcomes us in and gives us the confidence to enjoy the experience, but it doesn't mean that there aren't challenges ahead. The casual, "easy" read frequently becomes a thought-provoking compound of humor, irony, and unconventional wisdom. Humor is such an essential part of Collins's work that in 2004 he was the first recipient of the Poetry Foundation's Mark Twain Award for Humor in Poetry. Given this remarkable trifecta of humor, popularity, and book sales, it is hardly to be unexpected that Collins gives some of his colleagues—as Mark Twain might have put it—the "fantods," but his audiences and readers eagerly anticipate whatever poetic pleasures he will offer them next. In any case, Whitman made the point more than 150 years ago in his preface to *Leaves of Grass:* "The proof of a poet is that his country absorbs him as affectionately as he has absorbed it."

Chronology

1941	Born on March 22 in New York City.
1941–59	Raised in Queens, New York.
1963	Graduates from Holy Cross College with a B.A.
1965	Graduates from the University of California, Riverside, with an M.A.
1968	Begins teaching literature at Lehman College of the City University of New York.
1971	Receives Ph.D. from University of California, Riverside.
1978	*Pokerface* (Kenmore Press).
1980	*Video Poems* (Applezaba Press).
1988	*The Apple That Astonished Paris* (University of Arkansas Press).

BILLY COLLINS

Questions About Angels

POEMS

The poems "Nostalgia" (p. 447) and "Questions About Angels" (p. 450) are from *Questions About Angels,* published in 1991 by the University of Pittsburgh Press.

The cover art of *Questions About Angels,* by Billy Collins, © 1999, is reprinted by permission of the University of Pittsburgh Press.

1991	*Questions About Angels,* which wins the National Poetry Series award (William Morrow & Co.).
1995	*The Art of Drowning* (University of Pittsburgh Press).
1997	Releases a CD of thirty-three poems, *The Best Cigarette.*
1998	*Picnic, Lightning* (University of Pittsburgh Press).
2000	*Taking Off Emily Dickinson's Clothes* (Picador UK).
2000	Appointed Distinguished Professor at Lehman College.
2001	*Sailing Alone Around the Room* (Random House).
2001–03	Appointed United States poet laureate for two terms.
2002	*Nine Horses* (Random House).
2003	*Poetry 180: A Turning Back to Poetry* (Random House).
2004	First Recipient of the Poetry Foundation's Mark Twain Award for Humor in Poetry.
2004–06	Appointed New York State poet laureate.
2005	*The Trouble with Poetry and Other Poems* (Random House).
2006	*She Was Just Seventeen.* (Modern Haiku Press).
2008	*Ballistics* (Random House).
2008–09	Appointed the Irving Bacheller Chair at Rollins College.

The poem "Osso Buco" (p. 445) is from *The Art of Drowning,* published in 1995 by the University of Pittsburgh Press.

The cover art of *The Art of Drowning,* by Billy Collins, © 1995, is reprinted by permission of the University of Pittsburgh Press.

The poem "Litany" (p. 452) is from *Nine Horses,* published in 2002 by Random House. The poem "Building with Its Face Blown Off" (p. 454) is from *The Trouble with Poetry,* published in 2005 by Random House.

"Book cover," copyright © 2002, from *Nine Horses* by Billy Collins. Used by permission of Random House, Inc.

"Book cover," copyright © 2005, from *The Trouble with Poetry* by Billy Collins. Used by permission of Random House, Inc.

BILLY COLLINS

"How Do Poems Travel?"

2008

Asking a poet to examine his or her own work is a bit like trying to get a puppy interested in looking in a mirror. Parakeets take an interest in their own reflections but not puppies, who are too busy smelling everything and tumbling over themselves to have time for self-regard. Maybe the difficulty is that most imaginative poems issue largely from the intuitive right side of the brain, whereas literary criticism draws on the brain's more rational, analytic left side. So, writing about your own writing involves getting up, moving from one room of the brain to another, and taking all the furniture with you. When asked about the source of his work, one contemporary poet remarked that if he knew where his poems came from, he would go there and never come back. What he was implying is that much of what goes on in the creative moment takes place on a stealthy level beneath the writer's conscious awareness. If creative work did not offer access to this somewhat mysterious, less than rational region, we would all be writing annual reports or law briefs, not stories, plays, and poems.

Just because you don't know what you are doing doesn't mean you are not doing it; so let me say what I do know about the writing process. While writing a poem, I am also listening to it. As the poem gets underway, I am pushing it forward — after all, I am the one holding the pencil — but I am also ready to be pulled in the direction that the poem seems to want to go. I am willfully writing the poem, but I am also submitting to the poem's will. Emerson once compared writing poetry to ice-skating. I think he meant that both the skater on a frozen pond and the poet on the page might end up going places they didn't intend to go. And Mario Andretti, the Grand Prix driver, once remarked that "If you think everything is under control, you're just not driving fast enough."

Total control over any artistic material eliminates the possibility of surprise. I would not bother to start a poem if I already knew how it was going to end. I try to "maintain the benefits of my ignorance," as another poet put it, letting the poem work toward an understanding of itself (and of me) as I go along. In a student essay, the idea is to stick to the topic. In much imaginative poetry, the pleasure lies in finding a way to escape the initial topic, to transcend the subject and ride the poem into strange, unforeseen areas. As poet John Ashbery put it: "In the process of writing, all sorts of unexpected things happen that shift the poet away from his plan; these accidents are really what we mean whenever we talk about Poetry." Readers of poetry see only the finished product set confidently on the page; but the process of writing a poem involves uncertainty, ambiguity, improvisation, and surprise.

I think of poetry as the original travel literature in that a poem can take me to an imaginative place where I have never been. A good poem often progresses by a series of associative leaps, including sudden shifts in time and space, all of which results in a kind of mental journey. I never know the ending of the poem when I set out, but I am aware that I am moving the poem toward some destination, and when I find the ending, I recognize it right away. More interesting to me than what a poem means is how it travels. In the classroom, I like to substitute for the question, "What is the meaning of the poem?" other questions: "How does this poem go?" or "How does this poem travel through itself in search of its own ending?" Maybe a few of my poems that follow will serve as illustrations, and I hope what I have said so far will help you articulate how poems go and how they find their endings.

BILLY COLLINS

Osso Buco°   *1995*

I love the sound of the bone against the plate
and the fortress-like look of it
lying before me in a moat of risotto,
the meat soft as the leg of an angel
who has lived a purely airborne existence.   5
And best of all, the secret marrow,
the invaded privacy of the animal
prized out with a knife and swallowed down
with cold, exhilarating wine.

I am swaying now in the hour after dinner,   10
a citizen tilted back on his chair,
a creature with a full stomach—
something you don't hear much about in poetry,
that sanctuary of hunger and deprivation.
You know: the driving rain, the boots by the door,   15
small birds searching for berries in winter.

But tonight, the lion of contentment
has placed a warm, heavy paw on my chest,
and I can only close my eyes and listen
to the drums of woe throbbing in the distance   20
and the sound of my wife's laughter
on the telephone in the next room,
the woman who cooked the savory osso buco,
who pointed to show the butcher the ones she wanted.
She who talks to her faraway friend   25
while I linger here at the table
with a hot, companionable cup of tea,
feeling like one of the friendly natives,
a reliable guide, maybe even the chief's favorite son.

Somewhere, a man is crawling up a rocky hillside   30
on bleeding knees and palms, an Irish penitent
carrying the stone of the world in his stomach;
and elsewhere people of all nations stare
at one another across a long, empty table.

Osso Buco: An Italian veal dish; translated as "hole [*buco*] bone [*osso*]."

But here, the candles give off their warm glow,   35
the same light that Shakespeare and Izaak Walton wrote by,
the light that lit and shadowed the faces of history.
Only now it plays on the blue plates,
the crumpled napkins, the crossed knife and fork.

In a while, one of us will go up to bed   40
and the other one will follow.
Then we will slip below the surface of the night
into miles of water, drifting down and down
to the dark, soundless bottom
until the weight of dreams pulls us lower still,   45
below the shale and layered rock,
beneath the strata of hunger and pleasure,
into the broken bones of the earth itself,
into the marrow of the only place we know.

BILLY COLLINS

On Writing "Osso Buco"   *2008*

The critic Terry Eagleton pointed out that "writing is just language which can
function perfectly well in the physical absence of its author." In other words,
the author does not have to accompany his or her writing into the world to act
as its interpreter or chaperone. One way for a poem to achieve that kind of
independence is to exhibit a certain degree of clarity, at least in the opening
lines. The ideal progression of a poem is from the clear to the mysterious. A
poem that begins simply can engage the reader by establishing a common
ground and then lead the reader into more challenging, less familiar territory.
Robert Frost's poems are admirable models of this process of deepening. Of
course, if the initial engagement is not made early, it's hard to see how the participation of a reader can be counted on.

"Osso Buco" opens with a gourmand's appreciation of a favorite dish, one
commonly served up in Italian restaurants. The one thing I knew at the outset
was that the poem was going to be a meditation on the subject of contentment.
Misery, despondency, melancholy, and just plain human wretchedness are more
likely to be the moods of poetry. Indeed, happiness in serious literature is often
mistaken for a kind of cowlike stupidity. I thought I would address that imbalance by taking on the challenge of writing about the pleasures of a full stomach. Even the gloomiest of philosophers admits that there are occasional
interruptions in the despondency that is the human lot; so why not pay those
moments some poetic attention?

To me, the image of "the lion of contentment" suggested a larger set of
metaphors connected to African exploration that might add glue to the poem.
A metaphor can be deployed in one line of a poem and then dropped, but other
times the poem develops an interest in its own language and a metaphor can be
extended and explored. The result can bind together a number of disparate
thoughts by giving them a common vocabulary. Thus, in this extended metaphor

that begins with "the lion of contentment," "drums of woe" are heard "throbbing in the distance," and later the speaker feels like "one of the friendly natives" or "even the chief's favorite son."

In the fourth stanza, the camera pulls back from the domestic scene of the poem and its mood of contentment to survey examples of human suffering taking place elsewhere. The man with bleeding knees is a reference to the religious pilgrims who annually climb Croagh Patrick, a rocky mountain in the west of Ireland. The image of the "long, empty table" is meant to express the condition of world hunger and famine. But the poem offers those images only in contrast to its insistent theme: satisfaction. Back in the kitchen, there is the candle-lit scene of pleasures recently taken. The mention of Shakespeare and Izaak Walton, who wrote *The Compleat Angler*, a whimsical book on the pleasures of fly-fishing, adds some historic perspective and shows the speaker to be a person of some refinement, an appreciator of literature, history, and, of course, food.

The poem so far has made two noticeable maneuvers, shifting to a global then a historical perspective, but in the final stanza the poem takes its biggest turn when it hits upon the resolving metaphor of geology. The couple retires to bed—another pleasure—descends into sleep, then deeper into dreams, then deeper still through the layers of the earth and into its very center, a "marrow" which harkens back to the bone marrow of the eaten calf. Thus the poem travels from the domestic setting of a kitchen to the plains of Africa, a mountain in Ireland, then back to the kitchen before boring into the core of the earth itself—a fairly extensive journey for a poem of only fifty lines, but not untypical of the kind of ground a lyric poem can quickly cover.

BILLY COLLINS

Nostalgia   *1991*

Remember the 1340s? We were doing a dance called
    the Catapult.
You always wore brown, the color craze of the decade,
and I was draped in one of those capes that were popular,
the ones with unicorns and pomegranates in needlework.
Everyone would pause for beer and onions in the afternoon,   5
and at night we would play a game called "Find the Cow."
Everything was hand-lettered then, not like today.

Where has the summer of 1572 gone? Brocade and sonnet
marathons were the rage. We used to dress up in the flags
of rival baronies and conquer one another in cold rooms
    of stone.   10
Out on the dance floor we were all doing the Struggle
while your sister practiced the Daphne all alone in her room.
We borrowed the jargon of farriers for our slang.
These days language seems transparent, a badly broken code.

The 1790s will never come again. Childhood was big.   15
People would take walks to the very tops of hills
and write down what they saw in their journals without
        speaking.
Our collars were high and our hats were extremely soft.
We would surprise each other with alphabets made of twigs.
It was a wonderful time to be alive, or even dead.   20

I am very fond of the period between 1815 and 1821.
Europe trembled while we sat still for our portraits.
And I would love to return to 1901 if only for a moment,
time enough to wind up a music box and do a
        few dance steps,
or shoot me back to 1922 or 1941, or at least let me   25
recapture the serenity of last month when we picked
berries and glided through afternoons in a canoe.

Even this morning would be an improvement over
        the present.
I was in the garden then, surrounded by the hum of bees
and the Latin names of flowers, watching the early light   30
flash off the slanted windows of the greenhouse
and silver the limbs on the rows of dark hemlocks.

As usual, I was thinking about the moments of the past,
letting my memory rush over them like water
rushing over the stones on the bottom of a stream.   35
I was even thinking a little about the future, that place
where people are doing a dance we cannot imagine,
a dance whose name we can only guess.

BILLY COLLINS

On Writing "Nostalgia"   2008

"Nostalgia" offers me the opportunity to say something about poetic form. Broadly speaking, *form* can mean any feature of a poem that keeps it together and gives it unity. Form is the nails and glue that hold the emotions and thoughts of a poem in place. Naturally, poets are in the business of self-expression, but paradoxically they are always looking for limits. Form can be inherited — the sonnet is an enduring example — or the poet may make up his own rules as he goes along. He might even decide at some point to break the very rules he just imposed upon himself. In either case, formal rules give the poet an enclosed space in which to work, and they keep the poem from descending into chaos or tantrum. As poet Stephen Dunn put it, "form is the pressure that an artist puts on his material in order to see what it will bear."

The Irish poet W. B. Yeats felt that "all that is personal will rot unless it is packed in ice and salt." For a formalist poet like Yeats, "ice and salt," which were common food preservatives of his day, probably meant rhyme and meter. After Walt Whitman showed in *Leaves of Grass* (1855) that poems could be written without those two traditional supporting pillars, poets still had many other formal devices at their disposal. Just because poets could now write poems without a design of rhyme words at the ends of lines or a regular meter such as iambic pentameter did not mean they had abandoned form. Some of these alternative formal strategies would include line length, stanza choice, repetition, rhetorical development (beginning middle end), and thematic recurrence as well as patterns of sound and imagery. Focusing on form allows us to see that poetry can combine a high level of imaginative freedom with the imposition of boundaries and rules of procedure. For the reader, the coexistence of these two contrary elements—liberty and restriction—may be said to create a pleasurable tension found to a higher degree in poetry than in any other literary genre.

An apparent formal element in "Nostalgia," besides its use of stanza breaks, is the chronological sequence it obediently follows. After the absurd opening question (to which the only answer is no), the poem moves forward from the Middle Ages (the 1340s would place us smack in the middle of the Black Death) to the Renaissance, to the beginnings of English Romanticism, that being 1798, when the first edition of *Lyrical Ballads,* a poetic collaboration between Wordsworth and Coleridge, was published. The poem then continues to travel forward in time, but now more whimsically with dates that seem plucked out of the air—1901, 1922, 1941—before arriving rather abruptly at "last month" and then "this morning." If nothing else, the poem demonstrates poetry's freedom from normal time constraints as it manages to travel more than 600 years from the Middle Ages to the present in only twenty-eight lines.

When the poem does arrive at the present, the speaker morphs from a kind of thousand-year-old man into an actual person, a sympathetic fellow who likes to garden and who appreciates the sounds and sights of the natural world. The imaginary historical journey of the poem ends amid the bees and flowers of the speaker's garden, where he continues to dwell nostalgically on the past until his attention turns to the future, really the only place left for him to go. Having relinquished his power as an eyewitness to centuries of human civilization, the speaker trails off in a dreamy speculation about the unknowable dance crazes of the future.

The poem takes a lot of imaginative liberties in the oddness of its premise and its free-ranging images, yet, formally speaking, it is held together by a strict chronological line drawn from the distant historical past right through the present moment and into the future.

I don't recall how a lot of my poems got started, but I do remember that this poem arose out of a kind of annoyance. Just as a grain of sand can irritate an oyster into producing a pearl by coating it with a smooth surface, so a poem may be irked into being. What was bugging me in this case was the popular twentieth-century habit of breaking the past into decades ("the fifties," "the sixties," and so forth), constructs which amounted to little more than a collage of stereotypes. What a gross simplification of this mysterious, invisible thing we call the past, I thought. Even worse, each decade was so sentimentalized as to make one feel that its passing was cause for feelings of melancholy and regret. "Nostalgia," then, is a poem with a motive, that is, to satirize that kind of enforced nostalgia.

BILLY COLLINS

Questions About Angels

1991

Of all the questions you might want to ask
about angels, the only one you ever hear
is how many can dance on the head of a pin.

No curiosity about how they pass the eternal time
besides circling the Throne chanting in Latin
or delivering a crust of bread to a hermit on earth
or guiding a boy and girl across a rickety wooden bridge.

Do they fly through God's body and come out singing?
Do they swing like children from the hinges
of the spirit world saying their names backwards and
      forwards?
Do they sit alone in little gardens changing colors?

What about their sleeping habits, the fabric of their robes,
their diet of unfiltered divine light?
What goes on inside their luminous heads? Is there a wall
these tall presences can look over and see hell?

If an angel fell off a cloud, would he leave a hole
in a river and would the hole float along endlessly
filled with the silent letters of every angelic word?

If an angel delivered the mail, would he arrive
in a blinding rush of wings or would he just assume
the appearance of the regular mailman and
whistle up the driveway reading the postcards?

No, the medieval theologians control the court.
The only question you ever hear is about
the little dance floor on the head of a pin
where halos are meant to converge and drift invisibly.

It is designed to make us think in millions,
billions, to make us run out of numbers and collapse
into infinity, but perhaps the answer is simply one:
one female angel dancing alone in her stocking feet,
a small jazz combo working in the background.

She sways like a branch in the wind, her beautiful
eyes closed, and the tall thin bassist leans over
to glance at his watch because she has been dancing
forever, and now it is very late, even for musicians.

BILLY COLLINS

On Writing "Questions About Angels"   2008

I find that it doesn't take much to get a poem going. A poem can start casually with something trivial and then develop significance along the way. The first inkling may act as a keyhole that allows the poet to look into an imaginary room. When I started to write "Questions About Angels," I really had nothing on my mind except that odd, speculative question: How many angels can dance on the head of a pin? Seemingly unanswerable, the question originated as an attempt to mock certain medieval philosophers (notably Thomas Aquinas) who sought to solve arcane theological mysteries through the sheer application of reason. I had first heard the question when I was studying theology at a Jesuit college, but well before that, the phrase had made its way into the mainstream of modern parlance. It was typical of me to want to begin a poem with something everyone knows and then proceed from there. The poem found a direction to go in when it occurred to me to open up the discussion to include other questions. At that point, it was "Game on."

My investigation really begins in the second stanza, which draws on traditional images of angels in religious art, either worshipping God or paying helpful visits to earth, assisting the poor and protecting the innocent. Then the questions become more fanciful — off-the-wall, really: "Do they fly through God's body and come out singing?" No doubt you could come up with questions of your own about angel behavior; clearly, that has become the poem's game — an open inquiry into the spirit life of these creatures.

After the poem's most bizarre question, which involves a hole that a fallen angel has left in a river, the interrogation descends into the everyday with the image of an angel delivering mail, not gloriously "in a blinding rush of wings" but just like "the regular mailman." After a reminder of the monopoly "the medieval theologians" seem to have on questions about angels, the poem makes a sudden turn (one I did not see coming) by offering a simple, irreducible answer to that unanswerable question. On the little word "but" (line 29), the poem drops down abruptly from "billions" to "one," and the scene shrinks from heaven to a jazz club located in eternity.

In the process of composing a poem, the poet is mentally juggling many concerns, one of the most dominant and persistent being how the poem is going to find a place to end, a point where the journey of the poem was meant to stop, a point where the poet does not want to say any more, and the reader has heard just enough. In this case, the moment she appeared — rather miraculously, as I remember — I knew that this beautiful angel "dancing alone in her stocking feet" was how the poem would close. She was the hidden destination the poem was moving toward all along without my knowing it. I had only to add the detail of the bored bassist and the odd observation that even musicians playing in eternity cannot be expected to stay awake forever.

BILLY COLLINS

Litany   *2002*

You are the bread and the knife,
The crystal goblet and the wine.
            —*Jacques Crickillon*

You are the bread and the knife,
the crystal goblet and the wine.
You are the dew on the morning grass,
and the burning wheel of the sun.
You are the white apron of the baker,   5
and the marsh birds suddenly in flight.

However, you are not the wind in the orchard,
the plums on the counter,
or the house of cards.
And you are certainly not the pine-scented air.   10
There is no way you are the pine-scented air.

It is possible that you are the fish under the bridge,
maybe even the pigeon on the general's head,
but you are not even close
to being the field of cornflowers at dusk.   15

And a quick look in the mirror will show
that you are neither the boots in the corner
nor the boat asleep in its boathouse.

It might interest you to know,
speaking of the plentiful imagery of the world,   20
that I am the sound of rain on the roof.

I also happen to be the shooting star,
the evening paper blowing down an alley,
and the basket of chestnuts on the kitchen table.

I am also the moon in the trees   25
and the blind woman's teacup.
But don't worry, I am not the bread and the knife.
You are still the bread and the knife.
You will always be the bread and the knife,
not to mention the crystal goblet and—somehow—   30
      the wine.

BILLY COLLINS

On Writing "Litany" 2008

As the epigraph to this poem indicates, "Litany" was written in reaction to another poem, a love poem I came across in a literary magazine by a poet I had not heard of. What struck me about his poem was its reliance on a strategy that had its heyday in the love sonnets of the Elizabethan age, namely, the convention of flattering the beloved by comparing her to various aspects of nature. Typically, her eyes were like twin suns, her lips red as coral or rubies, her skin pure as milk, and her breath as sweet as flowers or perfume. Such exaggerations were part of the overall tendency to idealize women who were featured in the courtly love poetry of the time, each of whom was as unattainable as she was beautiful and as cruel as she was fair. It took Shakespeare to point out the ridiculousness of these hyperboles, questioning in one of his sonnets the very legitimacy of comparisons ("Shall I compare thee to a summer's day?" [p. 248]), then drenching the whole process with the cold water of realism ("My mistress' eyes are nothing like the sun" [p. 248]). You might think that would have put an end to the practice, but the habit of appealing to women's vanity through comparisons persists even in the poetry of today. That poem in the magazine prompted me to respond.

Starting with the same first two lines, "Litany" seeks to rewrite the earlier poem by offering a corrective. It aims to point out the latent silliness in such comparisons and perhaps the potential absurdity at the heart of metaphor itself. The poem even wants us to think about the kind of romantic relationships that would permit such discourse.

The poem opens by adding some new metaphors (morning dew, baker's apron, marsh birds) to the pile, but in the second stanza, the poem reverses direction by trading in flattery for a mock-serious investigation of what this woman might be and what she is not. Instead of appealing to her sense of her own beauty, the speaker is perfectly willing to insult her by bringing up her metaphoric shortcomings. By the time he informs her that "There is no way you are the pine-scented air" and "you are not even close / to being the field of cornflowers at dusk," we know that this is a different kind of love poem altogether.

The second big turn comes in the fifth stanza when the speaker unexpectedly begins comparing himself to such things as "the sound of rain on the roof." Notice that the earlier comparisons were not all positive. The "pigeon on the general's head" should remind us of an equestrian statue in a park, and we all know what pigeons like to do to statues. But the speaker is not the least bit ashamed to flatter himself with a string of appealing images including a "shooting star," a "basket of chestnuts," and "the moon in the trees." Turning attention away from the "you" of the poem to the speaker is part of the poem's impertinence — the attentive lover turns into an egomaniac — but it echoes a strategy used by Shakespeare himself. Several of his sonnets begin by being about the beloved but end by being about the poet, specifically about his power to bestow immortality on the beloved through his art. Thus, what begins as a love poem ends as a self-love poem.

The last thing to notice is that "Litany" has a circular structure: it ends by swinging back to its beginning, to the imagery of the epigraph. True to the cheekiness of the speaker, his last words are devoted to tossing the woman a bit of false reassurance that she is still and will always be "the bread and the knife." For whatever that's worth.

BILLY COLLINS

Building with Its Face Blown Off   *2005*

How suddenly the private
is revealed in a bombed-out city,
how the blue and white striped wallpaper

of a second story bedroom is now
exposed to the lightly falling snow   5
as if the room had answered the explosion

wearing only its striped pajamas.
Some neighbors and soldiers
poke around in the rubble below

and stare up at the hanging staircase,   10
the portrait of a grandfather,
a door dangling from a single hinge.

And the bathroom looks almost embarrassed
by its uncovered ochre walls,
the twisted mess of its plumbing,   15

the sink sinking to its knees,
the ripped shower curtain,
the torn goldfish trailing bubbles.

It's like a dollhouse view
as if a child on its knees could reach in   20
and pick up the bureau, straighten a picture.

Or it might be a room on a stage
in a play with no characters,
no dialogue or audience,

no beginning, middle and end —   25
just the broken furniture in the street,
a shoe among the cinder blocks,

a light snow still falling
on a distant steeple, and people
crossing a bridge that still stands.   30

And beyond that — crows in a tree,
the statue of a leader on a horse,
and clouds that look like smoke,

and even farther on, in another country
on a blanket under a shade tree,   35
a man pouring wine into two glasses

and a woman sliding out
the wooden pegs of a wicker hamper
filled with bread, cheese, and several kinds of olives.

Perspective

On "Building with Its Face Blown Off":
Michael Meyer Interviews Billy Collins   *2009*

Meyer: The subject matter of your poetry is well known for being typically about the patterns and rhythms of everyday life, along with its delights, humor, ironies, and inevitable pain. "Building with Its Face Blown Off," however, explicitly concerns war and is implicitly political. What prompted this minority report in your writing?

Collins: It's true that I usually steer away from big historical subjects in my poems. I don't want to assume a level of authority beyond what a reader might trust, nor do I want to appear ridiculous by taking a firm stand against some moral horror that any other humane person would naturally oppose. A few years back, I consciously avoided joining the movement called "Poets against the War" because I thought it was as self-obviating as "Generals for the War." A direct approach to subjects as enormous as war or slavery or genocide carries the risk that the poet will be smothered under the weight of the topic. Plus, readers are already morally wired to respond in a certain way to such things. As a writer, you want to *create* an emotion, not merely activate one that already exists in the reader. And who wants to preach to the choir? I have come across few readers of poetry who are all for war; and, besides, poets have enough work to do without trying to convert the lost. William Butler Yeats put it best in his "On Being Asked for a War Poem":

> I think it better that in times like these
> A poet's mouth be silent, for in truth
> We have no gift to set a statesman right;
> He has had enough of meddling who can please
> A young girl in the indolence of her youth,
> Or an old man upon a winter's night.

Before poetry can be political, it must be personal.

That's my dim view of poems that do little more than declare that the poet, walking the moral high road, is opposed to ethically reprehensible acts. But the world does press in on us, and I was stopped in my tracks one morning when I saw in a newspaper still another photograph of a bombed-out building, which echoed all the similar images I had seen for too many decades in too many conflicts around the world in Dresden, Sarajevo, or Baghdad, wherever shells happen to fall. That photograph revealed one personal aspect of the war: the apartment of a family blown wide open for all to see. "Building with Its Face Blown Off" was my response.

Meyer: The images in the poem have a photojournalistic quality, but they are snapped through the lens of personification rather than a camera. Isn't a picture better than a thousand words?

Collins: I wanted to avoid the moralistic antiwar rhetoric that the underlying subject invites, so I stuck to the visual. A photojournalist once observed that to capture the horrors of war, you don't have to go to the front lines and photograph actual armed conflict: just take a picture of a child's shoe lying on a road. That picture would be worth many words, but as a poet I must add, maybe not quite a thousand. In this poem, I wanted to downplay the horrible violence of the destruction by treating the event as a mere social embarrassment, an invasion of domestic privacy. As Chekhov put it, if you want to get the reader emotionally involved, write cold. For the same reason, I deployed nonviolent metaphors such as the dollhouse and the theater, where the fourth wall is absent. The poem finds a way to end by withdrawing from the scene like a camera pulling back to reveal a larger world. Finally, we are looking down as from a blimp on another country, one where the absence of war provides the tranquility that allows a man and a woman to have a picnic.

A reader once complimented me for ending this poem with olives, the olive branch being a traditional symbol of peace. Another reader heard an echo of Ernest Hemingway's short story "In Another Country," which concerns World War I. Just between you and me, neither of these references had ever occurred to me; but I am always glad to take credit for such happy accidents even if it is similar to drawing a target around a bullet hole. No writer can—or should want to—have absolute control over the reactions of his readers.

Meyer: In your essay on writing "Nostalgia," you point out that "formal rules give the poet an enclosed space in which to work, and they keep the poem from descending into chaos or tantrum" (p. 448). How does form in "Building with Its Face Blown Off" prevent its emotions and thoughts from being reduced to a prose bumper sticker such as "War is hell"?

Collins: I hope what keeps this poem from getting carried away with its traumatic subject is its concentration on the photograph so that the poem maintains a visual, even cinematic, focus throughout. You could think of the poem as a one-minute movie—a short subject about a big topic. Another sign of apparent form here is the division of the poem into three-line stanzas, or tercets, which slow down the reader's progress through the poem. Just as readers should pause slightly at the end of every poetic line (even an unpunctuated one—the equivalent of half a comma), they should also observe a little pause between stanzas. Poetry is famous for condensing large amounts of mental and emotional material into small packages, and it also encourages us to slow down from the speed at which we usually absorb information. The stanzas give the poem a look of regularity, and some of them make visible the grammatical structure of the poem's sentences. Regular stanzas suggest that the poem comes in sections, and they remind us that poetry is a spatial arrangement of words on the page. Think of such stanzas as stones in a stream; the reader steps from one to the next to get to other side.

Meyer: In a classroom discussion of the final two stanzas, one of my students read the couple's picnic scene as "offering an image of hope and peace in contrast to the reckless destruction that precedes it," while another student countered that the scene appeared to be a depiction of "smug indifference and apathy to suffering." Care to comment?

Billy Collins Action Poetry Web site.

In a 2003 interview with the American Booksellers Association, Billy Collins explained that his goal as United States poet laureate was for poetry "to pop up in unexpected places, like the daily announcement in high schools and on airplanes." At the Web site for the Billy Collins Action Poetry film project (www.bcactionpoet.org), you can view artful new interpretations of the poet's work and hear them read aloud by Collins himself, in what makes for an imaginative and elegant combination of poetry and technology.

Produced by the J. Walter Thompson ad agency and the Sundance Channel

Collins: I find it fascinating that such contrary views of the poem's ending could exist. Probably the most vexing question in poetry studies concerns interpretation. One thing to keep in mind is that readers of poetry, students especially, are much more preoccupied with "meaning" than poets are. While I am writing, I am not thinking about the poem's meaning; I am only trying to write a good poem, which involves securing the form of the poem and getting the poem to hold together so as to stay true to itself. Thinking about what my poem means would only distract me from the real work of poetry. Neurologically speaking, I am trying to inhabit the intuitive side of the brain, not the analytical side where critical thought and "study questions" come from. "Meaning," if I think of it at all, usually comes as an afterthought.

But the question remains: How do poets react to interpretations of their work? Generally speaking, once a poem is completed and then published, it is out of the writer's hands. I'm disposed to welcome interpretations that I did not consciously intend — that doesn't mean my unconscious didn't play a role — as long as those readings do not twist the poem out of shape. In "Building with Its Face Blown Off," I added the picnicking couple simply as a sharp contrast to the scene of destruction in the war-torn city. The man and woman are free to enjoy the luxury of each other's company, the countryside, wine, cheese, and even a choice of olives. Are they a sign of hope? Well, yes, insofar as they show us that the whole world is not at war. Smugness? Not so much to my mind, even though that strikes me as a sensible reaction. But if a reader claimed that the couple represented Adam and Eve, or more absurdly, Antony and Cleopatra, or Donny and Marie Osmond, then I would question the person's common sense or sanity. I might even ring for Security. Mainly, the couple is there simply to show us what is no longer available to the inhabitants of the beleaguered city and to give me a place to end the poem.

The Library of Congress   Poem # [ ] GO

POETRY 180

Poetry 180
a poem a day for american high schools

list of all 180 poems
poetry and literature center

RSS   RSS Feeds

Welcome to Poetry 180. Poetry can and should be an important part of our daily lives. Poems can inspire and make us think about what it means to be a member of the human race. By just spending a few minutes reading a poem each day, new worlds can be revealed.

Poetry 180 is designed to make it easy for students to hear or read a poem on each of the 180 days of the school year. I have selected the poems you will find here with high school students in mind. They are intended to be listened to, and I suggest that all members of the school community be included as readers. A great time for the readings would be following the end of daily announcements over the public address system.

Listening to poetry can encourage students and other learners to become members of the circle of readers for whom poetry is a vital source of pleasure. I hope Poetry 180 becomes an important and enriching part of the school day.

Billy Collins
Former Poet Laureate of the United States

more about this program | how to read a poem out loud | read our legal notices

Billy Collins writes: "Poetry can and should be an important part of our daily lives. Poems can inspire and make us think about what it means to be a member of the human race. By just spending a few minutes reading a poem each day, new worlds can be revealed." As United States poet laureate, Collins instituted an ongoing student program through the Library of Congress, called "Poetry 180: A Poem a Day for American High Schools." He chose 180 poems for the project — one for each day of the public school year — and offered some advice on reading poems aloud. (See loc.gov/poetry/180, where the poems can be read online.)
Library of Congress.

1st

DEC 14   tercets
08

Splash 3

The Bath

Nothing much to ~~really~~ tell really —

the soap resting in its soap dish,

hot water blasting from the spigot

hills of bubbles rising,
~~my ankles cro~~
my ankles crossed

and the mirror going blind ~~in the~~ with steam
But there is
~~and~~ the wish to apologize .
to R W B Lewis for letting his
American Adam
slip from my wet hands into the water

the book I propped up to dry

tub-side. like a diving bird

drying ~~its~~ its wings on the shore of
a volcanic Isle.
prehistoric, //

A draft of the unpublished poem "The Bath" from an entry in one of Collins's notebooks, dated December 14, 2008.
Courtesy of Billy Collins.

A draft of the unpublished poem "Busy Day" from an undated page of Collins's notebooks.
Courtesy of Billy Collins.

A draft page of "The Gathering" (working title) from an undated page in Collins's notebooks. Published in 2006 in *The New York Times* as "For Your Digestion; The Gathering."
Courtesy of Billy Collins.

CONSIDERATIONS FOR CRITICAL THINKING AND WRITING

1. In his commentary on "Osso Buco," Collins observes that "happiness in serious literature is often mistaken for a kind of cowlike stupidity" (p. 446). How does the language of the poem maneuver around that kind of sentimental quicksand?

2. What other "formal strategies" can you find in "Nostalgia" (p. 447) in addition to the use of stanza breaks and the chronological sequence that Collins discusses? What other poetic elements serve to unify this satiric poem?

3. **CREATIVE RESPONSE.** Collins explains that he began "Questions About Angels" by setting out to mock the medieval speculative question of how many angels can dance on the head of a pin. He also describes his discovery of how to end the poem in line 29 after the word "but" (p. 451) with the image of the female angel dancing by herself in a jazz club. That was his solution. Try writing your own final six lines as you discover them from the preceding twenty-nine.

4. As Collins indicates, the speaker in "Litany" writes a parodic love poem that "ends as a self-love poem" (p. 453). Is the "cheekiness" in his language appealing to you? Explain why or why not.

5. In his final paragraph "On 'Building with Its Face Blown Off'" (pp. 457–58), Collins offers some commonsense observations about literary interpretation and how to read a poem sensitively and sensibly. He also acknowledges that wild misreadings might cause him to "ring for Security." Write an essay on "How Not to Interpret a Poem" that articulates what you think are some of the most important problems to avoid.

CONNECTIONS TO OTHER SELECTIONS

1. Read carefully Robert Frost's "On the Figure a Poem Makes" (p. 388) and compare his views on how a poem begins, proceeds, and makes its way to an ending with Collins's perspective on how a poem "travel[s] through itself in search of its own ending" (p. 445).

2. Compare one of the commentaries by Collins on a poem of your choice with a commentary by Julia Alvarez on one of her poems in Chapter 16, "A Study of Julia Alvarez: The Author Reflects on Five Poems." How do the commentaries compare in their subject, tone, and emphasis on the art of composition? Describe how each poet's distinct voice emerges from the commentary.

SUGGESTED TOPICS FOR LONGER PAPERS

1. Analyze the humor in four of Collins's poems included in this anthology (see also "Introduction to Poetry" [p. 40] and "Marginalia" [p. 54]). What purpose does the humor serve? Does the humor appeal to you? Explain why or why not, giving examples.

2. View the poems available on the Billy Collins Action Poetry Web site (see page 457 and www.bcactionpoet.org), where you can find visual interpretations of individual poems and hear Collins read the poems aloud. Choose three of the poems and write an analysis of how the visual and auditory representations affect your response to the poems' language. Explain why you think this approach enhances or diminishes — or is simply different from — reading the poem on a page.

16

A Study of Julia Alvarez: The Author Reflects on Five Poems

When I'm asked what made me into a writer, I point to the watershed experience of coming to this country. Not understanding the language, I had to pay close attention to each word — great training for a writer.

— JULIA ALVAREZ

© Daniel Cima.

This chapter offers five poems, chosen by Julia Alvarez for this anthology, with commentaries written by the poet herself. Alvarez's insights on each work, in addition to accompanying images and documents, provide a variety of contexts — personal, cultural, and historical — for understanding and appreciating her poems.

In her introductions to each of the poems, Alvarez shares her reasons for writing, what was on her mind when she wrote each work, what she thinks now looking back at them, as well as a bird's-eye view into her writing process (see especially the drafts of the poem in progress on pp. 482–84). She also evokes the voices of those who have inspired her—muses that range from women talking and cooking in a kitchen to a character in *The Arabian Nights* to the poets Walt Whitman, Langston Hughes, and others. Alvarez writes, "A poem can be a resting place for the soul . . . a world teeming with discoveries and luminous little *ah-ha!* moments, a 'place for the genuine,' as Marianne Moore calls it." Read on and find out, for example, who her real "First Muse" was, and what, according to Alvarez, a famous American poet and the Chiquita Banana have in common.

In addition to Alvarez's inviting and richly detailed introductions, the chapter also presents a number of visual contexts, such as a photo of a 1963 civil rights demonstration in Queens, New York; the poet's passport photo taken at age ten, just before she moved back to the United States; a collection of draft manuscript pages; and an image of one of Alvarez's poems set in a bronze plaque in a sidewalk—part of "Library Way" in New York City. Further, a critical essay—which complements Alvarez's own perspectives throughout the chapter—by Kelli Lyon Johnson (p. 489) allows readers to consider Alvarez's work in a critical framework. (For a discussion on reading a work alongside critical theory, see Chapter 26, "Critical Strategies for Reading," p. 661.)

A BRIEF BIOGRAPHY

Although Julia Alvarez was born (1950) in New York City, she lived in the Dominican Republic until she was ten years old. She returned to New York after her father, a physician, was connected to a plot to overthrow the dictatorship of Rafael Trujillo, and the family had to flee. Growing up in Queens was radically different from the Latino Caribbean world she experienced during her early childhood. A new culture and new language sensitized Alvarez to her surroundings and her use of language so that emigration from the Dominican Republic to Queens was the beginning of her movement toward becoming a writer. Alvarez quotes the Polish poet Czeslaw Milosz's assertion that "Language is the only homeland" to explain her own sense that what she really settled into was not so much the United States as the English language.

Her fascination with English continued into high school and took shape in college as she became a serious writer—first at Connecticut College from 1967 to 1969 and then at Middlebury College, where she earned her B.A. in 1971. At Syracuse University she was awarded the American Academy of Poetry Prize and, in 1975, earned an M.A. in creative writing.

Since then Alvarez has served as a writer-in-residence for the Kentucky Arts Commission, the Delaware Arts Council, and the Arts Council of Fayetteville, North Carolina. She has taught at California State College (Fresno), College of Sequoias, Phillips Andover Academy, the University of

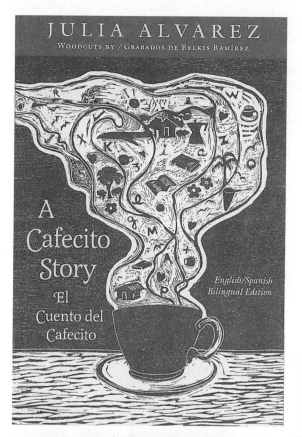

(*Left*) *A Cafecito Story* (2001), which Alvarez describes as a modern "eco-parable" or "green fable" and love story, was inspired by the author's work with local coffee growers in the Dominican Republic.

Cover image by Belkis Ramírez. Reprinted by permission.

(*Below*) Julia Alvarez with students from Middlebury College at her coffee farm, Alta Gracia, in the Dominican Republic.

Photograph courtesy of Fundación Finca Alta Gracia.

Vermont, George Washington University, the University of Illinois, and, since 1988, at Middlebury College, where she has been a professor of literature and creative writing and is currently a part-time writer-in-residence. Alvarez divides her time between Vermont and the Dominican Republic where she and her husband have set up an organic coffee farm, Alta Gracia, that supports a literacy school for children and adults. *A Cafecito Story* (2001), which Alvarez considers a "green fable" or "eco-parable," grew out of their experiences promoting fair trade and sustainability for coffee farmers in the Dominican Republic.

AN INTRODUCTION TO HER WORK

Alvarez's poetry has been widely published in journals and magazines ranging from the *New Yorker* to *Mirabella* to the *Kenyon Review*. Her first book of poems, *Homecoming* (1984; a new expanded verison, *Homecoming: New and Collected Poems*, was published in 1996 by Plume/Penguin), uses simple — yet incisive — language to explore issues related to love, domestic life, and work. Her second book of poetry, *The Other Side/El Otro Lado* (1995), is a collection of meditations on her childhood memories of immigrant life that shaped her adult identity and sensibilities. Some of these concerns are also manifested in her book of essays, titled *Something to Declare* (1998), a collection that describes her abiding concerns about how to respond to competing cultures. In her third poetry collection, *The Woman I Kept to Myself* (2004), Alvarez reflects on her personal life and development as a writer from the vantage point of her mid-fifties in seventy-five poems, each consisting of three ten-line stanzas.

In addition to writing a number of books for children and young adults, Alvarez has also published six novels. The first, *How the García Girls Lost Their Accents* (1991), is a collection of fifteen separate but interrelated stories that cover thirty years of the lives of the García sisters from the late 1950s to the late 1980s. Drawing on her own experiences, Alvarez describes the sisters fleeing the Dominican Republic and growing up Latina in the United States. *In the Time of the Butterflies* (1994) is a fictional account of a true story concerning four sisters who opposed Trujillo's dictatorship. Three of the sisters were murdered in 1960 by the government, and the surviving fourth sister recounts the events of their personal and political lives that led to her sisters' deaths. Shaped by the history of Dominican freedom and tyranny, the novel also explores the sisters' relationships to each other and their country.

In *¡Yo!* (1997), Alvarez focuses on Yolanda, one of the García sisters from her first novel, who is now a writer. Written in the different voices of Yo's friends and family members, this fractured narrative constructs a complete picture of a woman who uses her relationships as fodder for fiction, a woman who is self-centered, aggravating, and finally lovable — who is deeply embedded in American culture while remaining aware of her Dominican roots. *¡Yo!*, which means "I" in English, is a meditation on points of view and narrative.

In the Name of Salomé (2000) is a fictional account of Salomé Ureña, who was born in the 1850s and considered to be "the Emily Dickinson of the Dominican Republic," and her daughter's efforts late in life to reconcile her relationship to her mother's reputation and her own response to Castro's revolution in Cuba. Alvarez published her sixth and most recent novel, *Saving the World*, in 2006, a story that also links two women's lives, one from the past and one from the present, around personal and political issues concerning humanitarian efforts to end smallpox in the nineteenth century and the global AIDS epidemic in the twenty-first century.

Chronology

1950	Born on March 27 in New York City.
1950–60	Raised in the Dominican Republic.
1960	Alvarez family flees the Dominican Republic for New York City after her father joins efforts to overthrow the dictatorship of Rafael Trujillo.
1961	Rafael Trujillo is assassinated.
1967–69	Attends Connecticut College.
1971	Graduates from Middlebury College with a B.A.
1975	Graduates from Syracuse University with an M.A.
1979–80	Attends Bread Loaf School of English.
1979–81	Instructor at Phillips Andover Academy.
1981–83	Visiting assistant professor at University of Vermont.
1984	Publishes *Homecoming*, a volume of poems, and *The Housekeeping Book*, a handmade book of a series of "housekeeping poems," illustrated by Carol MacDonald and Rene Schall.
1984–85	Visiting writer-in-residence at George Washington University.
1985–88	Assistant professor of English at University of Illinois.
1987–88	Awarded a National Endowment for the Arts Fellowship.
1988–98	Professor of English at Middlebury College.
1988–Present	Writer-in-residence at Middlebury College.
1991	Publishes *How the García Girls Lost Their Accents*, a novel.
1994	Publishes *In the Time of the Butterflies*, a novel.
1995	Publishes *The Other Side/El Otro Lado*, a volume of poems.
1996	Publishes *Homecoming: New and Collected Poems*, a reissue of *Homecoming* (1984) with new work included.
1997	Publishes *¡Yo!*, a novel.
1998	Publishes *Something to Declare*, a collection of essays, and *Seven Trees*, a handmade volume of poems.
2000	Publishes *In the Name of Salomé*, a novel, and *The Secret Footprints*, a picture book for children.

2001	Publishes *A Cafecito Story*, a novel or "eco-parable," and *How Tía Lola Came to ~~Visit~~ Stay*, a novel for young adults.
2002	Publishes *The Woman I Kept to Myself*, a volume of poems, and *Before We Were Free*, a novel for young adults.
2004	Publishes *A Gift of Gracias: The Legend of Altagracia*, a picture book for children, and *Finding Miracles*, a novel for young adults.
2006	Publishes *Saving the World*, a novel.
2007	Publishes *Once Upon a Quinceañera: Coming of Age in the USA*, a memoir and cultural study of ceremonies for Latina girls when they turn fifteen.
2009	Publishes *Return to Sender*, a children's novel.

In "Queens, 1963" Alvarez remembers the neighborhood she lived in when she was a thirteen-year-old and how "Everyone seemed more American / than we, newly arrived." The tensions that arose when new immigrants and ethnic groups moved onto the block were mirrored in many American neighborhoods in 1963. Indeed, the entire nation was made keenly aware of such issues as integration when demonstrations were organized across the South and a massive march on Washington in support of civil rights for African Americans drew hundreds of thousands of demonstrators who listened to Martin Luther King Jr. deliver his electrifying "I have a dream" speech. But the issues were hardly resolved, as evidenced by 1963's two best-selling books: *Happiness Is a Warm Puppy* and *Security Is a Thumb and a Blanket*, by Charles M. Schulz of *Peanuts* cartoon fame. The popularity of these books is, perhaps, understandable given the tensions that moved across the country and which seemed to culminate on November 22, 1963, when President Kennedy was assassinated in Dallas, Texas. These events are not mentioned in "Queens, 1963," but they are certainly part of the context that helps us to understand Alvarez's particular neighborhood. In the following introductory essay, Alvarez reflects on the cultural moment of 1963 and her reasons for writing the poem.

JULIA ALVAREZ

On Writing "Queens, 1963"   *2006*

I remember when we finally bought our very own house after three years of living in rentals. Back then, Queens, New York, was not the multicultural, multilingual place it is today. But the process was beginning. Our neighborhood was sprinkled with ethnicities, some who had been here longer than others. The Germans down the block — now we would call them German Americans — had been Americans for a couple of generations as had our Jewish neighbors, and most definitely, the Midwesterners across the street. Meanwhile, the Greek family next door were newcomers as were we, our accents still heavy, our cooking

Julia Alvarez, age ten, in her 1960 passport photo.
Courtesy of Julia Alvarez.

smells commingling across our backyard fences during mealtimes: their Greek lamb with rosemary, our Dominican habichuelas with sofrito.°

It seemed a peaceable enough kingdom until a black family moved in across the street. What a ruckus got started! Of course, it was the early 1960s: the civil rights movement was just getting under way in this country. Suddenly, our neighborhood was faced with discrimination, but coming from the very same people who themselves had felt discrimination from other, more mainstream Americans. It was my first lesson in hypocrisy and in realizing that America was still an experiment in process. The words on the Statue of Liberty

habichuelas with sofrito: Kidney beans prepared with a sautéed mixture of spices, herbs, garlic, onion, pepper, and tomato.

(see "Sometimes the Words Are So Close," p. 481) were only a promise, not yet a practice in the deep South or in Queens, New York.

In writing this poem I wanted to suggest the many ethnic families in the neighborhood. Of course, I couldn't use their real names and risk being sued. (Though, come to think of it, I've never heard of a poem being sued, have you?) Plus, there is the matter of failing memory. (This was forty-two years ago!) So I chose names that suggested other languages, other places, and also — always the poet's ear at work — names that fit in with the rhythm and cadence of the lines.

JULIA ALVAREZ

Queens, 1963   1992

Everyone seemed more American
than we, newly arrived,
foreign dirt still on our soles.
By year's end, a sprinkler waving
like a flag on our mowed lawn,   5
we were blended into the block,
owned our own mock Tudor house.
Then the house across the street
sold to a black family.
Cop cars patrolled our block   10
from the Castellucci's at one end
to the Balakian's on the other.
We heard rumors of bomb threats,
a burning cross on their lawn.
(It turned out to be a sprinkler.)   15
Still the neighborhood buzzed.
The barber's family, Haralambides,
our left-side neighbors, didn't want trouble.
They'd come a long way to be free!
Mr. Scott, the retired plumber,   20
and his plump midwestern wife,
considered moving back home
where white and black got along
by staying where they belonged.
They had cultivated our street   25
like the garden she'd given up
on account of her ailing back,
bad knees, poor eyes, arthritic hands.
She went through her litany daily.
Politely, my mother listened —   30
¡Ay, Mrs. Scott, qué pena!°
— her Dominican good manners
still running on automatic.
The Jewish counselor next door,

31 *qué pena:* What a shame!

had a practice in her house;   35
clients hurried up her walk
ashamed to be seen needing.
(I watched from my upstairs window,
gloomy with adolescence,
and guessed how they too must have   40
hypocritical old-world parents.)
Mrs. Bernstein said it was time
the neighborhood opened up.
As the first Jew on the block,
she remembered the snubbing she got   45
a few years back from Mrs. Scott.
But real estate worried her,
our houses' plummeting value.
She shook her head as she might
at a client's grim disclosures.   50
Too bad the world works this way.
The German girl playing the piano
down the street abruptly stopped
in the middle of a note.
I completed the tune in my head   55
as I watched *their* front door open.
A dark man in a suit
with a girl about my age
walked quickly into a car.
My hand lifted but fell   60
before I made a welcoming gesture.
On her face I had seen a look
from the days before we had melted
into the United States of America.
It was hardness mixed with hurt.   65
It was knowing she never could be
the right kind of American.
A police car followed their car.
Down the street, curtains fell back.
Mrs. Scott swept her walk   70
as if it had just been dirtied.
Then the German piano commenced
downward scales as if tracking
the plummeting real estate.
One by one I imagined the houses   75
sinking into their lawns,
the grass grown wild and tall
in the past tense of this continent
before the first foreigners owned
any of this free country.   80

CONSIDERATIONS FOR CRITICAL THINKING AND WRITING

1. **FIRST RESPONSE.** What nationalities are the people in this neighborhood in
   the New York City borough of Queens? Are they neighborly to each other?

2. In line 3, why do you suppose Alvarez writes "foreign dirt still on our soles" rather than "foreign soil still on our shoes"? What does Alvarez's word choice suggest about her feelings for her native country?

3. Characterize the speaker. How old is she? How does she feel about having come from the Dominican Republic? About living in the United States?

4. Do you think this poem is optimistic or pessimistic about racial relations in the United States? Explain your answer by referring to specific details in the poem.

Connections to Other Selections

1. Compare the use of irony in "Queens, 1963" with that in John Ciardi's "Suburban" (p. 525). How does irony contribute to each poem?

2. Discuss the problems immigrants encounter in this poem and in Chitra Banerjee Divakaruni's "Indian Movie, New Jersey" (p. 562).

3. Write an essay comparing and contrasting the tone and theme in "Queens, 1963" and in Tato Laviera's "AmeRícan" (p. 292).

Queens Civil Rights Demonstration   1963

In this photograph police remove a Congress of Racial Equality (CORE) demonstrator from a Queens construction site. Demonstrators blocked the delivery entrance to the site because they wanted more African Americans and Puerto Ricans hired in the building-trade industry.
Reprinted by permission of AP/Wide World Photos.

CONSIDERATIONS FOR CRITICAL THINKING AND WRITING

1. Discuss the role played by the police in this photograph and in "Queens, 1963." What attitudes toward the police do the photograph and the poem display?

2. How do you think the Scotts and Mrs. Bernstein would have responded to this photograph in 1963?

3. Compare the tensions in "Queens, 1963" to those depicted in this photo. How do the speaker's private reflections relate to this public protest?

Perspective

MARNY REQUA (B. 1971)

From an Interview with Julia Alvarez   *1997*

M.R. What was it like when you came to the United States?

J.A. When we got to Queens, it was really a shock to go from a totally Latino, *familia* Caribbean world into this very cold and kind of forbidding one in which we didn't speak the language. I didn't grow up with a tradition of writing or reading books at all. People were always telling stories but it wasn't a tradition of literary . . . reading a book or doing something solitary like that. Coming to this country I discovered books, I discovered that it was a way to enter into a portable homeland that you could carry around in your head. You didn't have to suffer what was going on around you. I found in books a place to go. I became interested in language because I was learning a language intentionally at the age of ten. I was wondering, "Why is it that word and not another?" which any writer has to do with their language. I always say I came to English late but to the profession early. By high school I was pretty set: that's what I want to do, be a writer.

M.R. Did you have culture shock returning to the Dominican Republic as you were growing up?

J.A. The culture here had an effect on me — at the time this country was coming undone with protests and flower children and drugs. Here I was back in the Dominican Republic and I wouldn't keep my mouth shut. I had my own ideas and I had my own politics, and it, I just didn't gel anymore with the family. I didn't quite feel I ever belonged in this North American culture and I always had this nostalgia that when I went back I'd belong, and then I found out I didn't belong there either.

M.R. Was it a source of inspiration to have a foot in both cultures?

J.A. I only came to that later. [Then], it was a burden because I felt torn. I wanted to be part of one culture and then part of the other. It was a time when the model for the immigrant was that you came and you became an American and you cut off your ties and that was that. My parents had that frame of mind, because they were so afraid, and they were "Learn your English" and "Become one of them," and that left out so much. Now I see the richness. Part of what I want to do with my work is that complexity, that richness. I don't want it to be simplistic and either/or.

From "The Politics of Fiction," *Frontera* magazine 5 (1997)

CONSIDERATIONS FOR CRITICAL THINKING AND WRITING

1. What do you think Alvarez means when she describes books as "a portable homeland that you could carry around in your head"?

2. Why is it difficult for Alvarez to feel that she belongs in either the Dominican or the North American culture?

3. Alvarez says that in the 1960s "the model for the immigrant was that you came and you became an American and you cut off your ties and that was that." Do you think this model has changed in the United States since then? Explain your response.

4. How might this interview alter your understanding of "Queens, 1963"? What light is shed, for example, on the speaker's feeling that her family "blended into the block" in line 6?

JULIA ALVAREZ

On Writing "Housekeeping Cages" and Her Housekeeping Poems   *1998*

I can still remember the first time I heard my own voice on paper. It happened a few years after I graduated from a creative writing master's program. I had earned a short-term residency at Yaddo, the writer's colony, where I was assigned a studio in the big mansion — the tower room at the top of the stairs. The rules were clear: we artists and writers were to stick to our studios during the day and come out at night for supper and socializing. Nothing was to come between us and our work.

I sat up in my tower room, waiting for inspiration. All around me I could hear the typewriters going. Before me lay a blank sheet of paper, ready for the important work I had come there to write. That was the problem, you see. I was trying to do IMPORTANT work and so I couldn't hear myself think. I was trying to pitch my voice to "Turning and turning in the widening gyre," or, "Of man's first disobedience, and the fruit of that forbidden tree, " or, "Sing in me, Muse, and through me tell the story." I was tuning my voice to these men's voices because I thought that was the way I had to sound if I wanted to be a writer. After all, the writers I read and admired sounded like that.

But the voice I heard when I listened to myself think was the voice of a woman, sitting in her kitchen, gossiping with a friend over a cup of coffee. It was the voice of Gladys singing her sad boleros, Belkis putting color on my face with tales of her escapades, Tití naming the orchids, Ada telling me love stories as we made the beds. I had, however, never seen voices like these in print. So, I didn't know poems could be written in those voices, *my* voice.

So there I was at Yaddo, trying to write something important and coming up with nothing. And then, hallelujah — I heard the vacuum going up and down the hall. I opened the door and introduced myself to the friendly, sweating woman, wielding her vacuum cleaner. She invited me down to the kitchen so we wouldn't disturb the other guests. There I met the cook, and as we all sat, drinking coffee, I paged through her old cookbook, *knead, poach, stew, whip, score, julienne, whisk, sauté, sift.* Hmm. I began hearing a music in these words. I jotted down the names of implements:

> Cup, spoon, ladle, pot, kettle,
> grater and peeler,
> colander, corer,
> waffle iron, small funnel.

"You working on a poem there?" the cook asked me.
I shook my head.

A little later, I went upstairs and wrote down in my journal this beautiful vocabulary of my girlhood. As I wrote, I tapped my foot on the floor to the rhythm of the words. I could see Mami and the aunts with the cook in the kitchen bending their heads over a pot of habichuelas, arguing about what flavor was missing—what could it be they had missed putting in it? And then, the thought of Mami recalled Gladys, the maid who loved to sing, and that thought led me through the house, the mahogany furniture that needed dusting, the beds that needed making, the big bin of laundry that needed washing.

That day, I began working on a poem about dusting. Then another followed on sewing; then came a sweeping poem, an ironing poem. Later, I would collect these into a series I called "the housekeeping poems," poems using the metaphors, details, language of my first apprenticeship as a young girl. Even later, having found my woman's voice, I would gain confidence to explore my voice as a Latina and to write stories and poems using the metaphors, details, rhythms of that first world I had left behind in Spanish.

But it began, first, by discovering my woman's voice at Yaddo where I had found it as a child. Twenty years after learning to sing with Gladys, I was reminded of the lessons I had learned in childhood: that my voice would not be found up in a tower, in those upper reaches or important places, but down in the kitchen among the women who first taught me about service, about passion, about singing as if my life depended on it.

From *Something to Declare*

JULIA ALVAREZ

Housekeeping Cages   1994

Sometimes people ask me why I wrote a series of poems about housekeeping if I'm a feminist. Don't I want women to be liberated from the oppressive roles they were condemned to live? I don't see housekeeping that way. They were the crafts we women had, sewing, embroidering, cooking, spinning, sweeping, even the lowly dusting. And like Dylan Thomas said, we sang in our chains like the sea. Isn't it already thinking from the point of view of the oppressor to say to ourselves, what we did was nothing?

You use what you have, you learn to work the structure to create what you need. I don't feel that writing in traditional forms is giving up power, going over to the enemy. The word belongs to no one, the houses built of words belong to no one. We have to take them back from those who think they own them.

Sometimes I get in a mood. I tell myself I am taken over. I am writing under somebody else's thumb and tongue. See, English was not my first language. It was, in fact, a colonizing language to my Spanish Caribbean. But then Spanish was also a colonizer's language; after all, Spain colonized Quisqueya. There's no getting free. We are always writing in a form imposed on us. But then, I'm Scheherazade in the Sultan's room. I use structures to survive and triumph! To say what's important to me as a woman and as a Latina.

I think of form as territory that has been colonized, but that you can free. See, I feel subversive in formal verse. A voice is going to inhabit that form that was barred from entering it before! That's what I tried in the "33" poems, to use my woman's voice in a sonnet as I would use it sitting in the kitchen with a close friend, talking womanstuff. In school, I was always trying to inhabit those forms as the male writers had. To pitch my voice to "Of man's first disobedience, and the fruit. . . ." If it didn't hit the key of "Sing in me, Muse, and through me tell the story," how could it be important poetry? The only kind.

While I was in graduate school some of the women in the program started a Women's Writing Collective in Syracuse. We were musing each other into unknown writing territory. One woman advised me to listen to my own voice, deep inside, and put that down on paper. But what I heard when I listened were voices that said things like "Don't put so much salt on the lettuce, you'll wilt the salad!" I'd never heard that in a poem. So how could it be poetry? Then, with the "33" sonnet sequence, I said, I'm going to go in there and I'm going to sound like myself. I took on the whole kaboodle. I was going into form, sonnets no less. Wow.

What I wanted from the sonnet was the tradition that it offered as well as the structure. The sonnet tradition was one in which women were caged in golden cages of beloved, in perfumed gas chambers of stereotype. I wanted to go in that heavily mined and male labyrinth with the string of my own voice. I wanted to explore it and explode it too. I call my sonnets free verse sonnets. They have ten syllables per line, and the lines are in a loose iambic pentameter. But they are heavily enjambed and the rhymes are often slant-rhymes, and the rhyme scheme is peculiar to each sonnet. One friend read them and said, "I didn't know they were sonnets. They sounded like you talking!"

By learning to work the sonnet structure and yet remaining true to my own voice, I made myself at home in that form. When I was done with it, it was a totally different form from the one I learned in school. I have used other traditional forms. In my poem about sweeping, since you sweep with the broom and you dance — it's a coupling — I used rhyming couplets. I wrote a poem of advice mothers give to their daughters in a villanelle, because it's such a nagging form. But mostly the sonnet is the form I've worked with. It's the classic form in which we women were trapped, love objects, and I was trapped inside that voice and paradigm, and I wanted to work my way out of it.

My idea of traditional forms is that as women much of our heritage is trapped in them. But the cage can turn into a house if you housekeep it the right way. You housekeep it by working the words just so.

From *A Formal Feeling Comes: Poems in Form by Contemporary Women,*
edited by Annie Finch

CONSIDERATIONS FOR CRITICAL THINKING AND WRITING

1. How does Alvarez connect housekeeping to "writing in traditional forms"?

2. Compare "Sometimes the Words Are So Close" (Sonnet 42, p. 481) to Alvarez's description in her essay of how she writes sonnets. How closely does the poem's form follow her description?

3. Why does Alvarez consider "Dusting" (p. 478) and "Ironing Their Clothes" (p. 479) to be feminist poems? How can the poems be read as feminist in their sensibility?

JULIA ALVAREZ

On Writing "Dusting"   2006

Finally, I took the leap and began to write poems in my own voice and the voices of the women in my past, who inevitably were talking about their work, housekeeping. I had to trust that those voices, while not conventionally important, still had something to say. At school, I had been taught the formal canon of literature: epic poems with catalogues of ships, poems about wars and the rumors of wars. Why not write a poem in the voice of a mother cataloguing the fabrics, with names as beautiful as those of ships ("gabardine, organdy, wool, madras" from "Naming the Fabrics") or a poem about sweeping while watching a news report about the Vietnam War on TV ("How I Learned to Sweep")? Each time I delved into one of the housekeeping "arts," I discovered deeper, richer materials and metaphors than I had anticipated. This is wonderful news for a writer. As Robert Frost once said about rhymes in a poem, "No surprise for the writer, no surprise for the reader." The things we discover while writing what we write tingle with that special energy and delight of not just writing a poem, but enlarging our understanding.

Dusting is the lowliest of the housekeeping arts. Any little girl with a rag can dust. But rather than dust, the little girl in my poem is writing her name on the furniture, something her mother keeps correcting. What a perfect metaphor for the changing roles of women which I've experienced in my own life: the mother believing that a woman's place is in the home, not in the public sphere; the girl from a younger generation wanting to make a name for herself.

And in writing "Dusting," I also discovered a metaphor about writing. A complicated balancing act: like the mother, the artist has to disappear in her work; it's the poem that counts, not the name or celebrity of the writer. But the artist also needs the little girl's pluck and ambition to even imagine a public voice for herself. Otherwise, she'd be swallowed up in self-doubt, silenced by her mother's old-world way of viewing a woman's role.

Julia Alvarez

Dusting   *1981*

Each morning I wrote my name
on the dusty cabinet, then crossed
the dining table in script, scrawled
in capitals on the backs of chairs,
practicing signatures like scales   5
while Mother followed, squirting
linseed from a burping can
into a crumpled-up flannel.

She erased my fingerprints
from the bookshelf and rocker,   10
polished mirrors on the desk
scribbled with my alphabets.
My name was swallowed in the towel
with which she jeweled the table tops.
The grain surfaced in the oak   15
and the pine grew luminous.
But I refused with every mark
to be like her, anonymous.

Considerations for Critical Thinking and Writing

1. **FIRST RESPONSE.** Describe the central conflict between the speaker and the mother.
2. Explain why the image of dusting is a particularly appropriate metaphor for evoking the central conflict.
3. Discuss the effect of the rhymes in lines 15–18.
4. Consider the tone of each stanza. Explain why you see them as identical or not.

Connection to Another Selection

1. Discuss the mother-daughter relationships in "Dusting" and in Cathy Song's "The Youngest Daughter" (p. 92).

Julia Alvarez

On Writing "Ironing Their Clothes"   *2006*

Maybe because ironing is my favorite of all the housekeeping chores, this is my favorite of the housekeeping poems. In the apprenticeship of household arts, ironing is for the advanced apprentice. After all, think about it, you're wielding an instrument that could cause some damage: you could burn yourself, you could burn the clothes. I was not allowed to iron clothes until I was older and could be trusted to iron all different kinds of fabrics ("gabardine, organdy, wool, madras") just right.

Again, think of how ironing someone's clothes can be a metaphor for all kinds of things. You have this power to take out the wrinkles and worries from someone's outer skin! You can touch and caress and love someone and not be told that you are making a nuisance of yourself!

In writing this poem I wanted the language to mirror the process. I wanted the lines to suggest all the fussy complications of trying to get your iron into hard corners and places ("I stroked the yoke,/the breast pocket, collar and cuffs,/until the rumpled heap relaxed . . .") and then the smooth sailing of a line that sails over the line break into the next line ("into the shape/of my father's broad chest . . ."). I wanted to get the hiss of the iron in those last four lines. I revised and revised this poem, especially the verbs, most especially the verbs that have to do the actual work of the iron. When I finally got that last line with its double rhymes ("express/excess"; "love/cloth"), I felt as if I'd done a whole laundry basket worth of ironing just right.

Julia Alvarez

Ironing Their Clothes   *1981*

With a hot glide up, then down, his shirts,
I ironed out my father's back, cramped
and worried with work. I stroked the yoke,
the breast pocket, collar and cuffs,
until the rumpled heap relaxed into the shape   5
of my father's broad chest, the shoulders shrugged off
the world, the collapsed arms spread for a hug.
And if there'd been a face above the buttondown neck,
I would have pressed the forehead out, I would
have made a boy again out of that tired man!   10

If I clung to her skirt as she sorted the wash
or put out a line, my mother frowned,
a crease down each side of her mouth.
This is no time for love! But here
I could linger over her wrinkled bedjacket,   15
kiss at the damp puckers of her wrists
with the hot tip. Here I caressed
collars, scallops, ties, pleats which made
her outfits test of the patience of my passion.
Here I could lay my dreaming iron on her lap.   20

The smell of baked cotton rose from the board
and blew with a breeze out the window
to the family wardrobe drying on the clothesline,
all needing a touch of my iron. Here I could tickle
the underarms of my big sister's petticoat   25

or secretly pat the backside of her pajamas.
For she too would have warned me not to muss
her fresh blouses, starched jumpers, and smocks,
all that my careful hand had ironed out,
forced to express my excess love on cloth.   30

CONSIDERATIONS FOR CRITICAL THINKING AND WRITING

1. **FIRST RESPONSE.** Explain how the speaker expresses her love for her family in the extended metaphor of ironing.

2. How are ironing and the poem itself expressions of the speaker's "excess love" (line 30)? In what sense is her love excessive?

3. Explain how the speaker's relationship to her father differs from how she relates to her mother.

CONNECTION TO ANOTHER SELECTION

1. **CREATIVE RESPONSE.** Compare the descriptions of mothers in this poem and in Alvarez's "Dusting" (p. 478). Write a one-paragraph character sketch that uses vivid details and metaphoric language to describe them.

JULIA ALVAREZ

On Writing "Sometimes the Words Are So Close"   2006
From the "33" Sonnet Sequence

I really believe that being a reader turns you into a writer. You connect with the voice in a poem at a deeper and more intimate level than you do with practically anyone in your everyday life. Seems like the years fall away, differences fall away, and when George Herbert asks in his poem, "The Flower,"

> Who would have thought my shrivel'd heart
> Could have recover'd greennesse?

You want to stroke the page and answer him, "I did, George." Instead you write a poem that responds to the feelings in his poem; you recover greenness for him and for yourself.

With the "33" sonnet sequence, I wanted the voice of the speaker to sound like a real woman speaking. A voice at once intimate and also somehow universal, essential. This sonnet #42 ["Sometimes the Words Are So Close"] is the last one in the sequence, a kind of final "testimony" about what writing is all about.

I mentioned that when you love something you read, you want to respond to it. You want to say it again, in fresh new language. Robert Frost speaks to this impulse in the poet when he says, "Don't borrow, steal!" Well, I borrowed/ stole two favorite passages. One of them is from the poem on the Statue of

Liberty, which was written by Emma Lazarus (1849–1887), titled "The New Colossus" [p. 637]. These lines will sound familiar to you, I'm sure:

> "Give me your tired, your poor,
> Your huddled masses yearning to breathe free,
> The wretched refuse of your teeming shore.
> Send these, the homeless, tempest-tost to me,
> I lift my lamp beside the golden door!"

I think of these lines, not just as an invitation to the land of the brave and home of the free, but an invitation to poetry! A poem can be a resting place for the soul yearning to breathe free, a form that won't tolerate the misuses and abuses of language, a world teeming with discoveries and luminous little *ah-ha!* moments, a "place for the genuine," as Marianne Moore calls it in her poem, "On Poetry." William Carlos Williams said that we can't get the news from poems, practical information, hard facts, but "men die daily for lack of what is found there."

I not only agreed with this idea, but I wanted to say so in my own words, and so I echoed those lines from the Statue of Liberty in my sonnet:

> Those of you lost and yearning to be free,
> who hear these words, take heart from me.

Another favorite line comes from Walt Whitman's book-length "Leaves of Grass": "Who touches this [book] touches a man." As a young, lonely immigrant girl reading Whitman, those words made me feel so accompanied, so connected. And so I borrowed / stole that line and made it my own at the end of this poem.

JULIA ALVAREZ

Sometimes the Words Are So Close   1982
From the "33" Sonnet Sequence

Sometimes the words are so close I am
more who I am when I'm down on paper
than anywhere else as if my life were
practicing for the real me I become
unbuttoned from the anecdotal and   5
unnecessary and undressed down
to the figure of the poem, line by line,
the real text a child could understand.
Why do I get confused living it through?
Those of you lost and yearning to be free,   10
who hear these words, take heart from me.
I once was in as many drafts as you.
But briefly, essentially, here I am.
Who touches this poem touches a woman.

Drafts of "Sometimes the Words Are So Close": A Poet's Writing Process

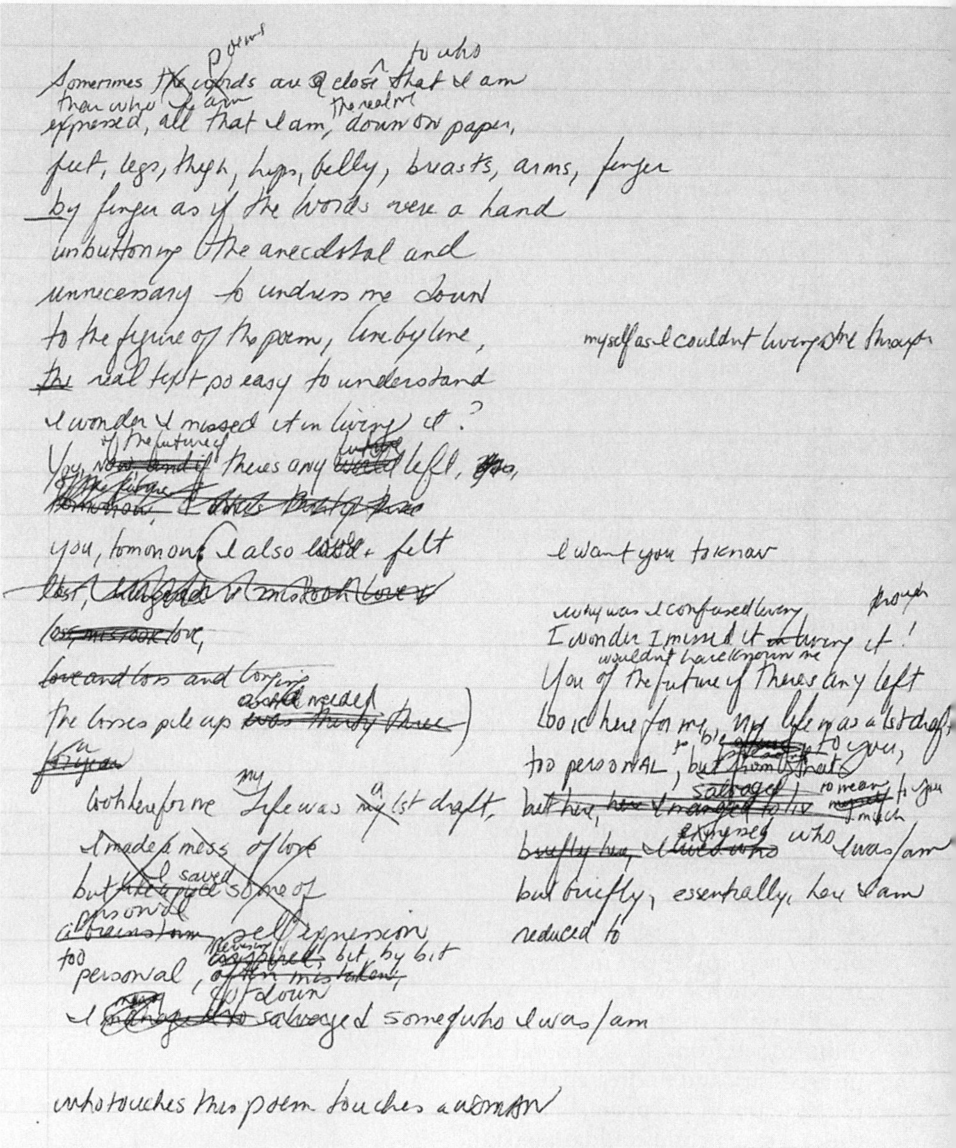

[Handwritten manuscript draft of the poem "Sometimes the Words Are So Close," with numerous revisions, crossings-out, and marginal notes.]

Manuscript on pages 482–84 reprinted with permission from the Henry W. and Albert A. Berg Collection of English and American Literature, The New York Public Library, Astor, Lenox, and Tilden Foundations.

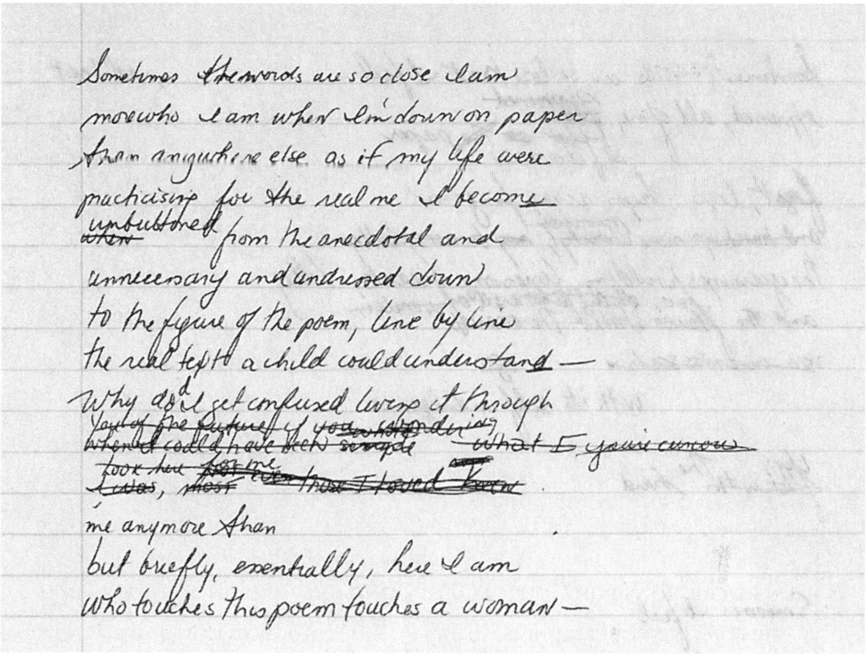

[handwritten draft]

Sometimes the words are so close I am
more who I am when I'm down on paper
than anywhere else, as if my life were
practising for the real me I become
unbuttoned ~~when~~ from the anecdotal and
unnecessary and undressed down
to the figure of the poem, line by line
the real text a child could understand —
Why do I get confused living it through
~~Those of you [illegible] of you [illegible]~~
~~intend could have been scraps~~ what I you're curious
~~took her [illegible] those I loved [illegible]~~
me anymore than
but briefly, essentially, here I am
Who touches this poem touches a woman —

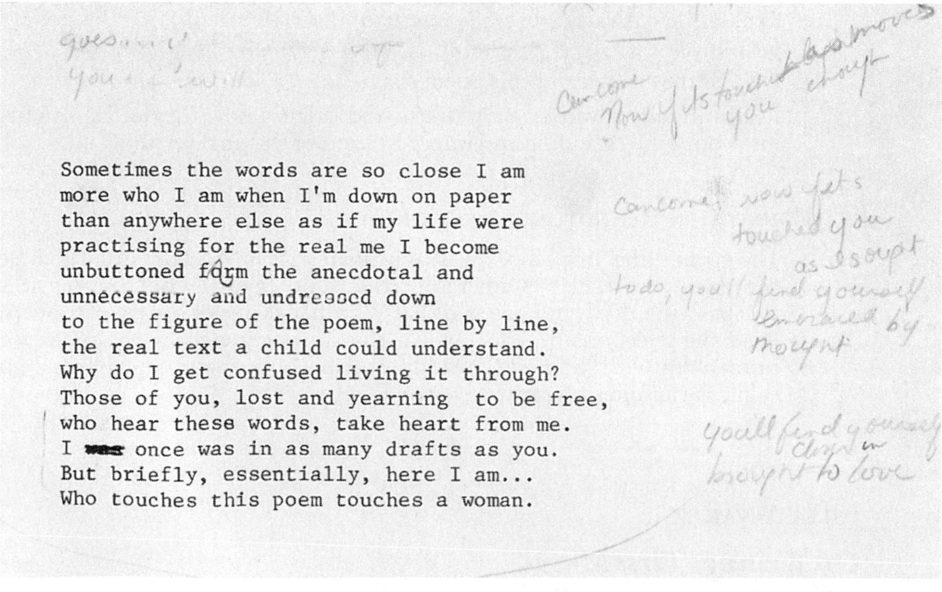

[typed draft]

Sometimes the words are so close I am
more who I am when I'm down on paper
than anywhere else as if my life were
practising for the real me I become
unbuttoned form the anecdotal and
unnecessary and undressed down
to the figure of the poem, line by line,
the real text a child could understand.
Why do I get confused living it through?
Those of you, lost and yearning to be free,
who hear these words, take heart from me.
I ~~was~~ once was in as many drafts as you.
But briefly, essentially, here I am...
Who touches this poem touches a woman.

[handwritten marginalia]

goes...
you ...will

Overcome
Now if its touched ... lifts ... moves
you ...

Overcome now lifts
touched you
as I sought
to do, you'll find yourself
embraced by
thought

you'll find yourself
drawn in
brought to love

```
Sometimes the words are so close I am
more who I am when I'm down on paper
than anywhere else as if my life were
practising for the real me I become
unbuttoned from the anecdotal and
unnecessary and undressed down
to the figure of the poem, line by line,
the real text a child could understand.
Why do I get confused living it through?
Those of you, lost and yearning to be free,
who hear these words, take heart from me.
I once was in as many drafts as you.
But briefly, essentially, here I am...
Who touches this poem touches a woman.
```

pretentious

CONSIDERATIONS FOR CRITICAL THINKING AND WRITING

1. **FIRST RESPONSE.** Paraphrase lines 1–9. What produces the speaker's sense of frustration?

2. How do lines 10–14 resolve the question raised in line 9?

3. Explain how Alvarez's use of punctuation serves to reinforce the poem's meanings.

4. Discuss the elements of this poem that make it a sonnet.

5. Read carefully Alvarez's early drafts and discuss how they offer insights into your understanding and interpretation of the final version.

CONNECTION TO ANOTHER SELECTION

1. The poem's final line echoes Walt Whitman's poem "So Long" in which he addresses the reader: "Camerado, this is no book,/Who touches this touches a man." Alvarez has said that Whitman is one of her favorite poets. Read the selections by Whitman in this anthology (check the index for titles) along with "So Long" (readily available online) and explain why you think she admires his poetry.

JULIA ALVAREZ

On Writing "First Muse"   2006

I have to come clean about calling this poem, "First Muse."

I had another first muse in Spanish. Her name was Scheherazade and I read about her in a book my aunt gave me called *The Arabian Nights*. Scheherazade saves her life by telling the murderous sultan incredible tales night after night for 1001 nights. Listening to her stories, the sultan is transformed. He no

Those of you, lost and yearning to be free,
who hear these words, take heart from me.
I once was in as many drafts as you.
But briefly, essentially, here I am....
Who touches this poem touches a woman.

—Julia Alvarez
(1950-), "33"

An excerpt from Alvarez's poem "Sometimes the Words Are So Close" is set by sculptor Gregg LeFevre in a bronze plaque on 41st Street in New York City, and is part of the "Library Way"—a display sponsored by Grand Central Partnership of sidewalk plaques leading to the landmark New York Public Library's Humanities and Social Sciences Library on Fifth Avenue literary quotations from forty-four artists and writers including Lucille Clifton, John Milton, and Pablo Picasso.

Courtesy of the Grand Central Partnership, New York and Gregg LeFevre.

longer wants to kill all the women in his kingdom. In fact, he falls in love with Scheherazade. This young lady saves her own life, the lives of all the women in her kingdom, and by changing him, she also saves the sultan's soul just by telling stories. Right then, I knew what I wanted to be when I grew up. You bet. A storyteller.

Of course, back then, I was growing up in the Dominican Republic, living in a cruel and dangerous dictatorship myself. My own father was a member of an underground freedom movement to depose this dictator. Like Scheherazade, my life and the life of many Dominicans was in danger. But stories like the ones in *The Arabian Nights* helped me dream that the world was a more exciting and mysterious place than I could even imagine. That I was free to travel on the magic carpet of Scheherazade's tales even if the dictatorship did not allow me to drive one town over without inspection and permission.

When I came into English and became a reader, I had new dreams. I wanted to be an American writer. But as I mentioned earlier, the United States of the early '60s was still a long way off from the multicultural "revolution" of the late '80s and '90s. All the writers we read in my English class were Anglo Americans, and many of them were male. Still, the words they put down on paper invited everyone to partake of them. The authors were talking directly to me, asking me questions ("Who would have thought my shrivel'd heart . . . ?"), inviting me to be intimate with their words ("Who touches this [book] touches a man"). That's what I loved about reading: the great egalitarian democracy between the covers of books. The table set for all. The portable homeland. I wanted to be a part of that world. I often say that when I left the Dominican Republic in 1960, I landed, not in the United States, but in the English language, and that's where I put down deep roots by becoming a writer.

But the world beyond the covers of books did not mirror this great democracy. As you read in "Queens, 1963," the reality was disappointing. There were gated communities within this great free country. Places where immigrants and blacks need not apply. One of them was the guarded canon of literature. I still recall the famous writer who made the pronouncement that one could not write in English unless it was one's mother tongue. I was filled with self-doubt, and since I didn't have any examples in what we were reading in school that this pronouncement was wrong, I thought he was right.

Back then, Latino stories were the province of sociology, not literature. As for popular media, the only "Hispanics" on TV were Ricky Ricardo, with his laughable accent, and Chiquita Banana, selling fruit for the United Fruit Company. But as I said about writing in form, you find yourself caught in a structure or negative paradigm and you turn it on its head. You use it to get free. I listened to Chiquita singing, "I'm Chiquita Banana and I've come to say," and I began to get her message: *I'm a Latina woman, and I am claiming it openly, and what's more I've got something to say.* I felt the same rush of hope when I read Langston Hughes's "I, Too" [This poem appears on p. 407]. In that poem, Mr. Hughes promised himself that "Tomorrow, / I'll be at the table" of American literature. And there he was in my English textbook. He had made good on his promise to himself, to me!

The civil rights struggle didn't just happen on buses and in places of business or on picket lines in Birmingham, Alabama, or Queens, New York. It also happened on paper. Chiquita Banana and Langston Hughes were right. There is a place for all our voices in the great inclusive world of literature. I feel honored and privileged to be part of that great liberating movement of words on paper, springing us all free with their magic and power, connecting us with ourselves and with each other.

JULIA ALVAREZ

First Muse   1999

When I heard the famous poet pronounce
"One can only write poems in the tongue
in which one first said *Mother*," I was stunned.
Lately arrived in English, I slipped down

into my seat and fought back tears, thinking   5
of all those notebooks filled with bogus poems
I'd have to burn, thinking maybe there was
a little loophole, maybe just maybe
Mami had sung me lullabies she'd learned
from wives stationed at the embassy,   10

thinking maybe she'd left the radio on
beside my crib tuned to the BBC
or Voice of America, maybe her friend
from boarding school had sent a talking doll
who spoke in English? Maybe I could be   15
the one exception to this writing rule?
For months I suffered from bad writer's-block,
which I envisioned, not as a blank page,
but as a literary border guard
turning me back to Spanish on each line.   20

I gave up writing, watched lots of TV,
and you know how it happens that advice
comes from unlikely quarters? *She* came on,
sassy, olive-skinned, hula-hooping her hips,
a basket of bananas on her head,   25
her lilting accent so full of feeling
it seemed the way the heart would speak English
if it could speak. I touched the screen and sang
my own heart out with my new muse, *I am*
Chiquita Banana and I'm here to say . . .   30

CONSIDERATIONS FOR CRITICAL THINKING AND WRITING

1. **FIRST RESPONSE.** What do you think the "famous poet" had in mind by insisting that "'One can only write poems in the tongue / in which one first said *Mother*'" (lines 2–3)? Explain why you agree or disagree with this statement.

2. How does the speaker preserve the serious nature of her bilingualism while simultaneously treating the topic humorously?

3. How and why does Chiquita Banana serve as the speaker's "new muse"?

CONNECTIONS TO OTHER SELECTIONS

1. Discuss the speakers' passion for language as it is revealed in "First Muse," "Sometimes the Words Are So Close" (p. 481), and "Dusting" (p. 478).

2. Compare the themes concerning writing and ethnicity in "First Muse" and in Julio Marzán's "Ethnic Poetry" (p. 173).

3. Consider the speakers' reactions in "First Muse" and in Judy Page Heitzman's "The Schoolroom on the Second Floor of the Knitting Mill" (p. 147) to the authoritative voice each hears. What effects do these powerful voices have on the speakers' lives?

A songbook featuring an image of the Chiquita Banana character referenced in Alvarez's "First Muse."

Courtesy of Chiquita Brands, Inc.

Web   For more images of this character, go to bedfordstmartins .com/rewritinglit.

CONSIDERATIONS FOR CRITICAL THINKING AND WRITING

1. How does this cover for the sheet music of Chiquita Banana's song illustrate the character's "sassy" tone (line 24) alluded to in the final stanza of "First Muse"?

2. In "First Muse," Alvarez humorously contemplates that if her mother had "left the radio on/beside my crib tuned to the BBC/or Voice of America," she might have learned English as an infant (lines 11–13). How does a careful analysis of the sheet music illustration suggest the difference between Chiquita's voice and that of the BBC or Voice of America?

3. The Chiquita Brands International corporation maintains a Web site (www.chiquita.com) that provides a history of its advertisements from the 1940s to the present, including recordings of the Chiquita song. How do you think the images of "Miss Chiquita" and her song served as a "new muse" for Alvarez when she was starting out as a writer?

Perspective

KELLI LYON JOHNSON (B. 1969)

Mapping an Identity   *2005*

Alvarez poses the problem of how we are to understand and represent identity within the multiple migrations that characterize an increasingly global society. By "mapping a country that's not on the map," Alvarez, a Dominican immigrant forced into exile in the United States, is undertaking a journey that places her at the forefront of contemporary American letters.

The question of identity and agency is particularly acute for women, postcolonial peoples, and others upon whom an identity has traditionally been imposed. Given Alvarez's success, both commercial and artistic, a variety of groups have claimed her as a member of their communities: as woman, ethnic, exile, diaspora, Caribbean, Dominican, Latina, and American. In the keynote address at a conference for Caribbean Studies, Doña Aída Cartagena Portalatín, "the grand woman of letters in the Dominican Republic" (*Something*[1] 171) gently chides Alvarez for writing in English. "Come back to your country, to your language," she tells Alvarez. "You are a Dominican" (171). By conflating linguistic, national, and cultural identity, Portalatín underscores the importance of these factors for constructing a literary tradition that includes displaced writers like Alvarez, who quite consciously has not adopted for writing the language of her country of origin.

In response to such comments, Alvarez has asserted her own self-definition as both (and neither) Dominican and American by writing "a new place on the map" (*Something* 173). Placing herself among a multiethnic group of postcolonial authors who write in English — "Michael Ondaatje in Toronto, Maxine Hong Kingston in San Francisco, Seamus Heaney in Boston, Bharati Mukherjee in Berkeley, Marjorie Agosín in Wellesley, Edwidge Danticat in Brooklyn" (173) — Alvarez, like these authors, has altered contemporary American literature by stretching the literary cartography of the Americas. These authors have brought, through their writings, their own countries of origin into a body of work in which the word *American* expands across continents and seas and begins to recapture its original connotation.

Alvarez has also claimed membership among a *comunidad* of U.S. Latina writers — Sandra Cisneros, Ana Castillo, Judith Ortiz Cofer, Lorna Dee Cervantes, Cherríe Moraga, Helena María Viramontes, and Denise Chávez — despite her fears that "the cage of definition" will enclose her writing "with its 'Latino subject matter,' 'Latino style,' 'Latino concerns'" (169). Like these authors, Alvarez seeks to write women into a postcolonial tradition of literature that has historically excluded women, particularly in writings of exile. To counter imposed definitions and historical silences, Alvarez has found that "the best way to define myself is through stories and poems" (169). The space that Alvarez maps is thus a narrative space: the site of her emerging cartography of identity and exile.

From *Julia Alvarez: Writing a New Place on the Map*

[1] *Something to Declare*, Alvarez's collection of essays published in 1998.

CONSIDERATIONS FOR CRITICAL THINKING AND WRITING

1. Based on your reading of the poems in this chapter, which community identity — "woman, ethnic, exile, diaspora, Caribbean, Dominican, Latina, and American" — best describes Alvarez for you?

2. In what sense does Alvarez's poetry expand "the literary cartography of the Americas"?

3. Consider "First Muse" as Alvarez's response to Portalatín's suggestion that she should write in Spanish rather than English and "[c]ome back to your country, to your language."

17

A CRITICAL CASE STUDY

T. S. Eliot's "The Love Song of J. Alfred Prufrock"

Genuine poetry can communicate before it is understood.
— T. S. ELIOT

This chapter provides several critical approaches to a challenging but highly rewarding poem by T. S. Eliot. After studying this poem, you're likely to find yourself quoting bits of its striking imagery. At the very least, you'll recognize the lines when you hear other people fold them into their own conversations. This poem has elicited numerous critical approaches because it raises so many issues relating to history, biography, imagery, symbolism, irony, myth, and other matters. The following critical excerpts offer a small

Explore contexts
for T. S. Eliot
on *LiterActive*.

T. S. Eliot began writing poetry as a student. He is shown here in 1906 at age eighteen, during his first year at Harvard. In 1910, Eliot continued his studies abroad at the Sorbonne in Paris and at age twenty-three completed his first draft of "The Love Song of J. Alfred Prufrock" during the summer of 1911. Later in his life Eliot said, "Immature poets imitate; mature poets steal."

Reprinted by permission of the Houghton Library, Harvard University.

and partial sample of the possible formalist, biographical, historical, mythological, psychological, sociological, and other perspectives that have attempted to shed light on the poem (see Chapter 26, "Critical Strategies for Reading," for a discussion of a variety of critical methods). They should help you to enjoy the poem more by raising questions, providing insights, and inviting you further into the text.

A BRIEF BIOGRAPHY

Born into a prominent New England family that had moved to St. Louis, Missouri, Thomas Stearns Eliot (1888–1965) was a major figure in English literature between the two world wars. He studied literature and philosophy at Harvard and on the Continent, subsequently choosing to live in England for most of his life and becoming a citizen of that country in 1927. Many writers have been powerfully influenced by his allusive and challenging poetry, particularly his treatment of postwar life in *The Waste Land* (1922)

This portrait of T. S. Eliot is by the Modernist painter and writer Wyndham Lewis. The modernist movement of art and literature, dating from the late nineteenth to the mid-twentieth centuries, represented a rejection of tradition, a radical departure from Victorian sentimentality, and a move toward more experimental forms of expression. Modernist writers included T. S. Eliot, James Joyce, and Virginia Woolf. One of the themes explored by modernist authors like Eliot is alienation. He once said, "[Poetry] may make us from time to time a little more aware of the deeper unnamed feelings which form the substratum of our being, to which we rarely penetrate; for our lives are mostly a constant evasion of ourselves."

Courtesy of the Friends of the Durban Art Gallery, South Africa.

T. S. Eliot (November 10, 1959), in a pose that suggests the Prufrock persona, holding a book containing some of his earlier work during a press conference at the University of Chicago.
© Bettmann/CORBIS.

and his exploration of religious questions in *The Four Quartets* (1943). In addition, he wrote plays, including *Murder in the Cathedral* (1935) and *The Cocktail Party* (1950). He was awarded the Nobel Prize for Literature in 1948. In "The Love Song of J. Alfred Prufrock" Eliot presents a comic but serious figure who expresses through a series of fragmented images the futility, boredom, and meaninglessness associated with much of modern life.

T. S. ELIOT (1888–1965)

The Love Song of J. Alfred Prufrock   1917

S'io credesse che mia risposta fosse
A persona che mai tornasse al mondo,
Questa fiamma staria senza più scosse.
Ma perciocchè giammai di questo fondo

Non tornò vivo alcun, s'i'odo il vero,
Senza tema d'infamia ti rispondo.°

Let us go then, you and I,
When the evening is spread out against the sky
Like a patient etherized upon a table;
Let us go, through certain half-deserted streets,
The muttering retreats   5
Of restless nights in one-night cheap hotels
And sawdust restaurants with oyster-shells:
Streets that follow like a tedious argument
Of insidious intent
To lead you to an overwhelming question . . .   10

Oh, do not ask, "What is it?"
Let us go and make our visit.

In the room the women come and go
Talking of Michelangelo.

The yellow fog that rubs its back upon the window panes,   15
The yellow smoke that rubs its muzzle on the window panes
Licked its tongue into the corners of the evening,
Lingered upon the pools that stand in drains,
Let fall upon its back the soot that falls from chimneys,
Slipped by the terrace, made a sudden leap,   20
And seeing that it was a soft October night,
Curled once about the house, and fell asleep.

And indeed there will be time°
For the yellow smoke that slides along the street,
Rubbing its back upon the window panes;   25
There will be time, there will be time
To prepare a face to meet the faces that you meet;
There will be time to murder and create,
And time for all the works and days° of hands
That lift and drop a question on your plate: 30
Time for you and time for me,
And time yet for a hundred indecisions,
And for a hundred visions and revisions,
Before the taking of a toast and tea.

Epigraph: *S'io credesse . . . rispondo:* Dante's *Inferno,* 27:58–63. In the Eighth Chasm of the
Inferno, Dante and Virgil meet Guido da Montefeltro, one of the False Counselors, who is
punished by being enveloped in an eternal flame. When Dante asks Guido to tell his life
story, the spirit replies: "If I thought that my answer were to one who might ever return to
the world, this flame would shake no more; but since from this depth none ever returned
alive, if what I hear is true, I answer you without fear of infamy."

23 *there will be time:* An allusion to Ecclesiastes 3:1–8: "To everything there is a season, and a
time to every purpose under heaven. . . ."

29 *works and days:* Hesiod's eighth-century B.C. poem *Works and Days* gives practical advice
on how to conduct one's life in accordance with the seasons.

In the room the women come and go   35
Talking of Michelangelo.

    And indeed there will be time
To wonder, "Do I dare?" and, "Do I dare?" —
Time to turn back and descend the stair,
With a bald spot in the middle of my hair —   40
(They will say: "How his hair is growing thin!")
My morning coat, my collar mounting firmly to the chin,
My necktie rich and modest, but asserted by a simple pin —
(They will say: "But how his arms and legs are thin!")
Do I dare   45
Disturb the universe?
In a minute there is time
For decisions and revisions which a minute will reverse.

    For I have known them all already, known them all:
Have known the evenings, mornings, afternoons,   50
I have measured out my life with coffee spoons;
I know the voices dying with a dying fall
Beneath the music from a farther room.
    So how should I presume?

    And I have known the eyes already, known them all —   55
The eyes that fix you in a formulated phrase.
And when I am formulated, sprawling on a pin,
When I am pinned and wriggling on the wall,
Then how should I begin
To spit out all the butt-ends of my days and ways?   60
    And how should I presume?

    And I have known the arms already, known them all —
Arms that are braceleted and white and bare
(But in the lamplight, downed with light brown hair!)
    Is it perfume from a dress   65
    That makes me so digress?
Arms that lie along a table, or wrap about a shawl.
    And should I then presume?
    And how should I begin?

    Shall I say, I have gone at dusk through narrow streets,   70
And watched the smoke that rises from the pipes
Of lonely men in shirtsleeves, leaning out of windows? . . .

I should have been a pair of ragged claws
Scuttling across the floors of silent seas.

    And the afternoon, the evening, sleeps so peacefully!   75
Smoothed by long fingers,
Asleep . . . tired . . . or it malingers,
Stretched on the floor, here beside you and me.
Should I, after tea and cakes and ices,
Have the strength to force the moment to its crisis?   80
But though I have wept and fasted, wept and prayed,

Though I have seen my head (grown slightly bald) brought in upon a platter,°
I am no prophet — and here's no great matter;
I have seen the moment of my greatness flicker,
And I have seen the eternal Footman hold my coat, and snicker,   85
    And in short, I was afraid.

    And would it have been worth it, after all,
After the cups, the marmalade, the tea,
Among the porcelain, among some talk of you and me,
Would it have been worth while   90
To have bitten off the matter with a smile,
To have squeezed the universe into a ball°
To roll it toward some overwhelming question,
To say: "I am Lazarus,° come from the dead,
Come back to tell you all, I shall tell you all" —   95
If one, settling a pillow by her head,
    Should say: "That is not what I meant at all;
        That is not it, at all."

    And would it have been worth it, after all,
Would it have been worth while,   100
After the sunsets and the dooryards and the sprinkled streets,
After the novels, after the teacups, after the skirts that trail along the floor —
And this, and so much more? —
It is impossible to say just what I mean!
But as if a magic lantern threw the nerves in patterns on a screen: 105
Would it have been worth while
If one, settling a pillow or throwing off a shawl,
And turning toward the window, should say:
    "That is not it at all,
        That is not what I meant, at all."   110

No! I am not Prince Hamlet, nor was meant to be;
Am an attendant lord,° one that will do
To swell a progress,° start a scene or two,   *state procession*
Advise the prince: withal, an easy tool,
Deferential, glad to be of use,   115
Politic, cautious, and meticulous;
Full of high sentence, but a bit obtuse;
At times, indeed, almost ridiculous —
Almost, at times, the Fool.

I grow old . . . I grow old . . .   120
I shall wear the bottoms of my trousers rolled.

82 *head . . . upon a platter:* At Salome's request, Herod had John the Baptist decapitated and had the severed head delivered to her on a platter (see Matt. 14:1-12 and Mark 6:17-29).

92 *squeezed the universe into a ball:* See Andrew Marvell's "To His Coy Mistress" (p. 80), lines 41-42: "Let us roll all our strength and all / Our sweetness up into one ball."

94 *Lazarus:* The brother of Mary and Martha who was raised from the dead by Jesus (John 11:1-44). In Luke 16:19-31, a rich man asks that another Lazarus return from the dead to warn the living about their treatment of the poor.

112 *attendant lord:* Like Polonius in Shakespeare's *Hamlet*.

Shall I part my hair behind? Do I dare to eat a peach?
I shall wear white flannel trousers, and walk upon the beach.
I have heard the mermaids singing, each to each.

I do not think that they will sing to me.   125

I have seen them riding seaward on the waves,
Combing the white hair of the waves blown back
When the wind blows the water white and black.

We have lingered in the chambers of the sea
By seagirls wreathed with seaweed red and brown,   130
Till human voices wake us, and we drown.

CONSIDERATIONS FOR CRITICAL THINKING AND WRITING

1. **FIRST RESPONSE.** What does J. Alfred Prufrock's name connote? How would
   you characterize him?
2. What do you think is the purpose of the epigraph from Dante's *Inferno*?
3. What is it that Prufrock wants to do? How does he behave? What does he
   think of himself? Which parts of the poem answer these questions?
4. Who is the "you" of line 1 and the "we" in the final lines?
5. Discuss the poem's imagery. How does the imagery reveal Prufrock's character? Which images seem especially striking to you?

CONNECTIONS TO OTHER SELECTIONS

1. Write an essay comparing Prufrock's sense of himself as an individual with
   that of Walt Whitman's speaker in "One's-Self I Sing" (p. 650).
2. Discuss in an essay the tone of "The Love Song of J. Alfred Prufrock" and
   Robert Frost's "Acquainted with the Night" (p. 158).

Perspectives on T. S. Eliot

ELISABETH SCHNEIDER (1897–1984)

Schneider uses a biographical approach to the poem to suggest that part
of what went into the characterization of Prufrock were some of Eliot's
own sensibilities.

Hints of Eliot in Prufrock   *1952*

Perhaps never again did Eliot find an epigraph quite so happily suited to his
use as the passage from the *Inferno* which sets the underlying serious tone for
Prufrock and conveys more than one level of its meaning: "S'io credesse che mia
risposta . . . ," lines in which Guido da Montefeltro consents to tell his story to
Dante only because he believes that none ever returns to the world of the living

from his depth. One in Hell can bear to expose his shame only to another of the damned; Prufrock speaks to, will be understood only by, other Prufrocks (the "you and I" of the opening, perhaps), and, I imagine the epigraph also hints, Eliot himself is speaking to those who know this kind of hell. The poem, I need hardly say, is not in a literal sense autobiographical: for one thing, though it is clear that Prufrock will never marry, the poem was published in the year of Eliot's own first marriage. Nevertheless, friends who know the young Eliot almost all describe him, retrospectively but convincingly, in Prufrockian terms; and Eliot himself once said of dramatic monologue in general that what we normally hear in it "is the voice of the poet, who has put on the costume and make-up either of some historical character, or of one out of fiction." . . . I suppose it to be one of the many indirect clues to his own poetry planted with evident deliberation throughout his prose. "What every poet starts from," he also once said, "is his own emotions," and, writing of Dante, he asserted that the *Vita nuova* "could only have been written around a personal experience," a statement that, under the circumstances, must be equally applicable to Prufrock; Prufrock was Eliot, though Eliot was much more than Prufrock. We miss the whole tone of the poem, however, if we read it as social satire only. Eliot was not either the dedicated apostle in theory, or the great exemplar in practice, of complete "depersonalization" in poetry that one influential early essay of his for a time led readers to suppose.

From "Prufrock and After: The Theme of Change," *PMLA*, October 1952

CONSIDERATIONS FOR CRITICAL THINKING AND WRITING

1. Though Schneider concedes that the poem is not literally autobiographical, she does assert that "Prufrock was Eliot." How does she argue this point? Explain why you find her argument convincing or unconvincing.
2. Find information in the library or online about Eliot's early career when he was writing this poem. To what extent does the poem reveal his circumstances and concerns at that point in his life?

BARBARA EVERETT

Everett's discussion of tone is used to make a distinction between Eliot and his characterization of Prufrock.

The Problem of Tone in Prufrock   1974

Eliot's poetry presents a peculiar problem as far as tone is concerned. *Tone* really means the way the attitude of a speaker is manifested by the inflections of his speaking voice. Many critics have already recognized that for a mixture of reasons it is difficult, sometimes almost impossible, to ascertain Eliot's tone in this way. It is not that the poetry lacks "voice," for in fact Eliot has an extraordinarily recognizable poetic voice, often imitated and justifying his own comment in the . . . *Paris Review* that "in a poem you're writing for your own voice, which is very important. You're thinking in terms of your own voice." It is this authoritative, idiosyncratic, and exact voice that holds our complete attention in poem after poem, however uninterested we are in what opinions it may seem or happen to be expressing. But Eliot too seems uninterested in what opinions it may happen to be expressing, for he invariably dissociates himself from his poems before they are even finished — before they are hardly begun — by balancing a derisory name or title against an "I," by reminding us that there is always going to be a moment at which detachment will take place or has taken place, a retrospective angle from which, far in the future, critical judgment alters the scene, and the speaking voice of the past has fallen silent. "I have known them all already, known them all." Thus whatever started to take place in the beginning of a poem by Eliot cannot truly be said to be Eliot's opinion because at some extremely early stage he began that process of dissociation to be loosely called "dramatization," a process reflected in the peculiar distances of the tone, as though everything spoken was in inverted commas.

From "In Search of Prufrock," *Critical Quarterly,* Summer 1974

CONSIDERATIONS FOR CRITICAL THINKING AND WRITING

1. According to Everett, why is it difficult to describe Eliot's tone in his poetry?
2. How does Eliot's tone make it difficult to make an autobiographical connection between Prufrock and Eliot?
3. How does Everett's reading of the relationship between Prufrock and Eliot differ from Schneider's in the preceding Perspective?

MICHAEL L. BAUMANN (b. 1926)

Baumann takes a close look at the poem's images in his formalist efforts to make a point about Prufrock's character.

The "Overwhelming Question" for Prufrock   1981

Most critics . . . have seen the overwhelming question related to sex. . . . They have implicitly assumed — and given their readers to understand — that Prufrock's is the male's basic question: Can I?

The poet and critic Delmore Schwartz once said that "J. Alfred Prufrock is unable to make love to women of his own class and kind because of shyness, self-consciousness, and fear of rejection."[1] This is undoubtedly true, but

---

[1] "T. S. Eliot as the International Hero," *Partisan Review,* 12 (1945), 202; rpt. in *T. S. Eliot: A Selected Critique,* ed. Leonard Unger (New York: Rinehart & Company, Inc., 1948), 46.

Prufrock's inability to *feel* love has something to do with his inability to *make* love, too. . . . A simple desire, lust, is more than honest Prufrock can cope with as he mounts the stairs.

But Prufrock is coping with another, less simple desire as well. . . . If birth, copulation, and death is all there is, then, once we are born, once we have copulated, only death remains (for the male of the species, at least). Prufrock, having "known them all already, known them all," having "known the evenings, mornings, afternoons," having "measured out" his life "with coffee spoons," desires death. The "overwhelming question" that assails him would no longer be the romantic rhetorical "Is life worth living?" (to which the answer is obviously No), but the more immediate shocker: "Should one commit suicide?" which is to say: "Should I?" . . .

. . . The poem makes clear that Prufrock wants more than the "entire destruction of consciousness as we understand it," a notion Prufrock expresses by wishing he were "a pair of ragged claws, / Scuttling across the floors of silent seas." Prufrock wants death itself, physical death, and the poem, I believe, is explicit about this desire.

Not only does Prufrock seem to be tired of time — "time yet for a hundred indecisions" — a tiredness that goes far beyond the acedia Prufrock is generally credited with feeling, if only because "there will be time to murder and create," time, in other words (in one sense at least) to copulate, but Prufrock is also tired of his own endless vanities, from feeling he must "prepare a face to meet the faces that you meet," to having to summon up those ironies with which to contemplate his own thin arms and legs, and, indeed, to asking if, in the rather tedious enterprise of preparing for copulation, the moment is worth "forcing to its crisis." No wonder Prufrock compares himself to John the Baptist and, in conjuring up this first concrete image of his own death, sees his head brought in upon a platter. That would be the easy way out. He had, after all, "wept and fasted, wept and prayed," but he realizes he is no prophet — and no Salome will burst into passion, will ignite for him. When the eternal Footman, Death, who holds his coat, snickers, he does so because Prufrock has let "the moment" of his "greatness" flicker, because Prufrock was unable to comply with the one imperative greatness would have thrust upon him: to kill himself. Prufrock explains: "I was afraid." Yet the achievement of his vision at the end of the poem, his being able to linger "in the chambers of the sea / By sea-girls wreathed with seaweed red and brown," is an act of the imagination that only physical death can complete, unless Prufrock wants human voices to wake him, and drown him. His romantic vision demands the voluntary act: suicide. It is to be expected that he will fail in this too, as he has failed in everything else.

From "Let Us Ask 'What Is It,'" *Arizona Quarterly,* Spring 1981

CONSIDERATIONS FOR CRITICAL THINKING AND WRITING

1. Describe the evidence used by Baumann to argue that Prufrock contemplates suicide.
2. Explain in an essay why you do or do not find Baumann's argument convincing.

3. Later in his essay Baumann connects Prufrock's insistence that "No, I am not Prince Hamlet" with Hamlet's "To be or not to be" speech. How do you think this reference might be used to support Baumann's argument in this excerpt?

FREDERIK L. RUSCH (B. 1938)

Rusch makes use of the insights developed by Erich Fromm, a social psychologist who believed "psychic forces [are] a process of constant interaction between man's needs and the social and historical reality in which he participates."

Society and Character in "The Love Song of J. Alfred Prufrock" *1984*

In looking at fiction, drama, and poetry from the Frommian point of view, the critic understands literature to be social portrayal as well as character portrayal or personal statement. Society and character are inextricably joined. The Frommian approach opens up the study of literary work, giving a social context to its characters, which suggests why those characters behave as they do. The Frommian approach recognizes human beings for what they are—basically gregarious individuals who are interdependent upon each other, in need of each other, and thus, to a certain degree, products of their social environments, although those environments may be inimical to their mental well-being. That is, as stated earlier, the individual's needs and drives have a social component and are not purely biological. The Frommian approach to literature assumes that a writer is—at least by implication—analyzing society and its setting as well as character. . . .

In T. S. Eliot's "The Love Song of J. Alfred Prufrock," Prufrock is talking to himself, expressing a fantasy or daydream. In his monologue, Prufrock, as noted by Grover Smith, "is addressing, as if looking into a mirror, his whole public personality."[1] Throughout the poem, Prufrock is extremely self-conscious, believing that the people in his imaginary drawing room will examine him as a specimen insect, "sprawling on a pin, / . . . pinned and wriggling on the wall. . . ." Of course, self-consciousness—being conscious of one's self—is not necessarily neurotic. Indeed, it is part of being a human being. It is only when self-consciousness, which has always led man to feel a separation from nature, becomes obsessive that we have a problem. Prufrock is certainly obsessed with his self-consciousness, convinced that everyone notices his balding head, his clothes (his prudent frocks), his thin arms and legs.

---

[1] Grover Smith, *T. S. Eliot's Poetry and Plays: A Study in Sources and Meaning* (Chicago: U of Chicago P, 1962), 16.

On one level, however, Prufrock is merely expressing the pain that all human beings must feel. Although his problem is extreme, he is quite representative of the human race:

> Self-awareness, reason, and imagination have disrupted the "harmony" that characterizes animal existence. Their emergence has made man into an anomaly, the freak of the universe. He is part of nature, subject to her physical laws and unable to change them, yet he transcends nature. He is set apart while being a part; he is homeless, yet chained to the home he shares with all creatures. . . . Being aware of himself, he realizes his powerlessness and the limitations of his existence. He is never free from the dichotomy of his existence: he cannot rid himself of his mind, even if he would want to; he cannot rid himself of his body as long as he is alive—and his body makes him want to be alive.[2]

This is the predicament of the human being. His self-awareness has made him feel separate from nature. This causes pain and sorrow. What, then, is the solution to the predicament? Fromm believed that mankind filled the void of alienation from nature with the creation of a culture, a society: "Man's existential, and hence unavoidable disequilibrium can be relatively stable when he has found, with the support of his culture, a more or less adequate way of coping with his existential problems" (*Destructiveness* 225). But, unfortunately for Prufrock, his culture and society do not allow him to overcome his existential predicament. The fact is, he is bored by his modern, urban society.

In image after image, Prufrock's mind projects boredom:

> For I have known them all already, known them all:
> Have known the evenings, mornings, afternoons,
> I have measured out my life with coffee spoons. . . .
> . . . .
>
> And I have known the eyes already, known them all —
> . . . .
>
> Then how should I begin
> To spit out all the butt-ends of my days and ways?
> . . . .
>
> And I have known the arms already, known them all —. . . .

Prufrock is completely unstimulated by his social environment, to the point of near death. The evening in which he proposes to himself to make a social visit is "etherized upon a table." The fog, as a cat, falls asleep; it is "tired . . . or it malingers, / Stretched on the floor. . . ."

Prufrock, living in a city of "half-deserted streets, / . . . one-night cheap hotels / And sawdust restaurants with oyster-shells," gets no comfort, no nurturing from his environment. He is, in the words of Erich Fromm, a "modern mass man . . . isolated and lonely" (*Destructiveness* 107). He lives in a destructive environment. Instead of providing communion with fellow human beings, it alienates him through boredom. Such boredom leads to "a state of chronic depression" that can cause the pathology of "insufficient inner productivity"

---

[2] Erich Fromm, *The Anatomy of Human Destructiveness* (New York: Holt, Rinehart & Winston, 1973), 225.

in the individual (*Destructiveness* 243). Such a lack of productivity is voiced by Prufrock when he confesses that he is neither Hamlet nor John the Baptist.

An interesting tension in "The Love Song of J. Alfred Prufrock" is caused by the reader's knowledge that Prufrock understands his own predicament quite well. Although he calls himself a fool, he has wisdom about himself and his predicament. This, however, only reinforces his depression and frustration. In his daydream, he is able to reveal truths about himself that, while they lead to self-understanding, apparently cannot alleviate his problems in his waking life. The poem suggests no positive movement out of the predicament. Prufrock is like a patient cited by Fromm, who under hypnosis envisioned "a black barren place with many masks," and when asked what the vision meant said "that everything was dull, dull, dull; that the masks represent the different roles he takes to fool people into thinking he is feeling well" (*Destructiveness* 246). Likewise, Prufrock understands that "There will be time, there will be time / To prepare a face to meet the faces that you meet. . . ." But despite his understanding of the nature of his existence, he cannot attain a more productive life.

It was Fromm's belief that with boredom "the decisive conditions are to be found in the overall environmental situation. . . . It is highly probable that even cases of severe depression-boredom would be less frequent and less intense . . . in a society where a mood of hope and love of life predominated. But in recent decades the opposite is increasingly the case, and thus a fertile soil for the development of individual depressive states is provided" (*Destructiveness* 251). There is no "mood of hope and love of life" in Prufrock's society. Prufrock is a lonely man, as lonely as "the lonely men in shirt-sleeves, leaning out of windows" of his fantasy. His only solution is to return to the animal state that his race was in before evolving into human beings.

Animals are one with nature, not alienated from their environments. They *are* nature, unselfconscious. Prufrock would return to a preconscious existence in the extreme: "I should have been a pair of ragged claws / Scuttling across the floors of silent seas." Claws *without a head* surely would not be alienated, bored, or depressed. They would seek and would need no psychological nurturing from their environment. And in the end Prufrock's fantasy of becoming claws is definitely more positive for him than his life as a human being. He completes his monologue with depressing irony, to say the least: it is with human voices waking us, bringing us back to human society, that we drown.

> From "Approaching Literature through the Social Psychology of
> Erich Fromm" in *Psychological Perspectives on Literature:
> Freudian Dissidents and Non-Freudians,* edited by Joseph Natoli

Considerations for Critical Thinking and Writing

1. According to Rusch, why is Fromm's approach useful for understanding Prufrock's character as well as his social context?

2. In what ways is Prufrock "representative of the human race" (para. 3)? Is he like any other characters you have read about in this anthology? Explain your response.

3. In an essay consider how Rusch's analysis of Prufrock might be used to support Baumann's argument that Prufrock's "overwhelming question" is whether or not he should kill himself (p. 500).

ROBERT SWARD (B. 1933)

Sward, a poet, provides a detailed explication, framed by his own personal experiences during the Korean War.

A Personal Analysis of *"The Love Song of J. Alfred Prufrock"* 1996

In 1952, sailing to Korea as a U.S. Navy librarian for Landing Ship Tank 914, I read T. S. Eliot's "The Love Song of J. Alfred Prufrock." Ill-educated, a product of Chicago's public-school system, I was nineteen-years-old and, awakened by Whitman, Eliot, and Williams, had just begun writing poetry. I was also reading all the books I could get my hands on.

Eliot had won the Nobel Prize in 1948 and, curious, I was trying to make sense of poems like "Prufrock" and "The Waste Land."

"What do you know about T. S. Eliot?" I asked a young officer who'd been to college and studied English literature. I knew from earlier conversations that we shared an interest in what he called "modern poetry." A yeoman third class, two weeks at sea and bored, I longed for someone to talk to. "T. S. Eliot was born in St. Louis, Missouri, but he lives now in England and is studying to become an Englishman," the officer said, tapping tobacco into his pipe. "The 'T. S.' stands for 'tough shit.' You read Eliot's 'Love Song of J. Alfred Prufrock,' what one English prof called 'the first poem of the modern movement,' and if you don't understand it, 'tough shit.' All I can say is that's some love song."

An anthology of poetry open before us, we were sitting in the ship's all-metal, eight by eight-foot library eating bologna sandwiches and drinking coffee. Fortunately, the captain kept out of sight and life on the slow-moving (eight to ten knots), flat-bottomed amphibious ship was unhurried and anything but formal.

"Then why does Eliot bother calling it a love song?" I asked, as the ship rolled and the coffee sloshed onto a steel table. The tight metal room smelled like a cross between a diesel engine and a New York deli.

"Eliot's being ironic, sailor. 'Prufrock' is the love song of a sexually repressed and horny man who has no one but himself to sing to." Drawing on his pipe, the officer scratched his head. "Like you and I, Mr. Prufrock is a lonely man on his way to a war zone. We're sailing to Korea and we know the truth, don't we? We may never make it back. Prufrock marches like a brave soldier to a British drawing room that, he tells us, may be the death of him. He's a mock heroic figure who sings of mermaids and peaches and drowning."

Pointing to lines 129–31, the officer read aloud:

> We have lingered in the chambers of the sea
> By seagirls wreathed with seaweed red and brown,
> Till human voices wake us and we drown.

"Prufrock is also singing because he's a poet. Prufrock *is* T. S. Eliot and, the truth is, Eliot is so much like Prufrock that he has to distance himself from his creation. That's why he gives the man that pompous name. Did you know

'Tough Shit,' as a young man, sometimes signed himself 'T. Stearns Eliot'? You have to see the humor — the irony — in 'Prufrock' to understand the poem."

"I read it, I hear it in my head, but I still don't get it," I confessed. "What is 'Prufrock' about?"

"'Birth, death and copulation, that's all there is.' That's what Eliot himself says. Of course the poem also touches on aging, social status, and fashion."

"Aging and fashion?" I asked.

The officer threw back his head and recited:

(They will say: "How his hair is growing thin!")
My morning coat, my collar mounting firmly to the chin,
My necktie rich and modest, but asserted by a simple pin.

He paused, then went on:

I grow old . . . I grow old . . .
I shall wear the bottoms of my trousers rolled.

"At the time the poem was written it was fashionable for young men to roll their trousers. In lines 120–21, Thomas Stearns Prufrock is laughing at himself for being middle-aged and vain.

"Anyway, 'The Love Song of J. Alfred Prufrock' is an interior monologue," said the officer, finishing his bologna sandwich and washing it down with dark rum. Wiping mustard from his mouth, he continued. "The whole thing takes place in J. Alfred Prufrock's head. That's clear, isn't it?"

I had read [Robert] Browning's "My Last Duchess" and understood about interior monologues.

"Listen, sailor: Prufrock thinks about drawing rooms, but he never actually sets foot in one. Am I right?"

"Yeah," I said after rereading the first ten lines. "I think so."

"The poem is about what goes through Prufrock's mind on his way to some upper-class drawing room. It's a foggy evening in October, and what Mr. Prufrock really needs is a drink. He's a tightass Victorian, a lonely teetotaling intellectual. Anyone else would forget the toast and marmalade and step into a pub and ask for a pint of beer."

Setting down his pipe, the naval officer opened the flask and refilled our coffee mugs.

"Every time I think I know what 'Prufrock' means it turns out to mean something else," I said. "Eliot uses too many symbols. Why doesn't he just say what he means?"

"The city — 'the lonely men in shirt-sleeves' and the 'one-night cheap hotels' — are masculine," said the officer. "That's what cities are like, aren't they: ugly and oppressive. What's symbolic — or should I say, what's obscure — about that?"

"Nothing," I said. "That's the easy part — Prufrock walking along like that."

"Okay," said the officer. "And in contrast to city streets, you've got the oppressive drawing room that, in Prufrock's mind, is feminine — 'Arms that are braceleted and white and bare' and 'the marmalade, the tea, / Among the porcelain, among some talk of you and me.'" Using a pencil, the officer underlined those images in the paperback anthology.

"You ever been to a tea party, Sward?"

"No, sir, I haven't. Not like Prufrock's."

"Well," said the officer, "I have and I have a theory about that 'overwhelming question' Prufrock wants to ask in line 10 — and again in line 93. Twice in the poem we hear about an 'overwhelming question.' What do you think he's getting at with that 'overwhelming question,' sailor?"

"Prufrock wants to ask the women what they're doing with their lives, but he's afraid they'll laugh at him," I said.

"Guess again, Sward," he said leaning back in his chair, stretching his arms. "What's your theory, sir?"

"Sex," said the officer. "On the one hand, it's true, he wants to fit in and play the game because, after all, he's privileged. He belongs in the drawing room with the clever Englishwomen. At the same time he fantasizes. If he could, I think he'd like to shock them. Prufrock longs to put down his dainty porcelain teacup and shout, 'I am Lazarus, come from the dead, / Come back to tell you all, I shall tell you all.'"

"Why doesn't he do it?" I asked.

"Because Prufrock is convinced no matter what he says he won't reach them. He feels the English gentlewomen he's dealing with are unreachable. He believes his situation is as hopeless as theirs. He's dead and they're dead, too. That's why the poem begins with an image of sickness, 'a patient etherized upon a table,' and ends with people drowning. Prufrock is tough shit, man."

"You said you think there's a connection between Eliot the poet and J. Alfred Prufrock," I said.

"Of course there's a connection. Tommy Eliot from St. Louis, Missouri," said the officer. "Try as he will, he doesn't fit in. His English friends call him 'The American' and laugh. Tom Eliot the outsider with his rolled umbrella. T. S. Eliot is a self-conscious, make-believe Englishman and you have to understand that to understand 'Prufrock.'

"The poem is dark and funny at the same time. It's filled with humor and Prufrock is capable of laughing at himself. Just read those lines, 'Is it perfume from a dress / That makes me so digress?'"

"You were talking about Prufrock being sexually attracted to the women. How could that be if he is, as you say, 'dead.'" I asked.

"By 'dead' I mean desolate, inwardly barren, godforsaken. Inwardly, spiritually, Prufrock is a desolate creature. He's a moral man, he's a civilized man, but he's also hollow. But there's hope for him. In spite of himself, Prufrock is drawn to women.

"Look at line 64. He's attracted and repelled. Prufrock attends these teas, notices the women's arms 'downed with light brown hair!' and it scares the hell out of him because what he longs to do is to get them onto a drawing-room floor or a beach somewhere and bury his face in that same wonderfully tantalizing 'light brown hair.' What do you think of that, sailor?"

"I think you're right, sir."

"Then tell me this, Mr. Sward: Why doesn't he ask the overwhelming question? Hell, man, maybe it's not sexual. Maybe I'm wrong. Maybe what he wants to do is to ask some question like what you yourself suggested: 'What's the point in going on living when, in some sense, we're all already dead?'"

"I think he doesn't ask the question because he's so repressed, sir. He longs for physical contact, like you say, but he also wants another kind of intimacy, and he's afraid to ask for it and it's making him crazy."

"That's right, sailor. He's afraid. Eliot wrote the poem in 1911 when women were beginning to break free."

"Break free of what?" I asked.

"Of the prim and proper Victorian ideal. Suffragettes, feminists they called themselves. At the time Eliot wrote 'Prufrock,' women in England and America were catching on to the fact that they were disfranchised and had begun fighting for the right to vote, among other things, and for liberation, equality with men.

"Of course Prufrock is more prim and proper than the bored, overcivilized women in the poem. And it's ironic, isn't it, that he doesn't understand that the women are one step ahead of him. What you have in Prufrock is a man who tries to reconcile the image of real women with 'light brown hair' on their arms with some ideal, women who are a cross between the goddess Juno and a sweet Victorian maiden."

"Prufrock seems to know pretty well what he's feeling," I said. "He's not a liar and he's not a coward. To be honest, sir, I identify with Prufrock. He may try on one mask or another, but he ends up removing the mask and exposing himself."

"Now, about interior monologues: to understand 'Prufrock' you have to understand that most poems have one or more speakers and an audience, implied or otherwise. Let's go back to line 1. Who is this 'you and I' Eliot writes about?"

"Prufrock is talking to both his inner self and the reader," I said.

"How do you interpret the first ten lines?" the officer asked, pointing with his pencil.

" 'Let us go then, you and I,' he's saying, let us stroll, somnolent and numb as a sedated patient, through these seedy 'half-deserted streets, / The muttering retreats / Of restless nights in one-night cheap hotels.' "

"That's it, sailor. And while one might argue that Prufrock 'wakes' at the end of the poem, he is for the most part a ghostly inhabitant of a world that is, for him, a sort of hell. He is like the speaker in the Italian epigraph from Dante's *Inferno*, who says, essentially, 'Like you, reader, I'm in purgatory and there is no way out. Nobody ever escapes from this pit and, for that reason, I can speak the truth without fear of ill fame.'

"Despairing and sick of heart, Prufrock is a prisoner. Trapped in himself and trapped in society, he attends another and another in an endless series of effete, decorous teas.

> In the room the women come and go
> Talking of Michelangelo.

"Do you get it now? Do you see what I mean when I say 'tough shit'?" said the officer.

"Yeah, I'm beginning to," I said.

"T. S. Eliot's 'Prufrock' has become so much a part of the English language that people who have never read the poem are familiar with phrases like 'I have measured out my life with coffee spoons' and 'I grow old . . . I grow old . . . / I shall wear the bottoms of my trousers rolled' and 'Do I dare to eat a peach?' and 'In the room the women come and go.'

"Do you get it now? Eliot's irregularly rhymed, 131-line interior monologue has become part of the monologue all of us carry on in our heads. We are all of us, whether we know it or not, love-hungry, sex-crazed soldiers and sailors, brave, bored and lonely. At some level in our hearts, we are all J. Alfred Prufrock, every one of us, and we are all sailing into a war zone from which, as the last line of the poem implies, we may never return."

From "T. S. Eliot's 'Love Song of J. Alfred Prufrock'" in *Touchstones: American Poets on a Favorite Poem*, edited by Robert Pack and Jay Parini

CONSIDERATIONS FOR CRITICAL THINKING AND WRITING

1. How satisfactory is this reading of the poem? Are any significant portions of the poem left out of this reading?

2. Compare the tone of this critical approach to any other in this chapter. Explain why you prefer one over another.

3. Using Sward's personal approach, write an analysis of a poem of your choice in this anthology.

SUGGESTED TOPICS FOR LONGER PAPERS

1. "The Love Song of J. Alfred Prufrock" has proved to be popular among generations of college students who are fond of quoting bits of the poem. What do you think accounts for that popularity among your own generation? Alternatively, why doesn't this poem speak to your concerns or those of your generation?

2. Of the five critical perspectives on the poem provided in this chapter, which did you find to be the most satisfying reading? Explain your response by describing how your choice opened up the poem more than the other four perspectives.

18

A THEMATIC CASE STUDY
Love and Longing

For a man to become a poet . . .
he must be in love or miserable.

— GEORGE GORDON, LORD BYRON

National Portrait Gallery,
London.

Behind all of the elements that make up a poem, and even behind its cultural contexts and critical reception, lies its theme. Its idea and the point around which the entire poem revolves, the theme is ultimately what we respond to — or fail to respond to. All of the other elements, in fact, are typically there to contribute to the theme, whether or not that theme is explicitly stated. Reading thematically means extending what you have learned about the analysis of individual elements at work in the poem to make connections between the text and the world we inhabit.

This chapter, organized into a case study on love poems, focuses on a single theme as it reappears throughout various parts of poetic history. These poems have much to say about human experience — experience that is contradictory, confusing, complicated, and fascinating. You'll find diverse perspectives from different historical, cultural, generational, or political moments. You'll also discover writers who aim to entertain, to describe, to convince, and to complain. After reading these poems in the context of one another, you're

Web Research the
poets in this chapter at
bedfordstmartins.com/
rewritinglit.

likely to come away with a richer understanding of how the themes of love play out in your own life.

Poems about love have probably enchanted and intrigued their hearers since people began making poetry. Like poetry itself, love is, after all, about intensity, acute impressions, and powerful responsibilities. The emotional dimensions of love do not lend themselves to analytic expository essays. Although such writing can be satisfying intellectually, it is most inadequate for evoking and capturing the thick excitement and swooning reveries that love engenders. The poems in this section include spiritual as well as physical explorations of love that range over five centuries. As you'll see, poetic responses to love by men and women can be quite similar as well as different from one another, just as poems from different periods can reflect a variety of values and attitudes toward love. It is indeed an engaging theme — but as you read, don't forget to pay attention to the formal elements of each of these selections and how they work together to create the poem's particular points about love. Also, remember to read not only for the presence of love; many other themes can be found in these works, and many other connections can be made to the literature elsewhere in this anthology.

The oldest love poem in this case study, Christopher Marlowe's "The Passionate Shepherd to His Love," opens with the line, "Come live with me and be my love." This famous pastoral lyric set a tone for love poetry that has been replicated since its publication. Before concluding with "Then live with me and be my love," Marlowe embraces the kinds of generous pleasure that readers have traditionally and happily received for centuries. The feelings, if not the particular images, are likely to be quite familiar to you.

CHRISTOPHER MARLOWE (1564-1593)

The Passionate Shepherd to His Love   *1599?*

Come live with me and be my love,
And we will all the pleasure prove
That valleys, groves, hills, and fields,
Woods, or steepy mountain yields.

And we will sit upon the rocks,   5
Seeing the shepherds feed their flocks,
By shallow rivers to whose falls
Melodious birds sing madrigals.

And I will make thee beds of roses
And a thousand fragrant posies,   10
A cap of flowers, and a kirtle°   *dress or skirt*
Embroidered all with leaves of myrtle;

A gown made of the finest wool
Which from our pretty lambs we pull;
Fair lined slippers for the cold,   15
With buckles of the purest gold;

A belt of straw and ivy buds,
With coral clasps and amber studs:
And if these pleasures may thee move,
Come live with me, and be my love.   20

The shepherd swains shall dance and sing
For thy delight each May morning:
If these delights thy mind may move,
Then live with me and be my love.

CONSIDERATIONS FOR CRITICAL THINKING AND WRITING

1. **FIRST RESPONSE.** How persuasive do you find the shepherd's arguments to his potential lover?

2. What do you think might be the equivalent of the shepherd's arguments in the twenty-first century? What kinds of appeals and images of love would be made by a contemporary lover?

3. Try writing a response to the shepherd from the female's point of view using Marlowe's rhythms, rhyme scheme, and quatrains.

CONNECTION TO ANOTHER SELECTION

1. Read Sir Walter Raleigh's "The Nymph's Reply to the Shepherd" (p. 639). How does the nymph's response compare with your imagined reply?

While Marlowe's shepherd focuses his energies on convincing his potential love to join him (in the delights associated with love), the speaker in the following sonnet by William Shakespeare demonstrates his love for poetry as well and focuses on the beauty of the object of the poem. In doing so, he introduces a theme that has become a perennial challenge to love — the corrosive, destructive nature of what Shakespeare shockingly calls "sluttish time." His resolution of this issue is intriguing: see if you agree with it.

WILLIAM SHAKESPEARE (1564–1616)

Not marble, nor the gilded monuments   1609

Not marble, nor the gilded monuments
Of princes, shall outlive this powerful rhyme;
But you shall shine more bright in these conténts
Than unswept stone, besmeared with sluttish time.
When wasteful war shall statues overturn,   5

And broils root out the work of masonry,
Nor Mars his° swords nor war's quick fire shall burn   *possessive of Mars*
The living record of your memory.
'Gainst death and all-oblivious enmity
Shall you pace forth; your praise shall still find room   10
Even in the eyes of all posterity
That wear this world out to the ending doom.
   So, till the judgment that yourself arise,
   You live in this, and dwell in lovers' eyes.

CONSIDERATIONS FOR CRITICAL THINKING AND WRITING

1. **FIRST RESPONSE.** What do you think is the central point of this poem? Explain whether you agree or disagree with its theme.
2. How does "sluttish time" (line 4) represent the poem's major conflict?
3. Consider whether this poem is more about the poet's loved one or the poet's love of his own poetry.

CONNECTIONS TO OTHER SELECTIONS

1. Compare the theme of this poem with that of Andrew Marvell's "To His Coy Mistress" (p. 80), paying particular attention to the speaker's beliefs about how time affects love.
2. Discuss whether you find this love poem more or less appealing than Marlowe's "The Passionate Shepherd to His Love." As you make this comparison, explain what the criteria for an appealing love poem should be.

As Shakespeare's speaker presents a love that will withstand the destruction of time, Anne Bradstreet's "To My Dear and Loving Husband" evokes a marital love that confirms a connection that transcends space and matter as well as time. Although Bradstreet wrote more than three centuries ago, such devotion remains undated for many (but, of course, not all) readers of love poetry. She begins, naturally enough, with the pleasure and paradox of how two people can be one.

ANNE BRADSTREET (c. 1612–1672)

To My Dear and Loving Husband   *1678*

If ever two were one, then surely we.
If ever man were loved by wife, then thee;
If ever wife was happy in a man,
Compare with me, ye women, if you can.
I prize thy love more than whole mines of gold   5
Or all the riches that the East doth hold.

My love is such that rivers cannot quench,
Nor ought but love from thee, give recompense.
Thy love is such I can no way repay,
The heavens reward thee manifold, I pray.   10
Then while we live, in love let's so persevere
That when we live no more, we may live ever.

CONSIDERATIONS FOR CRITICAL THINKING AND WRITING

1. **FIRST RESPONSE.** Describe the poem's tone. Is it what you'd expect from a seventeenth-century Puritan? Why or why not?

2. Explain whether Bradstreet's devotion is directed more toward her husband here on earth or toward the eternal rewards of heaven.

3. What is the paradox of the final line? How is it resolved?

CONNECTION TO ANOTHER SELECTION

1. How does the theme of this poem compare with that of Bradstreet's "Before the Birth of One of Her Children" (p. 617)? Explain why you find the poems consistent or contradictory.

The remaining poems in this case study are modern and contemporary pieces that both maintain and revise the perspectives on love provided by Marlowe, Shakespeare, and Bradstreet. As you read them, consider what each adds to your understanding of the others and of love in general.

ELIZABETH BARRETT BROWNING (1806–1861)
How Do I Love Thee?
Let Me Count the Ways   *1850*

How do I love thee? Let me count the ways.
I love thee to the depth and breadth and height
My soul can reach, when feeling out of sight
For the ends of being and ideal grace.
I love thee to the level of every day's   5
Most quiet need, by sun and candle-light.
I love thee freely, as men strive for right.
I love thee purely, as they turn from praise.
I love thee with the passion put to use
In my old griefs, and with my childhood's faith.   10
I love thee with a love I seemed to lose
With my lost saints. I love thee with the breath,
Smiles, tears, of all my life; and, if God choose,
I shall but love thee better after death.

CONSIDERATIONS FOR CRITICAL THINKING AND WRITING

1. **FIRST RESPONSE.** This poem has remained extraordinarily popular for more than 150 years. Why do you think it has been so often included in collections of love poems? What is its appeal? Does it speak to a contemporary reader? To you?

2. Comment on the effect of the diction. What kind of tone does it create?

3. Would you characterize this poem as having a religious theme — or is love a substitute for religion?

CONNECTION TO ANOTHER SELECTION

1. Compare and contrast the images, tone, and theme of this poem with those of Christina Rossetti's "Promises Like Pie-Crust" (p. 641). Explain why you find one poem more promising than the other.

EDNA ST. VINCENT MILLAY (1892–1950)

Recuerdo°
1922

We were very tired, we were very merry —
We had gone back and forth all night on the
    ferry.
It was bare and bright, and smelled like a
    stable —
But we looked into a fire, we leaned across a
    table,
We lay on a hill-top underneath the moon;   5
And the whistles kept blowing, and the dawn
    came soon.

We were very tired, we were very merry —
We had gone back and forth all night on the ferry;
And you ate an apple, and I ate a pear,
From a dozen of each we had bought somewhere;   10
And the sky went wan, and the wind came cold,
And the sun rose dripping, a bucketful of gold.

We were very tired, we were very merry,
We had gone back and forth all night on the ferry.
We hailed, "Good morrow, mother!" to a shawl-covered head,   15
And bought a morning paper, which neither of us read;
And she wept, "God bless you!" for the apples and pears,
And we gave her all our money but our subway fares.

Recuerdo: I remember (Spanish).

CONSIDERATIONS FOR CRITICAL THINKING AND WRITING

1. **FIRST RESPONSE.** This poem was a very popular representation of New York City bohemian life in Greenwich Village during the 1920s. What do you think made "Recuerdo" so appealing then?

2. How does the repetition in the first two lines of each stanza connect sound to sense through the rhythm of the lines?

3. Explain how love and generosity are evoked in the poem.

CONNECTION TO ANOTHER SELECTION

1. Discuss how the couple in this poem essentially follows the advice provided in the next selection, E. E. Cummings's "since feeling is first."

E. E. CUMMINGS (1894–1962)

since feeling is first   *1926*

since feeling is first
who pays any attention
to the syntax of things
will never wholly kiss you;

wholly to be a fool   5
while Spring is in the world

my blood approves,
and kisses are a better fate
than wisdom
lady i swear by all flowers. Don't cry   10
— the best gesture of my brain is less than
your eyelids' flutter which says

we are for each other:then
laugh,leaning back in my arms
for life's not a paragraph   15

And death i think is no parenthesis

CONSIDERATIONS FOR CRITICAL THINKING AND WRITING

1. **FIRST RESPONSE.** What is the speaker's initial premise? Why is it crucial to his argument? What is his argument?

2. Does this poem fit into the *carpe diem* tradition? How?

3. How are nature and society presented as being in conflict? Why is this relevant to the speaker's argument?

4. List and describe the grammatical metaphors in the poem. How do they further the speaker's argument?

CONNECTIONS TO OTHER SELECTIONS

1. Contrast the theme of this poem with that of Marlowe's "The Passionate Shepherd to His Love" (p. 511). How do you account for the differences, in both style and content, between the two love poems?

2. Discuss attitudes toward "feeling" in this poem and in Molly Peacock's "Desire" (p. 251).

MARK DOTY (B. 1953)

The Embrace 1998

© Kenneth Chen.

You weren't well or really ill yet
      either;
just a little tired, your handsomeness
tinged by grief or anticipation,
      which brought
to your face a thoughtful, deepening
      grace.

I didn't for a moment doubt you
      were dead.   5
I knew that to be true still, even in
      the dream.
You'd been out — at work maybe? —
having a good day, almost energetic.

We seemed to be moving from some old house
where we'd lived, boxes everywhere, things   10
in disarray: that was the *story* of my dream,
but even asleep I was shocked out of narrative

by your face, the physical fact of your face:
inches from mine, smooth-shaven, loving, alert.
Why so difficult, remembering the actual look   15
of you? Without a photograph, without strain?

So when I saw your unguarded, reliable face,
your unmistakable gaze opening all the warmth
and clarity of you — warm brown tea — we held
each other for the time the dream allowed.   20

Bless you. You came back, so I could see you
once more, plainly, so I could rest against you
without thinking this happiness lessened anything,
without thinking you were alive again.

CONSIDERATIONS FOR CRITICAL THINKING AND WRITING

1. **FIRST RESPONSE.** In what sense can "The Embrace" be read as a love poem?
   Explain why it does or doesn't fit your definition of a love poem.
2. Describe the tone of each of the stanzas and trace your emotional response
   to them as you move through the poem. What is your emotional reaction
   to the entire poem?
3. Describe the relation between death and love in the poem. How is that relation central to the theme?

JOAN MURRAY (B. 1945)

Play-by-Play   *1997*

Yaddo°

Would it surprise the young men
playing softball on the hill to hear the women
on the terrace admiring their bodies:
the slim waist of the pitcher, the strength
of the runner's legs, the torso of the catcher   5
rising off his knees to toss the ball back to the mound?
Would it embarrass them
to hear two women, sitting together after dinner,
praising even their futile motions:
the flex of a batter's hips   10
before his missed swing, the wide-spread stride
of a man picked off his base, the intensity
on the new man's face
as he waits on deck and fans the air?

Would it annoy them, the way some women   15
take offense when men caress them with their eyes?
And why should it surprise me that these women,
well past sixty, haven't put aside desire
but sit at ease and in pleasure,
watching the young men move above the rose garden   20
where the marble Naiads
pose and yawn in their fountain?
Who better than these women, with their sweaters
draped across their shoulders, their perspectives
honed from years of lovers, to recognize   25
the beauty that would otherwise
go unnoticed on this hill?
And will it compromise their pleasure
if I sit down at their table to listen
to the play-by-play and see it through their eyes?   30

Would it distract the young men if they realized
that three women laughing softly on the terrace
above closed books and half-filled wineglasses
are moving beside them on the field?
Would they want to know how they've been   35
held to the light till some motion or expression
showed the unsuspected loveliness
in a common shape or face?
Wouldn't they have liked to see how they looked
down there, as they stood for a moment at the plate,   40

Yaddo: An artist's colony in Saratoga Springs, New York.

bathed in the light of perfect expectation,
before their shadows lengthened, before they
walked together up the darkened hill,
so beautiful they would not have
recognized themselves?   45

CONSIDERATIONS FOR CRITICAL THINKING AND WRITING

1. **FIRST RESPONSE.** How would you answer the series of nine questions posed by the speaker?
2. What do you think the young men would have to say to the older women gazing at them?
3. Explain how the "marble Naiads" (line 21) help to set the tone.
4. Discuss the significance of the title.

CONNECTION TO ANOTHER SELECTION

1. Write an essay on the nature of desire in this poem and in Molly Peacock's "Desire" (p. 251).

BILLIE BOLTON (B. 1950)

Memorandum   *2004*

Photograph courtesy of Ashley G. Stollar.

TO: My Boyfriend from Hell
FR: Me
RE: Shit I Never Want to Hear Another Word
          About as Long as I Live

1. Your Addled Thoughts. Anything about your ongoing interest in Lucy Liu's legs, Shania Twain's bellybutton, or Reese Witherspoon's whatever; your must-see TV dramas, your fantasy baseball addiction, or your addictions period. Anything about going anywhere with you at any time including, but not limited to: Sam's Club, Big Lots, Waffle House, church fish fries, local snake round-ups or Amvet turkey shoots, unless you promise to be the turkey.

2. Your Wireless Connection. Anything about your stage-four cell phone habit; the dames who have your cell phone number and why; who's on your speed-dial list or who left a voice mail message; anything about cell phone rebates, late fees, roaming charges, contracts or dropping your cell phone in the john by accident, even if you flush it and walk away.

3. Your Adolescent Only Child. Anything about his bed-wetting or fire-setting habits; his gang affiliation, court dates or swastika tattoo; anything about his tantrums, seizures or deep psychological need for video games and fruit roll-ups; anything about his pathological grudge against mankind or his particular beef against me.

4. Your Significant Others (female). Anything about the redneck redhead you banged in high school, the long-haired potheads you balled in your hippie days, the white trash airhead you married or the blue-haired battle-ax who pats you on the rump and pays for your dinner. Anything about your devotion to your long-suffering mother, your loopy sisters, or even the Blessed Virgin.

CONSIDERATIONS FOR CRITICAL THINKING AND WRITING

1. FIRST RESPONSE. What makes this a poem rather than simply a memo?
2. How does the speaker's diction and choice of details reveal her own personality?
3. CREATIVE RESPONSE. Using Bolton's style, tone, and form as inspiration, write a reply from the boyfriend's point of view.

CONNECTION TO ANOTHER SELECTION

1. Compare the use of descriptive detail to create tone in "Memorandum" and in Michelle Boisseau's "Self-Pity's Closet" (p. 587)

MICHAEL RYAN (B. 1946)

Bunny   2004

In the scarred desk behind me
in history class,
she lulled her nyloned knee
against my ass,

its message pressing home   5
as dully we went
from the interminable Fall of Rome
to the Council of Trent

and through the even duller
steel town afternoons,   10
locked in a collar
of dim green rooms,

old nuns, and ever new
bewilderment
1962.   15
Like the hood ornament

on some chopped down hot rod
of the apocalypse,
above the blackboard stood
the crucifix   20

flanked on either slope
of its tiny Calvary
by color headshots of the Pope
and John F. Kennedy—

an arrangement meant to convey   25
not thievery being done
but God's work every day
by The Two Johns

drawing us like dynamos
through them to heaven   30
while we shook in our rows
as if on toboggans.

So what if we had known
what JFK was doing
in Laos and Vietnam,   35
and who he was screwing

(including the teenage mistress
of the head of the Mafia,
delivered to the White House
like a midnight pizza)?   40

The greater world to me,
present and past,
was the space between Bunny's knee
and my ass,

and I needed it collapsed   45
as soon as class began.
So what that I thought she had
the brains of a pecan,

mascara so black and thick
she must have smeared it on   50
with a popsicle stick,
and a nickname incredibly dumb?

Each day when she had helped me
annihilate an hour,
and we were going away,   55
I'd stare at her,

and she'd stare back and wink
I know you live off it:
one flashlight blink
at the bottom of a pit.   60

CONSIDERATIONS FOR CRITICAL THINKING AND WRITING

1. **FIRST RESPONSE.** How does the speaker's diction reveal his sensibilities? How would you describe him?

2. How does the speaker characterize his Catholic school? Are the images he uses to describe it nostalgic and sentimental? Explain why or why not.

3. What do you think are his feelings for Bunny?

CONNECTIONS TO OTHER SELECTIONS

1. Discuss the treatment of time in this poem and in Shakespeare's "Not marble, nor the gilded monuments" (p. 512).

2. Compare the speaker's tribute to Bunny with the speaker's devotion in Browning's "How Do I Love Thee? Let Me Count the Ways" (p. 514). Which poem do you find more moving and convincing? Why?

SUGGESTED TOPICS FOR LONGER PAPERS

1. Choose one of the love poems in this chapter and compare its themes with the lyrics of a contemporary love song in terms of poetic elements such as diction, tone, images, figures of speech, sounds, and rhythms.

2. Select any two poems from this chapter that were published before 1900 and compare them in style and theme with two poems published after 1900. Which set of poems, the early or the later, comes closest to representing your own sensibilities concerning love? Explain why.

19

A THEMATIC CASE STUDY
Humor and Satire

I think like a poet, and behave like a poet. Occasionally I need to sit in the corner for bad behavior.

— GARY SOTO

© Beinecke Library, Yale University.

There is nothing wrong with a poetry that is entertaining and easy to understand.

— CHARLES BUKOWSKI

© Gary Soto.

Poetry can be a hoot. There are plenty of poets that leave you smiling, grinning, chuckling, and laughing out loud because they use language that is witty, surprising, teasing, or satirical. Occasionally, their subject matter is simply wacky. There's a poem in this chapter, for example, titled "Commercial Leech Farming Today" (p. 536), that deftly squeezes humor out of bloodsucking leeches grown for treating surgical patients. Although the material might not sound promising, Thomas Lux's treatment shapes this unlikely topic into a memorable satiric theme.

Sadly, however, poetry is too often burdened with a reputation for only being formal and serious, and readers sometimes show their deference by feeling intimidated and humbled in its earnest, weighty presence. After all, poetry frequently concerns itself with matters of great consequence: its themes contemplate subjects such as God and immortality, love and death, war and peace, injustice and outrage, racism and societal ills, deprivation and disease, alienation and angst, totalitarianism and terrorism, as well as a host of other tragic grievances and agonies that humanity might suffer. For readers of *The Onion*, a widely distributed satirical newspaper also available online, this prevailing grim reputation is humorously framed in a bogus story about National Poetry Month, celebrated each April to increase an awareness of the value of poetry in American life. The brief article (April 27, 2005) quotes a speaker at a fund-raising meeting of the "American Poetry Prevention Society" who cautions that "we must stop this scourge before more lives are exposed to poetry." He warns that "young people, particularly morose high-school and college students, are very susceptible to this terrible affliction." *The Onion's* satire peels away the erroneous assumption that sorrow and tears are the only appropriate responses to a poetry "infection."

Poetry — at least in its clichéd popular form — is nearly always morosely dressed in black and rarely smiles. This severe image of somber profundity unfortunately tailors our expectations so that we assume that serious poetry cannot be playful and even downright funny or, putting the issue another way, that humorous poetry cannot be thoughtful and significant. The poems in this chapter demonstrate that serious poems can be funny and that comic poems can be thoughtful. Their humor, sometimes subtle, occasionally even savage, will serve to remind you that laughter engenders thought as well as pleasure.

FLEUR ADCOCK (B. 1934)

The Video

When Laura was born, Ceri watched.
They all gathered around Mum's bed —
Dad and the midwife and Mum's sister
and Ceri. "Move over a bit," Dad said —
he was trying to focus the camcorder   5
on Mum's legs and the baby's head.

After she had a little sister,
and Mum had gone back to being thin,
and was twice as busy, Ceri played
the video again and again.   10
She watched Laura come out, and then,
in reverse, she made her go back in.

CONSIDERATIONS FOR CRITICAL THINKING AND WRITING

1. **FIRST RESPONSE.** How does the humor in the final line produce the theme?

2. Discuss the appropriateness of Adcock's choice of "watched" in lines 1 and 11. What does the word suggest about Ceri?

3. How does the rhyme scheme affect your reading of the poem?

JOHN CIARDI (1916–1986)

Suburban

1978

Yesterday Mrs. Friar phoned. "Mr. Ciardi,
   how do you do?" she said. "I am sorry to say
this isn't exactly a social call. The fact is
   your dog has just deposited — forgive me —
a large repulsive object in my petunias."   5

I thought to ask, "Have you checked the rectal grooving
   for a positive I.D.?" My dog, as it happened,
was in Vermont with my son, who had gone fishing —
   if that's what one does with a girl, two cases of beer,
and a borrowed camper. I guessed I'd get no trout.   10

But why lose out on organic gold for a wise crack?
   "Yes, Mrs. Friar," I said, "I understand."
"Most kind of you," she said. "Not at all," I said.
   I went with a spade. She pointed, looking away.
"I always have loved dogs," she said, "but really!"   15

I scooped it up and bowed. "The animal of it.
   I hope this hasn't upset you, Mrs. Friar."
"Not really," she said, "but really!" I bore the turd
   across the line to my own petunias
and buried it till the glorious resurrection   20

when even these suburbs shall give up their dead.

CONSIDERATIONS FOR CRITICAL THINKING AND WRITING

1. **FIRST RESPONSE.** How does the speaker transform Mrs. Friar into a symbolic figure of the suburbs?
2. Why do you suppose Ciardi focuses on this particular incident to make a comment on the suburbs? What is the speaker's attitude toward suburban life?
3. **CREATIVE RESPONSE.** Write a one-paragraph physical description of Mrs. Friar that captures her character.

CONNECTION TO ANOTHER SELECTION

1. Compare the speakers' voices in "Suburban" and in John Updike's "Dog's Death" (p. 22).

DAISY FRIED (B. 1967)

Wit's End

2000

My father says, "Face it, you live
   in a civilization of mirrors and sinks,"
      invading my real room, the bathroom.

I pull down an eyelid till I see the pained
    pink meniscus underneath. I *"O"*   5
        my mouth, poke the mascara wand

at my eyelashes, not missing
    by much. It's makeup's premonition
        of sex in the house he can't stand.

The bathroom's littered with eyeliners,   10
    tweezers, kisslipped tissues. I shed snarls
        of hair in the shower like saffron threads,

red kelp. In the mirror I paint myself a clownface
    copied from *Sassy, Seventeen, Glamour.* He
        stands in the doorway, loving   15

the used-to-be lovable 12-year-old
    formerly his. We look in the mirror:
        blush welts, orange, riding low

on my cheeks, pink lipstick leaking
    from my lip corners. Glitter-white   20
        chevrons for eyelids; Cover Girl fails

again to cover my nose-zits. Reflected, behind me,
    tangles of the unwashed bras I don't need
        trail from shower rod, shampoo rack,

hot-cold dial, soapdish, stopcock.   25
    He hates it: me mooning, me sighing,
        me incessantly hairbrushing, singing stupid

love songs. "I'll buy back the gunk!" he says.
    He'll pay twice what I spent if only I'll stop.
        I stand by the tub in the bathroom,   30

my real room. I prop up a leg, I pull up
    my skirt, start shaving thigh-stubble. I shove
        the door shut between us with my ass.

Considerations for Critical Thinking and Writing

1. **FIRST RESPONSE.** What images and figures of speech make Fried's description of this father-daughter relationship convincing?

2. In what sense is the bathroom for the speaker "my real room" (lines 3 and 31)?

3. How does the title sum up the poem's familial conflict?

4. Explain why you think Fried treats the speaker mostly satirically or sympathetically.

Connections to Other Selections

1. Compare the tone and theme of "Wit's End" with those of Li Ho's "A Beautiful Girl Combs Her Hair" (p. 53).

2. How might the daughter in "Wit's End" be considered a youthful version of the speaker in Sylvia Plath's "Mirror" (p. 148)?

RONALD WALLACE (B. 1945)

In a Rut

2002

She dogs me while
I try to take a catnap.
Of course, I'm playing possum but
I can feel her watching me,
eagle-eyed, like a hawk.   5
She snakes over to my side
of the bed, and continues to
badger me. I may be a rat, but
I won't let her get my goat.
I refuse to make an   10
ass of myself, no matter
how mulish I feel.
I'm trying to make a
bee-line for sleep, but
You're a turkey! she says, and   15
I'm thinking she's no
spring chicken. She *is* a busy beaver,
though, always trying to ferret
things out. She's a bit batty,
in fact, a bit cuckoo, but   20
What's your beef, now? I say.
*Get your head out
of the sand,* she replies. *What
are you—a man, or a mouse?*
That's a lot of bull, I think;   25
she can be a real bear.
Don't horse around, now, she says.
You know you can't weasel out of it!
She's having a whale of a time,
thinking she's got me skunked, thinking   30
that she's out-foxed me.
But I know she's just crying wolf,
and I won't be cowed. Feeling
my oats now, I merely look sheepish;
I give her the hang-dog look;   35
I give her the lion's share.
I give her something to crow about.
Oh, lovey-dove, I intone.
We're all odd ducks, strange
birds; this won't be my swan-   40
song, after all. She's in hog-

heaven now, ready to pig-out.
Oh, my stallion, she says, *Oh,*
my lambkin! You are
a real animal, you know!   45

CONSIDERATIONS FOR CRITICAL THINKING AND WRITING

1. **FIRST RESPONSE.** Explain whether or not Wallace's orchestration of over-used phrases redeems them from being simply clichés.

2. How does the title contribute to your understanding of the poem's plot?

3. **CREATIVE RESPONSE.** Choose a set of familiar related expressions from sports, school, politics, religion, or whatever comes naturally to you, and write your own version of a poem that imitates Wallace's playful use of clichés.

CONNECTION TO ANOTHER SELECTION

1. Compare Wallace's organizing strategy in this poem and E. E. Cummings's technique in "next to of course god america i" (p. 166).

HOWARD NEMEROV (1920–1991)

Walking the Dog   *1980*

Two universes mosey down the street
Connected by love and a leash and nothing else.
Mostly I look at lamplight through the leaves
While he mooches along with tail up and snout down,
Getting a secret knowledge through the nose   5
Almost entirely hidden from my sight.

We stand while he's enraptured by a bush
Till I can't stand our standing any more
And haul him off; for our relationship
Is patience balancing to this side tug   10
And that side drag; a pair of symbionts
Contented not to think each other's thoughts.

What else we have in common's what he taught,
Our interest in shit. We know its every state
From steaming fresh through stink to nature's way   15
Of sluicing it downstreet dissolved in rain
Or drying it to dust that blows away.
We move along the street inspecting it.

His sense of it is keener far than mine,
And only when he finds the place precise   20
He signifies by sniffing urgently
And circles thrice about, and squats, and shits.
Whereon we both with dignity walk home
And just to show who's master I write the poem.

CONSIDERATIONS FOR CRITICAL THINKING AND WRITING

1. **FIRST RESPONSE.** How does the form of this poem give it dignity despite its topic? Explain why you experience the poem as amusing or repugnant.
2. How might you read the poem differently if the last line were deleted?
3. Compare the tone of stanzas 1 and 2 with that of 3 and 4. Discuss whether or not the two sets of stanzas are consistent and compatible.
4. Who do you think is finally the master? Explain why.

CONNECTIONS TO OTHER SELECTIONS

1. Discuss the speakers' attitudes toward dogs in "Walking the Dog" and in John Ciardi's "Suburban" (p. 525). How does humor inform those attitudes?
2. Consider the subject matter of this poem and Ronald Wallace's "Building an Outhouse" (p. 153). Some readers might argue that the subject matter is tasteless and not suitable for poetic treatment. What do you think?

LINDA PASTAN (B. 1932)

Jump Cabling

1984

When our cars   touched,
When you lifted the hood   of mine
To see the intimate workings   underneath,
When we were bound   together
By a pulse of pure   energy,
When my car like the   princess
In the tale woke with a   start,
I thought why not ride the rest of the way together?

CONSIDERATIONS FOR CRITICAL THINKING AND WRITING

1. **FIRST RESPONSE.** How is the word spacing in the poem related to its meaning?
2. Discuss the diction. How does it enhance the theme?
3. **CREATIVE RESPONSE.** Using Pastan's word spacing as a jumping-off point, write an alternate version of "Jump Cabling" in which the car does not start.

CONNECTION TO ANOTHER SELECTION

1. Compare the style and theme of this poem with that of Pastan's "Marks." (p. 152).

PETER SCHMITT (B. 1958)

Friends with Numbers   1995

If you make friends with numbers,
you don't need any other friends.
  —Shakuntala Devi, math genius

They are not hard to get to know:
6 and 9 keep changing their minds,
8 cuts the most graceful figure
but sleeps for an eternity,
and 7, lucky 7, takes   5
an arrow to his heart always.
5, halfway to somewhere, only
wants to patch his unicycle
tire, and 4, who'd like to stand for
something solid, has never had   10
two feet on the ground, yet flutters
gamely in the breeze like a flag.
3, for all his literary
accomplishments and pretensions
to immortality, is still   15
(I can tell you) not half the man
8 is asleep or awake. 1,
little 1. I know him better
than all the others, these numbers
who are all my friends. Only 2,   20
that strange smallest prime, can I count
as just a passing acquaintance.
Divisible by only 1
and herself, she seems on the verge,
yet, of always coming apart.   25
And though she eludes me, swanlike,
though I'd love to know her better,
still I am fine, there are others,
many, I have friends in numbers.

CONSIDERATIONS FOR CRITICAL THINKING AND WRITING

1. **FIRST RESPONSE.** How does the personification of numbers create characters in the poem?

2. Explain how the speaker's use of language helps to characterize him.

3. Discuss the various ways in which the single digits are transformed into individual visual images.

CONNECTION TO ANOTHER SELECTION

1. Discuss the originality—the fresh and unusual approach to their respective subject matter—in Schmitt's poem and in Christian Bök's "Vowels" (p. 56). What makes these poems so interesting?

MARTÍN ESPADA (B. 1957)

The Community College Revises Its Curriculum in Response to Changing Demographics

2000

SPA 100 Conversational Spanish
2 credits

The course
is especially concerned
with giving police
the ability
to express themselves
tersely
in matters of interest
to them

CONSIDERATIONS FOR CRITICAL THINKING AND WRITING

1. **FIRST RESPONSE.** What sort of political comment do you think Espada makes in this poem?
2. Would this be a poem without the title? Explain your answer.
3. **CREATIVE RESPONSE.** Choose a course description from your school's catalog and organize the catalog copy into poetic lines. Provide your poem with a title that offers a provocative commentary about it.

CONNECTION TO ANOTHER SELECTION

1. Compare the themes in Espada's poem and in Donald Justice's "Order in the Streets" (p. 297).

DENISE DUHAMEL (B. 1961)

Language Police Report

2006

After Diane Ravitch's The Language Police

The busybody (banned as sexist, demeaning to older women) who lives next door called my daughter a tomboy (banned as sexist) when she climbed the jungle (banned; replaced with "rain forest") gym. Then she had the nerve to call her an egghead and a bookworm (both banned as offensive; replaced with "intellectual") because she read fairy (banned because suggests homosexuality; replace with "elf") tales.

I'm tired of the Language Police turning a deaf ear (banned as handicapism) to my complaints. I'm no Pollyanna (banned as sexist) and will not accept any lame (banned as offensive; replace with "walks with a cane") excuses at this time.

If Alanis Morissette can play God (banned) in *Dogma* (banned as ethnocentric; replace with "Doctrine" or "Belief"), why can't my daughter play stickball (banned as regional or ethnic bias) on boy's night out (banned as sexist)? Why can't she build a snowman (banned, replace with "snow person") without that fanatic (banned as ethnocentric; replace with "believer," "follower," or "adherent") next door telling her she's going to hell (banned; replaced with "heck" or "darn")?

Do you really think this is what the Founding Fathers (banned as sexist; replace with "the Founders" or "the Framers") had in mind? That we can't even enjoy our Devil (banned)-ed ham sandwiches in peace? I say put a stop to this cult (banned as ethnocentric) of PC old wives' tales (banned as sexist; replace with "folk wisdom") and extremist (banned as ethnocentric; replace with "believer," "follower," or "adherent") conservative duffers (banned as demeaning to older men).

As an heiress (banned as sexist; replace with "heir") to the first amendment, I feel that only a heretic (use with caution when comparing religions) would try to stop American vernacular from flourishing in all its inspirational (banned as patronizing when referring to a person with disabilities) splendor.

Considerations for Critical Thinking and Writing

1. **FIRST RESPONSE.** Duhamel has explained that she was inspired to write this prose poem after reading a list of words banned as "politically incorrect" in Diane Ravitch's study of editorial censorship, *The Language Police: How Pressure Groups Restrict What Students Learn*. She found this abuse of language both "horrifying and hilarious" (*The Best of American Poetry 2007*, p. 132). What do you think?

2. What is the speaker's basic argument against the "Language Police"?

3. **CREATIVE RESPONSE.** Write a stanza of your own that adds to the list.

Connection to Another Selection

1. Compare the attitudes expressed toward language in this poem and in Barbara Hamby's "Ode to American English" (p. 85).

M. Carl Holman (1919–1988)

Mr. Z   1967

Taught early that his mother's skin was the sign of error,
He dressed and spoke the perfect part of honor;
Won scholarships, attended the best schools,
Disclaimed kinship with jazz and spirituals;
Chose prudent, raceless views for each situation,   5
Or when he could not cleanly skirt dissension,
Faced up to the dilemma, firmly seized
Whatever ground was Anglo-Saxonized.

In diet, too, his practice was exemplary:
Of pork in its profane forms he was wary;   10

Expert in vintage wines, sauces and salads,
His palate shrank from cornbread, yams and collards.

He was as careful whom he chose to kiss:
His bride had somewhere lost her Jewishness,
But kept her blue eyes; an Episcopalian   15
Prelate proclaimed them matched chameleon.
Choosing the right addresses, here, abroad,
They shunned those places where they might be barred;
Even less anxious to be asked to dine
Where hosts catered to kosher accent or exotic skin.   20

And so he climbed, unclogged by ethnic weights,
An airborne plant, flourishing without roots.
Not one false note was struck — until he died:
His subtly grieving widow could have flayed
The obit writers, ringing crude changes on a clumsy phrase: 25
"One of the most distinguished members of his race."

CONSIDERATIONS FOR CRITICAL THINKING AND WRITING

1. **FIRST RESPONSE.** What is the central irony of Mr. Z's life? What do you think of him?
2. Explain whether you find Holman's satiric portrait to be fair or unfair.
3. Discuss the poem's rhythms and rhymes. How do they contribute to the tone?
4. What does Mr. Z's name suggest about his identity?

CONNECTIONS TO OTHER SELECTIONS

1. Compare the satirical treatment of race in "Mr. Z" and in Langston Hughes's "Dinner Guest: Me" (p. 426).
2. Discuss the preference for "Anglo-Saxonized" (line 8) appearances in "Mr. Z" and in Janice Mirikitani's "Recipe" (p. 565).

GARY SOTO (B. 1952)

Mexicans Begin Jogging   *1995*

At the factory I worked
In the fleck of rubber, under the press
Of an oven yellow with flame,
Until the border patrol opened
Their vans and my boss waved for us to run.   5
"Over the fence, Soto," he shouted,
And I shouted that I was American.
"No time for lies," he said, and pressed
A dollar in my palm, hurrying me
Through the back door.   10

Since I was on his time, I ran
And became the wag to a short tail of Mexicans—
Ran past the amazed crowds that lined
The street and blurred like photographs, in rain.
I ran from that industrial road to the soft   15
Houses where people paled at the turn of an autumn sky.
What could I do but yell *vivas*
To baseball, milkshakes, and those sociologists
Who would clock me
As I jog into the next century   20
On the power of a great, silly grin.

Explore contexts for Gary Soto on LiterActive.

CONSIDERATIONS FOR CRITICAL THINKING AND WRITING

1. **FIRST RESPONSE.** What ironies are present in this poem?

2. Soto was born and raised in Fresno, California. How does this fact affect your reading of the first stanza?

3. In what different ways does the speaker become "the wag" (line 12) in this poem? (You may want to look up the word to consider all possible meanings.)

4. Explain lines 17–21. What serious point is being made in these humorous lines?

CONNECTION TO ANOTHER SELECTION

1. Compare the speakers' ironic attitudes toward exercise in this poem and in Peter Meinke's "The ABC of Aerobics" (p. 295).

BOB HICOK (B. 1960)

Spam leaves an aftertaste   *2002*

What does the Internet know that it sends me
unbidden the offer of a larger penis?
I'm flattered by the energy devoted
to the architecture of my body.
Brain waves noodling on girth, length, curvature   5
possibly, pictures drawn on napkins
of the device, teeth for holding, cylinder—
pneumatic, hydraulic—for stretching
who I am into who I shall be. But of all
messages to drop from the digital ether,   10
hope lives in the communiqué that I can find
out anything about anyone. So I've asked:
who am I, why am I here, if a train
leaving Chicago is subsidized

by the feds, is the romance of travel   15
dead? I'd like the skinny on where I'll be
when I die, to have a map, a seismic map
of past and future emotions, to be told
how to keep the violence I do to myself
from becoming the grenades I pitch   20
at others. The likes of Snoop.com
never get back to me, though I need
to know most of all if any of this helps.
How we can scatter our prayers so wide,
if we've become more human or less   25
in being able to share the specific
in a random way, or was it better
to ask the stars for peace or rain,
to trust the litany of our need
to the air's imperceptible embrace? Just   30
this morning I got a message
asking is anyone out there. I replied
no, I am not, are you not there too,
needing me, and if not, come over, I have
a small penis but aspirations   35
for bigger things, faith among them,
and by that I mean you and I
face to face, mouths
making the sounds once known
as conversation.   40

Considerations for Critical Thinking and Writing

1. **FIRST RESPONSE.** Comment on the humor Hicok uses to satirize how our lives have been affected by the Internet.

2. What is the serious theme that the speaker's humor leads the reader to contemplate? How does this theme complicate the poem's tone?

3. How do your own experiences with spam compare with the speaker's?

Connections to Other Selections

1. How might Hicok's poem be considered a latter-day version of T. S. Eliot's "The Love Song of J. Alfred Prufrock" (p. 494)?

2. Discuss the perspective on American contemporary life implicit in "Spam leaves an aftertaste" with respect to the view offered in Tony Hoagland's "America" (p. 591).

THOMAS LUX (B. 1946)

Commercial Leech Farming Today   *1997*

—for Robert Sacherman

Although it never rivaled wheat, soybean,
cattle and so on farming
there was a living
in leeches
and after a period of decline   5
there is again
a living to be made
from this endeavor: they're used to reduce
the blood in tissues
after plastic surgery — eyelifts, tucks,   10
wrinkle erad, or in certain
microsurgeries — reattaching a finger, penis.
I love the capitalist
spirit. As in most businesses
the technology has improved: instead   15
of driving an elderly horse
into a leech pond, letting him die
by exsanguination,
and hauling him out
to pick the bloated blossoms   20
from his hide, it's now done at Biopharm
(the showcase operation in Swansea,
Wales) — temp control, tanks, aerator
pumps, several species,
each for a specific job. Once, 19th century,   25
they were applied to the temple
as a treatment for mental
illness. Today we know
their exact chemistry: hirudin,
a blood thinner in their saliva,   30
also an anesthesia
and dilators for the wound area.
Don't you love
the image: the Dr. lays a leech along
the tiny stitches of an eyelift.   35
Where they go after their work is done
I don't know
but I've heard no complaints
from Animal Rights
so perhaps they're retired   40
to a lake or adopted
as pets, maybe the best looking
kept to breed. I don't know. I like the story,
I like the going backwards

to ignorance 45
to come forward to vanity. I like
the small role they can play
in beauty
or the reattachment of a part,
I like the story because it's true. 50

CONSIDERATIONS FOR CRITICAL THINKING AND WRITING

1. **FIRST RESPONSE.** Why does the speaker "like the story" (line 43) about leech farming so much? What does it symbolize to him or her?

2. How does Lux characterize the nature of contemporary life?

3. Explain how the humor in this poem moves beyond the simply bizarre to the satirical.

CONNECTION TO ANOTHER SELECTION

1. Discuss the perspectives on human vanity offered in Lux's poem and in Alice Jones's "The Foot" (p. 226).

LEE UPTON (B. 1953)

Dyserotica 2007

There is utopia
and there is dystopia.
There is erotica

and there is . . .
what you've written. 5
Somehow —

as if what two
at a minimum
people might do

or could do 10
in another lifetime —
if suddenly shipwrecked, for instance,

or if it was the end of the world
and they alone were left to procreate —
as if your words must be 15

the antidote to desire,
the corrective trip to the morgue,
the inoculation we haven't been waiting for . . .

although even your dyserotica
becomes erotic for some of us: 20
what else are death bed

confessions for?
Forgive me for not being impressed
by your image of spiders

crawling the mouth of Aphrodite.   25
I know you don't love me,
but why do you have to brag about it?

CONSIDERATIONS FOR CRITICAL THINKING AND WRITING

1. **FIRST RESPONSE.** How is "dyserotica" (line 19) defined in this poem? Why is it so painful to the speaker?

2. Are you—in contrast to the speaker—impressed with the image in lines 24–25? Why or why not?

3. Discuss the tone of the final line.

CONNECTION TO ANOTHER SELECTION

1. Compare the theme and tone of "Dyserotica" with those of Billie Bolton's "Memorandum" (p. 519).

ANTHONY HECHT (1923–2004)

The Dover Bitch°   *1968*

A Criticism of Life

So there stood Matthew Arnold and this girl
With the cliffs of England crumbling away behind them,
And he said to her, "Try to be true to me,
And I'll do the same for you, for things are bad
All over, etc., etc."   5
Well now, I knew this girl. It's true she had read
Sophocles in a fairly good translation
And caught that bitter allusion to the sea,°
But all the time he was talking she had in mind
The notion of what his whiskers would feel like   10
On the back of her neck. She told me later on
That after a while she got to looking out
At the lights across the channel, and really felt sad,
Thinking of all the wine and enormous beds
And blandishments in French and the perfumes.   15
And then she got really angry. To have been brought
All the way down from London, and then be addressed
As a sort of mournful cosmic last resort
Is really tough on a girl, and she was pretty.
Anyway, she watched him pace the room   20

The Dover Bitch: A parody of Arnold's poem "Dover Beach" (see p. 112).   8 *allusion to the sea:* Lines 9–18 in "Dover Beach" refer to Sophocles' *Antigone,* lines 583–91.

And finger his watch-chain and seem to sweat a bit,
And then she said one or two unprintable things.
But you mustn't judge her by that. What I mean to say is,
She's really all right. I still see her once in a while
And she always treats me right. We have a drink   25
And I give her a good time, and perhaps it's a year
Before I see her again, but there she is,
Running to fat, but dependable as they come.
And sometimes I bring her a bottle of *Nuit d'Amour.*

CONSIDERATIONS FOR CRITICAL THINKING AND WRITING

1. **FIRST RESPONSE.** Is it possible to appreciate and make sense of this poem without being familiar with Matthew Arnold's "Dover Beach" (p. 112)?
2. What do you think is the central point of the poem?
3. The subtitle identifies the poem as "A Criticism of Life." How seriously do you think the subtitle should be taken?

CONNECTION TO ANOTHER SELECTION

1. What does a comparison of the speakers' diction in "The Dover Bitch" and in "Dover Beach" (p. 112) reveal about the tone of each poem?

X. J. KENNEDY (B. 1929)

On a Young Man's Remaining an Undergraduate for Twelve Years   2006

Sweet scent of pot, the mellow smell of beer,
　　Frat-house debates on sex, on God's existence
Lasting all night, vacations thrice a year,
　　Pliant coeds who put up no resistance

Are all life is. Who'd give a damn for earning,   5
　　Who'd struggle by degrees to lofty places
When he can loll, adrift in endless learning,
　　In a warm sea of academic stasis?

He's famous now: the everlasting kid.
　　After conducting an investigation,   10
Two deans resigned, to do just what he did.
　　They couldn't fault his ratiocination.

CONSIDERATIONS FOR CRITICAL THINKING AND WRITING

1. **FIRST RESPONSE.** Comment on the description of undergraduate life in the first stanza and the effect of the enjambment in lines 4 and 5.
2. Discuss the sound effects in stanza three. How are they related to sense?
3. Why is "ratiocination" (line 12) just the right word in this context?

20

A THEMATIC CASE STUDY
Milestones

I like to think of all good poetry as providing more oxygen into the atmosphere; it just makes it easier to breathe.

— KAY RYAN

Christopher Felver/CORBIS.

The thematic center of this chapter focuses on milestones in people's lives. The various literary elements that contribute to the idea or point of each poem are there to enhance moments that seem particularly striking, moving, or memorable. Not surprisingly, this type of moment is the frequent purview of the lyric, a poem that typically expresses the subjective mood, emotion, or idea of a single speaker. Taken together, the poems in this chapter represent a variety of poetic responses ranging from sly observations on young love to painful reflections on birth and death. These poems won't necessarily reflect the complicated and pivotal moments in your own life, but they might make you more sensitive to them and perhaps encourage you to think more deeply about what they mean to you.

Most of these poems have been published within the past ten years, and so their contemporary nature should allow you to make vivid and accessible connections to the world you inhabit and the language you speak and read. Your own experience will provide the necessary annotations. As you read, think about how each of the poems captures a moment charged with some kind of recollection, experience, emotion, energy, insight, or meaning that is somehow transformative.

Steeped in expectation and desire, the young couple in Allen Braden's "Sweethearts" seem like ideal pictures from a high school yearbook — almost.

ALLEN BRADEN (B. 1968)

Sweethearts   *2000*

One Friday late at night they grope their way
through the pale statuary and fallen leaves

for a hollow to lie in where they fit perfectly
the way their perfect bodies fit one another.

It seems quite natural that he is the star   5
this season and she the head cheerleader.

Once or twice she recalls something else
unforgettable she wants to say but does not.

They touch as if to say, *Don't ever forget this,*
are young enough to wring love from elegy   10

with the vertigo of their longing, the rush
of uncovering and pushing flesh against flesh.

One tiny act is all it takes to bury themselves
in some small excuse for somewhere else,

anywhere but right here where his ambitions   15
will be planed down on the graveyard shift

and hers will be spent waiting on tables
with trays of coffee, hot cakes and syrup.

CONSIDERATIONS FOR CRITICAL THINKING AND WRITING

1. **FIRST RESPONSE.** How is the stanzaic form of this poem especially appropriate for its subject matter?

2. How do you think the speaker regards the romantic relationship of this couple? What does his choice of words and images reveal?

3. In what sense can this Friday night be seen as a milestone in this couple's life together?

CONNECTION TO ANOTHER SELECTION

1. Discuss the treatment of love in "Sweethearts" and in Sharon Olds's "Sex without Love" (p. 9).

The remaining poems in this chapter depict a variety of milestones in people's lives. You'll notice that the moments don't necessarily have to be big and dramatic to be important and moving. No car chases; no explosions.

BARON WORMSER (B. 1948)

Shoplifting 1997

The store dick lays a hand on your shoulder
Three steps from the exit. He asks what's
In your pockets but it's more like a statement
Than a question. Two candy bars and a roll of film.

Your stomach melts and your heart starts to beat 5
Like when you used to race on the playground.
He tells you to sit down on the bench by the doors.
Usually there are some old people sitting there

Gabbling about bargains but no one's around
This late in the evening. You expect the manager 10
To show up and give you a lecture about kids
Nowadays but he doesn't

And when the cop appears he doesn't say
Anything special beyond you'll have to go to court.
When he gives you the paper he's almost smiling 15
Or he's not there at all, he's not seeing you.

Thoughts, thoughts . . . your head's raw dough
One moment, light as a balloon the next.
They're always playing a song in the background
In these stores that you can't quite identify. 20

Your foot's tapping to the vacant beat
And after the cop leaves and you
Can leave you don't for some minutes.
You don't even own a camera.

CONSIDERATIONS FOR CRITICAL THINKING AND WRITING

1. **FIRST RESPONSE.** What is the effect of the speaker's addressing the reader in the second person ("you")?
2. Identify the figurative language in the poem. Why do you think there is so little of it?
3. How convincing to you is this portrait of a young shoplifter being caught in the act?

CONNECTION TO ANOTHER SELECTION

1. Consider how Michelle Boisseau's "Self-Pity's Closet" (p. 587) offers a potential commentary on Wormser's shoplifter.

JAN BEATTY (B. 1952)

My Father Teaches Me to Dream   1996

You want to know what work is?
I'll tell you what work is:
Work is work.
You get up. You get on the bus.
You don't look from side to side.   5
You keep your eyes straight ahead.
That way nobody bothers you—see?
You get off the bus. You work all day.
You get back on the bus at night. Same thing.
You go to sleep. You get up.   10
You do the same thing again.
Nothing more. Nothing less.
There's no handouts in this life.
All this other stuff you're looking for—
it ain't there.   15
Work is work.

CONSIDERATIONS FOR CRITICAL THINKING AND WRITING

1. **FIRST RESPONSE.** How likely is it that the son or daughter of this father actually asked for a definition of work? What do you imagine prompted the start
   of this explanation?

2. Discuss the effect of the use of repeated words and phrases. How are they
   related to the father's message?

3. Consider what the title reveals about the "you" of the poem.

CONNECTION TO ANOTHER SELECTION

1. Compare this father's vision of work with the perspective of the young man
   in Baron Wormser's "Labor" (p. 267). How might the difference between the
   two be explained?

MARILYN NELSON (B. 1946)

How I Discovered Poetry   1997

It was like soul-kissing, the way the words
filled my mouth as Mrs. Purdy read from her desk.
All the other kids zoned an hour ahead to 3:15,
but Mrs. Purdy and I wandered lonely as clouds borne
by a breeze off Mount Parnassus. She must have seen   5
the darkest eyes in the room brim: The next day
she gave me a poem she'd chosen especially for me
to read to the all except for me white class.

She smiled when she told me to read it, smiled harder,
said oh yes I could. She smiled harder and harder   10
until I stood and opened my mouth to banjo playing
darkies, pickaninnies, disses and dats. When I finished
my classmates stared at the floor. We walked silent
to the buses, awed by the power of words.

CONSIDERATIONS FOR CRITICAL THINKING AND WRITING

1. **FIRST RESPONSE.** Trace your response to Miss Purdy from the beginning to
   the end of the poem.
2. What do the allusions to William Wordsworth's poem "I Wandered Lonely
   as a Cloud" (see p. 653) and Mount Parnassus (look it up) in lines 4 and 5
   suggest to you about the speaker?
3. How do you interpret the tone of the final two lines?

CONNECTION TO ANOTHER SELECTION

1. How does Nelson's description of discovering poetry compare with Ronald
   Wallace's in "Miss Goff" (p. 350)?

CHARLES SIMIC (B. 1938)

In the Library   2008

for Octavio

There's a book called
"A Dictionary of Angels."
No one has opened it in fifty years,
I know, because when I did,
The covers creaked, the pages   5
Crumbled. There I discovered

The angels were once as plentiful
As species of flies.
The sky at dusk
Used to be thick with them.   10
You had to wave both arms
Just to keep them away.

Now the sun is shining
Through the tall windows.
The library is a quiet place.   15
Angels and gods huddled
In dark unopened books.
The great secret lies
On some shelf Miss Jones
Passes every day on her rounds.   20

She's very tall, so she keeps
Her head tipped as if listening.
The books are whispering.
I hear nothing, but she does.

CONSIDERATIONS FOR CRITICAL THINKING AND WRITING

1. **FIRST RESPONSE.** What does the speaker discover about the library and Miss Jones that makes this a striking experience?
2. Why do you think Simic chooses a book of angels as the source of this discovery? And why does he mention the flies?
3. **CREATIVE RESPONSE.** What sort of poem do you think might be written with the title "In the Computer"?

CONNECTION TO ANOTHER SELECTION

1. Compare the book lovers from "In the Library" and Billy Collins's "Marginalia" (p. 54).

TREVOR WEST KNAPP (B. 1958)

Touch   2001

We speak of the pain of childbirth, referring,
of course, to the mother, but what is pain
to the mother, the one through whose body
the course unwinds? She understands already
what kind of world she must return to,   5
how it daily hones its many edges
against human skin, unlike the child whose
untried limbs inch toward it, pressing now
so firmly against her he feels for the first time
the pinch of bone against bone and is seared   10
by the friction. Isn't he the one
on whom the real burden falls, the one
to whom resilience means nothing yet? His
tender skin like a small measure of cloth
unfolding before the blade under which   15
he will, for a lifetime, bruise
and heal: Crush of the long descent, grip
of the steadying hands, brush of breath
against cheek, even the constant barrage
of the microscopic, the tiny plink-plink   20
of the dust motes knocking against him
before custom makes him numb to it. No wonder
the startled mouth cries out,
each pore suddenly hungry
in the withering, nourishing light.   25

CONSIDERATIONS FOR CRITICAL THINKING AND WRITING

1. **FIRST RESPONSE.** What kind of passage does the speaker envision birth to be for an infant?

2. Discuss the effectiveness of the imagery in evoking pain.

3. Is this a grim view of birth? Overly sensitive? Empathetic? Tender? What do you think?

CONNECTION TO ANOTHER SELECTION

1. Consider whether or not this poem on childbirth and Anne Bradstreet's "Before the Birth of One of Her Children" (p. 617) have anything to say to each other. What kind of dialogue emerges by placing them side by side?

SHARON OLDS (B. 1942)

Rite of Passage   *1983*

As the guests arrive at my son's party
they gather in the living room —
short men, men in first grade
with smooth jaws and chins.
Hands in pockets, they stand around   5
jostling, jockeying for place, small fights
breaking out and calming. One says to another
How old are you? Six. I'm seven. So?
They eye each other, seeing themselves
tiny in the other's pupils. They clear their   10
throats a lot, a room of small bankers,
they fold their arms and frown. *I could beat you
up,* a seven says to a six,
the dark cake, round and heavy as a
turret, behind them on the table. My son,   15
freckles like specks of nutmeg on his cheeks,
chest narrow as the balsa keel of a
model boat, long hands
cool and thin as the day they guided him
out of me, speaks up as a host   20
for the sake of the group.
We could easily kill a two-year-old,
he says in his clear voice. The other
men agree, they clear their throats
like Generals, they relax and get down to   25
playing war, celebrating my son's life.

CONSIDERATIONS FOR CRITICAL THINKING AND WRITING

1. **FIRST RESPONSE.** In what sense is this birthday party a "Rite of Passage"?

2. How does the speaker transform these six- and seven-year-old boys into men? What is the point of doing so?

3. Comment on the appropriateness of the image of the cake in lines 14–15.
4. Why does the son's claim that "We could easily kill a two-year-old" (line 22) come as such a shock at that point in the poem?

CONNECTION TO ANOTHER SELECTION

1. Discuss the use of irony in "Rite of Passage" and in Gary Soto's "Behind Grandma's House" (p. 184).

SANDRA M. GILBERT (B. 1936)

How We Didn't Tell Her   *2008*

that the housekeeper said that
the gardener said that
someone named

Jean or Jeannie or Jenny
who was his friend or maybe   5
his boss had said that

today that just
today he was hit by a car
& he was killed he died

at once in the prime   10
of his handsome youth he
who was her youngest her

onetime baby ice-cream
cone with dimpled arms
& scrumptious tummy he   15

who gardened & prayed
for purity on earth
but we said let's wait let's

wait to tell her till we're
sure & we called the gardener   20
the housekeeeper the irrigation lady

the police the coroner
the highway patrol the neighbors
we called everyone but her

until at last the gardener   25
said no no how could the housekeeper
get it so wrong it wasn't

him it was someone else who was
hit by a car and killed
today & we rejoiced & were   30

glad we hadn't told her because
his handsome flesh his pulsing
prime returned to us as a gift

more precious than before
& as for the other one, the other   35
mother's son who really died

today we let him go we
didn't give him
another thought.

CONSIDERATIONS FOR CRITICAL THINKING AND WRITING

1. **FIRST RESPONSE.** Read the poem aloud. How does the lack of punctuation (except for the final period) contribute to your reading and understanding of what happens in the narrative?
2. Comment on the rhythm of the lines and its relationship to their meaning.
3. How would the tone and theme of this poem shift if it ended at line 34?

CONNECTION TO ANOTHER SELECTION

1. Compare the ending of this poem and of Robert Frost's "'Out, Out—'" (p. 380) in terms of their attitudes toward mortality.

ANNE CARSON (B. 1950)

Father's Old Blue Cardigan   2000

Now it hangs on the back of the kitchen chair
where I always sit, as it did
on the back of the kitchen chair where he always sat.

I put it on whenever I come in,
as he did, stamping   5
the snow from his boots.

I put it on and sit in the dark.
He would not have done this.
Coldness comes paring down from the moonbone in the sky.

His laws were a secret.   10
But I remember the moment at which I knew
he was going mad inside his laws.

He was standing at the turn of the driveway when I arrived.
He had on the blue cardigan with the buttons done up all the way to the top.
Not only because it was a hot July afternoon   15

but the look on his face—
as a small child who has been dressed by some aunt early in the morning
for a long trip

on cold trains and windy platforms
will sit very straight at the edge of his seat   20
while the shadows like long fingers

over the haystacks that sweep past
keep shocking him
because he is riding backwards.

CONSIDERATIONS FOR CRITICAL THINKING AND WRITING

1. **FIRST RESPONSE.** What does the speaker realize in the moment when the father's face reveals that a profound change has come over him?

2. Describe the effect of the simile in lines 17–24. What kinds of emotions does it evoke?

3. Why do you suppose Carson titled the poem "Father's Old Blue Cardigan" rather than, for example, "The Look on His Face"?

CONNECTION TO ANOTHER SELECTION

1. Compare the ways in which the speakers in this poem and in Rachel Loden's "Locked Ward: Newtown, Connecticut" (p. 592) cope with madness in a parent.

BARBARA CROOKER (B. 1945)

On the Edge of Adolescence, My Middle Daughter Learns to Play the Saxophone   *2000*

For Rebecca

Her hair, that halo of red gold curls,
has thickened, coarsened,
lost its baby fineness,
and the sweet smell of childhood
that clung to her clothes   5
has just about vanished.
Now she's getting moody,
moaning about her hair,
clothes that aren't the right brands,
boys that tease.   10
She clicks over the saxophone keys
with gritty fingernails polished in pink pearl,
grass stains on the knees
of her sister's old designer jeans.
She's gone from sounding like the smoke detector   15
through Old MacDonald and Jingle Bells.
Soon she'll master these keys,
turn notes into liquid gold,

wail that reedy brass.
Soon, she'll be a woman.   20
She's gonna learn to play the blues.

CONSIDERATIONS FOR CRITICAL THINKING AND WRITING

1. **FIRST RESPONSE.** Do you think the title is too long or just right? Explain why.

2. Why do these observations about the daughter's pending transformation seem more like a mother's than a father's?

3. The last line couldn't be better. Why?

CONNECTION TO ANOTHER SELECTION

1. Discuss Daisy Fried's "Wit's End" (p. 525) as a kind of sequel to the story of the young girl in this poem.

LUISA LOPEZ (B. 1957)

Junior Year Abroad   2002

We were amateurs, that winter in Paris.

The summer before we agreed:
he would come over to keep me company at Christmas.
But the shelf life of my promise expired
before the date on his airline ticket.   5
So we ended up together under a French muslin sky.

Together alone.

Certainly I was alone, inside dark hair, inside foreign blankets,
against white sheets swirling like a cocoon,
covering my bare skin,   10
keeping me apart.
The invited man snored beside me not knowing
I didn't love him anymore.

At first I tried,
perky as a circus pony waiting at the airport gate   15
to be again as I once had been.
But even during the first night
betrayal, the snake under the evergreen,
threw me into nightmares
of floods and dying birds.   20

You see, a new boy just last month
had raised my shy hand to his warm mouth
and kissed the inside of my palm.
I thought "this is impossible,
too close to Christmas, too soon, too dangerous."   25

In Paris I concede:
deceiving my old lover, the one now stirring in his sleep
is even more dangerous.
See him opening his eyes, looking at my face,
dropping his eyes to my breasts and smiling   30
as if he were seeing two old friends? Dangerous.

When I move away and hold the sheet against
myself he,
sensing what this means,
refuses, adamant yet polite,   35
to traffic in the currency of my rejection.

He made a journey. I offered a welcome.
Why should he give me up?

CONSIDERATIONS FOR CRITICAL THINKING AND WRITING

1. **FIRST RESPONSE.** This poem is about strength and dominance as much as it is about love and attraction. Discuss the ways in which the two characters are vying for control.

2. Why is the setting important? How might the sense of the poem be different if this were happening during a typical school year as opposed to "Junior Year Abroad"?

3. Do you think the speaker has the right to reject her old boyfriend under these circumstances? Does the old boyfriend have the right to expect a "welcome" (line 37) since he was invited to visit?

4. The speaker is wrapped in sheets that are like a "cocoon" (line 9). What does this suggest about the changes she is experiencing during this encounter?

CONNECTION TO ANOTHER SELECTION

1. Compare this 2002 poem about young love with A. E. Housman's poem "When I was one-and-twenty" (p. 227), published in 1896. How much has the situation changed in a hundred years?

YUSEF KOMUNYAKAA (B. 1947)

Slam, Dunk, & Hook   *1992*

Fast breaks. Lay ups. With Mercury's
Insignia on our sneakers,
We outmaneuvered the footwork
Of bad angels. Nothing but a hot
Swish of strings like silk   5
Ten feet out. In the roundhouse
Labyrinth our bodies

Created, we could almost
Last forever, poised in midair
Like storybook sea monsters.   10
A high note hung there
A long second. Off
The rim. We'd corkscrew
Up & dunk balls that exploded
The skullcap of hope & good   15
Intention. Bug-eyed, lanky,
All hands & feet . . . sprung rhythm.
We were metaphysical when girls
Cheered on the sidelines.
Tangled up in a falling,   20
Muscles were a bright motor
Double-flashing to the metal hoop
Nailed to our oak.
When Sonny Boy's mama died
He played nonstop all day, so hard   25
Our backboard splintered.
Glistening with sweat, we jibed
& rolled the ball off our
Fingertips. Trouble
Was there slapping a blackjack   30
Against an open palm.
Dribble, drive to the inside, feint,
& glide like a sparrow hawk.
Layups. Fast breaks.
We had moves we didn't know   35
We had. Our bodies spun

On swivels of bone & faith,
Through a lyric slipknot
Of joy, & we knew we were
Beautiful & dangerous.   40

CONSIDERATIONS FOR CRITICAL THINKING AND WRITING

1. **FIRST RESPONSE.** Why and how is basketball more than just a game to these players? What kind of symbolic significance does it hold for them?

2. Explain how the rhythm of the lines follows the rhythm of the game.

3. Why do you think the nostalgic speaker characterizes the players as not only "beautiful" but "dangerous" (line 40)?

CONNECTION TO ANOTHER SELECTION

1. Contrast the team experience described in this poem with that in Gary Gildner's "First Practice" (p. 283).

SUGGESTED TOPICS FOR LONGER PAPERS

1. Choose one of the writers represented in this chapter and read more poems in his or her collections. Write an analysis of five poems that you think make an interesting and coherent thematic grouping that reveals important elements of the poet's style and characteristic content.

2. Put together a portfolio of several popular songs about the same "milestone" topic (romance, school, work, road tripping, or whatever interests you) and analyze them in terms of their style, themes, or historical context.

21

A THEMATIC CASE STUDY
Crossing Boundaries

Courtesy of the author and the
Sandra Dijkstra Literary Agency.

As immigrants we have this enormous
raw material. . . . We draw from a dual
culture, with two sets of worldviews
and paradigms juxtaposing each other.
— CHITRA BANERJEE DIVAKARUNI

This chapter brings together six poems and a variety of images that center upon the theme of crossing borders. The borders referred to in these poems mark not only geographic or political divisions but also the uncertain and indeterminate borders associated with culture, class, race, ethnicity, and gender. Even if we have never left our home state or country, we have all moved back and forth across such defining lines as we negotiate the margins and edges of our personal identities within the particular worlds we inhabit. Any first-year college student, for example, knows that college life and demanding course work represent a significant border crossing: increased academic challenges, responsibility, and autonomy likely reflect an entirely new culture for the student. By Thanksgiving vacation, students know (as do their parents and friends) that they've crossed an invisible border that causes a slight shift in their identity because they've done some growing and maturing.

The poems and visuals in this chapter explore a wide range of border crossings. Phillis Wheatley was kidnapped and forced across borders in

1761 when she was brought to America as a slave. Her poem "On Being Brought from Africa to America" offers a fascinating argument against racism. Wheatley's perspective is deepened by a diagram of a ship and an advertisement for an auction that vividly illustrate how slaves were transported and marketed. Racial tensions are internalized in Pat Mora's "Legal Alien" and Jacalyn López García's "I Just Wanted to Be Me," which describe the dilemma of being raised as a Mexican American. Sandra M. Gilbert examines the pain caused by ethnic stereotyping in "Mafioso," which is complemented by a revealing photograph of Italian immigrant children as they are processed at Ellis Island. The anxieties felt by new immigrants and their yearnings for the life they left behind are the subject of Chitra Banerjee Divakaruni's "Indian Movie, New Jersey," which is paired with an optimistic cover of a Bollywood film soundtrack. The prejudice that causes some of the anxiety in that poem is also evident in Janice Mirikitani's "Recipe," a satire commenting on the impact of Western beauty ideals on Japanese girls and women. The relevance of that problem is brought home in the accompanying photograph by Chiaki Tsukumo of a child holding one of Japan's most popular dolls. Finally, Thomas Lynch's "Liberty" provides an amusing but pointed look at an Irish American who finds suburban life to be a lamentable state compared to the life of his ancestors in Ireland. The photograph of a crowded, working-class Boston suburb that follows the poem tidily captures Lynch's themes.

A list of additional thematically related poems is located at the end of this chapter.

TRANSCENDENCE AND BORDERS

Born in West Africa, Phillis Wheatley was kidnapped and brought to America in 1761 and sold to John and Susannah Wheatley of Boston. She was taught to read and write and was then freed at about the age of thirteen. Her remarkable intelligence and talents led Susannah to help her publish *Poems on Various Subjects, Religious and Moral* in 1773. The influence of religion on her poetry is clearly evident in "On Being Brought from Africa to America." Wheatley's response to having been a slave in America is complicated by her acceptance of the religion, language, and even the literary style of the white culture that she found there. The harsh nature of slavery is apparent, however, in the diagram of a slave ship and a slave auction advertisement. Do these documents qualify Wheatley's description of her origins and the new world into which she was brought as a slave?

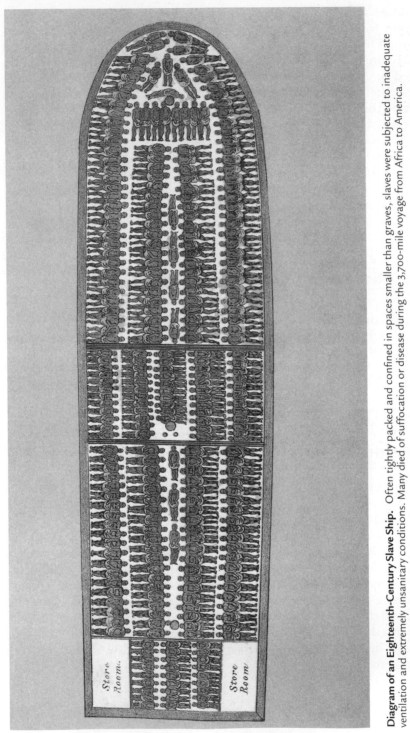

Diagram of an Eighteenth-Century Slave Ship. Often tightly packed and confined in spaces smaller than graves, slaves were subjected to inadequate ventilation and extremely unsanitary conditions. Many died of suffocation or disease during the 3,700-mile voyage from Africa to America.

Reprinted by permission of the Burstein Collection/CORBIS ©.

Store Room.

Store Room.

PHILLIS WHEATLEY (1753?–1784)

On Being Brought from Africa to America

1773

'Twas mercy brought me from my pagan land,
Taught my benighted soul to understand
That there's a God — that there's a Saviour too;
Once I redemption neither sought nor knew.
Some view our sable race with scornful eye —
"Their color is a diabolic dye."
Remember, Christians, Negroes black as Cain°
May be refined, and join the angelic train.

7 *Cain:* In the Bible, Cain murdered Abel and was therefore "marked" by God. That mark has been interpreted by some readers as the origin of dark-skinned people (see Genesis 4:1–15).

CONSIDERATIONS FOR CRITICAL THINKING AND WRITING

1. How does the speaker argue against the pervasive racist views concerning Africans in the eighteenth century?

2. Do you find the argument convincing? Explain whether your own refutation of racism would be argued on similar or other grounds.

3. What arguments are put forth on the slave-auction poster? What attitudes are revealed by its author's choice of words?

Negroes for Sale.

A Cargo of very fine stout Men and Women, in good order and fit for immediate service, just imported from the Windward Coast of Africa, in the Ship Two Brothers.—

Conditions are one half Cash or Produce, the other half payable the first of January next, giving Bond and Security if required.

The Sale to be opened at 10 o'Clock each Day, in Mr. Bourdeaux's Yard, at No. 48, on the Bay.

May 19, 1784. JOHN MITCHELL.

Thirty Seasoned Negroes

To be Sold for Credit, at Private Sale.

AMONGST which is a Carpenter, none of whom are known to be dishonest.

Also, to be sold for Cash, a regular bred young Negroe Man-Cook, born in this Country, who served several Years under an exceeding good French Cook abroad, and his Wife a middle aged Washer-Woman, (both very honest) and their two Children. Likewise, a young Man a Carpenter.

For Terms apply to the Printer.

1784 Slave-Auction Advertisement. In preparation for sale at auction, slaves were fed and washed by the ship's crew. Tar or palm oil was used to disguise sores or wounds caused by poor conditions on board.
© CORBIS.

4. Consider Wheatley's poem alongside the slave-ship diagram and the advertisement for a slave auction. How do you account for the speaker's attitude toward slavery and redemption in relation to the historical realities of slavery?

CONNECTION TO ANOTHER SELECTION

1. Compare the tone and theme of Wheatley's poem with those of Langston Hughes's "I, Too" (p. 407).

IDENTITY AND BORDERS

In "Legal Alien" Pat Mora explores the difficulties of living in two different cultures simultaneously. The poem's speaker, both Mexican and American, worries that each cultural identity displaces the other, leaving the speaker standing alone between both worlds. Similarly, Jacalyn López García, a multimedia artist who combines computer art, video, and music CD-ROMs to create complex images, explores the dilemmas that she encountered while being raised as a Mexican American. How do the poem and the image evoke the tensions produced by trying to assimilate into a new culture while trying to hold on to the cultural values brought from one's native country?

PAT MORA (B. 1942)

Legal Alien   *1985*

Bi-lingual, Bi-cultural,
able to slip from "How's life?"
to *"Me'stan volviendo loca,"*°
able to sit in a paneled office
drafting memos in smooth English,   5
able to order in fluent Spanish
at a Mexican restaurant,
American but hyphenated,
viewed by Anglos as perhaps exotic,
perhaps inferior, definitely different,   10
viewed by Mexicans as alien,
(their eyes say, "You may speak
Spanish but you're not like me")
an American to Mexicans
a Mexican to Americans   15

___

3 *Me'stan . . . loca:* They are driving me crazy.

NEVER

MY MOTHER'S STORY
"I raised my children speaking English only
because I did not want them to have an accent."

WANTED

"I thought it would be easier for them."

TO BE

"After all, I spoke English, having attended an
American school in Casas Grandes, Mexico."

" WHITE "

"But I never had the privileges of being "white".

"I Just Wanted to Be Me" (1997), by Jacalyn López García. In her multimedia exhibit *Glass Houses,* García explores family history and issues of identity. "As we crossed the Mexican border, the border patrol would ask me my citizenship. I would reply, 'American' because my parents taught me to say that. But in California, people would ask me 'What are you?' . . . I would proudly reply 'Mexican.' It wasn't until I became a teenager that I claimed I was 'Mexican-American.'" Once, a white neighbor reported to authorities that García's mother was undocumented. "I was only seven years old when my mother was deported, my brother was six. The Christmas tree stayed up until Mom returned home in April of the following year." Reprinted by permission of Jacalyn López García.

a handy token
sliding back and forth
between the fringes of both worlds
by smiling
by masking the discomfort   20
of being pre-judged
Bi-laterally.

CONSIDERATIONS FOR CRITICAL THINKING AND WRITING

1. **FIRST RESPONSE.** What is the nature of the discomfort the speaker experiences as an "American but hyphenated" (line 8)? Explain whether you think the advantages outweigh the disadvantages.

2. What qualities do you think make someone an American? How does your description compare with your classmates' views? How do you account for the differences or similarities?

3. Discuss the appropriateness of the poem's title. How does it encapsulate the speaker's emotional as well as official status?

4. How do poet Pat Mora and artist Jacalyn López García incorporate multiple voices into their work? Why do you think they do so?

CONNECTION TO ANOTHER SELECTION

1. Compare and contrast the speakers' responses to "sliding back and forth / between the fringes of both worlds" (lines 17–18) in Mora's "Legal Alien" and in Julia Alvarez's "Queens, 1963" (p. 470).

IMMIGRATION AND BORDERS

Ethnic stereotypes are the legacy Sandra M. Gilbert examines in "Mafioso." Her poem raises important questions about the way in which popular culture shapes our assumptions about and perceptions of ethnic groups. How much of what we regard as quintessentially Italian American is generated by films like *The Godfather* or television programs like *The Sopranos*? How did most immigrants actually work to become Americans once they arrived on the country's shores? A glimpse of the nature of that struggle is suggested by the 1911 photograph of three boys undergoing an examination at Ellis Island. Do you think the photograph supports or qualifies Gilbert's assessment of the difficulties immigrants faced upon their arrival in America?

SANDRA M. GILBERT (B. 1936)

Mafioso   1979

Frank Costello eating spaghetti in a cell at San Quentin,
Lucky Luciano mixing up a mess of bullets and
calling for parmesan cheese,
Al Capone baking a sawed-off shotgun into a
huge lasagna —   5
           are you my uncles, my
only uncles?

        O Mafiosi,
bad uncles of the barren
cliffs of Sicily — was it only you   10
that they transported in barrels
like pure olive oil
across the Atlantic?

          Was it only you
who got out at Ellis Island with   15
black scarves on your heads and cheap cigars
and no English and a dozen children?

No carts were waiting, gallant with paint,
no little donkeys plumed like the dreams of peacocks.
Only the evil eyes of a thousand buildings 20
stared across at the echoing debarkation center,
making it seem so much smaller than a piazza,

only a half dozen Puritan millionaires stood on the wharf,
in the wind colder than the impossible snows of the Abruzzi,
ready with country clubs and dynamos 25

to grind the organs out of you.

"Baggage Examined Here" (1911). Between 1880 and 1920, nearly four million Italian immigrants came to the United States, most arriving in New York City and settling in cities along the East Coast. While first- and second-class steamship passengers were quickly inspected onboard and allowed to disembark in Manhattan, third-class passengers, such as the boys in this photo, were taken to Ellis Island, where they were subjected to a series of medical examinations and interviews. Inspectors marked the immigrants' clothing with chalk, indicating the need for further examination: *Sc* for scalp disease, *G* for goiter, *H* for hernia, *L* for lameness, or *S* for senility.
© Bettmann/CORBIS.

CONSIDERATIONS FOR CRITICAL THINKING AND WRITING

1. **FIRST RESPONSE.** In what sense are the gangsters Frank Costello, Lucky Luciano, and Al Capone in the first stanza to be understood as "bad uncles" (line 9)? How does the speaker feel about the "uncles"?

2. Explain how nearly all of the images in the poem are associated with Italian life. Does the poem reinforce stereotypes about Italians or invoke images about them for some other purpose? If so, what other purpose?

3. What sort of people are the "Puritan millionaires" (line 23)? What is their relationship to the "bad uncles"?

4. Consider the photograph. Why was it taken? What does this image convey about attitudes toward working-class immigrants processed at Ellis Island? How do the words "Baggage Examined Here" function in the image? How do these words connect with the last line of Gilbert's poem ("to grind the organs out of you")? What comments are the photograph and poem making about the experience?

CONNECTIONS TO OTHER SELECTIONS

1. Discuss the ways in which ethnicity is used to create meaning in "Mafioso" and in Jimmy Santiago Baca's "Green Chile" (p. 114).

2. How do the attitudes conveyed in "Mafioso" and the photograph "Baggage Examined Here" compare with the sentiments expressed in Emma Lazarus's "The New Colossus" (p. 637), the poem inscribed at the base of the Statue of Liberty?

EXPECTATIONS AND BORDERS

The immigrants' dream of America is deeply present in Chitra Banerjee Divakaruni's "Indian Movie, New Jersey." The hopeful expectation that immigrants bring with them takes on a nostalgic and melancholy tone as the speaker contrasts America as imagined to the country that is experienced. The Indian movie offers yet another dream that suggests a powerful yearning for a different kind of life than the one found in New Jersey. Is the movie version of India any more or less real than the speaker's picture of America? Is this poem more about disillusionment or delusion?

CHITRA BANERJEE DIVAKARUNI (B. 1956)

Indian Movie, New Jersey   1990

Not like the white filmstars, all rib
and gaunt cheekbone, the Indian sex-goddess
smiles plumply from behind a flowery
branch. Below her brief red skirt, her thighs

are satisfying-solid, redeeming   5
as tree trunks. She swings her hips
and the men-viewers whistle. The lover-hero
dances in to a song, his lip-sync
a little off, but no matter, we
know the words already and sing along.   10
It is safe here, the day
golden and cool so no one sweats,
roses on every bush and the Dal Lake
clean again.
        The sex-goddess switches   15
to thickened English to emphasize
a joke. We laugh and clap. Here
we need not be embarrassed by words
dropping like lead pellets into foreign ears.
The flickering movie-light   20
wipes from our faces years of America, sons
who want mohawks and refuse to run
the family store, daughters who date
on the sly.
        When at the end the hero   25
dies for his friend who also
loves the sex-goddess and now can marry her,
we weep, understanding. Even the men
clear their throats to say, "What *qurbani!*°   *sacrifice*
What *dosti!*"° After, we mill around   *friendship* 30
unwilling to leave, exchange greetings
and good news: a new gold chain, a trip
to India. We do not speak
of motel raids, canceled permits, stones
thrown through glass windows, daughters and sons   35
raped by Dotbusters.°
        In this dim foyer
we can pull around us the faint, comforting smell
of incense and *pakoras,*° can arrange   *fried appetizers*
our children's marriages with hometown boys and girls,
open a franchise, win a million   40
in the mail. We can retire
in India, a yellow two-storied house
with wrought-iron gates, our own
Ambassador car. Or at least   45
move to a rich white suburb, Summerfield
or Fort Lee, with neighbors that will
talk to us. Here while the film-songs still echo
in the corridors and restrooms, we can trust
in movie truths: sacrifice, success, love and luck,   50
the America that was supposed to be.

36 *Dotbusters:* New Jersey gangs that attack Indians.

Rawal Films, *Ladki Pasand Hai (I Like This Girl)* (1971). India's massive Hindi-language film industry, known as Bollywood (a play on the word Hollywood, with the *B* representing Bombay), produces twice as many films as Hollywood each year, with a huge international audience. Bollywood films are churned out so quickly that sometimes scripts are handwritten and actors on set shoot scenes for multiple films. Traditionally, these colorful extravaganzas, chock full of singing, dancing, and multiple costume changes, stick to a "boy meets girl" formula — a hero and heroine fall in love and then struggle for family approval. This image is from the soundtrack to a 1971 film with a typical Bollywood plot.
Reprinted by permission of HMV/Odeon. Courtesy of Niall Richardson.

CONSIDERATIONS FOR CRITICAL THINKING AND WRITING

1. **FIRST RESPONSE.** Why does the speaker feel comfortable at the movies? How is the world inside the theater different from life outside in New Jersey?

2. Explain the differences portrayed by the speaker between life in India and life in New Jersey. What connotative values are associated with each location in the poem? Discuss the irony in the final two lines.

3. How do the ideas and values of the Bollywood poster contrast with the realities conveyed in the last part of the poem?

1. Explain how the speaker's idea of "the America that was supposed to be" (line 51) compares with the nation described in Florence Cassen Mayers's "All-American Sestina" (p. 256).

BEAUTY AND BORDERS

Janice Mirikitani, a third-generation Japanese American, reflects upon dominant cultural standards of beauty in "Recipe." Women who do not meet such standards — especially women of color — can be faced with complicated decisions about how they want to appear, decisions that go far more than skin deep. Chiaki Tsukumo's 2003 photograph of a young Tokyo girl holding a popular Western-style doll demonstrates how powerful Western concepts of beauty are, even among non-Western people. Why are "Round Eyes" so desirable? What kind of price is paid for such a desire?

JANICE MIRIKITANI (B. 1942)

Recipe   *1987*

Round Eyes

Ingredients: scissors, Scotch magic transparent tape,
               eyeliner — water based, black.
               Optional: false eyelashes.

Cleanse face thoroughly.   5

For best results, powder entire face, including eyelids.
    (lighter shades suited to total effect desired)

With scissors, cut magic tape $^1/_{16}$" wide, $^3/_4$"–$^1/_2$" long —
depending on length of eyelid.

Stick firmly onto mid–upper eyelid area   10
    (looking down into handmirror facilitates finding
    adequate surface)

If using false eyelashes, affix first on lid, folding any
excess lid over the base of eyelash with glue.

Paint black eyeliner on tape and entire lid.   15

Do not cry.

CONSIDERATIONS FOR CRITICAL THINKING AND WRITING

1. FIRST RESPONSE. Discuss your response to the poem's final line.
2. Why does Mirikitani write the poem in recipe form? What is the effect of the very specific details of this recipe?

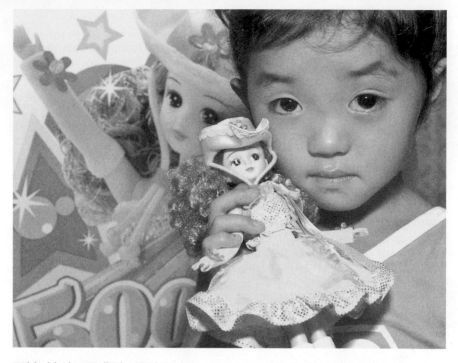

"Girl with Licca Doll," by Chiaki Tsukumo (2003). According to the Japanese toymaker Takara, "Licca-chan was developed to make girls' dreams and wishes come true" and "to nurture kindness, gentleness, and love in children." A fan's personal Web site notes that Licca-chan "hates arithmetic, but she's good at language, music, and art." Her favorite books are *Anne of Green Gables* and *A Little Princess*, and she loves eating ice cream and window-shopping. First introduced in 1967, the doll has since sold nearly fifty million units and become, according to the toymaker, a national character that has inspired a Licca-chan generation of women consumers.
Reprinted by permission of the Associated Press.

3. Why is "false eyelashes" (line 4) a particularly resonant phrase in the context of this poem?

4. Consider and note the Licca doll's hair, eyes, and costume in the photograph by Chiaki Tsukumo. How do you account for the success of the Licca doll? What do you make of the toymaker's claim that the doll makes "girls' dreams and wishes come true"? What dreams and wishes do you think the toymaker is selling? How do the ideals that the toymaker (Takara) associates with the Licca doll compare with those associated with Barbie?

5. How does the paragraph connect with Mirikitani's satirical poem?

CONNECTION TO ANOTHER SELECTION

1. How might the voice in Michelle Boisseau's "Self-Pity's Closet" (p. 587) be read as a version of the speaker in "Recipe"?

FREEDOM AND BORDERS

Thomas Lynch's "Liberty" is an amusing protest against conformity, the kind of middling placidity often associated with suburban life in America. The blustery Irish speaker in this poem laments the lost world his ancestors inhabited in Ireland and longs for the "form[s] of freedom" that they once enjoyed. Though the speaker may cause us to smile, his complaint is serious nonetheless. The potential validity of his assessment of suburban life is presented visually in the accompanying photograph of Somerville, Massachusetts, a suburb of Boston. How might Lynch's speaker be considered a resident of one of those houses? Does the arrangement of the streets and houses help to explain the attitudes expressed in the poem? What are your own views about the suburbs?

THOMAS LYNCH (B. 1948)

Liberty

1998

Some nights I go out and piss on the front lawn
as a form of freedom — liberty from
porcelain and plumbing and the Great Beyond
beyond the toilet and the sewage works.
Here is the statement I am trying to make: 5
to say I am from a fierce bloodline of men
who made their water in the old way, under stars
that overarched the North Atlantic where
the River Shannon empties into sea.
The ex-wife used to say, "Why can't you pee 10
in concert with the most of humankind
who do their business tidily indoors?"
It was gentility or envy, I suppose,
because I could do it anywhere, and do
whenever I begin to feel encumbered. 15
Still, there is nothing, here in the suburbs,
as dense as the darkness in West Clare
nor any equivalent to the nightlong wind
that rattles in the hedgerow of whitethorn there
on the east side of the cottage yard in Moveen. 20
It was market day in Kilrush, years ago:
my great-great-grandfather bargained with tinkers
who claimed it was whitethorn that Christ's crown was made from.
So he gave them two and six and brought them home —
mere saplings then — as a gift for the missus, 25
who planted them between the house and garden.
For years now, men have slipped out the back door

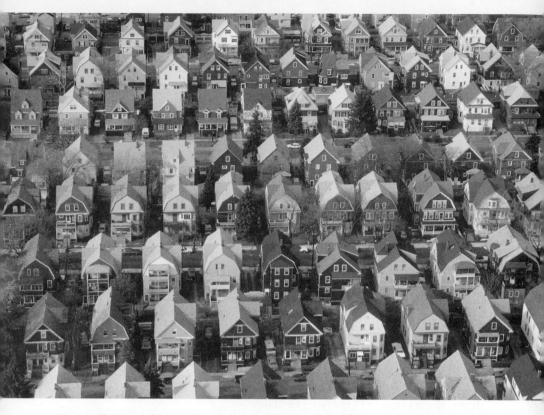

"Somerville, Massachusetts," by Alex MacLean (1993). Between 1870 and 1915, new streetcar lines in the Boston suburb of Somerville spurred major population growth in the area. Many of the newcomers were immigrants, including Irish workers attracted by plentiful jobs at the brickyards and in the slaughtering and meatpacking industry. The two-family houses in this photograph were built around 1910 to house the new population. By World War II, these neighborhoods swelled to a population density said to be greater than that of Calcutta.
Reprinted by permission of Alex S. MacLean / Landslides.

during wakes or wedding feasts or nights of song
to pay their homage to the holy trees
and, looking up into that vast firmament,   30
consider liberty in that last townland where
they have no crowns, no crappers and no ex-wives.

CONSIDERATIONS FOR CRITICAL THINKING AND WRITING

1. **FIRST RESPONSE.** Does "gentility or envy" (line 13) get in the way of your enjoyment and appreciation of this poem? Explain why or why not.

2. Characterize the speaker and explain why you find him engaging or not. What sort of "liberty" does he insist upon?

3. Consider Alex MacLean's aerial photograph of Somerville, Massachusetts. What strikes you about this landscape? What is the thinking behind this

example of city planning? How does such a plan affect personal freedoms, and how might it inspire rebellion such as that of the speaker in Lynch's poem?

CONNECTION TO ANOTHER SELECTION

1. Discuss Lynch's treatment of suburban life and compare it with that of John Ciardi in "Suburban" (p. 525). What similarities are there in the themes and metaphoric strategies of these two poems?

SUGGESTED TOPICS FOR LONGER PAPERS

1. Write an essay that develops a common theme or thread that you find in all six poems presented in this chapter. You may explore similarities or differences concerning any aspect of the border crossings they examine.
2. Choose one of the poems listed below and research at least three images that complement, extend, or qualify the poem. Select rich images that allow you to write an essay explaining how they are thematically connected to the idea of crossing borders in the poem.

Selections related to this chapter

22

A THEMATIC CASE STUDY
The Natural World

Writing is my salvation. If I didn't write,
what would I do?
—MAXINE KUMIN

© Bettmann/CORBIS.

This chapter is a collection of poems thematically related to the natural environment we inhabit. Though poets may have a popular (and mistaken) reputation for being somewhat ethereal in their concerns, they still breathe the same air as the rest of us. Not surprisingly, because poets instinctively draw inspiration from nature, they are often as delighted to praise its vivid joys as they are compelled to warn us when it is abused. Having neither the technical knowledge of scientists nor the political means of legislators to defend the environment, poets nevertheless lend a voice to remind us of its pleasures, importance, and urgent fragility. The celebration of nature has always, of course, been a major poetic genre, but only fairly recently has poetry treated nature as a cause célèbre.

The poems in this chapter provide some contemporary reflections on our relationship to nature. Though they are not representative of all of the kinds of environmental poetry being written today, these twelve poems do offer a range of voices and issues that can serve as prompts for seeing and responding to your own natural environment through poetic language. You'll find among them detailed and vivid observations of nature, as well as meditations on climate change, the sustainability of the wild, and, indeed, the future of the planet. Some of the voices are quietly thoughtful, while others are ironic or funny, and a couple will even holler at you.

The first poem, "Birdsong Interpreted" by Tom Disch, may not seem like an especially inviting welcome, but it helps to explain why you're invited in the first place.

Tom Disch (1940–2008)

Birdsong Interpreted

2007

Scuse me? Scuse M? This is *my* territory.
Didja hear what I said? I said, Go away!
No trespassing! Vamoose! Amscray!
Everything was hunky-dory
Till *you* disturbed the eco-balance.   5
I homestead here and you're Jack Palance
Terrorizing godly folk.
Leave! or I will have a stroke.
I will! I kid you not. I'll sing
My heart out, pop a valve, expire: 10
This nest will be my funeral pyre.
I'm warning you: if songs could sting,
If trills could kill, my dear sweet thing,
You wouldn't linger longer here.
Jug jug, pu-whee! — now, disappear!   15

Considerations for Critical Thinking and Writing

1. **First response.** Jack Palance (1919–2006) was famous for his film roles as a menacing villain dressed in black, especially in westerns, who disrupted peaceful towns. What does he symbolize in this poem?

2. How does the speaker's diction and speech pattern characterize the bird?

3. What serious point breaks through the poem's humor?

Connection to Another Selection

1. Compare the speaker's tone in "Birdsong Interpreted" and that in Herbert Lomas's "The Fly's Poem about Emily" (p. 98).

The rest of the poems in this chapter explore the natural world inhabited with human beings. What is never absent, however, is the human perception that creates the poems.

JANE HIRSHFIELD (B. 1953)

Happiness   1994

I think it was from the animals
that St. Francis learned
it is possible to cast yourself
on the earth's good mercy and live.
From the wolf who cast off   5
the deep fierceness of her first heart
and crept into the circle of sunlight
in full wariness and wolf-hunger,
and was fed, and lived; from the birds
who came fearless to him until he   10
had no choice but return that courage.
Even the least amoeba touched on all sides
by the opulent Other, even the baleened
plankton fully immersed in their fate—
for what else might happiness be   15
than to be porous, opened, rinsed through
by the beings and things?
Nor could he forget those other companions,
the shifting, ethereal, shapeless:
Hopelessness, Desperateness, Loneliness,   20
even the fire-tongued Anger—
for they too waited with the patient Lion,
the glossy Rooster, the drowsy Mule, to step
out of the trees' protection and come in.

CONSIDERATIONS FOR CRITICAL THINKING AND WRITING

1. **FIRST RESPONSE.** Look up some of the legends associated with St. Francis as the patron saint of animals and the environment. How do they inform the speaker's description of happiness?

2. Discuss the way nature is envisioned in the poem.

3. How is happiness defined by the speaker? To what extent does this definition match your own perspective?

CONNECTION TO ANOTHER SELECTION

1. Contrast the view of nature presented in "Happiness" with that in Emily Dickinson's "Apparently with no surprise" (p. 355) and Robert Frost's "Design" (p. 386).

LESLIE MARMON SILKO (B. 1948)

Love Poem 1970

© Christopher Felver/CORBIS.

Rain smell comes with the wind
     out of the southwest.

Smell of sand dunes
    tall grass glistening
       in the rain.
Warm raindrops that fall easy
      (this woman)

The summer is born.
Smell of her breathing new life
     small gray toads on
  damp sand.

(this woman)
    whispering to dark wide leaves
    white moon blossoms dripping
        tracks in the   15
  sand.

Rain smell
    I am full of hunger
   deep and longing to touch
wet tall grass, green and strong beneath.   20

This woman loved a man
and she breathed to him
     her damp earth song.

I am haunted by this story
I remember it in cottonwood leaves   25
      their fragrance in
  the shade.

I remember it in the wide blue sky
when the rain smell comes with the wind.

CONSIDERATIONS FOR CRITICAL THINKING AND WRITING

1. **FIRST RESPONSE.** How are the erotic and a sensitivity to the environment joined in the language of this poem's images?

2. Discuss the effects of Silko's use of line spacing on your reading.

3. Explain why this poem is both sensuous and sensual.

CONNECTION TO ANOTHER SELECTION

1. Compare how nature is used to express longing in "Love Poem" and in Molly Peacock's "Desire" (p. 251).

MARGARET ATWOOD   (B. 1939)

A Holiday   *1984*

My child in the smoke of the fire
playing at barbarism,
the burst meat dripping down her
chin, soot smearing
her cheek and her hair infested with twigs,   5
under a huge midsummer-leafed tree
in the rain, the shelter
of poles and canvas down
the road if needed:

This could be where we   10
end up, learning the minimal
with maybe no tree, no rain,
no shelter, no roast carcasses
of animals to renew us

at a time when language   15
will shrink to the word *hunger*
and the word *none.*

Mist lifts from the warm lake
hit by the cold drizzle:
too much dust in the stratosphere   20
this year, they say. Unseasonal.

Here comes the ice,
here comes something,
we can all feel it
like a breath, a footstep,   25
here comes nothing
with its calm eye of fire.

What we're having right
now is a cookout,
sausages on peeled sticks.   30
The blades of grass are still with us.
My daughter forages,
grace plumps the dusty berries,
two or three hot and squashed in her fist.

So far we do it.   35
for fun. So far is
where we've gone
and no farther.

CONSIDERATIONS FOR CRITICAL THINKING AND WRITING

1. **FIRST RESPONSE.** How does Atwood create suspense in this poem?
2. How does the imagery reveal the speaker's thoughts about society's relationship to nature?
3. Consider the potential ironies present in the title.

CONNECTION TO ANOTHER SELECTION

1. Discuss the treatment of air in "A Holiday" and in Mary Oliver's "Oxygen" (p. 92).

MAXINE KUMIN (B. 1925)

Though He Tarry   2007

© Bettmann/CORBIS.

I believe with perfect faith in
the coming of the Messiah
and though he tarry I will
wait daily for his coming
said Maimonides° in 1190
or so and 44 percent
of people polled in the USA
in 2007 are also waiting
for him to show up in person—
though of course he won't <u>be</u> a person.

Do we want to save our planet,
the only one we know of,
so the faithful 44 percent
can be in a state of high alert
in case he arrives in person   15
though of course he won't <u>be</u> a person?

According to Stephen Jay Gould
        science and religion are
        non-overlapping magisteria°
        See each elbowing the other   20
        to shove over on the bed
        they're condemned to share?
        See how they despise, shrink back
        from accidental touching?
It's no surprise that   25
60 percent of scientists
say they are nonbelievers.

But whether you're churchy or not
what about the planet?
Damn all of you with dumpsters.   30

---

5 *Maimonides* (c. 1135?–1204): A famous medieval Jewish philosopher.
19 *non-overlapping magisteria*: Stephen Jay Gould (1941–2002), an American evolutionary biologist and historian of science, published an article titled "Nonoverlapping Magisteria" in *Natural History* (March 1997) in which he described religion and science as two "magisteria" or domains of inquiry that neither overlap nor conflict with one another: "No such conflict should exist because each subject has a legitimate magisterium, or domain of teaching authority—and these do not overlap."

Damn all who do not compost.
Damn all who tie their dogs out
on bare ground, without water.
Damn all who debeak chickens
and all who eat them, damn   35
CEOs with bonuses,
corporate jets, trophy wives.

Damn venal human nature
lurching our way to a sorry
and probably fiery finale. . . .   40
If only he'd strap his angel wings on
in the ether and get his licensed
and guaranteed ass down here—
though of course he won't <u>be</u> a person—
if only he wouldn't tarry.   45

CONSIDERATIONS FOR CRITICAL THINKING AND WRITING

1. **FIRST RESPONSE.** Explain why you think this poem is more about the existence of God or the existence of the planet.

2. Describe the speaker's tone and whether or not you think it is appropriate for the poem's subject matter.

3. Comment on the significance of the title.

CONNECTION TO ANOTHER SELECTION

1. Compare the themes in this poem and in Gerard Manley Hopkins's "God's Grandeur" (p. 199).

GAIL WHITE (B. 1945)

Dead Armadillos   *2000*

The smart armadillo stays
on the side of the road
where it was born. The dumb ones
get a sudden urge to check the pickings
across the asphalt, and nine   5
times out of ten, collide
with a ton of moving metal.
They're on my daily route—soft shells
of land crustacea, small blind knights
in armor. No one cares.   10
There is no Save the Armadillo
Society. The Sierra Club and Greenpeace
take no interest. There are too
damned many armadillos, and beauty,
like money, is worth more when it's scarce.   15

Give us time. Let enough of them
try to cross the road.
When we're down to the last half dozen,
we'll see them with the eyes of God.

CONSIDERATIONS FOR CRITICAL THINKING AND WRITING

1. **FIRST RESPONSE.** Why do you think White chooses armadillos rather than, say, foxes to make her point?
2. What keeps this poem from becoming preachy?
3. How does the poem's language reveal the speaker's character?

CONNECTION TO ANOTHER SELECTION

1. Discuss the similarities in theme in "Dead Armadillos" and Margaret Atwood's "A Holiday" (p. 575).

DAVE LUCAS (B. 1980)

November   2007

October's brief, bright gush is over.
Leaf-lisp and fetch, their cold-tea smell
raked to the curb in copper- and shale-
stained piles, or the struck-match-sweet of sulfur

becoming smoke. The overcast
sky the same slight ambergris.
Hung across it, aghast surprise
of so many clotted, orphaned nests.

CONSIDERATIONS FOR CRITICAL THINKING AND WRITING

1. **FIRST RESPONSE.** What overall impression does this poem convey about the month of November? How does it serve as a dramatic contrast to October?
2. Carefully examine the diction in each line to determine how the poem's images achieve their effects.
3. **CREATIVE RESPONSE.** Choose two consecutive months that offer striking climatic environmental changes in the region where you live and write a two-stanza poem that includes vivid diction and images.

CONNECTION TO ANOTHER SELECTION

1. Consider the tone and theme of "November" and of Robert Frost's "Nothing Gold Can Stay" (p. 383).

WALT MCDONALD (B. 1934)

Coming Across It   *1988*

Cans rattle in the alley, a cat
prowling, or a man down on his luck
and starving. Neon on buildings

above us blinks like those eyes
in the dark, too slow for a cat,   5
lower than a man, like fangs,

yellow gold. Crowds shove us toward
something that crouches, this blind
alley like a cave. Someone shouts

Otter, and suddenly a sharp nose   10
wedges into focus, pelt shining,
webbed mammal feet begging for room.

Like a tribe, we huddle here
in the city and call *Here, otter,*
otter, asking how far to the river,   15

the police, the safest zoo. We call it
cute, call it ugly, maybe diseased
or lonely, amazed to find something wild

in the city. We wait for someone
with a gun or net to rescue it.   20
We talk to strangers like brothers,

puzzling what should be done
with dark alleys, with garbage,
with vermin that run free at night.

We keep our eyes on it, keep calling   25
softly to calm it. But if we had
clubs, we'd kill it.

CONSIDERATIONS FOR CRITICAL THINKING AND WRITING

1. **FIRST RESPONSE.** How is suspense created and sustained in the poem?
2. How do these city people respond to "something wild / in the city" (lines 18–19)?
3. How is the otter described? What is the effect of repeatedly referring to the animal as "it"?

CONNECTION TO ANOTHER SELECTION

1. Discuss how the unexpected encounter between civilization and nature produces anxiety in "Coming Across It" and in Alden Nowlan's "The Bull Moose" (below).

ALDEN NOWLAN (1933–1983)

The Bull Moose   *1962*

Down from the purple mist of trees on the mountain,
lurching through forests of white spruce and cedar,
stumbling through tamarack swamps,
came the bull moose
to be stopped at last by a pole-fenced pasture.   5

Too tired to turn or, perhaps, aware
there was no place left to go, he stood with the cattle.
They, scenting the musk of death, seeing his great head
like the ritual mask of a blood god, moved to the other end
of the field, and waited.   10

The neighbors heard of it, and by afternoon
cars lined the road. The children teased him
with alder switches and he gazed at them
like an old, tolerant collie. The women asked
if he could have escaped from a Fair.   15

The oldest man in the parish remembered seeing
a gelded moose yoked with an ox for plowing.
The young men snickered and tried to pour beer
down his throat, while their girl friends took their pictures.

The bull moose let them stroke his tick-ravaged flanks,   20
let them pry open his jaws with bottles, let a giggling girl
plant a little purple cap
of thistles on his head.

When the wardens came, everyone agreed it was a shame
to shoot anything so shaggy and cuddlesome.   25
He looked like the kind of pet
women put to bed with their sons.

So they held their fire. But just as the sun dropped in the river
the bull moose gathered his strength
like a scaffolded king, straightened and lifted his horns   30
so that even the wardens backed away as they raised their rifles.
When he roared, people ran to their cars. All the young men
leaned on their automobile horns as he toppled.

CONSIDERATIONS FOR CRITICAL THINKING AND WRITING

1. **FIRST RESPONSE.** How does the speaker present the moose and the townspeople? How are the moose and townspeople contrasted? Discuss specific
   lines to support your response.

2. Explain how the symbols in this poem point to a conflict between humanity
   and nature. What do you think the speaker's attitude toward this conflict is?

3. **CRITICAL STRATEGIES.** Read the section on mythological criticism (pp. 677–80)
   in Chapter 26, "Critical Strategies for Reading," and write an essay on "The Bull
   Moose" that approaches the poem from a mythological perspective.

CONNECTION TO ANOTHER SELECTION

1. In an essay compare and contrast how the animals portrayed in "The Bull Moose" and in Stafford's "Traveling through the Dark" (p. 172) are used as symbols.

ROBERT B. SHAW (B. 1947)

Wild Turkeys   2006

Out of the woods and into the side yard
they come in a slow march, a band of three,
dowdy, diaconal in somber plumes
that so englobe their awkward, ambling bodies
it is hard to believe their pipestem legs   5
truly support them as they promenade.
Their raw red necks and bare heads — slaty blue —
go with the legs, austere, deliberate, wiry,
seconding every step with a prim nod,
while now and then pausing to stoop and nip   10
whatever seeds or beetles their bead-eyes
have got a bead on. When they reach the foot
of the hill they advance gamely, helping themselves
with little hops and only a faint stirring
of wings, going up with uncanny lightness,   15
almost as though inflated (which in a sense
they are, given the air caught up inside
their fusty basketry of quills and pinions).
Whether on forage or reconnaissance,
they know where they are going with no hustle;   20
they are as much unwavering as wild.
Soon they pace out of sight, three emissaries
of shadow taking time to appraise sunshine
on a warm day two weeks before Thanksgiving,
intent as Pilgrims turning out for a hanging.   25

CONSIDERATIONS FOR CRITICAL THINKING AND WRITING

1. **FIRST RESPONSE.** These wild turkeys ultimately promenade through quite a lot of history. How does the appearance of Thanksgiving and the Pilgrims in the last two lines add to their "slow march" (line 2)?

2. Comment on the character of the turkeys that arises from Shaw's description of them.

3. Discuss the tone of the last line. What thoughts and feelings does it leave you contemplating?

CONNECTION TO ANOTHER SELECTION

1. Compare the elements of style used to characterize the birds in "Wild Turkeys" and in Tom Disch's "Birdsong Interpreted" (p. 572). How do the poetic styles match the birds' characters?

EDWARD HIRSCH (B. 1950)

First Snowfall: Intimations

1994

How long it has taken me to recall
That cold and radiant afternoon
                in late October, 1959,
When twenty-five squirming bundles
Of trouble were subdued
              and then transfixed
By a bright snowfall that drifted
                and gusted like leaves   5
Outside the prison-like windows of Peterson School.

To us, it seemed as if someone
Was dusting off the rooftops
              and high ceilings of winter,
Dropping sheets of paper, wet and unlined,
From a cloudy, invisible sky
              just beyond our reach . . .   10
It seemed as if someone was painting
              and repainting the air
Until the day shined blankly, like a white wall.

While the teacher droned on
About positive and negative numbers
We were stilled by the absolute
              stillness settling around us,   15
By the steady erasure of lawns
              and houses across the street,
And by the hushed fragility of the trees
Glistening in the distance,
              ghostly, inhuman . . .

Our gaze moved upward against the white light,
But by the time we were released   20
Into the chilly, untouched
              otherness of the day
There were smudges and wingbeats
              floating in the treetops
And a long string of footsteps —
              the animals before us —
Crossing and criss-crossing in the snow.

Our cries shattered the stillness
              like panes of glass   25
As we stomped over the playground
And lay down on our backs —
              our spines against the earth —
To outline the figure of angels in the snow.
What joy we took in flapping our arms
              up and down, like wings,
And sinking down lazily into the soft ground . . .   30

It was as if the heavens had cracked
                              and come floating down,
And I can still remember the giddy blankness
Of lying there and looking up dazed
                              by the luminous crystals
Spiraling out of an opaque white silence . . .
But then we rose up from the ground, noisily   35
Brushing off our bodies,
                    and raced each other for home.

CONSIDERATIONS FOR CRITICAL THINKING AND WRITING

1. **FIRST RESPONSE.** Why is it important that this experience with a first snowfall
   is told retrospectively rather than from the point of view of a child?

2. Trace how the emotions of the speaker change in the poem from beginning
   to end.

3. What kinds of "Intimations" are suggested by the speaker's description of
   the snow?

CONNECTIONS TO ANOTHER SELECTION

1. Discuss how snow has the power to transfix the speakers in this poem and
   in Robert Frost's "Stopping by Woods on a Snowy Evening" (p. 382).

PAUL ZIMMER (B. 1934)

What I Know about Owls   *1996*

They can break the night like glass.
They can hear a tick turn over in
The fur of a mouse thirty acres away.
Their eyes contain a tincture of magic
So potent they see cells dividing in   5
The hearts of their terrified victims.
You cannot hear their dismaying who,
You cannot speak their awesome name
Without ice clattering in your arteries.

But in daytime owls rest in blindness,   10
Their liquids no longer boiling.
There is a legend that if you are
Careful and foolishly ambitious,
You can gently stroke for luck and life
The delicate feathers on their foreheads,   15
Risking always that later on some
Quiet night when you least expect it,
The owl remembering your transgression,
Will slice into your lamplight like a razor,
Bring you down splayed from your easy chair,   20

Your ribcage pierced, organs raked
From their nests, and your head slowly
Rolling down its bloody pipe into
The fierce acids of its stomach.

CONSIDERATIONS FOR CRITICAL THINKING AND WRITING

1. **FIRST RESPONSE.** What does the speaker find both admirable and fearsome about owls?
2. As gruesome as this poem is, consider whether or not it qualifies as a celebration and appreciation of owls.
3. On a larger scale, what does this poem suggest about humanity's relationship to nature?

CONNECTION TO ANOTHER SELECTION

1. Write an essay comparing the views of nature offered in Zimmer's poem and in Andrew Hudgins's "The Cow" (p. 209).

SUGGESTED TOPICS FOR LONGER PAPERS

1. Write an analysis of Gail White's "Dead Armadillos" (p. 577), Walt McDonald's "Coming Across It" (p. 579), and Alden Nowlan's "The Bull Moose" (p. 580) as commentaries on our civilization's problematic relationship to the wild. How does each poem add to and extend a consideration of the issue?
2. Use the Internet to find the lyrics of popular songs written within the past five years about environmental issues. Choose three and write a comparative analysis of their style and themes.

An Anthology
of Poems

23

An Album of Contemporary Poems

© Jerry Bauer.

> Now the role of poetry is not simply to
> hold understanding in place but to help
> create and hold a realm of experience.
> Poetry has become a kind of tool for
> knowing the world in a particular way.
> —JANE HIRSHFIELD

MICHELLE BOISSEAU (B. 1955)

Born in Cincinnati, Michelle Boisseau earned a B.A. and M.A. from Ohio
University and a Ph.D. from the University of Houston. She teaches literature and writing courses at the University of Missouri,
Kansas City. She has received a National Endowment
for the Arts fellowship and prizes from the Poetry Society of America. Her poetry collections include *No Pri-
vate Life* (1990); *Understory* (1996), winner of the Morse Prize; and *Trembling
Air* (2003).

[Web] Research the
poets in this chapter at
bedfordstmartins.com/
rewritinglit.

Self-Pity's Closet

2003

Depression, loneliness, anger, shame, envy,
appetite without hunger, unquenchable
thirst, secret open wounds, long parades
of punishments, resentment honed and glinting

in the sun, the wind driving a few leaves,   5
an empty bird call, the grass bent down, far off
a dog barking and barking, the skin sticky,
the crotch itchy, the tongue stinking, the eyes,
words thrust from the mouth like bottles off a bridge,
tangy molasses of disgust, dank memory   10
of backs, of eyebrows raised and cool expressions
after your vast and painful declarations,
subtle humiliations creeping up
like the smell of wet upholstery, dial tone
in the brain, the conviction that your friends   15
never really loved you, the certitude
you deserved no better, never have, stains
in the carpet, the faucet drilling the sink,
the nights raining spears of stars, the days bland
and blank as newspapers eaten slowly   20
in the bathtub, the clock, the piano,
heavy impatient books, slippery pens,
the radio, a bug bouncing against
the window: go away, make it all go away.

CONNECTIONS TO OTHER SELECTIONS

1. Compare the pain experienced by the speaker in this poem with the speaker's pain in T. S. Eliot's "The Love Song of J. Alfred Prufrock" (p. 494). How do the images in each poem reveal the speaker's state of mind?

2. Discuss the themes you find in this poem and in Edgar Allan Poe's "The Haunted Palace" (p. 160). Explain whether or not you think the differences between these two poems are greater than their similarities.

EAMON GRENNAN (B. 1941)

Born in Dublin, Ireland, Eamon Grennan has lived most of his life in the United States since the early 1960s, though he is a frequent visitor to his homeland. After completing his education at University College, Dublin, and Harvard University, he began teaching at Vassar College, where he is a professor of English. His poetry has won him a number of honors and awards, including fellowships from the National Endowment for the Arts, the National Endowment for the Humanities, and the John Guggenheim Foundation. His most recent collections of poems include *Selected and New Poems* (2000), *Still Life with Waterfall* (2002), *Renvyle, Winter* (2003), *The Quick of It* (2005), and *Matter of Fact: Poems* (2008).

Herringbone

2007

By a dark green altar of moss
the ruffled herringbone twirl
of water: on its downstream
escalator two mallards snatch
a ride at the speed of water,   5
then take to air in a flurry of
flashes (brown, white, royal blue)
where the current crack-foams
over stone. Brisk thinkers
on the wing, they manage a   10
brusque trajectory to clear
the bridge, its one eye shining,
shivery with watershadow.

Time to weigh the few things
learned: the loud clean sound   15
the titmouse makes in April;
hearty whicker-whinny
of the flicker; the eight-note
plaintive song that says
somewhere inside the naked   20
network of hedges a white-
throated sparrow is uttering
something, letting silence settle,
then again saying it, finding it
right and sufficient   25
                    Isn't that
a lovely bit of herringbone tweed,
my mother would say, savoring
the word so you could see
and feel it. Likewise these simple   30
singers laying claim to space
make me feel the sturdy substance
of the air I walk through, the
life they make — as my mother
always did — a daily habit of.   35

CONNECTIONS TO OTHER SELECTIONS

1. Describe how sound is central to the effects and meanings of this poem
   and of Galway Kinnell's "Blackberry Eating" (p. 194).
2. Compare the themes of "Herringbone" and Mary Oliver's "The Poet with
   His Face in His Hands" (p. 48).

MARY STEWART HAMMOND (B. 1953)

Raised in Virginia and Maryland, Mary Stewart Hammond now lives in New York City, where she teaches master poetry classes for the New York Writer's Workshop. Her first book, *Out of Canaan* (1991), won the Great Lakes Colleges' Best First Collection of Poetry prize. Her poems have appeared in a variety of magazines and journals, such as *American Poetry Review, Atlantic Monthly,* the *New Yorker, Paris Review, Yale Review,* and *Shenandoah.* She has been awarded fellowships at the MacDowell Colony and Yaddo.

High Ground 2008

My husband and I sit in cones of electric light
reading in down-filled, chintz-covered armchairs
in our pretty little parlor in our pretty second home.
The tinnitus of crickets and the hiss of the sprinkler system
seep through screened doors and windows. 5
Thousands of miles away people are drowning.

In droves. For days. They stuff rags under their doors.
They perch on rooftops screaming, to us, to high heaven, to
anyone, for help. The water is rising. They dog-paddle
into our parlor exhausted. They are in despair. The wind 10
is roaring. They are the size of pixels. They can't be heard.
Bach's Brandenburg Concerto #6 fills the room.

Last night my husband dreamed we were standing in water.
The water was rising. It was clear. It was potable.
But it was rising. It was reaching our mouths. 15
We interpret his dream as empathy. But that's just a dream.
We, of course, can swim. Join us. Two hundred feet away
the sea kisses and kisses our shore.

CONNECTIONS TO OTHER SELECTIONS

1. Compare the narrative strategy of this poem with that in "Building with Its Face Blown Off" by Billy Collins (p. 454).
2. Discuss the speakers' responses to witnessing human suffering on television in "High Ground" and in James Merrill's "Casual Wear" (p. 176).

TONY HOAGLAND (B. 1953)

Born in Fort Bragg, North Carolina, Tony Hoagland has published collections of poetry that include *Sweet Rain* (1993), awarded the Brittingham Prize in Poetry; *Donkey Gospel* (1998), awarded the James Laughlin Award of the Academy of American Poets; *What Narcissism Means to Me* (2003); and *Hard*

Rain (2005). He has received writing grants from the Guggenheim Foundation, the National Endowment for the Arts, and the Academy of Arts and Letters. He teaches in the graduate program at the University of Houston.

America   *2003*

Then one of the students with blue hair and a tongue stud
Says that America is for him a maximum-security prison

Whose walls are made of RadioShacks and Burger Kings, and MTV episodes
Where you can't tell the show from the commercials,

And as I consider how to express how full of shit I think he is,   5
He says that even when he's driving to the mall in his Isuzu

Trooper with a gang of his friends, letting rap music pour over them
Like a boiling Jacuzzi full of ballpeen hammers, even then he feels

Buried alive, captured and suffocated in the folds
Of the thick satin quilt of America   10

And I wonder if this is a legitimate category of pain,
Or whether he is just spin doctoring a better grade,

And then I remember that when I stabbed my father in the dream last night,
It was not blood but money

That gushed out of him, bright green hundred-dollar bills   15
Spilling from his wounds, and — this is the weird part —,

He gasped, "Thank god — those Ben Franklins were
Clogging up my heart —

And so I perish happily,
Freed from that which kept me from my liberty" —   20

Which is when I knew it was a dream, since my dad
Would never speak in rhymed couplets,

And I look at the student with his acne and cell phone and phony ghetto
    clothes
And I think, "I am asleep in America too,

And I don't know how to wake myself either,"   25
And I remember what Marx said near the end of his life:

"I was listening to the cries of the past,
When I should have been listening to the cries of the future."

But how could he have imagined 100 channels of 24-hour cable
Or what kind of nightmare it might be   30

When each day you watch rivers of bright merchandise run past you
And you are floating in your pleasure boat upon this river

Even while others are drowning underneath you
And you see their faces twisting in the surface of the waters

And yet it seems to be your own hand   35
Which turns the volume higher?

CONNECTIONS TO OTHER SELECTIONS

1. Discuss the treatment of self-pity in "America" and in Michelle Boisseau's
   "Self-Pity's Closet" (p. 587).
2. Explain how "America" and Barbara Hamby's "Ode to American English"
   (p. 85) offer contrasting visions of American life and culture.

RACHEL LODEN (B. 1948)

Born in Washington, D.C., Rachel Loden
grew up in New York, Connecticut, and California. Her first book, *Hotel Imperium* (1999),
won the Contemporary Poetry Series Competition and was named one of the ten best
poetry books of the year by the *San Francisco
Chronicle*, which called it "quirky and beguil-
ing." Loden has also published four chap-
books, including *The Last Campaign* (1998)
and *The Richard Nixon Snow Globe* (2005). Her
second full-length book, *Dick of the Dead,*
was published by Ashahta Press in 2009.
Her work appears in numerous anthologies,
among them two editions of *The Best American Poetry* (1995 and 2005). Awards include a
Pushcart Prize, a fellowship in poetry from
the California Arts Council, and a grant
from the Fund for Poetry.

© Jussi Ketonen.

Locked Ward: Newtown, Connecticut   2005

Your tight-lipped jailer beckons
and I trail her like a moon.

The padding of her strange white shoes,
the doors she unlocks one by one—

then you are there on the edge of a cot   5
like a whipped child, with your eyes down.

There are no sharp objects in here,
only the malignant shapes

that dance out
when the strappings are undone. 10

I have brought you what you wanted
from home. A robe, a sweater —

an irony, as though what you wanted
could be mine to give so

easily. Oh I 15
would wrap you up and carry you away

to some all-powerful physician
or at least some place

they'd let you rave in peace.
Silence of the years, the sins against 20

the white page. Carried always out to sea
by the foul winds off the laundry,

the stains that cannot be removed
by any washing of the hands.

The years are mute. And yet 25
there is no end to the lament

of daughters, no end
to the sharp objects in the heart.

CONNECTIONS TO OTHER SELECTIONS

1. Discuss the parent-daughter relationship as it is revealed by the images in
   Loden's poem and in Cathy Song's "The Youngest Daughter" (p. 92).
2. Compare the themes in Loden's poem and in Emily Dickinson's "One need
   not be a Chamber — to be Haunted —" (p. 336).

SUSAN MINOT (B. 1956)

Born and raised in Massachusetts, Susan
Minot earned a B.A. at Brown University and
an M.F.A. at Columbia University. Before
devoting herself full-time to writing, Minot
worked as an assistant editor at *Grand Street*
magazine. Her stories have appeared in the
Atlantic Monthly, Harper's, the *New Yorker,*
Mademoiselle, and *Paris Review.* Her short stories have been collected in *Lust and Other*
Stories (1989), and she has published four
novels — *Monkeys* (1986), *Folly* (1992), *Evening*
(1998), and *Rapture* (2002), as well as one volume of poetry: *Poems 4 A.M.* (2002).

Courtesy of Dinah Minot Hubley.

My Husband's Back   2005

Sunday evening.
Breakdown hour. Weeping into
a pot of burnt rice. Sun dimmed
like a light bulb gone out
behind a gray lawn of snow.   5
The baby flushed with the flu
asleep on a pillow.
The fire won't catch.
The wet wood's caked
with ice. Sitting   10
on the couch my spine
collides with all its bones
and I watch my husband
peer past the glass grate
and blow.   15
His back in a snug plaid shirt
gray and white
leaning into the woodstove
is firm and compact
like a young man's back.   20

And the giant world which swirls
in my head
stopping most thought
suddenly ceases
to spin. It sits   25
right there, the back I love,
animal and gamine, leaning
on one arm.
I could crawl on it forever
the one point in the world   30
turns out
I have travelled everywhere
to get to.

CONNECTIONS TO OTHER SELECTIONS

1. Compare Minot's "My Husband's Back" and Anne Bradstreet's "To My Dear and Loving Husband" (p. 513) as love poems.
2. Discuss the speakers' tones and treatment of domestic life in Minot's poem and in Galway Kinnell's "After Making Love We Hear Footsteps" (p. 279).

ROBERT MORGAN (B. 1944)

Robert Morgan is a poet and novelist who has been widely praised as the poet laureate of Appalachia. Morgan was born and raised in North Carolina in a small, isolated valley in the Blue Ridge Mountains. He earned his B.A.

from the University of North Carolina at Chapel Hill and his M.A. from the University of North Carolina at Greensboro. He has published six books of fiction since 1969, including *The Hinterlands* (1994), *The Truest Pleasure* (1995), and *Brave Enemies* (2008). He has been widely published in such magazines as *Atlantic Monthly, New Republic, Poetry, Southern Review, Yale Review, Carolina Quarterly,* and *New England Review*. He has also published ten volumes of poetry, his latest titled *The Strange Attractor* (2004). In 1971 he began teaching at Cornell University, where, since 1992, he has been Kappa Alpha Professor of English. He has won several awards, including four National Endowment for the Arts fellowships and a Guggenheim Fellowship, and his poetry has appeared in *New Stories from the South* and *Prize Stories: The O. Henry Awards*. His novel *Gap Creek* (1999) was selected for Oprah's Book Club, and *Boone, A Biography* (2007) was awarded the Thomas Wolfe Prize.

Fever Wit

2000

If a child or young adult lay
near crisis with a temperature,
bedclothes hot as from an iron,
face swollen bright as a blown coal,
neighbors and kin would gather round,   5
sitting near the bedside, leaning
close, awaiting words uttered from
delirium, the scattered phrase
and mutter from hot throat and brain.
Every mumble seemed a message   10
to interpret, each groan and wince,
jerk and whisper, a report in
testimony from other tongues,
as though the sick child glowing with
infection could see beyond in   15
fever intoxication, become
a filament for lighting their
ordinary lives with lightning glimpse
burned through the secret boundary,
the ill one privileged to say   20
across and not distort or resist
the wisdom of sickness, the vision
from pain-fire's further peaks, before
the dreaded sweat, the chill descent.

CONNECTIONS TO OTHER SELECTIONS

1. Compare the theme of this poem with that of Emily Dickinson's "Tell all the Truth but tell it slant —" (p. 340).
2. Discuss the "neighbors and kin" (line 5) of this poem and "The people along the sand" in Robert Frost's "Neither Out Far nor In Deep" (p. 384).

ALBERTO RÍOS (B. 1952)

Born in Nogales, Arizona, Alberto Ríos grew up on the border between Mexico and Arizona, which is the subject of his memoir *Capriotoda* (1999). He earned a bachelor's degree and an M.F.A. from the University of Arizona. He has published several short story collections and a number of poetry collections, including *Whispering to Fool the Wind* (1982), *The Lime Orchard Woman* (1988), *Teodoro Luna's Two Kisses* (1990), *The Smallest Muscle in the Human Body* (2002), and *The Theater of Night* (2006). Among his many awards are the Arizona Governor's Arts Award and fellowships from the Guggenheim Foundation and the National Endowment for the Arts. He teaches at Arizona State University.

The Gathering Evening   *2002*

Shadows are the patient apprentices of everything.
They follow what might be followed,

Sit with what will not move.
They take notes all day long —

We don't pay attention, we don't see   5
The dark writing of the pencil, the black notebook.

Sometimes, if you are watching carefully,
A shadow will move. You will turn to see

What has made it move, but nothing.
The shadows transcribe all night.   10

Transcription is their sleep.
We mistake night as a setting of the sun:

Night is all of them comparing notes,
So many gathering that their crowd

Makes the darkness everything.   15
Patient, patient, quiet and still.

One day they will have learned it all.
One day they will step out, in front,

And we will follow them, be their shadows,
And work for our turn —   20

The centuries it takes
To learn what waiting has to teach.

CONNECTIONS TO OTHER SELECTIONS

1. Compare the treatment of shadows in this poem and in Emily Dickinson's "Presentiment — is that long Shadow — on the lawn —" (p. 136).
2. Discuss the significance of the night in this poem and in Robert Frost's "Acquainted with the Night" (p. 158).

CATHY SONG (B. 1955)

Of Chinese and Korean descent, Cathy Song was born in Honolulu, Hawaii. After receiving her B.A. from Wellesley College, she pursued an M.A. in creative writing at Boston University. The recipient of a number of grants and awards, including the Shelley Memorial Award from the Poetry Society of America and the Hawaii Award for Literature, she has taught creative writing at various universities. Her work frequently focuses on the world of family and ancestry. Among her collections of poetry are *Picture Bride* (1983), *Frameless Windows, Squares of Light* (1988), *School Figures* (1994), *The Land of Bliss* (2001), and *Cloud Moving Hands* (2007).

A Poet in the House   *2001*

© School Figures.

Emily's job was to think.
She was the only one of us
who had that to do.
    — Lavinia Dickinson

Seemingly small her work,
minute to the point of invisibility —
she vanished daily into paper, famished,
hungry for her next encounter —
but she opened with a string of humble
words necessity,
necessary as the humble work
of bringing well to water, roast to knife,
        cake to frost,
the coarse, loud, grunting labor of the rest of us
who complained not at all   10
for the noises she heard
we deemed divine, if
claustrophobic and esoteric —
and contented ourselves to the apparent,
the menial, set our heads   15
to the task of daily maintenance,
the simple order at the kitchen table,
while she struggled with a different thing —
the pressure seized upon her mind —
we could ourselves not bear such strain   20
and, in gratitude, heaved the bucket,
squeezed the rag, breathed the sweet,
homely odor of soap.
Lifting dirt from the floor
I swear   25
we could hear her thinking.

CONNECTIONS TO OTHER SELECTIONS

1. Compare Song's assessment of the life of a poet with the view expressed in Howard Nemerov's "Walking the Dog" (p. 528).

2. Discuss the perspective on Dickinson in this poem and in Ronald Wallace's "Miss Goff" (p. 350).

C. K. WILLIAMS (B. 1936)

Born in Newark, New Jersey, and educated at Bucknell University and the University of Pennsylvania, C. K. Williams has worked as a therapist, an editor, and a writer and has taught creative writing at a number of schools, including Boston, Columbia, Drexel, George Mason, and Princeton Universities. His collections of poetry include *A Dream of Mind* (1992); *Repair* (1999), awarded the Pulitzer Prize; *The Singing* (2003), awarded the National Book Award; and *Collected Poems* (2006). Among his other awards are a Guggenheim Fellowship, the National Book Critics Circle Award, *The Paris Review*'s Connor Prize, and the Ruth Lilly Poetry Prize.

The United States   2007

The rusting, decomposing hulk of the United States
is moored across Columbus Boulevard from Ikea,
rearing weirdly over the old municipal pier
on the mostly derelict docks in Philadelphia.

I'd forgotten how immense it is: I can't imagine   5
which of the hundreds of portholes looked in
on the four-man cabin five flights down
I shared that first time I ran away to France.

We were told we were the fastest thing afloat,
and we surely were; even from the tiny deck   10
where passengers from tourist were allowed
our wake boiled ever vaster out behind.

That such a monster could be lifted by mere waves
and in the storm that hit us halfway across
tossed left and right until we vomited   15
seemed a violation of some natural law.

At Le Havre we were out of scale with everything;
when a swarm of tiny tugs nudged like piglets
at the teat the towering mass of us in place,
all the continent of Europe looked small.   20

Now, behind its ravelling chain-link fence,
the ship's a somnolent carcass, cables lashed

like lilliputian leashes to its prow, its pocking,
once pure paint discoloring to blood.

Upstream, the shells of long-abandoned factories   25
crouch for miles beneath the interstate;
the other way the bridge named after Whitman
hums with traffic toward the suburbs past his grave;

and "America's mighty flagship" waits here,
to be auctioned, I suppose, stripped of anything   30
it might still have of worth, and towed away
and torched to pieces on a beach in Bangladesh.

CONNECTIONS TO OTHER SELECTIONS

1. Discuss Williams's symbolic use of the ship in "The United States" compared with Thomas Hardy's in "The Convergence of the Twain" (p. 86) and David R. Slavitt's in "Titanic" (p. 88).

2. Compare the images and attitudes expressed toward the United States in this poem and in Tony Hoagland's "America" (p. 591).

24

An Album of
World Literature

My poetry has passed through the same
stages of my life; from a solitary childhood and an adolescence cornered in
distant, isolated countries, I set out to
make myself a part of the great human
multitude.
— PABLO NERUDA

© Luis Poirot.

ANNA AKHMATOVA (RUSSIA / 1889–1966)

Born in Russia, Anna Akhmatova was a poet and translator who was
regarded as a major modern poet. Although she was expelled from the
Union of Soviet Writers during Stalin's rule, she was reclaimed by her
country in the 1960s. Her poetry is characterized by its
clarity, precision, and simplicity. Her work is translated
in *Complete Poems of Anna Akhmatova* (1990).

Web Research the
poets in this chapter at
bedfordstmartins.com/
rewritinglit.

Lot's Wife   1922

TRANSLATED BY RICHARD WILBUR

The just man followed then his angel guide
Where he strode on the black highway, hulking and bright;
But a wild grief in his wife's bosom cried,
Look back, it is not too late for a last sight

Of the red towers of your native Sodom, the square   5
Where once you sang, the gardens you shall mourn,
And the tall house with empty windows where
You loved your husband and your babes were born.

She turned, and looking on the bitter view
Her eyes were welded shut by mortal pain;   10
Into transparent salt her body grew,
And her quick feet were rooted in the plain.

Who would waste tears upon her? Is she not
The least of our losses, this unhappy wife?
Yet in my heart she will not be forgot   15
Who, for a single glance, gave up her life.

CONNECTIONS TO OTHER SELECTIONS

1. Discuss the use of biblical allusions in "Lot's Wife" and in William Butler
   Yeats's "The Second Coming" (p. 655). How is an understanding of the allusions crucial to interpreting each poem?
2. Consider the "unhappy wife" (line 14) in this poem and in Linda Pastan's
   "Marks" (p. 152). Discuss how you regard the wife in each poem.

CLARIBEL ALEGRÍA   (EL SALVADOR / B. 1924)

Born in Estelí, Nicaragua, Claribel Alegría moved with her family to El Salvador within a year of her birth. A 1948 graduate of George Washington
University, she considers herself a Salvadoran, and much of her writing reflects the political upheaval of recent Latin American history. In 1978 she
was awarded the Casa de las Americas Prize for her book *I Survive*. A bilin-
gual edition of her major works, *Flowers from the Volcano*, was published
in 1982. Recent translated collections of her poetry include *Sorrow* (1999)
and *Casting Off* (2003).

I Am Mirror   *1978*

TRANSLATED BY ELECTA ARENAL AND MARSHA GABRIELA DREYER

Water sparkles
on my skin
and I don't feel it
water streams
down my back   5
I don't feel it
I rub myself with a towel
I pinch myself in the arm

I don't feel
frightened I look at myself in the mirror   10
she also pricks herself
I begin to get dressed
stumbling
from the corners
shouts like lightning bolts   15
tortured eyes
scurrying rats
and teeth shoot forth
although I feel nothing
I wander through the streets: 20
children with dirty faces
ask me for charity
child prostitutes
who are not yet fifteen
the streets are paved with pain   25
tanks that approach
raised bayonets
bodies that fall
weeping
finally I feel my arm   30
I am no longer a phantom
I hurt
therefore I exist
I return to watch the scene:
children who run   35
bleeding
women with panic
in their faces
this time it hurts me less
I pinch myself again   40
and already I feel nothing
I simply reflect
what happens at my side
the tanks
are not tanks   45
nor are the shouts
shouts
I am a blank mirror
that nothing penetrates
my surface   50
is hard
is brilliant
is polished
I became a mirror
and I am fleshless   55
scarcely preserving
a vague memory
of pain.

1. Compare the ways in which Alegría uses mirror images to reflect life in El Salvador with Sylvia Plath's concerns in "Mirror" (p. 148).

2. Write an essay comparing the speaker's voice in this poem with that in William Blake's "London" (p. 119). How do the speakers evoke emotional responses to what they describe?

YEHUDA AMICHAI (ISRAEL / 1924–2000)

Considered a leading Hebrew poet, Yehuda Amichai was born in Germany in 1924 and later moved with his family to Jerusalem. Amichai fought with the Jewish Brigade of the British Army during World War II and in the War of Independence. After the war, he attended Hebrew University. His first volume of poetry, *Achshav Uve-Yamin HaAharim* (*Now and in Other Days*), appeared in 1955 and immediately attracted the interest of the poetry-reading public. Widely read and admired outside his country, his works have been translated into thirty-three languages. His *Collected Poems* appeared in 1963; he was also the author of two novels and a book of short stories. *The Selected Poems of Yehuda Amichai* was published in 1996.

Jerusalem, 1985   *1985*

TRANSLATED BY CHANA BLOCH

Scribbled wishes stuck between the stones
of the Wailing Wall:
bits of crumpled, wadded paper.

And across the way, stuck in an old iron gate
half-hidden by jasmine:
"Couldn't make it,
I hope you'll understand."

1. Consider the use of irony in this poem and in Emily Dickinson's "I know that He exists" (p. 354).

FAZIL HÜSNÜ DAĞLARCA (TURKEY / 1914–2008)

Born in Istanbul, Turkey, Fazil Hüsnü Dağlarca was one of Turkey's most important and prolific poets of the twentieth century. He began publishing poetry as a young military officer and continued throughout his career as a journal editor and book publisher. In 1968 he received the International Poetry Forum's Turkish Award. Over the course of his career he published more than fifty books for adults and children. The translator of this poem, Talât Sait Halman, translated some of Dağlarca's poetry in *Selected Poems* (1969).

Dead

1984

TRANSLATED FROM THE TURKISH BY TALÂT SAIT HALMAN

Whichever neighborhood has no clergyman
I shall die there.
Let no one see how beautiful
Are all the things I have, my feet, my hair.

In the name of the dead, free and immaculate,   5
A fish in unknown seas,
Am I not a Muslim, heaven knows,
Yet no crowds for me, please.

Don't let them make me wear a shroud,
In sky safeguard my darkness from misery,   10
Don't shake me as I go from shoulder to shoulder,
For all my parts are fancy free.

No prayer can turn my remoteness
From the other worlds into a reality.
Don't let them wash my body, don't: 15
I am madly in love with the warmth inside me.

CONNECTIONS TO OTHER SELECTIONS

1 Discuss the speaker's attitude toward religion in "Dead" and in the excerpt from Walt Whitman's "Song of Myself" (p. 182).

2. Compare the treatment of death in this poem and in Emily Dickinson's "I heard a Fly buzz—when I died—" (p. 335).

MAHMOUD DARWISH (PALESTINE / B. 1942)

Born in Al Birweh, a village near Galilee in what is now Israel, Mahmoud Darwish has devoted his life and writing to his Palestinian homeland, from which he has been exiled. His commitment to independence for Palestine is evident in his work for the Palestine Liberation Organization and in his publication of more than twenty books of poetry that include *Sand and Other Poems* (1986), *Adam of Two Edens* (2000), and *The Raven's Ink* (2001). In 2001 he was awarded the Lannan Prize for Cultural Freedom. Darwish remains a major literary voice for the Palestinians.

Identity Card   1980

TRANSLATED FROM THE ARABIC BY DENYS JOHNSON-DAVIES

Put it on record.
   I am an Arab
And the number of my card is fifty thousand
I have eight children
And the ninth is due after summer.   5
What's there to be angry about?

Put it on record.
   I am an Arab
Working with comrades of toil in a quarry.
I have eight children   10
For them I wrest the loaf of bread,
The clothes and exercise books
From the rocks
And beg for no alms at your door,
   Lower not myself at your doorstep.   15
   What's there to be angry about?

Put it on record.
   I am an Arab.
I am a name without a title,
Patient in a country where everything   20
Lives in a whirlpool of anger.
   My roots
   Took hold before the birth of time
   Before the burgeoning of the ages,
   Before cypress and olive trees,   25
   Before the proliferation of weeds.

My father is from the family of the plough
   Not from highborn nobles.
And my grandfather was a peasant
   Without line or genealogy.   30
My house is a watchman's hut
   Made of sticks and reeds.
Does my status satisfy you?
   I am a name without a surname.

Put it on record.   35
   I am an Arab.
Color of hair: jet black.
Color of eyes: brown.
My distinguishing features:
   On my head the *'iqal* cords over a *keffiyeh*   40
   Scratching him who touches it.
My address:
   I'm from a village, remote, forgotten,
   Its streets without name
   And all its men in the fields and quarry.   45

What's there to be angry about?

Put it on record.
  I am an Arab.
You stole my forefathers' vineyards
  And land I used to till,   50
  I and all my children,
  And you left us and all my grandchildren
  Nothing but these rocks.
  Will your government be taking them too
  As is being said?   55

So!
  Put it on record at the top of page one:
  I don't hate people,
  I trespass on no one's property.
And yet, if I were to become hungry   60
  I shall eat the flesh of my usurper.
  Beware, beware of my hunger
  And of my anger!

CONNECTIONS TO OTHER SELECTIONS

1. Discuss the relation between anger and political history in "Identity Card" and in Langston Hughes's "Harlem" (p. 422).
2. Consider "Identity Card" and Pablo Neruda's "The United Fruit Co." (p. 609) as two personal responses to political events. In what sense do the two poems speak to each other?

MARNE L. KILATES (PHILIPPINES / B. 1952)

Marne L. Kilates is a Filipino translator and poet. He has published three collections of poems: *Children of the Snarl and Other Poems* (1987), *Poems en Route* (1998), both of which won the Manila Critic Circle's National Book Award, and *Mostly in Monsoon Weather* (2006).

Python in the Mall   *1998*

A serpent-like creature has taken residence
in the dark recesses of a new shopping mall.
Supposedly the offspring of the mall tycoon
himself, the creature feeds, by preference,
on nubile virgins.
            —Tabloid story

She hatched in the dank
Basements of our gullibility,
Warmed in the gasp of our telling,

Curling in the tongues
Of housewives and clerks.   5

We gave her a body half-serpent,
Half-voluptuary, and a taste
For maidens and movie stars
Who began to vanish mysteriously
Behind the curtains of boutique   10
Fitting rooms and water closets,
Never to be seen again,
Or only to be found in the parking
Cellars, wandering dazed
Into the headlights of shoppers' cars.   15

How she fed on our thirst
For wonders, fattened on our fear
Of vacant places. Slowly
We embellished the patterns
On her scales and admired   20
The sinuous grace of her spine.

Avidly we filled our multifarious
Hungers at her belly, and lapped
The marvelous tales of her forked
Tongue. And as the gleaming temples   25
Of her worship rose in the midst
Of our squalor, how we trembled
At the seduction of her voice,
O what adoring victims we became.

CONNECTIONS TO OTHER SELECTIONS

1. Discuss the treatment of materialism in "Python in the Mall" and in Tony Hoagland's "America" (p. 591).

2. Compare the themes in this poem and in William Wordsworth's "The World Is Too Much with Us" (p. 247).

TASLIMA NASRIN (BANGLADESH / B. 1962)

Born in Mymensingh, East Pakistan (now Bangladesh), Taslima Nasrin earned her medical degree in 1984. In addition to working as a physician in Dacca hospitals, she has made a career as a prolific writer of fiction, poetry, and nonfiction, focusing particularly on women's oppression. Her widely translated writing has been condemned by conservative mullahs and religious fundamentalists, who have demanded that her books be banned and that she be executed. Since the early 1990s she has lived in the United States, Calcutta, and Europe, where the European Parliament awarded her the Sakharov Prize in Freedom of Thought in 1994. Her collections of poetry include *The Game in Reverse* (1995).

At the Back of Progress...   *1995*

TRANSLATED FROM THE BENGALI BY CAROLYNE WRIGHT AND MOHAMMAD NURUL HUDA

The fellow who sits in the air-conditioned office
is the one who in his youth raped
                          a dozen or so young girls
and at the cocktail party, he's secretly stricken with lust
fastening his eyes on the belly button of some lovely.   5
In the five-star hotels, this fellow frequently
                  tries out his different tastes
                  in sex acts with a variety of women.
This fellow goes home and beats his wife
                          over a handkerchief   10
                          or a shirt collar.
This fellow sits in his office and talks with people
                          puffing on a cigarette
                          and shuffling through his files.

            Ringing the bell he calls his employee   15
                                    shouts at him
                          orders the bearer to bring tea
                                    and drinks.
            This fellow gives out character references for people.

The employee who's speaking in such a low voice   20
that no one knows or would ever suspect
how much he could raise his voice at home,
                  how foul his language could be
                  how vile his behavior.
Gathering with his buddies, he buys some movie tickets   25
and kicking back on the porch outside, indulges
            in loud harangues on politics, art and literature.
Someone is committing suicide   his mother
                          or his grandmother
                          or his great-grandmother.   30
Returning home he beats his wife
                  over a bar of soap or
                  the baby's pneumonia.

The bearer who brings the tea
who keeps the lighter in his pocket   35
and who gets a couple of *tākā* as a tip:
he's divorced his first wife for her sterility,
his second wife for giving birth to a daughter,
he's divorced his third wife for not bringing dowry.
Returning home, this fellow beats his fourth wife   40
over a couple of green chiles or a handful of cooked rice.

1. Discuss the status of women in Nasrin's poem and in Marge Piercy's "The Secretary Chant" (p. 20).

2. Compare the treatment of men in Nasrin's poem and in Daisy Fried's "Wit's End" (p. 525). How do the cultural differences depicted in the poems result in divergent tones?

PABLO NERUDA (CHILE / 1904–1973)

Born in Chile, Pablo Neruda insisted all of his life on the connection between poetry and politics. He was an activist and a Chilean diplomat in a number of countries during the 1920s and 1930s and remained politically active until his death. Neruda was regarded as a great and influential poet (he was awarded the Nobel Prize in 1971) whose poetry ranged from specific political issues to the yearnings of romantic love. Among his many works are *Twenty Love Poems and a Song of Despair* (1924), *Residence on Earth* (three series, 1925–45), *Spain in the Heart* (1937), *The Captain's Verses* (1952), and *Memorial of Isla Negra* (1964).

The United Fruit Co. 1950

TRANSLATED BY ROBERT BLY

When the trumpet sounded, it was
all prepared on the earth,
and Jehovah parceled out the earth
to Coca-Cola, Inc., Anaconda,
Ford Motors, and other entities: 5
The Fruit Company, Inc.
reserved for itself the most succulent,
the central coast of my own land,
the delicate waist of America.
It rechristened its territories 10
as the "Banana Republics"
and over the sleeping dead,
over the restless heroes
who brought about the greatness,
the liberty and the flags, 15
it established the comic opera:
abolished the independencies,
presented crowns of Caesar,
unsheathed envy, attracted
the dictatorship of the flies, 20
Trujillo flies, Tacho flies,
Carias flies, Martinez flies,
Ubico flies, damp flies

of modest blood and marmalade,
drunken flies who zoom   25
over the ordinary graves,
circus flies, wise flies
well trained in tyranny.

Among the bloodthirsty flies
the Fruit Company lands its ships,   30
taking off the coffee and the fruit;
the treasure of our submerged
territories flows as though
on plates into the ships.

Meanwhile Indians are falling   35
into the sugared chasms
of the harbors, wrapped
for burial in the mist of the dawn:
a body rolls, a thing
that has no name, a fallen cipher,   40
a cluster of dead fruit
thrown down on the dump.

CONNECTIONS TO OTHER SELECTIONS

1. Discuss the political perspective in this poem and in Julio Marzán's "The Translator at the Reception for Latin American Writers" (p. 286). What significant similarities are there between the two poems?

2. Contrast the treatment of fruit in this poem and in Galway Kinnell's "Blackberry Eating" (p. 194).

OCTAVIO PAZ (MEXICO / 1914–1998)

Born in Mexico City, Octavio Paz studied at the National Autonomous University and in 1943 helped found one of Mexico's most important literary reviews, the *Prodigal Son*. He served in the Mexican diplomatic corps in Paris, New Delhi, and New York. Much of Paz's poetry reflects Hispanic traditions and European modernism as well as Buddhism. In 1990 he received the Nobel Prize for Literature. Paz's major works include *Sun Stone* (1958), *The Violent Season* (1958), *Salamander* (1962), *Blanco* (1966), *Eastern Rampart* (1968), *Renga* (1971), and *Collected Poems, 1957–1987* (1987).

The Street   1963

A long silent street.
I walk in blackness and I stumble and fall
and rise, and I walk blind, my feet
stepping on silent stones and dry leaves.

Someone behind me also stepping on stones, leaves: 5
if I slow down, he slows;
if I run, he runs. I turn: nobody.
Everything dark and doorless.
Turning and turning among these corners
which lead forever to the street   10
where nobody waits for, nobody follows me,
where I pursue a man who stumbles
and rises and says when he sees me: nobody.

CONNECTIONS TO OTHER SELECTIONS

1. How does the speaker's anxiety in this poem compare with that in Robert Frost's "Acquainted with the Night" (p. 158)?

2. Write an essay comparing the tone of this poem and that of Langston Hughes's "Lenox Avenue: Midnight" (p. 415).

YOUSIF AL-SÁ'IGH (IRAQ / B. 1932)

Born in Mousil, Yousif al-Sá'igh was educated at the University of Baghdad and is a teacher and writer of poetry, fiction, and nonfiction. His work has appeared in more than fourteen books. *Poems*, his collected poetry translated into English, was published in 1992. "An Iraqi Evening" offers a poignant glimpse of his country's home front during a war.

An Iraqi Evening   *1992*

TRANSLATED BY SAADI A SIMAWE, RALPH SAVARESE, AND CHUCK MILLER

Clips from the battlefield
in an Iraqi evening:
a peaceable home
two boys
preparing their homework   5
a little girl
absentmindedly drawing on scrap paper
funny pictures.
— breaking news coming shortly.
The entire house becomes ears   10
ten Iraqi eyes glued to the screen in frightened silence.
Smells mingle:
the smell of war
and the smell of just baked bread.
The mother raises her eyes to a photo on the wall   15

whispering
— May God protect you
and she begins preparing supper
quietly
and in her mind   20
clips float past of the battlefield
carefully selected for hope.

   [18 Feburary 1986]°

[18 February 1986]: The Iran-Iraq war was fought from 1980 to 1988 and claimed an estimated 150,000 Iraqis.

CONNECTIONS TO OTHER SELECTIONS

1. Compare the attitudes expressed toward war in "An Iraqi Evening" and in Alfred, Lord Tennyson's "The Charge of the Light Brigade" (p. 236).
2. Discuss how the images in "An Iraqi Evening" and in Dylan Thomas's "The Hand That Signed the Paper" (p. 140) create the respective tone for each poem.

SHU TING (CHINA / B. 1952)

Born in the Fujian Province of China, Shu Ting (whose real name is Gong Peiyu) was forced in 1969 to live in the countryside for three years because her father was accused of being hostile to the Cultural Revolution. There she began to read Western literature and write. On her return to the city of Xiamen in 1972, she worked in factories and continued writing poetry that made her one of China's most popular poets and a member of the Chinese Writers' Association. She has been a correspondent for the *Beijing Review* and continues to write poetry that has been translated into ten languages. Two of her poetry collections have been translated into English: *Selected Poems* (1994) and *The Mist of My Heart* (1995).

O Motherland, Dear Motherland   *1979*

TRANSLATED BY FANG DAI, DENNIS DING, AND EDWARD MORIN

I am the old broken waterwheel beside your river
That has composed a centuries-old song of weariness;
I'm the smoke-smudged miner's lamp on your forehead
That lights your snail-like crawl through the cave of history.
I'm the withered rice-ear, the washed-out roadbed,   5
The barge mired in a silt shoal
As the tow rope cuts

Deeply into your shoulder
— O Motherland.

I am poverty,   10
I'm sorrow,
I'm the bitterly painful hope
Of your generations.
I am the flowers strewn from Apsara's[n] flowing sleeves
That after thousands of years still have not reached earth   15
— O Motherland.

I am your untarnished ideal
Just broken away from the cobweb of myths;
I'm a bud of the ancient lotus blanketed under your snow,
I'm your smiling dimple wet with tears;   20
Your newly drawn lime-white starting line.
I'm the scarlet dawn emerging with long shimmering rays
— O Motherland.

I am numbered among your billions,
The sum of your nine million square kilometers.   25
You with the scar-blemished breast
Have nurtured me,
Me the confused, the ponderer, the seething,
So that from my body of flesh and blood
You might eke out   30
Your prosperity, your glory, and your freedom
— O Motherland,
My dear Motherland.

14 *Apsara's:* Flying Apsaras, or spirits, played music for the Buddhas.

Connections to Other Selections

1. Compare the speaker's tone in this poem and in Mahmoud Darwish's "Identity Card" (p. 605).
2. Discuss the view of China in this poem and the perspective on the United States in Florence Cassen Mayers's "All-American Sestina" (p. 256).

Tomas Tranströmer (Sweden / b. 1931)

Born in Stockholm, Tomas Tranströmer has had his work translated more than any other contemporary Scandinavian poet. He has worked as a psychologist with juvenile offenders and people with disabilities. His poetry collections include *Night Vision* (1971), *Windows and Stones: Selected Poems* (1972), *Truth Barriers* (1978), *Selected Poems* (1981), and *New Selected Poems* (1997). Among his awards are the Petrarch Prize (1981) and a lifetime subsidy from the government of Sweden.

April and Silence 1991

TRANSLATED BY ROBIN FULTON

Spring lies desolate.
The velvet-dark ditch
crawls by my side
without reflections.

The only thing that shines 5
is yellow flowers.

I am carried in my shadow
like a violin
in its black box.

The only thing I want to say 10
glitters out of reach
like the silver
in a pawnbroker's.

CONNECTIONS TO OTHER SELECTIONS

1. Discuss the description of spring in this poem and in William Carlos Williams's "Spring and All" (p. 651).

2. In an essay explain how the dictions used in this poem and in Martín Espada's "Latin Night at the Pawnshop" (p. 77) contribute to the poems' meanings and tone.

25

A Collection
of Poems

© Imogen Cunningham Trust.

If there were no poetry on any day in the world, poetry would be invented that day. For there would be an intolerable hunger.

— MURIEL RUKEYSER

ANONYMOUS (TRADITIONAL SCOTTISH BALLAD)

Bonny Barbara Allan

date unknown

It was in and about the Martinmas° time,
    When the green leaves were afalling,
That Sir John Graeme, in the West Country,
    Fell in love with Barbara Allan.

He sent his men down through the town,
    To the place where she was dwelling:
"Oh haste and come to my master dear,
    Gin° ye be Barbara Allan."

Web Research the poets in this chapter at bedfordstmartins.com/ rewritinglit.

5

if

1 *Martinmas:* St. Martin's Day, November 11.

O hooly,° hooly rose she up,   *slowly*
        To the place where he was lying,   10
And when she drew the curtain by:
        "Young man, I think you're dying."

"O it's I'm sick, and very, very sick,
        And 'tis a' for Barbara Allan." —
"O the better for me ye's never be,   15
        Tho your heart's blood were aspilling."

"O dinna ye mind,° young man," she said,   *don't you remember*
        "When ye was in the tavern adrinking,
That ye made the health° gae round and round,   *toasts*
        And slighted Barbara Allan?"   20

He turned his face unto the wall,
        And death was with him dealing:
"Adieu, adieu, my dear friends all,
        And be kind to Barbara Allan."

And slowly, slowly raise her up,   25
        And slowly, slowly left him,
And sighing said she could not stay,
        Since death of life had reft him.

She had not gane a mile but twa,
        When she heard the dead-bell ringing,   30
And every jow° that the dead-bell geid,   *stroke*
        It cried, "Woe to Barbara Allan!"

"O mother, mother, make my bed!
        O make it saft and narrow!
Since my love died for me today,   35
        I'll die for him tomorrow."

WILLIAM BLAKE (1757–1827)

The Garden of Love   *1794*

I went to the Garden of Love,
And saw what I never had seen: Explore contexts
A Chapel was built in the midst,   for William Blake on
Where I used to play on the green.   *LiterActive.*

And the gates of this Chapel were shut,   5
And "Thou shalt not" writ over the door;
So I turned to the Garden of Love
That so many sweet flowers bore;

And I saw it was filled with graves,
And tomb-stones where flowers should be;   10
And Priests in black gowns were walking their rounds,
And binding with briars my joys and desires.

WILLIAM BLAKE (1757–1827)

Infant Sorrow

1794

My mother groand! my father wept.
Into the dangerous world I leapt:
Helpless naked piping loud:
Like a fiend hid in a cloud.

Struggling in my father's hands:
Striving against my swadling bands
Bound and weary I thought best
To sulk upon my mother's breast.

ANNE BRADSTREET (CA. 1612–1672)

Before the Birth of One of Her Children

1678

All things within this fading world hath end,
Adversity doth still our joys attend;
No ties so strong, no friends so dear and sweet,
But with death's parting blow is sure to meet.
The sentence past is most irrevocable,   5
A common thing, yet oh, inevitable.
How soon, my Dear, death may my steps attend,
How soon't may be thy lot to lose thy friend,
We both are ignorant, yet love bids me
These farewell lines to recommend to thee,   10
That when that knot's untied that made us one,
I may seem thine, who in effect am none.
And if I see not half my days that's due,
What nature would, God grant to yours and you;
The many faults that well you know I have   15
Let be interred in my oblivious grave;
If any worth or virtue were in me,
Let that live freshly in thy memory
And when thou feel'st no grief, as I no harms,
Yet love thy dead, who long lay in thine arms,   20
And when thy loss shall be repaid with gains
Look to my little babes, my dear remains.
And if thou love thyself, or loved'st me,
These O protect from stepdame's° injury.   *stepmother's*
And if chance to thine eyes shall bring this verse,   25
With some sad sighs honor my absent hearse;
And kiss this paper for thy love's dear sake,
Who with salt tears this last farewell did take.

ELIZABETH BARRETT BROWNING (1806–1861)

When our two souls stand up erect and strong 1850

When our two souls stand up erect and strong,
Face to face, silent, drawing nigh and nigher,
Until the lengthening wings break into fire
At either curvèd point—what bitter wrong
Can the earth do to us, that we should not long   5
Be here contented? Think. In mounting higher,
The angels would press on us and aspire
To drop some golden orb of perfect song
Into our deep, dear silence. Let us stay
Rather on earth, Belovèd,—where the unfit   10
Contrarious moods of men recoil away
And isolate pure spirits, and permit
A place to stand and love in for a day,
With darkness and the death-hour rounding it.

ROBERT BROWNING (1812–1889)

Meeting at Night 1845

The gray sea and the long black land;
And the yellow half-moon large and low;
And the startled little waves that leap
In firey ringlets from their sleep,
As I gain the cove with pushing prow,   5
And quench its speed i' the slushy sand.

Then a mile of warm sea-scented beach;
Three fields to cross till a farm appears;
A tap at the pane, the quick sharp scratch
And blue spurt of a lighted match,   10
And a voice less loud, through its joys and fears,
Than the two hearts beating each to each!

ROBERT BROWNING (1812–1889)

Parting at Morning 1845

Round the cape of a sudden came the sea,
And the sun looked over the mountain's rim:
And straight was a path of gold for him,
And the need of a world of men for me.

ROBERT BURNS (1759–1796)
A Red, Red Rose   *1799*

O my luve's like a red, red rose
That's newly sprung in June;
O my luve's like the melodie
That's sweetly played in tune.

As fair art thou, my bonny lass,   5
So deep in luve am I;
And I will luve thee still my dear,
Till a' the seas gang° dry —   go

Till a' the seas gang dry, my dear,
And the rocks melt wi' the sun: 10
O I will luve thee still, my dear,
While the sands o' life shall run.

And fare thee weel, my only luve,
And fare thee weel awhile!
And I will come again, my luve,   15
Though it were a thousand mile.

GEORGE GORDON, LORD BYRON (1788–1824)
She Walks in Beauty   *1814*

From Hebrew Melodies

I

She walks in Beauty, like the night
   Of cloudless climes and starry skies;
And all that's best of dark and bright
   Meet in her aspect and her eyes:
Thus mellowed to that tender light   5
   Which Heaven to gaudy day denies.

II

One shade the more, one ray the less,
   Had half impaired the nameless grace
Which waves in every raven tress,
   Or softly lightens o'er her face;
Where thoughts serenely sweet express,   10
   How pure, how dear their dwelling-place.

III

And on that cheek, and o'er that brow,
  So soft, so calm, yet eloquent,
The smiles that win, the tints that glow,
  But tell of days in goodness spent,
A mind at peace with all below,
  A heart whose love is innocent!

15

LUCILLE CLIFTON (1936–2010)

this morning (for the girls of eastern high school)

1987

this morning
this morning
          i met myself

coming in

a bright
jungle girl
shining
quick as a snake
a tall
tree girl a
me girl

          i met myself
this morning
coming in

and all day
i have been
a black bell
ringing
i survive

          survive

survive

© Christopher Felver.

10

15

20

SAMUEL TAYLOR COLERIDGE (1772–1834)

Kubla Khan: or, a Vision in a Dream°

1798

In Xanadu did Kubla Khan°
   A stately pleasure-dome decree:
Where Alph, the sacred river, ran
Through caverns measureless to man
   Down to a sunless sea.   5

So twice five miles of fertile ground
With walls and towers were girdled round:
And here were gardens bright with sinuous rills
Where blossomed many an incense-bearing tree;
And there were forests ancient as the hills,   10
Enfolding sunny spots of greenery.

But oh! that deep romantic chasm which slanted
Down the green hill athwart a cedarn cover!°
A savage place! as holy and enchanted
As e'er beneath a waning moon was haunted   15
By woman wailing for her demon-lover!
And from this chasm, with ceaseless turmoil seething,
As if this earth in fast thick pants were breathing,
A mighty fountain momently was forced,
Amid whose swift half-intermitted burst   20
Huge fragments vaulted like rebounding hail,
Of chaffy grain beneath the thresher's flail:
And 'mid these dancing rocks at once and ever
It flung up momently the sacred river.
Five miles meandering with a mazy motion   25
Through wood and dale the sacred river ran,
Then reached the caverns measureless to man,
And sank in tumult to a lifeless ocean:
And 'mid this tumult Kubla heard from far
Ancestral voices prophesying war!   30
   The shadow of the dome of pleasure
   Floated midway on the waves;
   Where was heard the mingled measure
   From the fountain and the caves.
It was a miracle of rare device,   35
A sunny pleasure-dome with caves of ice!

Vision in a Dream: This poem came to Coleridge in an opium-induced dream, but he was interrupted by a visitor while writing it down. He was later unable to remember the rest of the poem.

1 *Kubla Khan:* The historical Kublai Khan (1216–1294, grandson of Genghis Khan) was the founder of the Mongol dynasty in China.

13 *athwart...cover:* Spanning a grove of cedar trees.

A damsel with a dulcimer
In a vision once I saw:
It was an Abyssinian maid,
And on her dulcimer she played,   40
Singing of Mount Abora.
Could I revive within me
Her symphony and song,
To such a deep delight 'twould win me,
That with music loud and long,   45
I would build that dome in air,
That sunny dome! those caves of ice!
And all who heard should see them there,
And all should cry, Beware! Beware!
His flashing eyes, his floating hair!   50
Weave a circle round him thrice,
And close your eyes with holy dread,
For he on honey-dew hath fed,
And drunk the milk of Paradise.

WYN COOPER (B. 1957)

Puritan Impulse   *1999*

I talk the least
of what I covet
most, seldom look
at what I wish to see,
turn my nose away   5
from what smells best,
refuse to listen
to my favorite opera,
La Traviata,
even when it's sung   10
in town for free.
The Van Gogh show
can't make me walk
the block to view it,
no chef can intuit   15
what I might want,
and handing me jars
of caviar while
popping Veuve Cliquot
is not what I call love.   20

The rain last night
froze on the birches,
and today they bend
almost to breaking.
The sun makes every   25

branch distinct, too bright
to look at for long.
And that's excuse
enough for me
to look back down   30
to the road
I walk on, ice
on the pavement
so clear it's blue.

E. E. CUMMINGS (1894–1962)

Buffalo Bill 's°   1923

Buffalo Bill 's
defunct
      who used to
      ride a watersmooth-silver
                  stallion   5
and break onetwothreefourfive pigeonsjustlikethat
                       Jesus

he was a handsome man
               and what i want to know is
how do you like your blueeyed boy   10
Mister Death

Explore contexts for E. E. Cummings on LiterActive.

Buffalo Bill: William Frederick Cody (1846–1917) was an American frontier scout and Indian killer turned international circus showman with his Wild West show, which employed Sitting Bull and Annie Oakley.

JOHN DONNE (1572–1631)

The Apparition   *c. 1600*

When by thy scorn, O murderess, I am dead,
     And that thou thinkst thee free
From all solicitation from me,
Then shall my ghost come to thy bed,
And thee, feigned vestal, in worse arms shall see;   5
Then thy sick taper° will begin to wink,   *candle*
And he, whose thou art then, being tired before,
Will, if thou stir, or pinch to wake him, think
     Thou call'st for more,
And in false sleep will from thee shrink.   10
And then, poor aspen wretch, neglected, thou,

Bathed in a cold quicksilver sweat, wilt lie
      A verier° ghost than I.   *truer*
What I will say, I will not tell thee now,
Lest that preserve thee; and since my love is spent,   15
I had rather thou shouldst painfully repent,
Than by my threatenings rest still innocent.

JOHN DONNE (1572–1631)

Batter My Heart   *1610*

Batter my heart, three-personed God; for You
As yet but knock, breathe, shine, and seek to mend;
That I may rise and stand, o'erthrow me, and bend
Your force, to break, blow, burn, and make me new.
I, like an usurped town, to another due,   5
Labor to admit You, but Oh, to no end!
Reason, Your viceroy in me, me should defend,
But is captived, and proves weak or untrue.
Yet dearly I love You, and would be loved fain.
But am betrothed unto Your enemy: 10
Divorce me, untie, or break that knot again,
Take me to You, imprison me, for I,
Except You enthrall me, never shall be free,
Nor ever chaste, except You ravish me.

JOHN DONNE (1572–1631)

The Flea   *1633*

Mark but this flea, and mark in this°
How little that which thou deny'st me is;
It sucked me first, and now sucks thee,
And in this flea our two bloods mingled be;
Thou know'st that this cannot be said   5
A sin, nor shame, nor loss of maidenhead,
    Yet this enjoys before it woo,
      And pampered swells with one blood made of two,
    And this, alas, is more than we would do.°

Oh stay, three lives in one flea spare,   10
Where we almost, yea more than, married are.
This flea is you and I, and this
Our marriage bed, and marriage temple is;

---

1 *mark in this:* Take note of the moral lesson in this object.   9 *more than we would do:* That is, if we do not join our blood in conceiving a child.

Though parents grudge, and you, we're met
And cloistered in these living walls of jet. 15
    Though use° make you apt to kill me, *habit*
    Let not to that, self-murder added be,
    And sacrilege, three sins in killing three.

Cruel and sudden, hast thou since
Purpled thy nail in blood of innocence? 20
Wherein could this flea guilty be,
Except in that drop which it sucked from thee?
Yet thou triumph'st, and say'st that thou
Find'st not thyself, nor me, the weaker now;
    'Tis true; then learn how false, fears be; 25
    Just so much honor, when thou yield'st to me,
    Will waste, as this flea's death took life from thee.

GEORGE ELIOT (MARY ANN EVANS / 1819–1880)

In a London Drawingroom 1865

The sky is cloudy, yellowed by the smoke.
For view there are the houses opposite,
Cutting the sky with one long line of wall
Like solid fog: far as the eye can stretch
Monotony of surface and of form 5
Without a break to hang a guess upon.
No bird can make a shadow as it flies,
For all its shadow, as in ways o'erhung
By thickest canvas, where the golden rays
Are clothed in hemp. No figure lingering 10
Pauses to feed the hunger of the eye
Or rest a little on the lap of life.
All hurry on and look upon the ground
Or glance unmarking at the passersby.
The wheels are hurrying, too, cabs, carriages 15
All closed, in multiplied identity.
The world seems one huge prison-house and court
Where men are punished at the slightest cost,
With lowest rate of color, warmth, and joy.

KATIE FORD (B. 1975)

Ark 2008

We love the stories of flood and the few
told to prepare in advance by their god.
In that story, the saved are
always us, meaning:
whoever holds the book.

DEBORAH GARRISON (B. 1965)
Unbidden Sonnet with Evergreen   2006

Round midnight we were drifting cheek to cheek
and you in sighing rhythmic beats pulled down
your milk; please, siphon off a bit of life —
what's mine is yours — and grow; you grow so you
can go from me, I know, yet I drink in   5
the sweet increase that will divide us.
The hand that kneads my breast, bell-pulls my hair,
is chubbier, more chubby as I stare.
And in the window stands the churchyard pine,
whose needled song must pierce through mine: *he may*   10
grow tall yet I'll be taller still than ten
of him, and year on year I'll stand in rain
and sun, still sentry here when he is gone —
The rosebud grip is loosed, the feeding's done.

CHARLOTTE PERKINS GILMAN (1860–1935)
Queer People   1899

The people people work with best
    Are often very queer
The people people own by birth
    Quite shock your first idea;
The people people choose for friends
    Your common sense appall,
But the people people marry
    Are the queerest folks of all.

THOMAS HARDY (1840–1928)
Hap   1866

If but some vengeful god would call to me
From up the sky, and laugh: "Thou suffering thing,
Know that thy sorrow is my ecstasy,
That thy love's loss is my hate's profiting!"

Then would I bear it, clench myself, and die,   5
Steeled by the sense of ire unmerited;
Half-eased in that a Powerfuller than I
Had willed and meted me the tears I shed.

But not so. How arrives it joy lies slain,
And why unblooms the best hope ever sown?   10
— Crass Casualty obstructs the sun and rain,

And dicing Time for gladness casts a moan. . . .
These purblind Doomsters had as readily strown
Blisses about my pilgrimage as pain.

THOMAS HARDY (1840–1928)
In Time of "The Breaking of Nations"°

1915

1

Only a man harrowing clods
    In a slow silent walk
With an old horse that stumbles and nods
    Half asleep as they stalk.

2

Only thin smoke without flame   5
    From the heaps of couch-grass;
Yet this will go onward the same
    Though Dynasties pass.

3

Yonder a maid and her wight°   *man*
    Come whispering by: 10
War's annals will cloud into night
    Ere their story die.

The Breaking of Nations: See Jeremiah 51:20: "Thou art my battle axe and weapons of war: for with thee will I break in pieces the nations, and with thee will I destroy kingdoms."

FRANCES E. W. HARPER (1825–1911)
Learning to Read

1872

Very soon the Yankee teachers
   Came down and set up school;
But oh! how the Rebs did hate it, —
   It was agin' their rule

Our masters always tried to hide   5
   Book learning from our eyes;
Knowledge did'nt agree with slavery —
   'Twould make us all too wise.

But some of us would try to steal
   A little from the book,   10
And put the words together,
   And learn by hook or crook.

I remember Uncle Caldwell,
   Who took pot-liquor fat
And greased the pages of his book,   15
   And hid it in his hat.

And had his master ever seen
   The leaves upon his head,
He'd have thought them greasy papers,
   But nothing to be read.   20

And there was Mr. Turner's Ben
   Who heard the children spell,
And picked the words right up by heart,
   And learned to read 'em well.

Well the Northern folks kept sending   25
   The Yankee teachers down
And they stood right up and helped us,
   Though Rebs did sneer and frown,

And, I longed to read my Bible,
   For precious words it said;   30
But when I begun to learn it,
   Folks just shook their heads,

And said there is no use trying,
   Oh! Chloe, you're too late;
But as I was rising sixty,   35
   I had no time to wait.

So I got a pair of glasses,
   And straight to work I went,
And never stopped till I could read
   The hymns and Testament.   40

Then I got a little cabin—
   A place to call my own—
And I felt as independent
   As the queen upon her throne.

George Herbert (1593–1633)

The Collar   *1633*

I struck the board° and cried, "No more;   *table*
            I will abroad!
What? shall I ever sigh and pine?
My lines and life are free, free as the road,
   Loose as the wind, as large as store.°   5
          Shall I be still in suit?°   *serving another*

5 *store:* A storehouse or warehouse.

Have I no harvest but a thorn
  To let me blood, and not restore
What I have lost with cordial° fruit?   *restorative*
      Sure there was wine   10
  Before my sighs did dry it; there was corn
      Before my tears did drown it.
  Is the year only lost to me?
      Have I no bays° to crown it,   *triumphal wreaths*
No flowers, no garlands gay? All blasted?   15
      All wasted?
  Not so, my heart; but there is fruit,
      And thou hast hands.
  Recover all thy sigh-blown age
On double pleasures: leave thy cold dispute   20
Of what is fit, and not. Forsake thy cage,
      Thy rope of sands,
Which petty thoughts have made, and made to thee
  Good cable, to enforce and draw,
      And be thy law,   25
  While thou didst wink and wouldst not see.
      Away! take heed;
      I will abroad.
Call in thy death's-head° there; tie up thy fears.
      He that forbears   30
  To suit and serve his need,
      Deserves his load."
But as I raved and grew more fierce and wild
      At every word,
Methought I heard one calling, *Child!*   35
      And I replied, *My Lord.*

29 *death's-head:* A skull, reminder of mortality.

GERARD MANLEY HOPKINS (1844–1889)

Hurrahing in Harvest   *1877*

Summer ends now; now, barbarous in beauty, the stooks° arise   *sheaves*
  Around; up above, what wind-walks! what lovely behaviour
  Of silk-sack clouds! has wilder, wilful-wavier
Meal-drift moulded ever and melted across skies?

I walk, I lift up, I lift up heart, eyes,   5
  Down all that glory in the heavens to glean our Saviour;
  And, éyes, heárt, what looks, what lips yet gave you a
Rapturous love's greeting of realer, of rounder replies?

And the azurous hung hills are his world-wielding shoulder
  Majestic — as a stallion stalwart, very-violet-sweet! —   10

These things, these things were here and but the beholder
    Wanting; which two when they once meet,
The heart rears wings bold and bolder
    And hurls for him, O half hurls earth for him off under his feet.

GERARD MANLEY HOPKINS (1844–1889)

Pied Beauty   *1877*

Glory be to God for dappled things —
    For skies of couple-color as a brinded cow;
        For rose-moles all in stipple upon trout that swim;
Fresh-firecoal chestnut-falls;° finches' wings;   *fallen chestnut*
    Landscape plotted and pieced — fold, fallow, and plow;   5
        And all trades, their gear and tackle and trim.

All things counter, original, spare, strange;
    Whatever is fickle, freckled (who knows how?)
        With swift, slow; sweet, sour; adazzle, dim;
He fathers-forth whose beauty is past change: 10
        Praise him.

GERARD MANLEY HOPKINS (1844–1889)

The Windhover°   *1877*

To Christ Our Lord

I caught this morning morning's minion,° king-   *favorite*
    dom of daylight's dauphin, dapple-dawn-drawn Falcon,
    in his riding
    Of the rolling level underneath him steady air, and striding
High there, how he rung upon the rein of a wimpling wing
In his ecstasy! then off, off forth on swing,   5
    As a skate's heel sweeps smooth on a bow-bend: the hurl and gliding
    Rebuffed the big wind. My heart in hiding
Stirred for a bird, — the achieve of, the mastery of the thing!

Brute beauty and valour and act, oh, air, pride, plume, here
    Buckle!° AND the fire that breaks from thee then, a billion   10
Times told lovelier, more dangerous, O my chevalier!

    No wonder of it: shéer plód makes plough down sillion°   *furrow*
Shine, and blue-bleak embers, ah my dear,
    Fall, gall themselves, and gash gold-vermilion.

The Windhover: "A name for the kestrel [a kind of small hawk], from its habit of hovering or hanging with its head to the wind" [*OED*].   10 *Buckle:* To join, to equip for battle, to crumple.

A. E. HOUSMAN (1859–1936)

Is my team ploughing   *1896*

"Is my team ploughing,
    That I was used to drive
And hear the harness jingle
    When I was man alive?"

Ay, the horses trample,   5
    The harness jingles now;
No change though you lie under
    The land you used to plough.

"Is football playing
    Along the river shore,   10
With lads to chase the leather,
    Now I stand up no more?"

Ay, the ball is flying,
    The lads play heart and soul;
The goal stands up, the keeper   15
    Stands up to keep the goal.

"Is my girl happy,
    That I thought hard to leave,
And has she tired of weeping
    As she lies down at eve?"   20

Ay, she lies down lightly,
    She lies not down to weep:
Your girl is well contented.
    Be still, my lad, and sleep.

"Is my friend hearty,   25
    Now I am thin and pine,
And has he found to sleep in
    A better bed than mine?"

Yes, lad, I lie easy,
    I lie as lads would choose;   30
I cheer a dead man's sweetheart,
    Never ask me whose.

A. E. HOUSMAN (1859–1936)

To an Athlete Dying Young   *1896*

The time you won your town the race
We chaired° you through the marketplace;
Man and boy stood cheering by,
And home we brought you shoulder-high.

2 *chaired:* Carried on the shoulders in triumphal parade.

Today, the road all runners come,   5
Shoulder-high we bring you home,
And set you at your threshold down,
Townsman of a stiller town.

Smart lad, to slip betimes away
From fields where glory does not stay,   10
And early though the laurel° grows
It withers quicker than the rose.

Eyes the shady night has shut
Cannot see the record cut,
And silence sounds no worse than cheers   15
After earth has stopped the ears:

Now you will not swell the rout
Of lads that wore their honors out,
Runners whom renown outran
And the name died before the man.   20

To set, before its echoes fade,
The fleet foot on the sill of shade,
And hold to the low lintel up
The still-defended challenge-cup.

And round that early-laureled head   25
Will flock to gaze the strengthless dead,
And find unwithered on its curls
The garland briefer than a girl's.

11 *laurel:* Flowering shrub traditionally used to fashion wreaths of honor.

JULIA WARD HOWE (1819–1910)

Battle-Hymn of the Republic   *1862*

Mine eyes have seen the glory of the coming of the Lord:
He is trampling out the vintage where the grapes of wrath are stored;
He hath loosed the fateful lightning of his terrible swift sword:
          His truth is marching on.

I have seen Him in the watch-fires of a hundred circling camps;   5
They have builded Him an altar in the evening dews and damps;
I can read His righteous sentence by the dim and flaring lamps.
          His day is marching on.

I have read a fiery gospel, writ in burnished rows of steel:
"As ye deal with my contemners, so with you my grace shall deal;   10
Let the Hero, born of woman, crush the serpent with his heel,
          Since God is marching on."

He has sounded forth the trumpet that shall never call retreat;
He is sifting out the hearts of men before his judgment-seat:

Oh! be swift, my soul, to answer Him! be jubilant, my feet!   15
    Our God is marching on.

In the beauty of the lilies Christ was born across the sea,
With a glory in his bosom that transfigures you and me:
As he died to make men holy, let us die to make men free,
    While God is marching on.   20

ANDREW HUDGINS (B. 1951)

The Cadillac in the Attic   *2003*

After the tenant moved out, died, disappeared —
the stories vary — the landlord
walked downstairs, bemused, and told his wife,
"There's a Cadillac in the attic,"

and there was. An old one, sure, and one   5
with sloppy paint, bald tires,
and orange rust chewing at the rocker panels,
but still and all, a Cadillac in the attic.

He'd battled transmission, chassis, engine block,
even the huge bench seats,   10
up the folding stairs, heaved them through the trapdoor,
and rebuilt a Cadillac in the attic.

Why'd he do it? we asked. But we know why.
For the reasons we would do it: for the looks
of astonishment he'd never see but could imagine.   15
For the joke. A Cadillac in the attic!

And for the meaning, though we aren't sure what it means.
And of course he did it for pleasure,
the pleasure on his lips of all those short vowels
and three hard clicks: the Cadillac in the attic.   20

BEN JONSON (1573–1637)

On My First Son   *1603*

Farewell, thou child of my right hand,° and joy.
My sin was too much hope of thee, loved boy;
Seven years thou wert lent to me, and I thee pay,
Exacted by thy fate, on the just day.°   *his birthday*
Oh, could I lose all father° now. For why   *fatherhood* 5

---

1 *child of my right hand:* This phrase translates the Hebrew name "Benjamin," Jonson's son.

Will man lament the state he should envỳ? —
To have so soon 'scaped world's and flesh's rage,
And, if no other misery, yet age.
Rest in soft peace, and asked, say, "Here doth lie
Ben Jonson his best piece of poetry,"   10
For whose sake henceforth all his vows be such
As what he loves may never like too much.

BEN JONSON (1573–1637)

To Celia   *1616*

Drink to me only with thine eyes,
    And I will pledge with mine;
Or leave a kiss but in the cup,
    And I'll not ask for wine.
The thirst that from the soul doth rise   5
    Doth ask a drink divine;
But might I of Jove's nectar sup,
    I would not change for thine.

I sent thee late a rosy wreath,
    Not so much honoring thee   10
As giving it a hope that there
    It could not withered be.
But thou thereon didst only breathe,
    And sent'st it back to me;
Since when it grows, and smells, I swear,   15
    Not of itself but thee.

JOHN KEATS (1795–1821)

To one who has been long in city pent   *1816*

To one who has been long in city pent,   Explore contexts
    'Tis very sweet to look into the fair   for John Keats
        And open face of heaven, — to breathe a prayer   on *LiterActive*.
Full in the smile of the blue firmament.
Who is more happy, when, with heart's content,   5
        Fatigued he sinks into some pleasant lair
        Of wavy grass, and reads a debonair
And gentle tale of love and languishment?

Returning home at evening, with an ear
        Catching the notes of Philomel,° — an eye   *A nightingale* 10
Watching the sailing cloudlet's bright career,
        He mourns that day so soon has glided by:
E'en like the passage of an angel's tear
        That falls through the clear ether silently.

JOHN KEATS (1795–1821)

When I have fears that I may cease to be   1818

When I have fears that I may cease to be
    Before my pen has gleaned my teeming brain,
Before high piled books, in charactery,°   *print*
    Hold like rich garners the full ripened grain;
When I behold, upon the night's starred face,   5
    Huge cloudy symbols of a high romance,
And think that I may never live to trace
    Their shadows, with the magic hand of chance;
And when I feel, fair creature of an hour,
    That I shall never look upon thee more,   10
Never have relish in the faery° power   *magic*
    Of unreflecting love; — then on the shore
Of the wide world I stand alone, and think
Till love and fame to nothingness do sink.

JOHN KEATS (1795–1821)

La Belle Dame sans Merci°   1819

O what can ail thee, knight-at-arms,
    Alone and palely loitering?
The sedge has withered from the lake,
    And no birds sing.

O what can ail thee, knight-at-arms,   5
    So haggard and so woe-begone?
The squirrel's granary is full,
    And the harvest's done.

I see a lily on thy brow,
    With anguish moist and fever dew,   10
And on thy cheeks a fading rose
    Fast withereth too.

I met a lady in the meads,
    Full beautiful — a faery's child,
Her hair was long, her foot was light,   15
    And her eyes were wild.

I made a garland for her head,
    And bracelets too, and fragrant zone;°   *belt*
She looked at me as she did love,
    And made sweet moan.   20

I set her on my pacing steed,
    And nothing else saw all day long,

La Belle Dame sans Merci: This title is borrowed from a medieval poem and means "The Beautiful Lady without Mercy."

For sidelong would she bend, and sing
    A faery's song.

She found me roots of relish sweet,   25
    And honey wild, and manna dew,
And sure in language strange she said,
    "I love thee true."

She took me to her elfin grot,
    And there she wept, and sighed full sore,   30
And there I shut her wild wild eyes
    With kisses four.

And there she lullèd me asleep,
    And there I dreamed — Ah! woe betide!
The latest° dream I ever dreamed   *last* 35
    On the cold hill side.

I saw pale kings and princes too,
    Pale warriors, death-pale were they all;
They cried — "La Belle Dame sans Merci
    Hath thee in thrall!"
                                    40

I saw their starved lips in the gloam,
    With horrid warning gapèd wide,
And I awoke and found me here,
    On the cold hill's side.

And this is why I sojourn here,   45
    Alone and palely loitering,
Though the sedge has withered from the lake,
    And no birds sing.

JOHN KEATS (1795–1821)

Written in Disgust of Vulgar Superstition   *1816*

The church bells toll a melancholy round,
    Calling the people to some other prayers,
    Some other gloominess, more dreadful cares,
More hearkening to the sermon's horrid sound.
Surely the mind of man is closely bound   5
    In some black spell; seeing that each one tears
    Himself from fireside joys, and Lydian° airs,
And converse high of those with glory crown'd.
Still, still they toll, and I should feel a damp, —
    A chill as from a tomb, did I not know   10
That they are dying like an outburnt lamp;
    That 'tis their sighing, wailing ere they go
    Into oblivion; — that fresh flowers will grow,
And many glories of immortal stamp.

7 *Lydian:* Soft, sweet music.

EMMA LAZARUS   (1849–1887)

The New Colossus   *1883*

Not like the brazen giant of Greek fame,
With conquering limbs astride from land to land;
Here at our sea-washed, sunset gates shall stand
A mighty woman with a torch, whose flame
Is the imprisoned lightning, and her name   5
Mother of Exiles. From her beacon-hand
Glows world-wide welcome; her mild eyes command
The air-bridged harbor that twin cities frame.
"Keep, ancient lands, your storied pomp!" cries she
With silent lips. "Give me your tired, your poor,   10
Your huddled masses yearning to breathe free,
The wretched refuse of your teeming shore.
Send these, the homeless, tempest-tost to me,
I lift my lamp beside the golden door!"

PHILLIS LEVIN   (B. 1954)

May Day   *2008*

I've decided to waste my life again,
Like I used to: get drunk on
The light in the leaves, find a wall
Against which something can happen,

Whatever may have happened   5
Long ago — let a bullet hole echoing
The will of an executioner, a crevice
In which a love note was hidden,

Be a cell where a struggling tendril
Utters a few spare syllables at dawn.   10
I've decided to waste my life
In a new way, to forget whoever

Touched a hair on my head, because
It doesn't matter what came to pass,
Only that it passed, because we repeat   15
Ourselves, we repeat ourselves.

I've decided to walk a long way
Out of the way, to allow something
Dreaded to waken for no good reason,
Let it go without saying,   20

Let it go as it will to the place
It will go without saying: a wall
Against which a body was pressed
For no good reason, other than this.

Henry Wadsworth Longfellow (1807–1882)

Snow-Flakes

1863

Out of the bosom of the Air,
   Out of the cloud-folds of her garments shaken,
Over the woodlands brown and bare
   Over the harvest-fields forsaken,
      Silent, and soft, and slow   5
      Descends the snow.

Even as our cloudy fancies take
   Suddenly shape in some divine expression,
Even as the troubled heart doth make
In the white countenance confession,   10
      The troubled sky reveals
      The grief it feels.

This is the poem of the air,
   Slowly in silent syllables recorded;
This is the secret of despair,   15
   Long in its cloudy bosom hoarded,
      Now whispered and revealed
      To wood and field.

John Milton (1608–1674)

On the Late Massacre in Piedmont°

1655

Avenge, O Lord, thy slaughtered saints, whose bones
   Lie scattered on the Alpine mountains cold;
   Even them who kept thy truth so pure of old,
When all our fathers worshiped stocks and stones,°
Forget not: in thy book record their groans   5
   Who were thy sheep, and in their ancient fold
   Slain by the bloody Piedmontese, that rolled
Mother with infant down the rocks.° Their moans
The vales redoubled to the hills, and they
   To heaven. Their martyred blood and ashes sow   10

On the Late Massacre . . . : Milton's protest against the treatment of the Waldenses, members of a Puritan sect living in the Piedmont region of northwest Italy, was not limited to this sonnet. It is thought that he wrote Oliver Cromwell's appeals to the duke of Savoy and to others to end the persecution.

4 *When . . . stones:* In Milton's Protestant view, English Catholics had worshipped their stone and wooden statues in the twelfth century, when the Waldensian sect was formed.

5-8 *in thy book . . . rocks:* On Easter Day, 1655, 1,700 members of the Waldensian sect were massacred in Piedmont by the duke of Savoy's forces.

O'er all the Italian fields, where still doth sway
    The triple Tyrant;° that from these may grow
    A hundredfold, who, having learnt thy way,
    Early may fly the Babylonian woe.°

12 *triple Tyrant:* The Pope, with his three-crowned tiara, has authority on earth and in Heaven and Hell.

14 *Babylonian woe:* The destruction of Babylon, symbol of vice and corruption, at the end of the world (see Rev. 17–18). Protestants interpreted the "Whore of Babylon" as the Roman Catholic Church.

John Milton (1608–1674)

When I consider how my light is spent   *c. 1655*

When I consider how my light is spent,°
    Ere half my days in this dark world and wide,
    And that one talent° which is death to hide
Lodged with me useless, though my soul more bent
To serve therewith my Maker, and present   5
    My true account, lest He returning chide;
    "Doth God exact day-labor, light denied?"
I fondly° ask. But Patience, to prevent   *foolishly*
That murmur, soon replies, "God doth not need
    Either man's work or His own gifts. Who best   10
    Bear His mild yoke, they serve Him best. His state
Is kingly: thousands at His bidding speed,
    And post o'er land and ocean without rest;
    They also serve who only stand and wait."

1 *how my light is spent:* Milton had been totally blind since 1651.   3 *that one talent:* Refers to Jesus's parable of the talents (units of money), in which a servant entrusted with a talent buries it rather than invests it and is punished on his master's return (Matt. 25:14–30).

Sir Walter Raleigh (1554–1618)

The Nymph's Reply to the Shepherd   *1600*

If all the world and love were young,
And truth in every shepherd's tongue,
These pretty pleasures might me move
To live with thee and be thy love.

Time drives the flocks from field to fold,   5
When rivers rage and rocks grow cold,
And Philomel° becometh dumb;   *nightingale*
The rest complains of cares to come.

The flowers do fade, and wanton fields
To wayward winter reckoning yields;   10

A honey tongue, a heart of gall,
Is fancy's spring, but sorrow's fall.

Thy gowns, thy shoes, thy beds of roses,
Thy cap, thy kirtle, and thy posies
Soon break, soon wither, soon forgotten —   15
In folly ripe, in reason rotten.

Thy belt of straw and ivy buds,
Thy coral clasps and amber studs,
All these in me no means can move
To come to thee and be thy love.   20

But could youth last and love still breed,
Had joys no date° nor age no need,   *end*
Then these delights my mind might move
To live with thee and be thy love.

CHRISTINA GEORGINA ROSSETTI
(1830–1894)

Some Ladies Dress in Muslin Full and White   *c. 1848*

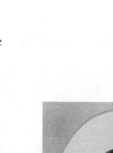

Some ladies dress in muslin full and
        white,
Some gentlemen in cloth succinct and black;
Some patronise a dog-cart, some a hack,
        Some think a painted clarence only
            right.
        Youth is not always such a pleasing
            sight:
Witness a man with tassels on his back;
Or woman in a great-coat like a sack,
        Towering above her sex with horrid height.
If all the world were water fit to drown,
        There are some whom you would not teach to swim,   10
    Rather enjoying if you saw them sink:
    Certain old ladies dressed in girlish pink,
With roses and geraniums on their gown.
        Go to the basin, poke them o'er the rim —

CHRISTINA GEORGINA ROSSETTI (1830–1894)

In Progress   *1862*

Ten years ago it seemed impossible
    That she should ever grow so calm as this,
    With self-remembrance in her warmest kiss
And dim dried eyes like an exhausted well.

Slow-speaking when she has some fact to tell, 5
    Silent with long-unbroken silences,
    Centred in self yet not unpleased to please,
Gravely monotonous like a passing bell.

Mindful of drudging daily common things,
    Patient at pastime, patient at her work, 10
Wearied perhaps but strenuous certainly.
Sometimes I fancy we may one day see
    Her head shoot forth seven stars from where they lurk
And her eyes lightnings and her shoulders wings.

CHRISTINA GEORGINA ROSSETTI (1830–1894)

The World   1862

By day she wooes me, soft, exceeding fair:
But all night as the moon so changeth she;
Loathsome and foul with hideous leprosy
    And subtle serpents gliding in her hair.
    By day she wooes me to the outer air, 5
Ripe fruits, sweet flowers, and full satiety:
But thro' the night, a beast she grins at me,
    A very monster void of love and prayer.
By day she stands a lie: by night she stands
    In all the naked horror of the truth 10
With pushing horns and clawed and clutching hands.
    Is this a friend indeed; that I should sell
My soul to her, give her my life and youth,
Till my feet, cloven too, take hold on hell?

CHRISTINA GEORGINA ROSSETTI (1830–1894)

Promises Like Pie-Crust°   1896

Promise me no promises,
    So will I not promise you;
Keep we both our liberties,
    Never false and never true:
Let us hold the die uncast, 5
    Free to come as free to go;
For I cannot know your past,
    And of mine what can you know?

You, so warm, may once have been
    Warmer towards another one; 10

Pie-Crust: An old English proverb: "Promises are like pie-crust, made to be broken."

I, so cold, may once have seen
   Sunlight, once have felt the sun:
Who shall show us if it was
   Thus indeed in time of old?
Fades the image from the glass   15
   And the fortune is not told.

If you promised, you might grieve
   For lost liberty again;
If I promised, I believe
   I should fret to break the chain: 20
Let us be the friends we were,
   Nothing more but nothing less;
Many thrive on frugal fare
   Who would perish of excess.

SIEGFRIED SASSOON (1886–1967)

"They"   *1917*

The Bishop tells us: "When the boys come back
They will not be the same; for they'll have fought
In a just cause: they lead the last attack
On Anti-Christ; their comrades' blood has bought
New right to breed an honourable race,   5
They have challenged Death and dared him face to face."

"We're none of us the same!" the boys reply.
"For George lost both his legs; and Bill's stone blind;
Poor Jim's shot through the lungs and like to die;
And Bert's gone syphilitic: you'll not find   10
A chap who's served that hasn't found *some* change."
And the Bishop said: "The ways of God are strange!"

WILLIAM SHAKESPEARE (1564–1616)

That time of year thou mayst in me behold   *1609*

That time of year thou mayst in me behold
When yellow leaves, or none, or few, do hang
Upon those boughs which shake against the cold,
Bare ruined choirs, where late the sweet birds sang.
In me thou see'st the twilight of such day   5
As after sunset fadeth in the west;
Which by and by black night doth take away,
Death's second self,° that seals up all in rest.   *sleep*
In me thou see'st the glowing of such fire,

Explore contexts
for William Shakespeare
on *LiterActive*.

That on the ashes of his youth doth lie,   10
As the deathbed whereon it must expire,
Consumed with that which it was nourished by.
   This thou perceiv'st, which makes thy love more strong,
   To love that well which thou must leave ere long.

WILLIAM SHAKESPEARE (1564–1616)

When forty winters shall besiege thy brow   *1609*

When forty winters shall besiege thy brow
And dig deep trenches in thy beauty's field,
Thy youth's proud livery, so gazed on now,
Will be a tattered weed,° of small worth held.   *garment*
Then being asked where all thy beauty lies,   5
Where all the treasure of thy lusty days,
To say within thine own deep-sunken eyes
Were an all-eating shame and thriftless praise.
How much more praise deserved thy beauty's use
If thou couldst answer, "This fair child of mine   10
Shall sum my count and make my old excuse,"
Proving his beauty by succession thine.
   This were to be new made when thou art old,
   And see thy blood warm when thou feel'st it cold.

WILLIAM SHAKESPEARE (1564–1616)

When, in disgrace with Fortune and men's eyes   *1609*

When, in disgrace with Fortune and men's eyes,
I all alone beweep my outcast state,
And trouble deaf heaven with my bootless cries,
And look upon myself and curse my fate,
Wishing me like to one more rich in hope,   5
Featured like him, like him with friends possessed,
Desiring this man's art, and that man's scope,
With what I most enjoy contented least,
Yet in these thoughts myself almost despising,
Haply I think on thee, and then my state,   10
Like to the lark at break of day arising
From sullen earth, sings hymns at heaven's gate;
   For thy sweet love remembered such wealth brings
   That then I scorn to change my state with kings.

Percy Bysshe Shelley (1792–1822)

Ozymandias°

1818

I met a traveler from an antique land
Who said: Two vast and trunkless legs of stone
Stand in the desert. . . . Near them, on the sand,
Half sunk, a shattered visage lies, whose frown,
And wrinkled lip, and sneer of cold command,   5
Tell that its sculptor well those passions read
Which yet survive, stamped on these lifeless things,
The hand that mocked them, and the heart that fed:
And on the pedestal these words appear:
"My name is Ozymandias, King of Kings: 10
Look on my works, ye Mighty, and despair!"
Nothing beside remains. Round the decay
Of that colossal wreck, boundless and bare
The lone and level sands stretch far away.

Ozymandias: Greek name for Ramses II, pharaoh of Egypt for sixty-seven years during the thirteenth century B.C. His colossal statue lies prostrate in the sands of Luxor. Napoleon's soldiers measured it (56 feet long, ear 3½ feet long, weight 1,000 tons). Its inscription, according to the Greek historian Diodorus Siculus, was "I am Ozymandias, King of Kings; if anyone wishes to know what I am and where I lie, let him surpass me in some of my exploits."

Sir Philip Sidney (1554–1586)

Loving in Truth, and Fain in Verse My Love to Show

1591

Loving in truth, and fain in verse my love to show,
That she, dear she, might take some pleasure of my pain,
Pleasure might cause her read, reading might make her know,
Knowledge might pity win, and pity grace obtain,
I sought fit words to paint the blackest face of woe,   5
Studying inventions fine, her wits to entertain,
Oft turning others' leaves, to see if thence would flow
Some fresh and fruitful showers upon my sunburnt brain.
But words came halting forth, wanting Invention's stay;
Invention, Nature's child, fled step-dame° Study's blows;   *stepmother* 10
And others' feet still seemed but strangers in my way.
Thus great with child to speak, and helpless in my throes,
Biting my truant pen, beating myself for spite:
"Fool," said my Muse to me, "look in thy heart and write."

LYDIA HUNTLEY SIGOURNEY (1791–1865)

Indian Names   *1834*

*"How can the red men be forgotten, while so many of
our states and territories, bays, lakes and rivers, are
indelibly stamped by names of their giving?"*

Ye say they all have passed away,
    That noble race and brave,
That their light canoes have vanished
    From off the crested wave;
That 'mid the forests where they roamed   5
    There rings no hunter shout,
But their name is on your waters,
    Ye may not wash it out.

'Tis where Ontario's billow
    Like Ocean's surge is curled,   10
Where strong Niagara's thunders wake
    The echo of the world.
Where red Missouri bringeth
    Rich tribute from the west,
And Rappahannock sweetly sleeps   15
    On green Virginia's breast.

Ye say their cone-like cabins,
    That clustered o'er the vale,
Have fled away like withered leaves
    Before the autumn gale,   20
But their memory liveth on your hills,
    Their baptism on your shore,
Your everlasting rivers speak
    Their dialect of yore.

Old Massachusetts wears it,   25
    Within her lordly crown,
And broad Ohio bears it,
    Amid his young renown;
Connecticut hath wreathed it
    Where her quiet foliage waves,   30
And bold Kentucky breathed it hoarse
    Through all her ancient caves.

Wachuset hides its lingering voice
    Within his rocky heart,
And Alleghany graves its tone   35
    Throughout his lofty chart;
Monadnock on his forehead hoar
    Doth seal the sacred trust,
Your mountains build their monument,
    Though ye destroy their dust.   40

Ye call these red-browed brethren
  The insects of an hour,
Crushed like the noteless worm amid
  The regions of their power;
Ye drive them from their father's lands,   45
  Ye break of faith the seal,
But can ye from the court of Heaven
  Exclude their last appeal?

Ye see their unresisting tribes,
  With toilsome step and slow,   50
On through the trackless desert pass,
  A caravan of woe;
Think ye the Eternal's ear is deaf?
  His sleepless vision dim?
Think ye the *soul's blood* may not cry   55
  From that far land to him?

WALLACE STEVENS (1879–1955)

The Emperor of Ice-Cream   *1923*

Call the roller of big cigars,
The muscular one, and bid him whip
In kitchen cups concupiscent curds.°
Let the wenches dawdle in such dress
As they are used to wear, and let the boys   5
Bring flowers in last month's newspapers.
Let be be finale of seem.°
The only emperor is the emperor of ice-cream.

Take from the dresser of deal,
Lacking the three glass knobs, that sheet   10
On which she embroidered fantails once
And spread it so as to cover her face.
If her horny feet protrude, they come
To show how cold she is, and dumb.
Let the lamp affix its beam.   15
The only emperor is the emperor of ice-cream.

3 *concupiscent curds:* "The words 'concupiscent curds' have no genealogy; they are merely
expressive: at least, I hope they are expressive. They express the concupiscence of life, but, by
contrast with the things in relation in the poem, they express or accentuate life's destitution,
and it is this that gives them something more than a cheap lustre" (Wallace Stevens, *Letters*
[New York: Knopf, 1960], p. 500).

7 *Let . . . seem:* "The true sense of 'Let be be finale of seem' is let being become the conclusion
or denouement of appearing to be: in short, ice cream is an absolute good. The poem is
obviously not about ice cream, but about being as distinguished from seeming to be"
(*Letters*, p. 341).

ALFRED, LORD TENNYSON (1809–1892)

Ulysses°   *1833*

    It little profits that an idle king,
By this still hearth, among these barren crags,
Matched with an agèd wife,° I mete and dole   *Penelope*
Unequal laws unto a savage race,
That hoard, and sleep, and feed, and know not me.   5
    I cannot rest from travel; I will drink
Life to the lees. All times I have enjoyed
Greatly, have suffered greatly, both with those
That loved me, and alone; on shore, and when
Through scudding drifts the rainy Hyades°   10
Vexed the dim sea. I am become a name;
For always roaming with a hungry heart
Much have I seen and known — cities of men
And manners, climates, councils, governments,
Myself not least, but honored of them all —   15
And drunk delight of battle with my peers,
Far on the ringing plains of windy Troy.
I am a part of all that I have met;
Yet all experience is an arch wherethrough
Gleams that untraveled world, whose margin fades   20
For ever and for ever when I move.
How dull it is to pause, to make an end,
To rust unburnished, not to shine in use!
As though to breathe were life. Life piled on life
Were all too little, and of one to me   25
Little remains; but every hour is saved
From that eternal silence, something more,
A bringer of new things; and vile it were
For some three suns to store and hoard myself,
And this gray spirit yearning in desire   30
To follow knowledge like a sinking star,
Beyond the utmost bound of human thought.

    This is my son, mine own Telemachus,
To whom I leave the scepter and the isle —
Well-loved of me, discerning to fulfill   35
This labor, by slow prudence to make mild
A rugged people, and through soft degrees
Subdue them to the useful and the good.
Most blameless is he, centered in the sphere

Ulysses: Ulysses, the hero of Homer's epic poem the *Odyssey*, is presented by Dante in *The Inferno,* XXVI, as restless after his return to Ithaca and eager for new adventures.

10 *Hyades:* Five stars in the constellation Taurus, supposed by the ancients to predict rain when they rose with the sun.

Of common duties, decent not to fail   40
In offices of tenderness, and pay
Meet adoration to my household gods,
When I am gone. He works his work, I mine.

    There lies the port; the vessel puffs her sail:
There gloom the dark, broad seas. My mariners,   45
Souls that have toiled, and wrought, and thought with me—
That ever with a frolic welcome took
The thunder and the sunshine, and opposed
Free hearts, free foreheads—you and I are old;
Old age hath yet his honor and his toil.   50
Death closes all; but something ere the end,
Some work of noble note, may yet be done,
Not unbecoming men that strove with Gods.
The lights begin to twinkle from the rocks;
The long day wanes; the slow moon climbs; the deep   55
Moans round with many voices. Come, my friends.
'Tis not too late to seek a newer world.
Push off, and sitting well in order smite
The sounding furrows; for my purpose holds
To sail beyond the sunset, and the baths   60
Of all the western stars, until I die.
It may be that the gulfs will wash us down;
It may be we shall touch the Happy Isles,°
And see the great Achilles,° whom we knew.
Though much is taken, much abides; and though   65
We are not now that strength which in old days
Moved earth and heaven, that which we are, we are:
One equal temper of heroic hearts,
Made weak by time and fate, but strong in will
To strive, to seek, to find, and not to yield.   70

63 *Happy Isles:* Elysium, the home after death of heroes and others favored by the gods. It
was thought by the ancients to lie beyond the sunset in the uncharted Atlantic. 64 *Achilles:*
The hero of Homer's *Iliad.*

ALFRED, LORD TENNYSON (1809–1892)

Tears, Idle Tears   *1847*

    Tears, idle tears, I know not what they mean,
Tears from the depth of some divine despair
Rise in the heart, and gather to the eyes,
In looking on the happy Autumn-fields,
And thinking of the days that are no more.   5

    Fresh as the first beam glittering on a sail,
That brings our friends up from the underworld,
Sad as the last which reddens over one

That sinks with all we love below the verge;
So sad, so fresh, the days that are no more.   10

    Ah, sad and strange as in dark summer dawns
The earliest pipe of half-awaken'd birds
To dying ears, when unto dying eyes
The casement° slowly grows a glimmering square;   *window*
So sad, so strange, the days that are no more.   15

    Dear as remember'd kisses after death,
And sweet as those by hopeless fancy feign'd
On lips that are for others; deep as love,
Deep as first love, and wild with all regret;
O Death in Life, the days that are no more.   20

RICHARD WAKEFIELD (B. 1952)

In a Poetry Workshop   *1999*

Let us begin with the basics of modern verse.
Meter, of course, is forbidden, and lines must be,
like life, broken arbitrarily
lest anyone mistake us for budding Wordsworths
(don't be alarmed if you've never heard of him).   5
Rhyme is allowed, but only in moderation
and preferably very slant. Alliteration
and assonance must only be used at whim
so the reader doesn't think we're playing God
by sneaking in a pattern of sounds and echoes.   10
As for subjects, the modern poet knows
that modern readers prefer the decidedly odd,
so flowers, except for weeds, are out, and love,
except the very weed-like, is also out.
So thistles and incest are fine to write about   15
but roses and happy marriage get the shove
into the editor's outbox with hardly a glance.
Now note that language matters, so "I" must be
in lower case, thus "i," to show that we
don't put on airs despite our government grants.   20
This also shows we've read our Marx and know
the self is a bourgeois fiction. We understand
the common speech, and so the ampersand,
pronounced "uhn," replaces "and," although
judicious use of allusions to classical thought   25
will keep the great unwashed from getting our drift,
while those outside of Plato's cave will lift
a knowing eyebrow, declaring our work "well-wrought."
And speaking of work, this is not a "class":
We modern poets roll up our sleeves and write   30
our verse in "workshops," no place for sissies, we fight

to find "a voice," and only the fittest pass.
I've summarized these rules in a convenient list,
it's wallet-sized, laminated, so keep
it handy, use it, recite it in your sleep.   35
First poems are due tomorrow. You're dismissed.

WALT WHITMAN (1819–1892)

I Heard You Solemn-Sweet Pipes of the Organ   1861

I heard you solemn-sweet pipes of the organ as last Sunday
    morn I pass'd the church,
Winds of autumn, as I walk'd the woods at dusk I heard your
    long-stretch'd sighs up above so mournful,
I heard the perfect Italian tenor singing at the opera, I heard
    the soprano in the midst of the quartet singing;
Heart of my love! you too I heard murmuring low through
    one of the wrists around my head,
Heard the pulse of you when all was still ringing little bells
    last night under my ear.

WALT WHITMAN (1819–1892)

When I Heard the Learn'd Astronomer   1865

When I heard the learn'd astronomer,
When the proofs, the figures, were ranged in columns before me,
When I was shown the charts and diagrams, to add, divide, and measure them,
When I sitting heard the astronomer where he lectured with much applause
    in the lecture-room,
How soon unaccountable I became tired and sick,
Till rising and gliding out I wandered off by myself,
In the mystical moist night-air, and from time to time,
Looked up in perfect silence at the stars.

WALT WHITMAN (1819–1892)

One's-Self I Sing   1867

One's-Self I sing, a simple separate person,
Yet utter the word Democratic, the word En-Masse.

Of physiology from top to toe I sing,
Not physiognomy alone nor brain alone is worthy for the Muse, I say the
    Form complete is worthier far,
The Female equally with the Male I sing.

Of Life immense in passion, pulse, and power,
Cheerful, for freest action formed under the laws divine,
The Modern Man I sing.

MILLER WILLIAMS (B. 1930)

Thinking about Bill, Dead of AIDS

1989

We did not know the first thing about
how blood surrenders to even the smallest threat
when old allergies turn inside out,

the body rescinding all its normal orders
to all defenders of flesh, betraying the head,   5
pulling its guards back from all its borders.

Thinking of friends afraid to shake your hand,
we think of your hand shaking, your mouth set,
your eyes drained of any reprimand.

Loving, we kissed you, partly to persuade   10
both you and us, seeing what eyes had said,
that we were loving and we were not afraid.

If we had had more, we would have given more.
As it was we stood next to your bed,
stopping, though, to set our smiles at the door.   15

Not because we were less sure at the last.
Only because, not knowing anything yet,
we didn't know what look would hurt you least.

WILLIAM CARLOS WILLIAMS (1883–1963)

Spring and All

1923

By the road to the contagious hospital
under the surge of the blue
mottled clouds driven from the
northeast — a cold wind. Beyond, the
waste of broad, muddy fields   5
brown with dried weeds, standing and fallen

patches of standing water
and scattering of tall trees

All along the road the reddish
purplish, forked, upstanding, twiggy   10
stuff of bushes and small trees
with dead, brown leaves under them
leafless vines —

Lifeless in appearance, sluggish
dazed spring approaches —   15

They enter the new world naked,
cold, uncertain of all
save that they enter. All about them
the cold, familiar wind —

Now the grass, tomorrow   20
the stiff curl of wildcarrot leaf
One by one objects are defined —
It quickens: clarity, outline of leaf

But now the stark dignity of
entrance — Still, the profound change   25
has come upon them: rooted, they
grip down and begin to awaken

WILLIAM CARLOS WILLIAMS (1883–1963)

This Is Just to Say   *1934*

I have eaten
the plums
that were in
the icebox

and which   5
you were probably
saving
for breakfast

Forgive me
they were delicious   10
so sweet
and so cold

WILLIAM WORDSWORTH (1770–1850)

A Slumber Did My Spirit Seal   *1800*

A slumber did my spirit seal;
  I had no human fears —
She seemed a thing that could not feel
  The touch of earthly years.

No motion has she now, no force;
  She neither hears nor sees;
Rolled round in earth's diurnal course.
  With rocks, and stones, and trees.

WILLIAM WORDSWORTH (1770–1850)

I Wandered Lonely as a Cloud   *1807*

I wandered lonely as a cloud
That floats on high o'er vales and hills,
When all at once I saw a crowd,
A host, of golden daffodils,
Beside the lake, beneath the trees,   5
Fluttering and dancing in the breeze.

Continuous as the stars that shine
And twinkle on the milky way,
They stretched in never-ending line
Along the margin of a bay;   10
Ten thousand saw I at a glance,
Tossing their heads in sprightly dance.

The waves beside them danced, but they
Outdid the sparkling waves in glee;
A poet could not but be gay,   15
In such a jocund company;
I gazed—and gazed—but little thought
What wealth the show to me had brought:

For oft, when on my couch I lie
In vacant or in pensive mood,   20
They flash upon that inward eye
Which is the bliss of solitude;
And then my heart with pleasure fills,
And dances with the daffodils.

WILLIAM WORDSWORTH (1770–1850)

It Is a Beauteous Evening, Calm and Free   *1807*

It is a beauteous evening, calm and free,
The holy time is quiet as a Nun
Breathless with adoration; the broad sun
Is sinking down in its tranquillity;
The gentleness of heaven broods o'er the Sea: 5
Listen! the mighty Being is awake,
And doth with his eternal motion make
A sound like thunder—everlastingly.
Dear Child! dear Girl! that walkest with me here,
If thou appear untouched by solemn thought,   10
Thy nature is not therefore less divine:
Thou liest in Abraham's bosom all the year;
And worshipp'st at the Temple's inner shrine,
God being with thee when we know it not.

WILLIAM WORDSWORTH (1770–1850)

The Solitary Reaper°

1807

Behold her, single in the field,
Yon solitary Highland lass!
Reaping and singing by herself;
Stop here, or gently pass!
Alone she cuts and binds the grain,   5
And sings a melancholy strain;
O listen! for the vale profound
Is overflowing with the sound.

No nightingale did ever chaunt
More welcome notes to weary bands   10
Of travelers in some shady haunt
Among Arabian sands.
A voice so thrilling ne'er was heard
In springtime from the cuckoo-bird,
Breaking the silence of the seas   15
Among the farthest Hebrides.

Will no one tell me what she sings? —
Perhaps the plaintive numbers flow
For old, unhappy, far-off things,
And battles long ago.   20
Or is it some more humble lay,
Familiar matter of today?
Some natural sorrow, loss, or pain,
That has been, and may be again?

Whate'er the theme, the maiden sang   25
As if her song could have no ending;
I saw her singing at her work,
And o'er the sickle bending —
I listened, motionless and still;
And, as I mounted up the hill,   30
The music in my heart I bore
Long after it was heard no more.

The Solitary Reaper: Dorothy Wordsworth (William's sister) wrote that the poem was suggested by this sentence in Thomas Wilkinson's *Tour of Scotland:* "Passed a female who was reaping alone; she sung in Erse, as she bended over her sickle; the sweetest human voice I ever heard; her strains were tenderly melancholy, and felt delicious, long after they were heard no more."

WILLIAM WORDSWORTH (1770–1850)

Mutability

1822

From low to high doth dissolution climb,
And sink from high to low, along a scale
Of awful° notes, whose concord shall not fail;   *awe-filled*

A musical but melancholy chime,
Which they can hear who meddle not with crime,   5
Nor avarice, nor over-anxious care.
Truth fails not; but her outward forms that bear
The longest date do melt like frosty rime,
That in the morning whitened hill and plain
And is no more; drop like the tower sublime   10
Of yesterday, which royally did wear
His crown of weeds, but could not even sustain
Some casual shout that broke the silent air,
Or the unimaginable touch of Time.

WILLIAM BUTLER YEATS (1865–1939)

The Second Coming°   *1921*

Turning and turning in the widening gyre°
The falcon cannot hear the falconer;
Things fall apart; the center cannot hold;
Mere anarchy is loosed upon the world,
The blood-dimmed tide is loosed, and
    everywhere
The ceremony of innocence is drowned;
The best lack all conviction, while the worst
Are full of passionate intensity.

Surely some revelation is at hand;
Surely the Second Coming is at hand.   10
The Second Coming! Hardly are those words out
When a vast image out of *Spiritus Mundi*°   *Soul of the world*
Troubles my sight: somewhere in sands of the desert
A shape with lion body and the head of a man,
A gaze blank and pitiless as the sun,   15
Is moving its slow thighs, while all about it
Reel shadows of the indignant desert birds.
The darkness drops again; but now I know
That twenty centuries of stony sleep
Were vexed to nightmare by a rocking cradle,   20
And what rough beast, its hour come round at last,
Slouches towards Bethlehem to be born?

Explore contexts for William Butler Yeats on *LiterActive*.

The Second Coming: According to Matthew 24:29–44, Christ will return to earth after a time of tribulation to reward the righteous and establish the millennium of heaven on earth. Yeats saw his troubled time as the end of the Christian era and feared the portents of the new cycle.

1 *gyre:* Widening spiral of a falcon's flight, used by Yeats to describe the cycling of history.

WILLIAM BUTLER YEATS (1865–1939)
Leda and the Swan°   *1924*

A sudden blow: the great wings beating still
Above the staggering girl, her thighs caressed
By the dark webs, her nape caught in his bill,
He holds her helpless breast upon his breast.

How can those terrified vague fingers push   5
The feathered glory from her loosening thighs?
And how can body, laid in that white rush,
But feel the strange heart beating where it lies?

A shudder in the loins engenders there
The broken wall, the burning roof and tower   10
And Agamemnon dead.
                            Being so caught up,
So mastered by the brute blood of the air,
Did she put on his knowledge with his power
Before the indifferent beak could let her drop?   15

Leda and the Swan: In Greek myth, Zeus in the form of a swan seduced Leda and fathered
Helen of Troy (whose abduction started the Trojan War) and Clytemnestra, Agamemnon's
wife and murderer. Yeats thought of Zeus's appearance to Leda as a type of annunciation,
like the angel appearing to Mary.

WILLIAM BUTLER YEATS (1865–1939)
Sailing to Byzantium°   *1927*

I

That is no country for old men.° The young
In one another's arms, birds in the trees
— Those dying generations — at their song,
The salmon-falls, the mackerel-crowded seas
Fish, flesh, or fowl, commend all summer long   5
Whatever is begotten, born and dies.
Caught in that sensual music all neglect
Monuments of unaging intellect.

Byzantium: Old name for the modern city of Istanbul, capital of the Eastern Roman Empire,
ancient artistic and intellectual center. Yeats uses Byzantium as a symbol for "artificial" (and
therefore, deathless) art and beauty, as opposed to the beauty of the natural world, which is
bound to time and death.
1 *That . . . men:* Ireland, part of the time-bound world.

II

An aged man is but a paltry thing,
A tattered coat upon a stick, unless   10
Soul clap its hands and sing, and louder sing
For every tatter in its mortal dress,
Nor is there singing school but studying
Monuments of its own magnificence;
And therefore I have sailed the seas and come   15
To the holy city of Byzantium.

III

O sages standing in God's holy fire
As in the gold mosaic of a wall,
Come from the holy fire, perne in a gyre,°
And be the singing-masters of my soul.   20
Consume my heart away; sick with desire
And fastened to a dying animal
It knows not what it is; and gather me
Into the artifice of eternity.

IV

Once out of nature I shall never take   25
My bodily form from any natural thing,
But such a form as Grecian goldsmiths make
Of hammered gold and gold enameling
To keep a drowsy Emperor awake;°
Or set upon a golden bough° to sing   30
To lords and ladies of Byzantium
Of what is past, or passing, or to come.

19 *perne in a gyre:* Bobbin making a spiral pattern.   27–29 *such . . . awake:* "I have read somewhere that in the Emperor's palace at Byzantium was a tree made of gold and silver, and artificial birds that sang." [Yeats's note.]   30 *golden bough:* In Greek legend, Aeneas had to pluck a golden bough from a tree in order to descend into Hades. As soon as the bough was plucked, another grew in its place.

WILLIAM BUTLER YEATS (1865–1939)

Crazy Jane Talks with the Bishop   *1933*

I met the Bishop on the road
And much said he and I.
"Those breasts are flat and fallen now,
Those veins must soon be dry;
Live in a heavenly mansion,   5
Not in some foul sty."

"Fair and foul are near of kin,
And fair needs foul," I cried.
"My friends are gone, but that's a truth
Nor grave nor bed denied,   10
Learned in bodily lowliness
And in the heart's pride.

"A woman can be proud and stiff
When on love intent;
But Love has pitched his mansion in   15
The place of excrement;
For nothing can be sole or whole
That has not been rent."

Critical Thinking and Writing about Poetry

26

Critical Strategies
for Reading

Great literature is simply language
charged with meaning to the utmost
possible degree.
— EZRA POUND

National Portrait
Gallery, London.

The answers you get from literature
depend upon the questions you pose.
— MARGARET ATWOOD

© Sophie Bassouls/CORBIS
SYGMA.

CRITICAL THINKING

Maybe this has happened to you: the assignment is to consider a work, let's
say Nathaniel Hawthorne's *The Scarlet Letter,* and write an analysis of some
aspect of it that interests you, taking into account critical sources that
comment on and interpret the work. You cheerfully
begin research in the library but quickly find yourself
bewildered by several seemingly unrelated articles. The
first traces the thematic significance of images of light
and darkness in the novel; the second makes a case for
Hester Prynne as a liberated woman; the third argues that Arthur Dimmes-
dale's guilt is a projection of Hawthorne's own emotions; and the fourth
analyzes the introduction, "The Custom House," as an attack on bourgeois

Web Explore
the critical approaches
in this chapter on
LiterActive or at
bedfordstmartins.com/
rewritinglit.

values. These disparate treatments may seem random and capricious — a confirmation of your worst suspicions that interpretations of literature are hit-or-miss excursions into areas that you know little about or didn't know even existed. But if you understand that the articles are written from different perspectives — formalist, feminist, psychological, and Marxist — and that the purpose of each is to enhance your understanding of the work by discussing a particular element of it, then you can see that their varying strategies represent potentially interesting ways of opening up the text that might otherwise never have occurred to you. There are many ways to approach a text, and a useful first step is to develop a sense of direction, an understanding of how a perspective — your own or a critic's — shapes a discussion of a text.

This chapter offers an introduction to critical approaches to literature by outlining a variety of strategies for reading poetry, fiction, or drama. The emphasis is, of course, on poetry, and to that end the approaches focus on Robert Frost's "Mending Wall" (p. 370); a rereading of that well-known poem will equip you for the discussions that follow. In addition to the emphasis on this poem to illustrate critical approaches, some fiction and drama examples are also included along the way to demonstrate how these critical approaches can be applied to any genre. These strategies include approaches that have long been practiced by readers who have used, for example, the insights gleaned from biography and history to illuminate literary works as well as more recent approaches, such as those used by feminist, reader-response, and deconstructionist critics. Each of these perspectives is sensitive to image, symbol, tone, irony, and other literary elements that you have been studying, but each also casts those elements in a special light. The formalist approach emphasizes how the elements within a work achieve their effects, whereas biographical and psychological approaches lead outward from the work to consider the author's life and other writings. Even broader approaches, such as historical and sociological perspectives, connect the work to historic, social, and economic forces. Mythological readings represent the broadest approach, because they discuss the cultural and universal responses readers have to a work.

Any given strategy raises its own types of questions and issues while seeking particular kinds of evidence to support itself. An awareness of the assumptions and methods that inform an approach can help you to understand better the validity and value of a given critic's strategy for making sense of a work. More important, such an understanding can widen and deepen the responses of your own reading.

The critical thinking that goes into understanding a professional critic's approach to a work should not be foreign to you because you have already used essentially the same kind of thinking to understand the work itself. The skills you have developed to produce a literary *analysis* that, for example, describes how a character, symbol, or rhyme scheme supports a theme are also useful for reading literary criticism, because such skills allow you to keep track of how the parts of a critical approach create a particular reading of a literary work. When you analyze a poem, story, or play by closely examining how its various elements relate to the whole, your *interpretation* — your articulation of what the work means to you as supported by an analysis of its elements — necessarily involves choosing what you focus on in the work. The same is true of professional critics.

Critical readings presuppose choices in the kinds of material that are discussed. An analysis of the setting of Robert Frost's "Home Burial" (p. 372) would probably bring into focus the oppressive environment of the couple's domestic life rather than, say, the economic history of New England farming. The economic history of New England farming might be useful to a Marxist critic concerned with how class is revealed in "Home Burial," but for a formalist critic interested in identifying the unifying structures of the poem such information would be irrelevant.

The Perspectives, Complementary Readings, and Critical Case Study in this anthology offer opportunities to read critics who are using a wide variety of approaches to analyze and interpret texts. In the critical case study on T. S. Eliot's "The Love Song of J. Alfred Prufrock" (Chapter 17), for instance, Elisabeth Schneider offers a biographical interpretation of Prufrock by suggesting that Eliot shared some of his character's sensibilities. In contrast, Michael L. Baumann argues that Prufrock's character can be understood through a close examination of the poem's images. Each of these critics raises different questions, examines different evidence, and makes different assumptions to interpret Prufrock's character. Being aware of those differences — teasing them out so that you can see how they lead to competing conclusions — is a useful way to analyze the analysis itself. What is left out of an interpretation is sometimes as significant as what is included. As you read the critics, it's worth reminding yourself that your own critical thinking skills can help you to determine the usefulness of a particular approach.

The following overview is neither exhaustive in the types of critical approaches covered nor complete in its presentation of the complexities inherent in them, but it should help you to develop an appreciation of the intriguing possibilities that attend literary interpretation. The emphasis in this chapter is on ways of thinking about literature rather than on daunting lists of terms, names, and movements. Although a working knowledge of critical schools may be valuable and necessary for a fully informed use of a given critical approach, the aim here is more modest and practical. This chapter is no substitute for the shelves of literary criticism that can be found in your library, but it does suggest how readers using different perspectives organize their responses to texts.

The summaries of critical approaches that follow are descriptive, not evaluative. Each approach has its advantages and limitations, but those matters are best left to further study. Like literary artists, critics have their personal values, tastes, and styles. The appropriateness of a specific critical approach will depend, at least in part, on the nature of the literary work under discussion as well as on your own sensibilities and experience. However, any approach, if it is to enhance understanding, requires sensitivity, tact, and an awareness of the various literary elements of the text, including, of course, its use of language.

Successful critical approaches avoid eccentric decodings that reveal so-called hidden meanings; if there is no apparent evidence of a given meaning, this is because it is nonexistent in the text, not because the author has attempted to hide it in some way. For a parody of this sort of critical excess, see "A Parodic Interpretation of 'Stopping by Woods on a Snowy Evening'" (p. 391), in which Herbert R. Coursen Jr. has some fun with a Robert Frost poem and Santa Claus while making a serious point about the dangers of overly ingenious readings. Literary criticism attempts, like any valid hypothesis, to account for phenomena — the text — without distorting or misrepresenting what it describes.

THE LITERARY CANON: DIVERSITY AND CONTROVERSY

Before looking at the various critical approaches discussed in this chapter, it makes sense to consider first which literature has been traditionally considered worthy of such analysis. The discussion in the Introduction called The Changing Literary Canon (p. 6) may have already alerted you to the fact that in recent years many more works by women, minorities, and writers from around the world have been considered by scholars, critics, and teachers to merit serious study and inclusion in what is known as the literary canon. This increasing diversity has been celebrated by those who believe that multiculturalism taps new sources for the discovery of great literature while raising significant questions about language, culture, and society. At the same time, others have perceived this diversity as a threat to the established, traditional canon of Western culture.

The debates concerning whose work should be read, taught, and written about have sometimes been acrimonious as well as lively and challenging. Bitter arguments have been waged on campuses and in the media over what has come to be called *political correctness*. Two main camps have formed around these debates: liberals and conservatives (the appropriateness of these terms is debatable but the oppositional positioning is unmistakable). The liberals are said to insist on encouraging tolerant attitudes about race, class, gender, and sexual orientation and opening up the curriculum to multicultural texts from Asia, Africa, Latin America, and elsewhere. These revisionists, seeking a change in traditional attitudes, are sometimes accused of intimidating the opposition into silence and substituting ideological dogma for reason and truth. The conservatives are also portrayed as ideologues; in their efforts to preserve what they regard as the best from the past, they refuse to admit that Western classics, mostly written by white male Europeans, represent only a portion of human experience. These traditionalists are seen as advocating values that are neither universal nor eternal but merely privileged and entrenched. Conservatives are charged with refusing to acknowledge that their values also represent a political agenda, which is implicit in their preference for the works of canonical authors such as Homer, Virgil, Shakespeare, Milton, Tolstoy, and Faulkner. The reductive and contradictory nature of this national debate between liberals and conservatives has been neatly summed up by Katha Pollitt: "Read the conservatives' list and produce a nation of sexists and racists — or a nation of philosopher kings. Read the liberals' list and produce a nation of spiritual relativists — or a nation of open-minded world citizens" ("Canon to the Right of Me . . . ," *The Nation,* Sept. 23, 1991, p. 330).

These troubling and extreme alternatives can be avoided, of course, if the issues are not approached from such absolutist positions. Solutions to these issues cannot be suggested in this limited space, and, no doubt, solutions will evolve over time, but we can at least provide a perspective. Books — regardless of what list they are about — are not likely to unite a fragmented nation or to disunite a unified one. It is perhaps more useful and accurate to see issues of canonicity as reflecting political changes rather than as the primary causes of them. This is not to say that books don't have an impact on readers — that *Uncle Tom's Cabin,* for instance, did not galvanize antislavery sentiments in nineteenth-century America — but that book lists do not by themselves preserve or destroy the status quo.

It's worth noting that the curricula of American universities have always undergone significant and, some would say, wrenching changes. Only a little more than one hundred years ago there was strong opposition to teaching English, as well as other modern languages, alongside programs dominated by Greek and Latin. Only since the 1920s has American literature been made a part of the curriculum, and just five decades ago writers such as Emily Dickinson, Robert Frost, W. H. Auden, and Marianne Moore were regarded with the same raised eyebrows that today might be raised about contemporary writers such as Sharon Olds, Martín Espada, Rita Dove, or Billy Collins. New voices do not drown out the past; they build on and eventually become part of it as newer writers take their place alongside them. Neither resistance to change nor a denial of the past will have its way with the canon. Though both impulses are widespread, neither is likely to dominate the other because there are too many reasonable, practical readers and teachers who instead of replacing Shakespeare, Frost, and other canonical writers have supplemented them with writers who have been neglected because they were from non-Western cultures or because they represented disenfranchised segments of the Western canon. These readers experience the current debates about the canon not as a binary opposition but as an opportunity to explore important questions about continuity and change in our literature, culture, and society.

FORMALIST STRATEGIES

Formalist critics focus on the formal elements of a work—its language, structure, and tone. A formalist reads literature as an independent work of art rather than as a reflection of the author's state of mind or as a representation of a moment in history. Historic influences on a work, an author's intentions, or anything else outside the work are generally not treated by formalists (this is particularly true of the most famous modern formalists, known as the ***New Critics,*** who dominated American criticism from the 1940s through the 1960s). Instead, formalists offer intense examinations of the relationship between form and meaning within a work, emphasizing the subtle complexity of how a work is arranged. This kind of close reading pays special attention to what are often described as *intrinsic* matters in a literary work—diction, irony, paradox, metaphor, and symbol, for instance—as well as larger elements, such as plot, characterization, and narrative technique. Formalists examine how these elements work together to give a coherent shape to a work while contributing to its meaning. The answers to the questions formalists raise about how the shape and effect of a work are related come from the work itself. Other kinds of information that go beyond the text—biography, history, politics, economics, and so on—are typically regarded by formalists as *extrinsic* matters, which are considerably less important than what goes on within the autonomous text.

Poetry especially lends itself to close readings, because a poem's relative brevity allows for detailed analyses of nearly all of its words and how they achieve their effects. For a sample formalist reading of how a pervasive sense of death is worked into a poem, see "A Reading of Dickinson's 'There's a certain Slant of light'" (p. 703).

Formalist strategies are also useful for analyzing drama and fiction. In his well-known essay "The World of *Hamlet*," Maynard Mack explores Hamlet's character and predicament by paying close attention to the words and images that Shakespeare uses to build a world in which appearances mask reality and mystery is embedded in scene after scene. Mack points to recurring terms, such as *apparition, seems, assume,* and *put on,* as well as repeated images of acting, clothing, disease, and painting, to indicate the treacherous surface world Hamlet must penetrate to get to the truth. This pattern of deception provides an organizing principle around which Mack offers a reading of the entire play:

> Hamlet's problem, in its crudest form, is simply the problem of the avenger: he must carry out the injunction of the ghost and kill the king. But this problem . . . is presented in terms of a certain kind of world. The ghost's injunction to act becomes so inextricably bound up for Hamlet with the character of the world in which the action must be taken—its mysteriousness, its baffling appearances, its deep consciousness of infection, frailty, and loss—that he cannot come to terms with either without coming to terms with both.

Although Mack places *Hamlet* in the tradition of revenge tragedy, his reading of the play emphasizes Shakespeare's arrangement of language rather than literary history as a means of providing an interpretation that accounts for various elements of the play. Mack's formalist strategy explores how diction reveals meaning and how repeated words and images evoke and reinforce important thematic significances.

A formalist reading of Robert Frost's "Mending Wall" leads to an examination of the tensions produced by the poem's diction, repetitions, and images that take us beyond a merely literal reading. The speaker describes how every spring he and his neighbor walk beside the stone wall bordering their respective farms to replace the stones that have fallen during winter. As they repair the wall, the speaker wonders what purpose the wall serves, given that "My apple trees will never get across / And eat the cones under his pines"; his neighbor, however, "only says, 'Good fences make good neighbors.'" The moment described in the poem is characteristic of the rural New England life that constitutes so much of Frost's poetry, but it is also typical of how he uses poetry as a means of "saying one thing in terms of another," as he once put it in an essay titled "Education by Poetry."

Just as the speaker teases his neighbor with the idea that the apple trees won't disturb the pines, so too does Frost tease the reader into looking at what it is "that doesn't love a wall." Frost's use of language in the poem does not simply consist of homespun casual phrases enlisted to characterize rural neighbors. From the opening lines, the "Something . . . that doesn't love a wall" and "That sends the frozen-ground-swell under it" is, on the literal level, a frost heave that causes the stones to tumble from the wall. But after several close readings of the poem, we can see the implicit pun in these lines suggesting that it is *Frost* who objects to the wall, thus aligning the poet's perspective with the speaker's. A careful examination of some of the other formal elements in the poem supports this reading.

In contrast to the imaginative wit of the speaker who raises fundamental questions about the purpose of any wall, the images associated with his neighbor indicate that he is a traditionalist who "will not go behind his father's saying." Moreover, the neighbor moves "like an old-stone savage" in "darkness" that is attributed to his rigid, tradition-bound, walled-in sensibilities rather than to "the shade of trees." Whereas the speaker's wit and intelligence are manifested by his willingness to question the necessity or desirability of "walling in or walling out" anything, his benighted neighbor can only repeat again that "good fences make good neighbors." The stone-heavy darkness of the neighbor's mind is emphasized by the contrasting light wit and agility of the speaker, who speculates: "Before I built a wall I'd ask to know . . . to whom I was like to give offense." The pun on the final word of this line makes a subtle but important connection between giving "offense" and creating "a fence." Frost's careful use of diction, repetition, and images deftly reveals and reinforces thematic significances suggesting that the stone wall serves as a symbol of isolation, confinement, fear, and even savagery. The neighbor's conservative, tradition-bound, mindless support of the wall is a foil to the speaker's — read Frost's — poetic, liberal response, which imagines and encourages the possibilities of greater freedom and brotherhood.

Although this brief discussion of some of the formal elements of Frost's poem does not describe all there is to say about how they produce an effect and create meaning, it does suggest the kinds of questions, issues, and evidence that a formalist strategy might raise in providing a close reading of the text itself.

BIOGRAPHICAL STRATEGIES

A knowledge of an author's life can help readers understand his or her work more fully. Events in a work might follow actual events in a writer's life just as characters might be based on people known by the author. Ernest Hemingway's "Soldier's Home" is a short story about the difficulties of a World War I veteran named Krebs returning to his small hometown in Oklahoma, where he cannot adjust to the pious assumptions of his family and neighbors. He refuses to accept their innocent blindness to the horrors he has witnessed during the war. They have no sense of the brutality of modern life; instead they insist he resume his life as if nothing has happened. There is plenty of biographical evidence to indicate that Krebs's unwillingness to lie about his war experiences reflects Hemingway's own responses on his return to Oak Park, Illinois, in 1919. Krebs, like Hemingway, finds he has to leave the sentimentality, repressiveness, and smug complacency that threaten to render his experiences unreal: "the world they were in was not the world he was in."

An awareness of Hemingway's own war experiences and subsequent disillusionment with his hometown can be readily developed through available biographies, letters, and other of his written works. Consider, for example, this passage from *By Force of Will: The Life and Art of Ernest Hemingway*, in which Scott Donaldson describes Hemingway's response to World War I:

> In poems, as in [*A Farewell to Arms*], Hemingway expressed his distaste for the first war. The men who had to fight the war did not die well:
>
> > Soldiers pitch and cough and twitch —
> > > All the world roars red and black;
> > Soldiers smother in a ditch,
> > > Choking through the whole attack.
>
> And what did they die for? They were "sucked in" by empty words and phrases —
>
> > King and country,
> > Christ Almighty,

And the rest,
Patriotism,
Democracy,
Honor—

which spelled death. The bitterness of these outbursts derived from the distinction Hemingway drew between the men on the line and those who started the wars that others had to fight

This kind of information can help to deepen our understanding of just how empathetically Krebs is presented in the story. Relevant facts about Hemingway's life will not make "Soldier's Home" a better written story than it is, but such information can make clearer the source of Hemingway's convictions and how his own experiences inform his major concerns as a storyteller.

Some formalist critics—some New Critics, for example—argue that interpretation should be based exclusively on internal evidence rather than on any biographical information outside the work. They argue that it is not possible to determine an author's intention and that the work must stand by itself. Although this is a useful caveat for keeping the work in focus, a reader who finds biography relevant would argue that biography can at the very least serve as a control on interpretation. A reader who, for example, finds Krebs at fault for not subscribing to the values of his hometown would be misreading the story, given both its tone and the biographical information available about the author. Although the narrator never *tells* the reader that Krebs is right or wrong for leaving town, the story's tone sides with his view of things. If, however, someone were to argue otherwise, insisting that the tone is not decisive and that Krebs's position is problematic, a reader familiar with Hemingway's own reactions could refute that argument with a powerful confirmation of Krebs's instincts to withdraw. Hence, many readers find biography useful for interpretation.

However, it is also worth noting that biographical information can complicate a work. For example, readers who interpret "Mending Wall" as a celebration of an iconoclastic sensibility that seeks to break down the psychological barriers and physical walls that separate human beings may be surprised to learn that very few of Frost's other writings support this view. His life was filled with emotional turmoil; it has been described by a number of biographers as egocentric and vindictive rather than generous and open to others. He once commented that "I always hold that we get forward as much by hating as by loving." Indeed, many facts about Frost's life—as well as many of the speakers in his poems—are typified by depression, alienation, tension, suspicion, jealous competitiveness, and suicidal tendencies. Instead of challenging wall-builders, Frost more characteristically built walls of distrust around himself among his family, friends, and colleagues. In this biographical context, it is especially noteworthy that it is the speaker of "Mending Wall" who alone repairs the damage done to the walls by hunters, and it is he who initiates each spring the rebuilding of the wall. However much he may question its value, the speaker does, after all, rebuild the wall between himself and his neighbor. This biographical approach raises provocative questions about the text. Does the poem suggest that boundaries and walls are, in fact, necessary? Are walls a desirable foundation for relationships between people? Although these and other questions raised by a biographical approach cannot be answered here, this kind of biographical perspective certainly adds to the possibilities of interpretation.

Sometimes biographical information does not change our understanding so much as it enriches our appreciation of a work. It matters, for instance, that much of John Milton's poetry, so rich in visual imagery, was written after he became blind; and it is just as significant — to shift to a musical example — that a number of Ludwig van Beethoven's greatest works, including the Ninth Symphony, were composed after he succumbed to total deafness.

PSYCHOLOGICAL STRATEGIES

Given the enormous influence that Sigmund Freud's psychoanalytic theories had on twentieth-century interpretations of human behavior, it is nearly inevitable that most people have some familiarity with his ideas about dreams, unconscious desires, and sexual repression, as well as his terms for different aspects of the psyche — the id, ego, and superego. Psychological approaches to literature draw on Freud's theories and other psychoanalytic theories to understand more fully the text, the writer, and the reader. Critics use such approaches to explore the motivations of characters and the symbolic meanings of events, while biographers speculate about a writer's own motivations — conscious or unconscious — in a literary work. Psychological approaches are also used to describe and analyze the reader's personal responses to a text.

Although it is not feasible to explain psychoanalytic terms and concepts in so brief a space as this, it is possible to suggest the nature of a psychological approach. It is a strategy based heavily on the idea of the existence of a human unconscious — those impulses, desires, and feelings about which a person is unaware but that influence emotions and behavior.

Central to a number of psychoanalytic critical readings is Freud's concept of what he called the *Oedipus complex,* a term derived from Sophocles' tragedy *Oedipus the King.* This complex is predicated on a boy's unconscious rivalry with his father for his mother's love and his desire to eliminate his father in order to take his father's place with his mother. The female version of the psychological conflict is known as the *Electra complex,* a term used to describe a daughter's unconscious rivalry for her father. The name comes from a Greek legend about Electra, who avenged the death of her father, Agamemnon, by killing her mother. In *The Interpretation of Dreams,*

Freud explains why *Oedipus the King* "moves a modern audience no less than it did the contemporary Greek one." What unites their powerful attraction to the play is an unconscious response:

> There must be something which makes a voice within us ready to recognize the compelling force of destiny in the *Oedipus*. . . . His destiny moves us only because it might have been ours — because the oracle laid the same curse upon us before our birth as upon him. It is the fate of all of us, perhaps, to direct our first sexual impulse towards our mother and our first hatred and our first murderous wish against our father. Our dreams convince us that this is so. King Oedipus, who slew his father Laius and married his mother Jocasta, merely shows us the fulfillment of our own childhood wishes . . . and we shrink back from him with the whole force of the repression by which those wishes have since that time been held down within us.

In this passage Freud interprets the unconscious motives of Sophocles in writing the play, Oedipus in acting within it, and the audience in responding to it.

A further application of the Oedipus complex can be observed in a classic interpretation of *Hamlet* by Ernest Jones, who used this concept to explain why Hamlet delays in avenging his father's death. This reading has been tightly summarized by Norman Holland, a recent psychoanalytic critic, in *The Shakespearean Imagination*. Holland shapes the issues into four major components:

> One, people over the centuries have been unable to say why Hamlet delays in killing the man who murdered his father and married his mother. Two, psychoanalytic experience shows that every child wants to do just exactly that. Three, Hamlet delays because he cannot punish Claudius for doing what he himself wished to do as a child and, unconsciously, still wishes to do: he would be punishing himself. Four, the fact that this wish is unconscious explains why people could not explain Hamlet's delay.

Although the Oedipus complex is, of course, not relevant to all psychological interpretations of literature, interpretations involving this complex do offer a useful example of how psychoanalytic critics tend to approach a text.

The situation in Frost's "Mending Wall" is not directly related to an Oedipus complex, but the poem has been read as a conflict in which the "father's saying" represents the repressiveness of a patriarchal order that challenges the speaker's individual poetic consciousness. "Mending Wall" has also been read as another kind of struggle with repression. In "Up against the 'Mending Wall': The Psychoanalysis of a Poem by Frost" Edward Jayne offers a detailed reading of the poem as "the overriding struggle to suppress latent homosexual attraction between two men separated by a wall" (*College English* 1973). Jayne reads the poem as the working out of "unconscious homosexual inclinations largely repugnant to Frost and his need to divert and sublimate them." Regardless of whether a reader finds these arguments convincing, it is clear that the poem does have something to do with powerful forms of repression. And what about the reader's response? How might a psychological approach account for different responses from readers who argue that the poem calls for either a world that includes walls or one that dismantles them? One needn't be versed in psychoanalytic terms to entertain this question.

HISTORICAL STRATEGIES

Historians sometimes use literature as a window onto the past, because literature frequently provides the nuances of a historic period that cannot be readily perceived through other sources. The characters in Harriet Beecher Stowe's novel *Uncle Tom's Cabin* (1852) display, for example, a complex set of white attitudes toward blacks in mid-nineteenth-century America that is absent from more traditional historic documents such as census statistics or state laws. Another way of approaching the relationship between literature and history, however, is to use history as a means of understanding a literary work more clearly. The plot pattern of pursuit, escape, and capture in nineteenth-century slave narratives had a significant influence on Stowe's plotting of action in *Uncle Tom's Cabin*. This relationship demonstrates that the writing contemporary to an author is an important element of the history that helps to shape a work. There are many ways to talk about a work's historical and cultural dimensions. Such readings treat a literary text as a document reflecting, producing, or being produced by the social conditions of its time, giving equal focus to the social milieu and the work itself. Four historical strategies that have been especially influential are literary history criticism, Marxist criticism, new historicist criticism, and cultural criticism.

Literary History Criticism

Literary historians situate work in the context in which it was written. Hence a literary historian might examine mid-nineteenth-century abolitionist attitudes toward blacks to determine whether Stowe's novel is representative of those views or significantly to the right or left of them. Such a study might even indicate how closely the book reflects racial attitudes of twentieth-century readers. A work of literature may transcend time to the extent that it addresses the concerns of readers over a span of decades or centuries, but it remains for the literary historian a part of the past in which it was composed, a past that can reveal more fully a work's language, ideas, and purposes.

Literary historians move beyond both the facts of an author's personal life and the text itself to the social and intellectual currents in which the author composed the work. They place the work in the context of its time (as do many critical biographers who write "life and times" studies), and sometimes they make connections with other literary works that may have influenced the author. The basic strategy of literary historians is to illuminate the historic background in order to shed light on some aspect of the work itself.

In Hemingway's "Soldier's Home" we learn that Krebs had been at Belleau Wood, Soissons, the Champagne, St. Mihiel, and the Argonne. Although nothing is said of these battles in the story, they were among the most bloody battles of the war; the wholesale butchery and staggering casualties incurred by both sides make credible the way Krebs's unstated but lingering memories have turned him into a psychological prisoner of war. Knowing something about the ferocity of those battles helps us account for Krebs's response in the story. Moreover, we can more fully appreciate Hemingway's refusal to have Krebs lie about the realities of war for the folks back home if we are aware of the numerous poems, stories, and plays published during World War I that presented war as a glorious, manly, transcendent sacrifice for God and country. Juxtaposing those works with "Soldier's Home" brings the differences into sharp focus.

Similarly, a reading of William Blake's poem "London" (p. 119) is less complete if we do not know of the horrific social conditions — the poverty, disease, exploitation, and hypocrisy — that characterized the city Blake laments in the late eighteenth century.

One last example: the potential historical meaning of the wall that is the subject of Frost's "Mending Wall" might be more distinctly seen if it is placed in the context of its publication date, 1914, when the world was on the verge of collapsing into the violent political landscape of World War I. The insistence that "Good fences make good neighbors" suggests a grim, ironic tone in the context of European nationalist hostilities that seemed to be moving inexorably toward war. The larger historical context for the poem would have been more apparent to its readers contemporary with World War I, but a historical reconstruction of the horrific tensions produced by shifting national borders and shattered walls during the war can shed some light on the larger issues that may be at stake in the poem. Moreover, an examination of Frost's attitudes toward the war and America's potential involvement in it could help to produce a reading of the meaning and value of a world with or without walls.

Marxist Criticism

Marxist readings developed from the heightened interest in radical reform during the 1930s, when many critics looked to literature as a means of furthering proletarian social and economic goals, based largely on the writings of Karl Marx. **Marxist critics** focus on the ideological content of a work — its explicit and implicit assumptions and values about matters such as culture, race, class, and power. Marxist studies typically aim at not only revealing and clarifying ideological issues but also correcting social injustices. Some Marxist critics have used literature to describe the competing socioeconomic interests that too often advance capitalist money and power rather than socialist morality and justice. They argue that criticism, like literature, is essentially political because it either challenges or supports economic oppression. Even if criticism attempts to ignore class conflicts, it is politicized, according to Marxists, because it supports the status quo.

It is not surprising that Marxist critics pay more attention to the content and themes of literature than to its form. A Marxist critic would more likely be concerned with the exploitive economic forces that cause Willy Loman to feel trapped in Arthur Miller's *Death of a Salesman* than with the playwright's use of nonrealistic dramatic techniques to reveal Loman's inner thoughts. Similarly, a Marxist reading of Frost's "Mending Wall" might draw on the poet's well-known conservative criticisms of President Franklin Delano Roosevelt's New Deal during the 1930s as a means of reading conservative ideology into the poem. Frost's deep suspicions of collective enterprise might suggest to a Marxist that the wall represents the status quo, that is, a capitalist construction that unnaturally divides individuals (in this case, the poem's speaker from his neighbor) and artificially defies nature. Complicit in their own oppression, both farmers, to a lesser and greater degree, accept the idea that "good fences make good neighbors," thereby maintaining and perpetuating an unnatural divisive order that oppresses and is mistakenly perceived as necessary and beneficial. A Marxist reading would see the speaker's and neighbor's conflict as not only an individual issue but also part of a larger class struggle.

New Historicist Criticism

Since the 1960s a development in historical approaches to literature known as **new historicism** has emphasized the interaction between the historic context of a work and a modern reader's understanding and interpretation of the work. In contrast to many traditional literary historians, however, new historicists attempt to describe the culture of a period by reading many different kinds of texts that traditional historians might have previously left for sociologists and anthropologists. New historicists attempt to define a period in all of its dimensions, including political, economic, social, and esthetic concerns. For a greater understanding of "Mending Wall," these considerations could be used to explain something about the nature of rural New England life early in the twentieth century. The process of mending the stone wall authentically suggests how this tedious job simultaneously draws the two men together and keeps them apart. Pamphlets and other contemporary writings about farming and maintaining property lines could offer insight into either the necessity or the uselessness of the spring wall-mending rituals. A new historicist might find useful how advice offered in texts about running a farm reflect or refute the speaker's or neighbor's competing points of view in the poem.

New historicist criticism acknowledges more fully than traditional historical approaches the competing nature of readings of the past and thereby tends to offer new emphases and perspectives. New historicism reminds us that there is not only one historic context for "Mending Wall." The year before Frost died, he visited Moscow as a cultural ambassador from the United States. During this 1962 visit — only one year after the Soviet Union's construction of the Berlin Wall — he read "Mending Wall" to his Russian audience. Like the speaker in that poem, Frost clearly enjoyed the "mischief" of that moment, and a new historicist would clearly find intriguing the way the poem was both intended and received in so volatile a context. By emphasizing that historical perceptions are governed, at least in part, by our own concerns and preoccupations, new historicists sensitize us to the fact that the history on which we choose to focus is colored by being reconstructed from our own present moment. This reconstructed history affects our reading of texts.

Cultural Criticism

Cultural critics, like new historicists, focus on the historical contexts of a literary work, but they pay particular attention to popular manifestations of social, political, and economic contexts. Popular culture — mass-produced and consumed cultural artifacts, today ranging from advertising to popular fiction to television to rock music — and "high" culture are given equal emphasis. A cultural critic might be interested in looking at how Baz Luhrmann's movie version of *Romeo and Juliet* (1996) was influenced by the fragmentary nature of MTV videos. Adding the "low" art of everyday life to "high" art opens up previously unexpected and unexplored areas of criticism. Cultural critics use widely eclectic strategies drawn from new historicism, psychology, gender studies, and deconstructionism (to name only a handful of approaches) to analyze not only literary texts but also radio talk shows, comic strips, calendar art, commercials, travel guides, and baseball cards. Because all human activity falls within the ken of cultural criticism, nothing is too minor or major, obscure or pervasive, to escape the range of its analytic vision.

Cultural criticism also includes *postcolonial criticism,* the study of cultural behavior and expression in relationship to the formerly colonized world. Postcolonial criticism refers to the analysis of literary works by writers from countries and cultures that at one time were controlled by colonizing powers — such as Indian writers during or after British colonial rule. The term also refers to the analysis of literary works written about colonial cultures by writers from the colonizing country. Many of these kinds of analyses point out how writers from colonial powers sometimes misrepresent colonized cultures by reflecting more of their own values: Joseph Conrad's *Heart of Darkness* (published in 1899) represents African culture differently from the way Chinua Achebe's *Things Fall Apart* (1958) does, for example. Cultural criticism and postcolonial criticism represent a broad range of approaches to examining race, gender, and class in historical contexts in a variety of cultures.

A cultural critic's approach to Frost's "Mending Wall" might emphasize how the poem reflects New England farmers' attitudes toward hunters, or it might examine how popular poems about stone walls contemporary to "Mending Wall" endorse such wall building instead of making problematic the building of walls between neighbors as Frost does. Each of these perspectives can serve to create a wider and more informed understanding of the poem.

GENDER STRATEGIES

Gender critics explore how ideas about men and women — what is masculine and feminine — can be regarded as socially constructed by particular cultures. According to some critics, sex is determined by simple biological and anatomical categories of male or female, and gender is determined by a culture's values. Thus ideas about gender and what constitutes masculine and feminine behavior are created by cultural institutions and conditioning. A gender critic might, for example, focus on Frost's characterization of the narrator's neighbor as an emotionally frozen son of a father who overshadowed his psychological and social development. The narrator's rigid masculinity would then be seen as a manifestation of socially constructed gender identity in the 1910s. Gender criticism expands categories and definitions of what is masculine or feminine and tends to regard sexuality as more complex than merely masculine or feminine, heterosexual or homosexual. Gender criticism, therefore, has come to include gay and lesbian criticism as well as feminist criticism. Although there are complex and sometimes problematic relationships among these approaches because some critics argue that heterosexuals and homosexuals are profoundly different biologically, gay and lesbian criticism, like feminist criticism, can be usefully regarded as a subset of gender criticism.

Feminist Criticism

Like Marxist critics, *feminist critics* would also be interested in examining the status quo in "Mending Wall," because they seek to correct or supplement what they regard as a predominantly male-dominated critical perspective with a feminist consciousness. Like other forms of sociological criticism, feminist criticism places literature in a social context, and, like those of Marxist criticism, its analyses often have sociopolitical purposes — purposes that might explain, for example, how images of women in literature reflect the patriarchal social forces that have impeded women's efforts to achieve full equality with men.

Feminists have analyzed literature by both men and women in an effort to understand literary representations of women as well as the writers and cultures that create them. Related to concerns about how gender affects the way men and women write about each other is an interest in whether women use language differently from the way men do. Consequently, feminist critics' approach to literature is characterized by the use of a broad range of disciplines — among them history, sociology, psychology, and linguistics — to provide a perspective sensitive to feminist issues.

A feminist approach to Frost's "Mending Wall" might initially appear to offer few possibilities, given that no women appear in the poem and that no mention or allusion is made about women. And that is precisely the point: the landscape presented in the poem is devoid of women. Traditional gender roles are evident in the poem because it is men, not women, who work outdoors building walls and who discuss the significance of their work. For a feminist critic, the wall might be read as a symbol of patriarchal boundaries that are defined exclusively by men. If the wall can be seen as a manifestation of the status quo built upon the "father's saying[s]," then mending the wall each year and keeping everything essentially the same — with women securely out of the picture — essentially benefits the established patriarchy. The boundaries are reconstructed and rationalized in the absence of any woman's potential efforts to offer an alternative to the boundaries imposed by the men's rebuilding of the wall. Perhaps one way of considering the value of a feminist perspective on this work can be discerned if a reader imagines the speaker or the neighbor as a woman and how that change might extend the parameters of their conversation about the value of the wall.

Gay and Lesbian Criticism

Gay and lesbian critics focus on a variety of issues, including how homosexuals are represented in literature, how they read literature, and whether sexuality and gender are culturally constructed or innate. Gay critics have produced new readings and discovered homosexual concerns in writers such as Herman Melville and Henry James, while lesbian critics have done the same with writers such as Emily Dickinson and Sylvia Plath. In "Mending Wall," some readers have found homosexual tensions between the narrator and his neighbor that are suppressed by both men as they build their wall to fence in forbidden and unbidden desires. Although gay and lesbian readings often raise significant interpretative controversies among critics, they have opened up provocative discussions of seemingly familiar texts.

MYTHOLOGICAL STRATEGIES

Mythological approaches to literature attempt to identify what in a work creates deep, universal responses in readers. Whereas psychological critics interpret the symbolic meanings of characters and actions in order to understand more fully the unconscious dimensions of an author's mind, a character's motivation, or a reader's response, mythological critics (also frequently referred to as archetypal critics) interpret the hopes, fears, and expectations of entire cultures.

In this context myth is not to be understood simply as referring to stories about imaginary gods who perform astonishing feats in the causes of love, jealousy, or hatred. Nor are myths to be judged as merely erroneous, primitive accounts of how nature runs its course and humanity its affairs. Instead, literary critics use myths as a strategy for understanding how human beings try to account for their lives symbolically. Myths can be a window onto a culture's deepest perceptions about itself, because myths attempt to explain what otherwise seems unexplainable: a people's origin, purpose, and destiny.

All human beings have a need to make sense of their lives, whether they are concerned about their natural surroundings, the seasons, sexuality, birth, death, or the very meaning of existence. Myths help people organize their experiences; these systems of belief (less formally held than religious or political tenets but no less important) embody a culture's assumptions and values. What is important to the mythological critic is not the validity or truth of those assumptions and values; what matters is that they reveal common human concerns.

It is not surprising that although the details of mythic stories vary enormously, the essential patterns are often similar, because these myths attempt to explain universal experiences. There are, for example, numerous myths that redeem humanity from permanent death through a hero's resurrection and rebirth. For Christians the resurrection of Jesus symbolizes the ultimate defeat of death and coincides with the rebirth of nature's fertility in spring. Features of this rebirth parallel the Greek myths of Adonis and Hyacinth, who die but are subsequently transformed into living flowers; there are also similarities that connect these stories to the reincarnation of the Indian Buddha or the rebirth of the Egyptian Osiris. To be sure, important differences exist among these stories, but each reflects a basic human need to limit the power of death and to hope for eternal life.

Mythological critics look for underlying, recurrent patterns in literature that reveal universal meanings and basic human experiences for readers regardless of when or where they live. The characters, images, and themes that symbolically embody these meanings and experiences are called ***archetypes.*** This term designates universal symbols, which evoke deep and perhaps unconscious responses in a reader because archetypes bring with them the heft of our hopes and fears since the beginning of human time. Surely one of the most powerfully compelling archetypes is the death/rebirth theme that relates the human life cycle to the cycle of the seasons. Many others could be cited and would be exhausted only after all human concerns were cataloged, but a few examples can suggest some of the range of plots, images, and characters addressed.

Among the most common literary archetypes are stories of quests, initiations, scapegoats, meditative withdrawals, descents to the underworld, and heavenly ascents. These stories are often filled with archetypal images: bodies of water that may symbolize the unconscious or eternity or baptismal rebirth; rising suns, suggesting reawakening and enlightenment; setting suns, pointing toward death; colors such as green, evocative of growth and fertility, or black, indicating chaos, evil, and death. Along the way are earth mothers, fatal women, wise old men, desert places, and paradisal gardens. No doubt your own reading has introduced you to any number of archetypal plots, images, and characters.

Mythological critics attempt to explain how archetypes are embodied in literary works. Employing various disciplines, these critics articulate the power a literary work has over us. Some critics are deeply grounded in classical literature, whereas others are more conversant with philology, anthropology, psychology, or cultural history. Whatever their emphases, however, mythological critics examine the elements of a work in order to make larger connections that explain the work's lasting appeal.

A mythological reading of Sophocles' *Oedipus the King*, for example, might focus on the relationship between Oedipus's role as a scapegoat and the plague and drought that threaten to destroy Thebes. The city is saved and the fertility of its fields restored only after the corruption is located in Oedipus. His subsequent atonement symbolically provides a kind of rebirth for the city. Thus the plot recapitulates ancient rites in which the well-being of a king was directly linked to the welfare of his people. If a leader were sick or corrupt, he had to be replaced in order to guarantee the health of the community.

A similar pattern can be seen in the rottenness that Shakespeare exposes in Hamlet's Denmark. *Hamlet* reveals an archetypal pattern similar to that of *Oedipus the King:* not until the hero sorts out the corruption in his world and in himself can vitality and health be restored in his world. Hamlet avenges his father's death and becomes a scapegoat in the process. When he fully accepts his responsibility to set things right, he is swept away along with the tide of intrigue and corruption that has polluted life in Denmark. The new order — established by Fortinbras at the play's end — is achieved precisely because Hamlet is willing and finally able to sacrifice himself in a necessary purgation of the diseased state.

These kinds of archetypal patterns exist potentially in any literary period. Frost's "Mending Wall," for example, is set in spring, an evocative season that marks the end of winter and earth's renewal. The action in the poem, however, does not lead to a celebration of new life and human community; instead there is for the poem's speaker and his neighbor an annual ritual to "set the wall between us once again" — a ritual that separates and divides human experience rather than unifying it. We can see that the rebuilding of the wall runs counter to nature itself because the stones are so round that "We have to use a spell to make them balance." The speaker also resists the wall and sets out to subvert it by toying with the idea of challenging his neighbor's assumption that "good fences make good neighbors," a seemingly ancient belief passed down through one "father's saying" to the next. The speaker, however, does not heroically overcome the neighbor's ritual; he merely points out that the wall is not needed where it is. The speaker's acquiescence results in the continuation of a ritual that confirms the old order rather than overthrowing the "old-stone savage," who demands the dark isolation and separateness associated with the "gaps" produced by winter's frost. The neighbor's old order prevails despite nature's and the speaker's protestations. From a mythological critic's perspective, the wall might itself be seen as a "gap," an unnatural disruption of nature and the human community.

READER-RESPONSE STRATEGIES

Reader-response criticism, as its name implies, focuses on the reader rather than the work itself. This approach to literature describes what goes on in the reader's mind during the process of reading a text. In a sense, all critical approaches (especially psychological and mythological criticism) concern themselves with a reader's response to literature, but there is a stronger emphasis in reader-response criticism on the reader's active construction of the text. Although many critical theories inform reader-response criticism, all ***reader-response critics*** aim to describe the reader's experience of a work: in effect we get a reading of the reader, who comes to the work with certain expectations and assumptions, which are either met or not met. Hence the consciousness of the reader — produced by reading the work — is the subject matter of reader-response critics. Just as writing is a creative act, so is reading, as it also produces a text.

Reader-response critics do not assume that a literary work is a finished product with fixed formal properties, as, for example, formalist critics do. Instead, the literary work is seen as an evolving creation of the reader's as he or she processes characters, plots, images, and other elements while reading. Some reader-response critics argue that this act of creative reading is, to a degree, controlled by the text, but it can produce many interpretations of the same text by different readers. There is no single definitive reading of a work, because the crucial assumption is that readers create rather than discover meanings in texts. Readers who have gone back to works they had read earlier in their lives often find that a later reading draws very different responses from them. What earlier seemed unimportant is now crucial; what at first seemed central is now barely worth noting. The reason, put simply, is that two different people have read the same text. Reader-response critics are not after the "correct" reading of the text or what the author presumably intended; instead they are interested in the reader's experience with the text.

These experiences change with readers; although the text remains the same, the readers do not. Social and cultural values influence readings, so that, for example, an avowed Marxist would be likely to come away from

Arthur Miller's *Death of a Salesman* with a very different view of American capitalism than that of, say, a successful sales representative, who might attribute Willy Loman's fall more to his character than to the American economic system. Moreover, readers from different time periods respond differently to texts. An Elizabethan — concerned perhaps with the stability of monarchical rule — might respond differently to Hamlet's problems than would a twenty-first-century reader well versed in psychology and concepts of what Freud called the Oedipus complex. This is not to say that anything goes, that Miller's play can be read as an amoral defense of cheating and rapacious business practices or that *Hamlet* is about the dangers of living away from home. The text does, after all, establish some limits that allow us to reject certain readings as erroneous. But reader-response critics do reject formalist approaches that describe a literary work as a self-contained object, the meaning of which can be determined without reference to any extrinsic matters, such as the social and cultural values assumed by either the author or the reader.

Reader-response criticism calls attention to how we read and what influences our readings. It does not attempt to define what a literary work means on the page but rather what it does to an informed reader — a reader who understands the language and conventions used in a given work. Reader-response criticism is not a rationale for mistaken or bizarre readings of works but an exploration of the possibilities for a plurality of readings shaped by the readers' experience with the text. This kind of strategy can help us understand how our responses are shaped by both the text and ourselves.

Frost's "Mending Wall" illustrates how reader-response critical strategies read the reader. Among the first readers of the poem in 1914, those who were eager to see the United States enter World War I might have been inclined to see the speaker as an imaginative thinker standing up for freedom rather than antiquated boundaries and sensibilities that don't know what they are "walling in or walling out." But for someone whose son could be sent to the trenches of France to fight the Germans, the phrase "Good fences make good neighbors" might sound less like an unthinking tradition and more like solid, prudent common sense. In each instance the reader's circumstances could have an effect on his or her assessment of the value of walls and fences. Certainly the Russians who listened to Frost's reading of "Mending Wall" in 1962, only one year after the construction of the Berlin Wall, had a very different response from the Americans who heard about Frost's reading and who relished the discomfort they thought the reading had caused the Russians.

By imagining different readers, we can imagine a variety of responses to the poem that are influenced by the readers' own impressions, memories, or experiences. Such imagining suggests the ways in which reader-response criticism opens up texts to a number of interpretations. As one final example, consider how readers' responses to "Mending Wall" would be affected if the poem were printed in two different magazines, read in the context of either the *Farmer's Almanac* or the *New Yorker.* What assumptions and beliefs would each magazine's readership be likely to bring to the poem? How do you think the respective experiences and values of each magazine's readers would influence their readings?

DECONSTRUCTIONIST STRATEGIES

Deconstructionist critics insist that literary works do not yield fixed, single meanings. They argue that there can be no absolute knowledge about anything because language can never say what we intend it to mean. Anything we write conveys meanings we did not intend, so the deconstructionist argument goes. Language is not a precise instrument but a power whose meanings are caught in an endless web of possibilities that cannot be untangled. Accordingly, any idea or statement that insists on being understood separately can ultimately be "deconstructed" to reveal its relations and connections to contradictory and opposite meanings.

Unlike other forms of criticism, deconstructionism seeks to destabilize meanings instead of establishing them. In contrast to formalists such as the New Critics, who closely examine a work in order to call attention to how its various components interact to establish a unified whole, deconstructionists try to show how a close examination of a text's language inevitably reveals conflicting, contradictory impulses that "deconstruct" or break down its apparent unity.

Although deconstructionists and New Critics both examine the language of a text closely, deconstructionists focus on the gaps and ambiguities that reveal a text's instability and indeterminacy, whereas New Critics look for patterns that explain how the text's fixed meaning is structured. Deconstructionists painstakingly examine the competing meanings within the text rather than attempt to resolve them into a unified whole.

The questions deconstructionists ask are aimed at discovering and describing how a variety of possible readings are generated by the elements of a text. In contrast to a New Critic's concerns about the ultimate meaning of a work, a deconstructionist's primary interest is in how the use of language — diction, tone, metaphor, symbol, and so on — yields only provisional, not definitive, meanings. Consider, for example, the following excerpt from an American Puritan poet, Anne Bradstreet. The excerpt is from "The Flesh and the Spirit" (1678), which consists of an allegorical debate between two sisters, the body and the soul. During the course of the debate, Flesh, a consummate materialist, insists that Spirit values ideas that do not exist and that her faith in idealism is both unwarranted and insubstantial in the face of the material values that earth has to offer — riches, fame, and physical pleasure. Spirit, however, rejects the materialistic worldly argument that the only ultimate reality is physical reality and pledges her faith in God:

Mine eye doth pierce the heavens and see
What is invisible to thee.
My garments are not silk nor gold,
Nor such like trash which earth doth hold,
But royal robes I shall have on,
More glorious than the glist'ring sun;
My crown not diamonds, pearls, and gold,
But such as angels' heads enfold.
The city where I hope to dwell,
There's none on earth can parallel;
The stately walls both high and strong,
Are made of precious jasper stone;
The gates of pearl, both rich and clear,
And angels are for porters there;
The streets thereof transparent gold,
Such as no eye did e'er behold;
A crystal river there doth run,
Which doth proceed from the Lamb's throne.

A deconstructionist would point out that Spirit's language — her use of material images such as jasper stone, pearl, gold, and crystal — cancels the explicit meaning of the passage by offering a supermaterialistic reward to the spiritually faithful. Her language, in short, deconstructs her intended meaning by using the same images that Flesh would use to describe the rewards of the physical world. A deconstructionist reading, then, reveals the impossibility of talking about the invisible and spiritual worlds without using materialistic (that is, metaphoric) language. Thus Spirit's very language demonstrates a contradiction and conflict in her conviction that the world of here and now must be rejected for the hereafter. Her language deconstructs her meaning.

Deconstructionists look for ways to question and extend the meanings of a text. In Frost's "Mending Wall," for example, the speaker presents himself as being on the side of the imaginative rather than hidebound, rigid responses to life. He seems to value freedom and openness rather than restrictions and narrowly defined limits. Yet his treatment of his Yankee farmer neighbor can be read as condescending and even smug in its superior attitude toward his neighbor's repeating his "father's saying," as if he were "an old-stone savage armed." The condescending attitude hardly suggests a robust sense of community and shared humanity. Moreover, for all the talk about unnecessary conventions and traditions, a deconstructionist would likely be quick to point out that Frost writes the poem in blank verse — unrhymed iambic pentameter — rather than free verse; hence the very regular rhythms of the narrator's speech may be seen to deconstruct its liberationist meaning. As difficult as it is controversial, deconstructionism is not easily summarized or paraphrased.

27

Reading and the
Writing Process

I can't write five words but that I change
seven.
— DOROTHY PARKER

© Bettmann/CORBIS.

THE PURPOSE AND VALUE
OF WRITING ABOUT LITERATURE

Introductory literature courses typically include three components: reading, discussion, and writing. Students usually find the readings a pleasure,
the class discussions a revelation, and the writing assignments — at least
initially — a little intimidating. Writing an analysis of the symbolic use of a
wall in Robert Frost's "Mending Wall" (p. 370) or in Herman Melville's
story "Bartleby, the Scrivener," for example, may seem considerably more
daunting than making a case for animal rights or analyzing a campus
newspaper editorial that calls for grade reforms. Like Bartleby, you might
want to respond with "I would prefer not to." Literary topics are not, however, all that different from the kinds of papers assigned in English composition courses; many of the same skills are required for both. Regardless of
the type of paper, you must develop a thesis and support it with evidence
in language that is clear and persuasive.

Whether the subject matter is a marketing survey, a political issue, or
a literary work, writing is a method of communicating information and
perceptions. Writing teaches. But before writing becomes an instrument

for informing the reader, it serves as a means of learning for the writer. An essay is a process of discovery as well as a record of what has been discovered. One of the chief benefits of writing is that we frequently realize what we want to say only after trying out ideas on a page and seeing our thoughts take shape in language.

More specifically, writing about a literary work encourages us to be better readers because it requires a close examination of the elements of a short story, poem, or play. To determine how plot, character, setting, point of view, style, tone, irony, or any number of other literary elements function in a work, we must study them in relation to one another as well as separately. Speed-reading won't do. To read a text accurately and validly — neither ignoring nor distorting significant details — we must return to the work repeatedly to test our responses and interpretations. By paying attention to details and being sensitive to the author's use of language, we develop a clearer understanding of how the work conveys its effects and meanings.

Nevertheless, students sometimes ask why it is necessary or desirable to write about a literary work. Why not allow stories, poems, and plays to speak for themselves? Isn't it presumptuous to interpret Hemingway, Dickinson, or Shakespeare? These writers do, of course, speak for themselves, but they do so indirectly. Literary criticism seeks not to replace the text by explaining it but to enhance our readings of works by calling attention to elements that we might have overlooked or only vaguely sensed.

Another misunderstanding about the purpose of literary criticism is that it crankily restricts itself to finding faults in a work. Critical essays are sometimes mistakenly equated with newspaper and magazine reviews of recently published works. Reviews typically include summaries and evaluations to inform readers about a work's nature and quality, but critical essays assume that readers are already familiar with a work. Although a critical essay may point out limitations and flaws, most criticism — and certainly the kind of essay usually written in an introductory literature course — is designed to explain, analyze, and reveal the complexities of a work. Such sensitive consideration increases our appreciation of the writer's achievement and significantly adds to our enjoyment of a short story, poem, or play. In short, the purpose and value of writing about literature are that doing so leads to greater understanding and pleasure.

READING THE WORK CLOSELY

Know the piece of literature you are writing about before you begin your essay. Think about how the work makes you feel and how it is put together. The more familiar you are with how the various elements of the text convey effects and meanings, the more confident you will be explaining whatever perspective on it you ultimately choose. Do not insist that everything make sense on a first reading. Relax and enjoy yourself; you can be attentive and still allow the author's words to work their magic on you. With subsequent readings, however, go more slowly and analytically as you try to establish relations between characters, actions, images, or whatever else seems important. Ask yourself why you respond as you do. Think as you read, and notice how the parts of a work contribute to its overall nature. Whether the work is a short story, poem, or play, you will read relevant portions of it over and over, and you will very likely find more to discuss in each review if the work is rich.

It's best to avoid reading other critical discussions of a work before you are thoroughly familiar with it. There are several good reasons for following this advice. By reading interpretations before you know a work, you deny yourself the pleasure of discovery. That is a bit like starting with the last chapter in a mystery novel. But perhaps even more important than protecting the surprise and delight that a work might offer is that a premature reading of a critical discussion will probably short-circuit your own responses. You will see the work through the critic's eyes and have to struggle with someone else's perceptions and ideas before you can develop your own.

Reading criticism can be useful, but not until you have thought through your own impressions of the text. A guide should not be permitted to become a tyrant. This does not mean, however, that you should avoid background information about a work—for example, that the title of Ann Lauinger's "Marvell Noir" (p. 82) alludes to Andrew Marvell's earlier *carpe diem* poem, "To His Coy Mistress" (p. 80). Knowing something about the author as well as historic and literary contexts can help to create expectations that enhance your reading.

ANNOTATING THE TEXT AND JOURNAL NOTE-TAKING

As you read, get in the habit of annotating your texts. Whether you write marginal notes, highlight, underline, or draw boxes and circles around important words and phrases, you'll eventually develop a system that allows you to retrieve significant ideas and elements from the text. Another way to record your impressions of a work—as with any other experience—is to keep a journal. By writing down your reactions to characters, images, language, actions, and other matters in a reading journal, you can often determine why you like or dislike a work or feel sympathetic or antagonistic to an author or discover paths into a work that might have eluded you if you hadn't preserved your impressions. Your journal notes and annotations may take whatever form you find useful; full sentences and grammatical correctness are not essential (unless they are to be handed in and your instructor requires that), though they might allow you to make better sense of your own reflections days later. The point is simply to put in writing thoughts that you can retrieve when you need them for class discussion or a writing assignment. Consider the following student annotation of the first twenty-four lines of Andrew Marvell's "To His Coy Mistress" and the journal entry that follows it:

Annotated Text

If we
had
time...

Had we but world enough, and time,
This coyness, lady, were no crime. — Waste life and you steal from yourself.
We would sit down, and think which way
To walk, and pass our long love's day.
Thou by the Indian Ganges' side   5
Shouldst rubies find; I by the tide
Of Humber would complain.° I would   *write love songs*
Love you ten years before the Flood,   Measurements
And you should, if you please, refuse   of time.
Till the conversion of the Jews.   10
My vegetable love should grow,°   *slow, unconscious growth*
Vaster than empires, and more slow;
An hundred years should go to praise
Thine eyes and on thy forehead gaze,
Two hundred to adore each breast,   15
But thirty thousand to the rest:
An age at least to every part,
And the last age should show your heart.

Contrast
river
and
desert
images.

For, lady, you deserve this state,
Nor would I love at lower rate.   20
But at my back I always hear   Lines move faster here —
Time's wingèd chariot hurrying near;   tone changes.
And yonder all before us lie
Deserts of vast eternity. — This eternity rushes in.

Journal Note

He'd be patient and wait for his "mistress" if they had the time--sing songs, praise her, adore her, etc. But they don't have that much time according to him. He seems to be patient but he actually begins by calling patience--her coyness--a "crime." Looks to me like he's got his mind made up from the beginning of the poem. Where's her response? I'm not sure about him.

This journal note responds to some of the effects noted in the annotations of the poem; it's an excellent beginning for making sense of the speaker's argument in the poem.

Taking notes will preserve your initial reactions to the work. Many times first impressions are the best. Your response to a peculiar character, a striking phrase, or a subtle pun might lead to larger perceptions. The student paper on "The Love Song of J. Alfred Prufrock" (p. 708), for example, began with the student making notes in the margins of the text about the disembodied images of eyes and arms that appear in the poem. This, along with the fragmentary thoughts and style of the speaker, eventually led her to examine the significance of the images and how they served to characterize Prufrock.

You should take detailed notes only after you've read through the work. If you write too many notes during the first reading, you're likely to disrupt your response. Moreover, until you have a sense of the entire work, it will be difficult to determine how connections can be made among its various elements. In addition to recording your first impressions and noting significant passages, images, diction, and so on, you should consult the Questions for Responsive Reading and Writing on page 59. These questions can assist you in getting inside a work as well as organizing your notes.

Inevitably, you will take more notes than you finally use in the paper. Note-taking is a form of thinking aloud, but because your ideas are on paper you don't have to worry about forgetting them. As you develop a better sense of a potential topic, your notes will become more focused and detailed.

CHOOSING A TOPIC

If your instructor assigns a topic or offers a choice from among an approved list of topics, some of your work is already completed. Instead of being asked to come up with a topic about Emily Dickinson's poems in this anthology, you may be assigned a three-page essay that specifically discusses "Dickinson's Treatment of Grief in 'The Bustle in a House.'" You also have the assurance that a specified topic will be manageable within the suggested number of pages. Unless you ask your instructor for permission to write on a different or related topic, be certain to address yourself to the assignment. An essay that does not discuss grief but instead describes Dickinson's relationship with her father would be missing the point. Notice, too, that there is room even in an assigned topic to develop your own approach. One question that immediately comes to mind is whether grief defeats or helps the speaker in the poem. Assigned topics do not relieve you of thinking about an aspect of a work, but they do focus your thinking.

At some point during the course, you may have to begin an essay from scratch. You might, for example, be asked to write about a poem that somehow impressed you or that seemed particularly well written or filled with insights. Before you start considering a topic, you should have a sense of how long the paper will be, because the assigned length can help to determine the extent to which you should develop your topic. Ideally, the paper's length should be based on how much space you deem necessary to present your discussion clearly and convincingly, but if you have any doubts and no specific guidelines have been indicated, ask. The question is important; a topic that might be appropriate for a three-page paper could be too narrow for ten pages. Three pages would probably be adequate for a discussion of the speaker's view of death in John Keats's "To Autumn." Conversely, it would be futile to try to summarize Keats's use of sensuality in his poetry in even ten pages; the topic would have to be narrowed to something like "Images of Sensuality in 'La Belle Dame sans Merci.'" Be sure that the topic you choose can be adequately covered in the assigned number of pages.

Once you have a firm sense of how much you are expected to write, you can begin to decide on your topic. If you are to choose what work to write about, select one that genuinely interests you. Too often students pick a poem because it is mercifully short or seems simple. Such works can certainly be the subjects of fine essays, but simplicity should not be the major reason for selecting them. Choose a work that has moved you so that you have something to say about it. The student who wrote about "The Love Song of J. Alfred Prufrock" was initially attracted to the poem's imagery because she had heard a friend (no doubt an English major) jokingly quote Prufrock's famous lament that "I should have been a pair of ragged claws / Scuttling across the floors of silent seas." Her paper then grew out of her curiosity about the meaning of the images. When a writer is engaged in a topic, the paper has a better chance of being interesting to a reader.

After you have settled on a particular work, your notes and annotations of the text should prove useful for generating a topic. The student paper on Prufrock developed naturally from the notes (p. 707) that the student jotted down about the images. If you think with a pen in your hand, you are likely to find when you review your notes that your thoughts have clustered into one or more topics. Perhaps there are patterns of imagery that seem to make a point about life. There may be symbols that are ironically paired or levels of diction that reveal certain qualities about the speaker. Your notes and annotations on such aspects can lead you to a particular effect or impression. Having chuckled your way through Peter Meinke's "The ABC of Aerobics" (p. 295), you may discover that your notations about the poem's humor point to a serious satire of society's values.

DEVELOPING A THESIS

When you are satisfied that you have something interesting to say about a work and that your notes have led you to a focused topic, you can formulate a *thesis,* the central idea of the paper. Whereas the topic indicates what the paper focuses on (the disembodied images in "Prufrock," for example), the thesis explains what you have to say about the topic (the frightening images of eyes, arms, and claws reflect Prufrock's disjointed, fragmentary response to life). The thesis should be a complete sentence (though sometimes it may require more than one sentence) that establishes your topic in clear, unambiguous language. The thesis may be revised as you get further into the topic and discover what you want to say about it, but once the thesis is firmly established it will serve as a guide for you and your reader, because all of the information and observations in your essay should be related to the thesis.

One student on an initial reading of Andrew Marvell's "To His Coy Mistress" (p. 80) saw that the male speaker of the poem urges a woman to love now before time runs out for them. This reading gave him the impression that the poem is a simple celebration of the pleasures of the flesh, but on subsequent readings he underlined or noted these images: "Time's wingèd chariot hurrying near"; "Deserts of vast eternity"; "marble vault"; "worms"; "dust"; "ashes"; and these two lines: "The grave's a fine and private place, / But none, I think, do there embrace."

By listing these images associated with time and death, he established an inventory that could be separated from the rest of his notes on point of view, character, sounds, and other subjects. Inventorying notes allows patterns to emerge that you might have only vaguely perceived otherwise. Once these images are grouped, they call attention to something darker and more complex in Marvell's poem than a first impression might suggest.

These images may create a different feeling about the poem, but they still don't explain very much. One simple way to generate a thesis about a literary work is to ask the question "why?" Why do these images appear in the poem? Why does the speaker in William Stafford's "Traveling through the Dark" (p. 172) push the dead deer into the river? Why does disorder appeal so much to the speaker in Robert Herrick's "Delight in Disorder" (p. 229)? Your responses to these kinds of questions can lead to a thesis.

Writers sometimes use freewriting to help themselves explore possible answers to such questions. It can be an effective way of generating ideas. Freewriting is exactly that: the technique calls for nonstop writing without concern for mechanics or editing of any kind. Freewriting for ten minutes or so on a question will result in fragments and repetitions, but it can also produce some ideas. Here's an example of a student's response to the question about the images in "To His Coy Mistress":

He wants her to make love. Love poem. There's little time. Her crime. He exaggerates. Sincere? Sly? What's he want? She says nothing — he says it all. What about deserts, ashes, graves, and worms? Some love poem. Sounds like an old Vincent Price movie. Full of sweetness but death creeps in. Death — hurry hurry! Tear pleasures. What passion! Where's death in this? How can a love poem be so ghoulish?

She does nothing. Maybe frightened? Convinced? Why death? Love and death — time — death.

This freewriting contains several ideas; it begins by alluding to the poem's plot and speaker, but the central idea seems to be death. This emphasis led the student to five potential thesis statements for his essay about the poem:

1. "To His Coy Mistress" is a difficult poem.
2. Death in "To His Coy Mistress."
3. There are many images of death in "To His Coy Mistress."
4. "To His Coy Mistress" celebrates the pleasures of the flesh but it also recognizes the power of death to end that pleasure.
5. On the surface, "To His Coy Mistress" is a celebration of the pleasures of the flesh, but this witty seduction is tempered by a chilling recognition of the reality of death.

The first statement is too vague to be useful. In what sense is the poem difficult? A more precise phrasing, indicating the nature of the difficulty, is needed. The second statement is a topic rather than a thesis. Because it is not a sentence, it does not express a complete idea about how the poem treats death. Although this could be an appropriate title, it is inadequate as a thesis statement. The third statement, like the first one, identifies the topic, but even though it is a sentence, it is not a complete idea that tells us anything significant beyond the fact it states. After these preliminary attempts to develop a thesis, the student remembered his first impression of the poem and incorporated it into his thesis statement. The fourth thesis is a useful approach to the poem because it limits the topic and indicates how it will be treated in the paper: the writer will begin with an initial impression of the poem and then go on to qualify it. However, the fifth thesis is better than the fourth because it indicates a shift in tone produced by the ironic relationship between death and flesh. An effective thesis, like this one, makes a clear statement about a manageable topic and provides a firm sense of direction for the paper.

Most writing assignments in a literature course require you to persuade readers that your thesis is reasonable and supported with evidence. Papers that report information without comment or evaluation are simply summaries. Similarly, a paper that merely pointed out the death images in "To His Coy Mistress" would not contain a thesis, but a paper that attempted to make a case for the death imagery as a grim reminder of how vulnerable flesh is would involve persuasion. In developing a thesis, remember that you are expected not merely to present information but to argue a point.

ARGUING ABOUT LITERATURE

An argumentative essay is designed to make persuasive your interpretation of a work. Arguing about literature doesn't mean that you're engaged in an angry, antagonistic dispute (though controversial topics do sometimes engender heated debates). Instead, argumentation requires that you present your interpretation of a work (or a portion of it) by supporting your discussion with clearly defined terms, ample evidence, and a detailed analysis of relevant portions of the text.

If you have a choice, it's generally best to write about a topic that you feel strongly about. Even if you don't like cats, you might find Jane Kenyon's "The Blue Bowl" (p. 125) just the sort of treatment that helps explain why you don't want one. On the other hand, if you're a cat fan, the poem may suggest something essential about cats that you've experienced but have never quite put your finger on. If your essay is to be interesting and convincing, what is important is that it be written from a strong point of view that persuasively argues your evaluation, analysis, and interpretation of a work. It is not enough to say that you like or dislike a work; instead you must give your reader some ideas and evidence that can be accepted or rejected based on the quality of the answers to the questions you raise.

One way to come up with persuasive answers is to generate good questions that will lead you further into the text and to critical issues related to it. Notice how the Perspectives, Complementary Readings, and Critical Case Study in this anthology raise significant questions and issues about texts from a variety of points of view. Moreover, the critical strategies for reading summarized in Chapter 26 can be a resource for raising questions that can be shaped into an argument. The following lists of questions for the critical approaches covered in Chapter 26 should be useful for discovering arguments you might make about a short story, poem, or play. The page number that follows each heading refers to the discussion in the anthology for that particular approach.

Questions for Arguing Critically about Literature

FORMALIST QUESTIONS (P. 666)

1. How do various elements of the work — plot, character, point of view, setting, tone, diction, images, symbol, and so on — reinforce its meanings?
2. How are the elements related to the whole?
3. What is the work's major organizing principle? How is its structure unified?
4. What issues does the work raise? How does the work's structure resolve those issues?

Biographical Questions (p. 668)

1. Are facts about the writer's life relevant to your understanding of the work?
2. Are characters and incidents in the work versions of the writer's own experiences? Are they treated factually or imaginatively?
3. How do you think the writer's values are reflected in the work?

Psychological Questions (p. 670)

1. How does the work reflect the author's personal psychology?
2. What do the characters' or speaker's emotions and behavior reveal about their psychological states? What types of personalities are they?
3. Are psychological matters such as repression, dreams, and desire presented consciously or unconsciously by the author?

Historical Questions (p. 672)

1. How does the work reflect the period in which it was written?
2. What literary or historical influences helped to shape the work's form and content?
3. How important is the historical context to interpreting the work?

Marxist Questions (p. 673)

1. How are class differences presented in the work? Are characters or speakers aware or unaware of the economic and social forces that affect their lives?
2. How do economic conditions determine the characters' or speaker's lives?
3. What ideological values are explicit or implicit?
4. Does the work challenge or affirm the social order it describes?

New Historicist Questions (p. 674)

1. What kinds of documents outside the work seem especially relevant for shedding light on the work?
2. How are social values contemporary to the work reflected or refuted in the work?
3. How does your own historical moment affect your reading of the work and its historical reconstruction?

Cultural Studies Questions (p. 675)

1. What does the work reveal about the cultural behavior contemporary to it?
2. How does popular culture contemporary to the work reflect or challenge the values implicit or explicit in the work?
3. What kinds of cultural documents contemporary to the work add to your reading of it?
4. How do your own cultural assumptions affect your reading of the work and the culture contemporary to it?

(continued)

GENDER STUDIES QUESTIONS (P. 676)

1. How are the lives of men and women portrayed in the work? Do the men and women in the work accept or reject these roles?

2. Is the work's form and content influenced by the author's gender?

3. What attitudes are explicit or implicit concerning heterosexual, homosexual, or lesbian relationships? Are these relationships sources of conflict? Do they provide resolutions to conflicts?

4. Does the work challenge or affirm traditional ideas about men and women and same-sex relationships?

MYTHOLOGICAL QUESTIONS (P. 677)

1. How does the work resemble other works in plot, character, setting, or use of symbols?

2. Does the work present archetypes such as quests, initiations, scapegoats, or withdrawals and returns?

3. Does the protagonist undergo any kind of transformation such as a movement from innocence to experience that seems archetypal?

4. Do any specific allusions to myths shed light on the text?

READER-RESPONSE QUESTIONS (P. 680)

1. How do you respond to the work?

2. How do your own experiences and expectations affect your reading and interpretation?

3. What is the work's original or intended audience? To what extent are you similar to or different from that audience?

4. Do you respond in the same way to the work after more than one reading?

DECONSTRUCTIONIST QUESTIONS (P. 682)

1. How are contradictory and opposing meanings expressed in the work?

2. How does meaning break down or deconstruct itself in the language of the text?

3. Would you say that ultimate definitive meanings are impossible to determine and establish in the text? Why? How does that affect your interpretation?

4. How are implicit ideological values revealed in the work?

These questions will not apply to all texts, and they are not mutually exclusive. They can be combined to explore a text from several critical perspectives simultaneously. A feminist approach to Anne Bradstreet's "The Author to Her Book" (p. 137) could also use Marxist concerns about class to make observations about the oppression of women's lives in the historical context of the seventeenth century. Your use of these questions should allow you to discover significant issues from which you can develop an argumentative essay that is organized around clearly defined terms, relevant evidence, and a persuasive analysis.

ORGANIZING A PAPER

After you have chosen a manageable topic and developed a thesis — a central idea about it — you can begin to organize your paper. Your thesis, even if it is still somewhat tentative, should help you decide what information will need to be included and provide you with a sense of direction.

Consider again the sample thesis in the section on developing a thesis:

On the surface, "To His Coy Mistress" is a celebration of the pleasures of the flesh,

but this witty seduction is tempered by a chilling recognition of the reality of

death.

This thesis indicates that the paper can be divided into two parts: the pleasures of the flesh and the reality of death. It also indicates an order: because the central point is to show that the poem is more than a simple celebration, the pleasures of the flesh should be discussed first so that another, more complex reading of the poem can follow. If the paper began with the reality of death, its point would be anticlimactic.

Having established such a broad and informal outline, you can draw on your underlinings, margin notations, and notecards for the subheadings and evidence required to explain the major sections of your paper. This next level of detail would look like the following:

1. Pleasures of the flesh

   Part of the traditional tone of love poetry

2. Recognition of death

   Ironic treatment of love

      Diction

      Images

      Figures of speech

      Symbols

      Tone

This list was initially a jumble of terms, but the student arranged the items so that each of the two major sections leads to a discussion of tone. (The student also found it necessary to drop some biographical information from his notes because it was irrelevant to the thesis.) The list indicates that the first part of the paper will establish the traditional tone of love poetry that celebrates the pleasures of the flesh, while the second part will present a more detailed discussion about the ironic recognition of death. The emphasis is on the latter because that is the point to be argued in the paper. Hence the thesis has helped to organize the parts of the paper, establish an order, and indicate the paper's proper proportions.

The next step is to fill in the subheadings with information from your notes. Many experienced writers find that making lists of information to be included under each subheading is an efficient way to develop paragraphs. For a longer paper (perhaps a research paper), you should be able to develop a paragraph or more on each subheading. On the other hand, a shorter paper may require that you combine several subheadings in a paragraph. You may also discover that while an informal list is adequate for a brief paper, a ten-page assignment could require a more detailed outline. Use the method that is most productive for you. Whatever the length of the essay, your presentation must be in a coherent and logical order that allows your reader to follow the argument and evaluate the evidence. The quality of your reading can be demonstrated only by the quality of your writing.

WRITING A DRAFT

The time for sharpening pencils, arranging your desk, surfing the Web, and doing almost anything else instead of writing has ended. The first draft will appear on the page only if you stop avoiding the inevitable and sit, stand up, or lie down to write. It makes no difference how you write, just that you do. Now that you have developed a topic into a tentative thesis, you can assemble your notes and begin to flesh out whatever outline you have made.

Be flexible. Your outline should smoothly conduct you from one point to the next, but do not permit it to railroad you. If a relevant and impor- tant idea occurs to you now, work it into the draft. By using the first draft as a means of thinking about what you want to say, you will very likely dis- cover more than your notes originally suggested. Plenty of good writers don't use outlines at all but discover ordering principles as they write. Do not attempt to compose a perfectly correct draft the first time around. Grammar, punctuation, and spelling can wait until you revise. Concen- trate on what you are saying. Good writing most often occurs when you are in hot pursuit of an idea rather than in a nervous search for errors.

To make revising easier, leave wide margins and extra space between lines so that you can easily add words, sentences, and corrections. Write on only one side of the paper. Your pages will be easier to keep track of that way, and, if you have to clip a paragraph to place it elsewhere, you will not lose any writing on the other side.

If you are working on a word processor, you can take advantage of its capacity to make additions and deletions as well as move entire paragraphs by making just a few simple keyboard commands. Many software programs can also check spelling and certain grammatical elements in your writing. It's worth remembering, however, that though a clean copy fresh off a printer may look terrific, it will read only as well as the thinking and writing that have gone into it. Many writers prudently store their data on disks and print their pages each time they finish a draft to avoid losing any material because of power failures or other problems. These printouts are also easier to read than the screen when you work on revisions.

Once you have a first draft on paper, you can delete material that is unrelated to your thesis and add material necessary to illustrate your points and make your paper convincing. The student who wrote "Disembodied Images in 'The Love Song of J. Alfred Prufrock'" (p. 707) wisely dropped a paragraph that questioned whether Prufrock displays chauvinistic attitudes toward women. Although this could be an interesting issue, it has nothing to do with the thesis, which explains how the images reflect Prufrock's inability to make a meaningful connection to his world.

Remember that your initial draft is only that. You should go through the paper many times — and then again — working to substantiate and clarify your ideas. You may even end up with several entire versions of the paper. Rewrite. The sentences within each paragraph should be related to a single topic. Transitions should connect one paragraph to the next so that there are no abrupt or confusing shifts. Awkward or wordy phrasing or unclear sentences and paragraphs should be mercilessly poked and prodded into shape.

Writing the Introduction and Conclusion

After you have clearly and adequately developed the body of your paper, pay particular attention to the introductory and concluding paragraphs. It's probably best to write the introduction — at least the final version of it — last, after you know precisely what you are introducing. Because this paragraph is crucial for generating interest in the topic, it should engage the reader and provide a sense of what the paper is about. There is no formula for writing effective introductory paragraphs, because each writing situation is different — depending on the audience, topic, and approach — but if you pay attention to the introductions of the essays you read, you will notice a variety of possibilities. The introductory paragraph to the Prufrock paper, for example, is a straightforward explanation of why the disembodied images are important for understanding Prufrock's character. The rest of the paper then offers evidence to support this point.

Concluding paragraphs demand equal attention because they leave the reader with a final impression. The conclusion should provide a sense of closure instead of starting a new topic or ending abruptly. In the final paragraph about the disembodied images in "Prufrock" the student explains their significance in characterizing Prufrock's inability to think of himself or others as complete and whole human beings. We now see that the images of eyes, arms, and claws are reflections of the fragmentary nature of Prufrock and his world. Of course, the body of your paper is the most important part of your presentation, but do remember that first and last impressions have a powerful impact on readers.

Using Quotations

Quotations can be a valuable means of marshaling evidence to illustrate and support your ideas. A judicious use of quoted material will make your points clearer and more convincing. Here are some guidelines that should help you use quotations effectively.

1. Brief quotations (four lines or fewer of prose or three lines or fewer of poetry) should be carefully introduced and integrated into the text of your paper with quotation marks around them.

> According to the narrator, Bertha "had a reputation for strictness." He tells us that she always "wore dark clothes, dressed her hair simply, and expected contrition and obedience from her pupils" (quoted in Jackson).

For brief poetry quotations, use a slash to indicate a division between lines.

> The concluding lines of Blake's "The Tyger" pose a disturbing question: "What immortal hand or eye / Dare frame thy fearful symmetry?" (Meyer 232).

Lengthy quotations should be separated from the text of your paper. More than three lines of poetry should be double-spaced and centered on the page. More than four lines of prose should be double-spaced and indented ten spaces from the left margin, with the right margin the same as for the text. Do *not* use quotation marks for the passage; the indentation indicates that the passage is a quotation. Lengthy quotations should not be used in place of your own writing. Use them only if they are absolutely necessary.

2. If any words are added to a quotation, use brackets to distinguish your addition from the original source.

> "He [Young Goodman Brown] is portrayed as self-righteous and disillusioned."

Any words inside quotation marks and not in brackets must be precisely those of the author. Brackets can also be used to change the grammatical structure of a quotation so that it fits into your sentence.

> Smith argues that Chekhov "present[s] the narrator in an ambivalent light."

If you drop any words from the source, use an ellipsis (three spaced periods) to indicate that the omission is yours.

> "Early to bed . . . makes a man healthy, wealthy, and wise."

Use an ellipsis preceding a period to indicate an omission at the end of a sentence.

Franklin wrote "Early to bed and early to rise makes a man healthy . . . ."

Use a single line of spaced periods to indicate the omission of a line or more of poetry or more than one paragraph of prose.

Nothing would sleep in that cellar, dank as a ditch,

Bulbs broke out of boxes hunting for chinks in the dark,

. . . .

Nothing would give up life:

Even the dirt kept breathing a small breath.

3. You will be able to punctuate quoted material accurately and confidently if you observe these conventions.

Place commas and periods inside quotation marks.

"Even the dirt," Roethke insists, "kept breathing a small breath."

Even though a comma does not appear after "dirt" in the original quotation, it is placed inside the quotation mark. The exception to this rule occurs when a parenthetical reference to a source follows the quotation.

"Even the dirt," Roethke insists, "kept breathing a small breath" (11).

Punctuation marks other than commas or periods go outside the quotation marks unless they are part of the material quoted.

What does Roethke mean when he writes that "the dirt kept breathing a small breath"?

Yeats asked, "How can we know the dancer from the dance?"

REVISING AND EDITING

Put some distance—a day or so if you can—between yourself and each draft of your paper. The phrase that seemed just right on Wednesday may be revealed as all wrong on Friday. You'll have a better chance of detecting lumbering sentences and thin paragraphs if you plan ahead and give yourself the time to read your paper from a fresh perspective. Through the process of revision, you can transform a competent paper into an excellent one.

Begin by asking yourself if your approach to the topic requires any re-thinking. Is the argument carefully thought out and logically presented? Are there any gaps in the presentation? How well is the paper organized? Do the paragraphs lead into one another? Does the body of the paper deliver what the thesis promises? Is the interpretation sound? Are any relevant and important elements of the work ignored or distorted to advance the thesis? Are the points supported with evidence? These large questions should be addressed before you focus on more detailed matters. If you uncover serious problems as a result of considering these questions, you'll probably have quite a lot of rewriting to do, but at least you will have the opportunity to correct the problems — even if doing so takes several drafts.

A useful technique for spotting awkward or unclear moments in the paper is to read it aloud. You might also try having a friend read it aloud to you. Your friend's reading — perhaps accompanied by hesitations and puzzled expressions — could alert you to passages that need reworking. Having identified problems, you can readily correct them on a word processor or on the draft provided you've skipped lines and used wide margins. The final draft you hand in should be neat and carefully proofread for any inadvertent errors.

The following checklist offers questions to ask about your paper as you revise and edit it. Most of these questions will be familiar to you; however, if you need help with any of them, ask your instructor or review the appropriate section in a composition handbook.

Questions for Revising and Editing

1. Is the topic manageable? Is it too narrow or too broad?
2. Is the thesis clear? Is it based on a careful reading of the work?
3. Is the paper logically organized? Does it have a firm sense of direction?
4. Is your argument persuasive? Do you use evidence from the text to support your main points?
5. Should any material be deleted? Do any important points require further illustration or evidence?
6. Does the opening paragraph introduce the topic in an interesting manner?
7. Are the paragraphs developed, unified, and coherent? Are any too short or long?
8. Are there transitions linking the paragraphs?
9. Does the concluding paragraph provide a sense of closure?
10. Is the tone appropriate? Is it unduly flippant or pretentious?
11. Is the title engaging and suggestive?
12. Are the sentences clear, concise, and complete?

13. Are simple, complex, and compound sentences used for variety?

14. Have technical terms been used correctly? Are you certain of the meanings of all of the words in the paper? Are they spelled correctly?

15. Have you documented any information borrowed from books, articles, or other sources? Have you quoted too much instead of summarizing or paraphrasing secondary material?

16. Have you used a standard format for citing sources (see p. 723)?

17. Have you followed your instructor's guidelines for the manuscript format of the final draft?

18. Have you carefully proofread the final draft?

When you proofread your final draft, you may find a few typographical errors that must be corrected but do not warrant printing an entire page again. Provided there are not more than a handful of such errors throughout the page, they can be corrected as shown in the following passage. This example condenses a short paper's worth of errors; no single passage should be this shabby in your essay.

To add a letter or word, use a caret on the line where the addition *is* needed. To delete a word draw a single line through ~~through~~ it. Run-on words are separated by a vertical|line, and inadvertent spaces are closed like t his. Transposed letters are indicated this way. New paragraphs are noted with the sign ¶ in front of where the next paragraph is to begin. ¶ Unless you . . .

These sorts of errors can be minimized by proofreading on the screen and simply entering corrections as you go along.

MANUSCRIPT FORM

The novelist and poet Peter De Vries once observed in his characteristically humorous way that he very much enjoyed writing but that he couldn't bear the "paper work." Behind this playful pun is a half-serious impatience with the mechanics of it all. You may feel some of that too, but this is not the time to allow a thoughtful, carefully revised paper to trip over minor details that can be easily accommodated. The final draft you hand in to your instructor should not only read well but look neat. If your instructor does not provide specific instructions concerning the paper's format, follow these guidelines.

1. Papers (particularly long ones) should be typed, double-spaced, on 8½ × 11–inch paper. Avoid transparent paper such as onionskin; it is difficult to read and write comments on. If you compose on a word processor,

be certain that the print is legible. If your instructor accepts handwritten papers, write legibly in ink on only one side of a wide-lined page.

2. Use a one-inch margin at the top, bottom, and sides of each page. Unless you are instructed to include a separate title page, type your name, instructor's name, course number and section, and date on separate lines one inch below the upper-left corner of the first page. Double-space between these lines and then center the title below the date. Do not italicize or put quotation marks around your paper's title, but do use quotation marks around the titles of poems, short stories, or other brief works, and italicize the titles of books and plays (a sample paper title: "Mending Wall" and Other Boundaries in Frost's *North of Boston*). Begin the text of your paper two spaces below the title. If you have used secondary sources, center the heading "Notes" or "Works Cited" one inch from the top of a separate page and then double-space between it and the entries.

3. Number each page consecutively, beginning with page 1, a half inch from the top of the page in the upper-right corner.

4. Gather the pages with a paper clip rather than staples, folders, or some other device. That will make it easier for your instructor to handle the paper.

TYPES OF WRITING ASSIGNMENTS

The types of papers most frequently assigned in literature classes are explication, analysis, and comparison and contrast. Most writing about literature involves some combination of these skills. This section includes a sample explication, an analysis, and a comparison and contrast paper. For a sample research paper that demonstrates a variety of strategies for documenting outside sources, see page 734. For other examples of student papers, see pages 704, 707, and 714.

Explication

The purpose of this approach to a literary work is to make the implicit explicit. *Explication* is a detailed explanation of a passage of poetry or prose. Because explication is an intensive examination of a text line by line, it is mostly used to interpret a short poem in its entirety or a brief passage from a long poem, short story, or play. Explication can be used in any kind of paper when you want to be specific about how a writer achieves a certain effect. An explication pays careful attention to language: the connotations of words, allusions, figurative language, irony, symbol, rhythm, sound, and so on. These elements are examined in relation to one another and to the work's overall effect and meaning.

The simplest way to organize an explication is to move through the passage line by line, explaining whatever seems significant. It is wise to avoid, however, an assembly-line approach that begins each sentence with "In line one. . . ." Instead, organize your paper in whatever way best serves your thesis. You might find that the right place to start is with the final lines, working your way back to the beginning of the poem or passage. The following sample explication on Emily Dickinson's "There's a certain Slant of light" does just that. The student's opening paragraph refers to the final line of the poem in order to present her thesis. She explains that though the poem begins with an image of light, it is not a bright or cheery poem but one concerned with "the look of Death." Because the last line prompted her thesis, that is where she begins the explication.

You might also find it useful to structure a paper by discussing various elements of literature, so that you have a paragraph on connotative words followed by one on figurative language and so on. However your paper is organized, keep in mind that the aim of an explication is not simply to summarize the passage but to comment on the effects and meanings produced by the author's use of language in it. An effective explication (the Latin word *explicare* means "to unfold") displays a text to reveal how it works and what it signifies. Although writing an explication requires some patience and sensitivity, it is an excellent method for coming to understand and appreciate the elements and qualities that constitute literary art.

A SAMPLE EXPLICATION

A Reading of Dickinson's "There's a certain Slant of light"

The sample paper by Bonnie Katz is the result of an assignment calling for an explication of about 750 words on any poem by Emily Dickinson. Katz selected "There's a certain Slant of light."

EMILY DICKINSON (1830–1886)

There's a certain Slant of light
c. 1861

There's a certain Slant of light,
Winter Afternoons —
That oppresses, like the Heft
Of Cathedral Tunes —

Heavenly Hurt, it gives us —   5
We can find no scar,
But internal difference,
Where the Meanings, are —

None may teach it — Any —
'Tis the Seal Despair —   10

An imperial affliction
Sent us of the Air —

When it comes, the Landscape listens —
Shadows — hold their breath —
When it goes, 'tis like the Distance   15
On the look of Death —

    This essay comments on every line of the poem and provides a coherent reading that relates each line to the speaker's intense awareness of death. Although the essay discusses each stanza in the order that it appears, the introductory paragraph provides a brief overview explaining how the poem's images contribute to its total meaning. In addition, the student does not hesitate to discuss a line out of sequence when it can be usefully connected to another phrase. This is especially apparent in the third paragraph, in her discussion of stanzas 2 and 3. The final paragraph describes some of the poem's formal elements. It might be argued that this discussion could have been integrated into the previous paragraphs rather than placed at the end, but the student does make a connection in her concluding sentence between the pattern of language and its meaning.

    Several other matters are worth noticing. The student works quotations into her own sentences to support her points. She quotes exactly as the words appear in the poem, even Dickinson's irregular use of capital letters. When something is added to a quotation to clarify it, it is enclosed in brackets so that the essayist's words will not be mistaken for the poet's: "Seal [of] Despair." A slash is used to separate line divisions as in "imperial affliction / Sent us of the Air."

Katz 1

Bonnie Katz

Professor Quiello

English 109–2

October 26, 2009

A Reading of Dickinson's

"There's a certain Slant of light"

    Because Emily Dickinson did not provide titles for her poetry, editors follow the customary practice of using the first line of a poem as its title. However, a more appropriate title for "There's a certain Slant of light," one

Thesis providing overview of explication

that suggests what the speaker in the poem is most concerned about, can be drawn from the poem's last line, which ends with "the look of Death."

Katz 2

Although the first line begins with an image of light, nothing bright, care-free, or cheerful appears in the poem. Instead, the predominant mood and images are darkened by a sense of despair resulting from the speaker's awareness of death.

In the first stanza, the "certain Slant of light" is associated with "Winter Afternoons" (lines 1-2), a phrase that connotes the end of a day, a season, and even life itself. Such light is hardly warm or comforting. Not a ray or beam, this slanting light suggests something unusual or distorted and creates in the speaker a certain slant on life that is consistent with the cold, dark mood that winter afternoons can produce. Like the speaker, most of us have seen and felt this sort of light: it "oppresses" (3) and pervades our sense of things when we encounter it. Dickinson uses the senses of hearing and touch as well as sight to describe the overwhelming oppressiveness that the speaker experiences. The light is transformed into sound by a simile that tells us it is "like the Heft / Of Cathedral Tunes" (3-4). Moreover, the "Heft" of that sound—the slow, solemn measures of tolling church bells and organ music—weighs heavily on our spirits. Through the use of shifting imagery, Dickinson evokes a kind of spiritual numbness that we keenly feel and perceive through our senses.

Line-by-line explication of first stanza, focusing on connotations of words and imagery, in relation to mood and meaning of poem as a whole; supported with references to the text

By associating the winter light with "Cathedral Tunes," Dickinson lets us know that the speaker is concerned about more than the weather. What-ever it is that "oppresses" is related by connotation to faith, mortality, and God. The second and third stanzas offer several suggestions about this con-nection. The pain caused by the light is a "Heavenly Hurt" (5). This "imperial affliction / Sent us of the Air—" (11-12) apparently comes from God above, and yet it seems to be part of the very nature of life. The oppressiveness we feel is in the air, and it can neither be specifically identified at this point in the poem nor be eliminated, for "None may teach it—Any" (9). All we know is that existence itself seems depressing under the weight of this "Seal [of] Despair" (10). The impression left by this "Seal" is stamped within the mind or soul rather than externally. "We can find no scar" (6), but once experienced this oppressiveness challenges our faith in life and its "Meanings" (8).

Explication of second, third, and fourth stanzas, focusing on connotations of words and imagery in relation to mood and meaning of poem as a whole; supported with references to the text

The final stanza does not explain what those "Meanings" are, but it does make clear that the speaker is acutely aware of death. As the winter daylight fades, Dickinson projects the speaker's anxiety onto the surrounding landscape and shadows, which will soon be engulfed by the darkness that follows this light: "the Landscape listens— / Shadows—hold their breath" (13-14). This image firmly aligns the winter light in the first stanza with darkness. Paradoxically, the light in this poem illuminates the nature of darkness. Tension is released when the light is completely gone, but what remains is the despair that the "imperial affliction" has imprinted on the speaker's sensibilities, for it is "like the Distance / On the look of Death" (15-16). There can be no relief from what that "certain Slant of light" has revealed because what has been experienced is permanent—like the fixed stare in the eyes of someone who is dead.

Explication of
the elements
of rhythm
and sound
throughout
poem

The speaker's awareness of death is conveyed in a thoughtful, hushed tone. The lines are filled with fluid *l* and *s* sounds that are appropriate for the quiet, meditative voice in the poem. The voice sounds tentative and uncertain—perhaps a little frightened. This seems to be reflected in the slightly irregular meter of the lines. The stanzas are trochaic with the second and fourth lines of each stanza having five syllables, but no stanza is identical because each works a slight variation on the first stanza's seven syllables in the first and third lines. The rhymes also combine exact patterns with varia-

Conclusion
tying
explication
of rhythm and
sound with
explication of
words and
imagery in
previous
paragraphs

tions. The first and third lines of each stanza are not exact rhymes, but the second and fourth lines are exact so that the paired words are more closely related: *Afternoons, Tunes*; *scar, are*; *Despair, Air*; and *breath, Death*. There is a pattern to the poem, but it is unobtrusively woven into the speaker's voice in much the same way that "the look of Death" is subtly present in the images and language of the poem.

Work Cited

Dickinson, Emily. "There's a certain Slant of light." *Poetry: An Introduction*.
   Ed. Michael Meyer. 6th ed. Boston: Bedford/St. Martin's 2010. 703.
   Print.

Analysis

The preceding sample essay shows how an explication examines in detail the important elements in a work and relates them to the whole. An ***analysis,*** however, usually examines only a single element — such as diction, character, point of view, symbol, tone, or irony — and relates it to the entire work. An analytic topic separates the work into parts and focuses on a specific one; you might consider "Point of View in 'The Love Song of J. Alfred Prufrock,'" "Patterns of Rhythm in Robert Browning's 'My Last Duchess,'" or "Irony in 'The Road Not Taken.'" The specific element must be related to the work as a whole or it will appear irrelevant. It is not enough to point out that there are many death images in Andrew Marvell's "To His Coy Mistress"; the images must somehow be connected to the poem's overall effect.

Whether an analytic paper is just a few pages or many, it cannot attempt to discuss everything about the work it is considering. Only those elements that are relevant to the topic can be treated. This kind of focusing makes the topic manageable; this is why most papers that you write will probably be some form of analysis. Explications are useful for a short passage, but a line-by-line commentary on a story, play, or long poem simply isn't practical. Because analysis allows you to consider the central effect or meaning of an entire work by studying a single important element, it is a useful and common approach to longer works.

A SAMPLE ANALYSIS

Disembodied Images in "The Love Song of J. Alfred Prufrock"

Beth Hart's paper analyzes some of the images in T. S. Eliot's "The Love Song of J. Alfred Prufrock" (the poem appears on p. 494). The assignment simply called for an essay of approximately 750 words on a poem written in the twentieth century. The approach was left to the student.

The idea for this essay began with Hart asking herself why there are so many fragmentary, disjointed images in the poem. The initial answer to this question was that "The disjointed images are important for understanding Prufrock's character." This answer was the rough beginning of a tentative thesis. What still had to be explained, though, was how the images are important. To determine the significance of the disjointed images, Hart jotted down some notes based on her underlinings and marginal notations.

Prufrock	Images
odd name--nervous, timid?	fog
"indecisions," "revisions"	lost, wandering

confessional tone, self-conscious	watching eyes
"bald spot"	ladies' arms
"afraid"	polite talk, meaningless talk
questioning, tentative	"ragged claws" that scuttle
"I am not Prince Hamlet"	oppressive
"I grow old"	distorted
wake--to drown	weary longing
	entrapped--staircase

From these notes Hart saw that the images — mostly fragmented and disjointed — suggested something about Prufrock's way of describing himself and his world. This insight led eventually to the final version of her thesis statement: "Eliot's use of frightening disembodied images such as eyes, arms, and claws reflects Prufrock's terror at having to face a world to which he feels no meaningful connection." Her introductory paragraph concludes with this sentence so that her reader can fully comprehend why she then discusses the images of eyes, arms, and claws that follow.

The remaining paragraphs present details that explain the significance of the images of eyes in the second paragraph, the arms in the third, the claws in the fourth, and in the final paragraph all three images are the basis for concluding that Prufrock's vision of the world is disconnected and disjointed.

Hart's notes certainly do not constitute a formal outline, but they were useful to her in establishing a thesis and recognizing what elements of the poem she needed to cover in her discussion. Her essay is sharply focused, well organized, and generally well written (though some readers might wish for a more engaging introductory paragraph that captures a glint of Prufrock's "bald spot" or some other small detail in order to generate some immediate interest in his character).

Hart 1

Beth Hart

Professor Lucas

English 110–3

March 30, 2009

Disembodied Images in

"The Love Song of J. Alfred Prufrock"

T. S. Eliot's poem "The Love Song of J. Alfred Prufrock" addresses the dilemma of a man who finds himself trapped on the margins of the social world, unable to make any meaningful interpersonal contact because of his deep-seated fear of rejection and misunderstanding. Prufrock feels acutely disconnected from society, which makes him so self-conscious that he is frightened into a state of social paralysis. His overwhelming self-consciousness, disillusionment with social circles, and lack of connection with those around him are revealed through Eliot's use of fragmented imagery. Many of the predominant images are disembodied pieces of a whole, revealing that Prufrock sees the world not as fully whole or complete, but as disjointed, fragmented parts of the whole. Eliot's use of frightening disembodied images such as eyes, arms, and claws reflects Prufrock's terror at having to face a world to which he feels no meaningful connection.

> *Thesis providing overview of writer's analysis*

> *Analysis of the meaning of fragmented imagery in the poem*

Eliot suggests Prufrock's acute self-consciousness through the fragmentary image of eyes. Literally, these eyes merely represent the people who surround Prufrock, but this disembodied image reveals his obsessive fear of being watched and judged by others. His confession that "I have known the eyes already, known them all— / The eyes that fix you in a formulated phrase" (lines 55-56) suggests how deeply he resists being watched, and how uncomfortable he is with himself, both externally—referring in part to his sensitivity to the "bald spot in the middle of my hair" (40)—and internally—his relentless self-questioning "'Do I dare?' and, 'Do I dare?'" (38). The disembodied eyes force the reader to recognize the oppression of being closely watched, and so to share in Prufrock's painful self-awareness. Prufrock's belief that the eyes have the terrifying and violent power to trap him like a specimen insect "pinned and wriggling on the wall" (58), to be scrutinized in its agony, further reveals the terror of the floating, accusatory image of the eyes.

> *Close analysis of "eyes" supported with references to the text*

The disembodied image of arms also reflects Prufrock's distorted vision of both himself and others around him. His acknowledgment that he has "known the arms already, known them all— / Arms that are braceleted and white and bare" (62-63) relates to the image of the eyes, yet focuses on a very different aspect of the people surrounding Prufrock. Clearly, the braceleted arms belong to women, and that these arms are attached to a perfumed dress (65) suggests that these arms belong to upper-class, privileged women. This is partially what makes the disembodied image of the arms so frightening for Prufrock: he is incapable of connecting with a woman the way he, as a man, is expected to. The image of the arms, close enough to Prufrock to reveal their

> *Close analysis of "arms" supported with references to the text*

down of "light brown hair" (64), suggests the potential for reaching out and possibly touching Prufrock. The terrified self-consciousness that the image elicits in him leads Prufrock to wish that he could leave his own body and take on the characteristics of yet another disembodied image.

Prufrock's despairing declaration, "I should have been a pair of ragged claws / Scuttling across the floors of silent seas" (73-74), offers yet another example of his vision of the world as fragmented and incomplete. The "pair of claws" that he longs to be not only connotes a complete separation from the earthly life that he finds so threatening, so painful, and so meaningless, but also suggests an isolation from others that would allow Prufrock some freedom and relief from social pressures. However, this image of the claws as a form of salvation for Prufrock in fact offers little suggestion of actual progress from his present circumstances; crabs can only "scuttle" from side to side and are incapable of moving directly forward or backward. Similarly, Prufrock is trapped in a situation in which he feels incapable of moving either up or down the staircase (39). Thus, this disembodied image of the claws serves to remind the reader that Prufrock is genuinely trapped in a life that offers him virtually no hope of real connection or wholeness.

The fragmented imagery that pervades "The Love Song of J. Alfred Prufrock" emphasizes and clarifies Prufrock's vision of the world as disconnected and disjointed. The fact that Prufrock thinks of people in terms of their individual component parts (specifically, eyes and arms) suggests his lack of understanding of people as whole and complete beings. This reflects his vision of himself as a fragmentary self, culminating in his wish to be not a whole crab, but merely a pair of disembodied claws. By use of these troubling images, Eliot infuses the poem with the pain of Prufrock's self-awareness and his confusion at the lack of wholeness he feels in his world.

[Margin note: Close analysis of "claws" supported with references to the text]

[Margin note: Conclusion of analysis echoes the thesis and draws in points made in previous paragraphs]

Work Cited

Eliot, T. S. "The Love Song of J. Alfred Prufrock." *Poetry: An Introduction.* Ed. Michael Meyer. 6th ed. Boston: Bedford/St. Martin's. 2010. 494. Print.

Hart's essay suggests a number of useful guidelines for analytic papers:

1. Only those points related to the thesis are included. In another type of paper the significance of Eliot's epigraph from Dante, for example, might have been more important than the imagery.
2. The analysis keeps the images in focus while at the same time indicating how they are significant in revealing Prufrock's character.
3. The title is a useful lead into the paper; it provides a sense of what the topic is.
4. The introductory paragraph is direct and clearly indicates that the paper will argue that the images serve to reveal Prufrock's character.
5. Brief quotations are deftly incorporated into the text of the paper to illustrate points. We are told what we need to know about the poem as evidence is provided to support ideas. There is no unnecessary summary.
6. The paragraphs are well developed, unified, and coherent. They flow naturally from one to another. Notice, for example, the smooth transition worked into the final sentence of the third paragraph and the first sentence of the fourth paragraph.
7. Hart makes excellent use of her careful reading and notes by finding revealing connections among the details she has observed.
8. As events in the poem are described, the present tense is used. This avoids awkward tense shifts and lends an immediacy to the discussion.
9. The concluding paragraph establishes the significance of why the images should be seen as a reflection of Prufrock's character and provides a sense of closure by relating the images of Prufrock's disjointed world with the images of his fragmentary self.
10. In short, Hart has demonstrated that she has read the work closely, has understood the function of the images in the revelation of Prufrock's sensibilities, and has argued her thesis convincingly by using evidence from the poem.

Comparison and Contrast

Another essay assignment in literature courses often combined with analytic topics is the type that requires you to write about similarities and differences between or within works. You might be asked to discuss "How Sounds Express Meanings in May Swenson's 'A Nosty Fright' and Lewis Carroll's 'Jabberwocky'" or "Love and Hate in Robert Frost's 'Fire and Ice.'" A *comparison* of either topic would emphasize their similarities, while a *contrast* would stress their differences. It is possible, of course, to include both perspectives in a paper if you find significant likenesses and differences. A comparison of Andrew Marvell's "To His Coy Mistress" (p. 80) and Ann Lauinger's "Marvell Noir" (p. 82) would, for example, yield similarities, because each poem describes a man urging his lover to make the most of their precious time together; however, important differences also exist in the tone and theme of each poem that would constitute a contrast. (You should, incidentally, be aware that the term *comparison* is sometimes used inclusively to refer to both similarities and differences as it is in the discussion and writing suggestions in this book. If you are assigned a comparison of two works, be sure that you understand what your instructor's expectations are; you may be required to include both approaches in the essay.)

When you choose your own topic, the paper will be more successful—more manageable—if you write on works that can be meaningfully related to each other. Although Robert Herrick's "To the Virgins, to Make Much of Time" (p. 79) and T. S. Eliot's "The Love Song of J. Alfred Prufrock" (p. 494) both have something to do with hesitation, the likelihood of anyone making a connection between the two that reveals something interesting and important is remote—though perhaps not impossible if the topic were conceived imaginatively and tactfully. Choose a topic that encourages you to ask significant questions about each work; the purpose of a comparison or contrast is to understand the works more clearly for having examined them together.

Choose works to compare or contrast that intersect with each other in some significant way. They may, for example, be written by the same author or about the same subject. Perhaps you can compare their use of some technique, such as irony or point of view. Regardless of the specific topic, be sure to have a thesis that allows you to organize your paper around a central idea that argues a point about the two works. If you merely draw up a list of similarities or differences without a thesis in mind, your paper will be little more than a series of observations with no apparent purpose. Keep in the foreground of your thinking what the comparison or contrast reveals about the works.

There is no single way to organize comparative papers as each topic is likely to have its own particular issues to resolve, but it is useful to be aware of two basic patterns that can be helpful with a comparison, a contrast, or a combination of both. One method that can be effective for relatively short papers consists of dividing the paper in half, first discussing one work and then the other. Here, for example, is a partial informal outline for a discussion of Langston Hughes's "Un-American Investigators" (p. 423) and Tato Laviera's "AmeRícan" (p. 292); the topic is a comparison and contrast:

"Two Views of America by Hughes and Laviera"

1. "Un-American Investigators"

   a. Diction

   b. Images

   c. Allusions

   d. Themes

2. "AmeRícan"

   a. Diction

   b. Images

   c. Allusions

   d. Themes

This organizational strategy can be effective provided that the second part of the paper combines the discussion of "AmeRícan" with references to "Un-American Investigators" so that the thesis is made clear and the paper is unified without being repetitive. If the two poems were treated entirely separately, then the discussion would be merely parallel rather than integrated. In a lengthy paper, this organization probably would not work well because a reader would have difficulty remembering the points made in the first half as he or she reads on.

Thus for a longer paper it is usually better to create a more integrated structure that discusses both works as you take up each item in your outline. Shown here in partial outline is the second basic pattern using the elements just cited.

1. Diction
   a. "Un-American Investigators"
   b. "AmeRícan"
2. Images
   a. "Un-American Investigators"
   b. "AmeRícan"
3. Allusions
   a. "Un-American Investigators"
   b. "AmeRícan"
4. Themes
   a. "Un-American Investigators"
   b. "AmeRícan"

This pattern allows you to discuss any number of topics without requiring that your reader recall what you first said about the diction of "Un-American Investigators" before you discuss the diction of "AmeRícan" many pages later. However you structure your comparison or contrast paper, make certain that a reader can follow its elements and keep track of its thesis.

A SAMPLE COMPARISON

Andrew Marvell and Sharon Olds Seize the Day

The following paper responds to an assignment that required a comparison and contrast — about 1,000 words — of two assigned poems. The student chose to write an analysis of two very different *carpe diem* poems.

In the following comparison essay, Christina Smith focuses on the male and female *carpe diem* voices of Andrew Marvell's "To His Coy Mistress" (p. 80) and Sharon Olds's "Last Night" (p. 84). After introducing the topic in the first paragraph, she takes up the two poems in a pattern similar to the first outline suggested for "Two Views of America by Hughes and Laviera." Notice how Smith works in subsequent references to Marvell's poem as she discusses Olds's so that her treatment is integrated and we are reminded why she is comparing the two works. Her final paragraph sums up her points without being repetitive and reiterates the thesis with which she began.

Christina Smith

English 109-10

Professor Monroe

April 2, 2009

Andrew Marvell and Sharon Olds Seize the Day

In her 1996 poem "Last Night," Sharon Olds never mentions Andrew Marvell's 1681 poem "To His Coy Mistress." Through a contemporary lens, however, she firmly qualifies Marvell's seventeenth-century masculine perspective. Marvell's speaker attempts to woo a young woman and convince her to have sexual relations with him. His seize-the-day rhetoric argues that "his mistress" should let down her conventional purity and enjoy the moment, his logic being that we are grave-bound anyway, so why not? Although his poetic pleading is effective, both stylistically and argumentatively, Marvell's speaker obviously assumes that the coy mistress will succumb to his grasps at her sexuality. Further, and most important, the speaker takes for granted that the female must be persuaded to love. His smooth talk leaves no room for a feminine perspective, be it a slap in the face or a sharing of his *carpe diem* attitudes. Olds accommodates Marvell's masculine speaker but also deftly takes poetic license in the cause of female freedom and sensuously lays out her own scenario. Through describing a personal sexual encounter both erotically and with jarring rawness, Olds's female speaker demonstrates that women have just as many lustful urges as the men who would seduce them; she presents sex as neither solely a male quest nor a female sacrifice. "Last Night" takes a female perspective on sex and fully explores it at its most raw and basic level.

"To His Coy Mistress" is in a regular rhyme scheme, as each line rhymes with the next—almost like a compilation of couplets. And this, accompanied by traditional iambic pentameter, lays the foundation for a forcefully flowing speech, a command for the couple to just do it. By the end of the poem the speaker seems to expect his mistress to capitulate. Marvell's speaker declares at the start that if eternity were upon them, he would not mind putting sex aside and paying her unending homage:

> Had we but world enough, and time,
>
> This coyness, lady, were no crime.
>
> We would sit down, and think which way
>
> To walk, and pass our long love's day. (lines 1-4)

He proclaims that he would love her "ten years before the Flood" (8) and concedes that she "should, if you please, refuse / Till the conversion of the Jews" (9-10). This eternal love-land expands as Marvell asserts that his "vegetable love should grow / Vaster than empires, and more slow" (11-12). Every part of her body would be admired for an entire "age" (17) because "lady, you deserve this state, / Nor would I love at lower rate" (19-20). He would willingly wait but, alas, circumstances won't let him. She'll have to settle for the here and now, and he must show her that life is not an eternity but rather an alarm clock.

The speaker laments that "at my back I always hear / Time's wingèd chariot hurrying near" (21-22). He then cleverly draws a picture of what exactly eternity does have in store for them, namely barren "Deserts" where her "beauty shall no more be found" (24, 25) while "worms shall try / That long preserved virginity" (27-28) and her "quaint honor turn to dust" (29). This death imagery is meant to frighten her for not having lived enough. He astutely concedes that "The grave's a fine and private place, / But none, I think, do there embrace" (31-32), thereby making even more vivid the nightmare he has just laid before her. Although he must make his grim argument, he does not want to dampen the mood, so he quickly returns to her fair features.

"Now," the speaker proclaims,

    while the youthful hue

    Sits on thy skin like morning dew,

    And while thy willing soul transpires

    At every pore with instant fires,

    Now let us sport us while we may. (33-37)

The speaker has already made the decision for her. Through sex, their energies will become one—they will "roll" their "strength" and "sweetness up into one ball" (41-42) as they "tear [their] pleasures with rough strife" (43). If the two of them cannot have eternity and make the "sun / Stand still" (45-46), then they will seize the day, combine and celebrate their humanity, and "make [the sun] run" (46). The speaker makes a vivid case in favor of living for the moment. His elaborate images of the devotion his mistress deserves, the inevitability of death, and the vivaciousness of human life are compelling. Three hundred years later, however, Sharon Olds demonstrates that women no longer need—or may never have needed—this lesson, because they share the same desires.

Olds's poem may be read as a contemporary response, though likely unintentional, to "To His Coy Mistress." This poet's "fine and private place" is not the grave, as it was in Marvell's poetic persuasion (31), but rather her own sexual encounter. The hard language of the poem, describing this act of sex as a "death-grip / holding to life" (Olds 13-14), suggests a familiarity with Marvell's own implications of death. More importantly, her speaker needs no rationale to live fully; she just does. She has sex on her own, willingly, knowingly, and thoroughly.

Unlike "To His Coy Mistress," "Last Night" has no rhyme scheme and has little meter or conventional form. The free verse tells the sexual story in an unconfined, open way. The poem flows together with urgent, sexual images drawn from a place in which nothing exists but biological instinct. It is organic at its most raw, basic level. The speaker and her lover unite "like dragonflies / in the sun, 100 degrees at noon, / the ends of their abdomens stuck together" (Olds 2-4). Whereas Marvell's lovers race against time, Olds's seem unaware of it altogether. The only sense of time in the poem is in reference to the morning after sex; the act itself is suspended in an unmeasured space in the speaker's memory. Any descriptive details are reserved for the encounter itself, and the setting is undefined. So it is the language of biology—

> something twisting and
> twisting out of a chrysalis,
> enormous, without language, all
> head, all shut eyes (6-9)

—that evokes erotic images. There is no foreplay, "No kiss, / no tenderness" (12-13), but the poem does not hint at a power struggle either. The speaker suggests mutuality, describing the lovers as "like violent hands clasped tight" (15). The two are "barely moving" (16), and when they "[start] / to die" (18-19), they do so together.

Afterwards, they return to themselves, away from the sensual, all-consuming world in which they reveled. However, the speaker has not literally or figuratively exhausted the natural world yet. She describes their hairlines as "wet as the arc of a gateway after / a cloudburst" (25-26). The cloudburst is itself a sudden, almost violent phenomenon, not unlike this sexual moment, and though she emerges from the encounter, it stays with her as a vivid memory.

Revisiting memories of the experience the next day allows the speaker to examine the moment, and she reflects in line 26 that it ended in peaceful sleep. The last lines stand in contrast to those of Marvell's speaker, whose desperate, pleading tone is filled with tension rather than the relief of consummation. As Olds's poem draws to a close (26-29), we see that this sexual encounter is an experience that, however raw, is rooted in tenderness. The erotic language of biology is in her own voice as she describes the two waking in the morning "clasped, fragrant, buoyant" (28). Olds's subject does not have to be persuaded by an excited man to be a sexual being; her sexuality seeps into her normal life, she wakes the next morning "almost afraid" (1) of it, and we marvel at its depth. Unlike Marvell's speaker, who remains eternally poised to "tear our pleasures" (43), Olds's speaker is steeped in those pleasures.

Smith 5

Works Cited

Marvell, Andrew. "To His Coy Mistress." *Poetry: An Introduction*. Ed. Michael
     Meyer. 6th ed. Boston: Bedford/St. Martin's, 2010. 80. Print.
Olds, Sharon. "Last Night." *Poetry: An Introduction*. Ed. Michael Meyer. 6th
     ed. Boston: Bedford/St. Martin's. 2010, 84. Print.

28

The Literary Research Paper

Does anyone know a good poet who's a vegetarian?
— DONALD HALL

© Nancy Crampton.

WRITING A LITERARY RESEARCH PAPER

A close reading of a primary source such as a short story, poem, or play can give insights into a work's themes and effects, but sometimes you will want to know more. A published commentary by a critic who knows the work well and is familiar with the author's life and times can provide insights that otherwise may not be available. Such comments and interpretations — known as *secondary sources* — are, of course, not a substitute for the work itself, but they often can take you into a work further than if you made the journey by yourself.

After imagination, good sense, and energy, perhaps the next most important quality for writing a research paper is the ability to organize material. A research paper on a literary topic requires a writer to take account of quite a lot at once: the text, ideas, sources, and documentation techniques all make demands on one's efforts to present a topic clearly and convincingly.

719

The following list should give you a sense of what goes into creating a research paper. Although some steps on the list can be folded into one another, they offer an overview of the work that will involve you.

1. Choosing a topic
2. Finding sources
3. Evaluating sources
4. Taking notes
5. Developing a thesis
6. Organizing an outline
7. Writing drafts
8. Revising
9. Documenting sources
10. Preparing the final draft and proofreading

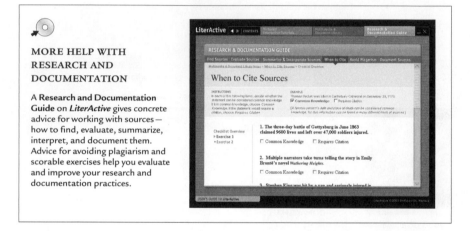

MORE HELP WITH RESEARCH AND DOCUMENTATION

A **Research and Documentation Guide** on *LiterActive* gives concrete advice for working with sources — how to find, evaluate, summarize, interpret, and document them. Advice for avoiding plagiarism and scorable exercises help you evaluate and improve your research and documentation practices.

Even if you have never written a research paper, you most likely have already had experience choosing a topic, developing a thesis, organizing an outline, and writing a draft that you then revised, proofread, and handed in. Those skills represent six of the ten items on the list. This chapter briefly reviews some of these steps and focuses on the remaining tasks, unique to research paper assignments.

CHOOSING A TOPIC

Chapter 27 discusses the importance of reading a work closely and taking careful notes as a means of generating topics for writing about literature. If you know a work well and record your understanding of it in notes, you'll have impressions and ideas to choose from for potential topics. You may find it useful to review the information on pages 686–88 before reading the advice in this chapter about putting together a research paper.

The student author of the sample research paper "Individuality and Community in Frost's 'Mowing' and 'Mending Wall'" (p. 735) was asked to write a five-page paper that demonstrated some familiarity with published critical perspectives on two Robert Frost poems of her choice. Before looking into critical discussions of the poems, she read them several times, taking notes and making comments in the margin of her textbook on each reading.

What prompted her choice of "Mending Wall," for example, was a class discussion that focused on the poem's speaker's questioning the value and necessity of the wall in contrast to his neighbor's insistence on it. At one point, however, the boundaries of the discussion opened up to the possibility that the wall is important to both characters in the poem rather than only the neighbor. It is, after all, the speaker, not the neighbor, who repairs the damage to the wall caused by hunters and who initiates the rebuilding of the wall. Why would he do that if he wanted the wall down? Only after having thoroughly examined the poem did the student go to the library to see what professional critics had to say about this question.

FINDING SOURCES

Whether your college library is large or small, its reference librarians can usually help you locate secondary sources about a particular work or author. Unless you choose a very recently published poem, play, or essay about which little or nothing has been written, you should be able to find out more about a literary work efficiently and quickly. Even if a work has been published recently, you can probably find relevant information on the Internet.

Electronic Sources

You can locate materials in a variety of sources, including card catalogs, specialized encyclopedias, bibliographies, and indexes to periodicals. Library Web sites also provide online databases that you can access from home. This can be an efficient way to establish a bibliography on a specific topic. Consult a reference librarian about how to use your library's online resources to determine how they will help you research your topic.

In addition to the many electronic databases ranging from your library's computerized holdings to the many specialized CD-ROMs available, such as *MLA International Bibliography* (a major source for articles and books on literary topics), the Internet also connects millions of sites with primary sources (the full texts of stories, poems, plays, and essays) and secondary sources (biography or criticism). If you have not had practice with research on the Web, it is a good idea to get guidance from your instructor or a librarian, and by using your library's home page as a starting point. Browsing on the Internet can be absorbing as well as informative, but unless you have plenty of time to spare, don't wait until the last minute to locate your electronic sources. You might find yourself trying to find reliable, professional sources among thousands of sites if you enter an unqualified entry such as "Charles Dickens."

Here are several especially useful electronic databases that will provide you with bibliographic information in literature studies. Your school's English Department home page may offer online support as well.

Internet Public Library Online Criticism. <http:www.ipl.org/div/litcrit>. Maintained by the University of Michigan, this site provides links to literary criticism by author, work, country, or period.

JSTOR. An index as well as abstracts of journal articles on language and literature.

A Literary Index. <http:www.vanderbilt.edu/AnS/english/flackcj/Litindex .html>. An extensive list of Internet literary resources for students and scholars.

MLA International Bibliography. This is a standard resource for articles and books on literary subjects that allow topical and keyword searches.

Voice of the Shuttle. <http://vos.ucsb.edu7>. Maintained by the University of California, this site is a wide-ranging resource for British and American literature studies.

Do remember that your own college library offers a broad range of electronic sources. If you're feeling uncertain, intimidated, and profoundly unplugged, your reference librarians are there to help you to get started.

EVALUATING SOURCES AND TAKING NOTES

Evaluate your sources for their reliability and the quality of their evidence. Check to see if an article or a book has been superseded by later studies; try to use up-to-date sources. A popular magazine article will probably not be as authoritative as an article in a scholarly journal. Sources that are well documented with primary and secondary materials usually indicate that the author has done his or her homework. Books printed by university presses and established trade presses are preferable to books privately printed. But there are always exceptions. If you are uncertain about how to assess a book, try to find out something about the author. Are there any other books listed in the catalog that indicate the author's expertise? What do book reviews say about the work? Three valuable indexes to book reviews of literary studies are *Book Review Digest, Book Review Index,* and *Index to Book Reviews in the Humanities.* Your reference librarian can show you how to use these important tools for evaluating books. Reviews can be a quick means to get a broad perspective on writers and their works because reviewers often survey previous approaches to the topic under discussion.

A cautionary note: assessing online sources can be more problematic than evaluating print sources because anyone with a computer and online access can publish on the Internet. Be sure to determine the nature of your sources and their authority. Is the site the work of a professional or an amateur? Is the information likely to be reliable? Is it biased? Is it documented? Before placing your trust in an Internet source, make sure that it warrants your confidence.

As you prepare a list of reliable sources relevant to your topic, record the necessary bibliographic information so that it will be available when you make up the list of works cited for your paper. For a book include the author, complete title, place of publication, publisher, and date. For an article include author, complete title, name of periodical, volume number, date of issue, and page numbers. For an Internet source, include the author, complete title, database title, periodical or site name, date of posting of the site (or last update), name of institution or organization, date when you accessed the source, and the network address (URL).

Once you have assembled a tentative bibliography, you will need to take notes on your readings. Be sure to keep track of where the information comes from by recording the author's name and page number. If you use more than one work by the same author, include a brief title as well as the author's name.

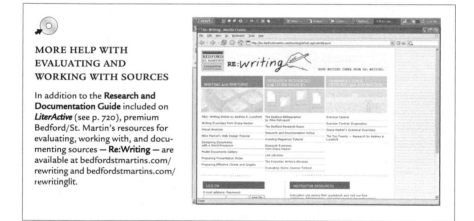

MORE HELP WITH EVALUATING AND WORKING WITH SOURCES

In addition to the **Research and Documentation Guide** included on *LiterActive* (see p. 720), premium Bedford/St. Martin's resources for evaluating, working with, and documenting sources — **Re:Writing** — are available at bedfordstmartins.com/rewriting and bedfordstmartins.com/rewritinglit.

DOCUMENTING SOURCES AND AVOIDING PLAGIARISM

You must acknowledge the use of a source when you (1) quote someone's exact words, (2) summarize or borrow someone's opinions or ideas, or (3) use information and facts that are not considered to be common knowledge. The purpose of this documentation is to acknowledge your sources, to demonstrate that you are familiar with what others have thought about the topic, and to provide your reader access to the same sources. If your paper is not adequately documented, it will be vulnerable to a charge of *plagiarism*—the presentation of someone else's work as your own. Conscious plagiarism is easy to avoid; honesty takes care of that for most people. However, there is a more problematic form of plagiarism that is often inadvertent. Whether inadequate documentation is conscious or not, plagiarism is a serious matter and must be avoided. Papers can be evaluated only by what is on the page, not by their writers' intentions.

Let's look more closely at what constitutes plagiarism. Consider the following passage quoted from A. R. Coulthard, "Frost's 'Mending Wall,'" *Explicator* 45 (Winter 1987): 40:

> "Mending Wall" has many of the features of an "easy" poem aimed at high-minded readers. Its central symbol is the accessible stone wall to represent separation, and it appears to oppose isolating barriers and favor love and trust, the stuff of Golden Treasury of Inspirational Verse.

Now read this plagiarized version:

> "Mending Wall" is an easy poem that appeals to high-minded readers who take inspiration from its symbolism of the stone wall, which seems to oppose isolating barriers and support trusting love.

Though the writer has shortened the passage and made some changes in the wording, this paragraph is basically the same as Coulthard's. Indeed, several of his phrases are lifted almost intact. (Notice, however, that the plagiarized version seems to have missed Coulthard's irony and, therefore, misinterpreted and misrepresented the passage.) Even if a parenthetical reference had been included at the end of the passage and the source included in "Works Cited," the language of this passage would still be plagiarism because it is presented as the writer's own. Both language and ideas must be acknowledged.

Here is an adequately documented version of the passage:

> A. R. Coulthard points out that "high-minded readers" mistakenly assume that "Mending Wall" is a simple inspirational poem that uses the symbolic wall to reject isolationism and to support, instead, a sense of human community (40).

This passage makes absolutely clear that the observation is Coulthard's, and it is written in the student's own language with the exception of one quoted phrase. Had Coulthard not been named in the passage, the parenthetical reference would have included his name: (Coulthard 40).

Some mention should be made of the notion of common knowledge before we turn to the standard format for documenting sources. Observations and facts that are widely known and routinely included in many of your sources do not require documentation. It is not necessary to cite a source for the fact that Alfred, Lord Tennyson, was born in 1809 or that Frost writes about New England. Sometimes it will be difficult for you to determine what common knowledge is for a topic that you know little about. If you are in doubt, the best strategy is to supply a reference.

There are two basic ways to document sources. Traditionally, sources have been cited in footnotes at the bottom of each page or in endnotes grouped together at the end of the paper. Here is how a portion of the sample paper on "Mending Wall" would look if footnotes were used instead of parenthetical documentation:

> It remains one of Frost's more popular poems, and, as Douglas Wilson notes, "one of the most famous in all of American poetry."[1]

> [1]Douglas L. Wilson, "The Other Side of the Wall," *Iowa Review* 10 (Winter 1979): 65. Print.

Unlike endnotes, which are double-spaced throughout and grouped under the title "Notes" at the end of the paper, footnotes appear four spaces below the text. They are single-spaced, with an extra space between notes.

No doubt you will have encountered these documentation methods in your reading. A different style is recommended, however, in the Modern Language Association's *MLA Handbook for Writers of Research Papers,* 7th ed. (2010). The MLA style uses parenthetical references within the text of the paper; these are keyed to an alphabetical list of works cited at the end of the paper. This method is designed to be less distracting for the reader. Unless you are instructed to follow the footnote or endnote style for documentation, use the parenthetical method explained in the next section.

The List of Works Cited

Items in the list of works cited are arranged alphabetically according to the author's last name and indented five spaces after the first line. This allows the reader to locate quickly the complete bibliographic information for the author's name cited within the parenthetical reference in the text. The following are common entries for literature papers and should be used as models. If some of your sources are of a different nature, consult the *MLA Handbook for Writers of Research Papers,* 7th ed. (New York: MLA, 2009); or, for the latest updates, check MLA's Web site at mlahandbook.org.

The following entries include examples to follow when citing electronic sources. For electronic sources, include as many of the following elements as apply and as are available:

- Author's name
- Title of work (if it's a book, italicize; if it's a short work, such as an article or a poem, use quotation marks)

- Title of the site (or of the publication, if you're citing an online periodical, for example), italicized
- Sponsor or publisher of the site (if not named as the author)
- Date of publication or last update
- Medium of publication.
- Date you accessed the source

A BOOK BY ONE AUTHOR

Hendrickson, Robert. *The Literary Life and Other Curiosities*. New York: Viking, 1981. Print.

AN ONLINE BOOK

Frost, Robert. *A Boy's Will*. New York: Holt, 1915. *Bartleby.com: Great Books Online*. 1999.
    Web. 4 Feb. 2009.

PART OF AN ONLINE BOOK

Frost, Robert. "Into My Own." *A Boy's Will*. New York: Holt, 1915. *Bartleby.com: Great
    Books Online*. Web. 4 Feb. 2009.

Notice that the author's name is in reverse order. This information, along with the full title, place of publication, publisher, and date, should be taken from the title and copyright pages of the book. The title is italicized and is also followed by a period. If the city of publication is well known, it is unnecessary to include the state. Use the publication date on the title page; if none appears there, use the copyright date (after ©) on the back of the title page. Include the medium of publication.

A BOOK BY TWO AUTHORS

Horton, Rod W., and Herbert W. Edwards. *Backgrounds of American Literary Thought*. 3rd
    ed. Englewood Cliffs: Prentice, 1974. Print.

Only the first author's name is given in reverse order. The edition number appears after the title.

A BOOK WITH MORE THAN THREE AUTHORS

Gates, Henry Louis, Jr., et al., eds. *The Norton Anthology of African American Literature*.
    New York: Norton, 1997. Print.

(Note: The abbreviation *et al.* means "and others.")

A WORK IN A COLLECTION BY THE SAME AUTHOR

O'Connor, Flannery. "Greenleaf." *The Complete Stories*. By O'Connor. New York: Farrar,
1971. 311-34. Print.

Page numbers are given because the reference is to only a single story in the collection.

A WORK IN A COLLECTION BY DIFFERENT WRITERS

Frost, Robert. "Design." *Poetry: An Introduction*. Ed. Michael Meyer. 6th ed. Boston:
Bedford/St. Martin's, 2010. 386. Print.

A TRANSLATED BOOK

Grass, Günter. *The Tin Drum*. Trans. Ralph Manheim. New York: Vintage-Random, 1962.
Print.

AN INTRODUCTION, PREFACE, FOREWORD, OR AFTERWORD

Johnson, Thomas H. Introduction. *Final Harvest: Emily Dickinson's Poems*. By Emily
Dickinson. Boston: Little, Brown, 1961. vii-xiv. Print.

This cites the introduction by Johnson. Notice that a colon is used between the
book's main title and subtitle. To cite a poem in this book, use this method:

Dickinson, Emily. "A Tooth upon Our Peace." *Final Harvest: Emily Dickinson's Poems*. Ed.
Thomas H. Johnson. Boston: Little, Brown, 1961. 110. Print.

AN ENTRY IN AN ENCYCLOPEDIA

"Wordsworth, William." *The New Encyclopedia Britannica*. 1984 ed. Print.

Because this encyclopedia is organized alphabetically, no page number or
other information is given, only the edition number (if available) and date.

AN ARTICLE IN A MAGAZINE

Morrow, Lance. "Scribble, Scribble, Eh, Mr. Toad." *Time* 24 Feb. 1986: 84. Print.

AN ARTICLE FROM AN ONLINE MAGAZINE

Wasserman, Elizabeth. "The Byron Complex." *Atlantic Online*. The Atlantic Monthly Group,
22 Sept. 2002. Web. 4 Feb. 2004.

The citation for an unsigned article would begin with the title and be alpha-
betized by the first word of the title other than "a," "an," or "the."

AN ARTICLE IN A SCHOLARLY JOURNAL WITH CONTINUOUS
PAGINATION BEYOND A SINGLE ISSUE

Mahar, William J. "Black English in Early Blackface Minstrelsy: A New Interpretation

of the Sources of Minstrel Show Dialect." *American Quarterly* 37 (1985): 260-85.

Print.

Because this journal uses continuous pagination instead of separate pagination for each issue, it is not necessary to include the month, season, or number of the issue. Only one of the quarterly issues will have pages numbered 260–85. If you are not certain whether a journal's pages are numbered continuously throughout a volume, supply the month, season, or issue number, as in the next entry.

AN ARTICLE IN A SCHOLARLY JOURNAL WITH SEPARATE
PAGINATION FOR EACH ISSUE

Updike, John. "The Cultural Situation of the American Writer." *American Studies*

International 15 (Spring 1977): 19-28. Print.

By noting the spring issue, the entry saves a reader from looking through each issue of the 1977 volume for the correct article on pages 19 to 28.

AN ARTICLE FROM AN ONLINE SCHOLARLY JOURNAL

Mamet, David. "Secret Names." *The Threepenny Review* 96 (Winter 2004): n. pag. Web.

4 Feb. 2004.

The following citation indicates that the article appears on page 1 of section 7 and continues onto another page.

AN ARTICLE IN A NEWSPAPER

Ziegler, Philip. "The Lure of Gossip, the Rules of History." *New York Times* 23 Feb. 1986:

sec. 7: 1+. Print.

AN ARTICLE FROM AN ONLINE NEWSPAPER

Brantley, Ben. "Souls Lost and Doomed Enliven London Stages." *New York Times*. New York

Times, 4 Feb. 2004. Web. 5 Feb. 2004.

A LECTURE

Tilton, Robert. "The Beginnings of American Studies." English 270 class lecture.

University of Connecticut, Storrs. 12 Mar. 2004. Lecture.

LETTER, E-MAIL, OR INTERVIEW

Vellenga, Carolyn. Letter to the author. 9 Oct. 1997.

Harter, Stephen P. E-mail to the author. 28 Dec. 1997.

McConagha, Bill. Personal interview. 6 March 2009.

Following are additional examples for citing electronic sources.

WORK FROM A SUBSCRIPTION SERVICE

Libraries pay for access to databases such as *Lexis-Nexis, ProQuest Direct,* and *Expanded Academic ASAP.* When you retrieve an article or other work from a subscription database, cite your source based on this model:

Vendler, Helen Hennessey. "The Passion of Emily Dickinson." *The New Republic* 3 Aug.
     1992: 34-38. *Expanded Academic ASAP.* Web. 4 Feb. 2004.

A DOCUMENT FROM A WEB SITE

When citing sources from the Internet, include as much publication information as possible (see guidelines on page 725). In some cases, as in the following example, a date of publication for the document "Dickens in America" is not available. The entry provides the author, title of document, title of site, access date, and URL:

Perdue, David. "Dickens in America." *David Perdue's Charles Dickens Page*. David A. Perdue,
     1 Apr. 2009. Web. 13 Apr. 2009.

AN ENTIRE WEB SITE

Perdue, David. *David Perdue's Charles Dickens Page*. David A. Perdue, 1 Apr. 2009. Web.
     13 Apr. 2009.

Treat a CD-ROM as you would any other source, but name the medium before the publication information.

A WORK FROM A CD-ROM

Aaron, Belèn V. "The Death of Theory." *Scholarly Book Reviews* 4.3 (1997): 146-47. CD-ROM.
     ERIC. SilverPlatter. Dec. 1997.

AN ONLINE POSTING

Shuck, John. "Hamlet." PBS Discussions. PBS, 16 May 2005. Web. 13 Apr. 2009.

Parenthetical References

A list of works cited is not an adequate indication of how you have used sources in your paper. You must also provide the precise location of quotations and other information by using parenthetical references within the text of the paper. You do this by citing the author's name (or the source's title if the work is anonymous) and the page number.

> Collins points out that "Nabokov was misunderstood by early reviewers of his work" (28).

or

> Nabokov's first critics misinterpreted his stories (Collins 28).

Either way a reader will find the complete bibliographic entry in the list of works cited under Collins's name and know that the information cited in the paper appears on page 28. Notice that the end punctuation comes after the parentheses.

If you have listed more than one work by the same author, you would add a brief title to the parenthetical reference to distinguish between them. You could also include the full title in your text.

> Nabokov's first critics misinterpreted his stories (Collins, "Early Reviews" 28).

or

> Collins points out in "Early Reviews of Nabokov's Fiction" that his early work was misinterpreted by reviewers (28).

There can be many variations on what is included in a parenthetical reference, depending on the nature of the entry in the list of works cited. But the general principle is simple enough: provide enough parenthetical information for a reader to find the work in "Works Cited." Examine the sample research paper for more examples of works cited and strategies for including parenthetical references. If you are puzzled by a given situation, ask your reference librarian to show you the *MLA Handbook*.

Incorporating Secondary Sources

The questions on page 731 can help you to incorporate materials from critical or biographical essays into your own writing about a literary work. You may initially feel intimidated by the prospect of responding to the arguments of professional writers in your own paper. However, the process will not defeat you if you have clearly formulated your own response to the literary work and are able to distinguish it from the critics' perspectives.

Reading what other people have said about a work can help you to develop your own ideas—perhaps, to cite just two examples, by using their ideas as supporting evidence or by arguing with them in order to clarify or qualify their points about the literary work. As you write and discover how to advance your thesis, you'll find yourself participating in a dialogue with the critics. This sort of conversation will help you to improve your thinking and hone your argument.

Keep in mind that the work of professional critics is a means of enriching your understanding of a literary work rather than a substitution for your own analysis and interpretation of that work. Quoting, paraphrasing, or summarizing someone else's perspective does not relieve you of the obligation of choosing a topic, organizing information, developing a thesis, and arguing your point of view by citing sufficient evidence from the text you are examining. These matters are discussed in further detail in Chapter 27. You should also be familiar with the methods for documenting sources that are explained in this chapter, and keep in mind how important it is to avoid plagiarism.

No doubt you won't find everything you read about a work equally useful: some critics' arguments won't address your own areas of concern; some will be too difficult for you to get a handle on; and some will seem wrongheaded. However, much of the criticism you read will serve to make a literary work more accessible and interesting to you, and disagreeing with others' arguments will often help you to develop your own ideas about a work. When you use the work of critics in your own writing, you should consider the following questions. Responding to these questions will help you to develop a clear understanding of what a critic is arguing about a work, to decide to what extent you agree with that argument, and to plan how to incorporate and respond to the critic's reading in your own paper. The more questions you can ask yourself in response to this list or as a result of your own reading, the more you'll be able to think critically about how you are approaching both the critics and the literary work under consideration.

Questions for Incorporating Secondary Sources

1. Have you read the poem carefully and taken notes of your own impressions before reading any critical perspectives so that your initial insights are not lost to the arguments made by the critics? Have you articulated your own responses to the work in a journal entry prior to reading the critics?

2. Are you sufficiently familiar with the poem that you can determine the accuracy, fairness, and thoroughness of the critic's use of evidence from the work?

3. Have you read the critic's piece carefully? Try summarizing the critic's argument in a brief paragraph. Do you understand the nature and purpose of the critic's argument? Which passages are especially helpful to you? Which seem unclear? Why?

(continued)

4. Is the critic's reading of the poem similar to or different from your own reading? Why do you agree or disagree? What generational, historical, cultural, or biographical considerations might help to account for any differences between the critic's responses and your own?

5. How has your reading of the critic influenced your understanding of the poem? Do issues that previously seemed unimportant now seem significant? What are these issues, and how does a consideration of them affect your reading of the work?

6. Are you too quickly revising or even discarding your own reading because the critic's perspective seems so polished and persuasive? Are you making use of your reading notes and the responses in your journal entries?

7. How would you classify the critic's approach? Through what kind of lens does the critic view the poem? Is the critical approach formalist, biographical, psychological, historical, mythological, reader-response, deconstructionist, or some combination of these or possibly other strategies? (For a discussion of these approaches, see Chapter 26.)

8. What biases, if any, can you detect in the critic's approach? How might, for example, a southern critic's reading of "Mending Wall" differ from a northern critic's?

9. Can you determine how other critics have responded to the critic's work? Is the critic's work cited and taken seriously in other critics' books and articles? Is the work dated by having been superseded by subsequent studies?

10. Are any passages or topics that you deem important left out by the critic? Do these omissions qualify or refute the critic's argument?

11. What judgments does the critic seem to make about the work? Is the work regarded, for example, as significant, unified, representative, trivial, inept, or irresponsible? Do you agree with these judgments? If not, can you develop and support a thesis about your difference of opinion?

12. What important disagreements do critics reveal in their approaches to the work? Do you find one perspective more convincing than another? Why? Is there a way of resolving their conflicting views that could serve as a thesis for your paper?

13. Can you extend or qualify the critic's argument to matters in the literary text that are not covered by the critic's perspective? Will this allow you to develop your own topic while acknowledging the critic's useful insights?

14. Have you quoted, paraphrased, or summarized the critic accurately and fairly? Have you avoided misrepresenting the critic's arguments in any way?

15. Are the critic's words, ideas, opinions, and insights adequately acknowledged and documented in the correct format? Do you understand the difference between common knowledge and plagiarism? Have you avoided quoting excessively? Are the quotations smoothly integrated into your own text?

16. Are you certain that your incorporation of the critic's work is for the purpose of developing your paper's thesis rather than for name-dropping or padding your paper? How can you explain to yourself why the critic's work is useful for your argument?

DEVELOPING A THESIS AND ORGANIZING THE PAPER

As the notes on "Mowing" and "Mending Wall" accumulated, the student sorted them into topics including

1. Publication history of the poems
2. Frost's experiences as a farmer
3. Critics' readings of the poems
4. The speaker's attitude toward the wall
5. The neighbor's attitude toward the wall
6. Mythic elements in the poems
7. Does the wall have any positive value?
8. How do the speaker and neighbor characterize themselves?
9. Humor and tone in the poems
10. Frost as a regional poet

The student quickly saw that items 1, 2, 6, and 10 were not directly related to her topic concerning why the speaker initiates the rebuilding of the wall. The remaining numbers (3–5, 7–9) are the topics taken up in the paper. The student had begun her reading of secondary sources with a tentative thesis that stemmed from her question about why the poem's speaker helps his neighbor to rebuild the wall. That "why" shaped itself into the expectation that she would have a thesis something like this: "The speaker helps to rebuild the wall because . . ."

She assumed she would find information that indicated some specific reason. But the more she read, the more she discovered that there was no single explanation provided by the poem or by critics' readings of the poem. Instead, through the insights provided by her sources, she began to see that the wall had several important functions in the poem. The perspective she developed into her thesis — that the wall "provided a foundation upon which the men build a personal sense of identity" — allowed her to incorporate a number of the critics' insights into her paper in order to shed light on why the speaker helps to rebuild the wall.

Because the assignment was relatively brief, the student did not write up a formal outline but instead organized her stacks of usable notecards and proceeded to write the first draft from them.

REVISING

After writing your first draft, you should review the advice and the Questions for Revising and Editing on pages 700–01 so that you can read your paper with an objective eye. Two days after writing her next-to-last draft, the writer of "Individuality and Community in Frost's 'Mowing' and 'Mending Wall'" realized that she had allotted too much space for critical discussions of the humor in the poem that were not directly related to her approach. She realized that it was not essential to point out and discuss the puns in the poem; hence she corrected this by simply deleting most references to the poem's humor. The point is that she saw this herself after she took some time to approach the paper from a fresh perspective.

A SAMPLE RESEARCH PAPER

Individuality and Community in Frost's "Mowing" and "Mending Wall"

As you read the paper by Stephanie Tobin on Robert Frost's "Mowing" (p. 368) and "Mending Wall" (p. 370), pay special attention to how she documents outside sources and incorporates other people's ideas into her own argument. How strong do you think her final thesis is? Is it effectively supported by the sources? Has she integrated the sources fully into the paper? How does the paper enhance your understanding of the two poems?

Stephanie's paper follows the format described in the *MLA Handbook for Writers of Research Papers,* 7th ed. This format is discussed in the preceding section on documentation in this chapter (p. 723) and in Chapter 27 in the section on manuscript form (p. 701). Though the sample paper is short, it illustrates many of the techniques and strategies useful for writing an essay that includes secondary sources — including a CD-ROM, a Web site, books, and journals.

Tobin 1

Stephanie Tobin
Professor Bass
Poetry 100
November 17, 2009

Individuality and Community in

Frost's "Mowing" and "Mending Wall"

We think of Robert Frost as a poet of New England who provides portraits of the rural landscape and communities. But it was not until Frost's
second book, *North of Boston* (1914), that he truly gave voice to a community—in dramatic monologues, dialogues, and narrative poems. The poems in
his first book, *A Boy's Will* (1913), are mainly personal lyrics in which the
poet encounters the world and defines it for himself through the writing of
poetry, establishing both an individual perspective and an aesthetic. A poem
from the first book, "Mowing," illustrates the theme of individualism, against
which a poem from the second book, "Mending Wall," can be seen as a widening of the thematic lens to include other perspectives.

In *A Boy's Will*, Frost explores the idea of man as a solitary creature,
alone, at work in the natural world. Poems such as "Mowing" capture the
essence of this perspective in the very first lines: "There was never a sound
beside the wood but one, / And that was my long scythe whispering to the
ground" (lines 1-2). Jay Parini describes "Mowing" as a poem in which the
"poet cultivates a private motion" (121)—the motions both of farm work,
done to support oneself, and the motion of the individual mind expressed in
the poem as it moves down the page. The sense of privacy and of an individually defined world captured in "Mowing" is central to the book itself.

The dramatic change in perspective evident in *North of Boston* illustrates Frost's development as a writer. Although the second collection was
published just one year later, Frost expresses a different perception and
understanding of human nature in *North of Boston*. W. S. Braithwaite wrote in
1915, in a review of the two books, that *A Boy's Will* and *North of Boston*
"represent a divergent period of development. The earlier book expresses an
individuality, the later interprets a community" (2). The focus on community
is best demonstrated by the poem "Mending Wall," which presents the reader

with an image of two men, separated literally and metaphorically by a wall, yet joined by their dedication to the task they must undertake and the basic human need for boundaries that compels them. The speaker in "Mending Wall" does not forfeit his own individuality, but rather comes to understand it more fully in the context of the society in which he lives, with its traditions and requirements, some of which he tries to see as a game: "Oh, just another kind of outdoor game, / One on a side" (21-22), while still allowing for deeper implications.

Individuality can be defined by one's differences from others, as well as by the creative work of defining, and self-defining, done in poetry. Frost's own experience of life in New England helped shape the perspectives of both individualism and community exemplified in his first two books. When Frost wrote "Mowing," his perspective on life in New England leaned more toward isolation than community. The first few years of farm life were arduous and lonely, and the stark environment provided an atmosphere far more suitable for self-realization than socialization. Prior to the publication of *A Boy's Will*, Frost had spent "five years of self-enforced solitude" (Meyers 99). "Mowing," which Frost considered to be the best poem in the collection, exemplifies this feeling of isolation and the need for self-exploration. While the poem is, in the literal sense, about the act of cutting grass in order to make hay, it is metaphorically rooted in the idea that man finds meaning and beauty in the world alone. Parini suggests that the idea that "a man's complete meaning is derived alone, at work . . . is a consistent theme in Frost and one that could be explored at length in all his work" (14).

"Mowing" begins with the speaker's observation of the silence that surrounds him as he works. The only sound is the hushed whisper of his scythe as he mows. He writes, "What was it it whispered? I knew not well myself" (3). The possibility that its meaning could be found in some fanciful imagination of the task is dismissed: "It was no dream of the gift of idle hours, / Or easy gold at the hand of fay or elf" (Frost, "Mowing" 7-8). For Frost, an exaggeration of the action would imply that meaning cannot be found in objective reality, an idea continually argued by his poems.

Instead, this poem asserts a faith in nature as it is, and in the labor necessary to support and define oneself—labor in the natural world, and in the making of poems. This idea is brought forth in the next lines: "Anything more than the truth would have seemed too weak / To the earnest love that laid the swale in rows" (9-10). Whether the "fact" that is "the sweetest dream that labour knows" (13) is the actual act of cutting the grass or the verse that is inspired by the simple action, it is something that must be achieved in solitude.

This faith in the work of the individual demonstrated in *A Boy's Will* is not lost in *North of Boston* but is redefined. Meyers writes that *North of Boston* "signaled Frost's change of emphasis from solitary to social beings" (112). In Frost's dedication to his wife, he called *North of Boston* "This Book of People." The poems in this collection demonstrate an understanding of the individual as well as the community in which he lives. This shift seems a natural development after a book in which Frost so carefully established his sense of self and his particular poetic vision and aims.

"Mending Wall," a poem in *North of Boston*, illustrates Frost's shift in focus from the solitary individual to the interacting society. In the poem, the speaker and his neighbor set out to perform the annual task of mending a wall that divides their properties. From the very beginning, the speaker's tone—at once humorous and serious—indicates that the real subject of the poem is not the mending of the wall, which he describes almost lightheart-edly, but the "mending" of the subtle boundaries between the speaker and his neighbor. The poem begins, "Something there is that doesn't love a wall, / That sends the frozen-ground-swell under it" (Frost, "Mending" 1-2), yet this "something," mentioned twice in the poem, refers to more than the seasonal frost that "spills the upper boulders in the sun" (3). Peter Stanlis writes in a commentary on "Mending Wall" that "the central theme falls within the philosophical polarities of the speaker and his neighbor" (1). The man's state-ment that "good fences make good neighbors" (Frost, "Mending" 27) implies his belief that boundaries between people will maintain the peace between them, but the speaker questions this need for boundaries: "Before I built a wall I'd ask to know / What I was walling in or walling out" (32-33). With this he brings the wall into the figurative realm to decipher its meaning.

His neighbor feels no need for such analysis. But while articulating a figurative barrier of noncommunication and different values between the men, the poem is as much about community as individuality; the wall is what connects as well as separates them. Marie Borroff argues that "the story told in the poem is not about a one-man rebellion against wall mending but about an attempt to communicate" (66). However individuated the men may perceive themselves to be, the common task they must undertake and the ethos it represents join them in a particular social community, the assumptions of which Frost articulates in this poem by both participating in and questioning them.

For the speaker, the task of mending the wall provides an opportunity for thought and questioning rather than serving a utilitarian purpose. While the tradition unites the men "by marking their claims to private property through mutual respect," it is still a barrier (Stanlis 3). Both joined and separated by the fence, the two neighbors walk together and alone, isolated by the physical boundary but connected by their maintenance of the relationship and tradition that created it. As James R. Dawes points out, these "men can only interact when reassured by the constructed alienation of the wall" (300). They keep the wall in place, and thereby keep in place their separate senses of self.

While the speaker is explicitly and lightheartedly critical of the ritual, it is he who "insists on the yearly ritual, as if civilization depends upon the collective activity of making barriers. . . . One senses a profound commitment to the act of creating community in the speaker" (Parini 139). Unwilling to placate his neighbor by performing the task in silence, the speaker makes a playful attempt at communication. Explaining that "My apple trees will never get across / And eat the cones under his pines" (Frost, "Mending" 25–26), he asks why the wall is necessary. But rather than contemplate the logic behind the boundary, the neighbor rejects the invitation to communicate: "He only says, 'Good fences make good neighbors'" (27). By refusing to think about the speaker's question, and choosing to hide behind his own father's words, he closes any possible window of communication between them (Monteiro 127), not crossing the barrier of the wall literally or psychologically. And even while the speaker jokes about the wall's uselessness, he keeps his deeper questions to himself. Rather than threaten the agreed-upon terms of community, he is complicit in keeping them there in actuality, only privately articulating and upending them, in poetry.

Mark Van Doren wrote in 1951 that Robert Frost's poems "are the work of a man who has never stopped exploring himself" (2); he never stopped exploring the psychology of others, either. "Mowing," which illustrates his initial focus on individualism, was only a starting point in Frost's understanding of his place in the world as a poet. The change of perspective evident in "Mending Wall" demonstrates his enriched idea of man as an individual within a community. Having established a singular voice and his own moral aesthetic—"The fact is the sweetest dream that labour knows" ("Mowing" 13)—Frost has the confidence to incorporate different voices into his poems and to allow his "facts" and values to encounter those of others, as the two men in "Mending Wall" do across the wall, each maintaining his own and the other's sense of personal identity.

Works Cited

Borroff, Marie. "Robert Frost's New Testament: The Uses of Simplicity." *Modern Critical Views: Robert Frost*. Ed. Harold Bloom. New York: Chelsea House, 1986. 63-83. Print.

Braithwaite, W. S. "A Poet of New England." *The Boston Evening Transcript* 28 April 1915: *Robert Frost: Poems, Life, Legacy*. CD-ROM. New York: Holt, 1997.

Dawes, James R. "Masculinity and Transgression in Robert Frost." *American Literature* 65 (June 1993): 297-312. Print.

Frost, Robert. "Mending Wall." *Poetry: An Introduction*. Ed. Michael Meyer. 6th ed. Boston: Bedford/St. Martin's, 2010. 370–71. Print.

---. "Mowing." *Poetry: An Introduction*. Ed. Michael Meyer. 6th ed. Boston: Bedford/St. Martin's, 2010. 368–69. Print.

Meyers, Jeffrey. *Robert Frost: A Biography*. New York: Houghton, 1996. Print.

Monteiro, George. *Robert Frost and the New England Renaissance*. Lexington: UP of Kentucky, 1988. Print.

Parini, Jay. *Robert Frost: A Life*. New York: Holt, 1999. Print.

Stanlis, Peter J. "Commentary: 'Mending Wall.'" *Robert Frost: Poems, Life, Legacy*. CD-ROM. New York: Holt, 1997.

Van Doren, Mark. "Robert Frost's America." *Atlantic Monthly*. Atlantic Unbound, June 1951. Web. 26 October 2009.

29

Taking Essay
Examinations

It is the function of the liberal arts
education not to give right answers, but
to ask right questions.
— CYNTHIA OZICK

By permission of Alfred
A. Knopf, Inc.

PREPARING FOR AN ESSAY EXAM

Keep Up with the Reading

The best way to prepare for an examination is to keep up with the reading. If you begin the course with a commitment to completing the reading assignments on time, you will not have to read in a frenzy and cram just days before the test. The readings will be a pleasure, not a frantic ordeal. Moreover, you will find that your instructor's comments and class discussion will make more sense to you and that you'll be able to participate in class discussion. As you prepare for the exam, you should be rereading texts rather than reading for the first time. It may not be possible to reread everything, but you'll at least be able to scan a familiar text and reread passages that are particularly important.

Take Notes and Annotate the Text

Don't rely exclusively on your memory. The typical literature class includes a hefty amount of reading, so unless you take notes, annotate the text with your own comments, and underline important passages, you're likely to forget material that could be useful for responding to an examination question (see pp. 686–88 for a discussion of these matters). The more you can retrieve from your reading the more prepared you'll be for reviewing significant material for the exam. Your notes can be used to illustrate points that were made in class. By briefly quoting an important phrase or line from the text, you can provide supporting evidence that will make your argument convincing. Consider, for example, the difference between writing that "Marvell's speaker in 'To His Coy Mistress' says that they won't be able to love after they die" and writing that "the speaker intones that 'The grave's a fine and private place, / But none, I think, do there embrace.'" No one expects you to memorize the entire poem, but recalling a few lines here and there can transform a sleepy generality into an illustrative, persuasive argument.

Anticipate Questions

As you review the readings, keep in mind the class discussions and the focus provided by your instructor. Very often class discussions and the instructor's emphasis become the basis for essay questions. You may not see the exact same topics on the exam, but you might find that the matters you've discussed in class will serve as a means of responding to an essay question. If, for example, class discussion of Robert Frost's "Mending Wall" (see p. 370) centered on the poem's rural New England setting, you could use that conservative, traditional setting to answer a question such as "Discuss how the conflicts between the speaker and his neighbor are related to the poem's theme." A discussion of the neighbor's rigidity and his firmly entrenched conservative New England attitudes could be connected to his impulse to rebuild the wall between himself and the poem's speaker. The point is that you'll be well prepared for an essay exam when you can shape the material you've studied so that it is responsive to whatever kinds of reasonable questions you encounter on the exam. Reasonable questions? Yes, your instructor is more likely to offer you an opportunity to demonstrate your familiarity with and understanding of the text than to set a trap that, for instance, demands that you discuss how Frost's work experience as an adolescent informs the poem when no mention was ever made of that in class or in your reading.

You can also anticipate questions by considering the Questions for Responsive Reading and Writing about poetry (p. 59) and the questions in Arguing about Literature (p. 692), along with the Questions for Writing about an Author in Depth (p. 352). Not all of these questions will necessarily be relevant to every work that you read, but they cover a wide range of concerns that should allow you to organize your reading, note-taking, and reviewing so that you're not taken by surprise during the exam.

Studying with a classmate or a small group from class can be a stimulating and fruitful means of discovering and organizing the course's major topics and themes. This method of brainstorming can be useful not only for studying for exams, but also through the semester as a way to understand and review course readings. And, finally, you needn't be shy about asking your instructor what types of questions might appear on the exam and how best to study for them. You may not get a very specific reply, but almost any information is more useful than none.

TYPES OF EXAMS

Closed-Book versus Open-Book Exams

Closed-book exams require more memorization and recall than open-book exams, which permit you to use your text and perhaps even your notes to answer questions. Obviously, dates, names, definitions, and other details play less of a role in an open-book exam. An open-book exam requires no less preparation, however, because you'll need to be intimately familiar with the texts and the major ideas, themes, and issues that you've studied in order to quickly and efficiently support your points with relevant, specific evidence. Because every student has the same advantage of having access to the text, preparation remains the key to answering the questions. Some students find open-book exams more difficult than closed-book tests, because they risk spending too much time reading, scanning, and searching for material and not enough time writing a response that draws on the knowledge and understanding that their reading and studying has provided them. It's best to limit the time you allow yourself to review the text or notes so that you devote an adequate amount of time to getting your ideas down on paper.

Essay Questions

Essay questions generally fall within one of the following categories. If you can recognize quickly what is being asked of you, you will be able to respond to the question more efficiently.

1. **Explication.** Explication calls for a line-by-line explanation of a passage of poetry or prose that considers, for example, diction, figures of speech, symbolism, sound, form, and theme in an effort to describe how language creates meaning. (For a more detailed discussion of explication, see p. 702.)

2. **Definition.** Defining a term and then applying it to a writer or work is a frequent exam exercise. Consider: "Define *Romanticism*. To what extent can Keats's 'Ode on a Grecian Urn' (p. 94) be regarded as a Romantic poem?" This sort of question requires that you first describe what constitutes a Romantic literary work and then explain how "Ode on a Grecian Urn" does (or doesn't) fit the bill.

3. **Analysis.** An analytical question focuses on a particular part of a literary work. You might be asked, for example, to analyze the significance of images in Sharon Olds's poem "Last Night" (p. 84). This sort of question requires you not only to discuss a specific element of the poem but also to explain how that element contributes to the poem's overall effect. (For a more detailed discussion of analysis, see p. 707.)

4. **Comparison and Contrast.** Comparison and contrast calls for a discussion of the similarities or differences between writers, works, or elements of works. For example: "Compare and contrast the tone of the *carpe diem* arguments made by the speaker in Ann Lauinger's 'Marvell Noir' and in Andrew Marvell's 'To His Coy Mistress.'" Despite the nearly three hundred years that separate these two poems in setting and circumstances, a discussion of the tone of the speakers' arguments reveals some intriguing similarities and differences. (For a more detailed discussion of comparison and contrast, see p. 711.)

5. **Discussion of a Critical Perspective.** A brief quotation by a critic about a work is usually designed to stimulate a response that requires you to agree with, disagree with, or qualify a critic's perspective. Usually it is not so important whether you agree or disagree with the critic; what matters is the quality of your argument. Think about how you might wrestle with this assessment of Robert Frost written by Lionel Trilling: "The manifest America of Mr. Frost's poems may be pastoral; the actual America is tragic." With some qualifications (surely not all of Frost's poems are "tragic"), this could provide a useful way of talking about a poem such as "Mending Wall" (p. 370).

6. **Imaginative Questions.** To a degree, every question requires imagination regardless of whether it's being asked or answered. However, some questions require more imaginative leaps to arrive at the center of an issue than others do. Consider, for example, the intellectual agility needed to respond to this question: "Discuss the speakers' attitudes toward the power of imagination in Emily Dickinson's 'To make a prairie it takes a clover and one bee,' Robert Frost's 'Mending Wall,' and Philip Larkin's 'A Study of Reading Habits.'" As tricky as this thematic triangulation may seem, there is plenty to say about the speakers' varied, complicated, and contradictory attitudes toward the power of an individual's imagination. Or try a simpler but no less interesting version: "How do you think Frost would review Marvell's 'To His Coy Mistress' and Olds's 'Last Night'?" Such questions certainly require detailed, reasoned responses, but they also leave room for creativity and even wit.

STRATEGIES FOR WRITING ESSAY EXAMS

Your hands may be sweaty and your heart pounding as you begin the exam, but as long as you're prepared and you keep in mind some basic strategies for writing essay exams, you should be able to respond to questions with confidence and a genuine sense of accomplishment.

1. Before you begin writing, read through the entire exam. If there are choices to be made, make certain you know how many questions must be answered (for instance, only one out of four, not two). Note how many points each question is worth; spend more time on the two worth forty points each and perhaps leave the twenty-point question for last.

2. Budget your time. If there are short-answer questions, do not allow them to absorb you so that you cannot do justice to the longer essay questions. Follow the suggested time limits for each question; if none is offered, then create your own schedule in proportion to the points allotted for each question.

3. Depending on your own sensibilities, you may want to begin with the easiest or hardest questions. It doesn't really matter which you begin with as long as you pace yourself to avoid running out of time.

4. Be sure that you understand the question. Does it ask you to compare or contrast, define, analyze, explicate, or use some other approach? Determine how many elements there are to the question so that you don't inadvertently miss part of the question. Do not spend time copying the question.

5. Make some brief notes about how you plan to answer the question; even a simple list of what you'll need to cover can serve as a useful outline.

6. Address the question; avoid unnecessary summaries or irrelevant asides. Focus on the particular elements enumerated or implied by the question.

7. After beginning the essay, write a clear thesis that describes the major topics you will discuss: "Mending Wall" is typical of Frost's concerns as a writer owing to its treatment of setting, tone, and theme.

8. Support and illustrate your answer with specific, relevant references to the text. The more specificity — the more you demonstrate a familiarity with the text (rather than simply providing a summary) — the better the answer.

9. Don't overlap and repeat responses to questions; your instructor will recognize such padding. If two different questions are about the same work or writer, demonstrate the breadth and depth of your knowledge of the subject.

10. Allow time to proofread and to qualify and to add more supporting material if necessary. At this final stage, too, it's worth remembering that Mark Twain liked to remind his readers that the difference between the right word and the almost right word is the difference between lightning and a lightning bug.

Glossary of Literary Terms

Accent The emphasis, or STRESS, given a syllable in pronunciation. We say "*syllable*" not "syl*lable*," "*em*phasis" not "em*pha*sis." Accents can also be used to emphasize a particular word in a sentence: *Is* she con*tent* with the *contents* of the *yellow pack*age? See also METER.

Allegory A narration or description usually restricted to a single meaning because its events, actions, characters, settings, and objects represent specific abstractions or ideas. Although the elements in an allegory may be interesting in themselves, the emphasis tends to be on what they ultimately mean. Characters may be given names such as Hope, Pride, Youth, and Charity; they have few if any personal qualities beyond their abstract meanings. These personifications are not symbols because, for instance, the meaning of a character named Charity is precisely that virtue. See also SYMBOL.

Alliteration The repetition of the same consonant sounds in a sequence of words, usually at the beginning of a word or stressed syllable: "*descending dew drops*"; "*luscious lemons*." Alliteration is based on the sounds of letters, rather than the spelling of words; for example, "*keen*" and "*car*" alliterate, but "*car*" and "*cite*" do not. Used sparingly, alliteration can intensify ideas by emphasizing key words, but when used too self-consciously, it can be distracting, even ridiculous, rather than effective. See also ASSONANCE, CONSONANCE.

Allusion A brief reference to a person, place, thing, event, or idea in history or literature. Allusions conjure up biblical authority, scenes from Shakespeare's plays, historic figures, wars, great love stories, and anything else that might enrich an author's work. Allusions imply reading and cultural experiences shared by the writer and reader, functioning as a kind of shorthand whereby the recalling of something outside the work supplies an emotional or intellectual context, such as a poem about current racial struggles calling up the memory of Abraham Lincoln.

Ambiguity Allows for two or more simultaneous interpretations of a word, phrase, action, or situation, all of which can be supported by the context of a work. Deliberate ambiguity can contribute to the effectiveness and richness of a work. However, unintentional ambiguity obscures meaning and can confuse readers.

Anagram A word or phrase made from the letters of another word or phrase, as *heart* is an anagram of *earth*. Anagrams have often been considered merely an exercise of one's ingenuity, but sometimes writers use anagrams

745

to conceal proper names or veiled messages or to suggest important connections between words, as in *hated* and *death*.

Anapestic meter See FOOT.

Apostrophe An address, either to someone who is absent and therefore cannot hear the speaker or to something nonhuman that cannot comprehend. Apostrophe often provides a speaker the opportunity to think aloud.

Approximate rhyme See RHYME.

Archetype A term used to describe universal symbols that evoke deep and sometimes unconscious responses in a reader. In literature, characters, images, and themes that symbolically embody universal meanings and the basic experiences of humans, regardless of when or where they live, are considered archetypes. Common literary archetypes include stories of quests, initiations, scapegoats, descents to the underworld, and ascents to heaven. See also MYTHOLOGICAL CRITICISM.

Assonance The repetition of internal vowel sounds in nearby words that do not end the same, for example, "asleep under a tr*ee*," or "*ea*ch evening." Similar endings result in rhyme, as in "asleep in the deep." Assonance is a strong means of emphasizing important words in a line. See also ALLITERATION, CONSONANCE.

Ballad Traditionally, a ballad is a song, transmitted orally from generation to generation, that tells a story and that eventually is written down. As such, ballads usually cannot be traced to a particular author or group of authors. Typically, ballads are dramatic, condensed, and impersonal narratives, such as "Bonny Barbara Allan." A **literary ballad** is a narrative poem written in deliberate imitation of the language, form, and spirit of the traditional ballad, such as John Keats's "La Belle Dame sans Merci." See also BALLAD STANZA, QUATRAIN.

Ballad stanza A four-line stanza, known as a QUATRAIN, consisting of alternating eight- and six-syllable lines. Usually only the second and fourth lines rhyme (an *abcb* pattern). Coleridge adopted the ballad stanza in "The Rime of the Ancient Mariner":

All in a hot and copper sky
The bloody Sun, at noon,
Right up above the mast did stand,
No bigger than the Moon.

See also BALLAD, QUATRAIN.

Biographical criticism An approach to literature that suggests that knowledge of the author's life experiences can aid in the understanding of his or her work. While biographical information can sometimes complicate one's interpretation of a work, and some formalist critics (such as the New Critics) disparage the use of the author's biography as a tool for textual interpretation, learning about the life of the author can often enrich a reader's appreciation for that author's work. See also FORMALIST CRITICISM, NEW CRITICISM.

Blank verse Unrhymed iambic pentameter. Blank verse is the English verse form closest to the natural rhythms of English speech and therefore is the most common pattern found in traditional English narrative and dramatic poetry from Shakespeare to the early twentieth century. Shakespeare's plays use blank verse extensively. See also IAMBIC PENTAMETER.

Cacophony Language that is discordant and difficult to pronounce, such as this line from John Updike's "Player Piano": "never my numb plunker fumbles." Cacophony ("bad sound") may be unintentional in the writer's sense of music, or it may be used consciously for deliberate dramatic effect. See also EUPHONY.

Caesura A pause within a line of poetry that contributes to the rhythm of the line. A caesura can occur anywhere within a line and need not be indicated by punctuation. In scanning a line, we indicate caesuras by a double vertical line (||). See also METER, RHYTHM, SCANSION.

Canon Those works generally considered by scholars, critics, and teachers to be the most important to read and study, which collectively constitute the "masterpieces" of literature. Since the 1960s, the traditional English and American literary canon, consisting mostly of works by white male writers, has been rapidly expanding to include many female writers and writers of varying ethnic backgrounds.

Carpe diem The Latin phrase meaning "seize the day." This is a very common literary theme, especially in lyric poetry, which emphasizes that life is short, time is fleeting, and one should make the most of present pleasures. Robert Herrick's poem "To the Virgins, to Make Much of Time" uses the *carpe diem* theme.

Cliché An idea or expression that has become tired and trite from overuse, its freshness and clarity having worn off. Clichés often anesthetize readers and are usually a sign of weak writing. See also SENTIMENTALITY, STOCK RESPONSES.

Colloquial Refers to a type of informal diction that reflects casual, conversational language and often includes slang expressions. See also DICTION.

Connotation Associations and implications that go beyond a word's literal meaning and deriving from how the word has been commonly used and the associations people make with it. For example, the word *eagle* connotes ideas of liberty and freedom that have little to do with the word's literal meaning. See also DENOTATION.

Consonance A common type of near rhyme that consists of identical consonant sounds preceded by different vowel sounds: *home, same; worth, breath.* See also RHYME.

Contextual symbol See SYMBOL.

Controlling metaphor See METAPHOR.

Convention A characteristic of a literary genre (often unrealistic) that is understood and accepted by readers because it has come, through usage and time, to be recognized as a familiar technique. For example, the use of meter and rhyme are poetic conventions.

Conventional symbol See SYMBOL.

Cosmic irony See IRONY.

Couplet Two consecutive lines of poetry that usually rhyme and have the same meter. A **heroic couplet** is a couplet written in rhymed iambic pentameter.

Cultural criticism An approach to literature that focuses on the historical as well as social, political, and economic contexts of a work. Popular culture — mass-produced and -consumed cultural artifacts ranging from advertising and popular fiction to television to rock music — is given the same emphasis as "high culture." Cultural critics use widely eclectic strategies such as new historicism, psychology, gender studies, and deconstructionism to analyze not only literary texts but everything from radio talk shows, comic strips, calendar art, commercials, to travel guides and baseball cards. See also HISTORICAL CRITICISM, MARXIST CRITICISM, POSTCOLONIAL CRITICISM.

Dactylic meter See FOOT.

Deconstructionism An approach to literature that suggests that literary works do not yield fixed, single meanings, because language can never say exactly what we intend it to mean. Deconstructionism seeks to destabilize meaning by examining the gaps and ambiguities of a text's language. Deconstructionists pay close attention to language in order to discover and describe how a variety of possible readings are generated by the elements of a text. See also NEW CRITICISM.

Denotation The dictionary meaning of a word. See also CONNOTATION.

Dialect A type of informal diction. Dialects are spoken by definable groups of people from a particular geographic region, economic group, or social class. Writers use dialect to contrast and express differences in their characters' educational, class, social, and regional backgrounds. See also DICTION.

Diction A writer's choice of words, phrases, sentence structures, and figurative language, which combine to help create meaning. **Formal diction** consists of a dignified, impersonal, and elevated use of language; it follows the rules of syntax exactly and is often characterized by complex words and lofty tone. **Middle diction** maintains correct language usage but is less elevated than formal diction; it reflects the way most educated people speak. **Informal diction** represents the plain language of everyday use and often includes idiomatic expressions, slang, contractions, and many simple, common words. **Poetic diction** refers to the way poets sometimes use an elevated diction that deviates significantly from the common speech and writing of their time, choosing words for their supposedly inherent poetic qualities. Since the eighteenth century, however, poets have been incorporating all kinds of diction in their work, and so there is no longer an automatic distinction between the language of a poet and the language of everyday speech. See also DIALECT.

Didactic poetry Poetry designed to teach an ethical, moral, or religious lesson. Michael Wigglesworth's Puritan poem *Day of Doom* is an example of didactic poetry.

Doggerel A derogatory term used to describe poetry whose subject is trite and whose rhythm and sounds are monotonously heavy-handed.

Dramatic irony See IRONY.

Dramatic monologue A type of lyric poem in which a character (the speaker) addresses a distinct but silent audience imagined to be present in the poem in such a way as to reveal a dramatic situation and, often unintentionally, some aspect of his or her temperament or personality. See also LYRIC.

Electra complex The female version of the Oedipus complex. *Electra complex* is a term used to describe the psychological conflict of a daughter's unconscious rivalry with her mother for her father's attention. The name comes from the Greek legend of Electra, who avenged the death of her father, Agamemnon, by plotting the death of her mother. See also OEDIPUS COMPLEX, PSYCHOLOGICAL CRITICISM.

Elegy A mournful, contemplative lyric poem written to commemorate someone who is dead, often ending in a consolation. Tennyson's *In Memoriam,* written on the death of Arthur Hallam, is an elegy. *Elegy* may also refer to a serious meditative poem produced to express the speaker's melancholy thoughts. See also LYRIC.

End rhyme See RHYME.

End-stopped line A poetic line that has a pause at the end. End-stopped lines reflect normal speech patterns and are often marked by punctuation. The first line of John Keats's "Endymion" is an example of an end-stopped line; the natural pause coincides with the end of the line and is marked by a period:

A thing of beauty is a joy forever.

English sonnet See SONNET.

Enjambment In poetry, when one line ends without a pause and continues into the next line for its meaning. This is also called a **run-on line.** The transition between the first two lines of William Wordsworth's "My Heart Leaps Up" demonstrates enjambment:

My heart leaps up when I behold
    A rainbow in the sky:

Envoy See SESTINA.

Epic A long narrative poem, told in a formal, elevated style, that focuses on a serious subject and chronicles heroic deeds and events important to a culture or nation. John Milton's *Paradise Lost,* which attempts to "justify the ways of God to man," is an epic. See also NARRATIVE POEM.

Epigram A brief, pointed, and witty poem that usually makes a satiric or humorous point. Epigrams are most often written in couplets but take no prescribed form.

Euphony *Euphony* ("good sound") refers to language that is smooth and musically pleasant to the ear. See also CACOPHONY.

Exact rhyme See RHYME.

Extended metaphor See METAPHOR.

Eye rhyme See RHYME.

Falling meter See METER.

Feminine rhyme See RHYME.

Feminist criticism An approach to literature that seeks to correct or supplement what may be regarded as a predominantly male-dominated critical perspective with a feminist consciousness. Feminist criticism places literature in a social context and uses a broad range of disciplines, including history, sociology, psychology, and linguistics, to provide a perspective sensitive to feminist issues. Feminist theories also attempt to understand representation from a woman's point of view and to explain women's writing strategies as specific to their social conditions. See also GENDER CRITICISM.

Figures of speech Ways of using language that deviate from the literal, denotative meanings of words in order to suggest additional meanings or effects. Figures of speech say one thing in terms of something else, such as when an eager funeral director is described as a vulture. See also METAPHOR, SIMILE.

Fixed form A poem that may be categorized by the pattern of its lines, meter, rhythm, or stanzas. A SONNET is a fixed form of poetry because by definition it must have fourteen lines. Other fixed forms include LIMERICK, SESTINA, and VILLANELLE. However, poems written in a fixed form may not always fit into categories precisely, because writers sometimes vary traditional forms to create innovative effects. See also OPEN FORM.

Foot The metrical unit by which a line of poetry is measured. A foot usually consists of one stressed and one or two unstressed syllables. An **iambic** foot, which consists of one unstressed syllable followed by one stressed syllable (ăwáy), is the most common metrical foot in English poetry. A **trochaic** foot consists of one stressed syllable followed by an unstressed syllable (lóvelў). An **anapestic** foot is two unstressed syllables followed by one stressed syllable (ŭndĕrstánd). A **dactylic** foot is one stressed syllable followed by two unstressed syllables (déspĕrăte). A **spondee** is a foot consisting of two stressed syllables (dèad sèt) but is not a sustained metrical foot and is used mainly for variety or emphasis. See also IAMBIC PENTAMETER, LINE, METER.

Form The overall structure or shape of a work, which frequently follows an established design. Forms may refer to a literary type (narrative form, lyric form) or to patterns of meter, lines, and rhymes (stanza form, verse form). See also FIXED FORM, OPEN FORM.

Formal diction See DICTION.

Formalist criticism An approach to literature that focuses on the formal elements of a work, such as its language, structure, and TONE. Formalist critics offer intense examinations of the relationship between FORM and meaning in a work, emphasizing the subtle complexity in how a work is arranged. Formalists pay special attention to DICTION, IRONY, PARADOX, METAPHOR, and SYMBOL, as well as larger elements such as plot, characterization, and narrative technique. Formalist critics read literature as an independent work of art rather than as a reflection of the author's state of mind or as a representation of a moment in history. Therefore anything outside of the work, including historical influences and authorial intent, is generally not examined by formalist critics. See also NEW CRITICISM.

Found poem An unintentional poem discovered in a nonpoetic context, such as a conversation, news story, or advertisement. Found poems serve as reminders that everyday language often contains what can be considered poetry or that poetry is definable as any text read as a poem.

Free verse Also called *open form poetry,* free verse refers to poems characterized by their nonconformity to established patterns of meter, rhyme, and stanza. Free verse uses elements such as speech patterns, grammar, emphasis, and breath pauses to determine line breaks and usually does not rhyme. See OPEN FORM.

Gay and lesbian criticism An approach to literature that focuses on how homosexuals are represented in literature, how they read literature, and whether sexuality, as well as gender, is culturally constructed or innate. See also FEMINIST CRITICISM, GENDER CRITICISM.

Gender criticism An approach to literature that explores how ideas about men and women — what is masculine and feminine — can be regarded as socially constructed by particular cultures. Gender criticism expands categories and definitions of what is masculine or feminine and tends to regard sexuality as more complex than merely masculine or feminine, heterosexual or homosexual. See also FEMINIST CRITICISM, GAY AND LESBIAN CRITICISM.

Genre A French word meaning "kind" or "type." The major genres in literature are poetry, fiction, drama, and essays. *Genre* can also refer to more specific types of literature such as comedy, tragedy, epic poetry, or science fiction.

Haiku A style of lyric poetry borrowed from the Japanese that typically presents an intense emotion or vivid image of nature, which, traditionally, is designed to lead to a spiritual insight. Haiku is a fixed poetic form, consisting of seventeen syllables organized into three unrhymed lines of five, seven, and five syllables. Today, however, many poets vary the syllabic count in their haiku. See also FIXED FORM.

Heroic couplet See COUPLET.

Historical criticism An approach to literature that uses history as a means of understanding a literary work more clearly. Such criticism moves beyond both the facts of an author's personal life and the text itself in order to examine the social and intellectual currents in which the author composed the work. See also CULTURAL CRITICISM, MARXIST CRITICISM, NEW HISTORICISM, POSTCOLONIAL CRITICISM.

Hyperbole A boldly exaggerated statement that adds emphasis without intending to be literally true, as in the statement "He ate everything in the house." Hyperbole (also called *overstatement*) may be used for serious, comic, or ironic effect. See also FIGURES OF SPEECH.

Iambic meter See FOOT.

Iambic pentameter A metrical pattern in poetry that consists of five iambic feet per line. (An iamb, or iambic foot, consists of one unstressed syllable followed by a stressed syllable.) See also FOOT, METER.

Image A word, phrase, or figure of speech (especially a SIMILE or a METAPHOR) that addresses the senses, suggesting mental pictures of sights, sounds, smells, tastes, feelings, or actions. Images offer sensory impressions to the reader and also convey emotions and moods through their verbal pictures. See also FIGURES OF SPEECH.

Implied metaphor See METAPHOR.

Informal diction See DICTION.

Internal rhyme See RHYME.

Irony A literary device that uses contradictory statements or situations to reveal a reality different from what appears to be true. It is ironic for a firehouse to burn down or for a police station to be burglarized. **Verbal irony** is a figure of speech that occurs when a person says one thing but means the opposite. **Sarcasm** is a strong form of verbal irony that is calculated to hurt someone through, for example, false praise. **Dramatic irony** creates a discrepancy between what a character believes or says and what the reader or audience member knows to be true. **Situational irony** exists when there is an incongruity between what is expected to happen and what actually happens owing to forces beyond human comprehension or control. The suicide of the seemingly successful main character in Edwin Arlington Robinson's poem "Richard Cory" is an example of situational irony. **Cosmic irony** occurs when a writer uses God, destiny, or fate to dash the hopes and expectations of a character or of humankind in general. In cosmic irony, a discrepancy exists between what a character aspires to and what universal forces provide. Stephen Crane's poem "A Man Said to the Universe" is a good example of cosmic irony, because the universe acknowledges no obligation to the man's assertion of his own existence.

Italian sonnet See SONNET.

Limerick A light, humorous style of fixed form poetry. Its usual form consists of five lines with the rhyme scheme *aabba;* lines 1, 2, and 5 contain three feet, while lines 3 and 4 usually contain two feet. Limericks range in subject matter from the silly to the obscene, and since Edward Lear popularized them in the nineteenth century, children and adults have enjoyed these comic poems. See also FIXED FORM.

Line A sequence of words printed as a separate entity on the page. In poetry, lines are usually measured by the number of feet they contain. The names for various line lengths are as follows:

monometer: one foot	pentameter: five feet
dimeter: two feet	hexameter: six feet
trimeter: three feet	heptameter: seven feet
tetrameter: four feet	octameter: eight feet

The number of feet in a line, coupled with the name of the foot, describes the metrical qualities of that line. See also END-STOPPED LINE, ENJAMBMENT, FOOT, METER.

Literary ballad See BALLAD.

Literary symbol See SYMBOL.

Litotes See UNDERSTATEMENT.

Lyric A type of brief poem that expresses the personal emotions and thoughts of a single speaker. It is important to realize, however, that although the lyric is uttered in the first person, the SPEAKER is not necessarily the poet. There are many varieties of lyric poetry, including the DRAMATIC MONOLOGUE, ELEGY, HAIKU, ODE, and SONNET forms.

Marxist criticism An approach to literature that focuses on a work's ideological content — its explicit and implicit assumptions and values about matters such as culture, race, class, and power. Marxist criticism, based largely on the writings of Karl Marx, typically aims at not only revealing and clarifying ideological issues but also correcting social injustices. Some Marxist critics use literature to describe the competing socioeconomic interests that too often advance capitalist interests such as money and power rather than socialist interests such as morality and justice. They argue that literature and literary criticism are essentially political because they either challenge or support economic oppression. Because of this strong emphasis on the political aspects of texts, Marxist criticism focuses more on the content and themes of literature than on its form. See also CULTURAL CRITICISM, HISTORICAL CRITICISM, SOCIOLOGICAL CRITICISM.

Masculine rhyme See RHYME.

Metaphor A metaphor is a figure of speech that makes a comparison between two unlike things without using the words *like* or *as*. Metaphors assert the identity of dissimilar things, as when Macbeth asserts that life *is* a "brief candle." Metaphors can be subtle and powerful and can transform people, places, objects, and ideas into whatever the writer imagines them to be. An **implied metaphor** is a more subtle comparison; the terms being compared are not so specifically explained. For example, to describe a stubborn man unwilling to leave, one could say that he was "a mule standing his ground." This is a fairly explicit metaphor; the man is being compared to a mule. But to say that the man "brayed his refusal to leave" is to create an implied metaphor, because the subject (the man) is never overtly identified as a mule. Braying is associated with the mule, a notoriously stubborn creature, and so the comparison between the stubborn man and the mule is sustained. Implied metaphors can slip by inattentive readers who are not sensitive to such carefully chosen, highly concentrated language. An **extended metaphor** is a sustained comparison in which part or all of a poem consists of a series of related metaphors. Robert Francis's poem "Catch" relies on an extended metaphor that compares poetry to playing catch. A **controlling metaphor** runs through an entire work and determines its form or nature. The controlling metaphor in Anne Bradstreet's poem "The Author to Her Book" likens her book to a child. **Synecdoche** is a kind of metaphor in which a part of something is used to signify the whole, as when a gossip is called a "wagging tongue" or when ten ships are called "ten sails." Sometimes, synecdoche refers to the whole being used to signify the part, as in the phrase "Boston won the baseball game." Clearly, the entire city of Boston did not participate in the game; the whole of Boston is being used to signify the individuals who played and won the game. **Metonymy** is a type of metaphor in which something closely associated with a subject is substituted for it. In this way, we speak of the "silver screen" to mean motion pictures, "the crown" to stand for the king, "the White House" to stand for the activities of the president. See also FIGURES OF SPEECH, PERSONIFICATION, SIMILE.

Meter When a rhythmic pattern of stresses recurs in a poem, it is called *meter.* Metrical patterns are determined by the type and number of feet in a line of verse; combining the name of a line length with the name of a foot concisely describes the meter of the line. **Rising meter** refers to metrical feet that move from unstressed to stressed sounds, such as the iambic foot and the anapestic foot. **Falling meter** refers to metrical feet that move from stressed to unstressed sounds, such as the trochaic foot and the dactylic foot. See also ACCENT, FOOT, IAMBIC PENTAMETER, LINE.

Metonymy See METAPHOR.

Middle diction See DICTION.

Mythological criticism An approach to literature that seeks to identify what in a work creates deep, universal responses in readers, by paying close attention to the hopes, fears, and expectations of entire cultures. Mythological critics (sometimes called *archetypal critics*) analyze literature for underlying, recurrent patterns that reveal universal meanings and basic human experiences for readers regardless of when and where they live. These critics attempt to explain how archetypes (the characters, images, and themes that symbolically embody universal meanings and experiences) are embodied in literary works in order to make larger connections that explain a particular work's lasting appeal. Mythological critics may specialize in areas such as classical literature, philology, anthropology, psychology, and cultural history, but they all emphasize the assumptions and values of various cultures. See also ARCHETYPE.

Narrative poem A poem that tells a story. A narrative poem may be short or long, and the story it relates may be simple or complex. See also BALLAD, EPIC.

Near rhyme See RHYME.

New Criticism An approach to literature made popular between the 1940s and the 1960s that evolved out of formalist criticism. New Critics suggest that detailed analysis of the language of a literary text can uncover important layers of meaning in that work. New Criticism consciously downplays the historical influences, authorial intentions, and social contexts that surround texts in order to focus on explication — extremely close textual analysis. See also FORMALIST CRITICISM.

New historicism An approach to literature that emphasizes the interaction between a work's historical context and a modern reader's understanding and interpretation of the work. New historicists attempt to describe the culture of a period by reading many different kinds of texts and paying close attention to many different dimensions of a culture, including political, economic, social, and esthetic concerns. They regard texts not simply as a reflection of the culture that produced them but also as producing that culture by playing an active role in the social and political conflicts of an age. New historicism acknowledges and then explores various versions of "history," sensitizing us to the fact that the history on which we choose to focus has been reconstructed from our present circumstances. See also HISTORICAL CRITICISM.

Octave A poetic stanza of eight lines, usually forming one part of a sonnet. See also SONNET, STANZA.

Ode A relatively lengthy lyric poem that often expresses lofty emotions in a dignified style. Odes are characterized by a serious topic, such as truth, art, freedom, justice, or the meaning of life; their tone tends to be formal. There is no prescribed pattern that defines an ode; some odes repeat the same pattern in each stanza, while others introduce a new pattern in each stanza. See also LYRIC.

Oedipus complex A Freudian term derived from Sophocles' tragedy *Oedipus the King.* It describes a psychological complex that is predicated on a boy's unconscious rivalry with his father for his mother's love and his desire to eliminate his father in order to take his father's place with his mother. The female equivalent of this complex is called the *Electra complex.* See also ELECTRA COMPLEX, PSYCHOLOGICAL CRITICISM.

Off rhyme See RHYME.

Onomatopoeia A term referring to the use of a word that resembles the sound it denotes. *Buzz, rattle, bang,* and *sizzle* all reflect onomatopoeia. Onomatopoeia can also consist of more than one word; writers sometimes create lines or whole passages in which the sound of the words helps to convey their meanings.

Open form Sometimes called *free verse,* open form poetry does not conform to established patterns of METER, RHYME, and STANZA. Such poetry derives its rhythmic qualities from the repetition of words, phrases, or grammatical structures; from the arrangement of words on the printed page; or by some other means. The poet E. E. Cummings wrote open form poetry; his poems do not have measurable meters, but they do have RHYTHM. See also FIXED FORM.

Organic form Refers to works whose formal characteristics are not rigidly predetermined but follow the movement of thought or emotion being expressed. Such works are said to grow like living organisms, following their own individual patterns rather than external fixed rules that govern, for example, the form of a SONNET.

Overstatement See HYPERBOLE.

Oxymoron A condensed form of paradox in which two contradictory words are used together, as in "sweet sorrow" or "jumbo shrimp." See also PARADOX.

Paradox A statement that initially appears to be contradictory but then, on closer inspection, turns out to make sense. For example, John Donne ends his sonnet "Death, Be Not Proud" with the paradoxical statement "Death, thou shalt die." To solve the paradox, it is necessary to discover the sense that underlies the statement. Paradox is useful in poetry because it arrests a reader's attention by its seemingly stubborn refusal to make sense.

Paraphrase A prose restatement of the central ideas of a work, in your own language.

Parody A humorous imitation of another, usually serious, work. It can take any fixed or open form, because parodists imitate the tone, language, and shape of the original in order to deflate the subject matter, making the original work seem absurd. Anthony Hecht's poem "Dover Bitch" is a famous parody of Matthew Arnold's well-known "Dover Beach." Parody may also be used as a form of literary criticism to expose the defects in a work. But sometimes parody becomes an affectionate acknowledgment that a well-known work has become both institutionalized in our culture and fair game for some fun. For example, Ann Lauinger's "Marvell Noir" gently mocks Andrew Marvell's "To His Coy Mistress."

Persona Literally, a *persona* is a mask. In literature a *persona* is a speaker created by a writer to tell a story or to speak in a poem. A persona is not a character in a story or narrative nor does a persona necessarily directly reflect the author's personal voice. A persona is a separate self, created by and distinct from the author, through which he or she speaks.

Personification A form of metaphor in which human characteristics are attributed to nonhuman things. Personification offers the writer a way to give the world life and motion by assigning familiar human behaviors and emotions to animals, inanimate objects, and abstract ideas. For example, in John Keats's "Ode on a Grecian Urn," the speaker refers to the urn as an "unravished bride of quietness." See also METAPHOR.

Petrarchan sonnet See SONNET.

Picture poem A type of open form poetry in which the poet arranges the lines of the poem so as to create a particular shape on the page. The shape of the poem embodies its subject; the poem becomes a picture of what the poem is describing. Michael McFee's "In Medias Res" is an example of a picture poem. See also OPEN FORM.

Poetic diction See DICTION.

Postcolonial criticism An approach to literature that focuses on the study of cultural behavior and expression in relationship to the colonized world. Postcolonial criticism refers to the analysis of literary works by writers from countries and cultures that at one time have been controlled by colonizing powers — such as Indian writers during or after British colonial rule. Postcolonial criticism also refers to the analysis of literary works written about colonial cultures by writers from the colonizing country. Many of these kinds of analyses point out how writers from colonial powers sometimes misrepresent colonized cultures by reflecting their own values. See also CULTURAL CRITICISM, HISTORICAL CRITICISM, MARXIST CRITICISM.

Prose poem A kind of open form poetry that is printed as prose and represents the most clear opposite of fixed form poetry. Prose poems are densely compact and often make use of striking imagery and figures of speech. See also FIXED FORM, OPEN FORM.

Prosody The overall metrical structure of a poem. See also METER.

Psychological criticism An approach to literature that draws on psychoanalytic theories, especially those of Sigmund Freud or Jacques Lacan, to understand more fully the text, the writer, and the reader. The basis of this approach is the idea of the existence of a human unconscious — those impulses, desires, and feelings about which a person is unaware but which influence emotions and behavior. Critics use psychological approaches to explore the motivations of characters and the symbolic meanings of events, while biographers speculate about a writer's own motivations — conscious or unconscious — in a literary work. Psychological approaches are also used to describe and analyze the reader's personal responses to a text.

Pun A play on words that relies on a word's having more than one meaning or sounding like another word. Shakespeare and other writers use puns extensively for serious and comic purposes; in *Romeo and Juliet* (3.2.101) the dying Mercutio puns, "Ask for me tomorrow and you shall find me a grave man." Puns have serious literary uses, but since the eighteenth century they have been used almost purely for humorous effect.

Quatrain A four-line stanza. Quatrains are the most common stanzaic form in the English language; they can have various meters and rhyme schemes. See also METER, RHYME, STANZA.

Reader-response criticism An approach to literature that focuses on the reader rather than the work itself, by attempting to describe what goes on in the reader's mind during the reading of a text. Hence the consciousness of the reader — produced by reading the work — is the actual subject of reader-response criticism. These critics are not after a "correct" reading of the text or what the author presumably intended; instead, they are interested in the reader's individual experience with the text. Thus there is no single definitive reading of a work, because readers create rather than discover absolute meanings in texts. However, this approach is not a rationale for mistaken or bizarre readings but an exploration of the possibilities for a plurality of readings. This kind of strategy calls attention to how we read, what influences our readings, and what that reveals about ourselves.

Rhyme The repetition of identical or similar concluding syllables in different words, most often at the ends of lines. Rhyme is predominantly a function of sound rather than spelling; thus words that end with the same vowel sounds rhyme (for instance, *day, prey, bouquet, weigh*), and words with the same consonant ending rhyme (for instance *vain, feign, rein, lane*). Words do not have to be spelled the same way or look alike to rhyme. In fact, words may look alike but not rhyme at all. This is called **eye rhyme,** as with *bough* and *cough,* or *brow* and *blow.* **End rhyme** is the most common form of rhyme in poetry; the rhyme comes at the end of the lines:

It runs through the reeds
    And away it proceeds,
Through meadow and glade,
    In sun and in shade.

The **rhyme scheme** of a poem describes the pattern of end rhymes. Rhyme schemes are mapped out by noting patterns of rhyme with small letters: the first rhyme sound is designated *a,* the second becomes *b,* the third *c,* and so on. Thus the rhyme scheme of the preceding stanza is *aabb.* **Internal rhyme** places at least one of the rhymed words within the line, as in "Dividing and gliding and sliding" or "In mist or cloud, on mast or shroud." **Masculine rhyme** describes the rhyming of single-syllable words, such as *grade* or *shade.* Masculine rhyme also occurs in rhyming words of more than one syllable when the same sound occurs in a final stressed syllable, as in *defend* and *contend, betray* and *away.* **Feminine rhyme** consists of a rhymed stressed syllable followed by one or more identical unstressed syllables, as in *butter,* *clutter; gratitude, attitude; quivering, shivering.* All of the examples so far have illustrated **exact rhymes,** because they share the same stressed vowel sounds as well as sharing sounds that follow the vowel. In **near rhyme** (also called **off rhyme, slant rhyme,** and **approximate rhyme**) the sounds are almost but not exactly alike. A common form of near rhyme is CONSONANCE, which consists of identical consonant sounds preceded by different vowel sounds: *home, same; worth, breath.*

Rhyme scheme See RHYME.

Rhythm A term used to refer to the recurrence of stressed and unstressed sounds in poetry. Depending on how sounds are arranged, the rhythm of a poem may be fast or slow, choppy or smooth. Poets use rhythm to create pleasurable sound patterns and to reinforce meanings. Rhythm in prose arises from pattern repetitions of sounds and pauses that create looser rhythmic effects. See also METER.

Rising meter See METER.

Run-on line See ENJAMBMENT.

Sarcasm See IRONY.

Satire The literary art of ridiculing a folly or vice in order to expose or correct it. The object of satire is usually some human frailty; people, institutions, ideas, and things are all fair game for satirists. Satire evokes attitudes of amusement, contempt, scorn, or indignation toward its faulty subject in the hope of somehow improving it. See also IRONY, PARODY.

Scansion The process of measuring the stresses in a line of verse to determine the metrical pattern of the line. See also LINE, METER.

Sentimentality A pejorative term used to describe the effort by an author to induce emotional responses in the reader that exceed what the situation warrants. Sentimentality especially pertains to such emotions as pathos and sympathy; it cons readers into falling for the mass murderer who is devoted to stray cats, and it requires that readers do not examine such illogical responses. CLICHÉS and STOCK RESPONSES are the key ingredients of sentimentality in literature.

Sestet A STANZA consisting of exactly six lines.

Sestina A type of FIXED FORM poetry consisting of thirty-six lines of any length divided into six sestets and a three-line concluding stanza called an **envoy.** The six words at the end of the first sestet's lines must also appear at the ends of the other five sestets, in varying order. These six words must also appear in the envoy, where they often resonate important themes. An example of this highly demanding form of poetry is Algernon Charles Swinburne's "Sestina." See also SESTET.

Setting The physical and social context in which the action of a poem occurs. The major elements of setting are the time, the place, and the social environment that frame the poem. Setting can be used to evoke a mood or atmosphere that will prepare the reader for what is to come, as in Robert Frost's "Home Burial."

Shakespearean sonnet See SONNET.

Simile A common figure of speech that makes an explicit comparison between two things by using words such as *like, as, than, appears,* and *seems:* "A sip of Mrs. Cook's coffee is like a punch in the stomach." The effectiveness of this simile is created by the differences between the two things compared. There would be no simile if the comparison were stated this way: "Mrs. Cook's coffee is as strong as the cafeteria's coffee." This is a literal translation because Mrs. Cook's coffee is compared with something like it — another kind of coffee. See also FIGURES OF SPEECH, METAPHOR.

Situational irony See IRONY.

Slant rhyme See RHYME.

Sociological criticism An approach to literature that examines social groups, relationships, and values as they are manifested in literature. Sociological approaches emphasize the nature and effect of the social forces that shape power relationships between groups or classes of people. Such readings treat literature as either a document reflecting social conditions or a product of those conditions. The former view brings into focus the social milieu; the latter emphasizes the work. Two important forms of sociological criticism are Marxist and feminist approaches. See also FEMINIST CRITICISM, MARXIST CRITICISM.

Sonnet A fixed form of lyric poetry that consists of fourteen lines, usually written in iambic pentameter. There are two basic types of sonnets, the Italian and the English. The **Italian sonnet,** also known as the **Petrarchan sonnet,** is divided into an octave, which typically rhymes *abbaabba,* and a sestet, which may have varying rhyme schemes. Common rhyme patterns in the sestet are *cdecde, cdcdcd,* and *cdccdc.* Very often the octave presents a situation, attitude, or problem that the sestet comments on or resolves, as in John Keats's "On First Looking into Chapman's Homer." The **English sonnet,** also known as the **Shakespearean sonnet,** is organized into three quatrains and a couplet, which typically rhyme *abab cdcd efef gg.* This rhyme scheme is more suited to English poetry because English has fewer rhyming words than Italian. English sonnets, because of their four-part organization, also have more flexibility with respect to where thematic breaks can occur. Frequently, however, the most pronounced break or turn comes with the concluding couplet, as in Shakespeare's "Shall I compare thee to a summer's day?" See also COUPLET, IAMBIC PENTAMETER, LINE, OCTAVE, QUATRAIN, SESTET.

Speaker The voice used by an author to tell a story or speak a poem. The speaker is often a created identity and should not automatically be equated with the author's self. See also PERSONA.

Spondee See FOOT.

Stanza In poetry, *stanza* refers to a grouping of lines, set off by a space, that usually has a set pattern of meter and rhyme. See also LINE, METER, RHYME.

Stock responses Predictable, conventional reactions to language, characters, symbols, or situations. The flag, motherhood, puppies, God, and peace are common objects used to elicit stock responses from unsophisticated audiences. See also CLICHÉ, SENTIMENTALITY.

Stress The emphasis, or ACCENT, given a syllable in pronunciation.

Style The distinctive and unique manner in which a writer arranges words to achieve particular effects. Style essentially combines the idea to be expressed with the author's individuality. These arrangements include individual word choices as well as matters such as the length of sentences, their structure, tone, and use of irony. See also DICTION, IRONY, TONE.

Symbol A person, an object, an image, a word, or an event that evokes a range of additional meaning beyond and usually more abstract than its literal significance. Symbols are educational devices for evoking complex ideas without having to resort to painstaking explanations that would make a story more like an essay than an experience. **Conventional symbols** have meanings that are widely recognized by a society or culture. Some conventional symbols are the Christian cross, the Star of David, a swastika, or a nation's flag. Writers use conventional symbols to reinforce meanings. E. E. Cummings, for example, emphasizes the spring setting in "in Just-" as a way of suggesting a renewed sense of life. A **literary** or **contextual symbol** can be a setting, a character, an action, an object, a name, or anything else in a work that maintains its literal significance while suggesting other meanings. Such symbols go beyond conventional symbols; they gain their symbolic meaning within the context of a specific story. For example, the urn in John Keats's "Ode on a Grecian Urn" takes on multiple symbolic meanings in the work, but these meanings do not automatically carry over into other poems about urns. The meanings suggested by Keats's urn are specific to that text; therefore it becomes a contextual symbol. See also ALLEGORY.

Synecdoche See METAPHOR.

Syntax The ordering of words into meaningful verbal patterns such as phrases, clauses, and sentences. Poets often manipulate syntax, changing conventional word order, to place certain emphasis on particular words. Emily Dickinson, for instance, writes about being surprised by a snake in her poem "A narrow Fellow in the Grass" and includes this line: "His notice sudden is." In addition to the alliterative hissing *s*-sounds here, Dickinson also effectively manipulates the line's syntax so that the verb *is* appears unexpectedly at the end, making the snake's hissing presence all the more "sudden."

Tercet A three-line stanza. See also STANZA, TRIPLET.

Terza rima An interlocking three-line rhyme scheme: *aba, bcb, cdc, ded,* and so on. Dante's *Divine Comedy* and Robert Frost's "Acquainted with the Night" are written in terza rima. See also RHYME, TERCET.

Theme The central meaning or dominant idea in a literary work. A theme provides a unifying point around which the plot, characters, setting, point of view, symbols, and other elements of a work are organized. It is important not to mistake the theme for the work's actual subject; the theme refers to the abstract concept that is made concrete through the images, characterization, and action of the text. In nonfiction, however, the theme generally refers to the main topic of the discourse.

Thesis The central idea of an essay. The thesis is a complete sentence (although sometimes it may require more than one sentence) that establishes the topic of the essay in clear, unambiguous language.

Tone The author's implicit attitude toward the reader or the people, places, and events in a work as revealed by the elements of the author's style. Tone may be characterized as serious or ironic, sad or happy, private or public, angry or affectionate, bitter or nostalgic, or any other attitudes and feelings that human beings experience. See also STYLE.

Triplet A TERCET in which all three lines rhyme.

Trochaic meter See FOOT.

Understatement The opposite of hyperbole, *understatement* (or litotes) refers to a figure of speech that says less than is intended. Understatement usually has an ironic effect, and it sometimes may be used for comic purposes, as in Mark Twain's statement, "The reports of my death are greatly exaggerated." See also HYPERBOLE, IRONY.

Verbal irony See IRONY.

Verse A generic term used to describe poetic lines composed in a measured, rhythmical pattern that are often, but not necessarily, rhymed. See also LINE, METER, RHYME, RHYTHM.

Villanelle A type of fixed form poetry consisting of nineteen lines of any length divided into six stanzas: five tercets and a concluding quatrain. The first and third lines of the initial tercet rhyme; these rhymes are repeated in each subsequent tercet (*aba*) and in the final two lines of the quatrain (*abaa*). Line 1 appears in its entirety as lines 6, 12, and 18, while line 3 reappears as lines 9, 15, and 19. Dylan Thomas's "Do not go gentle into that good night" is a villanelle. See also FIXED FORM, QUATRAIN, RHYME, TERCET.

762 | *Acknowledgments*

Acknowledgments (continued from p. ii)

Julia Alvarez. "Dusting," "Ironing Their Clothes," and "Sometimes the Words Are So Close" [Sonnet 42], from *Homecoming*, copyright © 1984, 1996 by Julia Alvarez. Published by Plume, an imprint of the Penguin Group (USA), and originally published by Grove Press. "First Muse" from *The Woman I Kept to Myself*, copyright © 2004 by Julia Alvarez. Published by Algonquin Books of Chapel Hill in 2004. "Housekeeping Cages," copyright © 1994 by Julia Alvarez. First published in *A Formal Feeling Comes: Poems in Form by Contemporary Women*, edited by Annie Finch, published by Story Line Press. "On Writing 'Housekeeping Cages' and Her Housekeeping Poems" excerpted from "Of Maids and Muses" in *Something to Declare*. Copyright © 1998 by Julia Alvarez. Published by Plume, an imprint of the Penguin Group (USA), in 1999 and originally published in hardcover by Algonquin Books of Chapel Hill. "On Writing 'Dusting,' " "On Writing 'First Muse,' " "On Writing 'Ironing Their Clothes,' " "On Writing 'Queens, 1963,' " and "On Writing 'Sometimes the Words Are So Close' [Sonnet 42]," copyright © 2006 by Julia Alvarez. "Queens, 1963" from *The Other Side/El Otro Lado*, copyright © 1995 by Julia Alvarez. Published by Plume, an imprint of the Penguin Group (USA), and originally in hardcover by Dutton. All selections reprinted by permission of Susan Bergholz Literary Services, New York, NY, and Lamy, NM. All rights reserved.

Yehuda Amichai. "Jerusalem, 1985" from *The Selected Poetry of Yehuda Amichai*, translated and edited by Chana Bloch and Stephen Mitchell. Copyright © 1996 by the Regents of the University of California. Reprinted by permission of the Regents of the University of California and the publisher, the University of California Press.

A. R. Ammons. "Coward" from *Diversifications* by A. R. Ammons. Copyright © 1975 by A. R. Ammons. Used by permission of W. W. Norton & Company, Inc.

Charles R. Anderson. "Eroticism in 'Wild Nights—Wild Nights!' " from *Emily Dickinson's Poetry: Stairway of Surprise* (Holt, Rinehart, and Winston, 1960). Reprinted by permission.

Richard Armour. "Going to Extremes" from *Light Armour* by Richard Armour. Permission to reprint this material is given courtesy of the family of Richard Armour.

Margaret Atwood. "A Holiday" from *Interlunar* by Margaret Atwood. Originally published by Oxford University Press. Copyright © 1984 by Margaret Atwood. Reprinted by permission of the author. "February" from *Morning in the Burned House: New Poems* by Margaret Atwood. Copyright © 1995 by Margaret Atwood. Reprinted by permission of Houghton Mifflin Harcourt Publishing Company and McClelland & Stewart, Ltd. All rights reserved. "you fit into me" from *Power Politics* by Margaret Atwood. Copyright © 1971, 1996 by Margaret Atwood. Reprinted by permission of House of Anansi Press, Toronto.

Jimmy Santiago Baca. "Green Chile" from *Black Mesa Poems* by Jimmy Santiago Baca. Copyright © 1989 by Jimmy Santiago Baca. Reprinted by permission of New Directions Publishing Corp.

Mary Barnard. "Prayer to my lady of Paphos" (Fragment #38) from *Sappho: A New Translation* by Mary Barnard. Copyright © 1958 by the Regents of the University of California, renewed © 1986 by Mary Barnard. Reprinted by permission of the Regents of the University of California and the publisher, the University of California Press.

Jeannette Barnes. "Battle-Piece." Reprinted from *Shenandoah: The Washington and Lee University Review,* with the permission of the editor and the author.

Regina Barreca. "Nighttime Fires" from *The Minnesota Review* (Fall 1986). Reprinted by permission of the author.

Matsuo Bashō. "Under cherry trees" from *Japanese Haiku*, trans. by Peter Beilenson, Series I, © 1955–56, Peter Beilenson, Editor. Reprinted by permission of Peter Pauper Press.

Michael L. Baumann. "The 'Overwhelming Question' for Prufrock" excerpted from "Let Us Ask 'What Is It?' " *Arizona Quarterly* 37 (Spring 1981): 47–58. Reprinted by permission of Friederike Baumann.

Jan Beatty. "My Father Teaches Me To Dream" from *Boneshaker* by Jan Beatty. First published in *Witness* Vol. 10, no. 2 (1996). Copyright © 2002. Reprinted by permission of the University of Pittsburgh Press.

Marvin Bell. "The Uniform" from *Nightworks: Poems 1962–2000*. Copyright © 1994, 2000 by Marvin Bell. Reprinted with the permission of Copper Canyon Press, www.coppercanyonpress.org.

Paula Bennett. "On 'I heard a Fly buzz—when I died—' " excerpted from *Emily Dickinson: Woman Poet* by Paula Bennett (University of Iowa Press, 1991). Copyright © 1991 by Paula Bennett. Reprinted by permission of the author.

Elizabeth Bishop. "The Fish" and "Manners" from *The Complete Poems, 1927–1979* by Elizabeth Bishop. Copyright © 1979, 1983 by Alice Helen Methfessel. Reprinted by permission of Farrar, Straus and Giroux, LLC.

Michelle Boisseau. "Self-Pity's Closet" from *Trembling Air*. Copyright © 2003 by Michelle Boisseau. Reprinted with the permission of the University of Arkansas Press, www.uapress.com. The poem first appeared in *The Yale Review* 89, no. 3 (July 2001).

Christian Bök. "Vowels" from *Eunoia* by Christian Bök (Toronto: Coach House Books, 2001). Copyright © 2001. Reprinted by permission.

Billie Bolton. "Memorandum." Copyright © 2006 by Billie Bolton. Reprinted by permission of the author.

Todd Boss. "Advance" from *Yellowrocket* by Todd Boss. Copyright © 2008 by Todd Boss. Used by permission of W. W. Norton & Company, Inc.

Allen Braden. "Sweethearts" from *Poetry Northwest* 41, no. 4 (2001). Copyright © 2001 by Allen Braden. Reprinted by permission of the author.

Gwendolyn Brooks. "We Real Cool" from *Blacks* by Gwendolyn Brooks. Copyright © 1991 by Gwendolyn Brooks. Reprinted by consent of Brooks Permissions.

Charles Bukowski. Photograph of Charles Bukowski on page 523. © The Yale Collection of American Literature, Beinecke Rare Book and Manuscript Library, Yale University.

Anne Carson. "Father's Old Blue Cardigan" from *Men in the Off Hours* by Anne Carson. Copyright © 2000 by Anne Carson. Used by permission of Alfred A. Knopf, a division of Random House, Inc.

Keith Casto. "She Don't Bop," from *Light Year '87*, Robert Wallace, ed. Bits Press, Cleveland, 1986. Copyright © 1986 by Keith Casto. Reprinted by permission of the author.

Helen Chasin. "The Word *Plum*" from *Coming Close and Other Poems* by Helen Chasin. Copyright © 1968 by Yale University Press. Reprinted by permission of Yale University Press.

Kelly Cherry. "Alzheimer's" from *Death and Transfiguration* by Kelly Cherry. Copyright © 1997 by Kelly Cherry. Reprinted by permission of Louisiana State University Press.

David Chinitz. "The Romanticization of Africa in the 1920s" from "Rejuvenation through Joy: Langston Hughes, Primitivism, and Jazz," *American Literary History* 9, no. 1 (Spring 1997), pp. 60–78. Reprinted by permission of the author and Oxford University Press.

John Ciardi. "Suburban" from *For Instance* by John Ciardi. Copyright © 1979 by John Ciardi. Used by permission of W. W. Norton & Company, Inc.

Lucille Clifton. "this morning (for the girls of eastern high school)" from *Good Woman: Poems and a Memoir 1969–1980*. Copyright © 1987 by Lucille Clifton. Reprinted with the permission of BOA Editions, Ltd., www. boaeditions.org.

Judith Ortiz Cofer. "Common Ground" is reprinted with permission from the publisher of *Silent Dancing: A Partial Remembrance of a Puerto Rican Childhood* by Judith Ortiz Cofer (© 1990 Arte Público Press–University of Houston).

Billy Collins. "Building with Its Face Blown Off" from *The Trouble with Poetry and Other Poems* by Billy Collins. Copyright © 2005 by Billy Collins. Reprinted by permission of SLL/Sterling Lord Literistic, Inc. "On Writing 'Building with Its Face Blown Off,'" by Billy Collins. Printed by permission of Billy Collins and SLL/Sterling Lord Literistic, Inc. © 2008. "Introduction to Poetry" from *The Apple That Astonished Paris*. Copyright © 1988, 1996 by Billy Collins. Reprinted with the permission of the University of Arkansas Press, www.uapress.com. "Litany" from *Nine Horses* by Billy Collins. Copyright © 2002 by Billy Collins. Reprinted by permission of SLL/Sterling Lord Literistic, Inc. "On Writing 'Litany,'" by Billy Collins. Printed by permission of Billy Collins and SLL/Sterling Lord Literistic, Inc. © 2008. "Marginalia" from *Picnic, Lightning* by Billy Collins. Copyright © 1998. Reprinted by permission of the University of Pittsburgh Press. "Nostalgia" and "Questions About Angels" from *Questions About Angels* by Billy Collins. Copyright © 1991. Reprinted by permission of the University of Pittsburgh Press. "On Writing 'Nostalgia'" and "On Writing 'Questions About Angels,'" by Billy Collins. Printed by permission of Billy Collins and SLL/Sterling Lord Literistic, Inc. © 2008. "Osso Buco" from *The Art of Drowning* by Billy Collins. Copyright © 1995. Reprinted by permission of the University of Pittsburgh Press. "On Writing 'Osso Buco,'" by Billy Collins. Printed by permission of Billy Collins and SLL/Sterling Lord Literistic, Inc. © 2008.

Edmund Conti. "Pragmatist" from *Light Year '86*. Reprinted by permission of the author.

Wyn Cooper. "Puritan Impulse" from *The Way Back* (White Pine Press, 2000). Copyright © 2000 by Wyn Cooper. Reprinted with the permission of White Pine Press, www.whitepine.org. Originally appeared in the Winter 1999–2000 issue of *Ploughshares*.

Wendy Cope. "Lonely Hearts" from *Making Cocoa for Kingsley Amis* by Wendy Cope. Copyright © 1986 by Wendy Cope. Reprinted by permission of Faber and Faber Ltd. and by permission of United Agents on behalf of Wendy Cope.

Sally Croft. "Home-Baked Bread" from *Light Year '86*. Reprinted by permission of Bruce Croft.

Barbara Crooker. "On the Edge of Adolescence, My Middle Daughter Learns to Play the Saxophone" from *Line Dance* (Word Press, 2008). Copyright © 2008 by Barbara Crooker. Reprinted by permission of the author.

E. E. Cummings. "Buffalo Bill's" and "in Just-," copyright © 1923, 1951, 1991 by the Trustees for the E. E. Cummings Trust, copyright © 1976 by George James Firmage. "l(a," copyright © 1958, 1986, 1991 by the Trustees for the E. E. Cummings Trust. "next to of course god america i" and "since feeling is first," copyright © 1926, 1954, 1991 by the Trustees for the E. E. Cummings Trust, copyright © 1985 by George James Firmage. From *Complete Poems: 1904–1962* by E. E. Cummings, edited by George J. Firmage. Used by permission of Liveright Publishing Corporation.

Fazil Hüsnü Dağlarca. "Dead" from *The New Renaissance* 6, no. 1 (1984). Translated by Talât Sait Halman. Translation copyright © 1984 by Talât Sait Halman. Reprinted by permission of the translator.

Mahmoud Darwish. "Identity Card" from *The Music of Human Flesh*, translated by Denys Johnson-Davies (Three Continents Press, 1980). Copyright © 1980 by Denys Johnson-Davies. Reprinted by permission of Denys Johnson-Davies.

Joanne Diaz. "On My Father's Loss of Hearing," *The Southern Review* 42, no. 3 (Summer 2006). Copyright © 2006 by Joanne Diaz. Reprinted by permission of the author.

Emily Dickinson. "A Bird came down the Walk –," "After great pain, a formal feeling comes –," "A Light exists in Spring," "A narrow Fellow in the grass," "Because I could not stop for Death –," "Fame is the one that does not stay –," "'Heaven' – is what I cannot reach!," "'Hope' is the thing with feathers –," "I dwell in Possibility –," "I felt a Cleaving in my Mind –," "If I shouldn't be alive," "I heard a Fly buzz – when I died –," "I like a look of Agony," "I never saw a Moor –," "Much Madness is divinest Sense –," "One need not be a Chamber – to be Haunted –," "Pain – has an Element of Blank –," "Safe in their Alabaster Chambers –," "Some things that fly there be –," "Success is counted sweetest," "Tell all the Truth but tell it slant –," "The Morning after Wo –," "There is no Frigate like a Book," "There's a certain Slant of light," "The Robin's my Criterion for Tune –," "The Soul selects her own Society –," "They dropped like Flakes –," and "What Soft – Cherubic Creatures –." Reprinted by permission of the publishers and the Trustees of Amherst College from *The Poems of Emily Dickinson*, Thomas H. Johnson, ed., Cambridge, Mass.: The Belknap Press of Harvard University Press. Copyright © 1951, 1955, 1979, 1983 by the President and Fellows of Harvard College.

Tom Disch. "Birdsong Interpreted" from *About the Size of It* by Tom Disch. Copyright © 2007 by Tom Disch. Reprinted by permission of Anvil Press Poetry.

Chitra Banerjee Divakaruni. "Indian Movie, New Jersey" from the *Indiana Review*, 1990. Copyright © by Chitra Banerjee Divakaruni. Reprinted by permission of the author. Photo on page 554 copyright © by Chitra Banerjee Divakaruni. Photo by Anand Divakaruni. Reprinted by permission of the author and the Sandra Dijkstra Literary Agency.

Mark Doty. "The Embrace" from *Sweet Machine* by Mark Doty. Copyright © 1998 by Mark Doty. "Tunnel Music" from *Atlantis* by Mark Doty. Copyright © 1995 by Mark Doty. Reprinted by permission of HarperCollins Publishers.

Rita Dove. "Fox Trot Fridays," from *American Smooth: Poems* by Rita Dove. Copyright © 2004 by Rita Dove. Used by permission of W. W. Norton & Company, Inc.

Denise Duhamel. "Language Police Report" from *Ka-Ching!* by Denise Duhamel. First published in *Sentence: A Journal of Prose Poetics* No. 4 (2006). Copyright © 2009. Reprinted by permission of the University of Pittsburgh Press.

James A. Emanuel. "Hughes's Attitudes toward Religion" from "Christ in Alabama: Religion in the Poetry of Langston Hughes" in *Modern Black Poets,* ed. Donald B. Gibson. Reprinted by permission of the author.

Martín Espada. "Bully" and "Latin Night at the Pawnshop" from *Rebellion Is the Circle of a Lover's Hands / Rebelión es el giro de manos del amante* by Martín Espada. Curbstone Press, 1990. Copyright © 1990 by Martín Espada. Reprinted with permission of Curbstone Press. Distributed by Consortium. "The Community College Revises Its Curriculum in Response to Changing Demographics" from *A Mayan Astronomer in Hell's Kitchen* by Martín Espada. Copyright © 2000 by Martín Espada. Used by permission of W. W. Norton & Company, Inc.

Ruth Fainlight. "The Clarinettist." Reprinted by permission from *The Hudson Review* Vol. LV, No. 1 (Spring 2002). Copyright © 2002 by Ruth Fainlight. "Crocuses" from *Moon Wheels* by Ruth Fainlight (Bloodaxe Books, 2006). Copyright © 2006 by Ruth Fainlight. Reprinted by permission of Bloodaxe Books Ltd.

Blanche Farley. "The Lover Not Taken" from *Light Year '86*. Reprinted by permission of the author.

Kenneth Fearing. "AD" from *Kenneth Fearing Complete Poems,* ed. by Robert Ryely (Orono, ME: National Poetry Foundation, 1997). Copyright © 1938 by Kenneth Fearing, renewed in 1966 by the Estate of Kenneth Fearing. Reprinted by the permission of Russell & Volkening as agents for the author.

Karen Jackson Ford. "Hughes's Aesthetics of Simplicity," from "Do Right to Write Right: Langston Hughes's Aesthetics of Simplicity," *Twentieth Century Literature* 38, no. 4 (Winter 1992). Reprinted by permission.

Katie Ford. "Ark" from *Colosseum.* Copyright © 2008 by Katie Ford. Reprinted with the permission of Graywolf Press, Saint Paul, Minnesota, www.graywolfpress.org.

Robert Francis. "Catch" and "The Pitcher" from *The Orb Weaver.* Copyright © 1960 by Robert Francis. Reprinted by permission of Wesleyan University Press, www.wesleyan.edu/wespress. "On 'Hard' Poetry" reprinted from *The Satirical Rogue on Poetry* by Robert Francis (Amherst: University of Massachusetts Press, 1968), copyright © 1968 by Robert Francis. Used by permission.

Daisy Fried. "Wit's End" from *She Didn't Mean to Do It* by Daisy Fried. Copyright © 2001. Reprinted by permission of the University of Pittsburgh Press.

Robert Frost. "Acquainted with the Night," "Design," "Fire and Ice," "Neither Out Far nor In Deep," "Nothing Gold Can Stay," "Stopping by Woods on a Snowy Evening," and "Unharvested," from *The Poetry of Robert Frost,* edited by Edward Connery Lathem. Copyright © 1923, 1928, 1936, 1969 by Henry Holt and Company, copyright © 1936, 1951, 1956 by Robert Frost, copyright © 1964 by Lesley Frost Ballantine. Reprinted by arrangement with Henry Holt and Company, LLC. "On the Figure a Poem Makes" from *The Selected Prose of Robert Frost,* edited by Hyde Cox and Edward Connery Lathem, copyright 1939, 1967 by Henry Holt and Company. Reprinted by permission of Henry Holt and Company. "On the Way to Read a Poem" from "Poetry and School" by Robert Frost in *The Atlantic Monthly,* June, 1951. Reprinted by permission of the Estate of Robert Frost. Robert Frost signature on page 359 copyright © Robert Lee Frost Copyright Trust.

Brendan Galvin. "An Evel Knievel Elegy" from *Shenandoah* 58.2 (2008), p. 6. Copyright © 2008. Reprinted by permission of the author.

Deborah Garrison. "Unbidden Sonnet with Evergreen" from *The Second Child* by Deborah Garrison. Copyright © 2006 by Deborah Garrison. Used by permission of Random House, Inc.

Sandra M. Gilbert. "Chairlift" from *Belongings: Poems* by Sandra Gilbert. Copyright © 2005 by Sandra M. Gilbert. Used by permission of W. W. Norton & Company, Inc. "How We Didn't Tell Her" from *Southwest Review* 93, no. 4 (2008). Copyright © 2008 by Sandra M. Gilbert. Reprinted by permission of the author. "Mafioso" from *Kissing the Bread: New and Selected Poems, 1969–1999* by Sandra M. Gilbert. Copyright © 1979 by Sandra M. Gilbert. Reprinted by permission of the author.

Sandra M. Gilbert and Susan Gubar. "On Dickinson's White Dress" excerpted from *The Madwoman in the Attic,* Yale University Press, 1979. Reprinted by permission of Yale University Press.

Gary Gildner. "First Practice" from *Blue Like the Heavens: New and Selected Poems* by Gary Gildner. Copyright © 1984. Reprinted by permission of the University of Pittsburgh Press.

Louise Glück. "March" from *A Village Life* by Louise Glück. Copyright © 2009 by Louise Glück. Reprinted by permission of Farrar, Straus and Giroux, LLC.

Eamon Grennan. "Herringbone." Reprinted by permission from *The Hudson Review* Vol. LIX, No. 4 (Winter 2007). Copyright © 2007 by Eamon Grennan.

H.D. (Hilda Doolittle). "Heat" from *Collected Poems, 1912–1944.* Copyright 1982 by The Estate of Hilda Doolittle. Reprinted by permission of New Directions Publishing Corp.

Rachel Hadas. "The Compact" from *Laws* by Rachel Hadas (Zoo Press, 2004). Copyright © 2004 by Rachel Hadas. Reprinted by permission of the author. "The Red Hat" from *Halfway Down the Hall.* Copyright © 1998 by Rachel Hadas. Reprinted by permission of Wesleyan University Press, www.wesleyan.edu/wespress.

Richard Hague. "Directions for Resisting the SAT" from *Ohio Teachers Write* (Ohio Council of Teachers of English, 1996). Copyright © 1996 by Richard Hague. Reprinted by permission of the author.

Mark Halliday. "Graded Paper," *The Michigan Quarterly Review.* Reprinted by permission of the author.

Barbara Hamby. "Ode to American English" from *Babel* by Barbara Hamby. Copyright © 2004. Reprinted by permission of the University of Pittsburgh Press.

Mary Stewart Hammond. "The Big Fish Story." First published in *The New Yorker,* April 17, 2006. Copyright © 2006 by Mary Stewart Hammond. "High Ground." First published in *Shenandoah* 58, no. 1 (Spring/Summer 2008). Copyright © 2008 by Mary Stewart Hammond. Reprinted by permission of the author.

Jeffrey Harrison. "The Names of Things" from *Incomplete Knowledge.* Copyright © 2006 by Jeffrey Harrison. Reprinted with the permission of Four Way Books, www.fourwaybooks.com.

Robert Hass. "A Story about the Body" from *Human Wishes* by Robert Hass. Copyright © 1989 by Robert Hass. Reprinted by permission of HarperCollins Publishers.

William Hathaway. "Oh Oh" from *Light Year '86*. This poem was originally published in *The Cincinnati Poetry Review*. Reprinted by permission of the author.

Robert Hayden. "Those Winter Sundays," copyright © 1966 by Robert Hayden, from *Collected Poems of Robert Hayden* by Robert Hayden, edited by Frederick Glaysher. Used by permission of Liveright Publishing Corporation.

Anthony Hecht. "The Dover Bitch" from *Collected Earlier Poems* by Anthony Hecht. Copyright © 1990 by Anthony E. Hecht. Used by permission of Alfred A. Knopf, a division of Random House, Inc.

Judy Page Heitzman. "The Schoolroom on the Second Floor of the Knitting Mill." Copyright © 1991 by Judy Page Heitzman. Originally appeared in *The New Yorker*, December 2, 1992, p. 102. Reprinted by permission of the author.

William Heyen. "The Trains" from *The Host: Selected Poems 1965–1990* by William Heyen. Copyright © 1994 by Time Being Press. Reprinted by permission of Time Being Press. All rights reserved.

Bob Hicok. "Making it in poetry," copyright © 2004 by Bob Hicok. "Making it in poetry" first appeared in the *Georgia Review* 58, no. 2 (Summer 2004). "Spam leaves an aftertaste," copyright © 2002 by Bob Hicok. "Spam leaves an aftertaste" first appeared in the *Gettysburg Review* 15, no. 1 (Spring 2002). Both poems are reprinted here with the acknowledgment of the editors and the permission of the author.

Edward Hirsch. "First Snowfall: Intimations" from *Earthly Measures* by Edward Hirsch. Copyright © 1994 by Edward Hirsch. Used by permission of Alfred A. Knopf, a division of Random House, Inc.

Jane Hirshfield. "Happiness" from *The October Palace* by Jane Hirshfield. Copyright © 1994 by Jane Hirshfield. Reprinted by permission of HarperCollins Publishers.

Tony Hoagland. "America," from *What Narcissism Means to Me*. Copyright © 1993 by Tony Hoagland. Reprinted with the permission of Graywolf Press, Saint Paul, Minnesota, www.graywolfpress.org.

M. Carl Holman. "Mr. Z." Reprinted by permission of the Estate of M. Carl Holman.

Andrew Hudgins. "The Cadillac in the Attic" from *Ecstatic in the Poison: New Poems*. Copyright © 2003 by Andrew Hudgins. Reprinted by permission of the Overlook Press, New York, NY. "The Cow." First published in *Poetry*, vol. 188 (July/August 2006). Copyright © 2006 by Andrew Hudgins. Reprinted with the permission of the author. "Elegy for My Father, Who Is Not Dead" from *The Glass Hammer: A Southern Childhood* by Andrew Hudgins. Copyright © 1994 by Andrew Hudgins. Reprinted by permission of Houghton Mifflin Harcourt Publishing Company. All rights reserved.

Langston Hughes. "125th Street," "50-50," "Ballad of the Landlord," "Cross," "Danse Africaine," "Dinner Guest: Me," "Dream Boogie," "Dream Variations," "Esthete in Harlem," "Formula," "Frederick Douglass: 1817–1895," "Harlem," "Harlem Sweeties," "High to Low," "I, Too," "Jazzonia," "Ku Klux," "Lenox Avenue: Midnight," "Motto," "Negro," "The Negro Speaks of Rivers," "Old Walt," "Red Silk Stockings," "Rent-Party Shout: For a Lady Dancer," "Song for a Dark Girl," "Un-American Investigators," and "The Weary Blues," from *The Collected Poems of Langston Hughes* by Langston Hughes, edited by Arnold Rampersad with David Roessel, Associate Editor. Copyright © 1994 by the Estate of Langston Hughes. Used by permission of Alfred A. Knopf, a division of Random House, Inc. "On Harlem Rent Parties," excerpted from "When the Negro Was in Vogue" from *The Big Sea* by Langston Hughes. Copyright © 1940 by Langston Hughes. Copyright renewed © 1968 by Arna Bontemps and George Houston Bass. Reprinted by permission of Hill and Wang, a division of Farrar, Straus and Giroux, LLC. Langston Hughes signature on page 399 reprinted by permission of Harold Ober Associates, Incorporated.

Paul Humphrey. "Blow" from *Light Year '86*. Reprinted with the permission of Eleanor Humphrey.

Colette Inez. "Back When All Was Continuous Chuckles." Reprinted by permission from *The Hudson Review* Vol. LVII, No. 3 (Autumn 2004). Copyright © 2004 by Colette Inez.

Mark Jarman. "Unholy Sonnet" from *Questions for Ecclesiastes* by Mark Jarman (Story Line Press, 1997). Copyright © 1997 by Mark Jarman. Reprinted with permission of the author.

Randall Jarrell. "The Death of the Ball Turret Gunner" from *The Complete Poems* by Randall Jarrell. Copyright © 1969, renewed 1997 by Mary von S. Jarrell. Reprinted by permission of Farrar, Straus and Giroux, LLC.

Kelli Lyon Johnson. "Mapping an Identity" excerpted from *Julia Alvarez: Writing a New Place on the Map* by Kelli Lyon Johnson. Copyright © 2005 University of New Mexico Press. Reprinted by permission of the author and University of New Mexico Press.

Alice Jones. "The Foot" and "The Larynx" from *Anatomy* by Alice Jones (San Francisco: Bullnettle Press, 1997). Copyright © 1997 by Alice Jones. Reprinted by permission of the author.

Donald Justice. "Order in the Streets" from *Losers Weepers: Poems Found Practically Everywhere*, edited by George Hitchcock. Reprinted by permission of the Estate of Donald Justice.

Katherine Kearns, "On the Symbolic Setting of 'Home Burial,'" excerpted from "The Place Is the Asylum: Women and Nature in Robert Frost's Poetry" in *American Literature* 59:2 (May 1987), pp. 190–210. Copyright © 1987 by Duke University Press. All rights reserved. Used by permission of the publisher.

X. J. Kennedy. "On a Young Man's Remaining an Undergraduate for Twelve Years." First published in the *Sewanee Review* 114, no. 1 (Winter 2006). Copyright © 2006 by X. J. Kennedy. Reprinted with the permission of the editor and the author. "The Purpose of Time Is to Prevent Everything from Happening at Once" from *The Lords of Misrule*, p. 5. Copyright © 2002 by X. J. Kennedy. Reprinted with permission of The Johns Hopkins University Press.

Jane Kenyon. "The Blue Bowl" and "Surprise," copyright © 2005 by the Estate of Jane Kenyon. Reprinted from *Collected Poems* with the permission of Graywolf Press, Saint Paul, Minnesota, www.graywolfpress.org.

Marne L. Kilates. "Python in the Mall" from *Poems en Route* by Marne L. Kilates (University of Santo Tomas Publishing House, 1998). Copyright © 1998 by Marne L. Kilates. Reprinted with the permission of the author.

Maxine Hong Kingston. "Restaurant," copyright © 1981 by Maxine Hong Kingston. First appeared in the *Iowa Review*. Reprinted by permission of the author and the Sandra Dijkstra Literary Agency.

Galway Kinnell. "After Making Love We Hear Footsteps" and "Blackberry Eating" from *Three Books* by Galway Kinnell. Copyright © 1993 by Galway Kinnell. Reprinted by permission of Houghton Mifflin Harcourt Publishing Company. All rights reserved.

Carolyn Kizer. "After Bashō" from *Cool, Calm & Collected: Poems 1960–2000.* Copyright © 2001 by Carolyn Kizer. Reprinted with the permission of Copper Canyon Press, www.coppercanyonpress.org.

Trevor West Knapp. "Touch" from *Poetry* vol. 178 (August 2001), p. 268. Copyright © 2001 by Trevor West Knapp. Reprinted with the permission of the author.

Yusef Komunyakaa. "Slam, Dunk, & Hook" from *Magic City.* Copyright © 1992 by Yusef Komunyakaa. Reprinted by permission of Wesleyan University Press, www.wesleyan.edu/wespress.

Maxine Kumin. "Though He Tarry" from *Still to Mow: Poems* by Maxine Kumin. Copyright © 2007 by Maxine Kumin. Used by permission of W. W. Norton & Company, Inc.

Philip Larkin. "A Study of Reading Habits" from *Collected Poems* by Philip Larkin. Copyright © 1988, 1989 by the Estate of Philip Larkin. Reprinted by permission of Farrar, Straus and Giroux, LLC. Also from *The Whitsun Weddings.* Copyright © 1964 by Philip Larkin. Reprinted by permission of Faber and Faber Ltd.

Ann Lauinger. "Marvell Noir." First appeared in *Parnassus: Poetry in Review* 28, no. 1 & 2 (2005). Copyright © 2005 by Ann Lauinger. Reprinted by permission of the author.

Tato Laviera. "AmeRícan" is reprinted with permission from the publisher of *AmeRícan* by Tato Laviera (© 2003 Arte Público Press–University of Houston).

David Lenson. "On the Contemporary Use of Rhyme" from "The Battle Is Joined: Formalists Take On Defenders of Free Verse," *The Chronicle of Higher Education* (February 24, 1988). Reprinted by permission of the author.

Phillis Levin. "May Day" from *May Day* by Phillis Levin. Copyright © 2008 by Phillis Marna Levin. Used by permission of Penguin, a division of Penguin Group (USA) Inc.

J. Patrick Lewis. "The Unkindest Cut" from *Light 5* (Spring 1993). Reprinted with the permission of the author.

Li Ho. "A Beautiful Girl Combs Her Hair," translated by David Young, from *Five T'ang Poets.* Copyright © 1990 by Oberlin College. Reprinted with the permission of Oberlin College Press, www.oberlin.edu/ocpress/.

Rachel Loden. "Locked Ward, Newtown, Connecticut." Copyright © 2005 by Rachel Loden. Reprinted by permission of the author.

Herbert Lomas. "The Fly's Poem about Emily." Reprinted by permission from *The Hudson Review* Vol. LXI, No. 1 (Spring 2008). Copyright © 2008 by Herbert Lomas.

Dave Lucas. "November," originally appeared in *Shenandoah* 57.1 (Spring 2007). Copyright © 2007 by Dave Lucas. Reprinted by permission of the author.

Thomas Lux. "Commercial Leech Farming Today" and "Onomatopoeia" from *New and Selected Poems, 1975–1995* by Thomas Lux. Copyright © 1997 by Thomas Lux. Reprinted by permission of Houghton Mifflin Harcourt Publishing Company. All rights reserved.

Thomas Lynch. "Liberty" from *Still Life in Milford* by Thomas Lynch. Copyright © 1998 by Thomas Lynch. Used by permission of W. W. Norton & Company, Inc.

Katharyn Howd Machan. "Hazel Tells LaVerne" from *Light Year '85.* Reprinted by permission of the author.

Haki R. Madhubuti. "The B Network" from *HeartLove: Wedding and Love Poems* by Haki R. Madhubuti. Copyright © 1998 by Haki R. Madhubuti. Reprinted by permission of Third World Press Inc., Chicago, Illinois.

Elaine Magarrell. "The Joy of Cooking" from *Sometime the Cow Kick Your Head, Light Year 88/89.* Reprinted with the permission of the author.

Julio Marzán. "Ethnic Poetry." Originally appeared in *Parnassus: Poetry in Review.* Reprinted by permission of the author. "The Translator at the Reception for Latin American Writers." Reprinted by permission of the author.

Donna Masini. "Slowly" from *Turning to Fiction: Poems* by Donna Masini. Copyright © 2004 by Donna Masini. Used by permission of W. W. Norton & Company, Inc.

Florence Cassen Mayers. "All-American Sestina," © 1996 Florence Cassen Mayers, as first published in *The Atlantic Monthly.* Reprinted with permission of the author.

David McCord. "Epitaph on a Waiter" from *Odds Without Ends,* copyright © 1954 by David T. W. McCord. Reprinted by permission of Arthur B. Page, executor of the estate of David McCord.

Walt McDonald. "Coming Across It" from *Embers* 13, no. 1 (1988), p. 17. Copyright © 1988 by Walt McDonald. Reprinted with the permission of the author.

Michael McFee. "In Medias Res" from *Colander* by Michael McFee. Copyright © 1996 by Michael McFee. Reprinted by permission of the author.

Peter Meinke. "The ABC of Aerobics" from *Night Watch on the Chesapeake* by Peter Meinke. Copyright © 1987. "Unnatural Light" from *Scars* by Peter Meinke. Copyright © 1996. "(Untitled)" ["This is a poem to my son Peter"] from *Liquid Paper: New and Selected Poems* by Peter Meinke. Copyright © 1991. All poems reprinted by permission of the University of Pittsburgh Press.

James Merrill. "Casual Wear" from *Selected Poems, 1946–1985* by James Merrill. Copyright © 1992 by James Merrill. Used by permission of Alfred A. Knopf, a division of Random House, Inc.

Edna St. Vincent Millay. "I will put Chaos into fourteen lines" from *Collected Poems,* HarperCollins. Copyright © 1954, 1982 by Norma Millay Ellis. All rights reserved. Reprinted by permission of Elizabeth Barnett, literary executor.

Susan Minot. "My Husband's Back." Copyright © 2005 by Susan Minot. Originally appeared in *The New Yorker* (August 22, 2005). Reprinted by permission of Georges Borchardt, Inc., on behalf of the author.

Janice Mirikitani. "Recipe," reprinted with permission from *Shedding Silence* by Janice Mirikitani. Copyright © 1987 by Janice Mirikitani, Celestial Arts, Berkeley, CA, www.tenspeed.com.

Elaine Mitchell. "Form" from *Light 9* (Spring 1994). Reprinted by permission of the author.

Janice Townley Moore. "To a Wasp" first appeared in *Light Year,* Bits Press. Reprinted by permission of the author.

Pat Mora. "Legal Alien" is reprinted with permission from the publisher of *Chants* by Pat Mora (© 1986 Arte Público Press–University of Houston).

Robert Morgan. "Fever Wit" from *Topsoil Road: Poems* by Robert Morgan. Copyright © 2000 by Robert Morgan. Reprinted by permission of Louisiana State University Press. "Mountain Graveyard" and "Overalls" from *Sigodlin*. Copyright © 1990 by Robert Morgan. Reprinted by permission of Wesleyan University Press, www.wesleyan.edu/wespress.

Thylias Moss. "Tornados" from *Rainbow Remnants in Rock Bottom Ghetto Sky* by Thylias Moss. Copyright © 1991 by Thylias Moss. Reprinted by permission of Persea Books, Inc. (New York).

Harryette Mullen. "Blah-Blah" from *Sleeping with the Dictionary* by Harryette Mullen. Copyright © 2002 by Harryette Mullen. Reprinted by permission of the Regents of the University of California and the publisher, the University of California Press.

Joan Murray. "Play-By-Play," Reprinted by permission from *The Hudson Review* Vol. XLIX, no. 4 (Winter 1997). Copyright © 1997 by Joan Murray. "We Old Dudes," copyright © 2006 by Joan Murray. First appeared in the July/August 2006 issue of *Poetry* magazine. Reprinted by permission of the author.

Taslima Nasrin. "At the Back of Progress . . . ," translated by Carolyne Wright and Mohammad Nurul Huda, from *The Game in Reverse: Poems* by Taslima Nasrin. Copyright © 1995 by Taslima Nasrin. English translation © 1995 by Carolyne Wright. Reprinted with the permission of George Braziller, Inc.

Marilyn Nelson. "Emily Dickinson's Defunct" from *For the Body: Poems* by Marilyn Nelson Waniek. Copyright © 1978 by Marilyn Nelson Waniek. Reprinted by permission of the author and Louisiana State University Press. "How I Discovered Poetry" from *The Fields of Praise: New and Selected Poems* by Marilyn Nelson. Copyright © 1997 by Marilyn Nelson. Reprinted by permission of the author and Louisiana State University Press.

Howard Nemerov. "Because You Asked about the Line between Prose and Poetry" from *Sentences* by Howard Nemerov. Copyright © 1980. "Walking the Dog" from *Trying Conclusions: New and Selected Poems 1961–1991*. Copyright © 1991. Reprinted by permission.

Pablo Neruda. "The United Fruit Co." from *Neruda & Vallejo: Selected Poems*, ed. and translated by Robert Bly. Reprinted with the permission of Robert Bly. "Verbo," poem from the work *Las Manos del Dia*. © Fundación Pablo Neruda, 1968. Reprinted by permission of Carmen Balcells Literary Agency, Barcelona, Spain, on behalf of the Pablo Neruda Foundation of Chile. "Word" ("Verbo" in English) from *Five Decades: Poems, 1925–1970* by Pablo Neruda, translated by Ben Belitt. Copyright © 1974 by Grove Press, Inc. Translation copyright © 1974 by Ben Belitt. Used by permission of Grove/Atlantic, Inc. "Word," translation by Kristin Linklater and Gilda Orlandi-Sanchez, from *Freeing Shakespeare's Voice: The Actor's Guide to Talking the Text* by Kristin Linklater. Copyright © 1992. Used by permission.

John Frederick Nims. "Love Poem" from *Selected Poems*. Copyright © 1982 by the University of Chicago. Reprinted by permission of the University of Chicago Press.

Alden Nowlan. "The Bull Moose" from *Alden Nowlan: Selected Poems* by Alden Nowlan. Copyight © 1967. Reprinted by permission of House of Anansi Press, Toronto.

Adrian Oktenberg. "Memory in 'The Negro Speaks of Rivers,'" excerpted from "From the Bottom Up: Three Radicals of the Thirties" in *A Gift of Tongues: Critical Challenges in Contemporary American Poetry*, ed. Marie Harris and Kathleen Aguero. Copyright © 1987. Reprinted by permission of the University of Georgia Press. [pp. 95–96]

Sharon Olds. "Last Night" from *The Wellspring* by Sharon Olds. Copyright © 1996 by Sharon Olds. Used by permission of Alfred A. Knopf, a division of Random House, Inc. "Rite of Passage" and "Sex without Love" from *The Dead and the Living* by Sharon Olds. Copyright © 1987 by Sharon Olds. Used by permission of Alfred A. Knopf, a division of Random House, Inc.

Mary Oliver. "Oxygen" and "The Poet with His Face in His Hands" from *New and Selected Poems, Volume Two*, by Mary Oliver. Copyright © 2005 by Mary Oliver. Reprinted by permission of Beacon Press, Boston.

Lisa Parker. "Snapping Beans," from *Parnassus* 23, no. 2 (1998). Reprinted by permission of the author.

Linda Pastan. "Jump Cabling" from *Light Year: The Quarterly of Light Verse*. Copyright © 1984 by Linda Pastan. Reprinted by permission of Jean V. Naggar Literary Agency, Inc. "Marks" from *PM/AM: New and Selected Poems* by Linda Pastan. Copyright © 1978 by Linda Pastan. Used by permission of W. W. Norton & Company, Inc. "Pass/Fail" from *Aspects of Eve* by Linda Pastan. Copyright © 1970, 1971, 1972, 1973, 1974, 1975 by Linda Pastan. Used by permission of Liveright Publishing Corporation. "To a Daughter Leaving Home" from *Carnival Evening: New and Selected Poems 1968–1998* by Linda Pastan. Copyright © 1998 by Linda Pastan. Used by permission of W. W. Norton & Company, Inc.

Octavio Paz. "The Street" from *Early Poems 1935–1955*. Reprinted with permission of Indiana University Press.

Molly Peacock. "Desire" from *Cornucopia: New and Selected Poems* by Molly Peacock. Copyright © 2002 by Molly Peacock. Used by permission of W. W. Norton & Company, Inc. "Of Night" from *The Second Blush: Poems* by Molly Peacock. Copyright © 2008 by Molly Peacock. Used by permission of W. W. Norton & Company, Inc., and McClelland & Stewart Ltd.

Peter Pereira. "Anagrammer" from *What's Written on the Body*. Copyright © 2007 by Peter Pereira. Reprinted with the permission of Copper Canyon Press, www.coppercanyonpress.org

Laurence Perrine. "The limerick's never averse." Reprinted by permission of Douglas Perrine.

Kevin Pierce. "Proof of Origin" from *Light* 50 (Autumn 2005). Copyright © 2005 by Kevin Pierce. Reprinted with the permission of the author.

Marge Piercy. "The Secretary Chant" from *Circles on the Water* by Marge Piercy. Copyright © 1982 by Marge Piercy. Used by permission of Alfred A. Knopf, a division of Random House, Inc.

Sylvia Plath. "Mirror" from *Crossing the Water* by Sylvia Plath. Copyright © 1963 by Ted Hughes. Originally appeared in *The New Yorker*. Reprinted by permission of HarperCollins Publishers. Also from *Collected Poems* by Sylvia Plath, ed. Ted Hughes, reprinted by permission of Faber and Faber, Ltd.

Peter D. Poland. "On 'Neither Out Far nor In Deep,'" from *The Explicator* 52, no. 2 (Winter 1994). Reprinted with permission of the Helen Dwight Reid Educational Foundation. Published by Heldref Publications, 1319 Eighteenth Street, NW, Washington, DC, 20036-1802. Copyright © 1994.

Ezra Pound. "In a Station of the Metro" from *Personae*. Copyright © 1926 by Ezra Pound. Reprinted by permission of New Directions Publishing Corp.

Arnold Rampersad. "On the Persona in 'The Negro Speaks of Rivers'" from "The Origins of Poetry in Langston Hughes," *Southern Review* 21, no. 3 (1985), pp. 703-4. Copyright © 1985 by Arnold Rampersad. Reprinted by permission of the author.

Henry Reed. "Lessons of the War" (1. Naming of Parts) from *Henry Reed: Collected Poems,* ed. Jon Stallworthy. Copyright © 1946, 1947, 1970, 1991, 2007 by the Executor of Henry Reed's Estate. Reprinted by permission of Carcanet Press Ltd.

Marny Requa. "From an Interview with Julia Alvarez" excerpted from "The Politics of Fiction," *Frontera* 5 (1997). 29 January 1997, http://www.fronteramag.com/issue5/Alvarez/index.htm. Reprinted with the permission of Marny Requa.

David S. Reynolds. "Popular Literature and 'Wild Nights — Wild Nights!'" excerpted from *Beneath the American Renaissance* by David S. Reynolds. Copyright © 1988 by David S. Reynolds. Used by permission of Alfred A. Knopf, a division of Random House, Inc.

Rainer Maria Rilke. "The Panther" from *The Selected Poetry of Rainer Maria Rilke* by Rainer Maria Rilke, translated by Stephen Mitchell. Copyright © 1982 by Stephen Mitchell. Used by permission of Random House, Inc.

Alberto Ríos. "The Gathering Evening" from *The Smallest Muscle in the Human Body*. Copyright © 2002 by Alberto Ríos. Reprinted with the permission of Copper Canyon Press, www.coppercanyonpress.org. "Seniors" from *Five Indiscretions*. Copyright © 1985 by Alberto Ríos. Reprinted by permission of the author.

Theodore Roethke. "Elegy for Jane," copyright © 1950 by Theodore Roethke, "My Papa's Waltz," copyright 1942 by Hearst Magazines, Inc., "Root Cellar," copyright 1943 by Modern Poetry Association, Inc., from *Collected Poems of Theodore Roethke* by Theodore Roethke. Used by permission of Doubleday, a division of Random House, Inc.

Jay Rogoff. "Death's Theatre." First published in the *Sewanee Review* 114, no. 4 (Fall 2006). Copyright © 2006 by Jay Rogoff. Reprinted with the permission of the editor and the author.

Frederik L. Rusch. "Society and Character in 'The Love Song of J. Alfred Prufrock'" from "Approaching Literature through the Social Psychology of Erich Fromm" in *Psychological Perspectives on Literature: Freudian Dissidents and Non-Freudians,* edited by Joseph Natoli. Copyright © 1984. Reprinted by permission of the author.

Kay Ryan. "Hailstorm" from *The Niagara River* by Kay Ryan. Copyright © 2005 by Kay Ryan. Used by permission of Grove/Atlantic, Inc.

Michael Ryan. "Bunny" from *New and Selected Poems* by Michael Ryan. Copyright © 2004 by Michael Ryan. Reprinted by permission of Houghton Mifflin Harcourt Publishing Company. All rights reserved.

Yousif al-Sa'igh. "An Iraqi Evening," translated by Saadi A Simawe, Ralph Savarese, and Chuck Miller, from *Iraqi Poetry Today,* ed. Saadi Simawe (Modern Poetry in Translation, 2003). Copyright © 2003 by Modern Poetry in Translation. Reprinted by permission of Modern Poetry in Translation.

Sonia Sanchez. "c'mon man hold me" from *Like the Singing Coming Off the Drums: Love Poems* by Sonia Sanchez. Copyright © 1998 by Sonia Sanchez. Reprinted by permission of Beacon Press, Boston. "Summer Words of a Sistuh Addict" from *We a BaddDDD People* by Sonia Sanchez, copyright © 1970 by Sonia Sanchez and published by the Broadside Press. Reprinted by permission of the author.

Peter Schmitt. "Friends with Numbers" from *Hazard Duty*. Copyright © 1995 by Peter Schmitt. Used by permission of Copper Beech Press.

Elisabeth Schneider. "Hints of Eliot in Prufrock." Reprinted by permission of the Modern Language Association of America from "Prufrock and After: The Theme of Change," *PMLA* 87 (1982): 1103-1117.

S. Pearl Sharp. "It's the Law: A Rap Poem" from *Typing in the Dark* (Writers and Readers Publishing, Inc., 1991). Reprinted in *African American Literature* 1998. Used by permission of the author.

Shu Ting. "O Motherland, Dear Motherland" (translated by Fang Dai, Dennis Ding, and Edward Morin) from *The Red Azalea: Chinese Poetry Since the Cultural Revolution,* ed. Edward Morin (Honolulu: U Hawai'i Press, 1990). Reprinted by permission of the University of Hawai'i Press.

Leslie Marmon Silko. "Love Poem." Copyright © 1970 by Leslie Marmon Silko. Reprinted with permission of The Wylie Agency LLC.

Charles Simic. "In the Library" from *The Book of Gods and Devils*. Copyright © 1990 by Charles Simic. Reprinted by permission of Houghton Mifflin Harcourt Publishing Company. "The Storm" from *The Virginia Quarterly Review* 84, no. 2 (Spring 2008), p. 92. Copyright © 2008 by Charles Simic. Reprinted by permission of the author.

Louis Simpson. "In the Suburbs" from *At the End of the Open Road* by Louis Simpson. Wesleyan University Press, 1963. Reprinted by permission of the author.

Floyd Skloot. "Winter Solstice" from *Approximately Paradise* by Floyd Skloot, published by Tupelo Press. Copyright © 2005 by Floyd Skloot. All rights reserved. Reproduced by permission of Tupelo Press.

David R. Slavitt. "Titanic" from *Change of Address: Poems New and Selected* by David R. Slavitt. Copyright © 2005 by David R. Slavitt. Reprinted by permission of Louisiana State University Press.

Ernest Slyman. "Lightning Bugs" from *Sometime the Cow Kick Your Head, Light Year 88/89*. Reprinted by permission of the author.

Patricia Smith. "What It's Like to Be a Black Girl (for Those of You Who Aren't)" from *Life According to Motown* by Patricia Smith. Copyright © 1991 by Patricia Smith. Reprinted by permission of the author.

Gary Snyder. "How Poetry Comes to Me" from *No Nature* by Gary Snyder. Copyright © 1992 by Gary Snyder. Used by permission of Pantheon Books, a division of Random House, Inc.

David Solway. "Windsurfing." Reprinted by permission of the author.

Cathy Song. "A Poet in the House" from *The Land of Bliss* by Cathy Song. Copyright © 2001. Reprinted by permission of the University of Pittsburgh Press. "The White Porch" and "The Youngest Daughter" from *Picture Bride*. Copyright © 1983 by Yale University Press. Reprinted by permission of Yale University Press. Photograph of

Cathy Song on page 597 from School Figures, by Cathy Song, © 1994. Reprinted by permission of the University of Pittsburgh Press.

Gary Soto. "Behind Grandma's House" and "Mexicans Begin Jogging" from *New and Selected Poems* by Gary Soto. Copyright © 1995. Used with permission of Chronicle Books, LLC, San Francisco. Visit ChronicleBooks.com.

Bruce Springsteen. "Devils & Dust." Copyright © 2005 by Bruce Springsteen (ASCAP). Reprinted by permission. International copyright secured. All rights reserved.

William Stafford. "Traveling through the Dark," from *The Way It Is: New & Selected Poems*. Copyright © 1962, 1998 by the Estate of William Stafford. Reprinted with the permission of Graywolf Press, Saint Paul, Minnesota, www.graywolfpress.org.

Timothy Steele. "Waiting for the Storm" from *Sapphics and Uncertainties: Poems, 1970–1986*. Copyright © 1986, 1995 by Timothy Steele. Reprinted with the permission of the University of Arkansas Press, www.uapress.com.

Jim Stevens. "Schizophrenia." Originally appeared in *Light: The Quarterly of Light Verse* (Spring 1992). Copyright © 1992 by Jim Stevens. Reprinted by permission.

Wallace Stevens. "Anecdote of the Jar" and "The Emperor of Ice-Cream," from *The Collected Poems of Wallace Stevens* by Wallace Stevens. Copyright © 1954 by Wallace Stevens and renewed 1982 by Holly Stevens. Used by permission of Alfred A. Knopf, a division of Random House, Inc.

Robert Sward. "A Personal Analysis of 'The Love Song of J. Alfred Prufrock'" from *Touchstones: American Poets on a Favorite Poem*, ed. Robert Pack and Jay Parini, Middlebury College Press, published by UP New England. Copyright © 1995, 1997, 2000 by Robert Sward. Reprinted by permission of the author.

May Swenson. "All That Time" from *The Complete Love Poems of May Swenson*. Copyright © 1991, 2003 by the Literary Estate of May Swenson. Reprinted by permission of Houghton Mifflin Harcourt Publishing Company. All rights reserved. "A Nosty Fright" from *In Other Words* by May Swenson, 1987. Copyright © 1984 by May Swenson. Used with permission of the Literary Estate of May Swenson.

Dylan Thomas. "Do Not Go Gentle into That Good Night," copyright © 1952 by Dylan Thomas. Reprinted by permission of New Directions Publishing Corp. "The Hand That Signed the Paper," copyright © 1939 by New Directions Publishing Corporation, from *The Poems of Dylan Thomas*. Reprinted by permission of New Directions Publishing Corp.

Mabel Loomis Todd. "The Character of Amherst" from *The Years and Hours of Emily Dickinson*, volume 2, by Jay Leyda. Copyright © 1960 by Yale University Press. Reprinted by permission of Yale University Press.

Tomas Tranströmer. "April and Silence," trans. Robin Fulton, from *New Collected Poems* (Bloodaxe Books, 1997). Copyright © 1997 by Robin Fulton and Bloodaxe Books. Reprinted by permission of Bloodaxe Books Ltd.

Natasha Trethewey. "On Captivity." First published in *Five Points: A Journal of Literature and Art* vol. 11, no. 3 (2007). Copyright © 2007 by Natasha Trethewey. Reprinted by permission of the author.

Mark Turpin. "Sledgehammer's Song" from *Hammer: Poems*. Copyright © 2003 by Mark Turpin. Reprinted with the permission of Sarabande Books, www.sarabandebooks.org.

John Updike. "Dog's Death" from *Midpoint and Other Poems* by John Updike. Copyright © 1969 and renewed 1997 by John Updike. Used by permission of Alfred A. Knopf, a division of Random House, Inc. "Player Piano" from *Collected Poems, 1953–1993* by John Updike. Copyright © 1993 by John Updike. Used by permission of Alfred A. Knopf, a division of Random House, Inc.

Lee Upton. "Dyserotica" from *Undid in the Land of the Undone* by Lee Upton. Copyright © 2007. Reprinted by permission of New Issues Press.

Richard Wakefield. "The Bell Rope" from *East of Early Winters: Poems* by Richard Wakefield (University of Evansville Press, 2006). Copyright © 2006 by Richard Wakefield. Reprinted with permission from the author. "In a Poetry Workshop," *Light* (Winter 1999). Reprinted with permission from the author.

Derek Walcott. Excerpt from "The Road Taken" from *Homage to Robert Frost* by Joseph Brodsky, Seamus Heaney, and Derek Walcott. Copyright © 1996 by the Estate of Joseph Brodsky, Seamus Heaney, and Derek Walcott. Reprinted by permission of Farrar, Straus & Giroux, LLC.

Ronald Wallace. "Building an Outhouse" from *Makings of Happiness* by Ronald Wallace. Copyright © 1991. Reprinted by permission of the University of Pittsburgh Press. "In a Rut" from *The Best American Poetry 2003*, ed. Yusef Komunyakaa. Originally published in *Poetry Northwest*. Copyright © 2003. Reprinted by permission of the author. "Miss Goff" from the poem sequence "Teachers: A Primer," from *Time's Fancy* by Ronald Wallace. Copyright © 1994. Reprinted by permission of the University of Pittsburgh Press.

Bruce Weigl. "Snowy Egret" from *The Monkey Wars* by Bruce Weigl. Copyright © 1985. Reprinted by permission of the University of Georgia Press.

Gail White. "Dead Armadillos." Copyright © 2000 by Gail White. Reprinted by permission of the author.

C. K. Williams. "Shock" from *Repair* by C. K. Williams. Copyright © 1999 by C. K. Williams. Reprinted by permission of Farrar, Straus & Giroux, LLC. "The United States," *The New Yorker*, April 16, 2007. Copyright © 2007 by C. K. Williams. Reprinted by permission of the author.

Miller Williams. "Thinking about Bill, Dead of AIDS" from *Living on the Surface: New and Selected Poems* by Miller Williams. Copyright © 1972, 1975, 1976, 1979, 1980, 1987, 1988, 1989 by Miller Williams. Reprinted by permission of the author.

William Carlos Williams. "Poem," copyright © 1953 by William Carlos Williams, "The Red Wheelbarrow," copyright © 1938 by New Directions Publishing Corp., "Spring and All," copyright © 1938 by New Directions Publishing Corp, "This Is Just to Say," copyright © 1938 by New Directions Publishing Corp., from *Collected Poems: 1909–1939*, Volume I. Reprinted by permission of New Directions Publishing Corp.

Cynthia Griffin Wolff. "On the Many Voices in Dickinson's Poetry" excerpted from *Emily Dickinson* by Cynthia Griffin Wolff. Copyright © 1986 by Cynthia Griffin Wolff. Used by permission of Alfred A. Knopf, a division of Random House, Inc.

Index of First Lines

Index of Authors and Titles

INDEX OF TERMS

Boldface numbers refer to the Glossary of Literary Terms, pages 745–761

RESOURCES FOR READING AND WRITING ABOUT POETRY

SUPPLEMENTAL READING AND WRITING HELP

VirtuaLit Interactive Tutorials

Available on the *LiterActive* CD-ROM and at bedfordstmartins.com/rewritinglit, these tutorials offer close readings, coverage of literary elements, cultural contexts, and critical approaches for

- Elizabeth Bishop's "The Fish"
- Theodore Roethke's "My Papa's Waltz"
- Andrew Marvell's "To His Coy Mistress"

LiterActive CD-ROM

This rich and student-friendly resource provides

- *VirtuaLit Interactive Tutorials*
- *A Multimedia and Documents Gallery:* hundreds of images, audio and video clips, and contextual documents supporting 43 authors
- *A Research and Documentation Guide:* advice for working with sources — how to find, evaluate, summarize, interpret, and document them
- *LitLinks:* a wealth of biographical information on the poets in the anthology